Administrative Law

Administrative Law

Eighth edition

David Foulkes

Butterworths
London, Dublin, Edinburgh
1995

United Kingdom	Butterworths, a Division of Reed Elsevier (UK) Ltd, Halsbury House, 35 Chancery Lane, London WC2A 1EL and 4 Hill Street, Edinburgh EH2 3JZ
Australia	Butterworths, Sydney, Melbourne, Brisbane, Adelaide, Perth, Canberra and Hobart
Canada	Butterworths Canada Ltd, Toronto and Vancouver
Ireland	Butterworth (Ireland) Ltd, Dublin
Malaysia	Malayan Law Journal Sdn Bhd, Kuala Lumpur
New Zealand	Butterworths of New Zealand Ltd, Wellington and Auckland
Puerto Rico	Butterworth of Puerto Rico, Inc, San Juan
Singapore	Butterworths Asia, Singapore
South Africa	Butterworths Publishers (Pty) Ltd, Durban
USA	Butterworth Legal Publishers, Carlsbad, California and Salem, New Hampshire

A CIP Catalogue record for this book is available from the British Library.

ISBN 0 406 04648 4

Printed in England by Clays Ltd, St Ives plc,

Preface

Administrative law has been moving so fast in recent decades that new editions of this book have been called for with some frequency and regularity since its first appearance in 1964. It has not only been moving fast, but growing fast; the first edition, written in the immediate aftermath of *Ridge v Baldwin* is a slight thing compared with this – though not, as it turned out, fragile.

By and large this edition follows the general pattern of the previous one, though one short chapter has been absorbed elsewhere, and some other material has been shifted about to form a new chapter (that on statutory applications and appeals). The need to keep reasonably up to date has, however, required many changes within each chapter, some of which are as follows.

The headlong privatisation of many public activities has taken many forms and, in chapter 2, I have tried to give such account of it as might be found relevant to students of administrative law. I have reduced, but by no means excluded, the account of the nationalised industries. In the field of delegated legislation, in chapter 3, the increased use of Henry 8 clauses is critically noted, and there are the new Parliamentary committees which will hopefully be able to provide more adequate scrutiny of government orders. Chapter 5, on tribunals, has undergone considerable, and I trust beneficial, change, due largely to my closer acquaintance with them as a member of the Council on Tribunals. Tribunals often raise basic questions of policy and practice which have to be applied to a wide variety of circumstances and are a rich field of study of administrative law problems.

Developments in the requirements of fairness, in the enforceability of expectations, in the duty to give reasons, in the law relating to retrospectivity and to partial validity – these and others had to be taken into account. The development of the law of judicial review has continued, with some clarification following the confusion caused by *O'Reilly v Mackman*; and I have been lucky in the timing of this edition as the Law Commission's Report on Administrative Law was published just before I set about revising the relevant chapter.

A new edition not only requires an updating and a clearing out of the old stuff; it also gives a opportunity to revise earlier judgments. Many times have I said to myself, adopting the words of a Victorian judge, 'The matter does not appear to me now as it appears to have appeared to me then'.

DLF
Penarth
May 1995

Contents

Table of statutes

References in this Table to *Statutes* are to Halsbury's Statutes of England (Fourth Edition) showing the volume and page at which the annotated text of the Act may be found.

Page references printed in **bold** type indicate where the Act is set out in part or in full.

Table of Cases

PAGE

Chapter 1

Administrative law: content and context

Administrative law is the law relating to public administration. It is concerned with the legal forms and constitutional status of public authorities; with their powers and duties and with the procedures followed in exercising them; with their legal relationships with one another, with the public and with their employees; and with the wide range of institutions, both internal and external to themselves, which seek, in varied ways, to control their activities.[1]

It is now accepted as an important subject of study for the legal practitioner, the academic lawyer, and for the public administrator. The reason for this is clear. The basic and traditional functions of the state are those of securing the community against external aggression and internal strife and of keeping itself going by way of taxation. In addition, the modern state has, during the last 150 years, coincident with the extension of the franchise and the rise of modern political parties, an increased population and technological inventions, acquired many more functions. Taken together all these functions[2] evidence involvement by public authority in most aspects of the life of the community. This evolution of modern public administration led to the evolution of modern administrative law.[3]

Administrative law is to do with public authorities. Their functions are varied and the law concerning them is extensive. However, neither the teacher nor the student of administrative law can be familiar with all the details of all the law concerning those functions – town and country planning, education, housing, civil aviation, immigration, the supervision of companies, the administration of the health service, etc. He is concerned with the principles thrown up by the grant and exercise of such powers. The only proviso is that when considering general issues, he will usually have to concern himself with detail, for abstract principles of law have no

1 See Robson in Ginsberg (ed) *Law and Opinion in England in the 20th Century*, p 200.
2 Friedmann *The Rule of Law and the Welfare State* suggests five categories: the state as protector, provider, entrepreneur, economic controller and arbiter.
3 See Arthurs 'Jonah and the Whale' (1980) 30 U T LJ 225.

1

practical meaning until applied to concrete situations. Important principles of administrative law tend to arise out of and to be applied to the minutiae of administration.

Administrative law is concerned with public administration; public administration operates through institutions. A study of administrative law must therefore include some knowledge of the complex institutions that comprise public administration. The institutions exist to exercise powers and duties. Administrative law is therefore concerned with the way powers are acquired, how we are to distinguish between the proper and improper use of these powers, how the latter is to be prevented and remedied, and the proper distribution of powers – ie which institutions should exercise which powers. The institutions were created, principally by statute, because it was thought that there was need for them. The community having decided, through the political process, that certain goals are to be sought, the grant of the necessary powers to and the imposition of the necessary duties on existing or new institutions may be needed. As these institutions operate within the framework of the law, those other institutions which exist to give authoritative rulings on the extent and requirements of the law (which we call the courts) are called on to determine the legality of the actions of the former. The role of the courts of law in providing rulings on the legality of the exercise of public powers is naturally a major concern of administrative law. These rulings may, or may not, have the effect of preventing authorities from doing what they wish to do. Those who are not disposed to agree with the exercise of public power either generally or in a particular case, will see the role of the courts as controlling or inhibiting the actions of public authorities, and will see that also as *the* purpose of administrative law. But administrative law and indeed other branches of the law, is to be seen also as an instrument for *getting things done* by the creation through legal processes of institutions and granting them powers and imposing duties on them. The administrator is controlled by law, but at the same time sees it as something to be used to achieve those results he believes should be achieved. Administrative law is for the administrator as much as it is for the lawyer and must be seen also from the point of view of the administrator acting under political direction to get things done.[4] There is a need for public power and its efficient exercise: there is a need for protection against abuse of power. Administrative law is important and interesting precisely because it is to do with this problem of power. And for much the same reason it tends to be contentious. It is to do with laws, many of which raise fundamental constitutional and hence political issues.

The role of the courts is then to determine the *legality* of administrative action. Control over other aspects of administrative action, its effectiveness, efficiency or political acceptability, for example, is exercised by other institutions. Which control is the more important or useful? It is

---

4   See Daintith 'Legal Analysis of Economic Policy' 9 BJLS 191, Harlow and Rawlings *Law and Administration*. The government will of course resort to the courts, ie 'use administrative law' where it thinks it necessary.

impossible to answer that question at this stage. All that can be said now is that it is necessary to stress that, in a study of administrative law, those other institutions are not less important than the courts.

It is convenient to refer briefly at this point to some landmarks in the study of modern English administrative law. The first book devoted solely to this subject was C T Carr's *Delegated Legislation* published in 1921. In 1928 Robson published his *Justice and Administrative Law*,[5] an examination of the judicial powers exercised by tribunals and departments. In the following year came F J Port's *Administrative Law*. This was also the year in which Lord Hewart, then Chief Justice, published *The New Despotism*, an account of the 'pretensions and encroach-ments of the bureaucracy' upon the functions of legislation and of the judiciary, in other words an attack on delegated legislation and on the granting of judicial powers to tribunals and departments. In that same year, 1929, the government appointed the Committee on Ministers' Powers to consider these two problems and to report what safeguards were 'desirable or necessary to secure the constitutional principles of the sovereignty of Parliament and the supremacy of the Law'. Its report, published in 1932,[6] led to little practical result. The 1939–45 war gave great powers to the government over the life of the nation, and in 1945 C K Allen published his *Law and Orders*,[7] an enquiry into delegated legislation and executive powers. An important statute from the post-war period was the Crown Proceedings Act 1947 which in general terms, gave the right to sue the government. In 1952 the first student text covering the whole subject, by Griffith and Street[8] was published. The Crichel Down affair of 1953, which involved the alleged abuse by civil servants of their powers, had a considerable popular and political impact. It was followed by the appointment in 1955 of the Franks Committee on tribunals and inquiries. The Committee's report[9] speedily led to the Tribunals and Inquiries Act 1958 which gave legislative force to most of its recommendations, including the creation of the Council on Tribunals. Its report is still influential.

One area not looked into by the Franks Committee was examined by a committee appointed by JUSTICE[10] whose report[11] published in 1961 recommended the creation of the office of Parliamentary Commissioner, or Ombudsman as he is popularly known. The creation of the office, which investigates complaints of maladministration by central government, by

5 3rd edn, 1951. See Robson 'Justice and Administrative Law Reconsidered' [1979] CLP 107. 'In 1929–30 I gave the first course in any British university under the title the Principles of Administrative Law' –vol 23 Political Studies 193 at 195.
6 Cmnd 4060. The first chairman was the Earl of Donoughmore; the report is sometimes called the Donoughmore Report. See D G T Williams, 'The Donoughmore Report in Retrospect' (1982) 60 Pub Admin 215.
7 3rd edn, 1965.
8 *Principles of Administrative Law* (5th edn 1972).
9 Cmd 218.
10 The British section of the International Commission of Jurists, a non-governmental, non-political organisation of lawyers dedicated to the support of the rule of law.
11 *The Citizen and the Administration.*

the Parliamentary Commissioner Act 1967 was followed by the creation of similar offices for other areas of government. As for the courts, for a period of about fifty years up to the early 1960s, they showed a marked reluctance to intervene in the area of public administration. But there was then a change in the climate (evidenced or created by the matters just referred to) and a few key decisions showed that they had put that reluctance behind them. An important recent change was the alteration in the procedure for applying for judicial review of administrative decisions. It has been followed by a great increase in litigation in this area, and a much richer body of case law.

As administrative law is to do with government and public administration it must be seen in the setting of our constitutional arrangements and principles. This brief consideration starts with *the legislative supremacy of Parliament*. The accepted dogma is that Parliament can by an Act make or unmake any law. No matter is too small or too great for its attention. An Act can retrospectively validate an administrative decision invalidated by the courts.[12] The only thing an Act cannot do is to prevent its own repeal, or to put it another way, Parliament cannot bind itself: it can change its mind at any time. The government composed as it is of members of the majority party in the House of Commons is normally able to get through Parliament the legislation it wants. 'In normal times parliamentary sovereignty is effectively activated, steered and implemented by the closely integrated group of men who compose the Government.'[13] The negative aspect of the legislative supremacy of Parliament is that no other institution in the state, neither court nor government, can declare an Act invalid on any ground whatsoever. This was unanimously and vigorously affirmed by the House of Lords in *British Railways Board v Pickin*,[14] in which the argument that a court could disregard a section in a private Act was firmly rejected. Lord Reid said that such argument 'must seem strange and startling to anyone with any knowledge of the history and law of our constitution'.[15]

The courts are of course frequently required to say what meaning is to be given to Acts of Parliament. As the powers and duties of public authorities derive almost entirely from statute, the question of statutory interpretation is of special importance in administrative law.

The second matter it is appropriate to mention here is *the doctrine of the separation of powers*. This states that in every state there are *three sorts of power*, the legislative (making of laws), the executive (or administrative) (the carrying out of the laws) and the judicial (the interpretation and application of the laws in particular disputes). Now, even if it is easy to point to examples of functions which are clearly legislative, clearly administrative or clearly judicial, it is not always easy to draw a theoretical

---

12 Eg National Health Service (Invalid Direction) Act 1980.
13 Baker *Administrative Theories and Public Administration*, p 81.
14 [1974] AC 765, [1974] 1 All ER 609.
15 Such a person will now take into account UK membership of the EC. See the *Factortame* cases: Craig 3 ERPL 521.

line between them, or to distinguish between them in practice. The Committee on Ministers' Powers tried to clarify the distinction between the administrative and the judicial by saying that an administrative decision is wholly within the complete discretion of the minister: such a decision is determined by considerations of public policy. A 'true judicial decision', on the other hand, presupposes an existing dispute between the two or more parties, which dispute is disposed of by a finding on any facts in dispute 'and an application of the law of the land to the facts as found'.[16] The essential distinction in the Committee's view was, therefore, that between law and policy: a true judicial decision involving no policy considerations, and a true administrative decision no judicial element. The validity of this distinction has been challenged. Robson argued that the judicial is fundamentally indistinguishable from the administrative in view of the element of discretion involved in both. 'Judicial administration ... is merely a specialised form of general administration which "has acquired an air of detachment" '.[17] On the other hand Gordon[18] sees the essential difference to be between the judicial on the one hand and the legislative and the administrative on the other, in that the former applies a pre-existing objective standard laid down by the law, whereas legislative and administrative decisions are based, not on legal rights, but on policy and expediency, and a body which makes law according to its own will is a legislative body.

It would be wrong however to give the impression that the Committee on Ministers' Powers suggested that the classification was a rigid one. Thus it wrote,

It is indeed difficult in theory and impossible in practice to draw a precise dividing line between the legislative on the one hand and the purely administrative on the other ... [There is an] inseparable mingling ... of the theoretically separate functions of legislation and justice ... In practical politics an academic attempt to draw the theoretical line may be contrary to common sense.[19]

The idea of the quasi should also be noted. The Committee defined the quasi-judicial as 'only an administrative decision, some stage or element of which possesses judicial characteristics'.[20] The idea of quasi-legislation has also been suggested.[1] This need to resort to the quasi reinforces the view that a precise distinction between the three kinds of powers is 'difficult in theory and impossible in practice'.

Whatever the difficulties of distinguishing between the various kinds of powers, the doctrine of the *separation* of powers is that they ought to be in the hands of *separate institutions* for 'there would be an end of

16 Cmd 4060, p 73.
17 *Justice and Administrative Law* (3rd edn) pp 14 and 433.
18 'Administrative Tribunals and the Courts' 49 LQR 94.
19 Cmd 4060, pp 19 and 39 (note 129).
20 Cmd 4060, p 81. In *Cooper v Wilson* [1937] 2 KB 309 Scott LJ referred (at 340) to the Committee's definitions and said that in the case in question 'the quasi-judicial approached in point of degree very near to the judicial'. Scott LJ had succeeded the Earl of Donoughmore as chairman of the Committee (see p 3 fn 6, above).
1 Megarry 60 LQR 125, 218.

everything were the same man or body to exercise those three powers...'
Thus Montesquieu,[2] with whom the doctrine is particularly associated.
As is well known it is not part of our constitution (it is in any case quite
differently applied by constitutions which purport to rely on it). Under
our arrangements, whereby the executive is drawn from the majority party
in the House of Commons, it follows that the executive, except in extreme
cases, controls the legislative power.[3] Our adherence to a separation of
powers is said to reside in the independence of the judiciary. It is the case
that a strong statutory guarantee of security in office is given to (part of)
the judiciary, the judges of the Supreme Court.[4] The judiciary, in their
turn, may express concern at their need to avoid usurpation of the
executive[5] or legislative[6] function.

A third point to note in connection with the classification of powers is
that it is not at all uncommon for statute to delineate an institution's
functions by reference to this classification. Examples are the jurisdiction
of the Parliamentary Commissioner for Administration and of the Council
on Tribunals, the obligation on Ministers to give reasons for decisions,
the Crown's liability in tort – there are many others. They are referred to
at the appropriate places in this book.

The third constitutional issue to consider is *the doctrine of ministerial
responsibility*. This says that ministers, who have the job of directing the
work of the central government, are responsible to Parliament for the
exercise of the powers and duties allotted to their respective departments.[7]
Responsibility for the actions of a large organisation is thus pinned on to
a particular individual. This political responsibility includes subjection
to question, criticism and inquiry by the various well-known Parliamentary procedures. (The corollary of this is that civil servants are not
responsible to Parliament, and do not publicly criticise or support
ministerial policy.) The minister is responsible in these senses not only
for what he himself does, but for everything done by his department. Every
decision taken by civil servants is technically and in law his decision (with
the corollary that civil servants are not associated publicly with those

2   *L'Esprit des Lois* (1748) Hafner's edition, pp 151–152. Montesquieu was a very influential
    writer on comparative politics. *L'Esprit* was his major work in which he classified
    constitutions in various ways; he was concerned with many other matters such as jury
    trial, freedom of expression and the importance of political parties. This dictum might
    be considered. 'To prevent abuse of power, things must be so ordered that power checks
    power'. See R Shackleton, *Montesquieu*.
3   'The fact that the government of the day now controls both Parliament and the executive
    has profound implications both for the constitutional separation of powers, and less
    often recognised, for the political distinction between party and State' – Sedley 'The
    Sound of Silence' (1994) 110 LQR 270.
4   Note that a similar security is given to other high officials such as the Parliamentary
    Commissioner and the Comptroller and Auditor General.
5   See Lord Shaw in *Local Government Board v Arlidge* [1915] AC 120 at 138.
6   See Lord Bridge in *Brind v Secretary of State for the Home Department* [1991] 1 All ER
    720 at 723. And see *R v Home Secretary, ex p Fire Brigades Union* [1995] 2 All ER 245,
    HL
7   See Turpin in *The Changing Constitution* 3rd edn, Jowell and Oliver; Wheare *Malad-
    ministration and its Remedies* ch 3; Marshall 'Ministerial Responsibility' 34 Pol Q 256.

decisions). Of course a minister cannot personally supervise every activity of his department and only a very small percentage[8] of all the decisions taken in the department can be brought to him personally. But as he is responsible for the proper management of the department, he and senior civil servants must see to it that decisions are taken in accordance with ministerial policies and that those matters which should, because of their importance, be brought to him, are in fact brought to him. Ministerial responsibility does not however mean that because civil servants' decisions are technically his the minister must in all circumstances support the decision taken by a civil servant. He need not do so where the civil servant has contravened a clear instruction, though the minister would be guilty of mismanagement in failing to give a clear instruction, or in failing to prevent the repetition of such a contravention.

The doctrine of ministerial responsibility is of key importance in our constitutional arrangements. It has a profound effect on the work of civil servants: 'The actions of all civil servants are coloured, whether consciously or not, by the responsibility of ministers to Parliament for those actions.'[9] Their unquestioning subordination to political chiefs has been emphasised.[10] Similarly, it is the presumption underlying the organisation and management of the civil service and has consequences of the first importance for it, including a high degree of centralisation. We are told that delegation of decision-making is desirable for effective administration (and the legality of delegation is a topic we shall consider in a later chapter). Does the doctrine therefore militate against the achievement of the most effective administrative process?[11] It may be that the two are not completely incompatible. 'The successful combination of ministerial responsibility with delegation of authority is the most rewarding as well as the most difficult thing to bring off.'[12] Other consequences of the doctrine of ministerial responsibility are said to be an emphasis on equity and on the avoidance of errors, elaborate record-keeping and the displacement of long-term planning by short-term political pressure at the top.[13] The doctrine does not tell us what matters are appropriately left to ministers, but rather the consequences of doing so: the consequences may be such as to encourage ministers to divest themselves wholly or partially of their responsibilities.[14]

One, perhaps the main, function of Parliament is to seek the redress of grievances, and a person adversely affected by the action of a government may seek a remedy through political channels. Where the exercise of

8 'Well under 1 per cent'. The Report of the Tribunal of Inquiry into the Collapse of the Vehicle and General Insurance Co, 1971–2, HC 33, para 61.
9 Compton 'The Administrative Performance of Government' (1970) 48 Pub Admin 4.
10 Sisson *The Spirit of British Administration*.
11 D Keeling *Management in Government*, p 154 says that in some respects eg capital investment decisions, civil servants often enjoy a much higher degree of delegation than their opposite numbers in business corporations.
12 Compton 'The Administrative Performance of Government' (1970) 40 Pub Admin 4.
13 Report on the Civil Service (Cmnd 3638), vol 2, paras 20–27, 305–315. And see Brown and Steel, *The Administrative Process in Britain*.
14 Through privatisation or executive agencies, respectively: see ch 2.

ministerial power is challenged in the courts the existence or otherwise of Parliamentary, ie political, accountability may affect the court's willingness to intervene. In *Liversidge v Anderson*[15] the House of Lords held that an order made by the Home Secretary detaining the plaintiff without trial could not be challenged in the courts. Lord Maugham said, 'The person who is primarily entrusted with these most important duties is one of the principal Secretaries of State ... answerable to Parliament for the proper discharge of his duties'.[16] In *Local Government Board v Arlidge*[17] Arlidge unsuccessfully challenged the Minister's decision about his property. In his judgment the Lord Chancellor relied to some extent on the Minister's responsibility to Parliament. Dicey thought this reference 'somewhat unfortunate'.[18] In *Secretary of State for Employment v Amalgamated Society of Locomotive Engineers and Firemen* (No 2)[19] Lord Denning, observing that the courts will be vigilant to see that a minister acts lawfully, added, 'This is especially the case where, as here, there is no immediate control by Parliament'.[20]

The fourth matter to mention here is *rule of law*. Dicey said that the rule or supremacy of law as a characteristic of the English constitution has three meanings. It means, first, 'the absolute supremacy or predominance of regular law as opposed to the influence of arbitrary power, and excludes the existence of arbitrariness ... or even of wide discretionary authority on the part of the government'.[1] We shall see in this book many examples of what might be called wide discretionary powers. These powers derive from the 'regular law' of legislation and their use is subject to parliament and judicial controls. We would say today that what is required to ensure the 'rule of law' is that such powers should be subject to adequate controls. There is plenty of room here for political disagreement as to the necessity for such powers and the adequacy of the controls.

The second meaning of the rule of law, according to Dicey, is that 'every man, whatever be his rank or condition, is subject to the ordinary law of the realm and amenable to the jurisdiction of the ordinary tribunals'[2] (by which he meant the courts). This state of affairs was to be contrasted, he said, with that in France where a leading idea of the *droit administratif* is that the government and every servant of the government possesses a whole body of special rights and privileges as against private citizens, that the extent of these rights is determined on principles different from those which fix the legal rights and duties of one citizen against another, and that the ordinary courts have no jurisdiction over issues arising

15 [1942] AC 206; p 265 below.
16 Ibid at 222.
17 [1915] AC 120; p 284, below.
18 (1915) 31 LQR 148 at 152.
19 [1972] 2 QB 455, [1972] 2 All ER 949.
20 At 487 and 963. But neither court nor Parliament availed – see p 329 below. And see *Nottinghamshire County Council v Secretary of State for the Environment* [1986] 1 All ER 199, p 255 below.
 1 A V Dicey *The Law of the Constitution*, p 202. First edition, 1885, the current (10th), 1959.
 2 *The Law of the Constitution*, p 193.

between private persons and the state. There was, he said, no proper English equivalent for the term *droit administratif*; that the words 'administrative law', which were its most natural rendering, were unknown to English lawyers; and this absence of a satisfactory wording arose at bottom from our non-recognition of the thing – *droit administratif* – itself.[3] In 1915, Dicey published an article[4] entitled 'The Development of Administrative Law in England' in which he asked whether recent events had tended to introduce a body of law 'resembling in spirit, though certainly by no means identical with' administrative law in the sense just referred to. He concluded that the conferring of judicial and quasi-judicial authority on the executive was a considerable step towards the introduction of something like the *droit administratif* of France,

but the fact that the ordinary courts can deal with any actual or probable breach of the law committed by any servant of the Crown still preserves that rule of law which is fatal to the existence of true *droit administratif*.[5]

David has explained it this way.[6] The existence of *droit administratif* in France proceeds from a fundamental distinction which is not recognised in England. Continental lawyers regard the law as consisting of two distinct sets of rules: public law and private law. The rules which govern relations between private persons should not be held to apply automatically to relations in which the state or some public agency is involved. 'Other rules may indeed be then appropriate: these rules constitute our *droit administratif*.' Or perhaps, he suggested, another definition may be preferable: *droit administratif* is in France a special body of law which is applied by the special hierarchy of administrative courts created for the purpose. The contrast he makes with England is that the common law is a unitary system which applies both to relations between private persons and relations to which a public authority is a party. Certainly we do not have a special hierarchy of courts dealing with suits against the administration. However, we do have (as David acknowledges) some special rules that apply when a public authority is involved, and it is appreciated that rules of private law may be quite inappropriate in a public law situation. Government bodies have functions that have no parallel in private activities. It would be surprising therefore if the rules governing their exercise were not different from those regulating private relations. We shall come across many of them. In the field of substantive law we shall see differences in contract, tort, and in estoppel for example, and in procedure the rules of *locus standi*, and the effect of delay in bringing proceedings are necessarily affected where the defendant is a public authority. There is a whole range of remedies available only in respect of the exercise of public power and the *grounds* on which such exercise is

3 Op cit, pp 203, 320. But Maitland was using it at the same time. 'If you take up a modern volume of the report of the Queen's Bench Division you will find about half the cases reported have to do with rules of administrative law ...' *Constitutional History of England*, p 505.
4 31 LQR 148, also reprinted as Appendix 2 to his *The Law of the Constitution* (10th edn).
5 31 LQR at 152.
6 René David *English Law and French Law*, ch 7.

challengeable are special to it. Further, a special procedure known as the
'application for judicial review' has to be followed when the exercise of a
public power is being challenged in the courts. These rules and procedures
we can recognise as a body of public law, which has been built up
pragmatically. Though not applied by a special system of courts it is none
the less a body of public law. What matters of course is whether the
existence of such a body of law, and a view of the need to treat public and
private differently, provides a body of rules which is more satisfactory
than would otherwise be the case.[7] The recognition that public authorities
require a public law need not lead to the conclusion Dicey feared, that
government becomes arbitrary and above the law, in other words to an
absence of the rule of law. The opposite may be the case.

The third meaning Dicey gave to the rule of law was that whereas in
many countries private rights such as freedom from arrest are sought to
be guaranteed by a statement in a written constitution of the general
principles relating thereto, with the UK these rights are the result of
court decisions in particular cases which have actually arisen. The
constitution, he said, is not the source but the consequence of the right of
individuals.[8] Dicey admitted that if these rights are in fact enjoyed it
does not matter whether they are secured by one method or the other, but
suggested that they would be more likely to be secured if the problems
were approached from the point of view of the contrivance of remedies by
which those rights could be enforced (that is through the courts) than
from the mere declaration of rights in a document, and that rights secured
in the latter way can be more easily suspended or taken away. As with
the first two meanings he gave to the rule of law, Dicey is here emphasising
the role of the courts as guarantors of liberty (subject of course to the
supremacy of Parliament).

Dicey has been heavily criticised,[9] but his influence has been wide.[10]
His formulation of the rule of law was responsible for the fact that it was
concerned largely with the negative (but valuable) aim of protecting the
individual from arbitrary power. Others would emphasise more positive
requirements such as the need for legal aid, and more broadly, the
achieving of such social and economic conditions as will ensure a reasonable standard of economic security, social welfare and education for the
mass of the people.

Certainly students of this subject can expect to meet frequent
references to it. The following provide examples of its meaning and
application today.

7   Harlow (1978) Kingston L Rev 3; 43 MLR 241.
8   *Law of the Constitution*, pp 195, 203.
9   See Jennings *The Law and the Constitution*; cf Lawson 'Dicey Revisited' (1959) 7 Political
    Studies 109, 207, and Jowell in *The Changing Constitution* 3rd edn Jowell and Oliver,
    where he refers to the rule of law as 'a principle of institutional morality'.
10 C T Carr said of the terms of reference of the Committee on Ministers' Powers (p 3,
    above) that they were 'whether Britain had gone off the Dicey standard', *Concerning
    English Administrative Law* (1941) p 26. Britain went off the gold standard by the Gold
    Standard (Amendment) Act 1931. See [1985] PL 583–723.

The maintenance of the rule of law is in every way as important in a free society as the democratic franchise. In our society the rule of law rests upon twin foundations; the sovereignty of the Queen in Parliament in making the law and the sovereignty of the Queen's courts in interpreting and applying the law.[11]

The Law Commission has said that the relevant public policy interests that have to be taken into account in deciding on judicial review procedures and the remedies available include the importance of vindicating the rule of law 'so that public bodies take lawful decisions and are prevented from relying on invalid decisions'.[12]

Lord Diplock said that the rules of standing in relation to applications for judicial review have been changed to meet the need to preserve the integrity of the rule of law.[13]

One theme ... lies at the heart of progress towards government under the rule of law ... the amenability of the Crown to the legal process.[14]

There is a strong public interest in the prosecution of offenders, but where the prisoner has been brought into the jurisdiction by force, abducting him from another state in disregard of available extradition treaties, the maintenance of the rule of law requires that the court can inquire into the circumstances, and if satisfied that the authorities in this country were a knowing party to the abduction, the court can stay the proceedings and order the prisoner to be released.[15]

And finally, the Lord Chancellor's Department, in meeting its aim of ensuring the 'efficient and effective administration of justice at an affordable cost' assures us that it is guided by the need, amongst other things, 'to protect and advance the rule of law'.[16]

---

11 Lord Bridge in *X Ltd v Morgan Grampian (Publishers) Ltd* [1990] 2 All ER 1 at 13.
12 *Administrative Law: Judicial Review and Statutory Appeals*. Law Com No 226, para 2.3.
13 [1982] AC 617 at 639.
14 Sedley 'The Sound of Silence' (1994) 110 LQR 270 at 287.
15 *Bennett v Horseferry Road Magistrates Court* [1993] 3 All ER 138, HL.
16 Cm 2209. And see p 139 below (immigration appeals).

Chapter 2

Administrative authorities

State, Crown and government

Administrative law is the law relating to public administration. Knowledge of some of the institutions of public administration is therefore necessary: without institutions there is no public administration.

The State

While it may be possible in some sense to view the administrative system and all the institutions of public administration as a unity, as for example being as a whole organised to achieve some common goal, or to further the public interest, it is not a unity in the sense of being comprised in one legal institution. It consists rather, in law, of a large number of institutions or organisations with varied forms and functions. English law knows nothing of the State as a *legal entity*, and the word is infrequently to be found in statutes dealing with the domestic law, but sometimes the courts are required to consider it. Two cases involved the Official Secrets Act 1911. In both, the question was whether what had been done was in, or against, the interest(s) of the State. In *Chandler v DPP*[1] the defendants were charged with doing acts (trying to immobilise an airfield) 'prejudicial to the safety or interests of the State'. Lord Reid said, 'State is not an easy word. It does not mean the Government or the Executive ... And I do not think it means, as counsel argued, the individuals who inhabit these islands ... perhaps the country or the realm are as good synonyms as I can find and I would be prepared to accept the organised community as coming as near to a definition as one can get.' Lord Devlin said, 'The [use of the word state] which I am quite satisfied ... was intended in this statute is to denote the organs of government of a national community.' This case concerned the possession of nuclear weapons and it was inevitable that the judges would say that in that matter the 'interests of the State' were

1 [1964] AC 763, [1967] 3 All ER 142.

12

to be determined by the executive branch of government. In *R v Ponting*[2] the question was whether the person to whom the defendant, a civil servant, had communicated certain information (a member of Parliament) was a person 'to whom it [was] in the interest of the State his duty to communicate it'. The issue was wholly different from that in *Chandler*. Ponting's argument was that he acted in pursuance of his duty in the interest of the state, namely, protecting Parliament from being deliberately misled by a minister.[3] This raises fundamental questions as to the duty of public officers towards their employers which cannot be pursued here. We have to note, rather, the judge's notorious direction to the jury to the effect that the interests of the state mean the policies of the state, that is those laid down by the recognised organs of government and authority. (The jury, happily, returned a verdict of not guilty.)

Reference to 'the State' was made in *Ross v Lord Advocate*.[4] Trustee Savings Banks (TSBs) have long been regulated by statute. The Trustee Savings Bank Act 1985 abolished the 'statutory' TSBs and replaced them, as an act of privatisation, by limited liability companies created for that purpose. The TSBs had surplus assets amounting to £800m and the effect of the Act was to present this sum to the successor companies. Depositors in a TSB who disapproved of the policy of privatisation argued that they were entitled not only to the sums they had deposited with the bank (with interest) but also to those surplus assets, which would not therefore have passed to the successor companies – this would of course have effectively scuppered the privatisation. On examination of the Act the House of Lords ruled against them. However, in the course of his judgment Lord Templeman (with whom the other judges agreed) said, 'Statutory savings banks and their assets belong to the state subject to the contractual rights of depositors to the return of their deposits and interest and subject to the powers and duties [over them] from time to time conferred and imposed by Parliament on [various] institutions of the state.' (This was in response to the argument that if the TSBs' assets were not 'owned' by the depositors then the banks had no owners and their assets were in 'limbo'.) This raised some doubt whether, if there is indeed some equation between 'state' and 'government' the government's expressed view that the banks did not belong to it was correct; and whether Parliament had been properly informed by it on the issue. The Solicitor-General's view was:

It is commonplace to draw a distinction between the Crown or the Government on the one hand and the State on the other. 'The Crown' is used to describe a body which has legal personality, and the ability to hold and dispose of property; 'the State' on the other hand is used to refer to a broader concept, which lacks legal personality and to which assets may be said to belong in the different and more general sense that they are ultimately at the disposition of Parliament.

2 [1985] Crim LR 318.
3 It is acknowledged that ministers sometimes find it necessary to say things that are untrue to the Commons.
4 [1986] 3 All ER 79; [1986] 1 WLR 1077.

As it was necessary for Parliament to legislate for the disposal of their assets on the closure of the TSBs, '[their] assets ... can therefore aptly be described, in the language of Lord Templeman, as having belonged to the State'.

The Solicitor-General's attention had been drawn to the judge's direction to the jury in the *Ponting* case. He replied:

This seems to me wholly irrelevant to the question of how one should understand the reference to 'the State' in the relevant passage in Lord Templeman's judgment. A direction in the case of a prosecution under s 2 of the Official Secrets Act can have no possible bearing on the ownership of TSB assets in the context of very different legislation.[5]

Domestic legislation acknowledges 'the State' in other ways. The Contempt of Court Act 1981 refers to tribunals 'exercising the judicial power of the State'. (Thus we may refer to its legislative and executive powers.) Legislation also acknowledges that under statutory schemes officials may be 'State registered'.[6]

In European law, for the purpose of the application of Council Directives it may be important to determine whether an organisation is 'under the control of the State'. Its relationship with legislature and government then has to be considered.

The Crown
If we do not have in domestic law a clear concept of the State, what we do have is the Crown.[7] 'The Crown' is not an easy term. Maitland warned against its use by students.[8] But it is used – so we have to know what is meant by it, particularly because of problems about suing the Crown and of its immunities and exemptions, as for example when an Act says that it does, or does not, bind the Crown, or when some coercive order is sought against it. In general terms we can say that the word represents the sum total of the powers of central government; or we may say that the government is carried on in the name of the Crown. While 'the Crown' gives in that sense a legal unity to those powers, it is not the whole of public administration, as much of public administration is carried on by bodies which are not part of, or members of, the Crown.

In *Town Investments Ltd v Department of the Environment*[9] the question was whether the Crown was the tenant of certain premises: a lease had

5 See HC 237, 1986–87, Trustee Savings Banks: Rights of Ownership, a Report by the National Audit Office. The Comptroller and Auditor General was concerned to see (if the assets did indeed belong to the government) whether there had been any loss of income to the Exchequer. He concluded that there had not been; and that given the legal distinction between government and State, there was no reason for believing that Parliament had been misled.
6 Eg Professions Supplementary to Medicine Act 1960.
7 Maitland 'The State as Corporation' (1901) 17 LQR 131; Laski 'The Responsibility of the State in England' (1919) 32 HLR 447. The Channel Tunnel Agreement refers to land belonging to the French *State*, but to land vested in the British *Minister*: Cmnd 9769.
8 *The Constitutional History of England*, p 418. 'It is a convenient cover for ignorance.'
9 [1978] AC 359, [1977] 1 All ER 813.

been granted to the Secretary of State 'for and on behalf of Her Majesty' and the premises were occupied by civil servants of another Department. The House of Lords held that the use of the premises by government servants for government purposes constituted occupation of the premises by the Crown as a tenant. The status of those government servants was that of 'servants of the Crown' and of no-one else. Ministers and civil servants are all fellow-servants of the Crown.

However, when it comes to making coercive orders against the Crown (for example, an injunction or possible action for contempt of court) a distinction is made between making such an order against the Crown *directly* (which cannot be done) and against a government department or a minister in his official capacity (which can be done). The latter exercise Crown functions but are not, for *that* purpose 'the Crown': they act on its behalf. This distinction is underlined by the Crown Proceedings Act 1947 which, making the Crown liable in contract and tort, provides for actions to be brought not against the Crown itself but against the appropriate Department.[10]

It may, because of the Crown's various privileges and immunities, be important to know whether a body is a Crown body, that is, exercises Crown functions, so as to enjoy those privileges. Statute may put the matter beyond doubt.

For example, section 6(5) of the Post Office Act 1969 provides:

It is hereby declared that the Post Office is not to be regarded as the servant or agent of the Crown, or as enjoying any status, immunity or privilege of the Crown.

(Why then is it the *Royal* Mail?)[11] And it goes on to provide – thus indicating what some of the privileges of the Crown are – that the Post Office is not to be regarded:

as exempt from any tax, duty, rate, levy or other charge whatsoever, whether general or local, and that its property is not to be regarded as property of or property held on behalf of, the Crown.

The subsection just quoted is a commonly-used form of wording. A different form is used in the case of the Equal Opportunities Commission.[12]

(1) The Commission is not an emanation of the Crown, and shall not act or be treated as the servant or agent of the Crown.
(2) Accordingly –
    (a) neither the Commission nor a Commissioner or a member of its staff as such is entitled to any status, immunity, privilege or exemption enjoyed by the Crown;
    (b) the Commissioners and members of the staff of the Commission as such are not civil servants;

10 *M v Home Office* [1993] 3 All ER 537.
11 'Her Majesty the Queen has been pleased to approve that the title Royal Mail should continue, and that the Corporation should use the Crown and Royal Cypher as the Post Office does at present. The Sovereign's head will continue to be included in the design of stamps and postal orders.' Cmnd 3233, para 8.
12 Sex Discrimination Act 1975, Sch 3; and see Race Relations Act 1976, Sch 1.

(c) the Commission's property is not property of, or held on behalf of the Crown.

What if there is no clear statutory indication of the body's status, what test is to be applied?

In *Gilbert v Trinity House Corpn*[13] the defendant could not, as the law then was, be sued if it was a Crown body. Trinity House was, and is, a body corporate exercising powers conferred on it by statute. It was in effect the amalgamation, by the authority of the State, of other bodies which had provided lighthouses for the general convenience. This was not enough, the court said, to make it a Crown servant. Great officers of State, said Day J are 'emanations from the Crown. They are delegates by the Crown of its own authority to particular individuals.' Trinity House, he added was in no way 'a participant of any royal [ie Crown] authority.' In *Tamlin v Hannaford*[14] Denning LJ said that the test was not so much whether a body is 'an emanation of the Crown' as whether it is a servant or agent of the Crown. The body whose status was in issue in that case was the British Transport Commission, a nationalised undertaking. The only thing that could make it a Crown servant, said Denning LJ, was the *control* exercised over it by the minister, but that control, great though it was, was not enough to make the Commission his agent. The Commission was a public authority and its purposes were public purposes, but it was not, he said, a government department, 'nor do its powers fall within the province of government'. This was supported by the fact that on nationalisation:

all that has happened is that there has been an amalgamation of the previous railway companies into one concern which is expressly made subject to the same rights and liabilities as were the railway companies, including statutory duties, contractual obligations, and even some customary obligations ... The carriage of passengers and goods is a commercial concern ... and we do not think that its unification under state control is any ground for conferring Crown privileges upon it.

In *Bank voor Handel en Scheepvaart NV v Administrator of Hungarian Property*[15] the question was whether the defendant was a Crown servant and not therefore liable to income tax. The dominant factor in the House of Lords decision that he was a Crown servant was the degree of *control* exercised over him by the Board of Trade. Lord Asquith distinguished between 'an aggregate of commercial undertakings brought under some degree of public statutory control' and 'mere ministerial instruments of the Crown's will'. The Civil Service Pay Research Unit was held to be such an instrument in *Kendall v Morgan*.[16] The Unit gathered information on the pay of jobs comparable with those in the Civil Service. The director was appointed by the Prime Minister and he and his staff become civil servants on appointment: its cost was borne by the Exchequer. It was, the

13 1886 17 QBD 795.
14 [1950] 1 KB 18, [1949] 2 All ER 327.
15 [1954] AC 584, [1954] All ER 969.
16 (1980) Times, 4 December.

court said, an arm of government. Being a Crown body the government had the right to stop the Unit from carrying on with its comparability studies. (The unions wished it to do so and to make its information available to them so that they could use it in support of their pay claim.)

One of the immunities enjoyed by the Crown is that it is not bound by a statute unless the statute expressly provides or necessarily implies that it does. Referring to the Town and Country Planning Act 1947 Lord Denning said, 'I am satisfied that the Crown does not need to get planning permission in respect of its own interest in Crown lands. The reason why it is exempt is, not by virtue of any provisions in the Act itself, but by reason of the general principle that the Crown is not bound by an Act unless it is expressly or impliedly included.'[17] This is still the case, except that it is not only in respect of Crown lands that it does not need planning permission.[18] (Legislation to bring the Crown within planning law is expected.)

A statute may provide that it is to bind the Crown wholly, in part, or in certain respects. For example, the Race Relations Act 1968 stated 'This Act binds the Crown': but the Act of the same name of 1976 deals with the matter quite differently. Section 75 provides:

(1) This Act applies –
   (a) to an act done by or for the purposes of a Minister of the Crown or government department; or
   (b) to an act done on behalf of the Crown by a statutory body or by a person holding a statutory office,
as it applies to an act done by a private person.
(2) Parts II and IV [which concern discrimination in the employment field and other discriminatory acts] apply to (a) service for purposes of a Minister of the Crown ... as they apply to employment by a private person.

This means that acts of a governmental nature, as distinct from those which might be done by a private person, are outside the control of the race relations legislation (for example, acts of immigration officers,[19] and the making of ministerial regulations).[20]

When will an Act necessarily imply that it binds the Crown? In *Cooper v Hawkins*[1] the Locomotives Act 1865 said that, subject to regulations made by local authorities, it was an offence to drive a vehicle at more than 2 mph. The Act did not expressly bind the Crown. It was argued that as the object of the Act was to protect the public it was a necessary implication that it bound the Crown. The court disagreed. If it bound the Crown, the Crown would be bound by regulations made by local authorities

---

17 *Ministry of Agriculture, Fisheries and Food v Jenkins* [1963] 2 All ER 147 at 149. In addition the Crown could not *get* planning permission, but see now Town and Country Planning Act 1990 s 299.
18 *Lord Advocate v Dumbarton District Council* [1990] 2 AC 580, [1990] 1 All ER 1.
19 *Home Office v Commission for Racial Equality* [1982] QB 385, [1981] 1 All ER 1042. And see *Amin v Entry Clearance Officer, Bombay* [1983] 2 AC 818, [1983] 2 All ER 864 for the same wording in the Sex Discrimination Act 1975.
20 *R v Secretary of State for Social Security, ex p Nessa* (1994) Times, 15 November.
1 [1904] 2 KB 164.

and, second, it might hamper military operations. (Cooper was employed by the War Department as a civilian driver. In carrying out orders to deliver a load in a Crown vehicle by a stated time he necessarily broke the speed limit. In these circumstances his act was the act of the Crown, and as the Act did not bind the Crown he was immune from prosecution.) And more recently, '[I]t is clear that the mere fact that the statute in question has been passed for the public benefit is not in itself sufficient for that purpose [of finding a necessary implication that the Crown is bound]'[2]

The above cases contain illustrations of the effect of the Crown's immunity. Here are some more:

— Three-wheelers supplied to disabled persons by the government had Crown exemption from the requirements of the Construction and Use of Motor Vehicles Regulations.[3]
— It had been assumed for many years that the Crown Agents were exempt from the Moneylenders Acts as a Crown body. If they were not, large loans made by them might have been unenforceable. When doubt was cast on the assumption, legislation swiftly followed providing that the Acts were not to apply and were to be deemed never to have applied to them.[4]
— The Crown not being named in the relevant section of the Public Health Act was not liable in respect of property owned by it for the expenses of paving the street on which the property abutted.[5]

If the Crown is not bound by an Act it may undertake to act as though it were. Is this satisfactory? A Committee of Inquiry into the Prison Services reported:

We have received some criticism concerning the fact that the Crown, and thus penal establishments, are exempt from the provisions of legislation relating to health and safety at work and public health. The response from the relevant departments has been that, notwithstanding the exemption, they nevertheless seek to comply with all of the statutory obligations which are imposed on other uses of premises. We have no doubt that this attempt is genuinely made but we nonetheless think that the absence of inspection by the relevant public inspectors, who are of course able to compare standards with those obtaining elsewhere, may result not only in some short-comings being overlooked but may also create the impression that the departments are concealing something from the public gaze.[6]

The government
Reference is made above in various places to 'the government'. 'The government' is not a legal entity, and functions are not conferred by statute on it as such, that is, statute will not say 'the government' may do such

2   *Lord Advocate v Dumbarton District Council* [1990] 2 AC 580, [1990] 1 All ER 1.
3   Sixth Report of the Parliamentary Commissioner, 1974–5, HC 529, p 165.
4   Moneylenders (Crown Agents) Act 1975, s 1.
5   *Hornsey UDC v Hennell* [1902] 2 KB 73.
6   Cmnd 7673, para 11.30.

and such. As for the phrase 'government department' this has no general legal definition. We may think of a government department as an organisation which is part of central government, staffed by civil servants, headed by a minister, and whose money is provided directly by Parliament. In reality, though operating under the unity of the Crown, central government is 'a federation of separate departments with their own ministers and their own policies',[7] which may well conflict, and which compete with one another for scarce resources.

Nearly all major departments are headed by a 'Secretary of State'. In constitutional law the office of Secretary of State is one and indivisible. There are a number of holders of the office, and each of them carries out the duties allotted to him or her under the prerogative. Thus, nearly always, powers conferred on a Secretary of State are expressed as being conferred on 'the' Secretary of State and not on any particular Secretary of State; they are exercised by the appropriate one.[8] The exercise by him of his functions is a Crown function, as the Secretary of State is a Crown servant. Alternatively, a function may be conferred directly on the Crown, by conferring it on 'Her Majesty' as in 'Her Majesty may by Order in Council provide ...'. The exercise of such a function is solely the responsibility of ministers, though it is done in the name of the Crown.

Executive ('Next Steps') Agencies
There has for some time been a number of bodies analogous to departments, staffed by civil servants, which though not headed by, are under the control of a minister who is answerable for their actions in Parliament. They include the Royal Mint, the Stationery Office, and the Meteorological Office. In 1967 the Fulton Committee[9] argued that more efficient and accountable management of the civil service would be achieved by hiving-off a number of the executive activities undertaken by departments. Nothing came of this. But a more recent report[10] contended, again, that since much of the work of the civil service concerns the delivery of services rather than policy formulation, a number of such services could with benefit be hived off. As much as 95% of civil service work involved service delivery or executive functions and was eligible for hiving-off, leaving a small core of civil servants engaged in policy advice to ministers. The government agreed that to the greatest possible extent executive as opposed to policy functions should be carried out by Agencies. A considerable part of the work of departments is now carried out through these

7 *Relations between Central Government and Local Authorities* HMSO, 1977, p 21. For reference to departments as persons separate from other departments see Data Protection Act 1984, ss 38 and 41.

8 Under the Transport and Works Act 1992 the Secretary of State may be that for Transport, for the Environment, for Trade and Industry or for Wales depending on the subject matter and location of the order being sought. All applications for orders are dealt with by a unit in the Department of Transport.

9 Cmnd 3638 (1967).

10 'Improving Management in Government: The Next Steps' HMSO, 1988. And now, 'The Next Steps Agencies Review' Cm 2111. Drewry in *The Changing Constitution*, 3rd edn, Jowell and Oliver.

Agencies and some two-thirds of all civil servants work in them. (It will be noted that no legislation or any other form of Parliamentary approval was needed.) They include the bodies mentioned above and the Patent Office, Driver and Vehicle Licensing Agency, Forensic Science Service, Land Registry, Highways Agency, Vehicle Inspectorate and Planning Inspectorate. The biggest is the Benefits Agency which administers social security benefits (worth £50bn annually) through a countrywide network of offices, and a staff of 65,000.

It is important to appreciate the relationship between Agency and Department. They are Agencies 'of' or 'in' the relevant Department; they are a way of organising the work of the department. Those who work in them are civil servants. Each Agency is headed by a Chief Executive (some of whom are appointed by open competition and perhaps with a performance-related element in their pay). The Chief Executive is the Accounting Officer and as such accountable to the Public Accounts Committee. The minister determines the Agency's policy and is answerable to Parliament for it but does not normally become involved in its day-to-day management. In each case a Framework Document will set out the Agency's financial and management structure and the Key Performance Indicators, for example in the case of the Benefits Agency, claims for various benefits are to be cleared in x days with y percentage accuracy.

An important aspect of the effect of these arrangements is the minister's obligations to answer to Parliament. Initially, when an MP wrote to the minister for information about something done by an Agency, instead of getting a reply from the minister he was merely told that the question had been referred to the Agency. The answer was placed in the House of Commons Library but not otherwise publicly available. This led to the disappearance of what had been information generally available about the activity of Departments. In response to widespread criticism replies are now published in Hansard in the usual way.

These Agencies are thus Departmental bodies – and are to be contrasted with Non-Departmental Public Bodies of which there is a large number, some of which are referred to below, such as ACAS, the Health and Safety Commission and Executive, and NHS Trusts. The work of these bodies, being *non*-Departmental is in some degree removed from Departmental responsibility.[11] The 'hiving-off' of Departmental work into Agencies may of course be a politically-convenient first step towards removing its work altogether from the public sector, that is to its 'privatisation'.

Body corporate or not?
It is convenient to mention at this point that some institutions of public administration – including some government departments – are incorporated; others are not.

---

11 See the annual *Public Bodies* HMSO. There are about 1,400 NDPBs; also 600 NHS bodies (p 25 below), and more than 3,000 organisations including grant-maintained schools, housing associations etc. More than 42,000 appointments are made.

We recognise the existence of Parliament or of the Minister of Health as instruments of government whether incorporated or not. The process of incorporation happens to be convenient in English law, particularly in relation to property, but it is by no means essential. The vesting of executive functions in an unincorporated committee of a local authority has no effect on the nature of its function, and the committee is as real a piece of machinery as the incorporated council.[12]

Most of the bodies mentioned in the rest of this chapter are incorporated because it is necessary or convenient, or thought to be desirable. But the Council on Tribunals,[13] for example is not: it does not need to be; much more important in its case is that its existence is required by and its functions are determined by, statute. The Criminal Injuries Compensation Board is not: again there was no need for it to be. The Criminal Justice Act 1988 provides for it to be, but that Part of the Act has not been brought into force, initially because it was in such administrative difficulties in coping with its work that to have activated the Act would have set it back even further. The Board and the scheme remain within the 'prerogative' with the advantage to the government, if not to victims of crime, of ease of changing the scheme. On the other hand the incorporation of governing bodies of schools was necessary to give protection to governors, who might otherwise be exposed personally to financial liabilities and was also convenient in respect of long-term contracts, which will now be with the body corporate rather than the unincorporated association which governors would otherwise have been.[14]

Local government

Referring first to the *structure* of local government. There has, over the past four decades been continual change; and the structure differs as between each of the regions of the UK – England, Northern Ireland, Scotland and Wales. Structure cannot be divorced from *function*: what functions is it desired that local authorities should perform (if any), and what structure is the most appropriate to the exercise of those functions? One of the perennial problems of local government structure has been whether a two-tier or single-tier system is to be preferred. In the former the country would be divided into areas called counties, each with a county council exercising certain functions over the whole county. Within the county would be a number of 'districts' each with a council exercising within its area certain other functions. The thinking is that certain functions (say fire service or police) can only be exercised over the larger (county) area, whereas others (say housing) can be exercised over the smaller. Where related services are in different hands as a result of this split between the two levels, difficulties are likely to arise. In a single-tier

12 J D B Mitchell *The Contracts of Public Authorities*, p 14. For provision treating each House as body corporate see Copyright, Designs and Patents Act 1988, s 167.
13 See p 170 below.
14 Education Reform Act 1993, s 238.

system, the country would be divided into 'districts' each district council exercising the totality of functions exerciseable by local government; such bodies are referred to as 'all-purpose' or 'unitary' authorities. This too has its difficulties; in particular, areas may not be large enough to provide services efficiently, and joint working arrangements may be required: these have their own problems.

Another question is whether there ought to be uniformity over the region, say England, as a whole, or whether a distinction is necessary as between predominantly rural areas and metropolitan areas.

The connection between politics and structure is not to be overlooked. When central government is considering changing local government structure (through legislation) and deciding on the boundaries of each authority, the possible impact of such changes on party-political control of each authority will not be far from its mind (though this will not of course be mentioned in the justification it gives for the changes it proposes).

The present structure of local government in England was created by the Local Government Act 1972, but amended by later legislation. Major changes have been made, and are being made. Wales and Scotland have unitary authorities only, but England will have a mixture of two-tier and unitary authorities.

Local authorities it will be noted, are multi-functional. In addition to functions already mentioned there are highways, libraries, education, refuse collection, recreation, consumer protection and town and country planning. A local authority's power to operate these services is conferred not by the Local Government Act 1972, but by the relevant statutes dealing, separately, with those services. The powers differ widely from one statute to another. Each has to be examined to see what is the extent of the authority's power and the procedure to be followed in any particular case. A classification of importance is that between the service-providing functions on the one hand (eg libraries, highways) and regulatory functions on the other, of which the most prominent example is the development control function in town and country planning, that is, the determination of applications for permission to develop land. They exercise many other licensing functions.

Each local authority is a body corporate, created by statute. It can be dissolved only by statute, not by ministerial edict, nor by the will of its members. Each authority has a legal personality of its own, separate from that of every other authority. 'Local government' is not a unity in the sense that central government is, operating as an emanation from the Crown.

As statutory corporations, local authorities are affected by the *ultra vires* rule. That is to say they can in law do only those things they are permitted by statute to do. Anything else is ultra vires, beyond their powers. They cannot of course do those things they are expressly prohibited by statute from doing. In particular, the spending of money has to be shown to be justified as being in the pursuance of a statutory function. A large part of administrative law consists of the application of the ultra vires doctrine and is dealt with later, so there is no need to say much about it here. But as it applies to local authorities, it is sometimes seen as inhibiting them from doing what they wish to do in the interests of the inhabitants of their area. It seems that the idea that a local authority exists to advance the general welfare of its area may flow from the facts that it is an elected body, and that it is multifunctional. That is not however the statutory remit of a local authority: its job is to carry out the various functions required or permitted by statute.[15]

In addition to powers conferred on them by public general statutes, individual local authorities have obtained private Acts of Parliament conferring further powers on them.[16] There is a large number of such Acts and the likelihood of their existence must always be taken into account in any particular case.

Politically, the single most important fact about local authorities is that their members are elected by the population at large. Those Ministers appointed from the (elected) members of the House of Commons, and members of local authorities constitute the only elected element in our system of public administration (disregarding for this purpose the elected members of the European Parliament). Central and local government are also the only institutions with taxing powers: the connection between election and the grant of taxing power needs no emphasis. (In *Daymond v South West Water Authority*[17] the majority was influenced in its refusal to uphold a sewerage charge by the fact that the defendant was an ad hoc *un*elected body.) The fact that a local authority consists of elected members is also relevant in the context of judicial review.

The significance of local authorities' taxing powers was referred to by the (Layfield) Committee on Local Government Finance.[18] The Committee noted the advantages of local government: local authorities are the means by which people can take part in decisions concerning the services and amenities in their own area; local government therefore has a value in its own right in promoting democracy; by providing a large number of points where decisions can be taken by people of different political persuasion it acts as counterweight to the uniformity inherent in government decisions – it enhances accountability, promotes the effective use of resources by enabling their provision to be adjusted to local needs, and provides scope for local discretion in many fields, such as education. But, said the Committee, this role depends on local authorities being able to raise their own taxes. 'A body operating within a fixed budget [ie fixed by central government] may have delegated to it a good deal of discretion over the way money is spent but the limits of that delegation are set by whoever is providing the money.'[19]

For centuries the local government tax consisted of a levy calculated by reference to the rateable value of property occupied by the taxpayer. The 'rate' was an amount expressed as so many pence in each £ of rateable

15 See further p 206, below.
16 For private Acts see p 56.
17 [1976] AC 609, [1976] 1 All ER 39.
18 Local Government Finance (Cmnd 6453).
19 Ibid, pp 52, 53, paras 12–17.

value, that value being fixed by officials of the Inland Revenue. In 1988 *domestic* rating was abolished and replaced by the unmanageable and inequitable tax, the 'community charge', or poll tax as it was popularly known, and correctly – as the principle was that everyone paid the same. In the face of widespread protests the tax was replaced by the 'council tax' which, based as it is on the valuation of property, is a modified form of the rating system. *Non-domestic* rates are payable by occupiers of non-domestic property according to a national rate poundage (the 'uniform business rate') set by the government. This tax is collected by the local authority but accounted for entirely to central government which then distributes it to local authorities in proportion to their population.

Local authorities' income is thus derived directly from the council tax and from payment for its services. This is only a small proportion of the income it needs to pay for the services it provides; the balance is made up by grants from central government – so much so that central government now controls 80 per cent of all local government revenues through the 'revenue support grant' and the redirection of the business rate. The amount of grant to each authority is determined through the use of the 'standard spending assessment', that is, the assessment by government of the money needed to provide the appropriate level of service. This is calculated on the basis of certain 'indicators' such as the number of children of primary school age, the number of elderly people, the road mileage, unemployment, homelessness. This 'assessment' is also used to set a maximum which an authority's budget may not exceed, (the 'cap') thus limiting the amount which those liable to pay council tax can be required to pay.

Local authorities need to borrow money, particularly for works of a permanent nature. Generally speaking, they can do so only for purposes approved by the Secretary of State, and in accordance with any conditions laid down.[20] This 'loan sanction' was originally devised to ensure that authorities adhere to principles of sound finance: it can also be and is used as part of government's management of the economy.

It has been said that assumptions of guidance and control by central over local government pervade all areas of local government operations.[1] It is widely agreed that central government financial controls over local government put it in a more inferior position than it has ever been, and has had the effect of undermining its important contribution to the democratic process. Other long-standing and more specific techniques of control include the power to give directions to individual authorities, to declare them to be in default, the need for central government consent to certain acts and the approval of certain appointments, the right to hear an appeal by a person aggrieved by a local authority decision, and so on. Two points must be emphasised, first, that the degree and method of control differs from one service to another so that the relationship between central and local government is quite different in education from what it

20 Local Government Act 1972, Sch 13. For control by Ombudsman and Audit see ch 16.
 1 Buxton *Local Government*, p 60. Loughlin 'The restructuring of central–local government relations' in *The Changing Constitution* 3rd edn, Jowell and Oliver.

is in housing, for example. The second point is that central government intervention in the affairs of a local authority is determined by statute, and is legally valid only in so far as it falls within the powers given by the statute to central government.[2]

A further recent development in local government is to be noticed, that of 'compulsory competitive tendering', which requires authorities to put out to tender a wide range of its services. The ideology here is that a local authority is to provide services only if it can do so more cheaply than anyone else. Local authorities are thus being put in a position that they will no longer provide services themselves but through the agency of the successful tenderers, thus becoming 'enabling' councils. The parallel with the purchaser/provider split in the NHS, and with Executive Agencies of government departments providing services through the 'contract' of the Framework Document (noted above) will be seen.

Problems on reorganisation
On the transfer of an undertaking, not only on the reorganisation of local government, but of other organs of public administration, provision will have to be made by statute for the transfer of rights and liabilities. These can give rise to legal disputes. For example, was a loss of employ-ment attributable to reorganisation?[3] Was continuity of employment preserved?[4] Was the employee's position worsened by it?[5] Was a duty to consult still alive?[6] Did liabilities transferred include potential and inchoate liabilities as well as causes of action existing at the date of reorganisation?[7] Did obligations transferred include an undertaking given to the court?[8] Could a successor council determine what use had been made of premises by its predecessor?[9] Where a council's water undertaking was transferred to a water authority and later privatised what beneficial interest if any did the council retain in the assets?[10]

The national health service

The creation of a national health service[11] was provided for by the National Health Service Act 1946. (The current legislation is in the National Health Service Act 1977, as amended, especially by the National Health Service and Community Care Act 1990.) Section 1 of that Act imposed on the Minister of Health the duty to promote the establishment of a 'compre-hensive health service', and for that purpose to provide or secure the

2 See eg p 259 below.
3 *Walsh v Rother District Council* [1978] 3 All ER 881, [1978] ICR 1216.
4 *West Midlands Residuary Body v Deebank* [1990] ICR 349.
5 *Tuck v National Freight Corpn* [1979] 1 All ER 215, [1979] 1 WLR 37.
6 *Sinfield v London Transport Executive* [1970] Ch 550, 2 All ER 264.
7 *Walters v Babergh District Council and Andrews* (1984) 82 LGR 235.
8 *Re British Concrete Pipe Association's Agreement* [1983] 1 All ER 203.
9 *Sheffield Area Health Authority v Sheffield City Council* [1983] 2 All ER 384.
10 *Sheffield City Council v Yorkshire Water Services Ltd* [1991] 2 All ER 280.
11 Not a phrase used in the legislation, apart from the short title.

effective provision of certain services. Part II of the Act dealt with the provision of hospital services. The duty of providing hospital accommodation and the medical and nursing services required there was put on the minister. Accordingly the then existing hospitals were, by the Act, transferred to him. It was thought best however not to leave the local administration of these Part II services in his hands, so the Act required him to constitute Regional Hospital Boards for the purpose of administering those services within their respective areas. Each Board had to appoint Hospital Management Committees for the purpose of exercising certain functions with respect to the management of individual hospitals or a group of hospitals. By section 12 of the Act the Boards administered Part II services 'on behalf of the minister', and the Committees managed and controlled its hospitals 'on behalf of the Board'.[12] (Outside this structure were the 'teaching' hospitals, each run by a Board of Governors, acting on behalf of the minister.)

The NHS was reorganised in 1980 and again in 1990. The position now is that in England and Wales[13] District Health Authorities are responsible for providing certain services in their areas; in England there is also a tier of Regional Authorities with responsibility for planning those services best administered on a wider, regional, basis. Both types of authority are bodies corporate. They are financed almost entirely out of general taxation raised by central government and allocated by it to them.

The legal relationship between the three tiers – Secretary of State, Regional Health Authorities (RHAs) and District Health Authorities (DHAs) – is that the Secretary of State may direct RHAs to exercise on his behalf such of his functions relating to the health service as are specified in the direction, and it is the duty of the RHAs to comply with the directions. Such directions, containing a long list of functions identified by reference to specific statutory provisions, have been made.[14] The regulation in question goes on to provide that every RHA is to secure by written directions, that every DHA within its region shall, in turn, exercise such of the RHA functions as have been delegated to it, the RHA, by the Secretary of State, as are delegated to it, the DHA, by the RHA. So there is a delegation of certain (not all) of the Secretary of State's functions to RHAs, and a further delegation by it to DHAs.

As for finance, it is the duty of the Secretary of State to pay, in respect of each financial year, to each RHA etc 'sums not exceeding the amount allotted ... by him to the Authority for that year towards meeting their expenditure attributable to the performance by the Authority of their functions in that year'.[15] (It is in turn the duty of the RHA to pay the

12 In *Re Buzzacott* [1953] Ch 28, [1952] 2 All ER 1011 a testamentary gift to a hospital was to fail if its funds came 'under government control'. Gift failed as hospital was in NHS at time of death. But where a gift was not to be made if hospital was 'entirely under control or management of the state or a government department' it did not fail as the NHS hospital was not 'entirely' under that control. (Times 10 June 1972, news item.)
13 For Scotland see National Health Service (Scotland) Act 1978 as amended. For Northern Ireland see SI 1972/1265 (NI 14).
14 SI 1991/554 as amended.
15 National Health Service Act 1977, s 97.

necessary sums to the DHAs.) It is then the duty of the RHA in respect of each financial year 'so to perform their functions as to secure that the expenditure attributable to the performance by the RHA [and the DHAs whose districts are in their region] of their functions in that year does not exceed' the amounts allotted to it. In other words, they must keep within their allotted budget. The Secretary of State may give 'such directions ... as appear to him requisite' to ensure that they do so.

The constitutional status of the bodies managing the hospital service was considered in a number of cases in varying contexts. In *Pfizer Corpn v Minister of Health*,[16] the question (of patent law) was whether drugs supplied to hospital patients were used 'for the services of the Crown.' The House of Lords held, by a majority, that they were. The duty to provide hospital services is put by the legislation on the minister, that is, the Crown. The (then) Regional Hospital Boards (and Hospital Management Committees below them) expressly acted on the minister's behalf. They were therefore providing Crown service and their employees were Crown servants. It was argued that the phrase 'for the services of the Crown' meant for the Crown's *own* purposes and benefit, but the House of Lords rejected the idea that a thing is not used 'for' the services of the Crown if it is used by the government for the fulfilment of duties laid on it by the legislation creating the Ministry of Health, the purpose of which was the promotion of the health of the people of England and Wales. This decision was in respect of the hospital bodies as they existed in 1965: it continued to apply to RHAs and DHAs.

An argument on which *Pfizer* put considerable reliance was based on section 13(1) of the National Health Service Act 1946. This stated that RHBs (etc);

shall, notwithstanding that they are exercising functions on behalf of the Minister ... be entitled to enforce any rights acquired, and shall be liable in respect of any liabilities incurred (including liabilities in tort), in the exercise of these functions in all respects as if the Board ... were acting as a principal, and all proceedings for the enforcement of such rights of liabilities, shall be brought by or against the Board ... in their own name.

The argument was that this showed that the Boards exercised their functions as principals and not as agents for the minister. It does not say this. Rather it asserts that they do act on behalf of the minister, but says that as far as legal liability and litigation is concerned they are to be treated as if they were principals – 'as if' because they are not really that, merely deemed for that purpose to be so. Diplock LJ pointed out that at the time the Act became law, you could not as of right sue the Crown – the Crown Proceedings Act which gave that right was of the following year, 1947. The purpose of section 13(1) was therefore to make it possible to sue the Boards as of right even though they were Crown bodies.[17]

16 [1965] AC 512, [1965] 1 All ER 450. See Foulkes (1964) 114 NLJ 703, (1965) 115 NLJ 689, 903.
17 But such proceedings are not proceedings against the Crown for the purpose of the Crown Proceedings Act 1947, s 21: *British Medical Association v Greater Glasgow Health Board* [1989] AC 1211, [1989] 1 All ER 984.

Despite the Crown Proceedings Act 1947 the provision in question has been carried through succeeding NHS legislation and is currently to be found in the National Health Service Act 1977 (Sch 5, para 15).

The status of health authorities was in issue in an important sex discrimination case decided by the European Court of Justice, *Marshall v Southampton and South-West Hampshire Health Authority.*[18] M was employed by the AHA. She relied on an EC directive in arguing that her dismissal at the age of 62 was unlawful. A directive applies only to states. Was the AHA to be treated for this purpose as 'the state'? In referring the matter to the European Court the Court of Appeal stated that the AHA was 'an emanation of the state.'

Health Authorities as Crown bodies, and their hospitals as Crown property, were exempt from legislation that does not apply to the Crown. Following outbreaks of disease at hospitals the National Health Service (Amendment) Act 1986 applied 'food legislation' and 'health and safety legislation' to those Authorities. However, section 60 of the National Health Service and Community Care Act 1990 now provides that 'health service bodies' (which includes health authorities) are no longer Crown bodies. Some exceptions remain, including the point of patent law in issue in *Pfizer.*[19]

NHS Trusts
The National Health Service and Community Care Act 1990 made important structural changes to the NHS. To be noted first is the creation of 'NHS Trusts'. Section 5 of the Act provides that the Secretary of State may by order establish NHSTs whose function is to assume responsibility for the ownership and management of hospitals (or other establishments or facilities) previously managed by RHAs or DHAs (or to provide and manage hospitals etc). Facilities owned by a NHST are thus taken out of the ownership of the Secretary of State and of the management of the RHA and DHA. They have thus 'opted-out' of the Secretary of State→ RHA→DHA system of ownership and management. Precisely what property, rights and liabilities are to be transferred to a NHST on its creation is determined by ministerial order. Each NHST is a body corporate, and not a Crown body. It has a 'board of directors' consisting of a chairman and non-executive and executive directors, the former group appointed by the RHA or the Secretary of State, the latter by the NHST itself, being its employees. There are of course provisions in the Act for the transfer of staff to a NHST.

A NHST is required to carry out its functions 'effectively, efficiently and economically;' it must achieve the financial objectives set for it by the

18 [1986] QB 401, 1986] 2 All ER 584.
19 Some pre-1990 Act cases: In *R A Cullen Ltd v Nottingham Health Authority* (1986) 2 BCC 99 368 CA, NHA owed C £x. C owed Dept of Health more than £x. Held applying *Pfizer*, Crown was indebted to C, C was indebted to Crown; set-off therefore possible. *Linden v Dept of Health and Social Security* [1986] 1 All ER 691, a landlord and tenant case. For status of hospital staff as Crown servants see *Wood v Leeds Area Health Authority* [1974] ICR 535.

Secretary of State; it must ensure that 'its revenue is not less than sufficient, taking one financial year with another, to meet outgoings properly chargeable to revenue account.' It can acquire and dispose of its property (including land) and employ staff on such terms as it thinks fit (thus other than on terms agreed, nationally or otherwise, for other NHS staff). It can carry out its functions jointly with a Health Authority, another NHST, or with a private organisation. The Secretary of State can give it directions on a considerable range of matters; and it must submit an annual report to him. A NHST can be dissolved by ministerial order. In sum, apart from that last point, NHSTs are very like the boards which run nationalised undertakings, as will be seen in the next section, and are thus well structured for being sold off to private profit-making concerns of whatever national origin.

A high proportion of NHS hospital facilities are now provided by NHSTs which total about 500. Before they were created that provision was by DHAs (under their delegated powers). What then is the role of the DHA now? It is to decide what NHS services are needed in their area, and to procure them (not provide them themselves), by 'buying' them from NHSTs. DHAs are funded for that purpose, by the Secretary of State as before, but now on the basis of the weighted resident population of their area, not, as before on the basis of the services they provide. NHSTs get their money by 'selling' their services to whomsoever they can, including probably the DHA in whose area the NHST is located. This 'buying' and 'selling' within the NHS is by means of 'NHS contracts': see p 459.

As to RHAs they are, at the time of writing, in the process of being reduced in number (by statutory instrument) with the intention of being wholly abolished (for which legislation is necessary). Within the Department of Health itself the NHS is subject to the Secretary of State, managed by the NHS Executive a wholly Departmental and non-statutory and non-corporate body.

It must be emphasised at this point that section 1 of the National Health Service Act 1946, as re-enacted in the Act of 1977, is still in force, so that the duty set out in that section, noted above, is still on the Secretary of State.

General Medical Services
Nothing has been said so far about the provision of general medical etc services that is other than in hospitals, for example by 'family doctors'. The present position is that it is the general function of Family Health Services Authorities 'to administer the arrangements for the provision of general medical, dental, ophthalmic and pharmaceutical services for their locality'.[20] FHSAs are set up by ministerial order (in general one for each county). A FHSA consists of a chairman appointed by the Secretary of State and nine other members appointed by the RHA including four from specified medical and other interests. It is subject to directions from the RHA. It is not a Crown body.

20 National Health Service Act 1977, s 15, as amended.

Notice that the FHSA's duty is not to *provide* the services in question, but to 'administer the arrangements' for their provision. Specifically it is its duty to 'arrange with medical practitioners [etc] to provide personal medical services for all persons in the locality who wish to take advantage of the arrangements.' (Notice: 'who wish to take advantage'; patients are not obliged to use the NHS; nor are doctors obliged to be employed in it – it is not a monopoly.) What happens is that a general medical (etc) practitioner who wishes to be employed in the NHS applies to the appropriate FHSA for inclusion on the list kept by it, and if he meets the qualifications, he may be accepted. The arrangements between him and the FHSA including his 'terms of service' are set out in detail in a statutory instrument (thus in a ministerial, not FHSA, document) – for example, his duty to attend a patient, to keep records, his responsibility for anyone acting as his deputy, his entitlement to fees etc. The legal relationship between the practitioner and his FHSA has been considered by the House of Lords in *Roy v Kensington, Chelsea and Westminster FPC*[1] but is more appropriately considered in a later chapter.

Another ideological construct to be found in the NHS & CC Act 1990 (at section 14 onwards) is that of the *fund-holding practice*. General medical practitioners may apply to the RHA for recognition as a fund-holding practice (FHP); regulations lay down the conditions that have to be met. Where a FHP is approved the RHA pays it an annual sum of money, determined in accordance with ministerial regulations. With that money the practice buys goods and services 'necessary for the proper treatment of individuals on the lists of patients ...' Certain nursing or health visitor services must be 'bought' from a health authority or a NHST by means of a 'NHS contract' (referred to above); otherwise they may be bought from where they can be obtained at the price the FHP is prepared to pay; choice may of course be limited or non-existent. FHPs can renounce their status or it may be removed. Practitioners not in FHPs continue as before to seek appropriate facilities for their patients.

Thus DHAs and FHSAs are both 'commissioning agents'. Collaboration between them seems desirable, and some do collaborate through setting up non-statutory 'joint commissions'. It appears to be the intention to merge DHAs and FHSAs; legislation will be necessary.

Community Health Councils do not provide health services, but exist within the area of each DHA to represent the interests in the health service of the public in its district.

There is, it will have been noted, no local democratic ie elected, involvement in the bodies mentioned. Local (elected) authorities provide certain services which are an important influence on the health of the people. Joint commissioning by local authorities and health authorities, or commissioning of health services by local authorities are developments that are foreseen in some quarters.

1   [1992] 1 AC 624, [1992] 1 All ER 705.

The nationalised industries

Many formerly 'nationalised' industries and undertakings have been recently 'privatised' or are about to be. It is nevertheless important to understand the place in public law of such organisations, how they were created, and how they were dismantled.

The phrase 'nationalised industries' is not a term of art. It is a phrase commonly used to encompass industries which may be said to have been brought (in ways to be described) into 'public' or 'national' ownership by being vested in bodies corporate directed by persons appointed by a minister, and who have to manage the industry within a statutory framework of obligations to the minister, who in turn is accountable to Parliament for his decisions in relation to them. It is in that sense that industries may be said to have been 'nationalised'.

The organisations falling under that rubric include the British Railways Board, British Coal (formerly the National Coal Board), London Regional Transport and the Post Office.

The constitution of each organisation, its functions, duties and powers, depends on its own constituent statute. (Contrast local government.) One thing they have in common is that they are none of them Crown bodies.[2] It is clear that the boards running the nationalised industries are subject to the ordinary law of the land, civil and criminal. A common form provision is as follows:

For the avoidance of doubt it is hereby declared that the foregoing provisions of this section relate only to the capacity of the Post Office as a statutory corporation, and nothing in those provisions shall be construed as authorising the disregard by it of any enactment or rule of law.[3]

The legal framework

The body corporate created by the nationalisation statute may be named Board, Corporation, Authority etc. For convenience we refer to it as the board. One or more boards may be created to run the industry. In deciding the structure of each industry, account is taken of technological, economic and managerial factors. For example, when the gas industry was nationalised by the Gas Act 1948, the technological state of the industry was such that it was thought right to put responsibility for production and distribution of gas in the hands of the twelve statutory Area Gas Boards. There was a national body, the Gas Council, but it had virtually no operational functions: ownership and management were at area level. As new sources of supply and techniques became available this structure became outdated and a move towards the centralisation of the industry came with the Gas Act 1965. This was completed by the Gas Act 1972 by which the area boards were dissolved and their assets and liabilities transferred to the national body, renamed the British Gas Corporation.

2 See p 15 above.
3 Post Office Act 1969, s 7(3).

The technology of the electricity industry required a different structure. The Electricity Act 1947 provided for a central Authority generating electricity and selling it to (statutory) Area Boards confined to distributing it to customers. In the coal industry on the other hand there were good reasons why from the beginning the National Coal Board should have been the only statutory and corporate body.[4]

It has been observed that in many of the nationalised industries 'there has been a remarkable series of changes of structure within the last twenty years each with its Act of Parliament ... It is wise to set up the constitution so that change can easily be made within the organisation and without legislation.[5]

Technique of nationalisation
We come now to the technique of nationalisation. The method chosen depends on the pre-nationalisation structure of the industry in question. The way the coal industry was nationalised was that the Coal Industry Nationalisation Act 1946 transferred the *relevant physical assets* of the coal companies – their coal interests, brickworks, houses etc – to the National Coal Board, and the *companies* were compensated for the loss of their property. The shareholdings were not interfered with. The companies had other interests such as shipping which it was not desired to disturb, hence the technique not of taking over the companies as a whole but of plucking out their coal assets.

Before nationalisation gas was provided partly by local authority gas undertakings and partly by gas companies. Local authority *undertakings* vested in the Area Boards. The local authorities were not compensated for the loss of their undertakings, but the Boards took over the cost of servicing any loans raised by the authorities for gas purposes. As for the companies supplying gas, the Act provided that the *whole of their property* rights, liabilities and obligations vested in the appropriate Board, and for their dissolution on such vesting of the companies. The shareholders were given compensation. On the nationalisation of steel in 1950 on the other hand, a different technique was used.[6] The *shares* of certain key steel-making companies were transferred to a public corporation which thereby acquired control over the companies by becoming their sole shareholder. (The shareholders were compensated for the loss of their property, not the companies which had not of course lost anything. Compensation was usually calculated on the basis of the Stock Exchange valuation on certain dates before the announcement of the proposed nationalisation.)[7]

The problem was different where 'nationalisation' took the form of removing certain responsibilities from a government department and transferring them to a corporation of the kind now being considered. (This

4   See First Annual Report of the National Coal Board.
5   R Clarke *New Trends in Government*, p 75.
6   Iron and Steel Act 1949.
7   For challenge to legality of compensation terms, see *Yarrow v UK* ECHR 30 DR 155 (1983).

was hardly 'nationalisation' as the activity was already a Crown function.) Thus in the case of the Post Office, the Post Office Act 1969 abolished the ancient ministerial office of Master of the Posts (Postmaster General), created as a new public authority the 'Post Office' and gave it the former ministerial function of providing postal, telecommunications and other services, and created a new ministerial office of Minister of Posts and Telecommunications to exercise control over the Post Office.[8] Likewise in the case of atomic energy, responsibility for it was originally within a department. In 1954 the Atomic Energy Authority took over some of those responsibilities.[9] The Authority's work in the military defence programme necessarily involved it in commercial production activities. In 1971 those activities were hived off to British Nuclear Fuels Ltd and to the Radiochemical Centre Ltd. In 1973 the Authority weapons research establishments were transferred back to departmental responsibility.[10]

In 1965 the British Airports Authority was created to operate the four international airports previously managed by a government department.[11] In all these cases – Post Office, atomic energy, airports – the operations were taken away from the Civil Service as that was thought not to provide the most suitable conditions for their success.

Board membership

The nationalisation statute which created the body corporate which was to run the industry also provided for the appointment of the chairman and members of the board by, invariably, the minister. Board members were not elected either by the public at large or by affected interests such as local authorities, trade unions or consumer organisations. Nor was Parliamentary approval required. Nor were they appointed as representative of any specific interests. Members' pay is fixed by the minister with the consent of the Civil Service Department. Members are disqualified by the nationalisation statute from membership of the House of Commons. On appointment they are told what restraints on their political activities they are expected to observe. The circumstances in which a board member may be removed by the minister are specified in the legislation.

Board functions

Notice that the industry or undertaking is vested in the Board, and it is on it, not on the minister, that the obligation to run it is in law put. The boards will have such powers and duties as are conferred on or required of them by statute. There may be a general duty to run the industry efficiently: such a duty is unlikely to be enforceable in a court of law – the statute may expressly provide that it is not to be.[12] There will be other duties relating to various aspects of the bodies' activities. Particularly

8 See Foulkes 'The Post Office and its Services' [1980] Camb L Rev 11–13.
9 Atomic Energy Authority Act 1954.
10 Atomic Energy Authority (Weapons Group) Act 1973. See further Atomic Energy (Miscellaneous Provisions) Act 1981.
11 Airports Authority Act 1965.
12 The enforceability of duties is referred to in ch 6 below.

important are the boards' financial duties – the justification for regarding them as commercial undertakings will be found there if anywhere. The duty usually imposed is that the board must exercise its functions 'so as to secure that taking one year with another, the board's revenue is not less than sufficient to meet its outgoings chargeable to revenue account and to enable it to make adequate allocations to reserves.' A board subject to this duty – such as were the nationalised gas and electricity boards – is commercial in the sense that it is in the business of making or acquiring goods and selling its product and must ensure that it manages to 'break even': it is not commercial in the sense that its aim in life is to maximise its profits. The financial duties of some corporations could not even be ascertained from the statute. Thus the duties of the formerly nationalised British Aerospace and British Shipbuilders were 'such as may from time to time be determined by the Secretary of State with the approval of Treasury.'[13] A crucial point to an understanding of the constraints on the boards' freedom of (commercial) action is that they can borrow money only from or with the consent of the government: the government is their banker.

Being statutory corporations the boards are subject to the ultra vires rule, that is, they can do only those things that statute permits them to do and cannot do those things statute prohibits them from doing.[14] The boards' powers are expressed widely, so that the ultra vires rule is of little guidance: but here and there will be found specific prohibitions on activities that might have been thought to fall within a board's competence. There have been few challenges to the vires of these boards. (Indeed there has been very little litigation about the constitution and functions of these organisations: their problems have not been legal.)

The board and the minister

Nationalisation statutes invariably give ministers power to give directions to boards on specific matters, but also on general matters. The latter power is commonly expressed thus:

... to give directions of a general character as to the exercise and performance by the Board of their functions in relation to matters which appear to him to affect the national interest.

In addition to being subject to such power of direction, a board may be under an obligation to agree its programme of activities, either generally or in respect of particular activities, with the Secretary of State.

Very few general directions have been given to boards. The existence of the powers to give directions may be enough to ensure compliance with ministerial wishes. Thus in *Tamlin v Hannaford*[15] Denning LJ said that the power to give directions was 'lest they should not prove amenable to

13 Aircraft and Shipbuilding Industries Act 1977, s 10(1).
14 For ultra vires doctrine, see ch 7, below.
15 [1950] 1 KB 18, [1949] 2 All ER 327; and see p 16 above.

his [the Minister's] suggestions as to the policy they should adopt'. Clearly ministers do have, and ought to have, an influence over the boards commensurate with the responsibility which statute has put on them.

The form which nationalisation took was in fact an attempt to get the best of both worlds – the worlds of commercial management and of public responsibility. The former was to be achieved by giving the job of running the industry not to a government department but to a specialist board whose duty it is to seek within its statutory framework maximum commercial efficiency: the achievement of that efficiency was to be the board's contribution to the public interest. But a wider view of the public interest might require something other than efficiency. Accordingly the minister was given power to require the board to act otherwise than it might wish to do in pursuit of efficiency. Such a requirement would be contained in and could be ascertained publicly from a formal direction given by the minister to the board.

That that was the theory behind nationalisation could be inferred from a reading of the statutes. However, their wording is such that a wide range of relationships between minister and board was possible, and the tendency was for more rather than less ministerial intervention. Ministers can exercise a continuous and pervasive influence over the boards without the need to resort to directions.[16] Boards can be used as weapons of general economic policy as for example by being requested to hold down or put up prices, or to accede to or resist wage claims, contrary to their own commercial judgment.

The minister and Parliament

A related problem to that of the relationship between minister and board, and which also caused some difficulty, was that of the relationship between minister and Parliament.

Ministers are accountable to Parliament for matters that fall within their area of responsibility. Their responsibilities for nationalised industries are determined by the relevant statutes. From those it is clear that the legal responsibility for providing the goods or services in question is put on the appropriate board, not on the minister. What the minister is therefore accountable to Parliament for is the exercise of his powers in relation to the board, as for example where he fixes a limit on the board's borrowing powers ('external finance limits') as well as for a decision not to exercise a power available to him. But as a minister is not accountable for what he is not responsible for, he is not accountable for any matter of what is called the 'day-to-day management' of the industry. However, it was not always clear how far a board was acting in accordance with its own views or was influenced by informal ministerial suggestions which could of course be turned into formal directions if they were not complied

16 The Public Accounts Committee referred to the 'continuous intervention, with a daily dialogue' by ministers in the work of nationalised industries: Seventh Report from the Committee, 1983–84, HC 139, para 45.

with (a problem not confined to nationalised industries). If the relationship between minister and board was thus blurred, it was not possible to know who to praise or blame for the board's actions.[17]

Organs of the State

For the purpose of the enforcement of EC Directives a body is an organ of or to be identified with the state if it 'was made responsible, pursuant to a measure adopted by the state, for providing a public service under the control of the state and had for that purpose special powers beyond those which result from the normal rules applicable in relations between individuals'. Applying these criteria the nationalised British Gas Corporation, and bodies of the same status, were organs of the state (though not as we have seen, Crown bodies).[18]

The Bank of England

A note on the Bank of England is appropriate here as a nationalised undertaking. The Bank was incorporated by Royal Charter and statute in 1694; it was brought into public ownership, by the Bank of England Act 1946, by the transfer of its stock to a Treasury nominee (the stockholders were compensated). The Governor and Court of Directors were thenceforward appointed by the Crown. The Act further provides that the Treasury 'may from time to time give such directions to the Bank as, after consultation with the Governor of the Bank, they think necessary in the public interest'. This is the underlying basis of the Bank's legal subordination to the Treasury today. But from the very beginning the Bank stood in a special relationship to the government and it has been said that effectively the Bank had long ago ceased operating as a private institution.[19] In recent years there has been public discussion as to the desirability of the Bank being given 'independence'. Experience from other countries shows that there are several gradations of 'independence' possible for a central bank, which are closely linked with the question of political accountability. A possible position would be for the government to lay down the objectives of monetary policy, the means of achieving it to be left to the Bank, which would be accountable to government and Parliament for its actions. In the meantime the simple arrangement whereby the minutes of the monthly meeting between the Chancellor of the Exchequer and the Governor are now published, thus disclosing their respective views as to monetary policy, is regarded as significantly altering the balance of power between the two parties and constituting in effect a measure of independence.

17 For contemporary views see vol 29 Public Administration, p 317 (Citrine) vol 30, p 27 (Chester) p 71 (Vickers).
18 *Foster v British Gas plc* [1991] 2 AC 306, [1991] 2 All ER 705. *Fidge v Governing Body of St Marys* (1994) Times, 9 November.
19 Report of the Committee to Review the Functioning of Financial Institutions, Cmnd 7937.

Broadcasting authorities

The *British Broadcasting Corporation* (BBC) originated in 1922 in the British Broadcasting Company Ltd which was owned and controlled by private wireless firms. The creation of a public corporation to provide a public service was recommended by a committee of enquiry. The government decided that it would be inappropriate to create it by Act of Parliament for two reasons. First, that its activities would be strictly confined by the working of the Act, and if any changes were called for legislation would be necessary; second, that to do so would give the impression that it was 'a creature of Parliament and connected with political activity'. Nor, on the other hand, did the government think that it would be appropriate to create it as a registered company: if it had no capital, it would 'lack dignity', if it had capital, the government would have to hold the shares. The answer was to create it by Royal Charter, and that was what was done.[20]

It has no regulatory functions, that is, it does not regulate programmes provided by others; it itself provides the programmes except for a certain proportion it is now required to buy in. It is financed by the government, principally out of the licence fee payable by users of television sets.

The constitutional status of the BBC was considered in *British Broadcasting Corpn v Johns*.[1] The BBC claimed exemption from taxation on the ground that it was a body 'exercising within the province of government functions required and created for the purposes of government' ie that it was a Crown body. The Court of Appeal unanimously held that it is not. In the first place, the BBC operates under a licence under the Wireless Telegraphy Act 1904. The Court said that when Parliament came to deal in 1904 with the new activity of wireless communication, it did it by empowering the government to control wireless transmission and reception by a system of licensing: wireless telegraphy was thus treated in much the same way in which road traffic was treated after the invention of the internal combustion engine, or more recently, civil aviation. This, Diplock LJ pointed out, was in marked contrast with the way Parliament dealt with the transmission of messages *with* the use of wires, for there an 'exclusive privilege' was conferred on a minister (though he could license others to do so).[2] It was not the case therefore that a monopoly of wireless broadcasting had been given by statute to the Crown.

Secondly, the fact that a corporation is created by the exercise of Crown prerogative does not of itself make the corporation a Crown agent. Whether or not it is such depends on its relationship to the Crown. The BBC's charter states that the BBC's main object is to provide broadcast services in conformity with a *licence* to be acquired under the 1904 Act and with an *agreement* to be made with the minister. The BBC's obligation to provide services flows from the term of the licence and the agreement, breach of

20 H of C Official Report (5th series) col 448.
 1 [1965] Ch 32, [1964] 1 All ER 923.
 2 See Telegraph Act 1869, s 4, British Telecommunications Act 1981, s 12, but Telecommunications Act 1984, s 2 for repeal.

which could lead to revocation and a claim for damages. Willmer LJ thought that the imposition in this way – through a contractual relationship – of the BBC's obligation suggested that it is independent from and not a part of the government service. Diplock LJ said that the fact that the services are provided under the licence and agreement was not conclusive that the BBC was not a Crown agent: it would depend on the terms of the contract. He continued:

But I agree with my Lords that the licence and agreement is drafted so as to make clear and give effect to the intention of the parties that the broadcasting services are to be provided by the BBC as an independent contractor and not as agent for the executive government. It is true that it contains numerous provisions under which [the Minister] is entitled to exercise controls over the stations and transmissions of the BBC in their technical aspects, but so far as concerns general conduct and operation of their stations and the content of their broadcasts, the freedom of the BBC from the control of the executive government is scrupulously maintained.

Willmer LJ usefully contrasted the possible alternatives:

[Broadcasting] might have been left to be developed entirely by private enterprise … It might on the other hand have been specifically made a function of government … for instance by imposing a statutory duty on [a Minister] to organise a government broadcasting service. That was what was done in relation to certain aspects of the National Health Service, as was held by this court in *Pfizer Corpn v Ministry of Health*.[3] Had Parliament seen fit to deal with broadcasting in the same sort of way, it would no doubt have been made a function of government. Another possible alternative would have been to set up a public corporation like the British Transport Commission, with power to carry on broadcasting as a commercial enterprise; ie by entering into direct contractual relationship with those receiving the broadcasts. In fact none of these courses was taken.

A House of Commons Committee reported in 1969:

The powers of the government over the BBC are theoretically absolute … Even allowing for this self-imposed limitation [of permitting the BBC independence in its day-to-day management] the government's overall authority and powers of control remain very considerable.[4]

With regard to the commercial sector, there has been a succession of regulatory bodies – the ITA, the IBA, and now the *Independent Television Commission*. Its function is to regulate the provision of television programme services provided from places in the UK by persons other than the BBC and the Channel Four Authority. It awards licences to the highest bidder, subject to a 'quality threshold': this replaces the former 'programme contractor' system. It issues a code of guidance in respect of the depiction of violence, and of advertisements. The Channel Four Authority is, by virtue of the statute, licensed by the Commission.

The *Radio Authority* regulates sound broadcasting services. The members of all the bodies mentioned are appointed by the government.

3   [1965] AC 512, [1965] 1 All ER 450; see p 27, above.
4   Third Report from the Estimates Committee, 1968–9, HC 387.

The theoretically absolute government powers over the BBC have been noted. Likewise with regard to the former Independent Broadcasting Authority a House of Committee reported:

There is in fact considerable scope for Government direction and control ... There have been few occasions on which any of those powers have been invoked: but the IBA is very conscious that they are there, and is unlikely to provoke Government intervention in any of these areas.[5]

In 1988 the Home Secretary served notice on the IBA, under its statute, and on the BBC, under a clause of its licence and agreement, prohibiting the broadcasting of direct statements by representatives of proscribed organisations in Northern Ireland.[6]

The Advisory, Conciliation and Arbitration Service

This Service (ACAS) was created by the Employment Protection Act 1975. It succeeded the non-statutory Conciliation and Arbitration Service. ACAS is directed by a Council: the Council is a body corporate, the members of which are appointed by the Secretary of State, as to one-third representing workers, one-third employers, and one-third independents.

ACAS was given the 'general duty of promoting the improvement of industrial relations, and in particular of encouraging the extension of collective bargaining'.[7] Other more specific functions were conferred on it. (i) Where a trade dispute exists, it may offer the parties its assistance with a view to bringing about a settlement. This assistance may be by way of *conciliation* or by other means. ACAS must appoint conciliation officers for this and other purposes. (ii) ACAS may, on request, refer any matters arising out of a trade dispute for settlement to *arbitration*. (iii) It may offer *advice* to both sides of industry on any matter concerned with industrial relations. (iv) It may *inquire* into any question relating to industrial relations generally or in any particular undertaking. (v) ACAS issues *codes of practice* containing practical guidance for the purpose of promoting the improvement of industrial relations.[8] (vi) A 'recognition issue' may be referred by a trade union to ACAS. ('Recognition' means the recognition of a union by an employer for the purposes of collective bargaining.) Where such an issue is referred to it, ACAS is required to examine it, consult, and make appropriate inquiries, and prepare a written report setting out its findings, any recommendation for recognition and the reasons for it, or the reasons for not making any recommendation. In the course of its inquiries into a recognition issue, ACAS is to ascertain the opinions of workers to whom the issue relates by any means it thinks

---

5 Tenth Report from the Select Committee on Nationalised Industries, 1977–79 HC 637.
6 This censorship was challenged (but not by the broadcasting authorities) in *Brind v Secretary of State for the Home Department* .[1991] 1 AC 696, [1991] 1 All ER 720.
7 Employment Protection Act 1975, s 1(2).
8 For (i) to (v) see Employment Protection Act 1975, ss 2–6 respectively.

fit, including a formal ballot (in which case special procedural rules have to be observed).[9]

The *status* of the Advisory, Conciliation and Arbitration Service is of interest. The Employment Protection Act 1975 provides that 'the functions of the Service and of its officers and servants shall be performed on behalf of the Crown'.[10] This makes it a Crown body and may give it the look of a government service. But in view of its general duty of 'promoting the improvement of industrial relations', it was important to secure its independence from government. So the provision just quoted goes on to say, 'but ... the Service shall not be subject to directions of any kind from any Minister of the Crown as to the manner in which it is to exercise any of its functions under any enactment'. Further, although most or all of the 'officers and servants' of the Service are civil servants, the Service is directed by a Council the members of which are not. The Service is clearly not a government department (though for the purpose of any civil proceedings arising out of its functions it is to be treated as though it were). Thus, within the limits of the statute, the Service is autonomous in the discharge of its duty. 'In discharging this duty, the Service no doubt fulfils a public function, and in this, but only in this sense, it can be considered as part of the public administration.'[11]

Data Protection Registrar

The purpose of the Data Protection Act 1984 is to regulate the use of automatically-processed information relating to individuals and the provision of services in respect of such information. Very briefly (and selectively) the Act requires 'data users' (those who 'hold' 'data' as defined) to register with the Data Protection Registrar. The Registrar decides whether an application for registration is accepted or refused, and it is his duty to maintain the Register, entries in which are to contain the particulars specified in the Act.

An important feature of the Act for our purposes is the 'data protection principles'. They include the following:

(i)   Information to be contained in 'personal data' (that is data consisting of information which relates to a living individual who can be identified from the information) shall be obtained fairly and lawfully;

(ii) personal data is to be held only for specified and lawful purposes;

(iii) it is not to be used or disclosed in any manner incompatible with the purpose for which it is held;

(iv) it shall not be kept for longer than is necessary for the purpose for which it is held.

(The Act also contains rules for interpreting those principles.)

---

9 Ibid ss 11–14.
10 Employment Protection Act 1975, s 1(2).
11 Kahn-Freund *Labour and the Law* (2nd edn) p 78.

The significance of these principles is: it is the Registrar's duty so to perform his functions as to promote their observance; he may, and in some circumstances shall, consider any complaint that any of the principles has been contravened; it is his duty, where appropriate, to encourage trade associations to prepare codes of practice for guidance in complying with the principles; a reason for refusing registration is that the Registrar is satisfied that the applicant is likely to contravene any of the principles; if the Registrar is satisfied that a registered person has contravened any of the principles he may serve on him an 'enforcement notice' requiring him to take such steps as are specified. He may further serve him with a 'deregistration notice' stating that he proposes to remove the entry from the register.[12]

Registered companies

The registered company is a very flexible device. In this section we are concerned with its use in the public sector, particularly in connection with denationalisation.

Governing through the registered company. It is open to the government to create a registered company by simply following the generally available procedure laid down in the Companies Act. (Statutory authority is not necessary for this.) It may then, if it thinks it appropriate, arrange for some of its business to be carried on through the medium of the company as in the case of the student loans scheme under the Education (Student Loans) Act 1990.

Local authorities and the corporations running the nationalised industries can also create registered companies by following the same procedure, and both types of authority have done so. Being statutory bodies and therefore limited by the ultra vires rule, they can create registered companies only if expressly or impliedly empowered (or of course required) to do so. The powers of registered companies are determined by the objects clause of the company's memorandum of association, which is determined in the first place by those who form the company.[13]

Acquiring public control of a registered company. From what was said about the nationalisation of industries it will be appreciated that where it is desired to 'nationalise' a registered company this may be done by the government acquiring compulsorily or by agreement some or all of the shares of the company. For example Cable and Wireless Ltd had been created in 1929 through the merger of companies which owned submarine

12 For Data Protection Tribunal see p 148 below.
13 For companies controlled by, under influence of, and at arm's length from, local authority, see Local Government and Housing Act 1989, Pt V. For requirement that a local authority running an airport *shall* form a company for purpose of operating it as a commercial undertaking (a 'public airport company') see Airports Act 1986, Pt II; for vires see s 17(4), and for waste disposal company see Environmental Protection Act 1990, Sch 2 .

cables and telegraphic installations. In 1938 certain Post Office installations were transferred to the company in return for which the government
acquired some one-tenth of its share.[14] In 1946 the government acquired
the remainder of those shares.[15] The government had no specific powers
over the direction of the company – nor were any needed, for as the
government was (through Civil Service nominees) the sole shareholder it
could use the machinery of the Companies Act to get its way. In practice,
though the legal form was different, supervision over the company was
exercised on lines similar to those adopted for the nationalised industries.
However, it was said that the fact that the company was self-financing
led to a rather more detached relationship from the government. Cable
and Wireless was thus a case of an existing company being fully nationalised by the acquisition of its shares.

The acquisition of shares in British Petroleum was undertaken to
safeguard the national interest in securing fuel oil products for the Navy.
In 1914 the government acquired a majority shareholding in what was
then the Anglo Persian Oil Co (now BP), and the right to appoint two
directors. In the last two decades the government's shareholding was
gradually decreased, and from 1990 to 1994 it dropped from 32% of the
ordinary shares to 1.9%.

The device of the registered company has been used in rescue operations.
In 1971 Rolls-Royce Ltd were faced with financial collapse. The Conservative
government took the view that for reasons of defence and international
obligations, the company's aero-engine and related undertakings had to
be rescued. The Rolls-Royce (Purchase) Act 1971 authorised the acquisition
of those assets, and their operation by a publicly-owned company. That
Act did not contain compulsory powers, and the price paid for the assets
was negotiated. A new company, limited by shares, Rolls-Royce (1971)
Ltd, was formed by the government. (The memorandum of association
was subscribed to by two civil servants.) The company's main object was
'to acquire any part of the undertaking and assets of Rolls-Royce Ltd ...
and to carry on any undertaking so acquired'. Referring to the decision to
establish a limited liability company, the minister said, 'It follows ... that
the relationship of the new public organisation to ministers and to Parliament will be somewhat different from that of an ordinary nationalised
corporation. The exact degree of ministerial and Parliamentary control
over the affairs of the company will be determined largely by the provisions
of the memorandum and Articles of Association of the new company.'[16]

Registered companies, even if partially or wholly publicly owned
(through the 'public' ownership of their shares) are subject to the ordinary
rules of company law and procedure including for example those relating
to the appointment of directors, the publication of accounts, and fraudulent

14 Imperial Telegraphs Act 1938.
15 Cable and Wireless Act 1946.
16 H of C Official Report (5th series) col 814. In *Doughty v Rolls-Royce plc* [1992] ICR 538
   it was held that though all its shares were held by the Crown, it was not, for the purpose
   of an EC directive, an organ of the state carrying out a state function. See p 36 above.

trading. Special statutory exemption may be provided where the rules are thought inappropriate, as was the case with steel companies whose shares vested in the British Steel Corporation.[17]

Privatisation and the registered company. The Conservative governments elected since 1979 developed a programme of denationalisation, or privatisation. Just as there was various motives for nationalisation, so are there various motives for denationalisation. The former include the demands of technical efficiency, replacement of the private profit motive by consideration of social welfare, the desire to better the lot of the employees etc. The latter include the difficulties of ensuring accountability and control of the industries in question, leading to the view that efficient management of businesses in the public sector is impossible; and more fundamentally the view that 'public control is seen as illegitimate because political objectives are held to be less valid than market criteria'.[18]

When nationalisation or 'public ownership' consisted of the government holding all the shares in a registered company, some or all of those shares could be sold. Thus the government took power to sell its shares in Cable and Wireless Ltd[19] and sold half of them in 1981 declaring in the prospectus that it intended to retain a majority holding in the company for 'the foreseeable future'. In 1983 it allowed its holding to slip to less than 25 per cent and now holds only the 'special share' mentioned below. Likewise all the shares in Amersham International Ltd (the former Radio-chemical Centre Ltd)[20] were sold.

The principal or one might say, the conventional, technique of the main privatisation Acts was to provide by statute for the transfer of the assets of a public corporation managing a nationalised industry to a registered company, followed by the sale to the public of some or all of its shares. For example:

On the appointed day all the property, rights, liabilities and obligations to which British Aerospace was entitled or subject immediately before that day shall ... become by virtue of this section property, rights, liabilities and obligations of a company nominated for the purpose of this section by the Secretary of State ...[1]

Thus the British Gas Corporation became British Gas plc, and British Telecommunications became British Telecommunications plc and so on.

Where *all* the shares in a formerly public undertaking are sold to the public, no element of 'public ownership' remains (or rather one kind of 'public ownership' is replaced by another, where the shares are held by 'the public'). However, this has not always been done. In some cases the government decided to retain just under fifty per cent of the shares issued. What is then the government's relationship to the industry? A House of Commons Committee reported:

17 See Iron and Steel Act 1975, Sch 5; p 32, above.
18 Heald (1985) 63 Pub Admin 7.
19 British Telecommunications Act 1981, s 79.
20 See p 33, above.
 1 British Aerospace Act 1980, s 1.

The Department assured us that one of the purposes of flotation had been to ensure that British Aerospace operated in future as a private sector company with no special relationship with the government even though the government retained a forty-eight per cent shareholding. The shareholding conferred no special status on the company as a borrower in private sector markets and ordinary creditors had no ground for looking to the government should the company meet financial difficulties.[2]

When BT was privatised in 1984 the government initially held forty-nine per cent of the shares. This was gradually reduced so that by 1993 it was 1.5%.

Another relationship between government and industry in the context of the registered company is that created by the (£1) 'special share'. The rights it gave to the holder differed from case to case, depending on the interests sought to be protected. Certain matters might require the written consent of the holder; if the holder had voting rights his share could outvote all the other shareholders on certain matters, and so on.

The device of the government-appointed director (mentioned in connection with BP above) was used in some but not all cases (it was, for BT). Such directors have no special powers. Their obligations under company law are to the company and all its shareholders. It seems that current government policy is to relinquish the power to appoint such directors, and to abandon any 'special shares'.

Privatisation – other techniques

The above section referred to the conventional privatisation technique of transferring the assets of a public corporation to a registered company followed by the sale of its shares. Privatisation has other connotations and techniques; an act of privatisation may involve a combination of techniques, as in the case of the railways.

Privatisation of the railways, which is currently being brought about is, objectively, an interesting exercise (if absurd). Pre-privatisation British Rail (which still exists) owned and operated the railway system. The Railways Act 1993 distinguishes between the railway track itself and the services which run on it. The track and its associated facilities (signalling, stations etc) is now owned by *Railtrack*. This is a company formed by the government which is the sole shareholder and with the status of a nationalised industry. (This is not expressly provided for in the Act, but was set up under powers in the Act.) The government's intention is to sell off the company. With regard to railway services, a distinction is made between passenger and other services. With regard to the former: they were from 1994 the responsibility of 25 train operating companies (TOCs), subsidiaries of BR. From 1995 they will be offered to the private sector as franchises, probably for periods of 15 to 20 years. This will take some time to achieve. Some or all companies will receive government subsidies (as BR did). Franchisees will pay charges for use of the track; they will not own the locomotives and rolling stock they use: they are the property

2   Tenth Report of the Committee of Public Accounts, 1981–82, HC 189, para 16.

of three leasing companies owned by BR, until sold off. Tickets will be sold by TOCs, but more than one may use the same station with perhaps separate ticket booths. Stations will be operated by a TOC, normally the major user; the largest will become independent units, until sold off. Freight and parcel services are dealt with differently as it is said that the nature of their operations permits their transfer and sale to the private sector. This then is a highly fragmented structure, and complex legal arrangements are anticipated.

The 'market-testing' programme is as follows. Government departments have set up market-testing units with the job of identifying in each department what can be privatised, defining the criteria under which the private sector can tender for the work, and then if private sector involvement is thought appropriate, putting the plan into action. (An example is the £1bn deal with a subsidiary of the US firm General Motors for the computerisation of the records of the Inland Revenue.)

The possible privatisation of the work of Executive Agencies has been noted; as has compulsory competitive tendering; and the closure of Crown post offices and the transfer of their business to the private sub-post offices will be noted.

Where facilities are available in both public and private sector, the government can encourage the use of the latter by grants and tax allowances. And where there is a failure to provide adequate and efficient public services, those who are able to will turn to the private sector as in the fields of health, education and transport.

Regulatory bodies

The major public utilities, gas, electricity and water for example, have long been subject to various measures of public control and regulation, including public ownership.

Gas
The regime for the regulation of the industry is, in summary, this.[3] It is an offence for a person to supply gas through pipes unless authorised to do so (unless the supply does not exceed a certain amount). Where a person is authorised to supply gas to *any* premises in his area, he is a 'public gas supplier' but not if he is authorised to supply specific premises or classes of premises. It is the duty of such a supplier to develop and maintain an efficient, co-ordinated and economical system of gas supply, and to comply with any reasonable request to give a supply of gas to any premises. Detailed obligations on supplier and customer are set out in the Public Gas Supply Code. The standards of quality with which gas must comply – pressure, purity etc – are laid down by the Secretary of State. In all these matters a public gas supplier is under much the same obligations as the former British Gas Corporation and its predecessors. There is only one public gas supplier – British Gas plc which has thus a private monopoly

3   Gas Act 1986.

in domestic gas supply, replacing the public monopoly of its predecessor. (It is intended to remove the monopoly.)

The regulatory regime, as applied to the company, distinguishes between the tariff and contract sectors of the gas supply market. In view of the limited scope for competition associated with gas supply to consumers who take small quantities of gas, the tariff sector has been made subject to certain regulatory requirements, particularly a system of price control. In the contract sector the company is required to publish certain inform-ation on pricing, but otherwise is free to negotiate contracts, subject to general competition law. Any one has the right to apply to use a pipe-line belonging to a public gas supplier for the purposes of the conveyance of gas provided by him from his own sources for sale to his specific (industrial) customers. (This facility is being increasingly used.)

The Act provides for the appointment by the Secretary of State of a Director General of Gas Supply. (He heads a non-ministerial government department, staffed by civil servants.) Where the Director is satisfied that a public gas supplier is contravening certain of its obligations he is to make whatever order 'is requisite for the purpose of securing compliance' with that obligation. These obligations include the general duty to have an efficient etc system (above), the duty to avoid undue preference in the supply of gas to those entitled to demand a supply, and certain duties under the Supply Code (above). The Director General also decides on applications to use the public gas suppliers' pipe-line. He may also refer questions to the Monopoly and Merger Commissions. (British Gas has been required to make significant changes to its price schedules.)

The legislation also created the Gas Consumers' Council which is to investigate complaints and to advise the Director on certain matters.

Telecommunications

The regulatory regime of the industry is, in outline, this.[4] A person who runs a 'telecommunications system' within the UK commits an offence unless authorised by a licence to do so. A licence may be granted by the Secretary of State, or by the Director General of Telecommunications with the consent of the Secretary of State or in accordance with a general authorisation given by him. Where the licence includes conditions requiring the licensee to provide specified services, to permit the connection to it of other telecommunication systems, not to show undue preference nor to exercise undue discrimination against eg those living in rural areas, and to publish its scale of charges – then the licensee is a 'public telecommunications operator' and is subject to the 'telecommunications code' which gives the operator various powers, eg to install apparatus in streets. The operator can, subject to ministerial approval, compulsorily purchase land required for its operation. Price control is exercised through a condition in the licence.

4   Telecommunications Act 1984.

The Director is to exercise his functions in the way he considers is best calculated to secure that there are provided throughout the UK such telecommunications services as satisfy all reasonable demands for them, and to secure that any person providing these services is able to finance them. In particular he is concerned to promote the interests of consumers in respect of the price and quality of the services provided; to promote effective competition and efficiency and economy on the part of the providers of services, etc.

The Director's functions include the power to enforce licence conditions by order and to modify the terms of licence. He regulates, through approvals, contractors working on, and equipment that can be attached to, a telecommunications system and meters. He investigates complaints; and can require to be given, and can publish, information. An unusual power is that where proceedings are taken on a question arising out of the Code, the Director may, on an application of a party (other than a telecommunications operator) grant assistance to that party in respect of that proceeding. He may do this where the case raises a question of principle, or where it is unreasonable, given the complexity of the case, for the applicant not to have that assistance. The Act also provides for the establishment of Advisory Councils for each of the four countries of the United Kingdom.

There are currently 18 public telecommunications operator licences; the two major basic services are provided by British Telecomm-unications and Mercury owned by Cable and Wireless. A major piece of work for the Director was settling the exact rules by which the two networks are linked. (The interconnection of the two systems was necessary as it would be uneconomic if not impossible for a competitor – Mercury – to duplicate the BT network.) Over 1,000 other types of licences have been issued. BT is the only operator whose prices have to be approved by the Director General. These, in effect, impose a limit on what the others can charge.

The water and electricity industries are also subject to the control and oversight of their respective Director-General (all of whom have the same constitution and status as that for Gas Supply). These officers are clearly of the utmost importance to the economies of their industries and thus to the welfare of the country as a whole. The extent of their powers and the way they have been exercised, and the lack of accountability for their exercise are matters for criticism.[5]

Railways
Under the Railways Act 1993 no one can operate a 'railway asset' unless licensed to do so. (A 'railway asset' is any train, used for whatever purpose, station etc). Such a licence is granted by the Rail Regulator, who is appointed by the Secretary of State, or by the Secretary of State himself. The job of the Director of Passenger Franchising is to arrange for the

5   See McEldowney in *Constitutional Studies* ed Blackburn, on nationalisation and privatisation.

franchising of passenger services that is, for their provision through an agreement with the Director who decides whose bid is to succeed, the quality of service required etc. Because appointed by the Secretary of State, he must seek to meet the objectives given him by the minister, and act in accordance with his instructions and guidance. The Health and Safety Executive will be closely involved in safety of railway operations, with which franchisees may have had no experience.

Coal

The British Coal Corporation (BC), formerly the National Coal Board, closed most of its deep mines in pursuance of government policy. By the end of 1994 it had 17, together with (the more profitable) 42 open cast mines. They have now been sold.) A new (non-Crown) public body, the Coal Authority, has been created, its members appointed by the Secretary of State, who can give it 'directions of a general character'. Coal-mining operations are not to be carried out except in accordance with a licence granted by the Authority. BC, which had the exclusive right to get coal, could also licence private mines, and its interest in unworked coal vested in the Authority. As in the case of the railways, the Health and Safety Executive has a role in connection with safety in mines.

Prisons

The privatisation of prisons raises important questions. How is the coercive power of the state to be delegated to the private sector and controlled? The Criminal Justice Act 1991 provides for 'contracted-out prisons'. The Secretary of State may enter into a contract with another person for the running by him of a prison. That prison will be subject to the legislation relating to prisons; the contract will determine such things as the numbers of prisoners that may be held, facilities to be provided, the number of assaults permitted etc (financial details are 'commercially confidential' and withheld from public scrutiny). However, instead of a governor (on whom powers and duties are imposed by legislation) the prison has a director (appointed by the company subject to ministerial approval); he is not able to impose or mitigate any penalty – that is kept in public hands. Duties and powers are conferred on the company's prison employees – searching visitors for example. If the director loses control of the prison the minister can appoint a civil servant as governor, who then takes over the director's functions. There is also for each prison a controller, a Crown servant. His job is to keep under review and report to the minister on the running of the prison. He investigates and reports on any allegations made against a prison officer. These arrangements are contentious. One view is that the coercive powers of the state should not be contracted-out from the state to a profit-making company. The other view is what matters is the quality of the service provided, not who provides it: how far can one apply this argument to the police and the administration of justice?

Co-operation in public administration

The need for co-operation. Public administration is carried on by a large number of and different types of institutions. An example is the control of pollution. The machinery of pollution control has developed over the years in reference to new environmental hazards and to increased scientific awareness of their implications, and because of public concern at the potential effect on human health of various pollutants. At central government level a number of government departments are involved, the Department of the Environment, the Department of Trade, the Ministry of Agriculture and the Department of Health. The Health and Safety Commission, the National Rivers Authority and local authorities are also involved. Effective action clearly requires collaboration in many ways between these various bodies. Another problem requiring collaboration is the physical abuse of children (officially referred to as 'non-accidental injury to children'). Here the social services and education departments of local authorities, health service authorities, general medical practitioners, the NSPCC, the probation service and the police, and others, may be involved. Crime prevention generally requires inter-agency collaboration. In the case of a major prison riot co-operation may be required between the prison authorities (the Home Office), the police, the (local authority) fire brigade, and the army (the Ministry of Defence).[6] Effective consumer protection requires collaboration between the Office of Fair Trading and local authorities.[7]

What is the role of the law? It is to refrain from hindering and positively to facilitate a desirable co-operation between public authorities. A possible hindrance is the ultra vires doctrine. The activity of each authority is bounded by the ultra vires rule. However, it is not the case that boundaries between institutions are recognised by practical problems; nature knows nothing of the ultra vires doctrine. For there to be co-operation therefore each institution must have the power to do what is necessary to co-operate with others.[8] For example both Customs and Excise and Inland Revenue has its own enforcement powers granted by specific legislation. 'In general terms the legislation expects each Department to operate within its own powers and does not recognise that both Departments are revenue-collecting arms of the State.' However, specific enabling legislation has been introduced to provide for exchange of information between the two authorities.[9] But when customs officials are conducting a search, and are accompanied by police officers as a breach of the peace is feared, the members of each organisation are confined to its own powers.[10] And a report on the working of the Prevention of Terrorism (Temporary

---

6 See Report of an Inquiry into events at HM Prison Hull, 1976–7, HC 453.
7 Annual Report of the Director General of Fair Trading for 1982, p 10.
8 Consider vires of use of fire brigade hoses to dislodge rioting prisoners from roof: Report at fn 6 above.
9 Report on the Enforcement Powers of the Revenue Departments, Cmnd 8822, p 463.
10 Ibid, p 225.

Provisions) Act 1976 said, 'Liaison seemed satisfactory ... failings were on the whole institutional rather than personal; the [Police] Special Branch tended to feel that the Immigration Service was prevented by its basic statutory functions from being as helpful as it might be.'[11]

A duty to co-operate? While there is no general duty on authorities to assist one another there may be specific statutory duties to co-operate. Thus in exercising their respective functions health authorities and local authorities shall co-operate with one another in order to secure and advance the health and welfare of the people of England and Wales;[12] to that end joint consultative committees have to be appointed. Fire authorities have to make arrangements for mutual assistance to one another in dealing with fires.[13] Under Police Act regulations it is a condition of the Home Office grant that adequate co-operation is afforded by the police force to other police forces.[14] The police and members of the armed forces are under a duty to assist the Commissioners of Customs and Excise in the enforcement of the law.[15] The problem of ensuring proper housing for children requires co-operation between housing and social service authorities or, where both functions are exercised by the same authority, between its appropriate departments.[16] In the field of mental health a code of practice[17] says that good practice requires that health authorities, NHS Trusts and local social service authorities should co-operate in ensuring that regular meetings take place between the professionals concerned to promote understanding and provide a forum for the clarification of their respective responsibilities.

Some statutory provisions empower ministers to impose a duty on one authority to assist another as for example section 12 of the Post Office Act 1969 by which the minister can direct the Post Office to do certain work for departments and local authorities (for which payment is to be made). A ministerial direction was given to the Civil Aviation Authority[18] requiring it to collaborate with the Ministry of Defence in exercising its functions in providing air navigation services through a joint organisation.

One public authority may be able to require another to make facilities available to it; for example the Post Office has long been able to require the provision of railway services for the carriage of the mails.[19] There are many provisions enabling public authorities to use other authorities as agents in carrying out their functions. For example a local authority may arrange for the discharge of its functions by any other local authority, and local authorities may discharge their functions jointly acting, if needs

11 Cmnd 8803.
12 National Health Service Act 1977, s 22.
13 Fire Services Act 1947, s 2(1).
14 SI 1966/223.
15 Customs and Excise Management Act 1979, s 11.
16 *R v Northavon District Council ex p Smith* [1993] 4 All ER 731.
17 Issued under s 118 of the Mental Health Act 1983; see para 2.38.
18 Under Civil Aviation Act 1971, s 28(2); see Cmnd 6400, Annex D.
19 Railways (Conveyance of Mails) Act 1838; see now Post Office Act 1953, ss 33–42.

be, through a joint committee.[20] Under the Local Authorities (Goods and Services) Act 1970 a local authority may enter into an agreement with a public body (as defined) for the supply by one to the other of technical and other services, for the maintenance by it of the other's buildings etc.

A necessary collaboration may be hindered by the institutional structure or the distribution of powers, requiring it to be changed. The problem of homelessness originally fell between the two stools of social services (county council) and housing departments (district council).[1] Local authorities were urged by ministerial circular to collaborate in regarding homelessness as a joint problem, but legislation was necessary to put the obligation squarely on the housing authority.[2] Referring to the need for co-ordination in dealing with urban renewal problems, a Parliamentary Committee has spoken of 'the complex patchwork of overlapping areas and disparate powers constituting an unduly fragmented system of government'.[3] And the same Committee reported that 'the illogicality of one part of government offering financial inducement to someone to do something which another part of government then has to pay him not to do, is clear'.[4]

Failure to fulfil a legal duty to co-operate may lead to litigation. Failure to co-operate may also lead to a charge of maladministration being investigated by an Ombudsman. The Parliamentary Committee referred to above said that relations between some of the bodies concerned made coherent urban governance impossible.

---

20 Local Government Act 1972, s 101; and see Water Act 1973, s 15; Development of Rural Wales Act 1976.
 1 See also the (Robens) Committee on Safety and Health at Work, 1972 (Cmnd 5034), paras 33 ff, for 'fragmentation of administrative jurisdictions' and difficulties resulting.
 2 Housing (Homeless Persons) Act 1977.
 3 Third Report from the Environment Committee, 1982–83, HC 18.
 4 First Report from the Environment Committee, 1984–85, HC 6–1 on operation of Wildlife and Countryside Act.

Chapter 3

Legislation and administration

The legal framework

The government carries on the administration of public affairs within the framework of the existing laws. If any action it wishes to take requires the authority of a statute as it involves the change of an existing statute or an interference with other persons' legal rights, it will have to submit its proposals for the necessary change to Parliament in the form of a bill which to become law must get the consent of both Houses.[1] Thus a government's ability to administer the affairs of the country in accordance with its own policies depends on the whole range of statutory powers which it inherits when it takes office and on those which it acquires by means of the legislation whose enactment it procures.

But there are some things the government can do without statutory authority. It can conduct foreign affairs and sign treaties; it can direct the work of its employees, civil and military; it can enter into contracts; it can create new institutions by the grant of a charter[2] or by purely administrative action.[3] All these and other things it can do without having to get the authority of an Act of Parliament. The reason why statutory authority is not necessary is that no change in the law or adverse interference with anyone's legal rights is involved.[4] Take for example the Criminal Injuries Compensation Board. In 1964 the government took the view that it was right that compensation should be paid to victims of acts of criminal violence. So it decided that there should be a number of persons to constitute a Board, appointed persons as members of the Board, laid down the rules in accordance with which compensation was to be paid, and gave the Board the job of adjudicating on claims for compensation in accordance with those rules. No statutory authority was necessary for

1 *Case of Proclamations* (1611) 12 Co Rep 74.
2 For example a university.
3 As in the case of the former University Grants Committee.
4 For the many reasons why legislation was needed for the building of the Channel Tunnel see Cmnd 9735, *The Channel Fixed Link*. For the prerogative basis of payment of war pensions see Ogus and Barendt, *Law of Social Security*, 3rd edn p 313.

this: money is by this scheme given to, not taken from, citizens. Of course the expenditure of money on the scheme has to be approved by Parliament, but that is true of all government expenditure.[5] It has been possible for some years for the Board and the scheme to be made statutory.[6]

All governmental functions have their source either in statute or in the common law. It follows that the functions referred to in the preceding paragraph are common law functions: they are recognised by the courts to exist at common law. A distinction may be made between those governmental common law powers which are also enjoyed by or shared with citizens (for example, the power to enter into contracts or to issue information about oneself), and those which are exercisable only by government (for example, signing treaties, granting a charter, the disposition of the armed forces). The latter are sometimes spoken of as the Crown's prerogative powers, or as being at common law within the prerogative of the Crown. A different view is that all the Crown's common law powers are 'prerogative'.

The government has then a battery of powers, statutory and common law, at its disposal. In exercising the former it is limited by the provisions of the statute in question and as we shall see, it is a major function of the courts to determine whether the purported exercise of a statutory power is so authorised. For one thing is clear, that no action of the administration – no policy, no decision, rules or regulations made by it, no administrative practice or procedure – which exceeds or is inconsistent with statute, has legal validity.

What of the legality of the exercise of a common law power? Traditionally the role of the courts was only to say whether the power in question existed. If it did, the way it was exercised was for the government alone to determine. However, the decision of the House of Lords in the *GCHQ* case brought an important and welcome shift away from that position. The case, *Council of Civil Service Unions v Minister for the Civil Service*[7] concerned the government's management of its employees in the civil service. An Order in Council (made under its common law powers) provides that the defendant minister (the Prime Minister) may give instructions for providing for the conditions of service of civil servants. Exercising that power, the minister instructed, with immediate effect, new conditions of service for a particular group of civil servants (those employed at Government Communications Headquarters): they were no longer to be allowed to be members of a trade union of their choice, only of an association approved by the government. The legality of that instruction was challenged. This raised the question whether it was open to the court to challenge the legality of the exercise of this (prerogative) power in view of the traditional relationship between the courts and the executive in this field. Lord Diplock said:

5 See Appropriation Act 1993, Sch (B) – Part 2, Class IX, Vote 1.
6 Criminal Justice Act 1988, s 108. See p 150 below.
7 [1985] AC 374, [1984] 3 All ER 935. See Wade (1985) 101 LQR 180.

My Lords, I see no reason why simply because a decision-making power is derived from a common law and not a statutory source it should *for that reason only* be immune from judicial review.

Lord Roskill, after observing that of course the exercise of a statutory power is subject to judicial review, said:

If the executive instead of acting under a statutory power acts under a prerogative power ... I am unable to see ... that there is any logical reason why the fact that the source of the power is the prerogative and not statute should today deprive the citizen of that right of challenge to the manner of its exercise which he would possess were the source of that power statutory. In either case the act in question is the act of the executive.

In this particular case the court reviewed the exercise by the government of the power of employment – which has its source in the common law (and which it has along with citizens, and thus is not within the prerogative in the narrow sense referred to above).

Lord Roskill went on to suggest that the exercise of certain prerogative powers is beyond the court's reach.

Prerogative powers such as those relating to the making of treaties, the defence of the realm, the prerogative of mercy, the grant of honours, the dissolution of Parliament and the appointment of ministers as well as others are not, I think, susceptible to judicial review because their nature and subject matter is such as not to be amenable to the judicial process. The courts are not the place to determine [these matters].

However, this is so not because they have their source in the prerogative, but because of their nature and subject matter, for there are certain acts of the executive which the courts may be, at any one particular time, disinclined to review – *whatever their source*, as for example matters relating to national security, the disposition of the armed forces, or the appropriate level of taxation and expenditure.

Some functions falling within the government's common law powers which have been considered by the courts are the issue of passports,[8] telephone-tapping,[9] and the issue of riot-control equipment by the Home Office to chief constables against the wishes of police authorities,[10] and, with reference to one of the examples given by Lord Roskill, the legality of the exercise of the prerogative of mercy has been reviewed.[11]

Two well-established points concerning the exercise of common law powers may be noted. A common law power cannot be used so as to detract from a statutory right.[12] And where Parliament provides by statute for powers previously within the common law to be exercised in a particular

8 *R v Secretary of State for Foreign and Commonwealth Affairs, ex p Everett* [1989] QB 811, [1989] 1 All ER 655.
9 *R v Secretary of State for the Home Department, ex p Ruddock* [1987] 2 All ER 518, [1987] 1 WLR 1482.
10 *R v Secretary of State for the Home Department, ex p Northumbria Police Authority* [1989] QB 26, [1988] 1 All ER 556.
11 *R v Secretary of State for the Home Dept, ex p Bentley* [1993] 4 All ER 442.
12 *Laker Airways Ltd v Department of Trade* [1977] QB 643, [1977] 2 All ER 182, CA.

way and subject to limitations and provisions contained in the statute, those powers can only be so exercised. While the statute is in force, the thing it empowers the Crown to do can thenceforth only be done under the statute.[13]

Legislative procedures

Bills are of two kinds, public and private. The difference is that public bills relate to matters of public policy, whereas private bills are for the particular interest or benefit of any person, public company or corporation or local authority.

This difference is marked by the different manner of their introduction into Parliament. Public bills are introduced directly into Parliament by members – by far the greater number by members who are ministers, thus making them *government bills*, the others being *private members'* bills. Private bills on the other hand are solicited by the parties who seek their promotion (because they wish to have statutory powers over and above those given them by the general law) and are founded on petitions deposited in Parliament.[14]

The enactment of government bills

Before a government bill sees the light of parliamentary day a lot of work will have gone on behind the scenes. In brief the procedure is that the administrative civil servants in the initiating department, acting on ministerial instructions, themselves instruct the department's lawyers as to what has to be put into legislative form. These lawyers then instruct those civil servants known as Parliamentary Counsel – they are stationed in the Treasury – who draft the bill. After many drafts and much written and oral discussion between these groups of officials and with ministers and perhaps with affected interests, the final draft is agreed on. The bill is then introduced into Parliament by a minister in accordance with the legislative programme agreed on by the Cabinet. This drafting process is clearly an important part of the legislative process.[15] Once a bill is introduced into Parliament it cannot be altered except by Parliament.

The procedure of debate and voting on the bill in Parliament follows. Those matters are more the concern of constitutional than of administrative law. Suffice it to say here that the government can normally summon the voting power of its supporters to ensure the passage of the

---

13 *A-G v De Keyser's Royal Hotel Ltd* [1920] AC 508; *Herbert Berry Associates Ltd v IRC* [1978] 1 All ER 161, [1977] 1 WLR 1437, HL. See *R v Secretary of State for the Home Dept ex p Fire Brigades Union* [1995] 2 All ER 245, HL.

14 The distinction is thus procedural. Acts are classified as Public, General, Local and Personal.

15 See Graham 'Well in on the Act – a government lawyer's view of legislation' [1988] Stat LR 4.

bill.[16] The government's control of the machinery also means that it may get its way by threatening legislation to ensure compliance with its wishes.

However, the need for an Act to implement a policy may cause a government to modify that policy because of expected opposition or the lack of parliamentary time. Even where a bill has been introduced, opposition may cause the government to amend it or even in very exceptional cases to withdraw it altogether. Disapproval by members on the government side will be more significant in this respect than that of Opposition members.[17]

The point to be noticed however is that even if the government is able to secure the passage of the bill in exactly the same form in which it was introduced, it has to subject it to parliamentary criticism and, through the usual organs of publicity, to that of the country as a whole. We can therefore say that Parliament's function in the legislative process is to ensure publicity and detailed scrutiny and criticism of proposed Acts.[18] We can regard the whole of the legislative process from the drafting of the bill and consultation with affected interests to its eventual presentation for Royal Assent, as the responsibility of government, but an essential part of this process consists of the submission of the bill to parliamentary scrutiny. The government is there to govern, but in the enactment of bills it must submit to the parliamentary process and carry both Houses with it. Seen in this light the legislative activity of government is little different from any of its other activities, for it is in all matters liable to criticism in Parliament and must carry that body with it which it can normally do, as it has a majority in the Commons, otherwise it would not be the government.

It is sometimes said that Parliament makes the laws. It is true that Parliament makes the laws if by this we mean that its consent is necessary for the creation of Acts, but looking at the whole legislative process it would perhaps be more realistic to say that the government makes the laws subject to prior parliamentary consent.[19]

Private and hybrid bills

The parliamentary procedure for the enactment of a private bill is complex and expensive. In outline it is as follows.[20] The bill and related documents have to be deposited by certain dates, notices have to be given to persons affected etc. Petitions may be presented against a bill by those interests

16 See p 4 above.
17 As in the case of the government's inability to proceed with its proposal in 1994 to sell off the Post Office.
18 See Griffith *Parliamentary Scrutiny of Government Bills*.
19 Griffith 'The Place of Parliament in the Legislative Process' (1951) 14 MLR 279. 'New laws are made by the Ministry with the acquiescence of the majority ... in the House of Commons ... The modern MP understands the condition of his political existence so well that ... he hardly ever does vote against his party on any party issue ...' S Low, The *Governance of England* (1904) pp 60, 63.
20 See Foulkes 'The Enactment of the County of South Glamorgan Act 1976' [1977] PL 272; 'Study of Parliament Group Private Bill Procedure: a case for reform' [1981] PL 206.

adversely affected by it. A petition may be objected to by the promoter on the ground of the petitioner's lack of *locus standi*. The bill is then allocated to one or other House. As with public bills, to give second reading means that the House affirms the general principle of the bill, but in the case of a private bill only conditionally, that is, the actual need for the clauses has to be proved by evidence to the satisfaction of a committee. (A private bill is rarely rejected on second reading.) The Committee stage is quite unlike that on a public bill. Parties are represented by lawyers. When a bill is opposed, evidence in support of the clauses is given on oath, and witnesses may be cross-examined. A copy of a private bill must be deposited with certain departments. Although departments do not petition against bills, if thought necessary a department will make a report to the House on the bill drawing attention to what it regards as objectionable clauses, and the Committee may hear departmental representatives.

The Committee allows or disallows clauses on the basis of the evidence. A clause may for example be disallowed because local need for it is not shown, because the clause would not effectively deal with the problem, or because the general law is adequate to deal with it, etc. The Committee thus has a judicial look about it, but it has to take a view as to where the balance of public interest lies.

After report and third reading stages, the bill is considered by the other House, and is in due course presented for Royal Assent. On getting this it is as fully an Act of Parliament as a public act.[1]

Historically, private Acts played a very important part in the growth of local government, the railways, and other services. Holdsworth wrote of the 'large and important place' private bill legislation took in the sphere of local government. It was by means of these Acts that many towns and districts obtained the power to watch, light, cleanse and pave their streets.[2] But private bill legislation continued to be and remained of particular importance in connection also with railway, harbour and water undertakings.

The private bill procedure was examined some years ago.[3] A particular matter of concern was that some developments for which private bill authorisation was sought could have been dealt with under planning law – that is, administratively rather than through the legislative process, thus releasing members of both Houses from the not inconsiderable burden of considering private bills. The outcome was the Transport and Works Act 1992 which introduced a system whereby the authorisation of the construction and operation of certain schemes (railways, tramways, inland waterways etc) may now be given by ministerial order, usually following a public local[4] inquiry.

1 *British Railways Board v Pickin* [1974] AC 765, [1974] 1 All ER 609.
2 *History of English Law* vol xi, p 629.
3 HC 625, 1987–88.
4 A proposed development may be of more than local significance, and the Act provides that where the minister thinks proposals are of national significance he may not make an order unless Parliament has in advance of any public inquiry passed a resolution approving them. The purpose is to give 'policy protection' to such a scheme: the subsequent inquiry would be limited to consideration of local and detailed aspects of the scheme.

The distinction between the two classes of bill, public and private, may appear straightforward, but the boundary line is narrow and fluctuates. Private bills have on occasions been debarred on the ground that they should have been introduced as public bills. There is in fact another category, the *hybrid* bill. Private bill procedure gives an opportunity to those interests affected by the bill to object to it. It would be possible to by-pass that procedural safeguard by introducing the bill as a public bill. All public bills are therefore scrutinised to see whether they contain provisions which do not apply uniformly or which discriminate within a category of persons or cases. A bill containing such provisions is a hybrid bill, which must then follow the procedures applicable to both public and private bills, thus giving those affected an opportunity to object. An example of such a bill would be one which nationalised some but not all the companies within a particular industry.[5]

Provisional orders

Owing to the expense and delay of private bill procedure new procedures were evolved in the nineteenth century to enable powers to be acquired more simply. One of these is the *provisional order procedure*. This example will illustrate the procedure. A power to construct a light railway, eg a funicular or mineral railway, is contained in the Light Railways Act 1896. A local authority wishing to exercise this power must apply for an order to the minister. Public notice of the application must be given, and a local inquiry held by the minister at which objections can be heard. The minister then decides whether or not to make an order conferring the power sought: if he does so it is as yet provisional only, being of no effect until confirmed by Parliament. This confirmation is sought by the minister presenting to Parliament a 'provisional order confirmation bill' which contains the order (or more than one) in a schedule to the bill. If the bill is opposed it is dealt with like a private bill, with the opportunities for objection that this provides. The passage of such a bill through Parliament is however usually purely formal. It contains one section, viz 'The Provisional Order contained in the Schedule hereunto annexed is hereby confirmed'.[6]

Special procedure orders

Because of the defects of cost and delay the provisional order procedure has in turn been largely superseded by the *special parliamentary procedure*, which was introduced by the Statutory Orders (Special Procedure) Act 1945 amended in 1965. The purpose of the Act was to enable local and other public authorities to carry out public works expeditiously in the post-war period, but at the same time to provide a measure of

5 The bills nationalising the Bank of England and Cable and Wireless Ltd (see above) were hybrid, but none of the major nationalisation statutes were. The Channel Tunnel Act 1988 was hybrid. For hybrid instruments see p 100 below.
6 In England and Wales light railway orders have been replaced by orders under the Transport and Works Act 1992 (see p 57 above).

protection to those whose interests might be affected. The Act provides for the making of *special procedure orders*. Such orders mostly concern the properties or operations of public authorities and the acquisition by them of certain categories of land.

The procedure applies in any case where in an Act passed after 1 June 1946 power to make an order is stated to be subject to 'special parliamentary procedure'. In addition, by regulations made under the 1945 Act, this procedure has been substituted for the provisional order procedure specified under certain Acts passed before that date. And although a statutory order may not normally be subject to this 'special parliamentary procedure', statute may say that it is to be available on demand by a person affected by the order.[7]

In outline the procedure is that an authority desiring the order to be made applies to the minister for the order. If the minister agrees, the applicant publishes notices explaining the project. Objections may then be made by persons affected, and the minister must hold a public inquiry into them unless he thinks there are circumstances making it unnecessary. An inquiry is normally held. If, having considered the report of the inquiry, the minister thinks the order should be made, he lays it before Parliament.

The first part of the procedure provides therefore for the proper *publication* of the order, and the making of *objections* including the possibility of a local *inquiry*. The second part provides for *parliamentary* scrutiny. Petitions may be submitted against the order within a specified period by persons particularly affected by it, that is with *locus standi*. The order may be annulled by a resolution of either House. If it is not, and there is no petition, the order comes into force at the end of a stated period. If there is a petition, it is referred to a Joint Committee of three members from each House. The committee on considering the petition, may approve, reject or amend the order. If they approve it, the order comes into operation on a specified date. If they report that it be not approved then the order cannot take effect unless confirmed by Act of Parliament.[8] If the order is reported with amendments it may come into force as so amended on the date the minister decides on.[9]

Despite the general replacement of the provisional order procedure by the special parliamentary procedure (as mentioned above) the latter is not always found appropriate. For example, section 303 of the Public Health Act 1875 gave a wide power to the Secretary of State to repeal or amend certain local Acts. This was exercisable by the provisional order procedure but regulations made under the Statutory Orders (Special Procedure) Act 1945 substituted the special parliamentary procedure.

7 See eg *R v Minister of Agriculture, Fisheries and Food, ex p Wear Valley District Council* (1988) Times, 26 March: was council 'affected' by ministerial order?

8 See Okehampton Bye-Pass (Confirmation of Orders) Act 1985.

9 First Report from the Joint Committee on Delegated Legislation, 1972–3, HL 188. See HC 399 of 1993–94 for criticism. The *Guide to Procedure* for obtaining orders under the Transport and Works Act 1992 warns applicants for orders to seek to avoid as far as possible land subject to special parliamentary procedure not least to avoid the risks and delays that would arise if the procedure was invoked.

However, in 1962 it was decided that that procedure was inappropriate for the reason that 'the powers under section 303 are almost unlimited and might be regarded as legislative in character'. The provisional order procedure was therefore reverted to in respect of the exercise of powers under section 303.[10]

The devolution of legislative authority to departments

It can be seen that from the private bill procedure, through the provisional order procedure to the special parliamentary procedure, there is a gradual devolution of legislative authority and activity from Parliament to the government departments.[11] In this connection the difference between the private bill procedure and the provisional order procedure is that in the former it is a *parliamentary* committee that has to be satisfied of the need for the measure, and that interested parties are adequately protected,[12] whereas in the latter it is the *department* that has to be satisfied. A significant difference between the provisional order and the special parliamentary procedure is that under the provisional order procedure the minister's order is not effective until *confirmed by Act* of Parliament, while a special procedure order requires no such confirmation in order to have legal force: it is subject to parliamentary processes but *an Act is not required* to give it effect.

A parallel development[13] to the one just referred to was the granting of power by statute to government *departments* to authorise the carrying out of various schemes by other public authorities which, before, could only be authorised by *Act*. For example local authorities were empowered to clear slum areas by making an order; and various public authorities were empowered to purchase land compulsorily for their respective purposes by means of an order. In both cases the order is effective only on the minister's confirmation: in neither case is any form of parliamentary process necessarily involved. This is a very common administrative procedure today. And the procedure for obtaining ministerial orders under the Transport and Works Act 1992 will be noted.

The very extensive delegation of legislative functions to ministers is considered in the rest of this chapter.

Delegated legislation, administrative rules etc

It is, and has long been, common for Parliament to confer by Act on ministers and other executive bodies the power to make general rules with the force of law – to legislate. Parliament is said to delegate to such

10 Statutory Orders (Special Procedure) Orders of 1949 and 1962. H C Debs (5th series) vol 653, col 1453.
11 See Willis *Parliamentary Powers of English Government Departments*, ch 4; Laski (ed) *A Century of Municipal Progress*, ch xvii.
12 See *Re Morley* (1875) 20 LR Eq 17.
13 See K Davies *Law of Compulsory Purchase and Compensation*, ch 1.

bodies the power to legislate. Thus the phrase 'delegated legislation' covers every exercise of a power to legislate conferred by Act of Parliament. The phrase is not a term of art, it is not a technical term, it has no statutory definition. To decide whether the exercise of a power constitutes 'delegated legislation' we have to ask whether it is a *delegated* power that is being exercised and whether its exercise constitutes *legislation*. Clearly an Act, public or private, is not delegated: it is primary legislation. When a minister or other authority is given power by Act of Parliament to make rules, regulations etc the power has been *delegated* to him, and insofar as the rules made by that authority are *legislative* in their nature, they comprise delegated legislation. If the contents of the document (made under delegated powers) are not legislative the document will obviously not be a piece of (delegated) legislation. Ministers and others are in fact given power to make orders, give directions, issue approvals and notices etc which one would not, because of their lack of generality, classify as legislative but rather as administrative. This distinction between what is legislative and what is administrative (or executive) has a number of consequences which are referred to below.

Another term which will be found in use is 'subordinate legislation'. We can take this to mean legislation made by an authority subordinate to Parliament. The term has a statutory definition for the purposes of the Interpretation Act 1978.[14]

The use of delegated legislation

Resort to delegated legislation is no new thing; it is a 'constitutional device to which Parliament has continually resorted from the earliest times'.[15] Why?

(i) It is enough, it is said, for Parliament to concern itself in an Act with principles: their application in the detailed regulations can properly be left to the administration subject to adequate controls. For example, many regulations deal with technical matters such as the safety of consumer goods, safety at the work place, detailed precautions to be taken against the misuse of drugs, etc. A typical example is the Road Traffic Act 1972, under which the Secretary of State may make regulations generally as to the use of motor vehicles on roads, their construction and equipment, and the conditions under which they may be so used. The regulations made under this section are extensive and detailed.[16] But many go far beyond the merely 'technical'. By section 57 of the Town and Country Planning Act 1990 planning permission is required for the development of land. By section 59 the Secretary of State is to provide by order for the granting of

---

14 It means 'Orders in Council, orders, rules, regulations, schemes, warrants, byelaws and other instruments made or to be made under any Act' – s 21(1).

15 Graham-Harrison *Notes on the Delegation by Parliament of Legislative Powers*, p 2.

16 The Motor Vehicles (Construction and Use) Regulations 1978, SI 1978/1017, as amended. And see SI 1994/1519 re traffic signs (367 pages); cf SI 1994/1780 prohibiting use of gaps in central reservation of Sidcup Rd Greenwich.

planning permission. The important General Development Order made under that power[17] specifies over fifty classes of development for which planning permission is not required.

The Committee on Ministers' Powers acknowledged the advantage of this arrangement. The practice, it said,

is valuable because it provides for a power of constant adaptation to unknown future conditions without the necessity of amending legislation. Flexibility is essential. The method of delegated legislation permits of the rapid utilisation of experience ... The practice, again, permits of experiment being made and thus affords an opportunity, otherwise difficult to ensure, of utilising the lessons of experience.[18]

For these reasons it may be a matter for criticism that too much detail is put in the Act. The Committee on Safety and Health at Work[19] found this to be the case in the legislation it examined; there was too much technical detail in the statutes. In any new legislation it should be dealt with, the Committee said, by subordinate instruments. This was done. The Health and Safety at Work Act 1974 lays down broad principles and gives wide power to the Secretary of State to make regulations over an extensive area including the prohibition of the manufacture of any substance or the transport in or importation into the UK of substances of any specified description.

(ii) Another advantage of the use of delegated legislation is that the knowledge and experience available outside the legislature and the Civil Service can be utilised by appropriate consultation.[20] Indeed it may be necessary to leave matters to be dealt with in regulations because at the time when the bill is before Parliament the government does not know precisely how to handle the problem it has set itself. Thus, referring to regulations made under the Gaming Act 1968 a minister said:

A great many matters were left to be dealt with by regulations precisely for the reason that neither the government nor Parliament then had sufficient knowledge of gaming and its problems to be able to work out in detail some aspects of the control which would be needed. It was the deliberate intention to leave these matters until the Gaming Board [created by that Act] had been able to give the Home Secretary expert advice.[1]

The haste with which legislation is sometimes prepared may mean that the minister does not know how he is going to exercise the powers he is seeking, so will provide for them to be exercised by regulation. It may not be unduly cynical to suggest that in some cases the minister knows full well how he is going to use these powers, but prefers to leave their

---

17 SI 1988/1813.
18 Cmd 4060, pp 51–52. '[The delegation of legislative power] facilitates administration because every administrative change is in the nature of an experiment': Ilbert *Legislative Methods and Forms*, p 41.
19 Cmnd 5034.
20 For consultation generally see p 128 below.
1 791 H of C Official Report (5th series) col 1269.

exercise to regulations which will be subject to less scrutiny than if they were set out in the Bill.

(iii) A further justification for the resort to delegated powers is the need to arm the government with power to deal with emergencies. As the Committee on Ministers' Powers put it:

In a modern State there are many occasions when there is a sudden need of legislative action. For many such needs delegated legislation is the only convenient or even possible remedy.[2]

Departments thus properly have powers to make orders to prevent and check diseases of animals as, for example, when restrictions on the movement of livestock are imposed on an outbreak of disease[3] or on the destruction of a nuclear power station in the USSR.[4] In time of war of course it is necessary to arm the government with very wide powers. As Carr said, 'The problem then is ... how to compensate the government of the country for the loss of the prerogative powers'.[5] Thus section 1(1) of the Emergency Powers (Defence) Act 1939[6] authorised the government to make such regulations 'as appear to him to be necessary or expedient for securing the public safety, the defence of the realm, the maintenance of public order, and the efficient prosecution of the war'. The Emergency Powers Act 1920, is, by contrast, a permanent piece of legislation. (It was enacted at the time when the extensive wartime legislation was coming to an end, and followed a major coal strike.) Under this Act the government may by proclamation declare a state of emergency to exist if it appears that 'there have occurred or are about to occur events of such a nature as to be calculated by interfering with the supply and distribution of food [etc] to deprive the community ... of the essentials of life'. Such proclamations cannot be in force for more than one month, but may be issued in succession. So long as a proclamation is in force regulations may be made by Order in Council 'for securing the essentials of life to the community' but they cannot impose any form of compulsory military service or industrial conscription. Under such emergency legislation wide powers are given to ministers to authorise persons to disregard not only contractual but also statutory obligations.

In emergencies it is in the nature of things necessary to be able to act quickly, and regulations can of course be made more quickly than Acts in so far as Parliament is necessarily concerned in the enactment of a bill but not in the making of regulations. Further, Parliament is not always sitting. And regulations can be made in secrecy – sometimes a necessity, not only in war time.

(iv) Power is not infrequently given to ministers to make orders relating to the bringing into or continuing in force of Acts of Parliament. An Act

2 Cmd 4060, p 52.
3 Eg SI 1989/2077.
4 Eg SI 1990/1948.
5 *Concerning English Administrative Law*, p 44.
6 One of many Acts passed in a few days, some of which are still in force see eg SI 1990/1640.

comes into force on the day it receives the Royal Assent, unless the Act provides otherwise. It may be left to a minister to decide on what day an Act or a part of it is to come into force.[7] A justification for such a provision is that it may not be possible for the Act or parts of it to be brought into force until certain administrative steps have been taken and it may be uncertain how long these will take.[7a] Under such an arrangement the order bringing the Act into force is of course made under Act. This seems to involve an insuperable defect. How can the order bring the Act into force before the Act which empowers the order to be made is itself in force? The answer is that section 13 of the Interpretation Act 1978, enables this to be done.

An Act remains in force until it is repealed, unless the Act sets some time limit on itself, by saying that it shall expire on a certain date, or after a certain period. In that case it may go on to say that it may be continued in force by ministerial order for a certain period. For example see section 1 of the Armed Forces Act 1991.

(v) An underlying reason for the need to resort to delegated legislation is that governments have in the last hundred years increased their activities in many fields – health, housing, welfare, education etc. The Committee on Ministers' Powers drew a parallel with the Tudor period,

a period, like the nineteenth and twentieth centuries, when great political, social and economic changes were taking place. We think that the appearance of statutes which delegate large legislative powers at both these periods is more than a coincidence, and that it confirms our conclusion that the delegation of legislative powers is at the present day inevitable. Similar needs have given rise at these two very different periods to a similar expedient.[8]

There simply is not enough Parliamentary time to subject all the regulations required to the full legislative process. An example of the saving of Parliamentary time is that before the passing of the Ministers of the Crown (Transfer of Functions) Act 1946, where functions had been assigned by statute to particular ministers, they could not be transferred to other ministers except by statute.[9] This sometimes meant that readjustments between departments which were desirable were delayed. Further, as the issue was simply whether a function should be transferred from one department to another it was thought enough to put it before Parliament on a yes or no basis. The 1946 Act therefore provides that functions may be transferred by an Order in Council. An order may also cause a department to be dissolved: this requires an affirmative resolution.

7   See *R v Home Secretary, ex p Fire Brigades Union* [1995] 2 All ER 245, HL on this provision.
7a See reasons for delay in bringing Zoo Licensing Act 1981 into force: elaborate consultation necessary; qualified inspectors to be found and appointed; detailed standards of zoo practice to be established; guidelines to licensing authorities to be drawn up; charges to be fixed. 42 H of C Official Report (6th series) col 519.
8   Cmd 4060, p 15.
9   Not all ministerial functions are regulated by statute: these can be redistributed as administrative necessities require: Wilson *Cases and Materials on Constitutional and Administrative Law*, p 36.

The misuse of delegated legislation

We may conclude, with the Committee on Ministers' Powers, that delegated legislation is inevitable and indispensable. As a House of Lords committee reported sixty years later, 'The argument is not whether delegated legislation is ever justified, but what criteria can be used in determining whether particular proposals for delegation are acceptable.[10] Now while the administration has no inherent powers of legislation, enjoying only those which Parliament grants it, there are in the United Kingdom no constitutional that is, legal, limits on the extent to which powers to legislate may be delegated to ministers by statute. The House of Lords committee just referred to thought it would 'not be a profitable exercise' to try to list the criteria giving precision to the test of appropriateness. Each case had to be considered in its context. The following paragraphs suggest some necessary limitations.

First, it is proper for an Act to lay down principles to which detailed effect is to be given by regulations: it would be improper for the statement of principle to be so attenuated as to provide no effective limit to the details and in effect to allow the minister by such a 'skeleton' bill to legislate on matters of principle – but what are principles and what are details might be disputable.

Second, it is a constitutional principle that Parliamentary approval is necessary for the imposition of taxation. However, even here there has been some delegation to the executive. The Committee on Ministers' Powers referred in this context to the Import Duties Act 1932. Section 9 of the Value Added Tax Act 1983 permits the rate of that tax to be increased within certain limits. The House of Lords committee said it was not likely to think it appropriate to delegate power to increase or impose taxation except to take account of inflation or increased costs. Also of doubtful acceptability would be the removal or reduction of *benefits* conferred in primary legislation unless the legislation laid down clear criteria for determining how the power was to be exercised.

Third, an exceptional type of delegation in the eyes of the Committee on Ministers' Powers, and still so regarded is the authority to alter statute by ministerial regulation. It does indeed seem to be a constitutional anathema. Nevertheless that power is neither recent nor rare. Section 78 of the National Insurance Act 1911 provided:

If any difficulty arises ... in bringing into operation this part of this Act, the insurance commissioners with the consent of the Treasury may by order ... do anything which appears to them necessary or expedient for bringing this part of this Act into operation, and any such order *may modify the provisions of this Act* so far as may appear necessary or expedient for carrying the order into effect.

Such a clause is known as a Henry VIII clause because, said the Committee on Ministers' Powers, 'that King is regarded popularly as the

10 Delegated Powers Scrutiny Committee, 1992–3 HL 37.

impersonation of executive autocracy'. The Committee admitted that such a power is extremely convenient but said that 'it cannot but be regarded as inconsistent with the principle of parliamentary government'.[11]

Another type of Henry VIII clause is one which empowers a minister to make regulations repealing or amending some *other* Act. An unexceptionable example is where statute authorises a minister to repeal or amend local Acts which are found to be inconsistent with a general principle laid down in the statute. Carr explained it this way:

The device is partly a draftsman's insurance policy in case he has overlooked something and is partly due to the immense body of local Acts in England creating special difficulties in particular areas. These local Acts are very hard to trace, and the draftsman could never be confident that he has examined them all in advance.[12]

A very different example, and far from unexceptionable, is in section 1 of the Deregulation and Contracting Out Act 1994, as follows:

If, with respect to any provision made by an enactment, a Minister of the Crown is of the opinion:
(a)   that the effect of the provision is such as to impose ... a burden affecting any person in the carrying on of any trade, business or profession or otherwise, and
(b)   that, by amending or repealing the enactment concerned ... it would be possible without removing any necessary protection, to remove or reduce the burden ...
he may ... by order amend or repeal that enactment.

This, as will be seen later, caused acute Parliamentary concern.

The wide power to amend legislation given in the European Communities Act 1972 should be noted. Section 2 provides:

(2) ... Her Majesty may by Order in Council ... make provision
(a) for the purpose of implementing any Community obligation ...
(4) The provision that may be made under subsection (2) above includes ... any such provision (of any extent) as might be made by Act of Parliament ...

The constitutionally significant limitations to this power, set out in Schedule 2 to the Act should be noted. Section 2(2) does not include power

(a) to make any provisions imposing or increasing taxation; or
(b) to make any provision with retrospective effect; or
(c) to confer any power to legislate by means of any subordinate instrument (other than rules of procedure for any court or tribunal); or
(d) to create any new criminal offence [punishable beyond the limits prescribed].

We now go on to consider various forms of delegated legislation, dealing first with the statutory instrument.

---

11 Cmd 4060, p 36, 59 et seq. The Committee proposed strict limits on the use of the clause. They are to be strictly construed by the Courts: *Britnell v Secretary of State for Social Security* [1991] 2 All ER 726.
12 *Concerning English Administrative Law*, p 44. See, for example, Health and Safety at Work etc Act 1974, s 14; Employment Act 1988, s 26(2)(a); Water Act 1989, s 191.

Statutory instruments

The document by which a minister exercises a power to make regulations, rules, orders, directions etc may be referred to as a *statutory order*. Statutory orders fall into two classes, those which are, and those which are not, statutory instruments.

Section 1(1) of the Statutory Instruments Act 1946 says that where by any Act passed after 1 January 1948:

power to make, confirm or approve orders, rules, regulations or other subordinate legislation is conferred on His Majesty in Council or any Minister of the Crown then, if the power is expressed
(a)   in the case of a power conferred on His Majesty, to be exercisable by Order in Council;
(b)   in the case of a power conferred on a Minister of the Crown, to be exercisable by statutory instrument,
any document by which that power is exercised shall be known as a 'statutory instrument' ...

To deal first with section 1(1)(b): where a power to make (etc) rules (etc) is conferred on a Minister by an Act, and the Act says that the power is to be exercisable by statutory instrument, then the document by which that power is exercised is to be a statutory instrument. The statutory instrument is thus the *form* in which a document containing the exercise of the power is to be put. It is clear therefore that whether a document is a 'statutory instrument' depends on whether or not it is made under a statutory power which requires it to be made by statutory instrument.

As for the meaning of 'Minister', section 11 provides that where a power to make rules etc is conferred on a department it is deemed to be conferred on the minister in charge of that department. The Minister for the Civil Service decides whether for this purpose any particular body is a government department. Power to make statutory instruments is conferred by various statutes on the Forestry Commission, the Church Commissioners, the Commissioners of Customs and Excise, and on the Building Societies Commission.

Section 1(1)(a) of the Act, above, shows that power to make rules etc may be conferred on the Queen in Council, and that where that power is exercisable by Order in Council, the document exercising that power is also a 'statutory instrument'.[13] The sovereign's assent to a proposed order is given at a meeting of the Privy Council, but this is purely formal: there is no discussion or explanation at such a meeting.[14] Thus the effective decision to make the order is that of the appropriate minister. Why is the power in some cases conferred directly on a minister and in other cases

13 A power conferred expressly on the Privy Council will not fall under this provision, see eg Medical Act 1983, s 51. The exercise of such a power is by way of Order *of* Council. Powers, whether to make statutory instruments or otherwise, are not conferred by statute on government or Cabinet as such: see Maitland *Constitutional History of England*, pp 399 to 406; nor usually on the prime minister, but for an example see National Audit Act 1983, s 1(1).
14 Morrison 'The Privy Council Today' (1948) 2 Parliamentary Affairs 10; Carr *Delegated Legislation*, p 55. Alan Clark, *Diaries*, p 397.

on the Queen in Council? It seems that an Order in Council is thought necessary for matters which are formally of some constitutional importance, for example, the fixing of the dates of the 1975[15] and 1979[16] referendums, and the extending of the provisions of an Act to certain territories outside the United Kingdom.[17]

We have referred earlier to prerogative (or common law) powers. The exercise of certain prerogative powers is by way of Order in Council.[18] These prerogative Orders in Council must be contrasted with those referred to in the preceding paragraph, which are made under statutory powers. Prerogative Orders in Council are not statutory instruments: they are not made under and do not owe their existence to statute, so they do not of course constitute delegated legislation – prerogative powers, like Acts, do not legally owe their existence to any source outside themselves.

The title 'statutory instrument' replaced that of 'statutory rule' provided for in the Rules Publication Act 1893.[19] The Statutory Instruments Act provides in section 1(2) that where before the Statutory Instruments Act came into force there was a power under a statute to make a statutory rule, an exercise of that power in a document which is 'of legislative and not an executive character' is now by way of statutory instrument. Although 'statutory rules' cannot therefore be made today, there are many hundreds still in force.

The making, duration and repeal of statutory instruments

Making   The decision to exercise the power to make delegated legislation is taken at the appropriate level within the department. Consultation with affected interests follows, and conclusions reached in the light of the views expressed. Then 'the administrator dealing with the exercise of the power will instruct his legal counterpart as to the content of the proposed instrument. The draftsman's first task is to verify that any conditions precedent to the exercise of the power have been fulfilled ... the procedure to which the order is subject, and that the department's proposals are intra vires the enabling legislation'.[20] Advice, particularly on the question of vires, may be taken by the departmental lawyer from outside the department, perhaps from the law officers or, in special circumstances, from Parliamentary Counsel. When a draft is drawn up copies may be circulated to other concerned departments and perhaps to outside organisations for comments, in the light of which the draft may be amended. When a firm draft is arrived at it will be put to the minister for approval with suitable explanations – though he may have been involved at an

15 Referendum Act 1975, s 1(4).
16 Scotland Act 1978, Sch 17, para 1; Wales Act 1978, Sch 12, para 1.
17 Merchant Shipping Act 1979, s 47.
18 See eg SI 1982/1693 for order requisitioning ships at time of Falklands war. See the *GCHQ* case, p 53. And for nature of such Orders in Council see *Ibralebbe v R* p 107 below.
19 See p 128 below for this Act.
20 Joint Committee on Delegated Legislation, 1972–3, HL 184, Minutes of Evidence, Appendix 8, Annex D.

earlier stage. When his approval has been given printed copies are obtained and submitted to him[1] for signature, though routine instruments may be signed on his behalf by a civil servant.[2] The instrument is 'made' when signed. It is then sent for printing, and steps are taken to comply with any necessary Parliamentary procedure.

The degree of formality involved in the making of a statutory instrument may affect the decision as to whether a document should be required to be by way of statutory instrument or not. For example section 4 of the National Health Service Act 1946 empowered the minister to make rules concerning the payment to be made by hospital patients for 'amenity' beds. These rules had to be by way of statutory instrument. Section 4 of the Health Services and Public Health Act 1968 removed that requirement. (Under the 1946 Act charges were uniform; under the later Act they vary according to the type of hospital.) And under section 2 of the Administration of Justice Act 1977 expenses payable for carrying out certain judicial functions are 'to be determined administratively'; before that statutory instruments were necessary.

A bill is necessarily subject to parliamentary and public scrutiny before it can become law. This is not the case with delegated legislation which may become law on a purely departmental decision and signature. It follows that consultation with affected interests is an important feature in the making of delegated legislation and it is usual for departments to engage in it.[3]

Duration Delegated legislation continues in force until repealed, unless its duration is limited by the parent Act or by its own terms.[4] When the parent Act is repealed, any delegated legislation made under it falls with it unless it is expressly preserved and continued in force by the repealing statute.[5] Delegated legislation may be expressly repealed (or amended) by a later statute,[6] or where a statute expressly authorises the repeal by ministerial order of the earlier delegated legislation, by such an order.

Repeal Does a power to make delegated legislation carry with it a power to repeal it? The Interpretation Act 1889, section 32(3) provided that a power to make rules, regulations, or byelaws, was to be construed as including a power to rescind, revoke, amend or vary them. The power was strictly construed, and was not applied to a power to make an 'order' or

---

1 Or them; see eg SI 1993/430 signed by four ministers, signed and sealed by one ministry, and, Treasury consent being required, approved by two Lords Commissioners ie government whips.
2 Eg SI 1993/2302.
3 For consultation generally see p 128 below. For orders made only on representation being made to minister, see eg Conservation of Wild Creatures and Wild Plants Act 1975, s 7; Transport Act 1980, s 43(2); Level Crossings Act 1983, s 1.
4 See Transport Act 1981, s 27 re seat belt regulations; and now 89 H of C Official Rep (6th series) col 877.
5 *Watson v Winch* [1916] 1 KB 688. Eg Reservoirs Act 1975, s 23(2). For failure to do so, see 926 H of C Official Report (5th series) col 1599.
6 Eg Finance Act 1975, s 1(2). Water Act 1983, Sch 5, Pt 2 revokes all or part of 24 instruments.

'order in council', for example. Such powers to revoke etc had to be expressly conferred in the parent statute. However, the Interpretation Act 1978, section 14, now provides that:

Where an Act confers powers to make—
(a) Rules, regulations or byelaws; or
(b) Orders in Council, orders or other subordinate legislation to be made by statutory instrument,
it implies unless the contrary intention appears, a power, exercisable in the same manner and subject to the same conditions and limitations, to revoke, amend or re-enact any instrument made under the power.

That section applies to Acts passed after the commencement of the Act, that is after 1 January 1979. But the section applies to Acts passed after 1899 so far as it relates to rules, regulations and byelaws.[7]

Byelaws

Byelaws have been defined[8] as rules made by some authority subordinate to the legislature for the regulation, administration or management of a certain district, property, undertaking, etc, and binding on all persons who come within their scope. They are statutory instruments if the Act authorising them to be made says they are to be.

Ministers may be empowered to make byelaws. These may or may not be statutory instruments, eg those made under the Military Lands Act 1892 are.

Local authorities have power to make byelaws under a number of statutes. In particular section 235(1) of the Local Government Act 1972 says:

The council of a district and the council of a London borough may make byelaws for the good rule and government of the whole or any part of the district or borough, as the case may be, and for the prevention and suppression of nuisances therein.

A byelaw must be made under the seal of the council. It must then be submitted to the appropriate minister for confirmation: it is of no effect until confirmed. The council must publish in one or more local papers at least one month's notice of its intention to submit the byelaw for confirmation. During that period a copy is to be open to public inspection without payment. A copy of a confirmed byelaw must be available for free public inspection and be on sale at not more than twenty pence a copy. Local authority bye-laws are not statutory instruments.

The argument for local authority byelaws is that authorities need to be able to make laws suited to their particular circumstances. Flexibility can however mean lack of uniformity, and in this connection there was a significant change in the power to make building byelaws. These used to be made by local authorities but because of the considerable inconvenience

---

7   Section 22(1), Sch 2, para 3. 'Subordinate legislation' is defined in s 21(1). See p 61 above.
8   See Jowitt's *Dictionary of English Law*.

caused to large construction firms and others through their lack of uniformity local authorities were deprived of their power to make them and the Minister of Housing and Local Government was instead empowered to make building regulations by way of statutory instrument.[9] Likewise local authority byelaws concerning the employment of children varied considerably. The power to make them was replaced by the Employment of Children Act 1973 by a power in the Secretary of State to make regulations on that matter.[10]

Other bodies empowered to make regulations called byelaws include 'airports operators', under the Airports Act 1986. Such operators have a general power to make byelaws for regulating the use and operation of its aerodromes and for specified purposes including the prevention of obstruction, the securing of safety, and for restricting access. Where the 'operator' is the Secretary of State the byelaws are made by way of a statutory instrument, not otherwise. Byelaws not made by a minister are not effective until confirmed by a minister. This need for ministerial confirmation is an important aspect of the control exercised over byelaws: other aspects are referred to later.[11]

It is not uncommon for an organisation to have rules which it calls byelaws; these will not bind third parties, but only members of the organisation itself, unless statute gives them that quality, or unless the third party agrees.[12]

Codes of practice

The last two decades or so have seen increasing use made of codes of practice. They are now a major administrative tool. What we are concerned with is their juridical status. Who makes them; in what form; is any Parliamentary process required; how if at all are they given effect; is breach of itself unlawful; if not, what is their relevance in legal proceedings and to legal liability?

Their forerunner was the Highway Code, first issued under the Road Traffic Act 1930, now under section 37 of the Road Traffic Act 1972 as substituted by section 60 of the Transport Act 1982. It is made by the Secretary of State and may from time to time be revised by him. It is described, in section 37(8), as comprising 'directions for the guidance' of persons using roads. It is not *in* a statutory instrument, nor is one necessary *to bring it into force*. The effect of the Highway Code is stated to be as follows:

---

9 Public Health Act 1961, s 4. See now Building Act 1984, s 1. Inconsistency arising from differing local Acts can also cause inconvenience.
10 This power has not yet been exercised.
11 Examples can be found empowering a minister to revoke etc a byelaw made by another authority eg County of South Glamorgan Act 1976, s 47; Pilotage Act 1983, s 17; Civil Aviation Act 1982, s 40. Airports Act 1986, s 64.
12 *London Association of Shipowners and Brokers v London and India Joint Docks Committee* [1892] 3 Ch 242.

A failure on the part of a person to observe a provision of the Highway Code shall not of itself render that person liable to criminal proceedings of any kind but any such failure may in any [civil or criminal] proceedings ... be relied upon by any party to the proceedings as tending to establish or to negative any liability which is in question in those proceedings.

Thus failure to comply with the Highway Code is *made relevant evidence* in deciding whether there is liability for breach of a legal duty. This is the most common way of giving effect to a code of practice. It does not shift the burden of proof. Thus in a prosecution for careless driving the burden is on the prosecution. Observance or non-observance of the Code (eg as to the distance to be kept between moving vehicles) is relevant in determining liability.

The codes of practice issued by the Secretary of State under section 66 of the Police and Criminal Evidence Act 1984 are of the first importance in their field. The section provides that in all criminal and civil proceedings any such code shall be admissible in evidence; and if any provision of any such code (relating for example to the questioning of persons by police officers) appears to the court to be relevant to any question arising in the proceedings, it shall be taken into account in determining that question (eg as to the admissibility of confessions).

Another circumstance in which a code has to be taken into account is where it is *addressed to authorities* requiring them to have regard to it in exercising their functions in relation to third parties. For example, where work is being done on a construction site a local authority may serve a notice imposing requirements as to the way the work is to be carried out. In exercising that function the authority must 'take into account' the provisions of any 'noise' code made by the Secretary of State for 'giving guidance on appropriate methods ... for minimising noise'.[13] Under the Water Act 1989 water undertakers are empowered to carry out certain works on private land. Every undertaker must submit to the minister for approval a code of practice with respect to its exercise of those powers. (His approval is given in a statutory instrument. The code itself is published by the undertaker.) Any complaint about the exercise of the powers in question is investigated by the Director General of Water Services. If he is satisfied that the undertaker by acting unreasonably, caused the complainant loss, he may direct the undertaker to pay the complainant up to £5,000. Breach of the code does not entitle anyone to payment but the DGWS is to 'take into account' whether there has been any such breach in deciding whether to give any, and if so what, direction.[14]

Under section 43 of the Education (No 2) Act 1986 a University must act so as to ensure freedom of speech within the institution. To this end it must itself draw up and issue a code of practice setting out the procedures and conduct required at meetings, and everyone concerned must try to ensure that those requirements are complied with.

13 Control of Pollution Act 1974 ss 60, 71.
14 Water Act 1989, s 162.

A variation on the way effect may be given to a code of practice is found in the Food Safety Act 1990. Under section 40 ministers may issue 'codes of recommended practice' for the guidance of food authorities and to which they are to have regard. But more than this: ministers may give directions to authorities requiring them to take specified steps in order to comply with such a code; any such direction is enforceable by a mandamus on application to the court by the minister. This makes it little removed from a statutory instrument.

It was stated above that a code of practice, though relevant evidence, will not alter the burden of proof. An exception to that is in section 17 of the Health and Safety at Work etc Act 1974. Under that section, failure to observe a code issued by the Health and Safety Commission (and to which the minister has consented) is admissible evidence of contravention of a provision for which a code is in force. Proof of such a failure is proof of any matter to which the code is relevant, unless the defendant satisfies the court that the steps he took were as effective as if he had complied with the code. Thus the onus is put on the accused to satisfy the court that though he did not observe the code, he took steps to comply with the law which were as effective as if he had complied with the code.

Statute may provide that compliance with a code may constitute a defence in criminal proceedings. By section 31 of the Control of Pollution Act 1974 it is an offence to permit noxious matter to enter any river etc. However, it is a defence to show that such entry is attributable to an act which is in accordance with good agricultural practice – and any practice recommended in a code approved that that purpose is deemed to be a good agricultural practice.

Contrast the following, where adherence to the code does not provide a defence, but a guide to what the offence consists of. By section 20 of the Consumer Protection Act 1987 a person is guilty of an offence if he gives to any consumers an indication which is misleading as to the price (etc) at which any goods (etc) are available. By section 25 the Secretary of State may approve a code of practice for the purpose of giving practical guidance with respect to any of the requirements of section 20.[15] Breach of the code does not itself give rise to any civil or criminal liability. The government originally intended that compliance with it would be a complete defence, but gave way on this point in face of criticism. The result is that compliance or non-compliance is something to be taken into account by the court in deter-mining whether an offence has been committed (like the Highway Code). The Director General of Fair Trading has commented that it is important to appreciate that the code 'is not meant to detract in any way from the broad sweep of the new offence'. Nor is it intended to give a more detailed description of the offence. If it was sought to do that:

it would need to be written in a different style of English with a wording suitable to the description of criminal offences ... The code is intended instead to give

15 See SI 1988/2078. The code itself is in a Schedule.

clear practical guidance in plain English to traders to enable them to avoid being misleading.[16]

Another way in which a code of practice may evolve and operate is as follows. Each education authority has to set up an education appeal committee. Because of certain difficulties in the operation of these tribunals local authority associations drew up, with the help of the Council on Tribunals, a code of practice to help authorities in an area where statutory guidance left many questions unanswered. This is an advisory document only, and there is no legal obligation to follow it. Nevertheless the Local Government Ombudsman will refer to the code in investigating allegations of maladministration by an authority, and where its practice differs from that recommended in the code he will expect the authority to show good reason for doing so.

Grant-maintained schools are those which choose central rather than local government control. Each has its own appeal committee. In this case a code of practice was drawn up by central not local government.

It should be noticed that the title 'code of practice' is not a term of art unlike, say, 'statutory instrument' and is widely used in public and private organisations. Further, statute may provide that an effect similar to that of a code of practice, as described above, may be given to documents differently described. For example, under the Building Act 1984 the minister may make building regulations. By section 6(1) he may approve and issue documents 'for the purpose of providing practical guidance with respect to the requirements' of the regulations. Such 'approved documents', as they are called, are given the same effect as the Highway Code.

Guidance may be required or authorised by statute, but not in any specified form or issued merely as a matter of administration. In the following example an attempt is made to give the status of statutory guidance to an unofficial code of practice. By section 7 of the Local Authority Social Services Act 1980 local authorities 'shall in the exercise of their social services functions ... act under the general guidance of the Secretary of State'. (The guidance is not required to be in any particular form.) The government commissioned the (non-government) Centre for Policy on Ageing to produce a code of practice for residential care homes. The document produced has no formal legal status but in a foreword to it the Secretaries of State asked local authorities in carrying out their duties in relation to residential homes 'to regard [the code] in the same light as the general guidance that we issue from time to time under our powers' under the above section 7. In exercising their powers under the Registered Homes Act 1984 authorities' inspectors of registered homes are expected to have regard to the code of practice which in that indirect way will therefore affect the likelihood of such homes getting the necessary registration.

Codes of practice and similar documents are of course subordinate to any statute under which they are made, and are liable to be struck down

---

16 Borrie 'Consumer Protection for the 1990s' [1987] Law Teacher, 239.

if contrary to law.[17] Administrators are likely to concern themselves with the need to adhere to the relevant code rather than to the wording of the Act under which it is made. Caution may be necessary. In a foreword to a code issued under section 118 of the Mental Health Act 1983 (concerning care of those with mental disorder) ministers point out the need to guard against the tendency to ignore the requirements of the Act itself concerning the criteria for the admission of patients to hospital.

With regard to the making of codes, most of those mentioned are made by ministers. Those made other than by ministers mostly require approval by ministers. Parliamentary procedure is required in some cases – this is referred to later. No particular form is required for codes, and they can come into effect when issued, but in some cases a statutory instrument is necessary to bring one into force.

There is legislative provision for encouraging the adoption of codes of practice by private organisations.[18] Section 124(3) of the Fair Trading Act 1973 imposes a duty on the Director General of Fair Trading 'to encourage relevant [trade] associations to prepare and disseminate to their members codes of practice in safeguarding and promoting the interests of consumers in the United Kingdom'. Some twenty codes have been formulated under this provision covering areas as diverse as funeral directors, footwear, and the photographic industry. Codes are formulated in consultation with the Office of Fair Trading. They are all negotiated on the basis that they are in no way enforceable in the courts, but they invariably contain provision for conciliation of disputes and in most cases for independent arbitration as well. Implementation of a code is for the association concerned, but is monitored by the Office of Fair Trading. The Director General of Fair Trading has described them as 'intended to *supplement* the requirements of the law by obtaining the agreement of trade associations on behalf of their members to raise their standards of trading'.[19] Their advantages are that they are more flexible than legal regulation, can be more readily revised, their enforcement rests with those with knowledge of the trade and they have a relative informality of style which is advantageous when their requirements need to be readily and widely understood.[20] Their principal weaknesses are that they cannot be enforced against non-members and may be difficult to enforce even against members.[1]

Public pressure may persuade private interests to agree to a code of conduct even without the support of the legislative provision referred to in the preceding paragraph, as for example the City Code on Take-overs

17 Eg *R v Secretary of State for the Environment, ex p Tower Hamlets London Borough Council* [1993] 3 All ER 439.
18 See Page 'Self-Regulation and Codes of Practice' [1980] JBL 24.
19 Borrie 'Laws and Codes for Consumers' [1980] JBL 315 at 322, and *The Development of Consumer Law*.
20 *Review of legislation on false and misleading price information:* Department of Trade and Industry, 1984.
1 Annual Report of the Director General of Fair Trading 1982.

and Mergers.[2] The possibility of direct legal intervention in their affairs may be a powerful consideration in persuading private interests of the need to regulate their conduct through such codes.

Circulars and other informal documents

Now come a range of documents prominent amongst which are 'circulars'; there are also bulletins, notices, notes for guidance, guidance manuals, policy notices or whatever terminology is thought by the administration to be relevant, including 'letter'.

Dealing first with *circulars*, a well-established category – and to be handled with care because of their varying impact.[3] By a circular is meant no more than a document, copies of which are sent or made available to a number of people. It should be appreciated that statute never authorises or requires the issue of a circular; statutory authority is not required; they are issued as part of the administrative process.[4] What then will be found in circulars, and with what effect?

In the first place a circular may do no more than contain *information* as where it draws authorities' attention to a recently published report; or explains the purpose of new legislation.[5] The information may be about the government's policy coupled with a request to authorities to observe it. For example by circular 10/65 the Department of Education asked local authorities to prepare plans for the reorganisation of schools on the comprehensive principle. This imposed no legally-enforceable obligation.[6] (The circular was 'repealed' by a later government by another circular signed by the same civil servant.) Where the information is as to how the government intends to *exercise its powers* it will be necessary to pay close attention to it. For example, where an applicant is refused planning permission by the local authority, he may appeal to the Secretary of State who may decide the appeal as if the application had been made to him in the first place. Documents called 'circulars' and 'planning policy guidance notes'[7] stating the considerations the Secretary of State will take into account in deciding appeals are thus essential documents in the practice and law of town and country planning and must be taken into account by the local authority in deciding whether to grant planning permission, and by the Secretary of State in considering an appeal.

A circular may contain *advice* or *guidance* as to the *exercise by the recipients of their powers*. Department of the Environment circular 1/85

2 See p 345, below.
3 See Baldwin and Houghton, 'Circular Arguments' [1986] PL 239.
4 Lexis indicates that 'circular' is used in statutes only in connection with commercial advertisements, and with the shape of eg manholes. For rare example see National Health Service and Community Care Act 1990, Sch 2, para 6(2)(e).
5 'A dangerous course to follow' – Graham op cit, p 55 fn 15 at p 5.
6 The policy was to be achieved by the use of a statutory power to refuse approval of school building projects not based on that principle.
7 The former contain advice on legislation and procedures, the latter, policy guidance on planning matters. They may need careful interpretation: *Safeway Properties Ltd v Secretary of State for the Environment* (1992) 63 P & CR 73.

advises local authorities as to the conditions that can lawfully be attached to the grant of planning permission. This (or any such advice) is of course only the Department's view of the law, not the law itself, and furthermore it is only its views of the law as at the date of the issue of the circular.[8] But consider *Coleshill and District Investment Co Ltd v Minister of Housing and Local Government*.[9] Here a circular issued twenty years earlier had given the Department's view as to whether demolition constituted 'development' and therefore required planning permission. Lord Wilberforce said:

I accept of course, that as an interpretation of the [Town and Country Planning] Act of 1947, under which it was issued, the circular has no legal status but it acquired vitality and strength when, through the years, it passed, as it certainly did, into planning practice and textbooks, was acted on as it certainly was in planning decision, and when the Act of 1962 (and I may add [of] 1968) maintained the same definition of development under which it was issued.[10]

In *Bristol District Council v Clark*[11] the question was what were the relevant considerations a local authority was to take into account when deciding whether to evict a tenant. Scarman LJ referred to government circulars inviting local authorities exercising Housing Act functions to have regard to the problem of homelessness, alternatives to eviction etc. He continued:

I do not think it possible to rely on those circulars as imposing any direct statutory duty on a housing authority; but I think they are a good indication as to the purposes to be served by the Housing Acts and as to what are the relevant matters ... to be taken into account by a local authority serving a notice to quit on a tenant in arrears of rent.

In *Annison v District Auditor for Metropolitan Borough of St Pancras Borough Council*[12] a circular was ignored by councillors to their disadvantage. They applied to the court to be relieved from a surcharge imposed by the district auditor. One of the factors persuading the court not to grant relief was that they had had their attention drawn to a circular

---

8 Lord Scarman in *Newbury District Council v Secretary of State for the Environment* [1981] AC 578 at 621, [1980] 1 All ER 731 at 756. For challenge to circular advice see p 409 below.
9 [1969] 2 All ER 525, [1969] 1 WLR 746, HL.
10 The phrase 'under which it was issued' is not to be taken to mean that the Act authorised or required the publication of the document: it was done as a part of the administration of the department's affairs. On the other hand, the publication of documents giving information as to how a department is going to exercise its powers may be required by statute – see eg Animals (Scientific Procedures) Act 1986, s 21(1), Banking Act 1979, s 16(1). For attempt to rely on circulars for interpretation of statute see *McCarthy & Stone (Developments) Ltd v Richmond upon Thames London Borough Council* [1991] 4 All ER 897.
11 [1975] 3 All ER 976, [1975] 1 WLR 1443, CA.
12 [1962] 1 QB 489, [1961] 3 All ER 914.

suggesting the right course of action for local authorities to take but had acted otherwise.

In *R v Secretary of State for the Home Department, ex p Lancashire Police Authority*[13] one police force gave assistance to another, and was entitled to be paid for it. Payment was to be determined in the light of agreement by and set out in circulars issued by the Police Negotiating Board. As there was disagreement over payment, the amount had to be determined by the minister. The court said that the circular (recommendatory to the minister) was of 'central relevance' to his determination.

A circular may go further than this. It may be the vehicle for *conferring powers* or *imposing duties* on recipients. A grant of powers to local authorities (by for example the delegation under statutory authority of ministerial powers to them) may be notified and conferred by circular. And Department of the Environment circular 105/73 contained a general dispensation permitting local authority members who are tenants of their authority to speak and vote on any matter of general housing policy despite their pecuniary interest as tenants. Or a circular may contain a *direction* to authorities generally, as for example a direction to National Health Service authorities as to the charges to be made to patients for hospital accommodation. In that case, it will be noted, the circular affected the *legal position of third parties* – the patients. This possibility was brought out in a case investigated by the Parliamentary Commissioner. Grants for teacher-training students were paid by local authorities in accordance with arrangements approved by the Secretary of State. Approved arrangements were set out in a circular. Such a circular is:

something more than a document issuing information to the general public; it is (and this is its primary function) a document setting out arrangements approved by the Secretary of State in pursuance of a statutory provision. Those arrangements impose duties and confer rights and powers which are enforceable in the courts as statutory duties, powers and rights.[14]

In *Palmer v Inverness Hospitals Board*[15] a department had issued a circular to hospital authorities setting out the procedure they should follow in disciplinary cases. The court held that the circular was incorporated into the plaintiff's contract of service with the defendant authority.

It is clear therefore that we cannot say, simply because a document is headed 'circular' what its effect in law is. We must examine its contents (it may, for example, be the vehicle for publishing a code of practice). And of course a document designated 'bulletin' or even 'letter' may have consequences similar to those given to a circular.

Statements of departmental practice issued by the Inland Revenue are of great importance in the practical administration of the taxation system. These statements are of various sorts. First, there are the Extra-Statutory Concessions. They are published as a booklet. Some are of long standing.

---

13 [1992] COD 161.
14 First Report of the Parliamentary Commissioner, 1974, HC 2, case C117/T, p 6 at para 6.
15 1963 SC 311.

They are 'few, tightly-written and almost legislative in form'.[16] Of course, they cannot be legislative in substance. They cannot take away the citizens' legal rights. Nor can they add to them: they are *extra* statutory. They can be withdrawn or limited at the discretion of the authorities. The benefit of a concession cannot be claimed in the courts. Indeed, most of them are of doubtful legality.[17] In addition to the Concessions, there are also Statements of Practice and other less formal publications of the official view.[18]

Public Notices published by Customs and Excise concerning value added tax are of interest. It has been shown[19] that three types of provisions will be found in these Notices: there may be elements derived from legislative powers; they may contain interpretive guidance; and they may detail extra-statutory concessions. Naturally these are given different weight by the relevant tribunals, and it has been suggested that, in the interest of the public appearing before those tribunals, the department should clarify the differences between the various types of provisions contained in the Notices (though this is to a degree done by the use of different typefaces).

The important Youth Training Scheme had been promulgated by no more than leaflets.[20]

Announcements as to the administration of important schemes may be made in a ministerial Parliamentary[1] statement or written answer.

Immigration rules

By the Immigration Act 1971 certain categories of persons are entitled to enter the United Kingdom. Others can enter only if given leave to do so. By section 3(2) of the Act the Secretary of State is to lay down rules 'as to the practice to be followed in the administration of [the] Act for regulating the entry ... of persons required to have leave to enter'. The rules so made have to be laid before Parliament, and are subject to disapproval there. The rules are of course binding on those officials who administer the Act. Further, where an immigrant appeals to the tribunal set up under the Act against a decision adverse to him, the tribunal is to allow the appeal if it considers that the decision appealed against was not in accordance with any relevant rule. Clearly the rules are of the first importance in the administration of immigration control and many cases reaching the courts turn on their correct interpretation. What is their status? It will be noted that they are not contained *in* or *given effect by* statutory instrument but are subject to Parliamentary process. In *R v Chief Immigration Officer,*

16 Tiley *Revenue Law* 3rd edn, p 27.
17 Williams 'Extra-Statutory Concessions' [1979] BTR 137; Potter 'Extra-Statutory Concessions' [1980] BTR 270; Oliver [1984] PL 389. See *R v Inspector of Taxes, Reading, ex p Fulford-Dobson* [1987] QB 978.
18 Gammie ' "Revenue in Practice": a suitable case for treatment' [1980] BTR 304.
19 Mowbray [1987] BTR 381.
20 Freedland [1980] ILJ 254, [1983] ILJ 220.
 1 For after-dinner speech see Purdue et al *Planning Law and Procedure*, p 37.

Heathrow Airport, ex p Bibi[2] counsel argued that the immigration rules
are not law, but mere departmental circulars laying down no more than
good departmental practice. Roskill LJ 'profoundly disagreed'. The rules,
he said, are 'just as much delegated legislation as any other form of rule-
making activity of delegated legislation'. A later Court of Appeal in *R v
Secretary of State for the Home Department, ex p Hosenball*[3] demurred.
The 'curious amalgam' that the rules comprise was commented on. They
are rules of practice for immigration officials; explanatory notes on the
Act itself; of legal effect in the appellate process, and taken into account
by the courts in deciding whether an official has acted fairly. For Geoffrey
Lane LJ the rules are 'very difficult to categorise or clarify. They are in a
class of their own'. For Lord Denning MR 'they are not rules in the nature
of delegated legislation so as to amount to strict rules of law', and for
Cumming-Bruce LJ they are 'not ... in any sense of themselves of
legislative force'. Lord Roskill (apparently persuaded by those views) said
later,[4] 'The rules give guidance to the various officers concerned and
contained statements of general policy ...' They were therefore not to be
construed like statutes. Lord Fraser, emphasising the words 'practice'
and 'administration' in s 3(2), said that though the rules have Parliamentary approval, they are not contained in statutory instruments and
do not have the force of law.[5] And most recently, in another case involving
the interpretation of the rules and their nature,[6] Lord Bridge said,
'Immigration rules ... are quite unlike ordinary delegated legislation ...
The rules do not purport to enact a precise code having statutory force.
They are discursive in style, in part merely explanatory, and on their face
frequently offer no more than broad guidance as to how discretion is to be
exercised in different typical situations.'

Regulations, codes or circulars – the appropriate form

The object of these various documents, by whatever title called, is to
regulate behaviour in some way. The question now is, what is the
appropriate and effective way of doing so, and in what document should
it be contained? This can only be usefully considered by means of further
examples.

Circular appropriate, code of practice inappropriate. When the Prevention
of Terrorism (Temporary Provisions) Act 1984 was being considered by
the House of Lords an amendment was moved to provide that a policeman's
power of arrest under section 12 of the Act should not be exercisable until
a code of practice giving guidance as to how the power should be exercised
had been made by the Secretary of State by way of statutory instrument.

2 [1976] 3 All ER 843, [1976] 1 WLR 979.
3 [1977] 3 All ER 452, [1977] 1 WLR 766.
4 *Alexander v Immigration Appeal Tribunal* [1982] 2 All ER 766, [1982] 1 WLR 1076.
5 *Re Amin* [1983] 2 AC 818, [1983] 2 All ER 864.
6 *Singh v Immigration Appeal Tribunal* [1986] 2 All ER 721 at 727.

This was rejected on the ground that this 'guidance' would interfere with the operational independence of the police.[7] The government undertook to issue a circular to the police on the exercise of the power. This explains how the power in question 'should' be used. Clearly, guidance in a circular was thought less intrusive than guidance in a code of practice: if the latter form is used, there is some suggestion that it is, if only indirectly, in some way enforceable.

Contrast the codes of practice issued under the Police and Criminal Evidence Act 1984 in connection with the exercise by the police of certain powers of search and seizure. Failure by a police officer to comply with such a code will not of itself render him liable to civil or criminal proceedings, but a code is admissible in evidence in any such proceedings. And a police officer is liable to disciplinary proceedings for failure to comply with a code.

Code appropriate, rules unnecessary. Refer here to the code of practice which governs the holding of an 'examination in public' – compared with the planning appeal inquiry, which is governed by a statutory instrument.[8]

Code satisfactory, but rules held in reserve. The suspicion that a code may be ineffective to bring about desired results is illustrated by the following. The object of Part II of the Local Government Planning and Land Act 1980 is to require publication by local authorities of financial and other information about their activities. The original intention was to impose a duty to do so on authorities by regulations made by the Secretary of State, supplemented by a code of practice, but as enacted, section 2 of that Act makes a 'code of recommended practice' the main device for securing publication of the information – with however, reserve powers, as the Secretary of State can make regulations requiring publication of information specified in a code 'if in his opinion it is necessary to make such regulations in order to ensure that authorities give public information of that description'.

One of the codes that has been made concerns the publication by authorities of information about the time taken to handle planning applications. It provides that quarterly reports 'should' be made available to members of the public on demand; that publicity 'shall' be made available to members of the public on demand; that publicity 'shall' be given to the fact that they are available; that authorities 'should' provide copies to the local press, and 'may wish' to send copies to interested parties.

Code inappropriate, rules necessary. It had been suggested to the Keith Committee on the Enforcement Powers of the Revenue Departments that a code of practice should be introduced to deal with the use by inland revenue authorities of control visits and investigation procedures. The Committee reported:

7   449 HL Official Report (6th series) col 862.
8   See pp 124 and 126 below.

In our view a code of this nature is not an appropriate means of providing safeguards against abuse of essentially intrusive powers. We consider that such safeguards should be brought into existence by statute and applied, where necessary, by external judicial authority.[9]

Circular and code ineffective. The proved ineffectiveness of both a circular and a code is illustrated by the following episode concerning the problem of homelessness. In 1974 the Department of the Environment issued a circular to county and district councils urging them to co-operate (through their respective social services and housing departments) in dealing with homelessness setting out its views as to which group of persons were entitled to priority treatment. The response was inadequate. A combination of events (including a new Labour government and a private member's Bill) led to the Housing (Homeless Persons) Act 1977,[10] which, in general terms, imposes duties on district councils to provide accommodation for the homeless. Section 12 of that Act says that those authorities 'shall have regard in the exercise of their functions to such guidance as may from time to time be given by the Secretary of State'. A code of guidance was accordingly published. In *Pulhofer v Hillingdon London Borough Council*[11] Mr and Mrs P were living with two small children in one room which had no means of cooking or for washing clothes. They applied to the council for accommodation on the ground that they were homeless because the accommodation they were in was inadequate for their needs. They were denied it on the ground that they had accommodation. They argued that the duty was to provide 'appropriate' accommodation. The House of Lords declined to imply that requirement: what was properly to be regarded as accommodation was a question of fact to be decided by the council (though it was generously conceded that a barrel was not accommo-dation as it was not capable of accommodating). In arriving at that conclusion the House of Lords regarded the code of guidance as irrelevant as not providing any assistance on the point at issue. However, it was later argued in the House of Lords (in its legislative capacity) that it was indeed Parliament's intention that regard was to be had to the condition of the accommodation, an intention that was confirmed by the code of guidance which referred to housing conditions in which people could not reasonably be expected to remain because of a lack of basic amenities. The law now is (despite government resistance) that a person is not to be treated as having accommodation 'unless it is accommodation which would be reasonable for him to continue to occupy'.[12] We see therefore the failure of a circular to persuade, followed by a statutory code, that being rendered ineffective by the courts, and finally direct legislative intervention.

9 Cmnd 8822, p 119.
10 See now the Housing Act 1985.
11 [1986] AC 484, [1986] 1 All ER 467.
12 Housing Act 1985, s 58(2A).

Publication of delegated legislation etc

It is a fundamental principle that the public must have access to the law. Acts of Parliament are valid on receiving Royal Assent, even if not generally published. They are, or should be, available from the Stationery Office. What of delegated legislation?

As for *statutory instruments,* section 2 of the Statutory Instruments Act 1946 says that immediately after the making of any statutory instrument it must be sent to the Queen's Printer of Acts of Parliament ie the Controller of the Stationery Office, who is to *number* it and cause copies to be *printed* and *sold* by him as soon as possible.[13]

Certain instruments are however exempt from the requirements of printing and sale by HMSO.[14] They are as follows: (a) Statutory instruments are classified as local or general according to their subject matter. Local instruments are normally exempt from the requirements referred to.[15] (b) Where the minister considers that the printing and sale of an instrument 'is unnecessary having regard to the brevity of the period during which that instrument will remain in force and to any other steps taken or to be taken for bringing its substance to the notice of the public'. (c) Where the minister certifies that the printing and sale of any schedule (or other annexed document) is unnecessary or undesirable having regard to its nature or bulk and to any other steps taken to bring its substance to the notice of the public, such schedule etc will be exempt. (d) Where the minister certifies that the printing and sale of an instrument before the instrument comes into force would be contrary to the public interest, it will be exempt.

In addition to publication by HMSO some further public notification of the making of a statutory instrument may be required by the parent Act as, for example, in the *London Gazette.*[16]

The Stationery Office is required by section 3 of the Statutory Instruments Act to publish lists showing the date on which every instrument printed and sold by it was first *issued;* the list is conclusive evidence of the date on which an instrument was first issued. If anyone is prosecuted for contravening the provisions of a statutory instrument he can by section 3(2) set up the defence that the instrument, *though made,* had not been issued at the date of the alleged contravention. The prosecution will however succeed if it can prove that nevertheless reasonable steps had at that date been taken to bring the purport of the instrument to the notice of the public or of persons likely to be affected by it, or of the persons charged.

13 The section also applies, unusually, to a resolution of the House of Commons under the House of Commons Members Fund Act 1948, s 3: see eg SI 1994/631. Annual volumes of statutory instruments are published by HMSO. General instruments are printed in full: local instruments are listed. Certain instruments which are not SIs are printed in an Appendix.

14 Section 3, 8(1), and SI 1948/1.

15 About half all statutory instruments are local.

16 SIs and other documents made in connection with the Iraq–Kuwait war in 1990, concerning the export of goods, were published in full in newspapers.

There are two cases to be considered on these requirements. *Simmonds v Newell*[17] concerned requirement (c) above as to the ministerial certificate that the printing of a schedule is unnecessary. Two points were at issue: had there been a valid certification; if not, what was the effect of that omission? The facts were that S was convicted summarily of selling steel prices higher than those permitted and laid down in schedules to a ministerial order. The (97) schedules had not been printed and sold by HMSO. S argued that there was no valid certificate exempting the schedules from those requirements. The only document produced to the magistrates on the matter was a letter from a civil servant to the Editor of the Statutory Instruments which stated, inter alia, that the schedules had been certified. But no certificate was produced to that court. The Divisional Court ruled that there was no valid certificate. What was the effect of there being no such certificate? The Crown agreed that (while the lack of the certificate did not, it said, affect the validity of the order itself), it did throw on it the burden of proving that steps had been taken for bringing the purport of the instrument to the notice of those affected. It appears that such steps had in fact been taken, but no evidence to that effect was before the justices. As there was therefore no proof of the steps taken the defence succeeded and the conviction was quashed.

In *R v Sheer Metalcraft Ltd*[18] it was argued that as there was no ministerial certificate exempting the schedules, the price-fixing order was not validly made. (This was of course the point referred to but not decided on in *Simmonds v Newell* above.) The court ruled that the implication of section 3(2) is that the *making* of an instrument is one thing, its *issue* another. The very fact that subsection (2) of section 3 refers to a defence that the instrument has not been issued postulates that the instrument could be validly made even though not issued, otherwise it could never have been contravened. The failure to certify the exemption of the schedules did not, the court ruled, invalidate the order itself, but put on the Crown the burden of proving that they had taken reasonable steps for bringing the instrument to the notice of those affected. Evidence to that effect was then given, and the jury returned a guilty verdict.

The case just referred to indicates that under the Statutory Instruments Act an instrument may be effective and come into operation before it has been issued. What is the position at common law? Does it require an order to be issued before effect can be given to it? In *Johnson v Sargant & Sons*[19] an order was made on one day, but its effect made known on the next, and it was probably well known to all persons interested in the trade on the later date. Bailhache J said, 'I am unable to hold that this order came into operation before it was known.' The common law appears to be therefore that an order does not have effect until it is adequately published to those affected. In *Lim Chin Aik v R*[20] an order had been

17 [1953] 2 All ER 38, [1953] 1 WLR 826.
18 [1954] 1 QB 586, [1954] 1 All ER 542.
19 [1918] 1 KB 101.
20 [1963] AC 160, [1963] 1 All ER 223.

made barring the appellant from Singapore. The statute under which it had been made had no provision for the publishing of the order (though an order directed to a *class* of persons had to be published). There was no evidence of anything having been done to bring the order to the attention of the appellant or of anyone. Was the appellant bound by it? The Crown argued that the maxim 'ignorance of the law is no excuse' applied, and that once made the order became part of the law. The Judicial Committee of the Privy Council replied thus:

In their Lordships' opinion even if the making of the order by the minister be regarded as the exercise of the legislative as distinct from the executive or administrative function (which they do not concede), the maxim cannot apply to such a case as the present where it appears that there is in the State of Singapore no provision corresponding for example to that in section 3(2) of the English Statutory Instruments Act 1946, for the publication in any form of an order of the kind made in the present case or any other provision designed to enable a man by appropriate inquiry to find out what 'the law' is.

A conviction for breach of the order was therefore quashed.

Can *Johnson v Sargant & Sons* be reconciled with *R v Sheer Metalcraft Ltd*? One view is that the former was wrongly decided, and that the common law rule is that an order is valid when made, that this rule is modified in criminal cases by the defence provided by section 3(2) of the 1946 Act, so that that section is an exception to the general rule. A contrary view is that the general rule is that delegated legislation does not come into force until it is published and that section 3(2) is not an exception to that rule but 'a rather limited statutory declaration of that rule'.[1] The question, it has been said, is whether the principle of justice is to be preferred to that of administrative efficiency.[2]

Documents which are not statutory instruments do not of course fall within the requirements of the Statutory Instruments Act, but may be required by the Act authorising them to be made to be published in some specified way. If there is no such requirement they should in the interests of good government be published in the most appropriate way.

Concerning *codes of practice*, Cabinet Office guidance[3] is that 'departments should ensure that there are satisfactory arrangements for publication or other means of bringing the contents of a code of practice to the notice of those to whom it is directed. No specific statutory provision is required, although it is sometimes found, for the sale and publication of codes. In the case of codes addressed to authorities, it should be borne in mind that others may have a legitimate interest in the contents of the codes, for instance in order to challenge a decision taken in breach of the code'.

The need to publish *circulars* was shown in *Blackpool Corpn v Locker*.[4] The maxim 'ignorance of the law is no excuse' is, said Scott LJ, the working

---

1 Lanham 'Delegated Legislation and Publication' (1974) 37 MLR 510.
2 Lanham [1983] PL 395 replying to Campbell [1982] PL 569.
3 *Codes of Practice and Legislation* issued in 1987 with the approval of the English and Scottish Law Officers.
4 [1948] 1 All ER 85.

hypothesis on which the rule of law rests, but to operate it required that the whole of the law be accessible to the public. In that case a minister had delegated to local authorities by circular his power of requisitioning houses. Scott LJ regarded the circular as legislative in character. It was most important that the circular should have been made known to Locker, whose house was requisitioned, for it contained limits on the requisitioning power. The requisitioning was in fact held to be void as the corporation had ignored those limits – but how could Locker know that without seeing the circular? Yet the authorities refused for almost six months to disclose it, a fact which drew heavy criticism from the Court of Appeal. Scott LJ said that there was no common law or statutory duty to publish sub-delegated legislation, and suggested that the Statutory Instruments Act 1946 should be amended.[5]

The need to publish *changes in administrative rules* has been referred to in this way by the Select Committee of the Parliamentary Commissioner.

We accept that with the large number of administrative rules formulated by government every year, the extent to which changes should be made public must be a matter of judgment [but we] trust that consideration will be given to the need for immediate publicity where significant changes affecting the public are made in administrative rules.[6]

The need to make public certain *administrative practices* was referred to in *Legal Entitlements and Administrative Practices*.[7] This report states that although claims to which there is legal entitlement must be met in full, *de minimis* practices (under which small sums of money are not paid to, or small overpayments not reclaimed from, members of the public) are necessary in order to keep the costs of administration at a tolerable level. But such practices, the report said, should be made public: if publicity results in criticism, it may be necessary to consider whether legislative approval should be sought to maintain the effectiveness of the practice.

A good reason for publishing is to dispel suspicion. A House of Commons Committee suggested that a part of the Planning Inspectorates Handbook which gave guidance to inspectors on certain matters should be published. One of those matters was the meaning that should be given by inspectors to 'contrary to the public interest'. The Committee suggested that if the guidance given on that matter was not published there would be a natural suspicion that the phrase was being equated with 'contrary to the government's interest'.[8]

---

5 De Smith 'Sub-delegation and Circulars' (1949) 12 MLR 37. See *Bugg v DPP* [1993] 2 All ER 817 for difficulty in getting bye-laws.
6 First Report from the Select Committee, 1970–1 HC 240, paras 12–21. Govt reply Cmnd 4729.
7 A report by officials, 1979 (HMSO). See p 543 below.
8 First Report from the Energy Committee, 1987–88, HC 310.

Parliamentary consideration of ministerial regulations etc

Ministers are of course accountable for everything falling within their area of responsibility, and may therefore be called to account for the delegated legislation they make as for anything else they do. But in addition Parliament may, in the Act authorising the regulations to be made, require some specified parliamentary procedure to be followed – or, more realistically, the government when drafting its bill, may propose to subject the regulations it will make to a degree of Parliamentary scrutiny; it is possible, though not common, for it to be persuaded by Parliament that that degree of scrutiny is inadequate. This is important. Parliament has delegated legislative powers to ministers, and must have some means of scrutinising or controlling the exercise of that power.

Laying and related procedures
As far as statutory instruments are concerned there are various forms of parliamentary control that may be provided for by the parent statute.

(a) The parent Act may merely require an instrument made under it to be *laid before Parliament* after being made, but require no further parliamentary procedure.

Section 4 of the Statutory Instruments Act 1946 says that where this form of control is provided for the instrument must be laid before coming into operation. Thus an instrument subject to this bare laying procedure is *made*, then *laid*, then *comes into operation* on the date specified. (At the top of every instrument which falls within section 4 will be found the dates of making, laying, and coming into operation.) But if it is essential that an instrument should come into operation before copies can be laid this may be done provided the Lord Chancellor and the Speaker of the House are notified and reasons given as to why copies were not laid before coming into operation. This laying requirement means that the regulation is drawn to the notice of members but is not subjected to the negative or affirmative procedures to be mentioned below.

Normally the requirement in the parent Act is to lay the document before both Houses of Parliament, but in some cases, usually where taxation is involved, the obligation is to lay before the House of Commons only.[9]

An 'instrument' is 'laid' when the procedure required by Standing Orders is observed.[10] (It must be emphasised that the Statutory Instruments Act does not itself contain any laying requirements but merely prescribes the procedure to be followed where a parent Act requires certain forms of parliamentary control.)

(b) The parent Act may say that an instrument made under it is to be *subject to annulment* in pursuance of a resolution in either House (or in

9 Eg Car Tax Act 1983, s 8(3).
10 The Laying of Documents before Parliament Act 1948. A statutory instrument is 'laid' with the delivery of a copy to the Votes and Proceedings Office—SO 138 of the House of Commons, 1988. See *R v Immigration Appeal Tribunal, ex p Joyles* [1972] 3 All ER 213, [1972] 1 WLR 1390.

the Commons only). Section 5 of the Statutory Instruments Act then applies. It provides that the instrument must be laid before Parliament after being made and that it may be annulled by either House within the period of 40 days beginning with the day on which a copy of the instrument was laid before it. Thus the instrument is *made*, then *laid*, then *comes into operation*[11] on the date specified, and may be *annulled* within 40 days from the day on which it was *laid*. Any member may seek to annul an instrument by moving that 'an address be presented to Her Majesty praying that the instrument be annulled'. If this is agreed to then by section 5(1) 'no further proceedings shall be taken thereunder after the date of the resolution, and Her Majesty may by Order in Council revoke the instrument'. Notice therefore that the instrument is *not* annulled by the resolution: government action is necessary for that. The subsection goes on to say that such resolution and revocation 'shall be without prejudice to the validity of anything previously done under the instrument or to the making of a new statutory instrument'. Annulment is rare, as voting is whipped.[12]

Such 'prayers' for annulment, as they are called, can be considered in the House of Commons only after government business for the day has been dealt with, that is, after 10 pm. This used to mean that the House might sit late into and even through the night, and the procedure was used too with the intention of harassing the government. Following a recommendation of the Select Committee on Delegated Legislation in 1953[13] the procedure now is that if a prayer is under discussion at 11.30 pm the Speaker puts the question to the House at that hour, unless he thinks that, owing to the lateness of the time of starting the discussion on the prayer or owing to the importance of the issues raised by the instrument, the time for debate has not been adequate. In that case the debate is adjourned to the next sitting day of the House and is resumed at the end of government business on that day.

An important point to note is that a prayer cannot seek the amendment but only the total annulment of an instrument. (Amending regulations may of course be introduced by the government as the result of a prayer.) The argument against allowing amendments to be moved is that if this were permitted Parliament would then find itself engaged in matters of detail and this would run counter to the basic purpose of delegated legislation which is to relieve Parliament of the consideration of details.

(c) A third form of parliamentary control is the requirement that a regulation must have the *affirmative* approval of Parliament in order to be effective. The order is made, then laid, but cannot come into effect unless approved. This then is the affirmative procedure, to be contrasted with the *negative* procedure described in (b) above.

---

11 It is now established practice that instruments subject to the negative procedure are laid before Parliament at least 21 days before they come into operation.

12 For example see 34 H of C Official Report (6th series) col 355 (immigration rules). See Beith 'Prayers Unanswered ...' (1981) 34 Parly Affairs 165.

13 1952–3, HC 310.

The procedures described in the two following paragraphs, (d) and (e), both involve the laying of the instrument *in draft*.

(d) A statute may provide that a draft of the instrument made under it must be laid before Parliament for *affirmative* approval. If the draft is approved the instrument may then be made in the terms of the draft.

(e) The parent Act may provide for the draft of an instrument to be laid and that the instrument *cannot be made if the draft is disapproved*. The procedure in (d) above is affirmative, this is negative. Section 6 of the Statutory Instruments Act provides that where a draft of an instrument is to be laid before Parliament the instrument shall not be made until the expiration of a period of 40 days beginning with the day on which a copy of the draft is laid before Parliament. If within that period it is resolved that the instrument be not made, 'no further proceedings shall be taken thereon, but without prejudice to the laying before Parliament of a new draft'.

It will be noted that the 40-day period is relevant to both sections 5 and 6 (section 5 is referred to in (b) above). Section 7 says that in calculating that period 'no account shall be taken of any time during which Parliament is dissolved or prorogued or during which both Houses are adjourned for more than four days'. This means, first, that account is taken of weekends; secondly, that if Parliament is prorogued or dissolved, there is no need to re-lay the instrument: the days during which it is prorogued or dissolved do not count towards the 40 days; thirdly, that if only one House is adjourned, time runs.

(f) Another method of control is to say that an instrument which has been made *will expire* at the end of a specified period (usually twenty-eight or forty days) *unless within that period it is approved* by resolution of each House or, where the House of Commons only is involved, that House. In general the 28 or 40 days are calculated in the same way as the 40 days, (e) above. (This again is an affirmative procedure.)

(g) There may be *no laying requirement at all*. This is not uncommon. For example, commencement orders are invariably not required to be laid.

A Joint Committee on Delegated Legislation reviewed the various laying procedures.[14] It said that procedure (a), bare laying, is relatively uncommon. Procedure (b), laying subject to annulment, *is by far the most common*. Procedures (c) and (d), it pointed out, are both affirmative, but (d), the laying of a draft subject to affirmative procedure, is much more common than (c). An advantage of (d) is that the government is less firmly committed to a draft than to an instrument already made. Procedure (e) it seems is rarely used. Procedure (f) is not common – 28 (or 40) day orders – but 'serves an essential purpose in the case of instruments which call for something more than negative control but cannot be disclosed in advance of coming into operation'. (g) is the second largest class. As this involves no laying procedure at all, this would seem a serious matter. There is however another control to be referred to later which covers this class.

14 Second Report for 1972–3, HL 304.

It will be noted that the seven procedures – (a) to (g) set out above – can be put into four categories thus: affirmative, negative, laying only, no laying requirements at all. The Joint Committee said that with a few exceptions, no consistent pattern could be found in previous practice. Its recommendations for the future were these. The *negative* procedure should generally be selected unless the power is of a type which would normally require the affirmative procedure or unless it is of a type over which Parliament has generally been content to relinquish any further control – in other words, the negative procedure unless there is good reason for using the affirmative procedure or for using neither. The *affirmative* procedure, the Committee said, is normally appropriate for (i) powers substantially affecting provisions of Acts of Parliament, (ii) powers to impose taxation or other financial burdens on the subject or to raise statutory limits on the amounts which may be borrowed by or lent or granted to public bodies, (iii) powers involving considerations of special importance not falling under (i) or (ii), for example powers to create new varieties of criminal offence of a serious character. Instruments which need normally be subject to *neither affirmative nor negative* procedure include commencement orders, orders prescribing routine forms etc.[15]

The above discussion has been about laying and related procedures (in relation to statutory instruments). There are additional techniques to keep Parliament informed about ministerial orders. The minister may be required to provide Parliament with an explanation of the instrument,[16] or proposed regulations, or with his reasons for thinking that an order is not necessary;[17] or with a statement as to the effect of an order.[18] In addition the views of an independent non-parliamentary body may have to be laid before Parliament.[19]

Some unusual examples of parliamentary control can be found in the Emergency Powers Act 1920.[20] First, if at the time when the Proclamation is made Parliament is not to sit for five days, it must be recalled. Second, the regulations may be 'added to, altered or revoked' by resolution of both Houses. Third, the regulations continue in force for only seven days unless continued in force by resolution of both Houses.

Finally, we noted that an Act may provide that an instrument is to be subject to procedures in the Commons only. Where the consent of both Houses to a regulation is required, that of the Lords cannot be dispensed with: the provisions of the Parliament Acts 1911 and 1949 (which say that in some circumstances a bill can become law without the Lords' consent) do not apply to delegated legislation. The Lords have however refused consent to a regulation only once. The government then made an identical order which the Lords let through.

15 It is a rule that the exercise of powers to make instruments that are suitable to different forms of parliamentary control should not be combined in a single instrument.
16 Eg Local Government Act 1974, s 3(3) (repealed but example relevant).
17 Eg Social Security Act 1975, s 126.
18 Eg General Rate Act 1967, s 35(5) (repealed but example relevant).
19 See p 130 below for Social Security Advisory Committee.
20 See p 63 above; Morris 'The Emergency Powers Act 1920' [1979] PL 317.

It must be emphasised that controls of the kind considered do not apply only to statutory instruments. The considerations that apply in deciding what controls should apply to statutory instruments are relevant also in deciding what controls should apply to documents that are not statutory instruments. Here are examples of such controls:

— Immigration rules[1] have to be laid before Parliament and are subject to disapproval there.

— Codes of practice made under the Employment Protection Act 1975 (which are not delegated legislation) either have to have the affirmative approval of both Houses, or are liable to disapproval (expressed in either case by way of resolution) in either House depending on the subject matter of the code. Proposed alterations to the Highway Code have to be laid before both Houses. If either House within 40 days resolves that the proposed alterations be not made, the revision is not to be made. A code may merely have to be laid, or there may be no Parliamentary involvement at all.

— A 40-day period of objection will be found in connection with a 'notice of designation' under the Video Recordings Act 1984.

— Under section 21 of the Animals (Scientific Procedures) Act 1986 the minister is requires to 'publish information to serve as guidance with respect to the manner in which he proposes to exercise his power to grant licences ...' He must lay copies of such information before Parliament. Either House may pass a resolution requiring the information to be withdrawn; such a resolution must be passed within 40 days; if it is passed the minister must withdraw the information.

— But just as there may be no laying requirement for a statutory instrument, so there may not be for a non-statutory instrument. Under the rules about the Social Fund, payment may be made out of that Fund to meet certain needs 'in accordance with directions given and guidance issued by' the minister. In *R v Secretary of State for Social Security, ex p Stitt*[2] the legality of a general direction excluding all claims of a certain kind was challenged (unsuccessfully). In the High Court Woolf LJ said 'Directions ... have to be followed and are therefore equivalent to delegated legislation: unusual delegated legislation because they are not subject to any form of direct Parliamentary control' – neither laying nor the affirmative or negative resolution procedures. In the Court of Appeal Purchas LJ referred to 'unbridled', 'wholly exceptional and, it might be thought by some objectionable' powers which the government had acquired without any Parliamentary fetter or supervision (other than the minister's annual report to Parliament). (This, he thought, might have been because in the legislative process 'Homer nodded' or 'it may be an unwelcome feature of a dominating executive in a basically two-party democracy'.)

1 See p 79 above.
2 (1990) Times, 5 July. See Lexis.

Examination by parliamentary committee

The Committee on Ministers' Powers had recommended in 1932 that a standing committee should be set up every session to consider and report on every regulation made in exercise of delegated legislative powers and which had been laid before the House. In 1944 a committee having, in general, the same kind of functions as those proposed by the Committee on Ministers' Powers was established.

This committee was the House of Commons *Select Committee on Statutory Instruments* also known as the 'Scrutiny Committee'. Briefly, it considered every statutory instrument which was laid before Parliament and on which proceedings might be taken in Parliament, and every general statutory instrument whether or not it was subject to laying or other requirements. The Committee considered whether the attention of the House should be drawn to any such instrument on certain grounds.

In 1925 the House of Lords had set up its *Special Orders Committee*. It examined any Order in Council, departmental order, rule, regulation, scheme or similar instrument presented to or laid in draft before that House, but only where an affirmative order of the House was required before the instrument became effective. In addition if the instrument was 'hybrid' (that is, was public but affected private interests such that if it had been contained in a bill it would have been treated as a hybrid bill)[3] it was open to anyone who could have petitioned against it as a bill to petition against the merits of the instrument.

This system of separate scrutiny by the two Houses obviously had disadvantages: there was duplication of effort; the Lords did not scrutinise negative instruments; the Commons did not scrutinise some instruments which the Lords did; and you could petition against an instrument only in the Lords.

A Committee of both Houses[4] proposed a Joint Committee whose terms of reference should be those of the Commons and Lords Committees combined.

The Joint Committee on Statutory Instruments

Its recommendations were accepted. As from 1973 each House has appointed a Select Committee of seven members. They come together to form the *Joint Committee on Statutory Instruments* (the Joint Scrutiny Committee). The Committee's job is to consider:
(1) Every instrument which is laid before each House in Parliament and upon which proceedings may be or might have been taken in either House of Parliament in pursuance of an Act of Parliament; being:
　(a) a statutory instrument, or a draft of a statutory instrument;
　(b) a scheme, or an amendment of a scheme, or a draft thereof, requiring approval by statutory instrument;[5]

3　For hybrid bills see p 56 above.
4　Joint Committee on Delegated Legislation, 1971–2, HL 184.
5　Eg SI 1984/2064.

(c) any other instrument (whether or not in draft) where the proceedings in pursuance of an Act of Parliament are proceedings by
   way of an affirmative resolution;

(d) any order subject to special parliamentary procedure.

(2) Every general statutory instrument not within the foregoing classes.

What if the instrument is to be subject to proceedings in the Commons
only? In that case the instruction by the Commons to its Committee is
that it is to consider any instrument of classes (a) (b) and (c) above, and
that 'the Committee do not join with the Committee appointed by the
Lords'.

The appropriate Committee examines the instruments falling within
its terms of reference and decides whether the attention of each House
(or, in the case of a Commons Committee, the Commons) should be drawn
to any of them on one or more of the following grounds:

(a) that it *imposes a charge* on the public revenues or contains provisions
   requiring payments to be made to any public authority in consideration
   of any licence or consent or of any services to be rendered, or prescribes
   the amount of any such charge or payments;

(b) that it is made in pursuance of any enactment containing specific
   provisions *excluding it from challenge in the courts* either at all times
   or after the expiration of a specific period;

(c) that it purports to have *retrospective effect* where the parent Act confers
   no express authority so to provide;

(d) that there has been unjustifiable *delay* in the publication or the laying
   of it before Parliament;

(e) that there has been unjustifiable *delay* in sending notification to the
   Speaker under section 4 of the Statutory Instruments Act 1946 when
   the instrument comes into operation before it is laid;

(f) that there appears to be a doubt whether it is *intra vires* or that it
   appears to make some *unusual or unexpected use* of the powers
   conferred by the statute under which it is made;

(g) that for any special reason its form or purport calls for *elucidation*;

(h) that its *drafting appears to be defective*;

or *on any other ground* which does not impinge on its *merits* or on the
policy behind it: and to report their decision with the reason therefore in
any particular case.[6]

The phrase at the end of the list, 'or on any ground which does not
impinge on its merits or on the policy behind it', will be noticed. It draws
attention to an important distinction, that between merits, policy or
political content on the one hand, and technical defects on the other. The
Joint Committee on Delegated Legislation in its 1972 Report[7] referred
approvingly to the 'settled practice' of keeping considerations of merit
and technical scrutiny quite separate. Thus the former Commons Scrutiny

6 For similar terms of reference of the Examiners of Statutory Rules for Northern Ireland,
   see Maguire (1979) 30 NILQ 306.

7 1971–2, HL 184.

Committee and now the Joint Scrutiny Committee is concerned with technical scrutiny. It cannot concern itself with policy or ends, only means. Its narrowest function is to see that on the face of the instrument everything that should have been done has been done – eg, if the parent Act requires the minister who made the instrument to consult with a specified body before making it, the committee will look to see that the instrument says that the minister did consult with that body, and if the parent Act requires the instrument to contain provisions on a certain matter the committee will look to see that the matter is dealt with in the instrument. But as the examples which follow show, if 'merits' are out of bounds, the Committee goes much further than 'technicalities' might suggest.

An important ground of criticism available to the Committee is that an instrument makes *unusual or unexpected use* of the power conferred – ground (f). Here are some examples:

– An order made under section 3(1) of the Plant Health Act 1967 was reported for conferring on local authorities, without express statutory authority, a power to recover from occupiers of land costs incurred in combating Dutch Elm disease.[8]

– A statutory instrument withdrew from conductors of passenger service vehicles the right, which they had enjoyed for 40 years under earlier regulations, to a reward for handing in lost property.[9]

– The Committee has criticised the degree of parliamentary scrutiny to which regulations are subject. It has also drawn attention to the unique discretionary power of the Executive under the European Communities Act 1972 to choose either the affirmative or the negative procedure for instruments made under section 2(2) of that Act.[10]

– Under a power to make regulations to secure that goods are 'safe', regulations were made making it an offence to sell fireworks to someone appearing to be under 16. If a firework is unsafe, is it any the less so because the purchaser is over 16?[11] the Committee asked.

– The Committee will criticise regulations which put the burden of proof on the accused in criminal proceedings for breach of the regulations.[12]

– An instrument conferred concessions on 'Members of the London Gold Market'. Membership of the Market is determined by the Bank of England. This instrument therefore in effect left the granting of the concessions to the wide discretion of the Bank.[13]

– By section 9(4) of the Transport Act 1968 the minister can designate a Passenger Transport Area. The order doing so much include such

8 The Act was amended: see Agriculture (Miscellaneous Provisions) Act 1972, s 20.
9 Sixteenth Report from the Joint Committee on Statutory Instruments, 1978–9, HC 33–xv.
10 First Special Report from the Joint Committee on Statutory Instruments, 1977–8, HL 51.
11 Thirtieth Report from the Joint Committee, 1985–86, HC 31–xxxix.
12 Special Report from the Joint Committee, 1985–86, HC 31–xxxvii.
13 HC 147–xxv.

provision for the remuneration of the Chairman of the Passenger Transport Authority 'as appears to the Minister to be necessary or expedient'. An order made under this provision provided that the Authority could pay such remuneration as the *Authority* thought reasonable. The Committee reported that this made 'some unusual use of the powers conferred by the Statute under which they are made, in that they delegate to the Authority concerned the power to remunerate their chairman'.[14]

    — An Act provided that an application for a licence had to be made in the 'prescribed manner': this meant prescribed by regulations. Regulations set out the application form. Replacement regulations did not. The department justified this in the interest of flexibility: the details required of applicants could be varied without having to amend the regulations. The Committee commented that the Act did not give a discretion to the minister to delegate such matters beyond the instrument.[15]

It will be noted that under ground (f) now being considered, the Committee can express its doubts as to the vires of an instrument. (It cannot of course rule that it *is* ultra vires: that is for the courts.) The Committee has noted that there is no formal mechanism for ensuring that corrective measures are taken, and thus instruments of doubtful vires may take effect. In some cases the department will agree with the Committee's view as to possible ultra vires and undertake to make new regulations; in other cases it will not. '... some departments respond to points taken by the Committee in a truculent manner, and refuse to repair faults in instruments'.[16] In one case the Committee criticised a department for paying out money under what it admitted to be an ultra vires instrument in expectation of a retrospectively validating statute. (The Committee will not, incidentally, express an opinion as to the legal effect of an instrument.)

Common grounds for criticism are *defective drafting* and *form or purport calling for elucidation.* The former includes ambiguity of meaning, and, where an instrument replaced an earlier instrument, failure to revoke the earlier. Under the latter the Committee has criticised an instrument for a misleading title, for giving an incomplete reference to the statutory power under which it was made, for not stating the specific date on which it came into operation. It has criticised instruments for inadequate definitions or insufficiently comprehensive Explanatory Notes. It has drawn attention to the absence of a right of appeal in a scheme, and has even asked the department to what degree those consulted by it on draft regulations were satisfied with the regulations.

14 Sixth Report from the Select Committee on Statutory Instruments, 1968–9, HL 12–x.
15 Fifth Report from the Joint Committee, 1979–80, HC 146. Criticism of SI 1991/1889 under this heading raised interesting questions of delegation and natural justice: 3rd Report from the Joint Committee, 1991–92, HC 14–iii. The Department's reply referred to the view of the Council on Tribunals.
16 Select Committee on Procedure, 1989–90, HC 19–i, x/vii.

The Committee has drawn special attention to an important matter of principle, namely the recurring tendency of departments to seek to by-pass Parliament by omitting necessary details from instruments and thus to confer wide discretion on the minister to vary the provisions without making a further instrument. Delegated legislation the Committee has said, must be:

detailed, specific and self-explanatory, and should not depend on the exercise of ministerial or departmental discretion unless provision to that effect is expressly contained in the enabling Statute. Circulars explaining or amplifying the contents of either primary or delegated legislation can be very useful to the general public and to the administrators. But the Committee hope that Parliament will condemn subordinate legislation by Department Circular when Parliament has itself passed a parent Act which requires such legislation to be by statutory instrument.[17]

It is not uncommon practice for an instrument to refer to a publication *other than one made by the department* itself. The official publication *Statutory Instruments Practice* has this to say:

Unless there is a specific statutory authority to the contrary, ... such a reference must be to an existing publication and should give the publisher's name, the place and year of publication [etc]; otherwise, if the authors of the publication alter it, the effect of the instrument will be altered, which will constitute unauthorised sub-delegation.[18]

The Committee has also drawn attention to the increasing need to ensure that *codes of practice* receive the attention they deserve, which they do not at present get in Parliament.

The way the Committee works[19] is that the officials who assist it examine the instruments within its terms of reference and report to it any on which they have doubts. The Committee is entitled to require the department to provide an explanation of the whole or part of any instrument. It expects to be provided with a memorandum explaining the need for and effect of certain classes of instruments at the time when they are submitted to it.[20] Oral evidence can be taken from government officials and HMSO, but only from these, which is a disadvantage. The Joint Committee meets weekly when both Houses are in session.

If the Committee does report an instrument to the House, what happens? Subsequent action is for members of the House not for the

---

17 First Special Report from the Joint Committee, 1977–8, HL 51, para 12. See Education Reform Act 1988 s 4(4) and SI 1990/423.

18 See eg Health and Safety at Work etc Act 1974, s 15(4)(b). Where an instrument has to be laid, and it refers to another document, the question may arise whether the document is part of the instrument and so has to be laid: see *R v Secretary of State for Social Services, ex p Camden London Borough Council* [1987] 2 All ER 560, [1987] 1 WLR 819.

19 Hayhurst and Wallington, 'The Parliamentary Scrutiny of Delegated Legislation' [1988] PL 547.

20 Ibid, paras 4, 5. The memorandum may be published. In one case the Committee reported that they were 'unimpressed both by the weak grounds on which the department rested its case and by the inadequately briefed witnesses who appeared before the Committee ... When we asked for a note we got a derisory memorandum ...': Twenty-sixth Report from the Joint Committee on Statutory Instruments, 1985–86, HC 31–xxxiii.

Committee, which does not, for example, itself pray against an instrument. Inevitably, members must rely on the Committee's reports for advice on the technical validity and propriety of instruments. Instruments subject to the affirmative procedure are of particular importance. In the House of Lords a debate on them cannot proceed until the Joint Committee has reported. In the Commons there is an understanding to that effect, but it may be ignored if the circumstances of the instrument or the business of the House requires. In one case, at a time when the department knew that the Committee had doubts about the vires of an order, but had not had a chance of considering it fully, the order was debated in and approved by the House. The Committee later reported its doubts. The department then withdrew the order and a new one had to be approved afresh by the House. 'This makes a farce of the appointment of a Scrutiny Committee to assist the House in its consideration of statutory instruments.'[1] It has been suggested:

- that where the Committee has drawn attention to an instrument subject to the negative procedure, the praying time should be altered to ten days from the date of the Committee's report, if that would be longer than the 40-day period provided by the Statutory Instruments Act; or as an alternative to that,
- that where a 'negative' instrument has been drawn to the attention of the House it should be converted to the 'affirmative' procedure.

So far the government has not seen fit to agree to any of these suggestions. The 'farce' continues.

Within those limitations, the Committee does useful, thankless and unobtrusive work as a guardian of the constitutional proprieties. It keeps an eye not only on individual instruments but on general developments in delegated legislation. It has shown itself anxious to make full use of its powers and has suggested extensions to its jurisdiction.

The Standing (Merits) Committees on Statutory Instruments
Parliament is of course interested in the merits of instruments, and most motions to annul are on the grounds of merit, not technicalities. Following a suggestion from a Joint Committee on Delegated Legislation a new House of Commons Standing Order was agreed in 1973. Under this one or more standing committees of the House called *Standing Committees on Statutory Instruments* are appointed to consider the merits of such instruments or drafts as may be referred to them by the House. Such committees may therefore be referred to as the *Merits* Committees. The procedure is that a minister may move in the House that a particular instrument or draft be referred to a Merits Committee. This will be done only if it is so agreed 'through the usual channels' ie between the parliamentary parties. If not less than twenty members object, the motion is lost. An instrument or

---

1 First Special Report from the Joint Committee on Statutory Instruments, 1977–8, HL 51, para 21.

draft may be so referred (a) if it is one in respect of which a minister has given notice of a motion that it be approved (ie where it is subject to the affirmative procedure); or (b) if any member has given notice of a motion praying that it be annulled, or in the case of a draft that it be not made.

When the instrument or draft comes before the Committee it is discussed (for up to ninety minutes) on the motion, 'That the Committee has considered the (draft) instrument.' The purpose of referring an instrument to the Committee is to give an opportunity for the merits to be discussed, but it will be noted that the merits cannot be *voted* on. (Indeed it would not seem possible not to vote for the motion, though the Committee could show, and has, its disapproval of an instrument by refusing to agree to the motion.[2]) The government may take account of views expressed in the Committee, particularly on a draft. However no debate can take place on the floor of the House in relation to such an instrument. It must proceed immediately to any vote there may be on it.

The Select Committee on Procedure recommended in 1978 that new procedures should be adopted for the consideration of statutory instruments.[3] Standing Committees should, it thought, be empowered to consider substantive motions; and in certain cases further debates of limited duration could be held in the House. The government disagreed. Experienced members expressed their view that without such reforms proceedings in these Standing Committees are 'useless' and 'a farce'.[4]

In total, the amount of time spent by the House of Commons in debating statutory instruments is not inadequate.[5] The question is whether that time is put to the best possible use. In a Special Report published in 1986 the Joint Committee on Statutory Instruments reported that in the previous five years, while the number of statutory instruments in each session had not increased unduly,[6] their volume and complexity had. They expressed the general position thus:

Since the establishment of this Committee in 1973, secondary legislation has increased not only in volume, but in scope. Instead of simply implementing the 'nuts and bolts' of Government policy, statutory instruments have increasingly been used to change policy, sometimes in ways that were not envisaged when the enabling primary legislation was passed. In view of the volume and complexity of much modern legislation and the difficulty of finding time for its preparation and consideration by Parliament, we accept that this trend is not one which it will necessarily be easy to reverse. We feel strongly, however, that the procedures for scrutinising secondary legislation should, like all other Parliamentary procedures, evolve to take account of historic change.

2   Stg Cttees Vol IV, 1977–8, 6th Stg Cttee 31.1.78; and 943 H of C Official Report (5th series) col 256.
3   1977–8, HC 588.
4   991 H of C Official Report (5th series) vol 753 (Mr J E Powell), col 793 (Sir G Page).
5   Evidence to the Procedure Committee by the chairman of the Scrutiny Committee: 1985–86, HC 257–i.
6   In 1981 there were 1,893 SIs, in 1986 2,333, in 1993 3,282. Is this 'rolling back the frontiers of the state'?

The Deregulation Orders Committee
The Henry VIII clause in the Deregulation and Contracting Out Act 1994, giving ministers power to make orders revoking primary legislation has been noted at p 66 above. The procedure for making these deregulation orders (which are statutory instruments) is that an order is not to be made unless a *draft* has been laid before and approved by both Houses. This draft contains the *deregulation proposals*. The minister is required to consult with appropriate organisations and persons about those proposals. He will then lay the draft together with details of certain matters including the burden it is proposed to remove by the order, whether the provision to be removed affords any protection and how it is to be continued, and resultant savings in costs, what consultation he has had, and with what effect etc. Having laid the draft and those details, the minister cannot make an order giving effect to the draft until the expiry 'of the period for Parliamentary consideration', which is 60 (originally 40 in the bill) days beginning with the day on which the draft is laid.

What consideration will Parliament give to the draft? Acknowledging the exceptional nature of the orders – the equivalent of primary legislation – the government invited the House of Commons Select Committee on Procedure to consider how the draft should be scrutinised: the Committee thought that new and stringent procedures were needed and suggested a Deregulation Orders Committee consisting of 16 senior MPs. It would be concerned with both vires and merits: it should give an opportunity to those affected by the proposals to express their concerns; it would agree to the proposals, say that amendments were necessary, or that the order should not be made.[7] (The power to propose amendments – in the form of drafting instructions rather than textual amendments – was justified, unlike in the usual case of scrutiny of delegated legislation, because of the importance of these orders.) Such a Committee has now been set up. Notice (i) Being SIs these orders would fall within the remit of the Joint Scrutiny Committee. That Committee has therefore been relieved of considering draft deregulation orders. (ii) In the Lords such orders will be considered by the Delegated Powers Scrutiny Committee.

House of Lords Committees
It is acknowledged that Select Committees of the House of Lords make a major contribution to the role and work of the House. There are (as in the Commons) different kinds of committees; our concern here is with those to do with delegated legislation. We have already noted the contribution of the Lords to the work of the Joint Scrutiny Committee, and to the proposal for a Deregulation Orders Committee.

7   Fourth Report from the Select Committee on Procedure, 1993–94, HC 238.

The Delegated Powers Scrutiny Committee
Some concern had been expressed by members about the extent of the delegation of legislative powers to ministers. A Committee on the Committee Work of the House reported[8] that all the evidence it received for a committee 'to give closer and more systematic scrutiny to delegated powers sought in bills was enthusiastic'. It recommended that such a committee be set up on a limited and experimental basis. Accordingly the Select Committee on the Scrutiny of Delegated Powers was set up in 1992. Its terms of reference are:

To report whether the provisions of any bill inappropriately delegate legislative power; or whether they subject the exercise of legislative power to an inappropriate degree of Parliamentary scrutiny.

The government undertook to provide the committee (of eight members) with a memorandum on each bill, in the light of which the committee considers the appropriateness of the provisions for delegated legislation. The committee's aim is to ensure that its views are available to the House before the committee stage of the bill. In an early report the committee criticised the delegation of powers to interfere with the freedom of students to associate in their student unions. The proposal was dropped.

The Select Committee on Hybrid Instruments
When referring to the House of Lords Special Orders Committee (p 92 above) we noted the procedure for petitioning against a hybrid instrument which requires affirmative approval. The Joint Scrutiny Committee continued the functions previously performed by the Commons Scrutiny Committee and the House of Lords Special Orders Committee, but this petitioning procedure was not given to it. The Special Orders Committee was kept in existence for the purpose of exercising that procedure. The name of that Committee was, in 1975 (helpfully) changed to that of the Select Committee on Hybrid Instruments. The procedure is that if the Committee agrees that an order is hybrid it is open to any person affected by the order to present a petition praying to be heard on the merits. The Committee having satisfied itself as to the *locus standi* of the petitioner and having examined the petition has to decide whether there should be a further inquiry by a Select Committee of five Lords. The criteria on which the Committee decides whether an instrument should go to a select committee are designed to obviate further inquiry by that committee in the case of orders which have already been the subject of adequate local, departmental, or other inquiry or where there are in fact no substantial grounds of complaint. This select committee can only report to the House whether the order should or should not be approved and the House then considers the report.

8   Report of the Committee on the Committee Work of the House, 1991–92, HL 35; and Select Committee on the Procedure of the House, 1992–3, HL 11. See [1995] PL 34.

There are in fact few hybrid Special Orders, say three in a year, and few of these are petitioned against, say one in four.[9] The Joint Committee on Delegated Legislation nevertheless thought that the procedure 'has provided valuable safeguards for private interests affected by delegated legislation and should be retained'.[10]

We have considered the work of Committees of both Houses which are specifically concerned with delegated legislation. Notice (a) that other Parliamentary Committees may be concerned with ministerial regulations; (b) that instruments may also fall within the jurisdiction of non-Parliamentary bodies such as the Social Security Advisory Committee[11] and the Council on Tribunals.[12] An example is the Electricity Generating Stations and Overhead Lines (Inquiry Procedure) Rules 1987, which are to do with the building of power stations. The rules were considered by the House of Commons Energy Committee, the Joint Scrutiny Committee and the Council on Tribunals.

The courts and delegated legislation

Proof of delegated legislation
The courts take judicial notice of Acts of Parliament: it is not necessary to prove their existence when relying on them. As for other legislation the Documentary Evidence Acts 1868 and 1882 provide that Orders in Council and regulations, orders, etc, made by government departments may be proved by producing a copy printed or issued by the Stationery Office. *Scott v Baker*[13] concerned a prosecution under the Road Safety Act 1967 under which the breath-test device must be of a type 'approved' by the Home Secretary. The Home Secretary had sent a circular to the courts and to the police stating that he had approved the device used in this case. It was held that the circular was not admissible as evidence of the minister's approval. The minister then made an order signifying his approval. It was published by the Stationery Office. In *R v Clarke*[14] it was held to fall within the Documentary Evidence Acts.

Interpretation
The provisions of the Interpretation Act 1978 apply, unless a contrary intention appears, to subordinate legislation as they apply to Acts, but only in respect of subordinate legislation made after the commencement

9 An example is the London Docklands Development Corporation (Area and Constitution) Order 1980. The Committee heard evidence from 38 witnesses over 46 days. See 421 HL Official Report (5th series) col 194, 7 H of C Official Report (6th series) 959.
10 1971–2, HL 184, para 55. See the Report for reasons why the petitioning procedure was introduced and arguments for and against it being operated by the Houses jointly, and whether the procedure should be extended to negative instruments.
11 See p 130 below.
12 See p 170 below.
13 [1969] 1 QB 659, [1968] 2 All ER 993.
14 [1969] 2 QB 91, [1969] 1 All ER 924.

of that Act (1 January 1979).[15] The Act further provides, in section 11, that where an Act confers power to make subordinate legislation, expressions used in that legislation have, unless a contrary intention appears, the meaning which they bear in the Act. 'Subordinate legislation' means in both these cases, rules, Orders in Council, orders, rules, regulations, schemes, byelaws, and other instruments made under any Act.

The fact that it is delegated and not primary legislation that is being interpreted and that it has not therefore been subjected to the full legislative procedure may affect the court's attitude to its interpretation.[16] And in *Pickstone v Freemans plc*[17] the House of Lords was clear that it was in the special circumstances proper to take into account the explanations given by ministers and members in Parliament of the effect of the draft regulations, which had not been open to amendment. (The circumstances were that the regulations had been made under the European Communities Act in order to give effect to EEC Treaty obligations.)

A further question that arises is whether regulations made under an Act may be referred to to interpret the Act under which they were made. Six relevant propositions have been stated by Lord Lowry.[18]

The courts are also called on to interpret circulars, codes of practice, ministers' decision letters, White Papers, etc, that is, documents which do not fall within the classification of 'delegated legislation'. How are they to approach their interpretation? Such documents may well be subjected to 'meticulous scrutiny' by the courts as for example the minister's letters in *Padfield v Minister of Agriculture, Fisheries and Food*.[19] On the other hand it has been doubted whether the Criminal Injuries Compensation Scheme[20] should be interpreted as though contained in a statute and the House of Lords has said that the Immigration Rules are to be construed sensibly and not with the strictness applicable to a statute.[1]

Invalidation
The courts can declare delegated legislation to be void on the ground that it is ultra vires the authorising statute. This is however only an aspect of the wider rule that the courts can declare void any act or decision which is ultra vires a statute. The invalidation of delegated legislation is not therefore treated here as a separate topic: reference to it will be found in chapter 7. However, it is convenient to mention here some matters of particular though not exclusive relevance to delegated legislation. *First,*

15 Section 23(1), except that to the extent specified in Pt II of Sch 2 to the Act, they apply to such legislation made before that date.
16 *Porter v Honey* [1988] 3 All ER 1045, [1988] 1 WLR 1420.
17 [1989] AC 66, [1988] 2 All ER 803.
18 In *Hanlon v Law Society* [1981] AC 124 at 193, [1980] 2 All ER 199 at 218.
19 [1968] AC 997, [1968] 1 All ER 694; the (condemnatory) phrase is Lord Morris's, at 1043 and 708 respectively. See p 246 below.
20 *R v Criminal Injuries Compensation Board, ex p Tong* [1975] 3 All ER 678, [1976] 1 WLR 47; revsd [1977] 1 All ER 171, [1976] 1 WLR 1237. See also p 52 above.
 1 *Alexander v Immigration Appeal Tribunal* [1982] 2 All ER 766, [1982] 1 WLR 1076. See p 79 above.

where a ministerial order or regulation is required by statute to be approved by Parliamentary resolution, the court can intervene by way of a declaration before that approval has been given (though this power will be exercised circumspectly). It would not intervene in the decision to lay the order before Parliament, and it is doubtful whether it would, once Parliamentary approval to an Order in Council had been obtained, intervene to prevent the minister from submitting it to the Queen in Council.[2] *Second*, the courts *can* declare subordinate legislation invalid even though it has been approved by resolutions of both Houses of Parliament, but whether the court *will* intervene will depend, it seems, on the subject matter of the instrument and on the ground on which its illegality is challenged.[3] *Third*, until it has been set aside by a court, delegated legislation is to be treated as part of the law and obeyed and enforced accordingly.[4] *Fourth*, the argument that a regulation is ultra vires can be raised by way of defence to a prosecution for an offence of infringing the regulation or by way of defence of a civil action where the claim is based on the regulation (but not where the invalidity is said to be due to a procedural irregularity.[5])

Legislative or administrative?

Reference has been made in a number of places above to the distinction between what is legislative and what is administrative. That is the question now to be considered. What is the distinction and why may it be of importance? If, seeing virtue in a separation of powers we think it desirable that a particular job (legislating, or making laws) should be done by a particular body (the legislature), then we must have some idea of what we mean by legislating, and what we think it is appropriate for the legislature to do or at least to be in some way involved in, and likewise what the executive should do.

2 *R v HM Treasury, ex p Smedley* [1985] QB 657, [1985] 1 All ER 589, CA.
3 See *Nottinghamshire County Council v Secretary of State for the Environment* [1986] AC 240, [1986] 1 All ER 199, p 255 below. In *R v Secretary of State for the Environment, ex p Hackney London Borough Council* [1984] 1 All ER 956 the court refused leave to argue that a statutory instrument was invalid as it would be inconsistent with the principles of judicial review to allow a challenge to an instrument which had been approved by Parliament more than three years previously and had been acted on ever since. For judicial review see ch 11.
4 See *Hoffman La Roche & Co AG v Secretary of State for Trade and Industry* [1975] AC 295, [1974] 2 All ER 1128.
5 *Bugg v DPP* [1993] 2 All ER 815. See below. In *Davey Paxman & Co Ltd v Post Office* (1954) Times, 15 November, the facts were that under the Wireless Telegraphy Act 1904 regulations made by the Postmaster-General could provide for fees to be charged on the granting of licences for the use of radio transmitting and receiving stations. It was discovered in 1954 that no such regulations had ever been made, though fees had been charged. The Post Office was sued by one firm for the return of fees it had paid, and submitted to judgment for the amount in question. Counsel for the Post Office declined to argue that the regulations must have been made but had been lost! (Retrospective legislation was passed providing that fees paid should be deemed to have been lawfully demanded.)

(i) For example, at p 59 above (dealing with the distinction between the provisional order procedure and the special Parliamentary procedure) it was noted that the former procedure was thought more appropriate than the latter for the exercise of a power to repeal or amend local Acts, as that power 'might be regarded as legislative in character' (and therefore a procedure necessarily incurring a Parliamentary procedure was desirable).

(ii) Statute may distinguish between legislative and administrative decisions, requiring the former but not the latter to undergo a specified procedure. For example we have seen at p 68 above, that section 1(2) of the Statutory Instruments Act 1946 provides that where before that Act came into force there was power to make a 'statutory rule', an exercise of that power in a document which is 'of a legislative and not an executive character' is now to be by way of statutory instrument. It is officially acknowledged[6] that the distinction is not always easy to draw. It has been suggested[7] that, as a document classified as a statutory instrument has to be published, it may be that the answer to the question 'Is the document legislative?' is 'Yes' if it is thought desirable that the document should be published as a statutory instrument, 'No', if not.

(iii) Statute may give a body certain functions but expressly exclude that which is legislative, as for example section 2(4) of the National Heritage Act 1983 which gives a Board of Trustees certain powers but excludes that of 'making regulations or other instruments of a legislative character'. Some indication of the distinction in question is given in another statutory scheme. By section 115 of the Financial Services Act 1986 the Secretary of State may make an order transferring back to himself all legislative or all administrative functions previously exercised by another. 'Legislative functions' are said to mean the function of making rules or regulations; and administrative functions mean functions other than legislative functions. But the section goes on to say that the transfer of legislative functions shall not deprive the other of 'any function of prescribing fees to be paid or information to be furnished in connection with administrative functions retained'. The implication is that the function of prescribing (that is determining or laying down, so as to be generally applicable) fees or information would or might otherwise be considered to be legislative.[8]

(iv) In *McEldowney v Forde*[9] the statute does not itself distinguish between 'legislative' and 'administrative', but the court used that classification in interpreting the Minister's powers. Section 1(3) of the Act being considered provided that the Minister had power to make *regulations* for making further provision for the preservation of the peace. These regulations were to have effect and be enforced 'in like manner as regulations contained in the Schedule to this Act'. Section 1(1) of the Act gave the

6   See *Statutory Instruments Practice* (HMSO).
7   Griffith and Street *Principles of Administrative Law*, p 48.
8   And see Tribunals and Inquiries Act 1992, s 10(5)(b): no duty to give reasons in connection with legislative and not executive rules.
9   [1971] AC 632, [1969] 2 All ER 1039.

Minister power to take all such *steps* and issue all such *orders* as were necessary for preserving the peace: the exercise of *this* power was subject to a proviso. The question was whether the proviso applied to regulations made under the later subsection, section 1(3). The House of Lords was clear that the regulations were legislative in their nature, and the steps and orders, administrative. When making the regulations (that is, when acting legislatively) the Minister was not restricted by the proviso which applied to the exercise of administrative functions only. Lord Pearson was clear that the regulations were legislative because they were to have the same effect as regulations contained in the Act.

(v) The nature of the legislative was considered in connection with circulars in *Jackson, Stansfield & Sons v Butterworth*.[10] The Minister of Works was empowered under a defence regulation to grant licences for carrying out building work. He authorised local authorities to issue licences on his behalf. The authorisation was contained in circulars supplemented by 'Notes for Guidance'. What was the nature of these circulars and notes? Were they legislative or administrative? In the opinion of Scott LJ they were not merely administrative but legislative in their nature in that they contained an elaboration of the instructions as to the granting of licences which were intended to be enforced: 'in other words to bind the public, and that means legislation'. The same point had arisen earlier in *Blackpool Corpn v Locker*.[11] There the Minister had delegated to local authorities by means of circulars his statutory power of requisitioning houses. Scott LJ said that the circular constituted delegated legislation conferring powers on local authorities which they would not otherwise have had. In *Lewisham Metropolitan Borough and Town Clerk v Roberts*[12] the minister delegated to the clerk to the council by letter his power of requisitioning in respect of *one* house. Jenkins J said that the delegation was not an act of legislation, and that *Locker*'s case was to be distinguished in that there was a general delegation of powers and not merely in respect of one house. Denning LJ said however that the delegation by the Minister whether general or specific was an administrative and not legislative act.

(vi) The distinction between the legislative and the administrative is relevant in connection with the jurisdiction of the Parliamentary Commissioner for Administration. The work of the Commissioner is considered in some detail in chapter 16, but it is convenient to deal with this here. Section 5(1) of the Parliamentary Commissioner for Administration Act 1967 provides that the Commissioner may investigate complaints of maladministration arising out of the exercise by certain bodies (principally government departments) of their *administrative* functions. Is the Commissioner excluded from investigating complaints about delegated legislation because of the reference to administrative functions? Is the making of delegated legislation an administrative or a legislative function? The Select Committee on the Parliamentary

10 [1948] 2 All ER 558.
11 [1948] 1 KB 349, [1948] 1 All ER 85.
12 [1949] 2 KB 608, [1949] 1 All ER 815.

Commissioner[13] has distinguished between statutory orders which are and those which are not statutory instruments. As regards statutory instruments, it was in the Attorney-General's view (expressed in evidence to the Select Committee) clear that the making of a statutory instrument is a legislative process[14] and accordingly that the Commissioner has no power to examine its form, content or merits. Could it not be argued that the preliminary stages of the making of an instrument (collecting information, consulting etc) are administrative? The Attorney-General preferred the view that these 'administrative processes' are merely a subordinate part of a legislative function. What then of the process of reviewing the operation of a statutory instrument perhaps as the result of the receipt of complaints? The collection of such complaints was, in his view, an administrative process, but the decision whether or not to amend the instrument 'involves legislative processes and is not therefore for the Commissioner'. This means that the Commissioner could investigate complaints that evidence of hardship caused by the operation of an instrument had not been properly considered and reviewed, but that if he found they had been, he could not take the matter any further. A Commissioner has said that he could not question the contents or merits of statutory instruments, but 'I may examine the effect of a statutory instrument and inquire into the action taken by a government department to review its operation'.[15] He has considered a complaint that the date of the coming into force of an instrument gave those affected insufficient notice, that inadequate publicity was given to it, and that a requirement was added to the instrument after consultation on it.[16]

With regard to statutory orders which are not statutory instruments, the Select Committee has said that it is 'proper for the Commissioner to investigate any complaint of maladministration in the administrative processes leading to [their] making and subsequent reviewing'. The Commissioner is acting on this.

(vii) *R v Secretary of State for Social Security, ex p Cotton*[17] indicates what is legislative, but in contrast to what is adjudicative. Under the social security legislation the question whether any person is entitled to supplementary benefit, and how much, is determined by the adjudication officer and various appellate tribunals applying the relevant regulations. However, the minister has power to make regulations for the determination of 'prescribed questions' otherwise than by those bodies. Under that power the minister made regulations requiring himself to lay down rules of *general* application as to the maximum amount of benefit to be paid to claimants in certain areas, which areas he himself was also to delineate in those regulations, and the period for which it was payable.

13 HC 385, 1968–69.
14 And see *Bates v Lord Hailsham of St Marylebone*, p 302 below.
15 First Report, 1974–5, HC 749, p 63. The legality of the instrument was also queried. Commissioner said that was for courts, but that department had taken proper legal advice: but see *Daymond v South West Water Authority* p 202 below.
16 Third Report from the Commissioner, 1977–78, HC 246, p 240.
17 (1985) Times, 14 December.

But the power to make those regulations was stated (in the statute conferring it) to be in respect of the law relating to social security *adjudication*. The regulations could therefore relate only to adjudicative functions, that is, of applying fixed criteria to the relevant factual situations. But these regulations were legislative as they contained the criteria in question which would be applied by the adjudication officer to the facts of each case. They were therefore ultra vires.

(viii) This paragraph is concerned with the relationship between form and content. The content of a statutory instrument is normally what would be regarded as legislative: binding rules of some generality. However this is not necessarily the case: would we regard a statutory instrument relating to one local authority,[18] or prohibiting the flight of aircraft over a small area for a short period,[19] as legislative – assuming the test of generality? A document must be a statutory instrument if the parent Act says that it is to be, regardless of its contents, though of course, in deciding whether a document should be by way of statutory instrument, the generality of the contents will be a relevant factor in the mind of the draftsman. But this distinction between the form of a document and its contents is to be noted: after all, an Act of Parliament may refer to only one person. A case illustrating this distinction is *Ibralebbe v R*[20] which concerned the legality of an Order in Council. Lord Radcliffe, delivering the judgment of the Judicial Committee of the Privy Council, said that the Order in Council which gives effect to a decision of the Committee is in everything but form the equivalent of a legal judgment; it is a *judicial* order. As such it has no analogy with an Order in Council having *legislative* effect (eg granting a new constitution), or with an Order in Council that is part of the *administration* of government, except in the widest sense that each within its category derives its ultimate force from some form of sovereign authority and thus can be said to 'make law'. The question in issue was whether following the grant of independence to Ceylon in 1947 appeals still lay to the Committee. Lord Radcliffe observed that following that grant there was no power to *legislate* for Ceylon, nor to participate in its *government* by Order in Council, but as the structure of the courts had not been affected by the grant of independence, it was open to the Committee to consider an appeal: an Order in Council that was *judicial* in its nature could still be made.

18 Local Government Finance Act 1988, s 104(2)(8)(a).
19 SI 1981/1039 (St Paul's Cathedral: Prince of Wales' marriage).
20 [1964] AC 900, [1964] 1 All ER 251.

Chapter 4

Administrative procedures and sanctions

In this chapter we look at some administrative procedures, first some related to various controls and sanctions; then land-use inquiries, and finally consultation.

Controls and sanctions

Licensing

The licence (or permit, consent, approval or certificate) is one of the oldest[1] devices of administrative control. It is used for a variety of purposes.[2] It may be used solely for revenue raising purposes, as in the case of the vehicle excise licence. It may be used to control the use of natural resources, as for example oil, fish, water, and radio frequencies; to control socially undesirable activities, as in the case of liquor licensing and betting and gaming; to ensure technical competence, as in the driver's licence; to protect the public against dishonest persons, as in the licensing of house-to-house collections, and of consumer credit business; to prevent congestion of the streets, as where a licence is needed for street trading; to control potentially offensive activities as in the case of sex shops; and to control the development of land, by the need for planning permission. The licence is a central feature of the regulation of public utilities.

There are advantages to the administration in control by licensing. The onus for taking action (to get the licence) is put on the citizen, whereas if the activity is to be controllable only by an order or notice served by the administration, the onus will be on such administration. Delay in application will be to the citizen's detriment. The technique is simple. And where it is a criminal offence to undertake the action without a licence, a conviction can be readily obtained.[3]

---

1   See Ogus 'Regulatory law' 12 JLS 1; and *Regulation: Legal Form and Economic Theory.* See definition in Deregulation Act 1994, s 5(6).
2   See G L Williams 'Control by Licensing' [1967] CLP 81.
3   See *R v Edwards* [1975] QB 27, [1974] 2 All ER 1085.

Some licensing systems may carry disadvantages. A substantial bureaucracy may be required. Where economic activity is regulated, monopolies may be created.

If permission is inherent in the concept of the licence, then merely informing the authority of an activity – what may be called *registration* – is not to be equated with a licence. But if registration can be refused or granted subject to conditions, if it carries with it the right of inspection, or if it can be revoked it may amount to a licence. However, the word used, be it licence, registration, consent, certificate etc, is no safe guide to the rights and duties involved.

Another possible technique is, where the citizen is required to give notice of his proposed action: the authority is given a specified time to serve notice of objection; if it does not do so, the action can go ahead.[4]

A system of licensing (by whatever name) having been decided on, the administration will have to ask itself some questions. What is it that is being licensed, a person, the use of land, or a particular activity?[5] Who is to be the licensing authority, a minister (as for a licence for keeping a stallion), a local authority (as for residential homes and ice-cream factories), a magistrates' court (as in liquor licensing) or some other body for example the Bank of England (for deposit-taking), or a Director General (eg of Fair Trading for a consumer credit licence)?[6] What will the applicant have to show to get a licence? If fees are to be charged, what proportion of the costs of the administrative scheme are to be recovered by the fees? Is the licence to be subject to conditions; if so of what kind? Can conditions be varied or added to during the currency of the licence? Is there to be an appeal against a refusal of a licence or against the conditions? If so, to whom, and on what grounds? For how long is the licence to last – a year, indefinitely? Is it to be transferable? Is there to be a power of revocation or suspension, and should a procedure for doing so be specified? Should there be an appeal against the use of that power, and again to whom and on what grounds? Can the licence be surrendered? Should third parties be able to intervene in any of these matters as where on application for the grant or renewal of a justices' liquor licence any member of the public may object? The answers to these (and other) questions will of course differ from case to case.

Inspection

By inspection is meant the examination or scrutiny of a place, thing or person. To be effective it will generally need to carry the right to enter premises. Inspection often goes with licensing or registration, as in the case of persons engaged in the training or exhibition of performing animals. But there may be licensing without inspection, as in liquor licensing.[7]

4 Eg Town and Country Planning Act 1990, s 211(3).
5 Or all three: Anatomy Act 1984.
6 See Borrie 'Licensing under the Consumer Credit Act' [1982] JBL 91.
7 See generally Rhodes *Inspectorates in British Government*.

The function of 'inspecting' in the sense suggested may not be the sole activity of an inspectorate. Thus the Report of the (Robens) Committee on Safety and Health at Work,[8] reviewing the work of the various inspectorates then in existence said:

Inspectors at various levels assist in the framing and revision of legislation; undertake investigations surveys and research; participate in the preparation of advisory literature; liaise with manufacturers of plant and equipment; sit on various kinds of technical committees; deliver lectures; and participate in conferences at home and overseas. But the main day-to-day activity of the majority of inspectors is the inspection of workplaces.[9]

Having recommended a unified inspectorate the Report went on to ask what its primary role should be. It found that there were two main views. One saw the role in terms of improving standards of safety and health at work, rather than in terms of law enforcement as such; that while the threat of legal sanctions in the background is important, in most cases advice and persuasion achieve more than duress, which is rarely the most effective or apt means of achieving the objectives of safety legislation. The other view would seek a policy of rigorous enforcement. The Report thought the latter view misconceived, or even if the policy were feasible, it was inappropriate and undesirable. 'The provision of skilled and impartial advice and assistance should be the leading edge of the activities of the unified inspectorate.'[10] An opposing view is that the Report played down to an unacceptable degree the role of legal sanctions.

Historically a paid professional inspectorate was crucial to the success of the early factory legislation. It remains a most important device.[11]

The 'inspectors' who hold public inquiries in connection with planning appeals have power to inspect the land in question, but this is subsidiary, though necessary, to their main function.[12]

Inspection, as well as being a device of control of private activities, is also used by central government in relation to local authorities, as in the case of the police and education inspectorates.

Prohibition and other notices

Many examples could be given of the device of prohibition and similar notices. (They may of course follow an inspection.) Under section 13 of the Consumer Protection Act 1987 the Secretary of State may serve on any person a *prohibition notice* prohibiting him from supplying etc goods which the Secretary of State considers are unsafe. Under section 14 where the Secretary of State (or other enforcing authority) has reasonable

8 Cmnd 5034.
9 Cmnd 5304, para 201.
10 Ibid, para 211.
11 See Health and Safety at Work etc Act 1974, s 20, Public Passenger Vehicles Act 1981, s 8.
12 See p 123 below.

grounds for sus-pecting that any 'safety provision' has been contravened in respect of any goods, the authority may serve a *suspension notice* prohibiting that person from supplying the goods specified for the period specified ('safety provision' refers to safety regulations, a prohibition notice etc). Section 16 of the Act authorises the *forfeiture* of goods; for this an application to a court is necessary.

Under section 21 of the Health and Safety at Work etc Act 1974 if an inspector is of the opinion that a person is contravening a relevant statutory provision he may serve on him an *improvement notice*, requiring the person to remedy the contravention. Under section 22 if an inspector is of the opinion that activities are being or are about to be carried on which involve or will involve a risk of serious personal injury, he may serve on that person a *prohibition notice*. This, among other things, will direct that the activities are not to be carried on unless the matters specified in the notice have been remedied. The direction is to have immediate effect if the inspector states it to be his opinion that the risk is imminent; otherwise, it takes effect at the end of the period specified. An appeal lies to an industrial tribunal[13] against either notice. An additional power the inspector has, under section 25, is to seize *and render harmless* (by destruction if necessary) an article, found on premises he has the power to enter, which is a cause of imminent danger of serious personal injury.

Under the Estate Agents Act 1979 the Director General of Fair Trading, if satisfied of certain matters, can make an order *prohibiting* a person from doing any estate agency work at all or work of a specified description. In respect of some matters the Director may issue a *warning order*; breach of this leads to a prohibition order. The Act sets out the procedure that has to be followed in each case, and the available appeal.

A method of control sometimes found appropriate to achieve a desired standard of behaviour is the *assurance*. Under the Fair Trading Act 1973, where it appears to the Director General of Fair Trading that a person has persisted in a course of conduct which is detrimental to consumers' interests and is unfair to them (by reason of the disregard of obligations imposed by the civil or criminal law), the Director is to use his best endeavours to get from that person a satisfactory written assurance that he will refrain from continuing that course of conduct.[14] If the Director is unable to get such an assurance, or if a person has given an assurance and it appears to the Director that he has failed to observe it, the Director may bring proceedings against him before the court. Where the court finds against that person, he may offer an *undertaking* to the court. If this is not acceptable to the court, it may make an *order* against him. Breach of the order may result in contempt of court resulting in a fine or imprisonment.

13 See p 146 below.
14 See the Director General's Annual Report for examples.

Investigation of companies

The Department of Trade has had powers for over one hundred years to appoint inspectors to investigate companies. Today the appointment may be by the Department on its own initiative or on the request of a proportion of the company's members. In some circumstances the Department may be required to appoint inspectors. The main purpose of the inspection is to find the facts where some irregularity in the running of the company is suspected. The inspector's function is therefore *inquisitorial* – to make such inquiries as are necessary to find the facts – not judicial, that is to rule on the facts as uncovered by the parties appearing before him. He is free to conduct the inquiry as he thinks fit, but he must act fairly so that, for example, if the inspector is disposed to criticise anyone he must first give him an opportunity to correct the evidence against him. The powers and duties of investigation are put by statute on the inspector, not on the department, and in that sense the inspector is independent of the department. The inspector's report is available to the prosecuting authorities to consider whether criminal proceedings should be brought. It may also be published: publicity itself may be a sanction. Another sanction that may be available to the department is to petition the court for the winding-up of a company.[15]

Requiring information

The operation of governing requires the obtaining of information from the governed. A wide range of information about individuals and organisations is in the government's possession. Much is given voluntarily; but it is frequently obtained under statutory powers, as under the Census Act 1920, or has to be supplied if some benefit is to be obtained, for example a licence. Information may also be obtained in the course of an inspection or seizure. The validity of the exercise of a statutory power to demand information is challengeable in the courts,[16] which have asserted as a matter of public policy that the state having acquired information from a citizen under compulsory powers for one purpose, should not use it for another.[17] It may be a criminal offence to disclose information obtained from the citizen except in the circumstances specified. Misleading information about the use to which the informationis put could be the subject of a complaint to the Parliamentary Commissioner.[18]

15 See Companies Act 1985. *Investigation Handbook* HMSO 1990.
16 *Customs and Excise Comrs v Harz* [1967] 1 AC 760, [1967] 1 All ER 177; *Potato Marketing Board v Merrick* [1958] 2 QB 316, [1958] 2 All ER 538.
17 *Lonrho plc v Fayed* (No 4) [1994] 1 All ER 870; and *Marcel v Commissioner of Police of the Metropolis* [1992] Ch 225, [1991] 1 All ER 845. For privilege against self-incrimination see *Bank of England v Riley* [1992] 1 All ER 769, [1992] 2 WLR 840, CA.
18 Third Report from the Parliamentary Commissioner, 1971–72, HC 204.

Criminal sanctions

The operation of an administrative scheme or the achievement of required standards may require reliance on criminal penalties. Planning law provides examples. Planning permission has to be obtained from the local authority if it is proposed to develop land. It is not however a criminal offence to develop land without such permission. The position is that if land is developed without permission, the local authority may serve an enforcement notice, and it is the failure to comply with that notice that may lead to criminal prosecution. But it may be possible instead, or in addition, for the local authority to enter the land, carry out what the notice required to be done, and charge the cost to the defaulting occupier of the land. However, although it is not an offence to develop land without permission,[19] it is an offence to contravene the advertising regulations or a tree preservation order made under the planning legislation, or to demolish a 'listed' building. And there are many other uses of land other than under planning law which it is an offence to undertake without getting the authority's permission or notifying it of one's intention. The point being made is that the appropriateness of criminal penalties will differ from case to case.[20] Take the problem of improving insulation in existing dwelling houses. How is this to be achieved? A discussion paper has examined ten possible 'models' designed to bring about that improvement.[1] These include better public information, financial incentives, penal tariffs for excess consumption etc. Criminal sanctions would seem to have a small or no part to play in this case. Rewards rather than penalties might be more appropriate.

Where criminal sanctions are available it by no means follows that they are readily or widely resorted to. Consider the following examples.

(i) In pollution control, prosecution is consistently viewed as the last resort, and was employed by the water authorities in only a very few cases of those polluters which could be brought to court.[2] The Royal Commission on Environmental Pollution commented, in its Fifth Report, on Air Pollution:

The present system of control has achieved great advances in the reduction of emissions and we are satisfied that much of this progress may be attributed to the policy of persuasion and co-operation with industry that the Inspectorate have adopted. An aggressive policy of confrontation, involving prosecution for every lapse, would destroy this basis of co-operation.

'For every lapse' note. The Royal Commission went on to say,

There is a danger that infrequent inspections by the controlling authority, together with a known reluctance to prosecute, will encourage some works to be careless in their attitudes to the day-by-day control of emissions.[3]

19 For reason see *Enforcing Planning Control*, HMSO, 1989.
20 See Ogus, *Regulation*.
 1 'Improving insulation in existing dwellings': National Consumer Council, 1981. And see Daintith, 9 BJLS 191 at 201. Marshall, *Alternatives to Criminal Punishment*.
 2 K Hawkins, *Environment and Enforcement*.
 3 Cmnd 6371, para 227. In 1992 the National Rivers Authority attributed a big fall in severe pollution incidents to the imposition of heavy fines.

And,

We are clear that where infractions by a firm are frequent or severe prosecution should follow automatically. We do not think that such a reasonable but firm attitude to prosecution would harm the Alkali Inspectorate's co-operative relationship with industry; it is illogical to accept the measures required to reduce pollution but to deny the need for firm enforcement.

(ii) The Animals Procedures Committee commented in its Report for 1988 on the actions that could be taken to deal with infringements of the licensing procedures under the Animals (Scientific Procedures) Act 1986 (which are to do with experiments on living animals). The range of action includes a letter of admonition for minor breaches, the imposition of additional conditions on the licence, a change in the holder of the licence where the holder has shown lax control over his employees, and the revocation of a licence. Not to be overlooked, in the Committee's view, is the possibility of prosecution: the fact that there is a discretion to enforce the criminal law should not mean that it is never resorted to. The Secretary of State agreed.

(iii) The Comptroller and Auditor General has reported on the way the Ministry of Defence deals with 'procurement irregularities'.[4] The Ministry investigates all cases of suspected fraud committed by its contractors, but most cases are dealt with by administrative action rather than by recourse to the law. The options open to the Ministry were listed thus by the C & AG:
–   debar the company from receiving further contracts;
–   suspend the contractor from new MOD business for a stated period;
–   place new work with the contractor only as a result of effective competition;
–   seek financial redress for any loss suffered by the MOD, not necessarily confined to recovery of the financial loss directly sustained; and
–   inform the company that it may be preferable for certain named employees not to be retained on MOD work.

(iv) The most common method of enforcement for fraudulently obtaining welfare benefits is a warning, and recovery of sums obtained by deduction from future benefits. Small amounts are not usually prosecuted.[5]

(v) Inland Revenue deal with tax evasion mainly not by criminal proceedings against the taxpayer but by a settlement with him which when agreed is enforceable as a contract. Such a settlement depends not on the compounding of criminal proceedings but on the possibility of dealing with fraud and default under the provisions of the Taxes Management Act 1970 for imposing *civil penalties*. Where negotiations for such a settlement break down the Department will take civil proceedings for the recovery of sums due before the Tax Commissioners. The Keith Committee[6]

4   Committee of Public Accounts, Ministry of Defence: Procurement Irregularities, Minutes of Evidence, 18 January 1988, HC 450–i.
5   *R v Stewart* [1987] 2 All ER 383, [1987] 1 WLR 559.
6   The Report of the Committee on Enforcement Powers of the Revenue Departments Cmnd 8822.

was impressed by the many advantageous features of the approach. Although criminal prosecution is undertaken only in a small minority of cases it is the possibility of prosecution which prevents the spread of fraud to unacceptable limits.

To be noted is the recent strong movement towards decriminalisation of certain offences (by that is meant the replacing of *criminal proceedings* followed by a court-imposed penalty and a criminal record, by a *civil penalty* ie one imposed after civil proceedings).

Customs and Excise are one of the major prosecuting agencies. They have the unusual power to compound criminal proceedings for offences under Customs and Excise and VAT legislation. In VAT law, regulatory offences were decriminalised by the Finance Act 1985, and a civil fraud option introduced for offences of dishonesty.

Further steps away from reliance on criminal prosecution have been taken in the field of excise duties.[7] The more serious excise offences involving dishonest conduct have been retained as crimes, but as an alternative Customs and Excise can treat such offences as a civil matter. If this is done a penalty is imposed administratively (the penalty being limited to an amount equal to the duty assessed as due). Both the imposition of the penalty and its amount are appealable (to a VAT and Duties Tribunal). Less serious offences have been removed from the criminal law, and have become civil offences for which a fixed penalty is imposed, subject to an appeal (to the same tribunal) against the imposition of the penalty.[8]

Where the administration has an option of proceeding criminally or civilly then if it chooses the latter it must nevertheless be satisfied that the evidence is sufficient to meet the higher standard of proof applicable in criminal proceedings. This system 'place[s] a clear responsibility on the Department's officers to take great care that they have a proper case for prosecution before they offer compounding, since they are making quasi-legal judgments, most of which will never be tested in a court of law'. In the case in which that comment was made, Customs Officers agreed to compound the offence of 'recklessly' completing certain documents. The Parliamentary Commissioner found that the instructions to officers contained two different explanations of 'reckless', and he concluded that they were making 'what are tantamount to legal judgments with insufficient understanding of the legal issues involved'.[9]

The generally civil nature of Inland Revenue proceedings is one of the models used by those who argue for the de-criminalisation of many criminal offences. Additional examples of civil penalties imposed by the administration without the need to involve the criminal courts are the fixed-penalty system for certain road traffic offences,[10] to compound prosecutions for failure to renew vehicle excise licences.[11]

7 Finance Act 1994.
8 For exercise of power to forfeit goods see *Customs and Excise Comrs v Air Canada* [1991] 2 QB 446, [1991] 1 All ER 570.
9 First Report from the Parliamentary Commissioner, 1982–83, Selected Cases Vol 4, HC 8, p 6.
10 Transport Act 1982, s 32 'punishment without prosecution'.
11 Vehicles (Excise) Act 1971, s 3.

Criminal proceedings are of course in public, and may be widely reported. A private arrangement with the authorities may be very attractive to the defaulter as an alternative to prosecution, and the threat to publicise what would otherwise be a private arrangement may act as a deterrent to wrong doing.

Who can prosecute?
In principle, it is open to anyone to commence criminal proceedings but there are wide exceptions to that rule and in practice few such proceedings are brought other than by the police or by certain public authorities.[12] Those brought by the police are brought by police officers not by police authorities.

Local authorities are empowered to prosecute for certain offences. It seems that there too, very frequently techniques other than prosecution are employed with the aim of securing the intent of the law rather than the punishment of its breach.[13] And where it is open to the authority to prosecute, a threat to do so may be enough. Typically, it has been said, 'the law is enforced not by legal imposition of punishment but by administrative application of the fact that punishment is possible.'[14] This consideration does not apply only to local authorities. The Parliamentary Commissioner has said that where an official of the DHSS is investigating a suggestion that a person has by deception obtained from public funds more than his due, it is not improper to point out to the claimant that it is a criminal offence to make a false statement when claiming benefit.[15]

Government departments may be expressly (and in some cases solely) authorised to prosecute offences, including the Inland Revenue and Customs and Excise Departments.

Where an official is empowered by statute to prosecute, the question of his proper appointment may be raised by way of defence to a charge. Likewise, where an authority prosecutes, its vires to do so may be raised as a defence.

The inadequacy of, or the inefficient use of, resources devoted by an authority to enforcement procedures may be a ground for criticism as may failure to give the question of prosecution adequate consideration in a particular case.[16]

Inquiries

The inquiry is a very commonly used device. There are many statutory provisions under which an inquiry may or must be held. But the government may also cause an inquiry to be held under its common law powers,

---

12 For judicial reviewability of decision to prosecute see *R v Inland Revenue Comrs, ex p Mead* [1993] 1 All ER 772.
13 Dickens 'Discretion in local authority prosecutions' [1970] Crim LR 618.
14 Ibid. And G Richardson *Policing Pollution*, p 197.
15 Annual Report for 1982, 1982–83, HC 257.
16 Third Report from the Parliamentary Commissioner, 1975–76, HC 259, p 189.

without the need to rely on statute. In every case it is essential to be clear what the purpose of the inquiry is, and to provide a procedure appropriate to that purpose.

Examples of *non*-statutory inquiries are the Bingham inquiry into the supervision of the Bank of Credit and Commerce International, the inquiry of the (Blom-Cooper) departmental committee into allegations of ill-treatment of patients at a special hospital,[17] and the Scott inquiry.[18]

Statutory inquiries are now considered under various headings.

Inquiries into accidents
It is in the public interest that inquiries are held into certain accidents, as under the Nuclear Installations Act 1965 and the Gas Act 1965. They are also held into railway and aircraft accidents.

The aim of all such inquiries is to discover the cause of the accident with the intention presumably that steps shall be taken by the appropriate authority to prevent such an accident from happening again. The role is *inquisitorial*, the purpose to get at the truth. There is a danger that such a role may become confused with an accusatory role in which the inquiry concerns itself with ascribing blame.[19]

Under section 466 of the Merchant Shipping Act 1894, the Secretary of State can direct that a formal investigation be held into a collision between ships at sea. The questions to be considered by the inquiry – for example, why did the accident occur, and why did one of the ships capsize so rapidly? – are determined by the Secretary of State. The first purpose of the investigation is to answer those questions. The second purpose is 'to consider what lessons can be learnt from the casualty. Such an exercise is the primary justification for any formal investigation and that is particularly so in this case'. Although the parties to the accident may blame one another, and though the investigation decided which one was to blame, the investigation is not like a piece of litigation, or lis, between the contending parties, and is not therefore conclusive of civil liability.[20]

Land-use inquiries
The terms of reference of the Franks Committee required it to:

consider and make recommendations on the working of such administrative procedures as include the holding of an inquiry or hearing by or on behalf of a minister on an appeal or as a result of objections or representation, and in particular the procedure for the compulsory purchase of land.

The main procedures it dealt with were those relating to the acquisition of land and those arising under planning law. The Report[1] said that two strongly opposed views may be held about such procedures. These were

---

17 For challenge to grant of statutory powers to inquiry see *R v Secretary of State for Health ex p Prison Officers Association* (1991) Independent, 16 October.
18 Report to be published Summer 1995.
19 Craig 'Judicial Investigation of Aviation Disasters [1968] PL 217 and SI 1969/833, reg 4.
20 *Speedlink Vanguard and the European Gateway* [1986] 3 All ER 554.
1 Cmnd 218.

that the procedures were on the one hand *judicial* or on the other *administrative*. The Committee considered what was meant by such views and what was their implication for the role of the inquiry. However, it was not, the Committee thought, helpful to consider the inquiry in the light of those concepts 'because we do not think them satisfactory instruments for dealing with the actual nature of the subject matter'. Its approach was rather to ask what was the intention of the legislature in providing for an inquiry. What was that intention? It was, the Report said, two-fold: to ensure that the interests of the citizens closely affected should be protected by the grant of a right to be heard and, second, to ensure that the minister should be better informed of the facts of the case. Thus instead of classifying the inquiry as judicial or administrative and drawing conclusions from that classification, it saw its task as finding a reasonable balance between those interests.

On the one hand there are *ministers* and other administrative authorities enjoined by legislation to carry out certain duties. On the other hand there are the rights and feelings of individual *citizens* who find their possessions or plans interfered with by the administration. There is also the *public interest* which requires both that ministers should not be frustrated in carrying out their duties and also that their decisions should be subject to effective checks or controls, and these can no longer be applied by Parliament in the general run of cases.[2]

The three principles of openness, fairness and impartiality should as far as possible be applied here (as well as to tribunals).

One particular proposal the Report made was that statutory regulations should be made governing the procedure to be followed at these inquiries. Legislation provided for this – see below.

A particular issue on which there was a conflict of evidence before the Committee (and a Dissenting Note to the Report) was whether the report of the inspector who held the inquiry, and containing his recommendation to the minister, should be published. Effect was given to the Report's view that it should. Note that legislation was not necessary for this development.[3]

Compulsory purchase order inquiries

The inquiry into objections
Many public authorities are given statutory power to acquire land compulsorily to enable them to carry out their functions. (Note that the exercise of this power by any authority other than a minister is subject to authorisation by the appropriate minister.)

The *power* to acquire land compulsorily is given in various statutes. The *procedure* to be followed for most compulsory acquisitions is laid down in the (consolidating) Acquisition of Land Act 1981. Where the authority

2   Ibid paras 262–277. Emphasis added.
3   'The adoption of the three attributes of openness, fairness and impartiality had a profoundly beneficial effect on practice generally ... The publication of the inspector's report had far-reaching effects in practice.' Layfield *Planning for Recovery*, 1993, p 90.

seeking to acquire the land is a local authority the procedure is, in outline, as follows. The compulsory purchase order is made by the local authority – the 'acquiring authority'. It has to be submitted to the minister who has been given statutory power to authorise purchase for the purpose in question. (He is the 'confirming authority'.) But before submitting the order to the minister for confirmation, the acquiring authority must advertise it in the local press and serve notices on every owner, lessee or occupier of the land. Objections to the proposal can be made within the time allowed. If no objection is made, or if made is withdrawn, the minister may then confirm the order with or without modifications. But:

if any objection duly made as aforesaid is not withdrawn, the confirming authority shall, before confirming the order, either cause a *public local inquiry* to be held or afford to any person by whom any objection has been duly made as aforesaid and not withdrawn an opportunity of appearing before and *being heard by* a person appointed by the confirming authority for the purpose, and, after considering the objection and the report of the person who held the inquiry or the person appointed as aforesaid, may confirm the order either with or without modifications.[4]

The feature we are concerned with is the *public local inquiry*. The paragraph quoted provides an alternative – the opportunity of 'being heard': the alternative is thus the *hearing*. The choice is made by the confirming authority. An inquiry is normally held.

In *Bushell v Secretary of State for the Environment*,[5] Lord Diplock referred to the nature and object of the public local inquiry, (in the context of a motorway scheme).

Where it is proposed that land should be acquired by a government department or local authority and works constructed on it for the benefit of the public either as a whole or in a particular locality, the holding of a public inquiry before the acquisition of the land and the construction of the works are authorised has formed a familiar part of the administrative process ever since authorisation by ministerial order of compulsory acquisition of land for public purposes began to be used to replace Parliamentary authorisation by private Bill procedure in the nineteenth century.

The *essential characteristics* of a 'local inquiry', an expression which when appearing in a statute has by now acquired a special meaning as a term of legal art, are that it is held in public in the locality in which the works that are the subject of the proposed scheme are situated by a person appointed by the minister on whom the statute has conferred the power in his administrative discretion to decide whether to confirm the scheme.

The *subject matter* of the inquiry is the objections to the proposed scheme that have been received by the minister from local authorities and from private persons in the vicinity of the proposed stretch of motorway whose interests may be adversely affected, and in consequence of which he is required ... to hold the inquiry.

The *purpose* of the inquiry is to provide the minister with as much information about those objections as will ensure that in reaching his decision he will have weighed the harm to local interests and private persons who may be adversely

4 Section 13(2). Emphasis added.
5 [1981] AC 75, [1980] 2 All ER 608.

affected by the scheme against the public benefit which the scheme is likely to achieve and will not have failed to take into consideration any matters which he ought to have taken into consideration.[6]

Lord Diplock there referred to the inquiry as being *into objections.* The nature of an *inquiry into objections* had been earlier considered in *B Johnson & Co (Builders) Ltd v Minister of Health.*[7] Lord Greene MR there provided a 'neglected but luminous analysis'[8] of the minister's functions. In that case a local authority had made a compulsory purchase order. The minister considered the plaintiff's objection to the order, which he confirmed. In arriving at his decision the minister took account of certain letters written to him by the local authority before it made the order. The plaintiff contended that this vitiated the confirmation of the order on the ground that the minister should have disclosed the letters to the objectors, in other words, he should at that *stage* of the proceedings and in respect of the *matter* complained of have acted judicially, as though he were a judge. Lord Greene said that an analogy with litigation or a *lis* (the idea of an issue joined between parties to litigation) was misleading.

[T]he local authority and the objectors are not parties to anything that resembles litigation. A moment's thought will show that any such conception of the relationship must be fallacious, because on the substantive matter, viz, whether the order should be confirmed or not, there is a third party who is not present, viz, the public, and it is the function of the Minister to consider the rights and the interests of the public. That by itself shows that it is completely wrong to treat the controversy between objector and local authority as a controversy which covers the whole of the ground. It is in respect of the public interest that the discretion that Parliament has given to the Minister comes into operation. It may well be that, on considering the objections, the Minister may find that they are reasonable and that the facts alleged in them are true, but, nevertheless, he may decide that he will overrule them. His action in so deciding is a purely administrative action, based on his conceptions as to what public policy demands ... The objections, in other words, may fail to produce the result desired by the objector, not because the objector has been defeated by the local authority in a sort of litigation, but because the objections have been overruled by the Minister's decision as to what the public interest demands. Unless that aspect of this stage in the process is thoroughly appreciated the word lis may result in a completely fallacious approach to the type of problem with which we have to deal.[9]

In the result, the court ruled that while after the inquiry had closed, the minister could not hear one side without letting the other know and could not accept fresh evidence from one side without giving the other one an opportunity to comment on it, when the minister came to reach his decision he could, in applying his policy make use of any information or advice available to him in his department. The plaintiff's challenge to

6   At 94 and 612 respectively. Paragraphs and emphasis added. Note the reference to private Bill procedure: see p 56 above.
7   [1947] 2 All ER 395.
8   Per Lord Diplock in *Bushell v Secretary of State for the Environment* [1981] AC 75 at 94, [1980] 2 All ER 608 at 612.
9   [1947] 2 All ER 395 at 399.

the validity of the order therefore failed.

This approach was approved by the House of Lords in *Bushell v Secretary of State for the Environment*.[10] The motorway scheme had been made by the *minister* and under the Act it was *he* who had to consider the objections to it. Notice therefore a difference between this scheme and that in *B Johnson & Co (Builders) Ltd v Minister of Health*, where the scheme had been made by a local authority. Lord Diplock, referring in *Bushell's* case to Lord Greene's analysis in the earlier case said:

> If the analogy of a *lis inter partes* be a false analogy even when the scheme which is the subject of the local inquiry is not a departmental scheme but one of which a public authority other than the minister is the originator, the analogy is even farther from reflecting the essentially administrative nature of the minister's functions when, having considered in the light of the advice of his department the objections which have been the subject of a local inquiry and the report of the inspector, he makes his decision in a case where the scheme is one that has been prepared by his own department itself and which it is for him in his capacity as head of that department to decide whether it is in the general public interest that it should be made or not.[11]

Investigating alternative proposals

A question that is sometimes of importance for objectors is whether an inquiry into objections can *investigate alternative proposals*. It was raised in *Wednesbury Corpn v Minister of Housing and Local Government* (No 2).[12] Under the Local Government Act 1958 it was the job of the Local Government Commission to review the organisation of local government and submit proposals to the minister. The Commission submitted proposals for the reorganisation of local government having first consulted local authorities in the area. Some local authorities objected, and a 'local inquiry' was held into the objections. A week before the inquiry opened the authorities submitted to the Commission an *alternative scheme* of reorganisation. Following the inquiry the plaintiffs argued that the hearing did not constitute a 'local inquiry' by law. What was the alleged defect? It was that the inspectors were unwilling to form a judgment on the merits of the alternative scheme.

These contentions were said by Sellers LJ to misunderstand the purpose of the inquiry. It was not an inquiry into alternative schemes, but into objections to a scheme prepared by an expert body, the Commission. Had it been the former, the inspectors, having to consider the merits of various schemes would have to be at least as expert in the field of local government as members of the Commission itself, and nothing in the 1958 Act suggested that that was intended. The inquiry, said Sellers LJ might be described as 'one-sided'. There was no issue or *lis*. It did not raise issues between the Commission's proposals and counter-proposals. Had it been such the Commission would doubtless have been represented by counsel

10 [1981] AC 75, [1980] 2 All ER 608.
11 At 102 and 617 respectively.
12 [1966] 2 QB 275, [1965] 3 All ER 571.

at the inquiry, but it was not. However, with regard to proposed road schemes, arrangements have been made to allow consideration to be given to alternative proposals.[13]

The obligation to hold an inquiry into objections under the Act in question was subject to the following proviso:

provided that, except where the objection is one made by a local authority to a proposal that the area of that authority should cease to be a separate area of local government ... the Minister may dispense with an inquiry if he is satisfied that for the purpose of considering the Commission's proposals he is sufficiently informed as to the matters to which the objection relates.

Three things are to be noted about this. First, it is not uncommon for an inquiry to be mandatory where an objection is made by an affected public authority. Second, the ground on which the inquiry can be dispensed with shows that the main and official purpose of the inquiry in this context is to inform the minister of the nature and strength of objections. Third, power to dispense with an inquiry or hearing is not uncommonly given. Because of the importance of such procedure to those affected by the consequent decision, the circumstances in which the power can be exercised should be critically looked at.[14] The Council on Tribunals has more than once expressed its concern at the increasing number of cases in which departments have considered it necessary for one reason or other, in recent years, to provide for dispensing with inquiries.[15]

It is sometimes asserted that inquiries serve little purpose, as the proposed schemes inevitably go ahead if with some minor amendment. A counter-consideration is that the possibility of a public inquiry following objections may well influence an authority when it is drawing up the scheme. For example it has been said that:

If the inquiry does constrain the [Central Electricity Generating] Board [in its application for consent to build a power station] that constraint occurs long before the inquiry in the internal decisions made in contemplation of a possible public inquiry. The proceedings of the inquiry itself will probably not affect the outcome of the Board's application for consent.[16]

Inquiries under the Town and Country Planning Act

Development control: planning. A basic rule of planning law is that permission is required for the carrying out of any development of land.

---

13 And see *Guide to Procedure* for obtaining orders under the Transport and Works Act 1992, para 4.70.
14 Decision to dispense with inquiry struck down in *Binney and Anscomb v Secretary of State for the Environment* [1984] JPL 871 but not in *Waltham Forest BC v Secretary of State for the Environment*: relevant criteria – number of objectors, clarity of the issue, and, if issue straightforward, whether it had been covered in objectors' written submissions. (1993) Independent, 9 February.
15 Annual Report for 1976–7, para 4.13; for 1974–5, paras 13–17. See p 170 below for Council.
16 Drapkin 'Development, Electricity and Power Stations' [1974] PL 220.

This has to be sought from the local planning authority. (This is the *development control* aspect of planning law.) The authority may refuse planning permission or grant it unconditionally or subject to such conditions as it thinks fit. When planning permission is refused, or is granted subject to conditions, the applicant can appeal to the Secretary of State, who may dismiss or allow the appeal or reverse or vary any part of the authority's decision.[17] Before determining the appeal the minister must, at the request of the applicant or the planning authority, hold an *inquiry* into the matter, giving the applicant and the authority an opportunity to be heard.[18] It will be noticed that the nature of this inquiry – held in connection with an appeal against a decision – is different from those held in connection with compulsory purchase orders which are into objections to a proposed order.

How is the appeal decided? At the time when the Franks Committee was considering planning inquiries the position was that an inquiry held in connection with a planning appeal was conducted by a person appointed to do so by the Secretary of State called an 'inspector'. The role of the inspector was to make a report and recommendation to the minister, who then decided – though not necessarily or indeed in most cases personally: it was decided within the department. The Franks Committee considered whether appeals could be decided not within the Department but by a *tribunal* independent of it, but thought not, because of the impossibility of framing rules for application by the tribunal. But it was in its view necessary to reduce the amount of planning appeal work falling on the departments. It therefore recommended that the power to take decisions on certain appeals should be *delegated to inspectors*.

This would mean that the decision would be taken by the person holding the inquiry, with an obvious saving of time. It would have to be recognised that the minister could not be accountable for a decision so delegated. He would however be responsible to Parliament for the act of delegation.[19]

This was one of the few recommendations of the Franks Report which were rejected outright by the government. However, the question was reconsidered later in view of the excessive length of time taken to issue decisions on appeals which go to an inquiry. (The time taken to decide appeals had been a continuing worry.) The outcome was a decision to amend the law so as to enable the minister to delegate to selected inspectors the responsibility for deciding certain planning appeals in respect of specified minor forms of development.

Accordingly section 21 of the Town and Country Planning Act 1968 (now Sch 6 of the 1990 Act) provides that certain classes of planning appeal may be determined by a person appointed by the minister for the purpose instead of by the Secretary of State. It goes on to say that an appeal determined by an appointed person 'shall be treated as that of the

17 Town and Country Planning Act 1990, ss 57, 70.
18 Ibid, s 78.
19 Cmnd 218, para 392.

Secretary of State' so that its validity can be questioned in court proceedings to, but only to, the same extent as can the minister's. Such appeals are known as *transferred appeals*.

The classes of appeal which can be determined by appointed persons are set out in regulations, the current ones being in SI 1988/945. There has been, since the first regulations were made, a gradual extension of the classes of appeal which appointed persons can decide and the position now is that virtually *all appeals are decided by inspectors*. It remains the case however that the Secretary of State can direct that an appeal shall be determined by himself. He must give his reasons for doing this. This might be done in cases involving major or controversial developments, substantial departures from structure plans, or matters of direct concern to other government departments.

The Dobry Report referred to this development as 'a sharp break from tradition.'[20] The Council on Tribunals pointed out that a decision taken by an inspector 'becomes in effect a tribunal hearing'.[1] It is significant that appeals against compulsory purchase orders cannot be decided by inspectors.[2]

Detailed regulations have been made for both transferred and Secretary of State cases.[3] The main objective of the rules is to make the inquiry process at all stages as efficient and effective as possible without impairing the fairness of the procedure or the ability of participants to say whatever is relevant to the issue. In Secretary of State cases an important rule deals with the position where the minister intends to disagree with the inspector on any matter of fact relevant to the inspector's conclusion.

Another development is the *written representations procedure*. As many as 85 per cent of all planning appeals are decided by this procedure, where there is no inquiry. It is used both in 'transferred appeals' and 'Secretary of State cases' where the Department suggests recourse to it, and the parties agree. It is an extra-legal device whereby the appellant voluntarily waives his right to an inquiry. The appeal is settled after an exchange of correspondence and a site visit. Regulations[4] prescribe time-limits for various stages of this procedure. They are intended to speed up the processing of planning appeals without any loss of quality but lack the element of publicity and may be advantageous to the developer.

Yet another development is the *hearing*, held in place of an inquiry in simple appeals. Again, they are held only when the parties agree. The object is to enable the inspector to ask questions about previous written submissions without undue formality in respect of a small-scale development which seems unlikely to raise complex legal or policy issues and gives rise to little or no third party issues. The regulations applying to inquiries (see above) do not apply; a code of practice has been drawn up.

20 Review of the Development Control System. Final Report, ch 11.37.
1 Annual Report for 1979–80, para 6.41. For tribunals see ch 5, below.
2 Cf Transport and Works Act 1992 s 23(4).
3 SI 1992/2039 and SI 1992/2038.
4 SI 1987/701.

Inspectors and Inspectorate

The inspectors are within an organisation called the Planning Inspectorate, established in 1992 as an Executive Agency of the Department of the Environment.[5] The Framework Document explains. The function of the Inspector*ate* is to serve the Secretary of State on appeals and other casework under planning and related (eg highways) legislation, and it is through the work of the Agency that the Secretary of State's policies are carried forward. Thus in processing appeals the Inspector*ate* acts on his behalf. This includes the work of the inspect*ors* who, in deciding cases, exercise their independent judgment. They must of course apply not only the law but also ministerial policies laid down within the legislation. Although an inspector, in determining an appeal, acts on behalf of the minister, the decision is his, and is issued in his name, and the minister is not accountable for it (though in legal proceedings to challenge the decision, the Secretary of State, not the inspector, is the respondent). The Document expressly says that one of the objectives of the Inspectorate is 'to maintain the integrity of each Inspector as an independent tribunal, not subject to any improper influence'. Being a tribunal, and thus having to act 'judicially' it is basic that there should be no material relevant to the case before an inspector which is not also available to the parties. It follows, the Document says, that government policy in relation to any case before an inspector must be as presented to Parliament or published through the usual channels.

Structure plans – the examination in public

The procedures just referred to are in the context of 'development control' – the sharp end of planning law. But planning law is also about plans, and one kind of plan that has to be drawn up by the appropriate local authority is the structure plan.[6] The purpose of this is to lay down general lines of development for the area in question. It deals with land use but in terms of policies such as employment, housing and transport; it does not deal with individual properties. Before adopting the plan the local authority will cause an examination in public to be held of 'such matters affecting the consideration of the proposals as they consider ought to be so examined ... ' That is, the authority selects those issues on which they need to be more fully informed by means of public discussion in order to reach their decisions. No-one, apart from the authority itself, has the right to be heard. The EIP is held by a panel of two persons appointed by the authority. Unlike the inquiries referred to under development control it does not proceed by examination and cross-examination of witnesses, but is in the nature of a 'probing discussion' led by the Panel which draws attention to the issues on which clarification and information is required, and which itself takes an active part in the discussion. A very different animal from appeal inquiries, invented to deal with the real difficulties of

---

5   See p 19 above.
6   Town and Country Planning Act 1990, s 31 et seq.

the old-style inquiry especially that of delay caused by giving every objector the right to have his say. A Code of Practice governs the procedure.

Another kind of plan that is required is the *local plan*,[7] each of which covers a smaller area than the structure plan, and whose policies must conform with the latter. It gives in appropriate detail the authority's proposals for the development of land including measures for the management of traffic. The authority must hold a local inquiry into the proposals when objections have been made unless all objectors agree that they do not wish to appear.

Major public inquiries
The system whereby an inquiry is held in connection with an appeal to the minister against a refused or conditional planning permission is generally considered to work satisfactorily. However, it may not be a suitable mechanism for considering proposed developments that have a more than local impact or raise questions of technical complexity, for permitting the full issues to be thrashed out or to act as a basis for a decision which can take into account the whole range of practicable alternatives.

In 1967 the government appointed the non-statutory *Roskill Commission*, consisting of six members under the chairmanship of a High Court Judge. The Commission's job was to identify the best site for a third 'London' airport. It was not tied to considering the pros and cons of a particular proposal, as would be the case in a normal planning inquiry. It began with 78 possibilities which it narrowed down to four. It was empowered to undertake its own research and it was thus an *investigatory* body. (The government later abandoned the idea of a third airport.)

In the meantime the government had proposed and Parliament had provided for a new type of inquiry, the *Planning Inquiry Commission*.[8] This was to be used whenever in the minister's opinion a special inquiry into a proposed development was necessary because of the regional or national interests involved or because of the unfamiliar scientific or technical questions in issue. The Commission, of three to five members, would operate a two-stage procedure, the *investigatory* (as it would be concerned with policy and the need for the development), and the second being site-specific, *inquiring into objections* to a site proposed by the Commission. However, no such Commission has been appointed.

A major inquiry was into the planning application of British Nuclear Fuels Ltd for a nuclear fuel reprocessing plant at *Windscale*. The application appeared to meet the criteria for a Planning Inquiry Commission. But when the application was 'called-in' for ministerial decision it was decided to hold a normal inquiry governed by the standard Inquiry Procedure Rules, although in this case a High Court Judge was appointed as inspector with two assessors to assist him. The inquiry sat for a hundred days, and recommended that permission be granted. Inevitably there were

7 Ibid s 36 et seq.
8 Town and Country Planning Act 1968, now Town and Country Planning Act 1990, s 101.

demands for the fullest possible public and Parliamentary debate before the final decision was taken. This was thought to put the Secretary of State in difficulty, as a decision taken by him after participation in a parliamentary debate might have been challengeable in a court of law, or the inquiry might have had to be re-opened under the rule concerning the taking of new evidence after the close of the inquiry.[9] The solution found was for the Secretary of State to refuse permission, and at the same time to announce that permission would be granted in due course by means of a special development order which was subject to the negative resolution procedure in Parliament.[10] (There seems to be something amiss when it is necessary to resort to such a stratagem.)

The *Sizewell* inquiry was into the proposal of the Central Electricity Generating Board to build a station at Sizewell to generate electricity by nuclear energy. This required the consent of the Secretary of State under the Electric Lighting Act 1909. The inquiry was held under the Electricity Generating Stations and Overhead Lines (Inquiries Procedure) Rules 1981 – not technically a planning inquiry, but if consent was given under the 1909 Act deemed planning consent could be given. Hearings were held on 340 days between 1983 and 1985. The inspector reported in 1986; Parliamentary debates took place in 1987. In this case the minister said he was there to listen to what was said, but would not comment. Consent was given a few weeks later.

From a detailed account of the inquiry[11] we can select the following points. The main characteristic of the inquiry was its *investigative* nature; another was the use of *counsel to the inquiry*, whose role was to pursue inquiries on behalf of the inspector and to ensure that evidence put before him, which was very technical, was clear and complete. A third feature was the *pre-inquiry stage* which was regarded as contributing significantly to an orderly and efficient consideration of the issues.

The 1981 Rules, mentioned above, were, in the light of the Sizewell experience, replaced by Rules of the same name of 1987 (and now 1990). They refer to assessors and pre-inquiry meetings, and contain other new rules intended to streamline the procedure at future such inquiries.

The switch from Bill to administrative procedure and *inquiry* under the Transport and Works Act 1992 will be noted.[12]

Consultation

Consulting is a major government activity. Departments are frequently under a statutory duty to consult before taking certain action. They will often wish to consult, even if not so required; but a statutory requirement

9 945 H of C Official Report (5th series) col 981.

10 SI 1978/523 (a local instrument); 950 H of C Official Report (5th series) col 111; Annual Report of the Council on Tribunals for 1977–8, para 7.24.

11 O'Riordan, Kemp and Purdue, *Sizewell B*. For the later Hinkley Point Inquiry see Council on Tribunals Annual Report 1991–92 para 2.67.

12 See p 57 above.

is intended as a guarantee that they will do so. The purpose of consultation is to give those affected by the proposed action an opportunity to put their case; or where they have some special knowledge, experience or expertise, to ensure that it is put at the disposal of the authority; or both. It should ensure that the authority does not overlook matters it ought to have regard to. The resultant decision should be 'better' than it would otherwise have been: 'better' in such senses as being more effective, relevant, practical, and acceptable to those affected. An intention is to benefit the consulter; an effect may be to educate the consulted in the problem facing the consulter.[13] It has been put more widely.

Nor is this all. The process of being consulted gives [the citizen] a sense of being significant in the State. It makes him feel that he is more than the mere recipient of orders ... He comes to see that his needs will be met only as he contributes his instructed judgment to the experience out of which decisions are compounded. He gains the expectation of being consulted, the sense that he must form an opinion on public affairs.[14]

The obligations on the authority may be expressly to 'consult'; but the objectives of 'consultation' can be achieved by, for example, requiring the authority to invite representations or objections, to seek opinions, etc. There may also be a power or duty to hold an oral inquiry into the proposed action at which representations, objections etc may be put. Apart from such statutory obligations, the courts may impose on the administration a duty to act fairly which may carry with it a duty to hear what those affected have to say before the decision is taken, or may say that a duty to have regard to certain opinions or interests requires that they be consulted.[15]

Consultation takes place over the whole range of government action. It takes place on *broad issues* of policy – economic, educational, etc. The publication of Green Papers which invite comments on their contents is part of the process.[16] A duty to consult is generally imposed as part of the process of making *delegated legislation.*[17] One particular device is the obligation to publish notice of intention to make the rules. The Rules Publication Act 1893 said that at least 40 days before making certain statutory rules notice of the proposal to do so and of the place where copies of the draft rule could be obtained had to be published in the *London Gazette*. During those 40 days any public body could obtain copies and submit written representations on the draft to the relevant authority. Those representations had to be taken into account by the authority before finally settling the rules. These requirements applied however to a very limited range of statutory rules and the Act was repealed by the Statutory Instruments Act 1946.[18] There is now no general rule requiring notice of an

13 The Conduct of Local Authority Business, Research Vol 1, Cmnd 9798, ch 7.
14 H J Laski *Liberty in the Modern State*, p 83.
15 See ch 9, below.
16 See D Johnstone *A Tax shall be charged*, ch 4.
17 See p 68 above.
18 Contrast Allen *Law and Orders*, p 99 with Ilbert *Legislative Methods and Forms*, p 41 as to utility of 1893 Act.

intention to make orders, but there are many examples of specific require-ments. For example before making certain orders under the Fair Trading Act 1973 the minister must publish a notice stating the intention of making the order, the nature of the provisions to be embodied in it, and inviting written representations.[19] Another consultative device is the public inquiry referred to at p 117 above. Its use in connection with making delegated legislation is unusual. The Committee on Safety and Health at Work commented on the 'manifestly absurd' delays involved in the inquiry pro-cedure and recommended that it be replaced by a simple obligation to consult.[20] Provisions for local inquiries into proposed delegated legislation are to be found in other legislation eg Control of Pollution Act 1974, section 104(3).

Consultation may also be required before the taking of more *specific decisions* such as the designation of the site of a new town,[1] a decision to grant or refuse a licence,[2] the appointment of persons to a public office.[3]

Government departments constantly consult with one another, but the obligation to do so does not have to be imposed on them by statute: it is a matter of good administration – but statutory obligations to do so can be found.[4] Not uncommon is the obligation on other public authorities to consult with one another.[5] They may also be required to consult with employees or their representatives,[6] or with particular employees.[7]

The answer to the question *who is to be consulted?* is given by looking to the purpose of the consultation. If it is to ensure that technical expertise is made available, then those with that expertise; if it is to ensure that those affected can make their views known, then those likely to be affected and so on. But the matter is not always free from difficulties. Voluntary pressure groups will be eager to make their views known: but these are often foreseeable.[8] To ensure that the trawl of opinion is wide and deep,[9] government may appoint advisory committees on a temporary or per-manent basis, and in the latter case, perhaps through statute. The problem then is to ensure that opinion is adequately reflected in the membership and procedure of the committee.

---

19 And see Trade Marks Act 1938, s 40(3), and SI 1992/1069.
20 Cmnd 5034, para 141.
 1 New Towns Act 1981, s 1(1).
 2 Forestry Act 1967, s 33(3).
 3 Local Government Act 1974, s 23(4).
 4 Agricultural Marketing Act 1958, s 43(1).
 5 National Health Service Act 1977, s 22; Town and Country Planning Act 1990, s 30(4).
 6 Post Office Act 1969, Sch 1, para 11. *Gallaher v Post Office* [1970] 3 All ER 712; *R v Post Office, ex p Association of Scientific, Technical and Managerial Staffs* [1981] 1 All ER 139, CA. The duty to consult may be imposed in private law relationships.
 7 Local Government Act 1972, s 113(1).
 8 Eg 'Wind up the Country Landowners' Association and it will deplore the effects of legislation to facilitate succession to farms by children of tenants. Plug in the National Farmers' Union and it will ... Switch on the Economic Development Committee for Agriculture and it will ...': *The Times*, 25 January 1977. See Johnstone *A Tax shall be charged.*
 9 Some 250 organisations were consulted about metrication: 948 H of C Official Report (5th series) col 408 (written answer).

Special reference must be made to the *Social Security Advisory Committee*. The National Insurance Act 1946 provided for a comprehensive system of insurance administered by the Secretary of State for Social Services. The Act gave the minister wide powers to make regulations on many important matters. It also provided for the setting up of the National Insurance Advisory Committee now replaced by the Social Security Advisory Committee.[10] This consists of a chairman and not less than eight nor more than eleven members, all appointed by the minister. At least one of the members must be a person with experience of work among and of the needs of the chronically sick and disabled, one must be appointed after consultation with organisations representing employers, one after consultation with organisations representing workers. The *general* function of the Committee is to give advice and assistance to the minister in connection with his functions under the Act, and he may refer to it for consideration and advice such questions relating to the operation of relevant enactments as he thinks fit including the advisability of their amendment. But *in particular*, where the minister proposes to make regulations under the Act he shall (unless it appears to him that by reason of the urgency of the matter[11] it is inexpedient to do so) refer the proposals, whether in the form of draft regulations or otherwise, to the Committee. Where the proposals seem to the Committee technical or wholly beneficial it can agree not to be consulted, but where a significant change is involved it can ask for them to be formally referred to it.[12] The Committee's practice is to give public notice of the fact that it has received the draft and of the purport of the proposed regulations, and to invite written representations on the draft. After considering the draft and the representations, and perhaps questioning officials, the Committee reports to the minister. It may urge changes, or that the regulations be dropped entirely; it will not refrain from severe criticism.[13] When the regulations are laid before Parliament they must be accompanied by the Committee's report and by a statement from the minister showing the extent to which he has given effect to the Committee's recommendations, and his reasons for departing from them, if such be the case. The attention of Parliament is thereby drawn to the views of an independent body on the regulations. The scrutiny of regulations before they are made, that is, at the stage when administrative policy is being developed and can most easily be modified is particularly valuable.

Where there is a statutory duty to consult, the statute may name the body (or bodies) to be consulted (as in the example just given), or may require consultation with such bodies, persons, etc, as appear to the minister (etc) to be appropriate. Or there may be a combination of the two

10 Social Security Administration Act 1992, s 170.
11 A self-induced urgency does not excuse: *R v Secretary of State for Social Security ex p Association of Metropolitan Authorities* (1992) Times, 23 July.
12 See generally the Committee's Ninth Report, 1993.
13 See eg Report of the Social Security Advisory Committee on the Draft Housing Benefits Amendment Regulations 1984, Cmnd 9150.

requirements. A statutory *power* to consult is sometimes given. But this would not seem to be necessary, as a power to consult would seem to be exercisable without having to be expressly conferred.

In addition to the question of *whom* to consult, there may be the question of *when* to consult. For example, if there are a number of possible ways of dealing with a problem (say sewage disposal), is the authority to take a view of the best way to deal with it and then 'consult', saying in effect, 'This is what we propose to do. What do you think?' Or is it to make known the alternatives and invite comments, thus consulting at an earlier stage? The advantages to an applicant for an order under the Transport and Works Act 1992 in consulting early and widely have been emphasised.[14]

The question of when to consult may be tied in with the question of *what to consult about*, as in the example given. In the first case the authority would be consulting about the desirability of its preferred scheme, in the second, about the options open to it.

Consultation is generally regarded as a good thing. Are there any drawbacks?

Delay is acknowledged to be a possible disadvantage in all consultation: though the time taken over the consultation (which is what is meant by 'delay' here), has to be set against the hoped-for advantages.[15] And expectations may be disappointed. The Independent Broadcasting Authority referred to the problem thus.

Extensive consultation carries its own dangers. People may come to expect that a forcefully expressed view in favour of a particular change should carry the day. The Authority, on the other hand, has to assess the extent to which an energetic and vocal minority actually reflect a deeply and widely held view among the public in the area concerned ... it also has to assess the technical and financial feasibility of proposal for change.[16]

Nor is the majority view entitled to carry the day; but numbers are not irrelevant.

In *Westminster City Council v Greater London Council*[17] Lord Bridge cautioned against imposing too wide a duty to consult as this could be to the detriment of the efficient conduct of public business. A Report on the management of the National Health Service noted that a great importance was attached to ensuring that the views of the community at all levels were taken into account, but the reality was that 'by any business standards' the process of consultation was so labyrinthine, that the result in many cases was 'institutionalised stagnation.'[18]

In addition there is often a suspicion that consultation, like the public inquiry, is a purely formal exercise; that it is gone through for the sake of

14 Transport and Works Act – a Guide to Procedure, HMSO, para 2.2.
15 The obligation to consult may be lifted in the case of eg danger to the public, eg Consumer Safety Act 1978, Sch 1, paras 5 and 14 or where there is some other overriding public interest, eg SI 1985/304 reg 9(1)(2).
16 Annual Report 1978–9. For consultation by Law Commission, see North 101 LQR at 344.
17 [1986] 2 All ER 278, at 289.
18 The (Griffiths) Report of the NHS Management Inquiry, 1983, p 14.

appearance, and will have little or no significant effect on the decision or action proposed. A House of Commons Select Committee acknowledged that the government had consulted widely over changes in the rules concerning inquiries into proposals to build nuclear power stations, but observed that 'it seems to have paid particular attention to the arguments from what might be described as the establishment side'.[19]

Note finally that it is not to be assumed that because (for example) ministerial regulations state that they have been made 'after consultation with the Council on Tribunals' that the Council therefore approves of the regulations as made. It is consultation with, not the consent of, the Council, that is required, but such a statement may give the impression that approval has been given.

19 First Report from the Energy Committee, 1987–88, HC 310.

Chapter 5

Tribunals

What are they?

We can approach an answer to this question by looking at the terms of reference of the Franks Committee.[1] It was asked to consider and make recommendations on 'the constitution and working of tribunals other than the ordinary courts of law, constituted under any Act of Parliament by a Minister of the Crown or for the purposes of a Minister's functions'.

Thus:

− 'Tribunal' is not defined but the phrase 'other than the ordinary courts of law' indicates that their functions are akin to those of courts of law.

− The reference to Acts suggests that though tribunals are mostly constituted by statute, they may be established under the prerogative.

− The reference to Ministers suggests that a body may be a tribunal even if constituted by someone other than a Minister, say a local authority.

Note further:

− The Franks Committee decided to exclude certain tribunals from its consideration 'although many of them are or appear to be within the terms of reference'. These were (a) tribunals which do not make decisions (by which they meant tribunals which only make recommendations) and (b) tribunals in the industrial field (which they thought could not be examined in isolation from inter-related industrial questions).

Adding together tribunals which were and those which were not examined by the Franks Committee, we get some initial idea of the range of complexity of tribunals. But what do tribunals do? A tribunal is a body whose functions are akin to those of, or share some of the characteristics of, a court of law; to pick up a word used by Franks, it has an 'adjudicating' function. The kinds of decisions, Franks said, which tribunals make are those which might be considered suitable for the courts, but which Parliament had decided should not be remitted to the 'ordinary courts' − nor should they be left to be decided in the course of the administration of

---

1   Cmnd 218. See p 3 above.

the Department concerned. Instead, they are decided by a 'tribunal'. In a key phrase Franks said 'Tribunals are not ordinary courts, but neither are they appendages of Government Departments'. And, 'the essential point is that … Parliament has deliberately provided for a decision outside and independent of the department concerned'.[2] We may interpret these statements as meaning that the decisions allocated to a tribunal have, by definition, been given to a body independent of the department, that therefore the tribunal is not to be treated as a mere appendage of the department; and further while tribunals are not part of the ordinary courts of law, as they are not established as such by statutes which created them, in their independence of departments and in their functions they are akin to the regular courts.

The Tribunals and Inquiries Act 1958, acting on a recommendation of the Franks Report, established a Council on Tribunals, one of whose functions is to 'keep under review' the constitution and working of certain tribunals. The Act, in bringing tribunals under the Council's jurisdiction, did not proceed by defining 'tribunal' and thus bring under it any existing (or future) body which fell within that definition. This was because 'tribunals defy definition in general terms'. Rather the Act proceeded by listing in a Schedule those bodies which were considered to be tribunals and which were appropriately subjected to the Council's supervision. On what basis then was the Schedule compiled and what was deemed to be a tribunal for this purpose? The basis was 'broadly to include all tribunals of the type which the Franks Committee took to be within their purview, that is to say, bodies other than the ordinary courts which hear and determine disputes or differences and which are constituted under an Act of Parliament by a Minister or for the purposes of a Minister's functions'.[3]

When a new dispute-resolving body is created the question will arise whether it is a 'tribunal' and thus should be added to the Schedule to the Tribunals and Inquiries Act (now of 1992), and be brought within the Council's jurisdiction. This is considered below, but the following points can be conveniently noted here.

– A body may be a 'tribunal' – that is, have a tribunal function – though not called 'tribunal', as indeed many of them are not – but Board, Committee, Authority or even Ombudsman.

– Some bodies exercise tribunal and non-tribunal functions (and may thus be under the jurisdiction of the Council or Tribunals in respect only of the former).

– Most tribunals determine disputes between an individual and a public authority, but some determine disputes between individuals (or have both functions).

– Most tribunals are concerned with *appeals* against a decision adverse to the individual taken by a public official (generally about financial matters, but it could be about personal liberty), but some are concerned with the *initial* determination of a claim (as for a licence, for example).

2 Cmnd 218, para 40.
3 HC Debs (5th series) vol 590 col 1603 et seq.

– Sometimes tribunals are referred to as *administrative* tribunals. In so far as this implies that tribunals are mere appendages of departments, it is to be deplored. If it draws attention to the fact that tribunals are not courts of law, it is unnecessary. It is suggested that it should be discarded, as was the even more objectionable phrase 'ministerial tribunals' which was used by the Committee on Ministers' Powers.

– There are what are called *domestic* tribunals. (The Franks Report gave them as an example of bodies 'which are sometimes included in general studies of the subject [but which] are in fact outside the ambit of our enquiry'.[4]) Any club, organisation, association or profession may have rules for dealing with the discipline and expulsion of its members and may set up a body internal to itself to enforce those rules – a *domestic tribunal*. The exercise by such a private body of its powers may raise questions of legal rights and duties, for example the duty to give a fair hearing, and the workings of such bodies raise problems akin to those in public law. Where the organisation is given statutory recognition and its disciplinary body exercises statutory powers, the concern of public law is clear.[5]

What questions should be given to tribunals for decision?

Whether or not there is a tribunal to which an appeal or application lies depends on whether the Act establishing the scheme in question, in the administration of which disputes may arise, provides for one. It follows that when a scheme is being drafted the department will have to decide whether to propose in the Bill the creation of a tribunal to determine disputes which may arise. The question therefore is, what principles are to be applied when deciding whether a decision should be taken within a department or put in the hands of a body independent of it, that is of a tribunal? The question in each case is, who is to decide? Should it be the minister or some body independent of him? To whom are functions to be allocated? It will be agreed that under our political system certain actions and decisions should be in the hands of departments, for which ministers are accountable to Parliament and to public opinion. Whether a motorway system is needed, whether a particular motorway is required, whether in the light of projected demand for energy, and the availability of oil and coal, a series of nuclear power stations and whether a barrage across the Severn estuary should be built, are such questions. No one would say that foreign affairs and defence ought to be in anyone's hands other than ministers'; or on the other hand few would dispute (at least until recently) that there is properly an appeal from a departmental refusal of social security benefit to an independent tribunal. There are of course borderline cases, and the examples of these given below will suggest the principles acted on.

The Committee on Ministers' Powers, reporting in 1932, had approached this problem of the allocation of functions by way of the doctrine of the

4   Cmnd 218 Appendix II, para 3.
5   See eg Medical Act 1983.

separation of powers. That doctrine, said the Committee in its report:

is prima facie the guiding principle by which Parliament when legislating should allocate the executive and judicial tasks involved in its legislative plan.[6]

The approach suggested by the Committee was therefore that one should first classify the act in question as executive or judicial[7] and then allocate it accordingly: if executive, it should be given to the executive; if judicial it should be given to a judicial body, preferably to a court of law. Only on special grounds, it said, should a judicial decision be given to a tribunal. But it acknowledged that resort to tribunals did not mean that the constitution was developing in a fundamentally wrong direction though the system was capable of abuse and safeguards were essential 'if the rule of law and the liberty of the subject are to be maintained'.[8] Indeed the report recognised that tribunals have much to recommend them: they are likely to be cheaper than the courts, more readily accessible, freer from legal and procedural technicalities, and more expeditious. (Certainly one of the reasons for the resort to tribunals has been a disenchantment with the courts.)

The Report of the Franks Committee, published in 1957[9], took a different approach from that of the Committee on Ministers' Powers. It said that the distinction between the judicial and the administrative (like the distinction between what is according to the rule of law and what is arbitrary), while historic and important, did not:

yield a valid principle on which one can decide whether the duty of making a certain decision should be laid upon a tribunal or upon a minister or whether the existing allocation of decisions between tribunals and ministers is appropriate.[10]

Like its predecessor the Committee thought that if a decision was suitable for decision by either a court or a tribunal, it should be entrusted to a court 'in the absence of special considerations which make a tribunal more suitable'. But despite this expressed preference for the courts, the Committee agreed with its predecessor that tribunals have characteristics which often given them advantages over the courts, and made no recommendation for the transfer of the jurisdiction of any existing tribunal to the ordinary courts. Indeed it found positive advantage in not doing so, and concluded, 'the system of administrative tribunals has positively contributed to the preservation of our ordinary judicial system'.[11]

The Franks Report thus largely concerned itself with improvements and safeguards to the system of tribunals as it found it. In particular it said there should be two Councils on Tribunals to keep them under constant review, and that tribunals should show three basic characteristics, 'openness, fairness, and impartiality'.

---

6 Cmnd 4060, p 92.
7 This required it to define what it meant by 'judicial' 'executive' etc, see p 5 above.
8 Cmnd 4060, p 97.
9 Cmnd 218.
10 Ibid, para 30.
11 Ibid, para 39 quoting evidence from the Permanent Secretary to the Lord Chancellor.

It seems that an administrator working out a new administrative scheme will not get much practical assistance from the report of either the Committee on Ministers' Powers or the Franks Committee in deciding on the allocation of functions. The Council on Tribunals has said that the selection of subjects referred to tribunals does not form a regular pattern. 'Certain basic guidelines can be detected, but the choice is influenced by the interplay of various factors – the nature of the decisions, accidents of history, departmental preferences and political considerations – rather than by the application of a set of coherent principles'.[12] The following examples illustrate that interplay of factors and suggest some principles. The relevant factors are italicised.

Closed shop compensation

Section 2 of the Employment Act 1982 empowered the Secretary of State to make payments towards compensating persons dismissed for refusing to join a trade union where a closed shop agreement was in operation. The government rejected opposition proposals that would have allowed a tribunal to decide the amount of compensation, on the ground that this would have *emasculated the minister's discretionary power, which he desired to retain*. Further, the section gave no legal entitlement to compensation, and therefore *no obligations were imposed 'of a sort which a judicial tribunal was normally regarded as the appropriate forum* to determine'.[13]

Authorised vehicle examiners

Under the Road Traffic Act 1972, now 1988 and regulations made under it, certain vehicles have to be submitted for examination to ascertain whether they comply with technical requirements. If they do, a test certificate is granted. The tests are carried out by examiners authorised for the purpose by the Secretary of State. The authorisation may be withdrawn at any time where the Secretary of State is dissatisfied with the way tests have been carried out. The withdrawal could be a serious matter for the examining garage, but the regulations provide only that if the examiner makes representations to the Secretary of State he must take them into account and make such further inquiries as he thinks fit. It has been suggested that there should be a right of appeal to some independent tribunal. The Department's view was that 'under the present set-up with 19,000 garages it would not be justified ... [If there were] a great reduction in the number of vehicle testing stations and a different set-up then perhaps in that context one might consider someone other

12 The Function of the Council on Tribunals: special report by the Council, 1980 (Cmnd 7805), para 1.7.
13 HC Official Report, SCG, 23 February 1982.

than the Secretary of State being the final arbiter'.[14] This view is based on the *practicalities* of the matter and on a *rigorous policy* of weeding out unsatisfactory examiners, which it might not be possible to ensure if the department's decisions went on appeal to an independent tribunal.[15]

Sound insulation of houses

Regulations under the Land Compensation Act 1973 impose a duty on highway authorities to offer insulation against nuisance by sound to residents affected by the use of new highways. Before the regulations where made the advice of the Council on Tribunals was sought on the specific question of whether an appeal procedure should be provided for a resident who believed that his house was eligible for insulation but found it had not been included on the map which would identify the properties to be insulated. The Council on Tribunals said:

Having regard to the proposed statutory prescription of the qualifying noise level and the detailed arrangements for establishing and re-checking noise contour, we were inclined to agree with the Department that the provision for formal machinery for settling disputes might be unnecessary and we did not urge its introduction at this stage. We advised, however, that a review of the nature and extent of complaints received by the Department in connection with the operation of the schemes should be carried out after an initial period of (say) two years.[16]

The Council later decided in the light of experience gained, not to press for a formal appeal machinery.[17] Here there was *no need* for an adjudicative machinery, as the administrative arrangements for determining entitlement to grant were satisfactory.

Foreign compensation

When the interests of British subjects have been adversely affected by the actions of a foreign government, for example by the confiscation of their property, the Foreign and Commonwealth Office may seek to negotiate financial compensation for them by way of a lump sum payment to be paid by the foreign government to the British Government, and distributed amongst those affected. Who adjudicates on individual claims for compensation out of the sum received by the British Government?

The Foreign Compensation Commission, an independent body of lawyers, is normally required to adjudicate. This is done on the basis of

14 Report from the Select Committee on the Parliamentary Commissioner, 1972–3, HC 379 Minutes of Evidence, Q50.
15 For an account of a complaint to the Parliamentary Commissioner about the withdrawal of an authorisation, of the system of internal appeals and the 'rigid complexities' of the system, see 2nd Report, 1993–94 HC 157, Case C 524/92.
16 Annual Report for 1972–3, para 29.
17 Annual Report for 1978–9, para 2.18.

precise provisions contained in the Commission's terms of reference as laid down by the Foreign Office. However, some years ago the British government arrived at a settlement with the (West) German government whereby the latter paid £1,000,000 to the former for distribution to victims of its predecessor's persecution. In this case the Foreign Office decided that it would itself adjudicate on individual claims. It did this because it thought it could do the job more *quickly* and more *flexibly* and it also thought that claims that dealt, as these did, with death and imprisonment and disability perhaps should be *dealt with differently from property claims*, which the Commission had mainly concerned itself with previously. The way the Department administered the distribution led to complaints being made to the Parliamentary Commissioner. A senior civil servant said later, 'W could have handed [the decision] to some kind of tribunal. It would have taken *longer*, and it would have saved our ministers and officials a good deal of *agony*.'[18] As a result of this experience the Foreign Office decided that in future such adjudications would also go to the Commission. In this case therefore, the Department discovered that the disadvantages of keeping such decisions in its own hands outweighed the disadvantages of giving them to a tribunal.

The Commission has been brought under the supervision of the Council on Tribunals as it has 'a judicial role and many of the characteristics displayed by the tribunals under our general supervision'.[19]

Immigration appeals

The law used to be that aliens had no right of appeal from a Home Office decision concerning their presence here. In 1966 a Committee was appointed to consider whether any right of appeal should be available to those persons who are refused admission to or are required to leave the country. In its Report the Committee agreed with the view that it was 'wrong and *inconsistent with the rule of law* that power to take decisions affecting a man's whole future should be vested in officers of the executive, from whose findings there is no appeal'.[20] In due course a two-tier appeal system was set up, consisting of adjudicators (sitting singly) and, above them, a three man Immigration Appeal Tribunal with an appeal on a point of law to the Court of Appeal. An appeal can be made to those authorities, against, for example a deportation order made by the minister, but not, be it noted, where the order is made on the ground that deportation is conducive to the public good 'as being in the interests of national security

18 Report from the Select Committee on the Parliamentary Commissioner, 1967–8, HC 258. It used to be the case that when a police officer was disciplined he could appeal to the Home Secretary. This was a *burden* on him personally, and he had been *criticised* when he had to differ from the advice he had been given. The Police and Magistrates Courts Act 1994 now provides for such appeals to be heard by a police appeals tribunal.
19 Annual Report for 1983–84, para 2.17.
20 Report of the Committee on Immigration Appeals, Cmnd 3387, para 84.

... or for other *reasons of a political nature*.[1] On such matters the minister is given the right to decide. And by the Asylum and Immigration Appeals Act 1993 the right of visitors and certain students to appeal against adverse decisions was removed on grounds of the need to tackle *delays* in the system, and of *economy*.[2]

Some tribunals

This section provides an account of the constitution, procedure etc of some selected tribunals. In reading it the student should ask himself for example: What is in dispute, a financial matter, personal liberty, a licence to trade? Why was the dispute given to a tribunal? Could it properly be determined by the courts or within a department? How is the tribunal constituted? Is there an appeal and if so, to what body and on what grounds? If not, why not? Is legal representation required, or allowed? Does the tribunal sit in public? Is its procedure purely adversarial, or is it in some degree inquisitorial? Are the tribunals organised on a national or regional or on a purely local basis? and so on.

Social Security Appeal Tribunals

National insurance claims

From about the beginning of this century schemes were brought into existence which separately provided for insurance against sickness, unemployment, widowhood, old age and industrial accidents. Each of these schemes had its own statutory procedure for the determination of disputes arising in the administration of the scheme. Thus, claims for unemployment benefit were decided by officials at local offices of the Ministry of Labour, with a right of appeal to a court of *referees* and then to the *umpire*; claims for old age pensions were decided by the Ministry of Health with an appeal to an independent *referee*, whereas claims in respect of industrial accident were decided by the *county court* with appeal to the Court of Appeal and the House of Lords.

In July 1948 new schemes for National Insurance and for industrial injuries were brought into existence replacing the many separate schemes by one unified scheme of insurance except for industrial injuries and a new comprehensive system of adjudication of appeals was introduced.

Social Security Adjudication

There have been and continue to be many changes in social security law since then, and it is now a complex body of law requiring specialist attention to the range of benefits available. The legislation was consolidated in 1992 in the Social Security Administration Act, the Social Security

1   Immigration Act 1971, s 5.
2   For criticism see Council on Tribunals Annual Report 1992–93, para 2.45.

Contributions and Benefits Act, and the Social Security (Consequential Provisions) Act. The following is a brief account of the system of adjudication, to be found in the first-named of those Acts.

The handling of benefit claims now comes within the Benefits Agency (for which see p 20), or, for unemployment benefit, within the Employment Service. Claims for benefit are submitted to *adjudication officers*; these are civil servants appointed for this purpose by the Secretary of State, with the consent of the Treasury as to numbers.

Their role is to adjudicate on claims, but only a small minority of them do that full-time; the majority spend most or a large part of their time on duties such as supervising their sections or collecting evidence on claims. In adjudicating on claims the AOs act, it is said, independently of the Department, applying statute law and case law to the claims. The Secretary of State is not accountable for their decisions. When adjudicating, AOs appear to be exercising a judicial function, but the Court of Appeal has ruled that[3] the AO is acting administratively.

There is also a *Chief Adjudication Officer*. His duty is to advise (not therefore to direct) adjudication officers as to the performance of their duties. He also keeps under review the operation of the system of adjudication; he submits an annual written report to the Secretary of State on the standard of adjudication, and the report has to be published. The general impression gained from reading these reports is that standards of adjudication fall considerably short of what is acceptable; a common error reported on is that the AO act on insufficient evidence. The AOs themselves have complained of inadequate training and guidance.

Appeal lies to local *Social Security Appeal Tribunals* (of which there is a President, who is a Judge). Each Tribunal, of which there are 178, consists of a lawyer-chairman and two 'wing' members drawn from panels for the area to which have been appointed (by the President) persons appearing to have knowledge or experience of conditions in the area or to be representative of persons living or working there. The President himself is appointed by the Lord Chancellor.

Where a SSAT decision is by a majority, appeal lies without leave to a *Social Security Commissioner*. Where the decision is unanimous no appeal lies except with the leave of the person who was chairman of the tribunal or of a Commissioner. A Commissioner has to have a ten-year legal qualification. There is a Chief Social Security Commissioner and 15 full-time Commissioners. If any appeal appears to involve a question of law of special difficulty it may be dealt with by a tribunal of three Commissioners. Appeal lies on a question of law from any decision of a Commissioner. Leave of the Commissioner or of the court is necessary. Appeal is normally to the Court of Appeal.[4]

In claims for certain social security payments, medical questions can arise, for example, in industrial injuries a 'disablement question' such as

3 *Jones v Department of Employment* [1989] QB 1, [1989] 1 All ER 725; and see p 484 below.
4 Commissioners can determine vires of ministerial regulations: *Chief Adjudication Officer v Foster* [1993] AC 754, [1993] 1 All ER 705.

'Is the loss of faculty caused by the accident likely to be permanent?' Such questions are referred to an *adjudicating medical practitioner*. Appeals lie to a *Medical Appeal Tribunal* of which there are 32, consisting of a lawyer-chairman and two medical practitioners appointed by the Secretary of State. The workload of these tribunals is reducing and being absorbed by the *Disability Appeals Tribunals*, of which there are 137, to which appeals in respect of certain new allowances go. This tribunal consists again of a lawyer-chairman and two others, one a medical practitioner, the other a person experienced in dealing with the needs of disabled people. Appeal lies from the tribunals referred to in this paragraph to a Social Security Commissioner.

All the above are under the jurisdiction of the Council on Tribunals.

In a recent year SSATs decided 75,000 cases, Medical Appeal Tribunals 16,300, Disability Appeal Tribunals 15,000.

It is convenient to mention here the role of *assessors*, which arises elsewhere than in those tribunals.[5] When a SSAT is considering an appeal in respect of a claim to the new 'incapacity [from work] benefit' it sits with a medical assessor whose role is to comment on and explain the medical evidence and advise the tribunal on the weight to be given to it. The Council on Tribunals would have preferred the appeal to be a tribunal with a medically-qualified person as a *member*, and suggested the Disability Appeal Tribunal. The department disagreed. Not irrelevant is the fact that DATs cost more to run as all their members are paid, whereas on SSATs only the chairman is.

Two further matters should be specially noticed. Some questions arising under the social security legislation do not go to this tribunal system of adjudication, but to the Secretary of State, that is, they are decided by the administrative process. This includes questions whether the contribution conditions for any social security benefit are satisfied; over these the Secretary of State has exclusive jurisdiction.[6]

The arrangements in connection with the *Social Fund* are of interest. There used to be a 'supplementary benefits scheme' by which every person aged 16 or over whose resources were insufficient to meet his requirements was entitled to certain 'supplementary benefits'. Any appeal lay to a tribunal. In 1986 this scheme was replaced, by the Social Security Act, by a system of 'income support' and 'family credit' for regular payments – and by the Social Fund for special needs. This Fund is a sum of money, fixed by the government, out of which payments or loans are made on a *discretionary* basis. When the government announced the introduction of this scheme, it proposed that there should be no right of appeal to a tribunal against decisions made about payments and loans from the Fund. A dissatisfied claimant could have the decision in his case reviewed, which would mean first a check made by the official – the Social Fund officer – who made the original decision, followed by a review by a more senior official in the same office. The argument was that a formal system of

5   See eg SI 1980/941 (re legal assessors).
6   *Secretary of State for Social Security v Scully* [1992] 4 All ER 1, [1992] 1 WLR 927.

adjudication was inappropriate for reviewing the exercise of judgment by the Social Fund Officer, and that the reasonableness of giving or withholding help in any particular case was not suitable for external assessment. The Council on Tribunals, in a Special Report,[7] observed that this 'highly retrograde step' would abolish a right of appeal which had existed for over fifty years. The most the government felt able to do was to substitute a review of decisions of Social Fund officers by Social Fund *inspectors*[8] outside the local office management hierarchy. The Act also provides for a Social Fund Commissioner who appoints the Social Fund inspectors and checks their work, and reports annually to the Secretary of State. There is no power to review individual cases. (Note these arrangements as an example of the move away from a tribunal and towards a system of internal review within the administration – see p 155 below.)

It will be noted that the payments referred to are made on a *discretionary* basis, and are subject to budget constraints, ie the total sum available is limited. In these cases there is no appeal to an independent tribunal. However, two kinds of payment out of the Fund – maternity and funeral payments – are based on regulations which say who is *entitled* to them. Decisions in these matters are made by adjudication officers, and are not subject to budget constraints. Significantly, dissatisfied claimants can appeal against these decisions to a tribunal, the SSAT.

Vaccine Damage Tribunals

The government strongly recommends that children be vaccinated against certain serious diseases; the number suffering from such diseases has sharply declined as a result of that policy. However, doubts came to be raised as to the safety of some of the vaccines. Following a report from the Royal Commission on Civil Liability and Compensation for Personal Injury[9] the government accepted that it was right to set up a scheme to compensate those suffering very serious injury resulting from vaccination recommended by a public authority. The scheme is in the Vaccine Damage Payments Act 1979. Section 1 provides that if, on a claim being made to him, the Secretary of State is satisfied that a person is severely disabled as a result of vaccination against the diseases to which the Act applies, he is to make a lump sum payment of £30,000 to that person. If he is not satisfied that, though the claimant falls within other requirements of the scheme (for example as to age), he was not severely disabled as a result of vaccination, he is to tell the claimant that he may apply to him for a review of his case; in which case the matters of which the Secretary of State was not satisfied 'will be reviewed by an independent medical

7 Cmnd 9722.
8 Whose 'work involves applying the principles of administrative law, and requires an analytical mind, good drafting skills and the intellectual capacity to become familiar with a complex area of work very quickly.' – from a public advertisement; 2 A-levels required.
9 Cmnd 7054 (1978).

tribunal' set up under the Act. (These are the vaccine damage tribunals.) The Secretary of State then refers certain questions to the tribunal (eg the extent of the disablement and whether it was caused by the vaccination) and the decision of the tribunal is 'conclusive' on such questions. However, even after a matter has been determined by a tribunal the Secretary of State may reconsider his initial decision that a payment should not (or in the case of ignorance or a mistake as to the material fact should) be paid. This reconsideration may be as a result of an application made to the Secretary of State, or may be done of his own motion.

As to the tribunal, it consists of a chairman and two medically-qualified members. (The chairman is always legally qualified though the regulations do not require it.) The Secretary of State and the claimant have the right to be heard, to be represented, and to call and question witnesses at a hearing of the tribunal (which is to be in public except in so far as the chairman may for special reasons otherwise direct). It is, it seems, rare for the Secretary of State to be represented, and even where he is, he does not necessarily regard it as his role to be represented in an adversarial capacity. It is then the function of his representative to assist the tribunal rather than oppose the claimant. Thus the ordinary rules of adversarial litigation do not apply. This is further indicated by another regulation which provides that it may be proper not to disclose to the claimant some of the evidence put before the tribunal.

In the vast majority of cases, in which the Secretary of State is not represented, the proceedings will inevitably be investigative rather than adversarial and will no doubt be conducted in a relatively informal manner.[10]

The tribunals are under the supervision of the Council on Tribunals. They have been brought for administrative purposes under the jurisdiction of the President of Social Security Appeal Tribunals. There are six such tribunals. In 1993 they decided 22 cases.

To be briefly noted are the *Child Support Appeals Tribunals*, to which appeals lie from assessments by the Child Support Agency of maintenance payments for children of absent parents. Appeal lies to the Child Support Commissioner.

All the tribunals in this section are under the aegis of the President and are known as the Independent Tribunal Service – a non-statutory title.

Mental Health Review Tribunals

It is one of the main aims of the modern mental health legislation, beginning with the Mental Health Act 1959, now of 1983, to encourage the voluntary, rather than to insist on the compulsory, hospital treatment of those suffering from mental disorders. Compulsory powers are intended

10 *R v Vaccine Damage Tribunal, ex p Loveday* (1984) Times, 10 November. Lexis per Nolan J.

to be used only where no other appropriate method of treatment is available. It was to provide an independent review of the exercise of those compulsory powers that Mental Health Review Tribunals were set up by the 1959 Act. (Here then is a tribunal concerned not with money, but with personal liberty.) There are 15 Tribunals in England and Wales. Each consists of a number of 'legal members' appointed by the Lord Chancellor and having such legal experience as he considers suitable; of a number of 'medical members' being medical practitioners appointed by the Lord Chancellor after consultation with the Secretary of State; and of a number of persons similarly appointed and having such experience in admini-stration, such knowledge of the social services or such other qualifications as the Lord Chancellor considers suitable. The jurisdiction of a Tribunal may be exercised by any three or more of its members, a legal member presiding.

The 1983 Act specifies the circumstances in which a patient may apply to a Tribunal (as where he is detained in hospital for assessment or treatment) and in which the nearest relative may apply (as where his application to discharge the patient is refused). The patient is to be told of his right to apply to a Tribunal. However, the hospital managers must themselves in some circumstances refer a patient to a Tribunal: this is to ensure that patients who lack the ability themselves to apply to a Tribunal have the safeguard of an independent review of their case. Amongst the options open to it the Tribunal may, and in some cases must, direct the patient's discharge.

Detailed procedural rules have been made.[11] They provide, amongst other things, that the Tribunals 'may conduct the hearing in such a manner as it considers most suitable bearing in mind the health and interests of the patient and it shall, so far as appears to it appropriate, seek to avoid formality in proceedings'. The tribunal is to sit in private unless the patient requests a hearing in public and the tribunal is satisfied that a hearing in public would not be contrary to the interests of the patient. Before the hearing the tribunal's 'medical member' is to do what is necessary, including examining the patient and all his medical records, to enable him to form an opinion of the patient's mental condition (this caused the Council on Tribunals some concern). Before or during the hearing the tribunal may call for such information and reports as it may think desirable. It was these and other rules which caused Scott J in *W v Edgell*[12] to categorise the nature of a hearing before this tribunal as inquisitorial rather than adversarial. The tribunal must give a written decision, with reasons, but where it considers that the full disclosure to the patient of its reasons would adversely affect the health or welfare of the patient or others, the tribunal may instead 'communicate its decision to him in such manner as it thinks appropriate'.

A party may be represented by anyone whom he authorises; assistance by way of representation is available under the legal aid scheme; it is unusual for an applicant not to be legally represented.

11 SI 1983/942.
12 [1989] 1 All ER 1089 at 1095; Aff'd [1990] 1 All ER 835.

A tribunal may, and if so required by the High Court must, state in the form of a special case any question of law which may arise before them for determination by that Court. However, it is now accepted that judicial review is the more appropriate method of reviewing the legality of a decision.

The Council on Tribunals' main concern in recent years about these tribunals has been the delay in the determination of appeals, which is obviously important where a person's liberty is at stake. A significant cause of such delay has been inadequate staffing in the tribunals' offices. The Council has urged the acceptance of a Presidential system to help overcome some of the defects in the administration.[13]

Industrial Tribunals

These important tribunals originated in 1964 as tribunals hearing appeals against the imposition of levies by Industrial Training Boards on employers for the purpose of providing training for employees. Since then they have acquired jurisdiction to deal with a wide variety of complaints, claims, appeals and disputes, including the following:
– complaints of unfair dismissal under the Employment Protection (Consolidation) Act 1978. These account for more than half of all cases heard by these tribunals;
– under that Act employees are given the right to certain payments – maternity pay, remuneration on suspension from work on medical grounds, etc. Complaints by the employee about these go to these tribunals;
– disputes regarding entitlement to and amounts of redundancy payments under the 1978 Act;
– claims to be entitled to equal pay and conditions under the Equal Pay Act 1970;
– complaints under the provisions of the Sex Discrimination Act 1975 and of the Race Relations Act 1976;
– appeals against improvement and prohibition notices issued under the Health & Safety Act 1974 (referred to at p 111 above);
– very recently the tribunals have acquired power to hear claims for damages for breach of contract of employment (but not for personal injuries).[14]

Organisation and constitution
Industrial tribunals are organised and constituted as follows. There are three Central Offices, London, Glasgow and Belfast. There are 11 Regional Offices to which, after receipt by it, the administration of applications is delegated by the Central Office. Within each region hearings take place at a number of centres. The convenience of the parties and the availability of premises and personnel will be the determining factors.

13 The Department of Health now publishes an annual report by these Tribunals.
14 SI 1994/1623.

There is a President of the Industrial Tribunals (one for each Central Office), appointed (for England and Wales) by the Lord Chancellor. He must be a lawyer of not less than seven years' standing. He holds office for five years, is eligible for reappointment and may be removed by the Lord Chancellor in certain specified circumstances. He is responsible for the overall administration of the tribunals in this country, and himself sits as chairman of a tribunal.

A tribunal is constituted thus. The Lord Chancellor draws up a panel of lawyers of at least seven years' standing to act as chairmen. In 1993 there were 65 full-time chairmen and 95 part-time chairmen for England and Wales. In each region one of the full-time chairmen is appointed Regional Chairman. For each hearing the chairman is either the president or a regional chairman or one of the persons selected by him from the panel drawn up by the Lord Chancellor.

There are in addition two lay members appointed as follows. The Secretary of State for Employment draws up two panels, one of persons appointed by him after consultation with any organisation representing employers, the other after consultation with any organisation representing employed persons. The President or regional chairman selects one person from each panel to constitute, with the chairman, a tribunal. There are some 1,600 panel members. They are appointed for three years at a time and are paid a fee for each hearing.

Recent legislation permits certain categories of cases to be heard by a chairman sitting alone.

Procedure

Proceedings are initiated by the applicant sending to the Secretary of the Tribunals (at the Central Office) an 'originating application'. In view of the varied jurisdictions exercised by these tribunals, it would not be surprising to find the procedures relevant to those jurisdictions varying in some measure. And so it is that the regulations contain five schedules setting out relevant procedures.[15] Most hearings fall within the terms of Schedule 1.

The hearing is in public unless the tribunal thinks a private hearing is appropriate because it would be against the interests of national security to allow certain evidence to be given in public[16] or because the evidence would be likely to consist of (a) information which the person giving it could not disclose without contravening a statutory prohibition, (b) information communicated to him in confidence, or (c) information the disclosure of which would cause substantial injury to any undertaking of his or in which he works.

A person entitled to appear may be represented by counsel or by a solicitor, by a representative of a trade union or of an employer's association or by any other person whom he wants to represent him.

15 SI 1993/2687.
16 A minister may direct a tribunal to sit in private on grounds of national security.

The decision, which can be by a majority, may be announced at the end of the hearing, but has to be recorded in a document signed by the chairman. The tribunal must give its reasons in writing, stating whether the reasons are in summary or in full form – they are to be in summary form unless a request for full reasons is made by a party. A tribunal can, on certain grounds, review, vary or revoke a decision.[17]

A tribunal is not normally to award costs, but where in its opinion a party has acted frivolously, vexatiously or otherwise unreasonably, it may order him to pay another party's costs.

These tribunals decided 21,400 cases in 1993.

Appeal

Appeal lies on a question of law only, from a decision of an industrial tribunal either to the Employment Appeal Tribunal (EAT) or to the High Court, depending on which jurisdiction the tribunal was exercising.

The EAT consists of a certain number of nominated judges of the High Court and of 'appointed members'. The latter must appear to the Secretary of State and the Lord Chancellor to have special knowledge or experience of industrial relations as representatives of either workers or employers. An appeal is heard by a judge and two or four appointed members (with an equal number from each 'side'). The Tribunal has its central office in London, but may sit at any time and place within Great Britain. Appeal lies from it, with leave, on a point of law to the Court of Appeal and thence to the House of Lords. In 1987, 720 appeals were disposed of by EAT.

The tribunals are, but the EAT is not, under the jurisdiction of the Council on Tribunals.

Data Protection Tribunal

The work of the Data Protection Registrar under the Data Protection Act 1984 is referred to at page 40 above. The Act also requires there to be a Data Protection Tribunal. This consists of a chairman and a number of deputy chairmen (all to be lawyers) appointed by the Lord Chancellor, and other members appointed by the Secretary of State to represent the interests of data users and of data subjects. Appeal lies to the Tribunal against certain decisions of the Registrar eg to refuse an application for registration, or to serve an enforcement notice. Where the appeal is against the matters referred to the Tribunal will allow the appeal or substitute such other decision as the Registrar could have made if (a) the Registrar's action was not in accordance with the law or (b) he ought to have exercised his discretion differently. There is an appeal on a point of law to the High Court. It is under the jurisdiction of the Council on Tribunals. It decides a handful of cases each year.

17 See p 168 below.

The Pensions Ombudsman

The work of various Ombudsmen is considered in chapter 16 below. Generally, it is to investigate complaints. The role of the Pensions Ombudsman is to provide a means for resolving the grievances of members of pensions schemes. How then could he be a tribunal? When the Council on Tribunals examined the Bill intended to create his office it noted that in addition to investigating complaints the official was to have the function of determining disputes of fact and law, that his determinations were to be binding and enforceable in the County Court, and that procedural rules were contemplated for the investigation of disputes, including oral hearings. The Council's suggestion that, in the exercise of his function of determining disputes, the Pensions Ombudsman should be brought under its jurisdiction, was accepted by the government.[18]

The NHS Contracts Adjudicator

The nature of 'NHS Contracts' is referred to at p 459 below. If any dispute arises with respect to such a 'contract', either party may refer the matter to the Secretary of State for determination. He may himself determine the matter – or he may appoint a person to consider and determine it in accordance with regulations made by the Secretary of State. These[19] provide for the appointment of an adjudicator to determine the dispute, and prescribe the procedure. This may include an oral hearing. The adjudicator must give a written decision with reasons. Is this a tribunal? The question was not considered by the Council on Tribunals.

The Banking Appeal Tribunal

Under the Banking Act 1987 certain financial institutions require authorisation from the Bank of England. An institution aggrieved by certain decisions of the Bank (eg to refuse authorisation) may appeal to a Banking Appeal Tribunal. A tribunal consists of a chairman appointed by the Lord Chancellor (he must be a lawyer of at least seven years' standing) and two members appointed by the Chancellor of the Exchequer (one experienced in accountancy, one in banking practice). The details of appeals are complex. In outline, on an appeal against refusal of authorisation the question for the tribunal is whether, for the reasons adduced by the appellant, the decision was unlawful, or not justified by the evidence on which it was based. The tribunal may confirm or reverse the decision which is the subject of the appeal, but may not (with exceptions) vary it. An institution which has appealed (as well as the Bank itself) may appeal to the courts on a question of law arising from the decision of the appeal,

18 Social Security Act 1990. Council on Tribunals Annual Report 1989–90, para 2.43.
19 SI 1991/725.

and if the court finds the decision was wrong in law, it must remit the matter to the tribunal for re-hearing and determination by it.

A Banking Appeal Tribunal is under the jurisdiction of the Council on Tribunals. Few cases have been initiated before this tribunal: of those most have been settled or withdrawn before hearing.

The Criminal Injuries Compensation Scheme

This scheme was set up in 1964 not by Act, but by the government. It provides for the payment of compensation to persons suffering personal injury attributable to a criminal offence. The rules of the scheme state the circumstances in which compensation is payable and the principles on which it is to be calculated. Until recent changes, application for compensation was made to the Criminal Injuries Compensation Board which consisted of some forty QCs and senior solicitors acting part-time. If an application was refused an appeal lay to a committee of three Board members, sitting in private. (This was a 'tribunal'.) The Criminal Justice Act 1988 provided for the scheme to be made statutory, the Board to be a body corporate and brought under the jurisdiction of the Council on Tribunals, but the relevant provisions of the Act have never been brought into force.

The recent changes referred to above altered significantly the basis on which awards are calculated. These are no longer assessed on the basis of common law damages (including future loss of earnings) but are related only to the nature of the injury suffered and are based on a tariff (£x for a broken leg, £y for rape etc). The direct relevance of this to our concerns (the constitution and working of tribunals) is that 'the specialised skills of senior lawyers ... will no longer be needed and that cases can be decided administratively' (ie much less expensively). The scheme will be administered by the Criminal Injuries Compensation Authority, a non-departmental public authority (immediate privatisation was ruled out but is in mind). Appeals are expected, because of the tariff system, to be far fewer under this scheme. (One way of cutting down the cost of an appeal system is to make fewer decisions appealable). A dissatisfied applicant may require a *review* of his case; this would be conducted by a more senior member of the administration. If he remains dissatisfied he can *appeal* to the appeals panel independent of both the CICA and the Secretary of State (who would appoint them). There may be an oral hearing.

(Note: the introduction of the new scheme outlined above was struck down by the House of Lords in *R v Home Secretary, ex p Fire Brigades Union* [1995] 2 All ER 245. Legislation is expected.)

The Parole Board

The Parole Board was created by the Criminal Justice Act 1967 with the function of advising the Home Secretary as to the early release from prison of convicted persons. Clearly this was not a tribunal. However, the Criminal Justice Act 1991 while continuing the Board's *advisory role* also gives it power to *direct* the release of a discretionary life sentence prisoner once he has served a part of his sentence (ie that specified by the court as 'punitive', the rest of the sentence being necessary to protect the public). This change in the Board's function was brought in because of judgments of the European Court of Human Rights which held that Article 5(4) of the Convention had been breached by the then arrangements. The Court said that the lawfulness of continued detention beyond the 'punitive' period should be considered by an independent court with the power of release. This body did not have to be a court in the full sense – a regular court of law – but had to have power to decide; it had to have proper procedural rules, including the participation of the prisoner. Just as clearly, this is a tribunal when exercising that function. It has not however been brought under the jurisdiction of the Council on Tribunals.

Interception of Communications Tribunal

Under the Interception of Communications Act 1985 anyone who believes that communications sent to or by him have been intercepted in the course of their transmission by post etc, may apply to the Tribunal appointed under the Act for an investigation. The Tribunal investigates whether a relevant warrant (to intercept) exists. If it did, the Tribunal's concern is whether various authorisations required by the Act were properly carried out. In deciding whether there was a contravention of those requirements, the Tribunal is to apply 'principles applicable by a court on an application for judicial review'. If they find a contravention they are to report their findings to the Prime Minister and may make an order quashing the warrant, directing the destruction of copies of the intercepted material, or directing the payment of compensation to the applicant.

The Tribunal consists of five lawyers appointed by the Crown and removable on an address from both Houses of Parliament. Its decisions (including decisions as to jurisdiction) are not 'subject to appeal or liable to be questioned in any court'. When this tribunal was created the government told the Chairman of the Council on Tribunals that it should not be placed under the Council's jurisdiction as it would be dealing with highly sensitive and secret matters which would prevent it from conforming to the normal pattern of procedure expected by the Council. When analogous tribunals were set up under the Security Services Act 1989 and the Intelligence Services Act 1994 the Council decided that discretion was the better part of valour.

Education Appeal Committees

Education Appeal Committees were created by the Education Act 1980. Their role under that Act was to hear appeals by parents denied by the local education authority (LEA) the school of their choice for their children. Later legislation gave them jurisdiction to hear appeals concerning arrangements made by LEAs for children with special educational needs and to hear appeals by parents whose children have been permanently excluded from schools. A Committee consists of three, five or seven persons nominated by the LEA. The persons are to be appointed from: (a) members of the authority, and (b) persons who do not fall within (a) but have relevant experience or knowledge or are parents of pupils at an LEA school and a 'lay member' as defined. (LEA members may not now outnumber the others, as used to be the case.) The decision of a Committee on any such appeal 'shall be binding on the local education authority ... by or on whose behalf the decision under appeal was made ...'

The Act provides a few procedural rules which a Committee must follow: it must afford an appellant the opportunity of appearing and making representations and may allow him to be accompanied by a friend or be represented; appeals are to be in private unless otherwise directed, and the decision can be by a majority vote; the decision and the grounds on which it is made is to be communicated to the parties.

The Committees are under the supervision of the Council on Tribunals, and within the jurisdiction of the Local Ombudsmen. These Committees were long of substantial concern to the Council, and recent changes do not, in its view go far enough. At the instance of the Council and in co-operation with it, local authority associations prepared a Code of Practice for these Committees which set out the procedures which should be followed.

Grant Maintained Schools (ie those which are accountable to central rather than local government) each have their own Committee. A Code of Practice similar to that referred to was produced by the department and sent to the Council for its advice. The Council noted 'a high degree of ignorance' on appeal matters amongst some representatives of these schools.

Special Educational Needs Tribunal

LEAs have responsibility towards children with 'special educational needs', and appeal lay against certain of their decisions in respect of such children to Education Appeal Committees (EACs). However, in respect of certain other decisions in those matters an appeal or in other cases, a complaint lay to the Secretary of State, not the EAC. 'As a result of this confusion of approach, not only had the question of special educational needs become increasingly litigious, but the delays ... had become very substantial, with consequent adverse effects on the education of the children concerned'.[20] The various avenues of complaint and appeal have now been replaced by an appeal to a Special Educational Needs Tribunal. This is organised on a national rather than a local basis. The President and a panel of chairmen

20 Council on Tribunals Annual Report 1992–93, para 2.11.

are appointed by the Lord Chancellor and another panel – the 'lay panel' – is appointed by the Secretary of State from which two are selected to sit for each hearing with a chairman. There is an appeal on a point of law to the High Court.

Housing Benefit Review Boards

The Housing Benefit Scheme replaced the previous rate and rent rebate schemes. Under those schemes claimants had a right to have their case reviewed by officials. Under the new scheme they have new rights – to a written explanation of how their entitlement has been assessed; and if they are not satisfied, following a review by officials, to a 'further review'. The function of making this review 'shall not be that of the authority but that of a review board appointed by that authority'.[1] The Housing Benefit Review Board consists of not less than three members of the authority. It may confirm or alter the earlier decision. Notice that the only appeal system available to claimants is to a board consisting of members of the authority whose decision is being challenged. The Social Security Advisory Committee has commented that though this system is quick, cheap and simple to operate, it has many failings: it lacks the (Franks) virtues of openness, fairness and impartiality; there is an absence of legally-qualified chairmen or proper training for members, etc. It has commented that, by contrast, the social security appeals tribunal system under an independent president is proven and effective.

Although local authority councillors have a constituency interest in ensuring that the housing benefit scheme is fairly run, the present system of review boards is too close to the administration of the benefit to be seen to be independent.[2]

The Committee recommended that the scope of the social security appeal tribunals should be extended to cover housing benefit. The National Audit Office has compared the housing benefit scheme unfavourably with the social security appeals system for lack of consistency.[3] The Council on Tribunals has been critical and referred to 'compelling evidence' about the need for change.[4] The Boards are not under its jurisdiction, nor of that of the Local Ombudsmen. (Contrast the Education Appeal Committees.) Thus the only possibility of review of these Boards is by way of an application for judicial review.[5]

Student loans: no tribunal
If a dispute arises between a student and the Student Loans Company it will be investigated by an 'assessor' appointed by the company (with the

1 Housing Benefits Regulations 1982, SI 1982/1124, reg 47.
2 Sixth Report of the Committee, 1988, para 5.19.
3 National Audit Office: Report by the Comptroller and Auditor General, 1984, HC 638.
4 Annual Report for 1992–93, para 2.39.
5 An authority may obtain judicial review of its own Board's decision – *R v Housing Benefit Review Board of Birmingham City Council, ex p Birmingham City Council* [1992] COD 205.

approval of the minister) and paid by it. He will deal with complaints about certain actions of the company, including maladministration. He will not deal with issues of eligibility, which are resolved by the colleges themselves. The Council on Tribunals sees the arrangements as unsatisfactory: there should have been a tribunal to deal with questions of eligibility and the matters now within the scope of the assessor.

Appealing to a Tribunal

When we say that an appeal lies to another body, what is meant is that that other body can change, if it thinks fit, the decision appealed against. The grounds on which one can appeal may of course be limited and likewise the circumstances in which the appellate body can interfere (that is, the criteria which it is to apply in deciding whether the appeal succeeds) may be circumscribed as may be the action it can take on finding those circumstances or criteria to exist. (All these matters will have to be considered once it has been decided that an appeal should be allowed to be brought.) These considerations will be clear to anyone looking at appeals within the court system. And the range and variety of tribunals is such that there is no uniform pattern of appeal: the rules relating to each scheme have to be looked up. The account given above of selected tribunals provides examples. Additional examples are as follows. Many disputes arise between Customs & Excise and taxpayers in connection with the purchase by businesses of 'luxury' items eg racehorses. Appeals to VAT Tribunals were often successful. Section 46 of the Finance Act 1993 seeks to reduce the chance of such appeals succeeding by providing that the Tribunal can allow the appeal 'only if it determines that the determination was unreasonable except where genuinely fresh evidence is brought forward'. In respect of certain other disputes the same Tribunal where it finds a decision to have been unreasonable, but which has already been acted on, can give directions to Customs & Excise as to the steps to be taken for securing that repetitions of the unreasonableness do not occur when comparable circumstances arise in future. This is unusual.

Internal review

A recent tendency should be noted. It is that a person wishing to exercise a right of appeal to a tribunal may be required before doing so, to ask for a review by the body which took the decision, of the decision complained of. This is the case, for example in connection with child support payments. The grounds for review and the time within which it must be sought will be specified. In some cases a 'further review' may be required. (The purpose and effect will be to reduce the number of appeals.) The Council on Tribunal's view is that the introduction of a review stage is not objectionable in principle, but it is concerned that an *internal review* of this kind should not be referred to as an appeal or used as a substitute for a right of appeal to an independent adjudicatory body. 'Even where such a review is carried out by a more senior official it will not be seen as an impartial reconsideration of the case.'[6]

Note, too, the following points:

– the function of a body to which an appeal in the proper sense lies may be said in the regulations to be to review a decision (for example the Vaccine Damage Tribunals, p 143 above). It is nevertheless in that case an appeal.

– the internal review referred to above must be distinguished from a pre-hearing review, and also from the review which a tribunal may be authorised to make of its own decisions (see p 168 below).

Aspects of tribunal law, administration and procedure

Having considered above a selection of tribunals, we now look at some general considerations affecting tribunals, illustrated both by some of the tribunals already mentioned, and by others.

The Franks principles

Mention has been made above of the Franks espousal of the three virtues of openness, fairness and impartiality. 'Parliament, in deciding that certain decisions should be reached only after a special procedure must have been intended that they should manifest three basic characteristics: openness, fairness and impartiality'. What does the application of these require in relation to tribunals?

Openness appears to us to require the publicity of proceedings and knowledge of the essential reasoning underlying the decisions; *fairness* to require the adoption of a clear procedure which enables parties to know their rights, to present their case fully and to know the case which they have to meet; and *impartiality* to require the freedom of tribunals from the influence, real or apparent, of Departments concerned with the subject matter of their decisions.[7]

These Franks principles are still influential both generally and in their detailed application. Additional (not alternative) criteria may today be thought to be relevant, such as efficiency in the administration of the tribunal (including lack of delay) and accuracy of the decision-making process.

The constitution and administration of tribunals

It is trite to say that the constitution of a tribunal (as of any other public body) must be appropriate to its task. Thus a one-man tribunal will in

6 Annual Report 1989–90, para 1.9.
7 Cmnd 218, para 42.

some circumstances be acceptable. The three-man tribunal is regarded by the Council on Tribunals as the norm, with, in most cases, a lawyer-chairman and the members representing the interests or experience involved. Even with a three-man tribunal the chairman may be empowered to act alone in some cases. A two-man tribunal is sometimes possible. Some tribunals can consist of seven members. The Council on Tribunals is against tribunals of this size if only because an appellant, perhaps unrepresented, might find it intimidating or at least unwieldy.

The appointing authorities have been noted in the section on selected tribunals. They include the Lord Chancellor (in respect of certain chairmen), a Secretary of State or other minister in respect of the other members, and the relevant local authority in respect of certain 'local authority' tribunals. The Tribunals and Inquiries Act 1992 provides in section 7 that in respect of certain tribunals listed in Schedule 1 the Lord Chancellor is to draw up lists of persons competent to act as chairmen, and the appointing minister then selects chairmen from those lists. The Council on Tribunals can, by section 5 make general recommendations as to the making of appointments to Schedule 1 tribunals. The Franks Report had suggested that the Council should have the function of appointing tribunal members: this was not accepted.

The terms and conditions of service of tribunal members and chairmen vary widely. Some are full-time salaried and pensionable appointments. Others are paid fees for actual sittings. Yet others get no fees, but claim for loss of earnings. (Some tribunals are in constant session, some meet from time to time, others hardly ever.) The period of appointment also varies from between one to ten years. The qualifications required will naturally normally be that of some experience in and knowledge of the field of activity the tribunal is concerned with. Membership of a tribunal is normally inconsistent with being an MP. Disqualification may also arise where a member represents in his professional capacity the interest of a claimant before the tribunal.

The length of appointment and grounds for removal will have a bearing on the perceived independence of the tribunal.

Some tribunals exercise a jurisdiction over the whole country and sit in London, for example the Immigration Appeals Tribunal. Other tribunals exercise jurisdiction over an area or region of the country and sit at appropriate centres. Yet other tribunals are locally based, for example the social security tribunals. Factors influencing this include the number of cases the tribunals have to deal with and their subject matter. The staffing arrangements require mention. In most tribunals the staff – those who do the administrative jobs necessary for running a tribunal system – are civil servants employed in the 'sponsoring department' ie the government department concerned with the work of the tribunal, and seconded for work with the tribunal. It has been suggested that this 'places departments and staff alike in a potentially invidious position'.[8] Are tribunals too dependent on departments? Particularly important is the

---

8   Wraith and Hutchesson *Administrative Tribunals*, p 127.

role of the clerk to the tribunal. The Franks Report emphasised that the clerk's functions should be so confined that he could not influence the tribunal's decision.[9] The Council on Tribunals has said that the desirability for tribunals to be administered completely independently from government departments has been a constant theme throughout its history. It has therefore been in favour of some tribunals being administered by that department which is responsible for judicial appointments – the Lord Chancellor's Department (LCD). The Lord Chancellor, we have seen, is res-ponsible for or involved in certain tribunal appointments, and is now responsible for the administration of a number of tribunals. (In addition until recently the General Commissioners of Income Tax – who are appointed by the Lord Chancellor – and their clerks, were paid by the Inland Revenue; that is, one party to cases before the GCIT was their paymaster. Hardly satisfactory. Since April 1994 payment has been by the LCD.) In addition the LCD has within government a co-ordinating role in advising and guiding other departments about tribunal policy.

The LCD has indicated the standards of performance required of tribunals under its aegis – for example, the number of days within which 90% of cases should be listed, and within which determinations should be typed, and that the average length of a sitting day should be four and a half hours.

On the issue of which departments should run tribunals the Council on Tribunals has concluded[10] that the only criterion of any significance is that the independence of the tribunal has to be safeguarded and made clear. It acknowledges that it would not be realistic to propose that *all* tribunals be placed under the LCD: it might be impractical and even disadvantageous to do so. The LCD would not of course wish to take on the extra work unless extra resources were made available.

Some tribunals are organised on a 'presidential' basis. The Council on Tribunals has frequently recommended this system of organisation under which a particular class of tribunal has a national president or chairman and possibly regional chairmen as well.[11] There is, however, more than one model on which a presidential system of tribunal administration can be based. In the case of tribunals for which the LCD has assumed responsibility the president's functions are in general restricted to the judicial aspects of the tribunals' business. In other systems the president has responsibility for the administrative running of the tribunals (as in the case of the Independent Tribunal Service – see p 144 above). The Council on Tribunals believes there are advantages in the latter approach.

Procedural rules

Tribunals ought to halve statutory rules governing their procedure. It was one of the grounds of criticism of the General Commissioners of Income

9 Cmnd 218, para 60.
10 Annual Report for 1984–85, para 2.48.
11 Annual Report for 1982–83, para 2.15.

Tax by the Council on Tribunals that the Commissioners, founded in 1799, had no such rules. Eventually, in 1993 at the Council's urging, they were made.

Secondly, the rules must be appropriate to the issue, which may, as we saw in connection with the Industrial Tribunals for example, differ even before the same Tribunal. They must deal with matters that need to be dealt with, and the way they deal with them must be satisfactory. An important part of the work of the Council on Tribunals is the consideration of proposed procedural rules for tribunals, and it will apply the principles it espouses in doing so. These can be found in detail in its Annual Reports. (The work of the Council is referred to below.)

The Council has in fact produced a Report on Model Rules of Procedure for Tribunals.[12] This is designed to provide a comprehensive collection of rules for Departments and tribunals in drafting rules for tribunals. It is not a Code: it is rather a storehouse of precedents from which draftsmen may select, adopt (and adapt) what they need. While there are limitations to the extent to which simple common form procedural rules can be provided – in view of the great variety of tribunals – it is hoped that the Model Rules will help in providing a degree of harmonisation of procedures which should be advantageous. A feature of the Report is the extensive Notes provided for each Rule which explain the Rules and provide a comment on their purpose. Experience shows that some departments at least find the Report helpful.

Adversarial or inquisitorial?

In *adversarial* proceedings the court, tribunal or whatever, decides the issue between the adversaries on the basis of the evidence produced by them. It does not itself suggest lines of inquiry, seek evidence or call its own witnesses, but rules, on the basis of the evidence put before it whether the complaint, allegation or charge made by one party against the other has been made out. It does not act on its own information or knowledge. (Even here of course the 'court' can ask questions of witnesses in order to clarify evidence etc.) We may say that the court etc is *adjudicating* between the parties. The criminal trial is the classic case.

For this system to work properly both versions put before the court must be fully presented and tested, each having an opportunity to present his case, each being aware of his opponent's case with an opportunity to test and rebut it. Professional representation will often, if not usually, be necessary. The problem of the unrepresented party is well known. Where that problem is likely to arise before a tribunal, the Council on Tribunals has commended this: 'It shall be the duty of the Tribunal to assist any appellant who appears to it to be unable to make the best of his case'.[13]

---

12 Cm 1434 (1991). See also Deregulation ... Act 1994, s 6.
13 *Model Rules* (Cm 1434), p 69.

In the *inquisitorial* function there may well be conflicting interests represented before the 'inquiry' but the purpose here is, if necessary, to go further than the cases presented to it and to seek out the truth of whatever is in issue. To this end the 'inquiry' (or whatever it is called) can carry out its own research, call its own witnesses, suggest what issues can be profitably followed up. There is of course a spectrum of possibilities.

A tribunal may be designated by statute as an investigatory body as for example, the Insolvency Practitioners Tribunal which has the duty of investigating cases referred to it and carrying out such inquiries as it thinks fit, rather than as acting as an arbitrator in an adversarial procedure; the Tribunal is the master of what it proposes to look at, and the persons affected do not have the status of parties. Other tribunals, though more clearly adjudicatory, are given the power to summon witnesses or to order discovery of documents. The nature of insurance tribunals (now social security appeal tribunals) was referred to by Diplock, LJ in *R v Deputy Industrial Injuries Comr, ex p Moore*,[14] where what was an issue was the admissibility of evidence. He said:

There is an important distinction however, between the functions of an insurance tribunal and those of an ordinary court of law ... [A] claim by an insured person to benefit is not strictly analogous to a lis inter partes. Insurance tribunals form part of the statutory machinery for investigating claims, that is, for ascertaining whether the claimant has satisfied the statutory requirements which entitle him to be paid benefit out of the fund. In such an investigation neither the insurance officer nor the Minister (both of whom are entitled to be represented before the insurance tribunal) is a party adverse to the claimant ... The insurance tribunal is not restricted to accepting or rejecting the respective contentions of the claimant on the one hand and of the insurance officer and Minister on the other.

And Lord Denning has said that proceedings before such tribunals are not to be regarded as if they were a law suit between opposing parties. 'They are more in the nature of an inquiry before an investigating body charged with the task of finding out what happened.'[15] This, as in *Ex p Moore*, has implications as to the evidence admissible, the onus of proof etc as is shown by the contrasting views expressed in *Corpus Christi College, Oxford v Gloucestershire County Council*[16] as to the proper role of a Commons Commissioner. And the Chief Registrar of Friendly Societies in making his inquiries 'is not conducting an adversarial inquiry in which two sides lay out before him all the evidence they wish him to take into account. [He] makes his own inquiries and he has extensive powers and a large department at his disposal to do so'.[17]

14 [1965] 1 QB 456, [1965] 1 All ER 81.
15 *R v National Insurance Comr, ex p Viscusi* [1974] 2 All ER 724, [1974] 1 WLR 646.
16 [1983] QB 360, [1982] 3 All ER 995, CA.
17 *R v Chief Registrar of Friendly Societies, ex p New Cross Building Society* [1984] QB 227, [1984] 2 All ER 27.

Informality and an orderly procedure

The Franks Report[18] said that while informality of tribunal proceedings was desirable, it should not be at the expense of an orderly procedure: the object should be the combination of a formal procedure with an informal atmosphere, the latter meaning a sympathetic attitude on the part of the tribunal and the absence of the trappings of a court.

The achieving of an orderly procedure is likely to require proper rules of procedure; it is not the case, as is sometimes suggested, that such rules are incompatible with a degree of informality. The Council on Tribunal's *Model Rules* provide:

... the Tribunal shall conduct the hearing in such manner as it considers most suited to the clarification of the issues before it, and generally to the just handling of the proceedings; it shall so far as appears to it appropriate seek to avoid formality in its proceedings.[19]

The avoidance of formality does not of course mean a slap-dash attitude by the tribunal to its task by for example, failing to pay scrupulous attention to the substantive law it is required to apply; nor does it mean that the tribunal's deliberation in private of the issues can degenerate into an unstructured chat. It does mean a procedure as simple as possible in the light of the issues to be decided and, for example, being prepared when appropriate to vary the order of proceedings, and not insisting that a party distinguishes between asking questions and making a statement. The seating arrangements and mode of address also need to be considered. The administration of the oath is regarded as injecting a degree of formality: this may or may not be justified. The fact is that the complexity of the legislation affecting some tribunals and/or the financial value of the issues at stake may leave little room for departure from a high degree of formality. Finally, for a tribunal to refer, as some do, in the information it gives to appellants as to its procedure as 'informal' may mislead. The tribunal itself is confined to the law and the evidence, and the appellant must be aware that he must direct his case to those matters.

Tribunals and the rules of evidence

How far are tribunals bound to follow the strict rules of evidence applying in the courts? Some tribunals are specifically empowered by the relevant regulations to receive evidence that would not be admissible under those rules.[20] In *R v Deputy Industrial Injuries Comr, ex p Moore*[1] the Commissioner's decision was impugned on the ground that he let in inadmissible

---

18 Cmnd 218.
19 Cm 1434, p 66. See eg SI 1993/2687, Sch 1, reg 9.
20 The fact that a tribunal is not bound by the strict rules of evidence does not give it discretion to refuse to admit evidence which is admissible at common law and is relevant: *Rosedale Mouldings Ltd v Sibley* [1980] ICR 816.
 1 [1965] 1 QB 456, [1965] 1 All ER 81.

evidence. The regulations empowered him to follow the procedure he thought fit. It was not even contended that he was bound by strict rules of evidence. He could therefore (subject to the rules of natural justice) take into account any material which had probative value (that is, which tended to show the existence or otherwise of relevant facts).

But no body acting (like the Commissioner) judicially can act on evidence not disclosed to the parties. Thus it was improper for a person constituting the Lands Tribunal to act on evidence he collected for himself – that is, to be a witness giving evidence to himself which the parties concerned had not heard and had not an opportunity of challenging.[2] And where a member of a tribunal has specialised knowledge of the matter before the tribunal he can use it to weigh up or assess evidence given to the tribunal and to assist his fellow members to do so, but he must not himself 'give evidence' to them, telling them what he might have said in evidence.[3] Where the tribunal relies in this way on a member's personal knowledge and experience the parties must be informed, and the facts known to the member must be disclosed.[4]

A further consideration that may arise is whether the tribunal can take into account matters which have arisen since the decision appealed against (where eg the question is whether the appellant is 'fit' to hold a licence).

Finally the question of the burden of proof to be applied by the tribunal will have to be addressed.

Tribunals and precedent

Tribunals must of course follow relevant court decisions. But what about precedent within a particular hierarchy of tribunals? Take for example the social security tribunals where the first decision is taken by the adjudication officer with appeal to the local tribunal and then to a Social Security Commissioner. The latter gives reasons, decisions are written, and selected decisions are reported. Obviously the Commissioners' decisions bind those authorities below them, so it is necessary that their decisions should be known by those below them. The Chief Adjudication Officer[5] has reported that use of and reference to Commissioners' decisions was infrequent; even when new decisions were brought to their attention their relevance was not always appreciated. (The situation is, it is said, being remedied.)

Tribunal decisions must also be available for those who appear before them and their advisers.[6]

2   *Hickmott v Dorset County Council* (1977) 35 P & CR 195.
3   *Hammington v Berker Sportcraft Ltd* [1980] ICR 248, EAT.
4   *Dugdale v Kraft Foods Ltd* [1977] ICR 48, EAT.
5   See p 141 above.
6   See Oliver 'Tax Tribunal Reports' [1980] BTR 229.

Representation, legal aid, advice, assistance

Tribunals deal with many problems which the citizen is likely to meet with: employment, social security, tax, housing etc. It is important that potential applicants or appellants to tribunals are aware of their rights in these matters, and are capable of exercising them. This raises the questions of the right to be represented before a tribunal, whether by a lawyer or otherwise, the right to advice and assistance in preparing one's case, and to financial assistance in order to obtain those things.

Legal representation is permitted before all tribunals.[7] it is possible for a tribunal's rules to confine the right of representation before that tribunal to lawyers or other relevant professions. This should be done only in very special circumstances, apart from which there would seem to be no reason why a person should not be represented by anyone he pleases. It has been suggested[8] that (in the case of the four systems studied) the presence of a representative significantly and independently of other factors increases the probability of success at a tribunal hearing, that representation increases the accuracy of decision-making, and the fairness of the proceeding; that it can lead to the filtering out of unmeritorious cases and to pre-hearing resolution of disputes; that specialisation and experience, rather than legal qualifications as such, are the most important qualifications for good representation, but that some areas of law are so complex and adversarial that specialist lawyers are needed.

A person appearing before a court, and by implication a tribunal, is entitled to have assistance from anyone he pleases: the tribunal's permission is not needed. Such assistance is by way of taking notes, and giving suggestions and advice to the appellant – but not speaking for (ie representing) him.[9]

What of financial assistance from public funds? The provisions of the legal aid scheme (whereby finance is available for litigation) do not in general apply to tribunals. However, *assistance by way of representation* (the ABWOR scheme) is available in respect of proceedings before the Employment Appeal Tribunal, the Lands Tribunal, the Commons Commissioners and the Mental Health Review Tribunals. It means any assistance given to a person by taking on his behalf any step in the institution or conduct of any proceedings before the court or tribunal in question. Outside that scheme parties must pay for legal representation themselves or seek the assistance of others, such as trade union officials or the various advice agencies. The Council on Tribunals has consistently argued that legal aid should be available for all tribunals, but should be granted only in accordance with the following criteria: where a significant point of law is

7 The one exception is in respect of Service Committees of Family Health Service Authorities (see p 29 above). The whole area of complaints in the Health Service is currently being considered – see *Being Heard*, the report of a committee of inquiry, pub Dept of Health. Legislation is expected.
8 *The Effectiveness of Representation at Tribunals*, a report to the Lord Chancellor by Genn and Genn (1989).
9 *R v Leicester City JJ, ex p Barrow* [1991] 3 All ER 935.

in issue; where the evidence is likely to be so complex or specialised that the average layman could reasonably wish for expert help in assembling and evaluating evidence and in its testing or interpretation; where it is a test case; and where deprivation of liberty or the ability of an individual to follow his occupation is at stake.

Advice is also currently available from solicitors' offices which give advice under the 'Green Form' scheme. Eligibility for advice under that scheme, as for ABWOR, is dependent on an applicant's financial status. The advice is not uniformly available throughout the country. (It will be appreciated that both for advice and representation non-lawyers in advice agencies may well in some cases be more helpful than lawyers.)[10]

Under the Immigration Act 1971 the Secretary of State may, by section 23, make grants to any voluntary organisation which provides advice or assistance for, or other services for the welfare of, persons who have rights of appeal under that Act. The body set up to provide that service and funded by government was the UK Immigration Advisory Service, replaced in 1992 by the Immigration Appeals Advisory Service, and the Refugee Legal Centre, the latter assisting those seeking asylum here. Under the Race Relations Act 1976 section 66, the Commission for Racial Equality may grant assistance to an individual who is a complainant in proceedings under the Act, and this may include arrangements for representation before a tribunal or court. The Equal Opportunities Commission has somewhat similar powers in respect of proceedings under the Sex Discrimination Act 1975. And under the Equal Pay Act 1970 section 2(2) the Secretary of State may make a reference to an Industrial Tribunal where it appears to him that it is not reasonable to expect a person claiming equal treatment to make the reference him/herself.

Public hearings

The Franks Committee, reporting that not all tribunals sat in public, recommended that they should do so, for public hearings were 'an important constituent of openness'. But the Committee recognised that exceptions could properly be made to the requirement of publicity in three cases: where public security was involved, where intimate personal or financial circumstances had to be disclosed, and where questions of professional capacity and reputation were involved.[11]

Some tribunals are by their rules required always to sit in public, some always to sit in private. The most common provision is that they shall sit in public but can exclude the public in certain circumstances.

It is characteristic of the judicial process that it is done in public, in contrast with the administrative process which is done in private. The significance of a process being carried out in public is not merely that

10 See *Bruce v Legal Aid Board* [1992] 3 All ER 321 at 328: 'Few solicitors will have the incentive to master the intricacies of welfare benefit law ...'
11 Cmnd 218, para 76 et seq. See Council on Tribunals Model Rules, Cm 1434, p 61.

members of the public can attend, hear the evidence on which the decision is arrived at and publicise it[12] but that the person taking the decision is identified and his name is known or can be discovered. There seems no good reason for not, as a general rule, disclosing the names of tribunal members if they are asked for.[13]

Another aspect of a tribunal's publicness is that its decisions should be published. There is a number of specialist law reports of tribunal decisions. The Council on Tribunals has in the past expressed concern about the availability of Social Security Commissioners' decisions, and the use of unreported decisions.[14]

Privilege in defamation

Words spoken in the course of judicial proceedings, whether by judge, jury, parties, advocates or witnesses, are *absolutely* privileged in the law of defamation.[15] Are the proceedings of tribunals 'judicial' for this purpose? In *Royal Aquarium Society v Parkinson*[16] the Court of Appeal said that the rule of absolute privilege extends to, and only to, a body 'acting in a manner as nearly as possible similar to that on which a court of justice acts'. In that case the defendant, a *member* of the London County Council, had defamed the plaintiff at a meeting of the Council at which the plaintiff's application for a licence was being considered. The court held that the Council was neither as to its function, constitution or procedure analogous to a court of law. The fact that the Council had to act 'judicially' in the matter in question, that is, fairly and impartially, and to that extent to act like a court, did not make it a court for the purpose of this rule. In *Trapp v Mackie*[17] the House of Lords held that, provided that the body in question was one 'recognised by law', there was no single element which would be conclusive to show that it had attributes sufficiently similar to those of a court of law to create absolute privilege. Lord Diplock listed ten characteristics of the body in question – which was holding an inquiry into the dismissal of a teacher – which cumulatively were more than enough to justify the granting of absolute privilege within the rule laid down in *Royal Aquarium Society v Parkinson*. Two points about *Trapp v Mackie* will be noted: it concerned not a tribunal in the sense defined here but an inquiry (into the dismissal of a teacher); and the privilege of a witness, not a member, was in issue.

There is no doubt that proceedings before a tribunal attract *qualified* privilege. In the *Royal Aquarium* case (above) Lord Esher said,

12 For 'restricted reporting order' in 'sexual misconduct' cases, and alternative procedures considered see Council on Tribunals Annual Report 1992–93, para 2.3 and *R v Southampton Industrial Tribunal, ex p INS Group* (1995) Times, 22 April.
13 Annual Report for 1978–79, para 2.5
14 Annual Report for 1981–82, para 3.58; for 1982–83, para 3.41.
15 See further eg *Street on Torts*, Pt VI.
16 [1892] 1 QB 431.
17 [1979] 1 All ER 489, [1979] 1 WLR 377.

Where, as in this case, a body of persons are engaged in the performance of a duty imposed upon them, of deciding a matter of public administration, which interests not themselves, but the parties concerned and the public, it seems to be clear that the discussion is privileged.[18]

Also to be considered is protection from suit in defamation of a published report of proceedings before a tribunal. The Defamation Act 1952 gives qualified privilege to 'a fair and accurate report of proceedings at any meeting or sitting ... of any ... tribunal (etc)' but nothing protects 'the publication ... of any matter which is not of public concern and the publication of which is not for the public benefit'.[19]

Contempt of court

Contempt of court is conduct calculated to prejudice or interfere with the processes of the law. It can take a number of forms including the publication when proceedings are active of matter calculated to prejudice a fair trial.[20]

Does the law of contempt of course apply to tribunals? The Contempt of Court Act 1981 provides that for its purposes (including for example the prohibition of making tape recordings of court proceedings without consent),[1] court includes 'any tribunal or body exercising the judicial power of the State'. RSC Order 52, rule 1 provides that where contempt of court 'is committed in connection with proceedings in an inferior court' an order of committal may be made only by a Divisional Court of the Queen's Bench Division. The House of Lords has ruled that the jurisdiction of the Divisional Court in this matter did not extend to a local valuation court.[2] Though termed a court, the functions of the local valuation court were essentially administrative, and it was not a court of law established to exercise the judicial power of the state.

The status of Mental Health Review Tribunals[3] has arisen in this context. (Section 12(A)(B) of the Administration of Justice Act 1960 is also relevant.) In *Pickering v Liverpool Daily Post & Echo Newspapers plc*[4] the House of Lords ruled, overruling an earlier decision, that a MHRT is a court for this purpose. It was nevertheless not unlawful to publicise the fact that P, the patient, had made an application to the tribunal, the

18 [1892] 1 QB 431 at 443.
19 See *Kingshott v Associated Kent Newspapers Ltd* [1991] 2 All ER 99, [1991] 1 QB 88.
20 See Contempt of Court Act 1981.
 1 Section 19. For use of tape recorders, see Annual Report of the Council on Tribunals for 1981–82, Appendix D.
 2 *A-G v British Broadcasting Corpn* [1981] AC 303, [1980] 3 All ER 161. An appeal lay from a valuation officer's decision as to the rating valuation of property to this tribunal, now replaced by the Valuation Tribunals.
 3 See p 144 above.
 4 [1991] 2 AC 370, [1991] 1 All ER 622. For episode in which Council on Tribunals criticised Ministerial statement about P's application to MHRT see Annual Report 1985–86, para 4.21 and for 1988–89, para 2.68.

date and place of the hearing, and the nature of the order made. But this did not give unlimited freedom to comment on those matters; and the reasons for the tribunal's decision, or any conditions imposed by it could not be published.

Acting by a majority

The common law principle is that in the exercise of public power 'the majority will conclude the minority and their act will be the act of the whole'.[5] A Tribunal's rules may deal with the question; they are likely, in effect, to enshrine the common law. Where a tribunal consists of two persons, a rule may give the chairman a second vote.

It seems that it is not permitted to a member of a tribunal (or other judicial body) to abstain from deciding and voting (contrast political assemblies).

Reasons

The extent and meaning of the duty to give reasons for decisions is dealt with in chapter 10 below. Concerning tribunals, section 10(1) of the Tribunals and Inquiries Act 1992 says that where a tribunal listed in the First Schedule to the Act gives a decision it must give a written or oral statement of the reasons for the decision, if requested to do so or before the giving of notification of the decision. (The Act does not require tribunals to tell applicants of their right to ask for reasons but this may be done as a matter of practice.) The statement may be refused or the specification of reasons restricted on grounds of national security, and the tribunal may refuse to give the statement to a person not principally concerned with the decision if it thinks that to give it would be against the interests of any person primarily concerned. The statement of the reasons forms part of the record.[6] Furthermore the decisions of any particular tribunal, or any descriptions of such decisions, may be excluded from section 10(1) by the Lord Chancellor on the ground that the subject matter of such decisions, or the circumstances in which they are made, make the giving of reasons unnecessary or impracticable. The Lord Chancellor must consult the Council on Tribunals before making the necessary order. With few exceptions, dating from its earliest days, it has resisted exemption. It also believes section 10 is itself inadequate.[7]

It must be noted that the obligation under section 10 does not apply to decisions in respect of which some other statutory provision has effect as

5   *Grindley v Barker* (1798) 1 Bos & P 229; *Picea Holdings Ltd v London Rent Assessment Panel* [1971] 2 QB 216, [1971] 2 All ER 805 and SI 1971/1065, reg 10 – decision not to refer to it being by majority. See Council on Tribunals *Model Rules*, p 70. See Lanham [1984] PL 461.
6   For significance of this see p 198 below.
7   See Annual Report for 1992–93, para 2.94 et seq.

to the giving of reasons. It is necessary therefore to examine in every case the tribunal's rules of procedure to see what provision is made for the giving of reasons.

Appealing against a tribunal's decision

Should there be an appeal *from* a tribunal – bearing in mind that some tribunals are themselves hearing an appeal from an administrative decision? The Franks Report suggested that a right of appeal has these merits.

The existence of a right of appeal is salutary and makes for right adjudication. Provision for appeal is also important if decisions are to show reasonable consistency. Finally, the system of adjudication can hardly fail to appear fair to the applicant if he knows that he will normally be allowed two attempts to convince independent bodies of the soundness of his case.[8]

This recommendation was not accepted. In some cases there is, in other cases there is not, an appeal from one tribunal to another. Examples will be found in the previous section of this chapter.

The next question is whether there should be an appeal from a tribunal (or the appellate tribunal if there is one) to a court of law. The Franks Report thought that generally there should be a right of appeal on a point of law to the High Court, and thence to the Court of Appeal but no further. The Tribunals and Inquiries Act 1992 provides that if a party to proceedings before those Schedule 1 tribunals which are referred to in section 11(1) of the Act is 'dissatisfied in point of law with a decision of the tribunal, he may, according as rules of court may provide, either appeal from the tribunal to the High Court or require the tribunal to state and sign a case for the opinion of the High Court'.

What do the rules of court provide? RSC Order 94(8) provides that a party to proceedings before any tribunal mentioned in section 11(1) may appeal on a point of law to the High Court. Further, by Order 94(9) any of those tribunals may of its own motion or at the request of any party state in the course of proceedings before it, in the form of a special case for the decision of the High Court, any question of law arising in the proceedings.

What of those tribunals not specifically referred to in section 11(1)? Some are expressly dealt with in this respect by their parent legislation and in Order 94, for example Agricultural Land Tribunals and Mental Health Review Tribunals.

Order 55 applies to every appeal (except one by way of case stated) which by statute lies to the High Court from any court, tribunal or person. (Tribunal is defined as 'any tribunal constituted by or under an enactment other than any of the ordinary courts of law'.) Such an appeal is not confined to points of law. Amongst its other powers the court hearing the appeal may make any decision which ought to have been made by the tribunal or may remit the matter to it for re-hearing. However, the rules

---

8 Cmnd 218, para 104.

in this Order are subject to any provisions made in relation to the appeal in question by or under any enactment. Most statutory appeals, it seems, are thus affected, so that the statutory basis pertaining to any particular appeal must be examined. Tribunals which are subject to this Order seem to be bodies concerned with professional discipline – these do not fall under the aegis of the Council on Tribunals.

A further strand in this complex issue is that one body which is not listed in Schedule 1 to the 1992 Act is brought, by section 11(6), within section 11(1) of the Act, namely the Secretary of State when deciding an appeal from the Director General of Fair Trading in a consumer credit licensing matter.

If there is no appeal from an administrative decision, its legality can be challenged only by judicial review, as in local authority decisions in homelessness cases; likewise if there is no appeal from a tribunal to the court.

The view of the Council on Tribunals is that there should be an appeal on point of law to the court from all tribunals and that such an appeal is preferable to an appeal by way of case stated.

Notice that an appeal lies only if statute so provides, whereas judicial review is available unless taken away by statute. The Tribunals and Inquiries Act 1958 sought to strengthen the availability of one of the remedies available by way of judicial review, certiorari, in this way.

In some statutes attempts have been made to prevent review of decisions by certiorari by providing that a decision 'shall not be called into question in any court' or by some similar phrase.[9] Section 11 of the 1958 Act (section 12 of the 1992 Act) says that such wording found in any Act passed before 1 August 1958 (the day on which most sections of the Act came into force) shall not prevent the examination of the decision by means of certiorari. It does not apply to such words found in an Act passed on or after that date.

Review

The normal rule is that once a court has given its decision it cannot reconsider it. This applies to tribunals. However, tribunals are sometimes given power to review their own decisions. For example, Industrial Tribunals have the power on the application of a party or of its own motion to review any decision on the grounds that: (a) it was wrongly made as a result of an error on the part of the tribunal staff; (b) a party did not receive notice of the proceedings; (c) the decision was made in the absence of a party; (d) new evidence has become available provided its existence could not have been reasonably known of or foreseen at the time of the hearing; or (e) the interests of justice require such a review. On reviewing its decision the tribunal may confirm the decision, or vary or revoke it; if it revokes it there is to be a re-hearing.[10]

9 See p 427 below on this.
10 SI 1993/2687, Sch 1, reg 11.

What is relevant in exercising this power 'is whether or not a decision, alleged to be erroneous in law, has been reached after there had been a procedural mishap'. It would not normally be appropriate when the parties had a fair opportunity to present their case. In particular ground (e) needs to be exercised with caution.[11]

A note on conciliation etc

Courts and tribunals are provided by the state as machinery for the formal determination of disputes. An alternative is recourse to conciliation. By conciliation is meant a third party bringing together the parties to the dispute and assisting them to arrive at an agreement. The hoped-for outcome is thus an agreement arrived at by the parties themselves. Contrast arbitration. An arbitrator listens to what the parties have to say, and makes an award.

In the field of industrial relations the state has long provided machinery for both conciliation and arbitration, and we have previously noted the existence and status of the statutory Advisory, Conciliation and Arbitration Service.[12] In its conciliation work a distinction is made between collective and individual conciliation, the former being intended to prevent industrial action by bringing the parties together at as early a stage as possible. The bulk of ACAS's conciliation work is however in individual cases, the majority to do with unfair dismissal.

There is provision for conciliation where a complaint is made on certain matters to an industrial tribunal. For example, the Race Relations Act 1976 declares that it is unlawful to discriminate against a person on racial grounds both in employment and in other fields, such as education and the provision of goods and services. A complaint by an individual of discrimination against him in the field of employment may be presented to an industrial tribunal. It is the duty of the conciliation officer, if requested to do so by both parties (or if in the absence of such request he considers he could act with a reasonable prospect of success) to 'endeavour to promote a settlement of the complaint without its being determined by an industrial tribunal'.[13] The conciliation officer may on request so act even before a complaint is formally presented to the tribunal. (Claims of discrimination in fields other than employment are dealt with by different machinery.) The conciliation officer has a similar role in connection with a complaint of discrimination on sex grounds, and of unfair dismissal.[14]

Where a complaint is made to a Family Health Service Authority[15] of the conduct of a medical practitioner, the Authority is required to seek informal settlement of the matter by conciliation in the hope of preventing

11 See *Trimble v Supertravel Ltd* [1982] ICR 440. Council on Tribunals *Model Rules* p 74.
12 See p 39 above.
13 Section 55.
14 Sex Discrimination Act 1975, s 64; Employment Protection (Consolidation) Act 1978, s 133.
15 See p 29 above.

its referral to the formal Service Committee. An Authority may also under the regulations appoint a Dental Conciliation Committee for the purpose of investigating complaints about the fitness or efficiency of a denture. The object seems to be to get the patient to attend for and the dentist to undertake adjustment of the denture.

As to *arbitration*: any dispute may be submitted to this process under the provisions of the Arbitration Act 1950. Statute also provides for some disputes to be submitted to arbitration. In the field of agricultural tenancies the Agricultural Land Tribunals deal with certain disputes, principally about succession to land on the death of the tenant and certificates of bad husbandry. Agricultural Arbitrators on the other hand deal mainly with rent reviews, end of tenancy compensation etc. The Tribunals are under the jurisdiction of the Council on Tribunals, but it has jurisdiction over an arbitrator only when he has been appointed other than by agreement between the parties. These appear to be the only arbitrators under its jurisdiction.

The Council on Tribunals

The Franks Report recommended the setting up of two Councils on Tribunals, one for England and Wales and one for Scotland. The Tribunals and Inquiries Act 1958 set up one Council, with from ten to fifteen members appointed by the Lord Chancellor and the Lord Advocate.[16] As the Act requires, there is a Scottish Committee of the Council consisting of (two or) three members of the Council and (three or) four other persons, appointed by the Lord Advocate. In addition the Parliamentary Commissioner for Administration is by virtue of his office a member of the Council and of the Scottish Committee. Membership of the Council is incompatible with membership of the House of Commons.[17]

Appointments to the Council are all part-time, though the chairmanship is a half-full-time job. The chairman is paid a salary and members are entitled to a remuneration. It is assumed that members who accept remuneration work on Council business for 44 days a year. Appointment to the Council is for three years, with the possibility of re-appointment for the same period. Members' qualifications and experience are given in an Appendix to each annual report. The full Council meets eleven times a year; it also works through committees.

The Council has a staff of thirteen mostly seconded from the Lord Chancellor's Department. For budgetary purposes the Council is dealt with as part of that Department.

---

16 In making appointments regard is to be had to the need for representation of 'persons in Wales'. The Act extends to Northern Ireland but the Council cannot deal with any matter with respect to which the Parliament of that Province had power to make laws when it existed.

17 But not of the House of Lords. Of the Council's eight chairmen to date, six were or are members of that House; five of those had been ministers.

As required by statute, the Council makes an annual report to the Lord Chancellor which is laid before Parliament. This contains much information about the work done by the Council during the year, and draws attention to matters of a particular concern to the Council affecting tribunals and inquiries which fall under Council supervision. (The Scottish Committee also publishes an annual report.)

The Council has functions in respect of tribunals and despite its name, in respect of inquiries also. First, then, its function in respect of tribunals.

Tribunals

The council's general function in respect of tribunals is 'to keep under review the constitution and working of the tribunals specified in Schedule 1 [to the 1992 Act] ...' Reference has been made[18] to the principle on which tribunals were originally selected for subjection to the Council's jurisdiction. When a new administrative scheme is being created by statute which requires the resolution of disputes or differences, the government will have to decide whether to provide in the Bill for them to be submitted to the adjudication of a tribunal. Given that a new tribunal is created, the question then is whether it should be added to the list of tribunals in Schedule 1 so as to bring it under the Council. This is generally done, but reference is made above to examples of cases where this was not done.

For a body to be regarded as a tribunal, it must, as we have seen, have an adjudicatory function, and, as noted, it is possible for a body to have both adjudicatory and other (advisory, administrative, or executive) functions in which case it will be under the Council only in respect of the former. Section 14(1) of the Act provides that reference to the working of certain of the tribunals listed in the Schedule 'do not include reference to their working, decisions or procedure in the exercise of executive functions'. (These provide very useful examples for the student of this subject of the distinction, not in general terms but in the practical details of administration, between the classification of these powers and procedures.) Section 14(2) uses a different method to indicate the extent of the Council's jurisdiction over the body in question. It provides that references in the Act to the working of the Occupational Pensions Board 'are references to the working so far as relating to matters dealt with by the Board by means of a formal hearing or on review'. Yet another means of distinguishing between various functions of a body is made in the case of the Civil Aviation Authority.

There are cases where the Council has, on consideration, declined to seek jurisdiction over a body which appears to have adjudicatory functions; in one case where the adjudicator envisaged following principally a written rather than an oral procedure; in another where the Council thought the

18 See p 134 above.

adjudicative arrangement proposed within an organisation had an inadequate degree of independence from the rest of the organisation.[19]

In supervising tribunals, the Council concerns itself with such matters as: the need for non-statutory forms issued to applicants to be clear and simple; the need for legally-qualified chairmen, and for the proper training of chairmen and members (particularly in the general principles of fair adjudication); the low proportion of women tribunal members; the need for neutral venues for tribunal hearings, for legal aid, and for an appeal on a point of law; and the degree of independence from departments enjoyed by clerks of tribunals. The Council has commented on the inadequacy of reasons given by tribunals, and has made representations to the departments where a substantial back-log of cases waiting to be heard has led to an unacceptable delay in hearings. It has recommended the 'presidential'[20] system of organisation of tribunals and has concerned itself with the structure of the tribunal system as a whole. On that last point, the Franks Report had referred to the possibility of the amalgamation of tribunals. Since then tribunals have greatly increased in number, variety and importance. The Council has spoken of the need to avoid an undue proliferation of tribunals by, wherever possible, organising them into fewer and stronger units and ensuring that each group has a proper structure and, where necessary, adequate arrangements for appeal. Proposals for new tribunals should be closely examined in the context of the overall structure of the system to see whether the work proposed for them could be done by existing tribunals. The Council also makes special studies of particular tribunals.

By section 8(1) of the Act a minister (and certain other bodies) must before making, confirming etc procedural rules for any Schedule 1 tribunal consult with the Council. This is an important and valuable part of the Council's work which requires its members and staff to give detailed scrutiny to the proposed rules. The Council's Annual Reports list the considerable number of regulations scrutinised. Sometimes departments consult the Council at an early stage, before the rules are even in draft, finding it helpful to do so. On other occasions departments, perhaps overlooking their obligations, leave it to the last minute, thus verging on the unlawful. The *Model Rules* indicate the sort of points the Council will be looking at when examining the rules – the right of appearance and representation, time-limits, the quorum, the rules of evidence etc.

Apart from such obligatory consultation, departments will sometimes seek the Council's advice on a voluntary basis. This is welcomed.

By section 5 the Council may make to the appropriate minister 'general recommendations as to the making of appointments to membership of any [Schedule 1] tribunals ...' This power is rarely exercised. (The Council was not given the function recommended by the Franks Report of appointing tribunal members.)

19 For further details of the matters referred to in the preceding paragraphs see Foulkes 'Executive or Judicial? The jurisdiction of the Council on Tribunals'. 13 ERPL 263. See Council on Tribunals Annual Report 1993-94, p 6.
20 See p 157 above.

By section 1(1)(b) the Council has to consider and report on 'such particular matters as may be referred [to it by the Lord Chancellor] with respect to tribunals other than the ordinary courts of law whether or not specified in Schedule 1 ...' There have been few such references. In its early days the Council was asked to consider the degree of privilege that ought to be granted to witnesses before tribunals, and the issue of subpoenas.

By section 10 the Council must be consulted before the giving of reasons is dispensed with. This is referred to above.

Inquiries

The Council's main function in connection with inquiries is, by section 1(1)(c) 'to consider and report on such matters as may be referred to the Council ... or as the Council may determine to be of special importance, with respect to administrative procedures involving or which may involve, the holding by or on behalf of a Minister, of a statutory inquiry ...'

What is a statutory inquiry? It is: (a) an inquiry or hearing held in pursuance of a statutory *duty*; or (b) an inquiry or hearing held under a *power* to do so and which has been designated by an order made by the Lord Chancellor for this purpose. This, it will be noted, is quite different from the terms in which the Council's functions in respect of tribunals are expressed. There is no duty to 'keep under review' the working of inquiries; and there is no express power in respect of tribunals to report on 'such matters as the Council may determine to be of special importance', but neither point could be said to inhibit the Council's work. The reason for this distinction doubtless lies in the fact that the Franks Report recommended that the Council should have jurisdiction over tribunals only: it did not mention inquiries in that connection. Indeed section 1(1)(c) of the Act was not in the Bill as laid before Parliament.

With regard to inquiries, the Council has concerned itself with the principles to be applied in the deployment of inspectors to hold inquiries on behalf of various ministers. It has also considered the practice of the appointment as assessors, at inquiries held by the Department of the Environment, of technical officers from that Department, and the role of such assessors. As the Council can consider 'administrative procedures involving ... an inquiry', it does not regard itself as confined to what happens at the inquiry itself, but can also look at what happens before and after the inquiry. It has thus concerned itself with delays on disposing of planning appeals after inquiries. It collaborated with departments in a review of Highway Inquiry Procedures undertaken in 1979. It issued a special report in the Award of Costs at Statutory Inquiries:[1] its recommendation, extending the circumstances in which costs are awarded to objectors to compulsory purchase orders, was accepted by the government. Its report recommending that the Special Development Order authorising the

1 Cmnd 2471.

development of Stansted Airport should be the subject of a statutory inquiry was also accepted. And the rule determining the action to be taken by a minister when new evidence is received after the holding of a public inquiry was recommended by the Council. It has been concerned about the independence of planning inspectors,[2] about proposals to remove an obligation to hold an inquiry or to restrict the right to be heard; it commented extensively on proposed changes to Planning Inquiry Rules.[3]

Section 9 of the Act empowers the Lord Chancellor to make rules regulating the procedure to be followed in connection with statutory inquiries held by Ministers, but he must consult the Council before doing so. (A duty to consult is not therefore imposed by this Act on ministers other than the Lord Chancellor.)

The exemption of ministers from the duty to give reasons is subject to consultation with the Council, as it is in the case of tribunals.

An important aspect of the Council's work in respect of both tribunals and inquiries is the visits made by individual members to those proceedings.[4] Not less than one hundred visits are made each year (plus those made by members of the Scottish Committee). The visiting member makes a written report on his visit to the Council. Visits enable members to watch in operation the procedures on which the Council has advised, and give an opportunity to discuss matters relevant to the Council's interests with those visited. Over a period of time a considerable amount of information uniquely available to the Council is accumulated, and enables the Council to advise departments. (A tribunal's procedural rules will normally authorise the presence of a Council member even when it is sitting in private.)

The following limitations will be noted

(i) It is of course clear that the Council's functions are advisory and consultative only. It has no executive powers. It cannot override, review or require reconsideration of tribunal decisions or inquiry recommendations, (and a member visiting a tribunal takes no part in, though he may observe, its deliberations).

(ii) There is nothing in the Council's terms of reference about the handling of any complaints it may receive. On receiving a complaint the Council explains to its correspondent the Council's role, tells him that the information he sent may be useful in supplementing the other information about the tribunal or inquiry it has, even though the Council can take no action on the complaint itself.

(iii) There is no obligation on ministers to consult with the Council at the stage *when bills are being drafted* which may establish new tribunals or inquiry procedures or may fail to provide tribunals or inquiries in circumstances in which the Council would think them desirable. The

2   See p 125 above.
3   Annual Report for 1987–88, para 2.76.
4   See Foulkes [1994] PL 564.

Council can of course, and does, comment on the published bill, but wishes to make its views known before that stage is reached. The Council has commented on this:

Thus we welcome, and indeed have come to expect, consultation by Government departments while new procedures are still in the formative stage, and before officials or ministers are firmly committed to their design and scope ... [O]ur consideration of draft primary legislation is carried out without any specific authority and we should be considerably strength-ened in this part of our work if consultation with us in such legislation were clearly provided for by statute.[5]

The government's response was that it would be constitutionally inappropriate for statutory *obligations to* be imposed on ministers to consult the Council about legislation they were promoting. The Council accepts this and has proposed instead that the Council be given an express *power* to advise, thus acknowledging in statute what it already does. In addition a Code for Consultation with the Council has been drawn up by the Council and the Lord Chancellor's Department and circulated to departments, most recently in 1992. The Code is principally concerned with the need to consult the Council in good time on draft tribunal rules of procedure. Consultation on other matters is referred to thus:

Consultation on proposals for primary legislation affecting scheduled tribunals or statutory inquiries ... is not mandatory, but usually takes place and is welcomed by the Council. ... Consultation on proposals for primary legislation affecting the rights of the citizen which may require consideration of whether, and in what form, new adjudicating procedures are necessary or desirable is again welcomed by the Council.[6]

A good part of the Council's time and of its Secretariat is in fact spent in advising government departments on the matters referred to in that extract from the Code.

(iv) The Council has been making the following point with some persistence and frequency, and regards it as of particular importance. It accepts that while ministers are fully entitled to disregard the Council's recommendations, it is misleading for them to say for example in the preface to a statutory instrument containing a tribunal's procedural rules that action was taken 'after consultation with the Council' as this gives the impression that the Council agreed with the action taken. In 1972 and again in 1980 and 1994 the Council suggested that a procedure similar to that in regard to advice given by the National Insurance Advisory Committee (now the Social Security Advisory Committee)[7] be adopted in respect of the Council's recommendations 'as being entirely consistent with the present-day ideas of more open government and the need to inform Parliament fully about legislative proposals'.[8] The government disagreed on every occasion.

5 The Functions of the Council on Tribunals; special report by the Council (Cmnd 7805), paras 6.4, 6.5. For government response see 419 HL Official Report (5th series) col 1118.
6 See Annual Report for 1991–92, Appendix I.
7 See p 130 above.
8 The Functions of the Council on Tribunals, Cmnd 7805.

Apart from the question of having its powers extended, the Council took the view in 1980 that it was 'not fully equipped' to carry out the functions it had. It did not, it said, have the resources to carry out what was needed by way of the collection of information on a methodical basis about the operation of the tribunal and inquiry system, and suggested the type of work that was necessary. This could be done by its own (extended) staff, or by commissioning research by others. The Council had 'potentialities as yet unrealised'. They remain unrealised. It may be concluded that, within its limitations, the Council does useful work, unobtrusively, in bringing about some important and desirable changes in administrative law and practice.

Administrative Review Commission

The Justice—All Souls Report[9] of 1988 considered it to be a problem that there is no single institution in the UK 'the function of which is to keep under constant review all the procedures and institutions whereby the individual may challenge administrative action'. There was in its view, a need for an independent body, separate from the executive functions of government, charged with the duty of reviewing all aspects of administrative law and the process of administrative decision-making throughout the UK. It could be set up by legislation, or as a standing Royal Commission. Membership would be of persons of 'recognised stature'. It would have to have 'first-class research capability'.

What about the relationship of the proposed Commission to the Council on Tribunals? The Council, the Report points out, covers only part of the ground, and further, the government declined to accept the Council's proposal that it be given power to act as an advisory body over the whole area of administrative adjudication. While this was regrettable, the Report thought that it would be very difficult to convert a body which has existed for many years and which has had a limited remit into the kind of body the Report proposed. Nevertheless it would be desirable in its view, to keep the Council in being: it would work in close collaboration with the Commission, and there could be some common membership.

How much power and influence would this Commission have, the Report asked:

We ask the question because we heard complaints from so many quarters about the treatment accorded to the Council on Tribunals. It has been starved of resources and the recommendations which it has made appear to have been summarily rejected. We have compared this with the influence acquired by the Parliamentary Commissioner for Administration ... Much of his strength derives from his links with Parliament, in particular from the Select Committee of the House of Commons.

It proposed that the Commission's Annual Report to Parliament should be backed up by a Select Committee procedure.

9   *Administrative Justice: some necessary reforms* ch 4.

The following comments can be made.

– As it stands the Report's proposal is insufficiently detailed to be persuasive.[10] Its recommendations appear to have been summarily rejected – certainly ignored, by the government.

– The proposal that the Council should continue alongside the Commission is probably misconceived. If the Council's work was subsumed by that of the Commission the Council's expertise would not be lost if some of the Council's members and Secretariat were transferred to the Commission; whereas if the Council were continued alongside the Commission there might be difficulties of jurisdiction.

– A Parliamentary link has now been established through the oversight by the Home Affairs Committee of the Lord Chancellor's Department.[11]

10 See Williams 'The Tribunal System – its Future Control and Supervision' [1990] CJQ 27.
11 For Select Committees see p 562, fn 14 below.

Chapter 6

Duties in administrative law

Administrative law is sometimes spoken of as to do with 'controlling' the administration. This may carry the suggestion of preventing action. Control is of course a much wider concept than that and certainly embraces ensuring that a body does what it is required to do, as well as ensuring that it does not do what it is not empowered to do. If we are interested in public authorities getting things done, in providing services for the community at large, whether it be defence, prosecuting for breach of the criminal law, medical treatment, education or social security benefits, then our focus of interest will be on duties: whether duties are imposed or mere powers granted, the terms in which those duties are expressed, whether they are enforceable and by whom. Our concern is not only with the courts but with any institution which can effectively ensure the carrying out of those duties.[1]

The creation of duties

There is obviously an important distinction to be made between having a *discretion* whether or not to take or to refrain from taking certain action, and having an *obligation* to take or not to take it; between, that is, having a power and being under a duty.[2] Whether, in any particular case, it is a power that is conferred or a duty that is imposed, will depend on the wording of the statute or other relevant document.

Shall, will etc

A statutory duty may be expressly imposed by saying 'It is the duty of X to ... ' or 'X is under a duty to ... ' The terminology most commonly used is

1 See generally A J Harding *Public Duties and Public Law*.
2 In *McCarthy & Stone (Developments) Ltd v Richmond-upon-Thames LBC* [1991] 4 All ER 897 'functions' was held to mean the totality of duties and powers, and a distinction was made between discretionary functions and duty functions.

178

to say that X 'shall' do such-and-such. The word 'will' is uncommonly used. In *Jackson v Secretary of State for Scotland*[3] civil service conditions of service (not statutory) said that J's case 'will be referred to ... ' It meant that that event 'will occur' – it envisaged a future certain event. 'Must', occasionally used, seems stronger than 'shall'. The word 'should' is rarely if ever found in statutes but will be found in subordinate documents such as circulars, and immigration rules.[4]

It may be possible to imply a substantive duty from an examination of the statutory scheme. In *R v Secretary of State for the Environment, ex p Greater London Council*[5] the GLC was entitled to submit alterations to its structure plan to the Secretary of State for his approval. In doing so it had to consider any representations which were made to it 'within the prescribed period' about the proposed alterations. 'Prescribed' meant 'prescribed by ministerial regulations'. The Secretary of State had not made the regulations, and on being asked to do so by the GLC, so that it would know which representations it was bound to consider, and therefore lawfully do what it was entitled to do, refused to do so. The court ruled that he was bound to make them. In *South Hams District Council v Shough*[6] it was held that although the council, unlike a county council, was under no statutory duty to provide sites for gypsies, it might be under a duty not to evict them from its land if it was aware of the county's failure to provide sites.

May, entitled, it shall be lawful etc

It is very common to find that an authority 'may' do such-and-such. The word 'may' prima facie confers a power but taken in its context may be interpreted as imposing a duty.

In *R v Roberts*[7] statute provided that a weights and measures inspector 'may take ... the fees specified in the First Schedule and no other'. The Schedule was headed 'Fees to be taken'. The court held, on this application for a certiorari to quash a district auditor's surcharge for not collecting the fees, that the council had no discretion in the matter, it had to collect the fees. 'May' meant that it had to take those fees and not any others.

In *R v Metropolitan Police Comr ex p Holloway*[8] an order made under an Act of 1869 provided that 'a licence for a cab may be granted to any person by the Commissioners of Police of the Metropolis ... subject to the

3   1992 SLT 572.
4   For 'must' see eg National Lottery Act 1993 s 1. For 'should' see eg *Liberto & Immigration Officer* [1975] Imm AR 61, *Howard v Department for National Savings* [1981] 1 All ER 675. *R v Home Secretary, ex p Okello* (1994) Times, 21 December. The Guidance to Procedure under the Transport and Works Act 1992 says which bodies 'must' be consulted who 'should', who 'ought' to be consulted, whom it would be 'sensible' or 'wise' to consult, and whom applicants are 'advised' to consult.
5   (1983) Times, 2 December, Lexis.
6   (1992) 65 P & CR 148.
7   [1901] 2 KB 117.
8   [1911] 2 KB 1131.

following exceptions' [a licence could not be granted to a person under 21; and could be refused to persons with previous convictions]. Holloway fell into neither class. He was entitled to a licence and to a mandamus. The effect of the order, said Farwell LJ was that, apart from those exceptions 'the whole of the rest of the world is entitled to apply for and obtain licences ... Any other construction would allow the [Commissioner] to debar mero motu any one of whom he disapproved from exercising the common law right of using the street ... The word "may" here must be read "shall" ... '

In *Pargan Singh v Secretary of State for the Home Dept*[9] an Act gave certain rights of appeal and empowered ('may') the Secretary of State to make regulations relating to notices etc to be given to an appellant. The House of Lords was clear that as the right of appeal could not be exercised unless notice was given in accordance with the regulations, the Secretary of State had a duty to make them.

The phrase 'it shall be lawful' was considered in the leading case of *Julius v Lord Bishop of Oxford*.[10] Statute provided that where a priest was charged with an offence 'it shall be lawful for the bishop of the diocese on the application of any party complaining thereof ... to [cause the matter to be inquired into]'. The House of Lords was very clear that 'it shall be lawful' is plain and unequivocal. The effect of the phrase is to authorise and empower only; its meaning is permissive and enabling only. Thus the bishop was not, as was argued, required to set up an inquiry into a complaint against a priest. However, the judgments recognised that in some circumstances *a power may be coupled with a duty* so that the donee of the power would be obliged to exercise it. Lord Cairns LC said:

There may be something in the nature of the thing empowered to be done, something in the object for which it is done, something the conditions under which it is to be done, something in the titles of the person or persons for whose benefit the power is to be exercised, which may couple the power with a duty, and make it the duty of the person in whom the power is reposed, to exercise that power when called upon to do so.

Reviewing the cases he concluded:

Where a power is deposited with a public officer for the purpose of being used for the benefit of persons who are specifically pointed out and with regard to whom a definition is supplied by the legislature of the conditions upon which they are entitled to call for its exercise, that power ought to be exercised, and the court will require it to be exercised.[11]

Lord Blackburn put it this way:

If the object for which the power is conferred is for the purpose of enforcing a right, there may be a duty cast on the donee of the power, to exercise it for the benefit of those who have that right, when required in that behalf.[12]

9 [1992] 4 All ER 673.
10 (1880) 5 App Cas 214.
11 Ibid p 225.
12 Ibid p 241. He noted: 'It is very true that bishops are but men and being human may misuse any discretion entrusted to them; but so are judges and so are parties who make a complaint' – p 247.

That was not the situation here. The complainant's interest might be very slight ('any party'); the matter complained of might be trifling; and it might be remedied to the satisfaction of the bishop. It was right therefore to leave the matter to the discretion of the bishop in each case.

In *Alderman Backwell's Case*[13] an Act provided that the Lord Chancellor, on a complaint being made to him against a bankrupt 'shall have full power and authority' to issue a commission. On a complaint by the alderman's creditors the court ruled that 'though the words in the Act of Parliament were that the Chancellor *may* grant a commission of bankrupt yet that may was in effect *must* ... and the granting of a commission was not a matter discretionary in him, but he was bound to do it'.

Even though a power is not coupled with a duty (such that the discretion must be exercised in one particular way), it must nevertheless be exercised in accordance with correct legal principles. For example, in *Padfield v Minister of Agriculture, Fisheries and Food*[14] the minister was empowered to refer a complaint to a committee of investigation. It was argued that the minister was bound to refer the complaint as the power was coupled with a duty. The House was clear that, applying the rule in *Julius*, the minister was not under a duty to refer the complaint to the committee. Nevertheless, as his exercise of the power was based on a misunderstanding of the purpose for which the power had been given to him, he was ordered to consider the complaint in accordance with the correct understanding of the law, as indicated by the court. The result was that the minister referred the complaint to the committee. The question raised in this paragraph – the correct way to exercise a power – is considered in later chapters.

Trust or governmental obligation?

A true trust exists when one person, the trustee, is under a duty to hold the trust property vested in him for the benefit of other persons, the beneficiaries. The term 'trust' is, however, used in a much wider sense. We may speak of government being 'entrusted' with power, of Parliament as 'the trustee which the nation has authorised to act on its behalf'.[15] Other public authorities may be spoken of in these terms. The Railways Department of the Board of Trade spoke of a 'trust which ... is imposed upon the Board by the general understanding of Parliament and the public, of watching the proceedings of railway companies [to ensure that they did not misuse the powers Parliament gave them]'.[16] The British Broadcasting Corporation was referred to on its creation as 'acting as trustee

13 (1683) 1 Vern 152.
14 [1968] AC 997, [1968] 1 All ER 694.
15 E Barker *Essays on government*, p 56. 'Government is not a trade ... it is altogether a trust in right of those by whom the trust is delegated and by whom it is always resumable. It has, of itself no rights; they are altogether duties.' Paine, *Rights of Man*, p 63 (pub Watts).
16 Quoted in H Parris *Government and the Railways in Nineteenth-Century Britain*, p 37.

for the national interest'.[17] In *Rowning v Goodchild*[18] the duty put on a postmaster to deliver mail to the house of the addressee (rather than to keep it for collection at the Post Office) was said to 'arise out of a great public trust since the legislative establishment of the Post Office ... '. The purpose of the use of the concept in such contexts is of course to emphasise that the powers and duties of such bodies should be exercised not for the advancement of their own interests, but that of others, to underline their obligations to others.[19] Those obligations are not of course the obligations of a trustee of a true trust to his beneficiaries. Dicey showed (if demonstration were needed) that Parliament is not in a legal sense a trustee,[20] and the 'trust' of an elected representative of which J S Mill spoke is enforced through the ballot box, not in the Chancery Division.[1] And despite the reference to a trust in *Rowning v Goodchild*, the extent of the duty on the postmaster depended, as the court acknowledged, on the interpretation of the meaning of 'delivery' in the statute.

It is of course possible for a public authority to be a trustee in the full sense. Thus Lord Atkin said, in *Civilian War Claimants Association v R*,[2] 'there is nothing so far as I know, to prevent the Crown acting as agent or trustee, if it deliberately chooses to do so'. However, when it is alleged that the Crown is a trustee a possible alternative explanation has to be considered. This arises from the fact that the Crown has obligations put on it because of its governmental functions. Megarry VC said in *Tito v Waddell (No 2)*:[3]

These [sc governmental powers and obligations] readily provide an explanation which is an alternative to a trust. If money or other property is vested in the Crown and is used for the benefit of others, one explanation can be that the Crown holds on a true trust for those others. Another explanation can be that, without holding the property on a true trust, the Crown is nevertheless administering that property in the exercise of the Crown's governmental functions. This latter possible explanation, which does not exist in the case of an ordinary individual, makes it necessary to scrutinise with greater care the words and circumstances which are alleged to impose a trust.

In the case in question Megarry VC held that the relationship between the inhabitants of a Pacific island and the Crown was governmental and not enforceable by him, a judge sitting in the Chancery Division.

The inaptness of the reliance on private law concepts in a public law situation was also emphasised in *Town Investments Ltd v Department of*

17 H of C Official Report (5th series) vol 198, col 448.
18 (1773) 2 Wm Bl 906.
19 The Royal Commission on Environmental Pollution, 10th Report, para 2.51: 'The public must be considered to have a right analogous to the beneficial interest in the condition of the air and water and to be able to obtain information on how far they are being degraded.'
20 *Law of the Constitution*, p 48.
1 '[The electors] are the judges of the manner in which he fulfils his trust', *Representative Government*, ch 12.
2 [1932] AC 14.
3 [1977] Ch 106, [1977] 3 All ER 129.

the Environment.[4] It was argued that as, when land to be used for government purposes is conveyed to an official is said to be held by him 'in trust for' (or on behalf of) 'Her Majesty', the interest so conveyed is subject to all the incidents of a trust in private law, and that therefore the legal estate is vested in the official, and only an equitable interest is vested in the Crown. Lord Diplock, while not excluding the possibility that an official may hold property subject to a private law trust said:

But clear words would be required to do this and even where the person to be benefited is a subject, the use of the expression 'in trust' to describe the capacity in which the property is granted to an officer of state is not conclusive that a trust in private law was intended; for 'trust' is not a term of art in public law and when used in relation to matters which lie within the field of public law the words 'in trust' may do no more than indicate the existence of a duty owed to the Crown by the officer of state, a servant of the Crown, to deal with the property for the benefit of the subject for whom it is to be held in trust, any duty being enforceable administratively by disciplinary sanctions and not otherwise.

The need to distinguish between public and private law in this context was further emphasised by the House of Lords (through the judgments of Lords Diplock and Brightman) in *Swain v Law Society*.[5] The Law Society, acting on behalf of all solicitors required to be insured, had taken out insurance to provide indemnity against loss arising from claims made against solicitors in respect of liability for professional negligence. The plaintiff, a solicitor, argued that the Law Society was accountable, on the basis of a fiduciary relationship to the solicitors concerned, for the share of the commission it secured from the brokers. This turned on whether the Society was a trustee of that share. The House of Lords said it was not. The Law Society (incorporated by Royal Charter) has both private and public functions. When acting in its private capacity it is subject to private law (when for example 'facilitating the acquisition of legal knowledge'). But when exercising public functions it is subject to public law, and in this case it was exercising such functions, as the insurance arrangement it made was entered into under a power under the Solicitors Act relating to the compulsory insurance of solicitors, the principal purpose of which is to safeguard the public. This fundamental distinction, said Lord Brightman, had important consequences because:

the nature of a public duty and the remedies of those who seek to challenge the manner in which it is performed differ markedly from the nature of a private duty and the remedies of those who say that the private duty has been breached. If a public duty has been breached there are remedies of judicial review ... There is no remedy in breach of trust or equitable account. The latter remedies are available, and available only, where a private trust has been created. The duty enforced on the possessor of a statutory power for public purposes is not accurately described as fiduciary because there is no beneficiary in the equitable sense.

Since the function being exercised in this case was statutory the relationship created between the parties by the insurance arrangement

---

4 [1978] AC 359, [1977] 1 All ER 813. And see p 14, above.
5 [1983] 1 AC 598, [1982] 2 All ER 827.

was statutory, and on that basis there was no case for saying that the Law Society held the commission on behalf of solicitors on whose behalf the insurance arrangements had been made.

It is in the field of local government that the concept of the trust and of a resulting fiduciary duty has been most noticeably and contentiously used. The ultra vires doctrine – that local authorities are confined to their statutory functions – imposes limits on the actions of local authorities and on the purposes for which they may dispose of their funds. The fiduciary duty has been relied on to impose additional limits. It is more conveniently dealt with in another context, but here it is convenient to briefly note a historical point. Municipal corporations were transformed by the Municipal Corporations Act 1835 from private to public, governmental, institutions.[6] As private chartered organisations based on the trust they could use their corporate funds for the benefit of the members of the corporation. But when they became public bodies all money was paid into a corporate fund which had to be used for public purposes. The courts took the view that in the exercise of their powers and in the expenditure of their money the authorities owed a duty, trust-like or fiduciary in its nature, towards those, the ratepayers, who had contributed to its funds.

Where a public authority is created with the word 'trust' as part of its name, it is not to be assumed that it is a trustee in the full, equitable, sense. Consider, for example, the Housing Action Trusts created by ministerial order under the Housing Act 1988. The purpose of such bodies is, in general terms, to improve the stock of housing in inner city areas. Their powers and duties are those set out in the Act. They may be said to be in a broad sense 'trusts' in that their functions could be said to be exercisable so as to benefit the populace affected – as was said of the Post Office and the BBC in the examples given above. National Health Service Trusts have been referred to elsewhere.[7]

What the duty requires

Duties imposed on public authorities are of a wide variety. The duty may be purely 'ministerial' requiring no exercise of discretion on its part, as where for example it is required to issue a licence on the mere payment of money. On the other hand the existence of the duty may depend on the judgment of the person on whom it is put as to whether a certain state of affairs exists: for example a housing authority is under a duty to provide accommodation for a person where they are satisfied that he is homeless. The enforceability of duties is referred to later in this chapter, and in

6   Jennings said that what made them governmental institutions was the granting of functions about police and lighting, the power to make byelaws for the good rule and government of the borough, and their role in the appointment of magistrates and the provision of courts – ch 3 of *A Century of Municipal Progress* (ed Laski, Robson and Jennings).
7   See p 28 above.

chapter 3 on judicial remedies and torts. In the meantime, the following examples will show that the extent of a duty can be determined only in the context of the administrative scheme as a whole.

(i) Section 3(1) of the National Health Service Act 1977 imposes a duty on the Secretary of State 'to provide [certain services] throughout England and Wales to such extent as he considers necessary to meet all reasonable requirements'. The requirement imposed by this duty was considered in *R v Secretary of State for Social Services, ex p Hincks*.[8] In 1971 the Department approved plans for the extension of a hospital to provide orthopaedic services, but the work was put off from time to time as the tenders exceeded the estimated cost, and in 1978 the scheme was shelved for ten years for financial reasons. In 1979 Hincks and others who needed orthopaedic services sought a declaration that the Secretary of State was in breach of his duty. The Court of Appeal held that the section does not impose an absolute duty. The Secretary of State is not bound to meet all demands for hospital facilities, but to do what he can within resources made available to him by Parliament. He is not under a duty to see to it that Parliament gives him the necessary funds. (What Parliament gives is of course determined by the government of which he is a member.) In any particular year he is limited by the money available for that year, and in calculating the amount of money necessary in future years he can pay regard to current government financial policy. Bridge LJ noted the ineffectiveness of judicial action.

I can only hope that [the applicants] have not been encouraged to think that these proceedings offered any real prospect that this court could enhance the standard of the National Health Service, because any such encouragement would be based on a manifest illusion.

(ii) In *R v Secretary of State for Social Services, ex p Child Poverty Action Group*[9] the minister had a duty to make arrangements with a view to securing that benefit officers exercised their functions in such a way as shall best promote the welfare of those affected – another 'general' or 'target' duty as in *Hincks*. It was shown that the staff had failed to pay many claimants the full benefit they were entitled to. In these proceedings it was held that the duty in question did not require the minister to go hunting through millions of cases no longer current in order to discover all past underpayments. His duty was rather to decide how best to allocate his resources so as to take reasonable steps to identify claimants (as by advertisements) without impairing the efficiency of the processing of current claims.

(iii) In *R v Bristol Corpn, ex p Hendy*[10] a closing order was made in respect of the applicant's flat. The Corporation was thereupon under a statutory duty to secure that he be provided with 'suitable alternative accommodation'. The Corporation had provided him with temporary

8 (1980) 1 BMLR 93.
9 (1985) Times, 8 August, Lexis.
10 [1974] 1 All ER 1047, [1974] 1 WLR 498.

accommodation until suitable council housing was available. The Court of Appeal said that was a fulfilment of the Corporation's duty, and rejected the applicant's argument that the duty entitled him to go to the head of the council's waiting list. The council's duty was to do their best, as soon as practicable, to get him other accommodation, acting fairly as between him and all the others on the list.[11]

These three cases are, note, all to do with allocation of resources.

(iv) In *R v Camden London Borough Council, ex p Gilla*[12] the council had a duty to consider applications from persons claiming to be homeless. This meant, the court said, that there was a duty on the authority to take reasonable steps to actually adjudicate on applications made. This duty included the prior duty to actually receive the applications.

It is no use homeless applicants making applications for accommodation ... if their applications are not going to reach the ears of the authority to whom the application is made.

In heavily populated areas, this might, the court said, require 24-hour cover, though not in country areas. Camden (heavily populated) had an office which dealt with the homeless. It was open from 9.30 am to 12.30 pm, Monday to Friday. Only those who arrived at 9.30 would be seen. The office was not open at weekends. It was possible to telephone in, but the phone was frequently not answered. This was a clear breach of Camden's duty.

(v) *R v Secretary of State for Social Services, ex p Child Poverty Action Group* (1988) concerned the payment of supplementary benefit. The Social Security Act 1975, section 2, provides that the question whether any person is entitled to that benefit 'shall be determined by an adjudication officer appointed under section 97' of that Act. That section provides that adjudication officers (AO) 'shall be appointed by the Secretary of State subject to the consent of the Treasury as to numbers'. Section 98 provides that any claim for benefit 'shall be submitted forthwith to an adjudication officer for determination'. And section 99 provides that an AO to whom a claim is submitted 'shall take it into consideration and, so far as practicable dispose of it ... within 14 days of its submission to him'.

Concern was felt by the applicants, the CPAG and others, at the length of time taken over the determination of claims to the detriment of claimants. They therefore argued (in respect of section 98) that the duty on the respondent Department to refer a claim to the AO arose as soon as it was received by the Department, that it was not therefore proper for the Department itself to investigate the claim (thereby delaying its consideration). The Court of Appeal observed that the claim is submitted by the Department to the AO for his 'determination'. It followed that what the Department had to do was to submit the claim only when it was in a

11 And see *West Glamorgan County Council v Rafferty* [1987] 1 All ER 1005, [1987] 1 WLR 457 for criteria to apply in deciding whether council has fulfilled its duty to exercise its powers so as to provide 'adequate accommodation' for gypsies in its area.
12 (1988) Independent 12 October. Note: there is no appeal to a tribunal against homelessness decisions; see Law Com No 226, para 2.26.

fit state to be determined. Thus the duty to submit it did not arise until the Department was in possession of all the information necessary to enable the claim to be determined (which might for example require it to make inquiries or hold an interview). It was therefore proper for it to take steps to get that information before submitting the claim. Once that information was available the Department could not delay submitting the claim; and the need for verification of information did not by itself justify delay in submission (the verification could be undertaken by the AO). (The Court acknowledged that it was difficult to draw a precise line here.) The duty to submit the claim 'forthwith' meant that the Department was under a duty to bear in mind the need for expedition in deciding what steps to take in order to make the claim suitable for determination.

There was also argument about the extent of the duty to dispose of the claim within 14 days in view of the phrase 'so far as practicable' (see section 99). The court ruled that in deciding whether or not it was 'practicable' to do so, account could be taken of the volume of cases waiting to be determined and the number of officers available to deal with claims. This, CPAG said, made the requirement meaningless. This raised their third point, that as the claim had to be submitted forthwith to the AO and as he had 14 days to determine it, the Secretary of State was under a duty to appoint such numbers of AOs as would enable an officer to be available to consider a claim promptly. The Court pointed out that the Secretary of State's power to appoint AOs was expressly subject to the Treasury's approval as to numbers. This was quite inconsistent with some open-ended commitment on the Secretary of State to ensure that there was always an AO available to deal immediately with any claim. But apart from that, it would be absurd to say that the number of AOs to be appointed was to be dictated by the largest conceivable number of difficult claims that could arise at any one time. This did not mean that the Secretary of State had no obligation as to the number of AOs appointed; his discretion had to be exercised reasonably taking into account the fact that the legislation required the expeditious disposal of cases. It followed that his decision was challengeable on the grounds of unreasonableness, but there was no justification for arguing that here.[13]

Conflicting duties

The law may impose on an authority a number of related duties, and the question may arise whether there is any conflict between them,[14] which is to have priority,[15] or whether the authority has to balance one against the other.[16]

---

13 See *Vince v Chief Constable of Dorset Police* [1993] 2 All ER 321 for defendant's duty to appoint custody officer for designated police stations.
14 *R v Cleveland County Council, ex p Commission for Racial Equality* [1992] COD 116.
15 *R v Kingston-upon-Thames Royal Borough Council, ex p Kingswell* [1992] 1 FLR 182; and see side-note to s 4 National Lottery Act 1993: 'overriding duties'.
16 *R v Newcastle upon Tyne City Council, ex p Dixon* (1993) 17 BMLR 82.

Exemption from duty

It is up to the court to say whether a duty exists, to whom it is owed, and what it requires. Having found that a duty exists towards the plaintiff, it cannot decline to enforce it, as that would be to dispense with the statute. There is however an exception – of uncertain scope. Public policy requires, it is said, a statute to be interpreted as *not* requiring the performance of a duty if to do so would enable a person to benefit from a serious crime committed by him or which he intended to commit, or if the circumstances were such that there was a justified apprehension of a significant risk that the enforcement of a statutory duty would facilitate a crime resulting in danger to life. Thus in the circumstances a public official acted lawfully in declining to perform his duty to provide information to an adopted person about his natural mother.[17]

The enforcement of duties in administrative law

We are now concerned with the different techniques by which duties imposed on public authorities and others may be enforced. Some, which are dealt with elsewhere in this book, are merely noted here.

(a)   *Criminal penalties.*
Public authorities except the Crown are subject to the general criminal law and may be subject to criminal penalties. Criminal penalties may also be available against members of the public who are in breach of duties owed to the administration. Some reference to these matters are found elsewhere.[18]

(b)   *Civil Penalties.*
By a civil penalty is meant the imposition by statute, for failure to carry out a statutory duty, of a penalty that can be sued for in the courts by the person empowered by the statute to do so. For example, the Electric Lighting (Clauses) Act 1899[19] imposed a duty on electricity boards to supply those persons stated in the Act to be entitled to a supply. The Act imposed civil penalties on a Board for failure to give and maintain a proper supply.

(c)   *Administrative Penalties.*
Where a duty is put on a public authority other than a government department the statute may, as for example in the case of *Pasmore v Oswaldwistle UDC*[20] provide for it to be enforced by a mandamus made on the application of a government department. But in a desire to avoid the disadvantages of resort to the courts, central government evolved other methods of enforcing such duties. For example the National Health Service Act 1977 provides in section 85 that where the Secretary of State is of opinion that an NHS authority have failed to carry out any functions conferred or imposed on them

17 *R v Registrar General, ex p Smith* [1991] 2 All ER 88.
18 See p113 and ch 14.
19 Repealed by the Electricity Act 1989.
20 [1898] AC 387.

by that Act, he may make an order declaring them to be in default. The members of the body forthwith vacate their office, and the order provides for the appointment of new members to the body. The penalty in this case is *removal from office*.[1] Another penalty is *removal of functions*, as under section 42 of the Food Act 1990: where there is default in the discharge of its duty by a food authority, the minister may empower *another authority* or *one of his officers* to discharge that duty in place of the authority in default.

Another form of administrative penalty is the *financial*. For example a registered local bus service (that is, one registered with the Traffic Commissioner) must be run exactly in accordance with its terms of registration (as to route, frequency of service etc). Failure to do so may lead to the Secretary of State reducing by 20 per cent any fuel duty rebate payable for the previous three months for all local services provided by the operator.[2] This can be a very significant sum.

An unusual type of penalty is found in section 77 of the Local Govern-ment Finance Act 1988. This is in the context of the payment of revenue support grant by central government to certain local authorities. By the section the Secretary of State may serve notice on such an authority requiring it to supply him with such *infor-mation* as is specified in the notice and is required by him for carrying out certain functions under the Act. If the authority fails in its duty to supply that information the Secretary of State may assume the information to be such as he sees fit (if he informs the authority of his intention to make that assumption – thus giving it a chance to comply). The penalty here is ultimately financial.

(d)   A contrast with the imposition of penalties for breach of duty is the *granting of rewards* for carrying out a desired act – the carrot rather than the stick. Failure to carry out the act will then result in the withholding or withdrawal of the reward. An old example is found in the Railways Regulation Act 1842. This imposed a duty on railway companies to run one second-class stopping train a day (with adequate protection against the weather, at not less than 12 mph and at a charge of not more than a penny a mile).[3] This duty was sought to be enforced by a daily penalty payable to the Crown, but also by exemption from taxes on the receipts from such trains: the carrot *and* the stick.

The granting of rewards[4] by the State goes much further than for the performance of specific duties, witness for example the grant of immunity from prosecution, the imposition of a lesser sentence

---

1   And see Professions Supplementary to Medicine Act 1960, s 11 for mandamus and alternatives.
2   Transport Act 1985, s 111.
3   Such trains were known as 'Parliamentary trains'; for their suggested use as punishment to fit the crime see *The Mikado*. (For 'parliamentary contracts' see p 447 below. For 'unparliamentary smoke' see E Gaskell *North and South*, chs 7 and 10.)
4   See Freiberg, 'Reward, Law and Power: toward a jurisprudence of the carrot' (1986) 19 ANZJ Crim 91.

in return for a plea of guilty, tax relief for expenditure regarded for some reason as desirable, and the award of honours. Notice finally a statutory power to reward informers. Section 32 of the Inland Revenue Regulation Act 1890 provides that the Commissioners of Inland Revenue may at their discretion:

reward any person who informs them of any offence against any Act relating to inland revenue or assists in the recovery of any fine or penalty provided that a reward exceeding fifty pounds shall not be paid in any case without the consent of the Treasury.

(e) *By Judicial Review.*

This brief section merely notes certain remedies relevant to the enforcement of duties. They are dealt with in detail later.[5]

A 'mandamus' is the name commonly given to an order or document containing an order, by which the court requires a body or person to carry out its public duty. It will be clear that one of the issues that may arise on an application for a mandamus is what the precise requirements of the duty are.

Another remedy that may be sought by way of judicial review is the declaration, or declaratory judgment, by which the court declares the public body in question failed, in taking the decision, to have regard to a relevant duty.

Certiorari is the name given to the court order which quashes a decision taken in the exercise of public power. One of the grounds for quashing is that the public body in question failed, in taking the decision, to have regard to a relevant duty.

In the above three cases, the public authority is the defendant – strictly, the respondent to the application for judicial review of its decision. A contrasting situation is where the authority is the instigator of legal proceedings but is denied a remedy because it is shown that it had failed to take sufficient account of its own breach of duty. An example is *West Glamorgan County Council v Rafferty*.[6] For some ten years the County Council was in breach of its duty to provide adequate accommodation for gipsies. The Council decided to bring legal proceedings to evict trespassing gipsies from a site it owned: it did this because it intended to develop the site. The fact that the Council was in breach of its duty to provide sites did not by itself afford the gipsies right to possession. The decision to evict was however unlawful as it could be explained only as one made by a Council which was either not thinking of its duties or was by some error mistaken as to their nature and extent.[7]

(f) *Action for breach of statutory duty.*

An action in tort may lie for failure to carry out a statutory duty at the instance of a person affected by that failure. This is considered in chapter 15.

5 Ch 11, below.
6 [1987] 1 All ER 1005, [1987] 1 WLR 457.
7 Cf *R v Essex County Council, ex p Curtis* [1991] COD 9.

(g) *Ombudsmen and others.*
The function of the various British Ombudsmen is to investigate complaints of maladministration by certain public bodies. Their work is considered in chapter 16. Suffice it to say here that a complaint may be of a failure to carry out satisfactorily a statutory obligation. In the same chapter will be found an account of other officials who may also be empowered to act against certain public authorities which are thought to be in breach of their duties.

Enforcing a duty: examine the statute

The above paragraphs indicate the various statutory and common law remedies which seek to ensure performance of duties. It is of course open to the statute which imposes a duty to detail with some precision what penalties are or are not to be available. Some recent examples are of interest.

(i) Section 17 of the Local Government Act 1988 imposes on certain public authorities the duty when exercising certain contractual functions not to take into account 'non-commercial matters'. Section 19(7) provides that that duty is not enforceable by *criminal* proceedings. It goes on to say however that an action in *tort* can be brought by anyone who in consequence of such a breach suffers loss or damage. In addition it envisages the possibility of a *judicial review* of a decision taken in breach of that duty by providing that a potential contractor has a sufficient interest to bring such proceedings.

(ii) Section 6 of the Representation of the People Act 1983 refers to the breach of duty imposed on certain public officials in connection with parliamentary and local government elections. It provides that such a person guilty of any act or omission in breach of official duty shall be liable to a *fine* on summary conviction. It further provides that there is no liability to any *civil penalty*, or to any action for *damages*.

(iii) Section 21 of the Gas Act 1986 concerns the use of a pipe-line belonging to a 'public gas supplier'. If a person other than the supplier makes representation to the Director General of Gas Supply that a pipe-line should be adapted by installing in it a junction through which another pipe-line may be connected with the pipe-line (thus enabling the applicant to use the suppliers' pipe-line), and the Director agrees, the Director may give directions to the supplier. Obviously the supplier is under a duty to comply with the directions, but the obligation to comply is owed to any person who may be affected by contravention of the directions; and any breach of that duty is actionable civilly at the suit of any such person.

(iv) Contrast with the above section 43 of the Education (No 2) Act 1986. This provides that those persons concerned in the government of universities and polytechnics 'shall take such steps as are reasonably practicable to ensure that freedom of speech is secured' in those institutions. This is followed by certain particular duties. Nothing is said in the section about the enforcement of such duties. This does not mean that no effect can be given to them in court proceedings.[8]

8 See *R v University of Liverpool, ex p Caesar-Gordon* [1990] 3 All ER 821 – declaration that university decision to ban meetings was ultra vires.

Chapter 7

Powers and their use

Most administrative powers are statutory: they owe their existence to, and the limitations on their use are determined by, Act of Parliament. A person or body acting under statutory powers can do only those things permitted by the statute to be done, and cannot do those things forbidden to be done: that is the ultra vires doctrine. That doctrine is applied by the courts, which are therefore in a position of importance and influence in determining the scope and the validity of the exercise of administrative powers. It is for the courts, not the body whose act is in question, to say whether the act is within the powers given to it by statute: if it were otherwise a public authority could determine the extent of its own powers. The role of the lawyer is to warn of the limitations imposed by the doctrine, and to advise how they can be overcome. He is the 'geographer of policy space',[1] mapping out where the authority can and cannot go; the court gives an authoritative ruling on the accuracy of the map – subject always to the government through its control of the legislative process.

Statute and common law

Before considering the ultra vires doctrine some related matters must be referred to.

(i) Not all administrative powers are statutory: some exist at common law. The prerogative consists of those powers which the Crown enjoys not under statute, but at common law. We have noted this previously, at p 52.

(ii) An administrative authority may, in dealing with a particular issue, have both statutory and common law powers available to it. Where the extent or the consequence of the use of those powers differs, or one is subject to conditions the other is free from, the question may arise whether it was, in that particular case, acting under its statutory or common law power. This possibility can certainly arise when it is the Crown that is

---

1 Stewart in Leach and Stewart *Approaches in Public Policy*, p 28.

acting. In *A-G v de Keyser's Royal Hotel Ltd*[2] the question was whether the Crown had requisitioned property using statutory or common law powers; in the former case compensation was payable, in the latter, possibly not. Examining the letters sent by the Crown to the company, the court had no doubt that possession had been taken under statutory powers. A police officer has both statutory and common law powers, and the nature of the power being exercised may determine the legality of his action.[3] In contrast, the ambulance and fire services do not, unlike the police, have a common law basis.[4]

(iii) Most but not all institutions of public administration are bodies corporate created either by statute or by Charter.[5] As bodies corporate they are, at law, persons. Jennings pointed out that the primary purpose of a body corporate in the governmental sphere is not to do those things which a *natural* person may do. A governmental institution is likely to require special powers of compulsion which an ordinary person does not have. In particular it wants to tax, to inspect, to acquire other peoples' land and do what would otherwise be a nuisance. These things cannot be done by ordinary persons. Hence a public corporation's powers derive principally not from its capacity as a legal person but from statute.[6]

(iv) If a corporation is created by statute, has it any residual or common law powers? To what extent can it act as a private person? The question has been raised in connection with an authority's right to exclude the public from its premises, as in *Cinnamond v British Airports Authority*.[7] Under its Act the BAA had 'power to do anything which is calculated to facilitate the discharge of its duties ... ' In addition it had exercised its statutory power to make byelaws for regulating the use of its aerodromes. Acting under those byelaws, the Authority prohibited the plaintiffs, six minicab drivers, from entering Heathrow Airport except as bona fide passengers. (They had been convicted many times of touting for passengers and not paid the fines.) The plaintiffs sought a declaration that, on various grounds, the notices prohibiting them were invalid. The point we are concerned with here is whether the authority in excluding the plaintiffs could be said to be exercising the ordinary private landowners' power of excluding whom he wishes from his premises, so that – be it noted – the rights of the individuals seeking entry to the airport were to be determined according to that relationship. Nineteenth-century cases concerning railway companies were relied on in support of that proposition.[8] Lord Denning MR thought that those cases had no application to this statutory authority which was of a different character altogether from those companies. It followed that the power of the Authority and the rights of

2   [1920] AC 508.
3   *Beard v Wood* [1980] RTR 454.
4   *George v Garland* [1980] RTR 77.
5   See p 20 above.
6   Jennings *The Law relating to Local Authorities*, p 20.
7   [1980] 2 All ER 368, [1980] 1 WLR 582, CA. Case note by Samuel 97 LQR 19.
8   For railway companies formed by or under statutory powers see 27 Halsbury's Laws of England (2nd edn).

the individuals concerned were to be determined by reference only to the statute. The court agreed. It therefore treated the relationship in question as existing in public rather than in private law. And in *British Airports Authority v Ashton*[9] the Authority's position concerning the exclusion of the public was contrasted with that of a private landowner, as its ownership is subject to the right of the public to have access for the purpose of taking advantage of the services provided by it in pursuance of its statutory duty.

The right to exclude members of the public was raised in *Hall v Beckenham Corpn*[10] where it was argued that the corporation, as owners of a recreation ground could, like any landowner, eject from it whom it pleased (and was therefore liable in nuisance for the actions of people flying model aircraft there). However, the land had been acquired under statutory powers for the purpose of being used by the public, and the authority could make byelaws to control people's conduct there. It could therefore eject only those whom the byelaws permitted it to eject. It was, in other words, confined to its statutory powers.

(Notice that, in other fields, public authorities have been able to rely on private law rights of property and confidentiality in order to prevent the disclosure of information to the public.)[11]

It is then clear that a corporation created by statute has, when limiting the rights of third parties, only those powers given it by statute. If, on the other hand, it is created under the prerogative (by a charter) it has all the powers of a natural person except in so far as the charter provides otherwise (that is it may have those powers). What if the corporation is created by a charter which is itself issued under authority of a statute? In that case the extent of the corporation's powers depends on the construction of the statute. In *Hazell v Hammersmith and Fulham London BC*[12] it was held that the combined effect of the two documents was such as to confine the defendant local authority to the statutory powers enjoyed by any other such authority.

'Under statutory authority'

The fact that an act is done 'under statutory authority', or 'in pursuance of an enactment' or some similar phrase may have significant consequences. In *Harwich Dock Co Ltd v IRC*,[13] a rate rebate was available in respect of a hereditament comprising a dock undertaking and occupied by a person carrying on the undertaking 'under authority conferred by or under any enactment'. The plaintiff dock company had been formed under the Companies Act. The hereditament it occupied was a wharf 'approved' by the Commissioners of Customs and Excise under relevant legislation.

9 [1983] 3 All ER 6, [1983] 1 WLR 1079.
10 [1949] 1 KB 716, [1949] 1 All ER 423. See *Ex p Fewings*, p 245 below.
11 See A Lester in *The Changing Constitution* (2nd edn Jowell and Oliver) p 287, et seq.
12 [1992] 2 AC 1, [1990] 3 All ER 33.
13 (1977) 75 LGR 632.

The company could not have carried on its business in that place without that approval. It argued that the significance of that approval was that it carried on its undertaking under 'authority conferred by [an] enactment'. The House of Lords held that the company got its *authority* to carry on its dock undertaking from its own Memorandum and Articles of Association. True, it could carry on its business only in a *place* 'approved' by the Commissioners, but the company did not get its authority to carry on its business from that approval. (That approval was to be seen as akin to planning permission and was available to anyone who carried on his business in that place.) 'Authority conferred by or under any enactment' meant authority conferred by Act of Parliament, statutory instrument or provisional order.[14]

The Race Relations Act 1976 makes certain acts of racial discrimination unlawful. However, it provides that 'nothing [in this Act] shall render unlawful any act done: (a) in pursuance of any enactment or Order in Council; or (b) in pursuance of any instrument made under any enactment by a Minister of the Crown'. In *Hampson v Department of Education and Science*[15] the facts were that acting under a power given to him by regulations made under a statute the minister refused 'qualified teacher status' to H on the ground that the teacher training course she had undergone in Hong Kong was not comparable to one in the UK. H alleged racial discrimination. The House of Lords held that the exemption of racial discriminatory acts (ie those done 'in pursuance of an enactment') was restricted to those specified in and required by the instrument. What was done in this case was not so specified but decided on by the Minister in the exercise of his discretion under the regulations. Two points should be noted: (a) The House noted that if the provision which led to racial discrimination was a requirement in the instrument itself (which they said it had to be) it would (as delegated legislation) be subject to Parliamentary scrutiny, whereas the exercise of ministerial discretion could be challengeable only by way of judicial review which was an unsatisfactory alternative to the application an Industrial Tribunal which is available for an allegation of racial discrimination. (The case was remitted by the House to the Industrial Tribunal.) (b) The House also noted that the phrase 'in pursuance of an enactment' occurs in such different contexts that interpretation of the phrase in one context may not be much use in another.

Power and jurisdiction

Jurisdiction can be equated with power, but the word is used in preference to power in respect of certain bodies which may perhaps be identified as those which decide disputes, or may be said to 'hear and determine' an issue, or which act in some sense judicially. For example, we would speak

14 See p 58 above.
15 [1990] 3 WLR 42. Applied in *Hertfordshire County Council v Ozanne* [1991] 1 All ER 769, HL.

of a local authority's 'power' to build houses, but of its education appeals committee's 'jurisdiction' to determine an appeal. If it built houses where it had no statutory authority to do so, we would say it acted ultra vires, without the power to do so; if its committee heard an appeal when it had no statutory authority to do so, we would say that it acted without jurisdiction.

There are two issues to be considered. First: suppose a tribunal has jurisdiction to fix the fair rent of houses. The main, ultimate, or central issue for the tribunal is, what is the fair rent for this house? But what of the question, is this building a house (or, say, a shop)? The tribunal will have to decide, if the issue is raised before it, whether or not it is a house. If it decides that it is, it can then go on to consider the rent; if not, not. But is the tribunal's decision on the classification of the building to be final? It would seem, in this example, that its statutory authority is limited to houses and that it cannot give itself jurisdiction over what is not in law a house by classifying it as such. The status of the building would thus be a *jurisdictional fact* (or issue), a matter 'collateral' to the main issues. The question whether the building is a house 'goes to' the tribunal's jurisdiction. Where that is the case, the tribunal's decision on the issue cannot, it would seem, be conclusive; if it were, the tribunal would be able to determine its own jurisdiction. And, it is said, just as a body cannot determine its own powers, so it cannot determine its own jurisdiction.

The concept of jurisdictional fact was consistently attacked by Gordon.[16] His view was that a tribunal having been given a job to do, all that can be expected of it is that it gives a decision which is reasonable on all the matters presented to it for decision, and that to distinguish between some questions and others is illogical. It would mean for example that the tribunal decision that a building was a house would be conclusive, which in general would not be the case at present.

This problem is not confined to tribunals, though in respect of administrative authorities we may use language of vires. For example in *Re Ripon (Highfield) Housing Confirmation Order 1938, White and Collins v Minister of Health*,[17] a local authority had power to acquire land compulsorily for housing but not land which formed part of a park. It made an order in respect of 23 acres which were part of the grounds of a house. The minister took the view that the grounds did not constitute a park and confirmed the order. The order was quashed: there was, the court said, no evidence on which the minister could conclude that the land was not a park. It was not within his power to finally decide whether it was a park.

But the possibility that Parliament may 'entrust a tribunal [or other body] with the power of deciding whether or not they have jurisdiction, because they are empowered to decide the preliminary facts which alone will give it to him'[18] must be acknowledged. Lord Esher MR contrasted the two possibilities thus:

16 (1929) 45 LQR 459, (1960) 76 LQR 306, (1966) 82 LQR 515.
17 [1939] 2 KB 838, [1939] 3 All ER 548, CA.
18 Per Lord Goddard CJ in *R v Ludlow, ex p Barnsley Corpn* [1947] KB 634, [1947] 1 All ER 880.

Where an inferior court or tribunal, which has to exercise the power of deciding facts, is first established by Act of Parliament, the legislature has to consider what powers it will give that tribunal or body. It may in effect say that if a certain state of facts exists and it is shown to such tribunal or body to exist before it proceeds to do certain things, it shall have jurisdiction to do such things, but not otherwise. There it is not for them conclusively to decide whether that state of facts exists, and if they exercise the jurisdiction without its existence, what they do may be questioned, and it will be held that they have acted without jurisdiction. But there is another state of things which may exist. The legislature may entrust the tribunal or body with a jurisdiction which includes the jurisdiction to determine whether the preliminary state of affairs exists, as well as the jurisdiction, on finding that it does exist, to proceed further or do something more.[19]

The second issue is this. Where a power is improperly exercised we say that the body in question acted without power, ultra vires, in respect of that matter. For example a local authority *has*, say, a power to revoke a licence it has granted. If, in revoking it, it acts on irrelevant considerations, it acts ultra vires. Likewise a body which exercises 'jurisdiction' may have jurisdiction to determine a particular matter, but whilst determining it, may act in such a way as to deprive itself of that jurisdiction, just as the local authority had no power to act in the way it did, or deprived itself of the power to revoke the licence. One long-standing ground for quashing a decision is where there is displayed an 'error of law on the face of the record' of the proceedings being queried. It used to be thought that the 'error on the face' had to be such as to deprive the body of jurisdiction but in *Ex p Shaw*[20] it was held that any determination which on the face of it offends against the law (such as in that case the misinterpretation of regulations) can be quashed. However, it is not the case that an error of law must be on the 'face' in order to enable a court to intervene. And any error of law renders a decision void, whether it deprives of jurisdiction or not. Thus the distinction between errors of law within and those which deprive of jurisdiction has been undermined as has the importance of 'error of law on the face' as a ground of challenge.[1]

The ultra vires doctrine

The essence of the ultra vires doctrine, as already stated, is that a person or body acting under statutory power can only do those things the statute authorises him or it to do; an act will be ultra vires if the person or body doing it did not have the statutory power to do it.[2] (And of course it cannot

19 *R v Income Tax Special Purposes Comrs* (1888) 21 QBD 313 at 319.
20 *R v Northumberland Compensation Appeal Tribunal, ex p Shaw* [1952] 1 KB 338, [1952] 1 All ER 122, CA.
 1 For an example see *R v Minister of Housing, ex p Chichester RDC* [1960] 2 All ER 407, [1960] 1 WLR 587.
 2 Statute may say what the *object* of a body is to be, as in the case of an urban development corporation whose object 'shall be to secure the regeneration of its area'. But in seeking to achieve that object it can exercise only those powers which are given it for the purpose stated. Eg Local Government, Planning and Land Act 1980, s 136.

do what it is forbidden to do.) It follows that the more widely expressed powers are, the less will there be for the doctrine to bite on.

But notice the two uses of the phrase 'ultra vires'. There is the use just mentioned: there was no power to do the act. But an act may also be ultra vires not because there was no power to do it, but because of the way the power was exercised. Thus, a challenge to the legality of an act may be either on the ground that there was no power to do it, or on the ground that though, or if, there was power to do it, the power was exercised in an unlawful manner. A challenge on the first ground is that the body in question acted ultra vires in the narrow, or strict, sense of that doctrine – that there was no power to do it. A challenge on the second ground is that though the body had the power in question, and was thus acting intra, not ultra, vires (in the narrow sense), it exercised the power in a way not permitted by legal rules; and thus acted ultra vires in the wider sense of that doctrine.[3] The distinction was crucial in *Page v Hull University Visitor*[4] where it was held that if a University visitor acts within his jurisdiction in the narrow sense he is not subject to judicial review, but is if he acts outside its narrow meaning. And in *R v Secretary of State, ex p Mahli*[5] an appeal tribunal was entitled only to inquire whether the respondent's power existed, not whether it had been improperly exercised.

As the most basic concept in the judicial review of administrative action, ultra vires, even in its narrow sense, has many applications, as the following pages show.

(i) The administration exercises its statutory functions within *a hierarchy of powers*. At the top is the Act of Parliament which cannot be ultra vires in domestic law. Regulations, orders or decisions of whatever name or form must be within the powers given by the Act and not repugnant to it. Any further act authorised or required to be taken by such regulations etc must likewise be within the regulations and within the Act and not repugnant to either. For example, section 47 of the Prison Act 1952 empowers the Secretary of State to make Rules for the discipline and control of prisoners. Under the authority of the Rules the Secretary of State has made standing orders; and has issued circulars. The Rules must be intra vires the Act; the standing orders must be intra vires the Rules and the Act. The Rules cannot confer any greater power than the Act; nor the standing orders any greater powers than the Rules; and the circulars must be warranted by the terms of the statutory documents.

(ii) *The doctrine applied.* In *A-G v Fulham Corpn*[6] the defendant had statutory power to provide 'wash-houses' which were to be supplied with facilities for washing and drying clothes. Acting under that power, it provided facilities where members of the public came to wash their clothes except that the 'hydro-extractors' (ie the wringers) were operated by its employees. It was limited to providing those facilities: it could not

3 See Oliver, 'Is the ultra vires rule the basis of judicial review?' [1987] PL 543.
4 [1993] AC 682, [1993] 1 All ER 97.
5 [1991] 1 QB 194, [1990] 2 All ER 357.
6 [1921] 1 Ch 440.

therefore, the court said, do all or most of the washing through its employees, that is provide 'something in the nature of a laundry' and provide a collection and delivery service. The scheme of the Act was to provide facilities for persons who did not themselves have them, so that they could do their own washing. A laundry operation was for the benefit of classes not intended by the Act to be benefited (that is, for other than the 'labouring classes').

That is the simplest kind of case. Even there the words in question had to be construed in their statutory context.[7] Thus a statutory power to 'regulate' an activity may or may not[8] give the right to prohibit the activity in question. Was an area in and around South Yorkshire a 'substantial part' of the UK for the purpose of the Act in question?[9] There may be cases of considerable complexity, as for example *Bromley London Borough Council v Greater London Council*[10] (the *Fare's Fair* case). The defendant, the (Labour controlled) GLC, had power to make grants to the London Transport Executive (LTE) 'for any purpose'. The GLC, which had a duty to develop policies which promoted the provision of integrated efficient and economic transport facilities in the GLC area, decided that all fares in the area should be reduced by twenty five per cent. This would have caused LTE an annual operating loss of some £69 million. GLC proposed to make up this sum by way of a grant to LTE; to raise that sum GLC issued a supplementary precept for rates to all London boroughs. One of those boroughs, (Conservative controlled) Bromley, applied for a certiorari to quash the supplementary rate. Was there a power to make this grant (and to issue the precept)? The House of Lords held that while the power to make a grant 'for any purpose' included a power to supplement by grant the revenue received by LTE from fares, including anticipated deficits, the power was subject to other statutory provisions which in effect required LTE to operate on what the House of Lords called 'ordinary business principles'. The proposed reduction in fares had not been based on those principles and was therefore ultra vires. The grant was therefore for an ultra vires purpose: in the result the supplementary rate was quashed. Bromley had argued that even if there was the power in question it had been unlawfully used. Whichever way the case was put, the issue was one involving the interpretation of a statute, and this was to be done not 'in isolation [but with regard to] the legal structure and status of the GLC as a local authority and the means that are available to it for raising the moneys necessary to enable it to perform its functions'.

7 For cases in which Parliamentary materials may be used to assist interpretation see *Pepper v Hart* [1993] AC 593, [1993] 1 All ER 42. Familiarity with such materials is thus required of students of this subject. See Practice Direction at [1995] 1 All ER 234.
8 Thus in *R v British Airports Authority, ex p Wheatley* (1983) 81 LGR 794 the regulating of the use of an airport was said to require that certain activities be prohibited. Cf *Birmingham and Midland Omnibus Co Ltd v Worcestershire County Council* [1967] 1 All ER 544, [1967] 1 WLR 409. *Anderson v Alnwick DC* [1993] 3 All ER 613: was byelaw regulatory or prohibitory?
9 *South Yorkshire Transport Ltd v Monopolies and Mergers Commission* [1993] 1 All ER 289, [1993] 1 WLR 23.
10 [1983] 1 AC 768, [1982] 1 All ER 129.

The judgment in this *cause célèbre* attached much criticism.[11] A year later an amended scheme, permitting subsidisation but within the ruling in the *Bromley* case, was agreed between GLC and LTE, and held to be lawful.[12] Shortly afterwards the Transport Act 1983 changed the financial duties of the LTE. In the meantime the subsidisation of public transport in another part of the country had been held to be lawful, on the interpretation of different statutory provisions from those in issue in the *Bromley* case.[13]

Where a power to make regulations is stated to be in respect of the law relating to the *adjudication* of social security claims, it cannot be used to *legislate* in respect of such claims.[14]

Where the Secretary of State could reduce a grant by reference to 'guidance' issued by him, it was argued[15] that guidance is something given with the object of assisting the recipient to arrive at the destination to which he is guided – in this case, to achieve a reduction in expenditure which, it was said, was not possible in this case; with the result that the reduction in grant was unlawful. The argument did not succeed. Where statute gave the minister power to give directions as to the needs that can be met out of the Social Fund, the argument that there was no power to exclude categories of needs (in this case domestic help) was rejected.[16]

(iii) *The 'fairly incidental' rule.* The ultra vires doctrine, it is said:

ought to be reasonably and not unreasonably understood and applied, and whatsoever may fairly be regarded as incidental to or consequential upon those things which the legislature has authorised ought not (unless expressly prohibited) to be held, by judicial construction, to be ultra vires.[17]

An example is *A-G v Crayford UDC*.[18] Section 111(1) of the Housing Act 1957 gave a local authority powers of 'general management' of houses provided by it. Under this power the defendant made arrangements with the Municipal Mutual Insurance Ltd for the issue of a policy under which the council's tenants could, if they chose, insure their effects against fire, storm, etc. The Prudential Staff Union (a competitor) sought an injunction and a declaration that the scheme was ultra vires the council. The council

---

11 Eg Loughlin *Local Government, the Law and the Constitution*; Dignan 'Policy Making and the Courts' 99 LQR at 630. Griffith 'Judicial Decision-making ...' [1985] PL 564. The Times commented that the decision was 'not an instructed framework for a transport policy. By ruling out budgeting for a general deficit as an objective of policy it ruled out an instrument which has been found necessary by most of the world's major urban transport authorities', 30 June, 1982.
12 *R v London Transport Executive, ex p Greater London Council* [1983] QB 484, [1983] 2 All ER 262.
13 *R v Merseyside County Council, ex p Great Universal Stores Ltd* (1982) 80 LGR 639.
14 *R v Secretary of State for Social Security, ex p Cotton* (1985) Times, 14 December, CA; *Britnell v Secretary of State for Social Security* [1991] 2 All ER 726 – power to make 'transitional' regulations: were they?
15 *R v Secretary of State for the Environment, ex p Hackney London Borough Council* [1984] 1 All ER 956.
16 *R v Secretary of State for Social Security, ex p Stitt* [1991] COD 68.
17 Per Lord Selbourne in *A-G v Great Eastern Rly Co* (1880) 5 App Cas 473 at 478.
18 [1962] Ch 575, [1962] 2 All ER 147.

showed that council tenants do not generally insure their effects, and that if they lose them are likely to default on their rent. The court said that, that being so, a prudent landlord may reasonably seek to protect his rent by facilitating insurance against such loss. The council's scheme was therefore within its powers of 'general management' and intra vires. (Notice that the court emphasised that it was not concerned with the standards of management appropriate to private landlords concerned to maximise their profit.)

Contrast *A-G v Fulham Corpn.*[19] The court was clear that the laundry operation was not directly authorised by statute: but neither could it be fairly regarded as incidental to what had been authorised, as it was a 'completely different undertaking'. But there was no need to rely on the 'fairly incidental' rule in *Wansbeck District Council v Charlton.*[20] A statute said, 'A notice under this section must be in a form prescribed by regulations made by the Secretary of State'. There is there no express power to make regulations, but the court had no doubt that the power was there, not because it was to be fairly regarded as incidental, but because it was clearly implied.

(iv) *Some presumptions*. If the wording of the statute gives room for manoeuvre in its interpretation, the court's attitude to the nature of the power in question and the function of the body exercising it may well affect the outcome.

A strong presumption applied by the courts when interpreting legislation is that a tax is not to be levied without the clear authority of Parliament. In *A-G v Wilts United Dairies*[1] the Food Controller was empowered to make orders regulating the production, distribution etc of milk, and fixing prices. A licensing system for trading in milk was introduced, and maximum prices fixed. To ensure equitable distribution the country was divided into zones, and differing maxima fixed. To prevent milk being taken from a zone where it was 2d a gallon cheaper than in a neighbouring zone for sale there, it was made a condition of the licence to trade in the first zone, that the trader pay the Food Controller 2d a gallon. The defendant agreed to do so, but later refused to pay. The High Court regarded the 2d as a valid administrative method of regulating the market. The Court of Appeal and House of Lords regarded it as tax for the imposition of which no clear and definite statutory power could be found. The condition to pay was unlawful, and the agreement to pay unenforceable.

In *Daymond v South West Water Authority*[2] the Authority had power to fix and recover 'such charges for the services ... performed by them' as it thought fit. The demand served on the plaintiff included a sewerage charge: but his house was not connected to the public sewers. The House of Lords held, by a bare majority, that in the absence of an express power as to

19 [1921] 1 Ch 440; p 199 above.
20 (1981) 79 LGR 523.
  1 (1922) 38 TLR 781; applied in *Congreve v Home Office* [1976] QB 629, [1976] 1 All ER 697. And see *Liverpool Corpn v Arthur Maiden Ltd* [1939] 4 All ER 200.
  2 [1976] AC 609, [1976] 1 All ER 39; p 23 above.

who was liable to be charged, only those persons who actually availed themselves of the services provided by the authority could be charged. Lord Kilbrandon said that he did not consider the words adequate 'to empower an ad hoc non-representative body to impose what is in truth a tax namely an impost under the head of charges for services ... on persons who do not directly receive such advantages'.[3]

In view of the constitutional relationship between legislature and administration, a power to amend, modify etc an Act by ministerial regulation should, it is said, be narrowly and strictly construed.[4] Another presumption applied by the courts in interpreting statutes is that Parliament does not intend to deny access to the courts. In *Chester v Bateson*[5] there was a very wide statutory power:

during the continuance of the present war to issue regulations for securing the public safety and the defence of the realm ... and to prevent ... the successful prosecution of the war being endangered.

Under this power a regulation was made to prevent munition workers from being ejected from their homes: whilst it was in force no one could, without the minister's consent, take any court proceedings for the recovery of a house occupied by such a person. To do so was an offence. The High Court held that the regulation was ultra vires. Access to the courts was not to be taken away by regulation unless the Act clearly authorised it, the court said. On the other hand, in *R v Halliday*[6] the House of Lords held that a regulation made under the same statutory power which provided for the imprisonment without trial of persons of hostile origin or associations was valid.

The same presumptive right of access to the courts was also in issue in *Raymond v Honey*.[7] Section 47 of the Prison Act 1952 empowers the Secretary of State to make rules for the regulation and management of prisons. This wording was quite insufficient, the House of Lords said, to authorise hindrance with so basic a right, which could be taken away only by express enactment and in *R v Secretary of State for the Home Dept, ex p Leech*[8] that whilst the section authorises some interference with the confidentiality of prisoners' correspondence, in so far as it in effect authorises the stopping of correspondence with his solicitor, it is ultra vires.

Customs and Excise Comrs v Cure and Deeley Ltd[9] raised a number of the points considered here. Section 31 of an Act provided that purchase tax was to be accounted for and paid in accordance with regulations made under section 33 by the Commissioners. Section 33 says:

3 The charge to the plaintiff was £4.89, but about £30 million a year was at stake in the country as a whole.
4 *Britnell v Secretary of State for Social Security* [1991] 2 All ER 726 at 732. See p 201 above.
5 [1920] 1 KB 829.
6 [1917] AC 260.
7 [1983] 1 AC 1, [1982] 1 All ER 756.
8 [1994] QB 198, [1993] 4 All ER 539.
9 [1962] 1 QB 340, [1961] 3 All ER 641.

The Commissioners may make regulations providing for any matter for which provision appears to them to be necessary for the purpose of giving effect to the provisions of this Part of this Act and of enabling them to discharge their functions thereunder ...

Regulation 12 made under section 33 said:

If any person fails to furnish a return as required by these regulations the Commissioners may ... determine the amount of tax appearing to them to be due from such person ... which amount shall be deemed to be the proper tax due.

In these proceedings for the recovery of tax, the defendant argued that regulation 12 was ultra vires. The High Court agreed. First, the Commissioners were empowered to make regulations to enable them to discharge 'their functions': by the regulation they had taken on themselves the functions of a High Court judge in purporting to decide issues of fact and law as between Crown and subject. Second, the regulation was capable of excluding the subject from access to the courts. And third, the Act imposed a duty to pay such tax such as was due in law, whereas the regulation imposed a duty to pay such tax as the Commissioners believed to be due: it was thus repugnant to the Act.

Will a power to create a criminal offence by ministerial order be implied? Such a power may be expressly granted[10] or withheld[11] by statute. In *R v Marlow (Bucks) Justices, ex p Schiller*[12] it was argued that a minister could not by regulation turn a civil obligation into a criminal obligation. It was held, however, that the section of the Act under which the regulation was made did authorise the provision which was challenged. Schedule 2 of the European Communities Act 1972 (p 66 above) limits the wide power given in section 2 of the Act by excluding from it the power to create any new criminal offence carrying penalties greater than those stated in the Schedule.

(v) Although then in some cases the court will take a strict view of the powers granted, in others they may be ready to give a generous interpretation of an authority's powers in the light of its status and the importance to the public interest of the functions conferred – as, for example, the Chief Registrar of Friendly Societies,[13] the Monopolies and Mergers Commission,[14] and the Bank of England.[15]

(vi) *Ultra vires by omission.* An act of the administration will be ultra vires where it deals with a matter it is not authorised by statute to deal with. It will also be unlawful where it does not deal with a matter it is expressly or implicitly required to deal with.

---

10 Eg Petroleum and Submarine Pipelines Act 1975, s 32.
11 Eg Consumer Protection Act 1987, s 11(4).
12 [1957] 2 QB 508, [1957] 2 All ER 783.
13 *R v Chief Registrar of Friendly Societies, ex p New Cross Building Society* [1984] QB 227, [1984] 2 All ER 27.
14 *South Yorkshire Transport Ltd v Monopolies and Mergers Commission* [1993] 1 All ER 289, [1993] 1 WLR 23, *R v Monopolies and Mergers Commission, ex p Visa International* [1991] COD 29.
15 *A v B Bank* [1992] 1 All ER 778.

Under the Agricultural Marketing Acts the minister could make a scheme concerning the marketing of an agricultural product. The scheme itself had to regulate the marketing of the product. If therefore a scheme merely empowered the board to be set up under it to regulate marketing, it was not a valid scheme.[16]

In *Utah Construction and Engineering Pty Ltd v Pataky*[17] the government had statutory powers to make regulations relating to 'safeguards and measures to be taken for securing the safety and health of persons engaged in excavation work'. A regulation made under this power said, 'Every drive and tunnel shall be securely protected and made safe for persons employed therein'. The court held that the statute authorised only regulations stating the specific means which persons bound by the regulations had to adopt. These regulations did not tell the employer what measures he had to take to safeguard the workers' safety and were therefore void.

It was the statutory duty of a local authority to formulate in a plan its land use proposals. It excluded from the plan its proposals for office development in part of the area in question, and set them out in non-statutory guidelines (The effect of this was to deprive objectors of the right to secure a public inquiry into their objections to those proposals.) The plan was to that extent ultra vires.[18]

In *R v Secretary of State for the Environment, ex p Brent London Borough Council*[19] it was argued that an order did not, as required by statute, specify the 'principles' on which a formula contained in it was made. The argument did not succeed on the facts.

An act may be ultra vires because it lacks some statutorily-required pre-condition, be it document, decision, recommendation, report etc. If the report etc could be shown to be legally defective then the act following it might fall for lack of legal support. The report might be flawed on the ground that it did not deal with a matter it was required to deal with (or dealt with matters it was not authorised to deal with). What is required depends on the statutory provisions and their interpretation. For example every local education authority had to consider a report from its education committee before exercising any of its education functions. The implied purpose of this seems clearly to be to ensure that the authority had the benefit of the views of the expert committee. It follows, it is said, that the report had to contain an evaluation by the committee of the matter in question. How detailed this must be would depend on the particular educational function which the council were exercising, the complexity and novelty of the situation, the difficulty of the problem, the gravity of the consequences and all the circumstances of the case. In the case in

---

16 *Tuker v Ministry of Agriculture, Fisheries and Food* [1960] 2 All ER 834, [1960] 1 WLR 819.
17 [1966] AC 629, [1965] 3 All ER 650.
18 *Great Portland Estates plc v Westminster City Council* [1984] 3 All ER 744.
19 [1982] QB 593, [1983] 3 All ER 321. *Re A barrister* [1993] 3 All ER 429: court order required to specify costs: ultra vires for not doing so.

question, *R v Kirklees Metropolitan Borough Council, ex p Molloy*,[20] the Court of Appeal said that a bare recommendation (that a school be closed) could not constitute a 'report'; there must be at least some explanation of the reasons for it. A recommendation is not necessarily required (a 'report' is called for), but whether or not one is made the principal reasons relied on should be reported, and also the variety of views expressed. The courts did not think this would lead to any practical administrative difficulties. (It should be noted too that the council is to 'consider' the report, not merely 'receive' or 'note' it.)

Not uncommonly A can by statute act only with B's consent. B's consent may be ineffective, and thus A's act ultra vires, unless A makes full disclosure to B of all the facts within his knowledge which could properly influence B in giving his consent.[1]

(vii) *Ultra vires and local authorities*. The effect of the ultra vires rule on local authorities has been much debated. The (Maud) Committee on the Management of Local Government (1967) thought that the doctrine 'has a deleterious effect on local government because of the narrowness of the legislation governing local authorities' activities, and recommended that local authorities should have a 'general competence', that is, a general power to act for the good of the community.[2]

The Local Government Act 1972 did not accept the recommendation. Instead it provides in section 111(1) that a local authority has power to do any thing 'which is calculated to facilitate or is conducive or incidental to the discharge of any of their functions'. This seems to do no more than to give statutory effect to Lord Selbourne's dictum quoted above.[3]

This section has been considered in two recent House of Lords cases. In *Hazell v Hammersmith and Fulham London BC*[4] the council having borrowed money, entered into 'interest rate swap transactions' (by which one swaps one's interest obligations with another – fixed for variable rate, for example). The hope was that profits accruing – if any – would mitigate the burden of interest on the borrowing. The auditor challenged the legality of the transactions. The banks argued that they were lawful by virtue of section 111(1): as they replaced existing interest obligations they were 'incidental' to their borrowing function. However, an exercise of a section 111(1) power is 'subject to the provisions of this Act' and Schedule 13 to the Act sets out a council's borrowing powers in detail, and this, the House said, was inconsistent with any incidental power to enter into the transaction in question. *McCarthy & Stone Ltd v Richmond-upon-Thames*

---

20 (1988) 86 LGR 115.
 1 *T C Coombs & Co v Inland Revenue Commissioners* [1991] 3 All ER 623.
 2 Management of Local Government, Report, vol 1, paras 283–286.
 3 Page 201. A power similar to that in s 111(1) is commonly given to other statutory bodies. In *R v Midlands Electricity Board, ex p Busby* there was no express power in the statute to give time to pay (ie to give an interest-free loan) but it was 'conducive' to its duty in respect of economic and efficient distribution, and to ensure that revenue matched outgoings (1987) Times, 28 October.
 4 [1992] 2 AC 1, [1990] 3 All ER 33.

London BC[5] involved the legality of a charge. The council had the function of deter-mining planning applications. It is not uncommon for would-be developers to seek the council's advice in pre-application discussions and this council had a policy of charging a fee for such advice. Was this lawful? The principle exemplified by *A-G v Wilts United Dairies*[6] applies to local as it does to central government, so where was the authority to charge? It was argued that pre-application discussions were incidental to the function of determining applications. The House agreed, but said that this did not mean that the *charge* for that advice was conducive etc to the function of determining the application, which by section 111(1) it had to be. 'A charge cannot be made unless the power to charge is given by express words or by necessary implication. These last words impose a rigorous test going far beyond the proposition that it would be reasonable or even conducive or incidental to charge for the provision of a service.'[7]

Power to be exercised only by the person authorised

It must be a basic principle that a power can be exercised only by the person on whom it is conferred. It is to be assumed that the recipient of a statutory power has been chosen for its qualities and suitability for the task in hand. In each case the statute has to be looked at to see on whom the power is conferred, and whether it can, by the statute, be exercised by anyone else. If the statute contains express powers of delegation and in their exercise the statutory limits are observed, all well and good. If there are no such express powers, and the power has been used by someone who, on the face of it, has not been authorised, it will be for the court to rule.

(i) The first group of cases deal with the situation where a body permits a subordinate part of itself to exercise functions conferred on it. The first-mentioned state some general principles. It is also convenient to put them under the heading of 'a body and its committee'.

A body and its committee

In *Vine v National Dock Labour Board*[8] a local board on which disciplinary powers had been lawfully conferred had in turn transferred (or, sub-delegated or, conveyed) these powers to a disciplinary committee. Vine was dismissed from his employment by that committee. The question was whether that transfer was valid: if it was not his dismissal was ultra vires. The judgment of the House of Lords shows that in deciding whether a power to delegate or transfer is lawful one has to consider the *nature* of the function in question and the *character* of the person on whom it is

5 [1992] 2 AC 48, [1991] 4 All ER 897.
6 (1922) 38 TLR 781; see p 202 above.
7 At pp 70 and 903 respectively. See *R v Elmbridge BC, ex p Health Care Corpn* 63 P & CR 260. For non-application of s 111 at one remove see 911 HC Debs (5th series) col 41.
8 [1957] AC 488, [1956] 3 All ER 939. See Lanham (1985) 101 LQR 587.

put. As to the former, the House was clear that disciplinary powers cannot be delegated. As to the latter, the Board had been 'clearly constituted so as to inspire confidence and weigh fairly the interests of employers and employed.'[9]

There had been in *Vine* a complete divesting of its discretion by the local Board to the committee. Had the committee been appointed merely to take evidence and report, that would not have constituted such a divesting, and the House suggested that if its decision caused administrative difficulties some such arrangement might be an answer to them.[10]

In *Vine* the House of Lords also made it clear that a judicial function cannot be delegated. There may be a degree of delegation of administrative functions leading up to the judicial decision, but the decision itself must remain in the hands of the body specifically indicated. For example, in *Jeffs v New Zealand Dairy Production and Marketing Board*[11] the Board had to determine applications for zoning orders (to trade in a product in the zoned area). The Board conceded that this was a judicial function; this required *it* to hear the evidence submitted by the parties. The Judicial Committee said that it would have been proper, at least when the credibility of witnesses was not involved, for the Board to appoint a committee to hear evidence for the purpose of informing the Board of it. If the committee's report was such that it could be said that the Board was thereby informed of the evidence, it could not be said that it had not 'heard' the parties. An adequate summary of the evidence might suffice. On the facts of the case however the committee's report did not state what the evidence was: the Board thus reached its decision in ignorance of the evidence and its decision was set aside.[12]

A body and its chairman

In *R v Monopolies and Mergers Commission, ex p Argyll Group plc*[13] a take-over bid had been referred to the Commission which was empowered by the statute not to proceed with the reference if the bid was abandoned. The chairman (the one full-time member of the Commission) decided, in the events that happened, not to proceed with the reference. The Court of Appeal held, reluctantly, that such a power could not be found in the Act to be available to the chairman alone (reluctantly, because it was a sensible and practical way of dealing with the question).

---

9 Per Lord Somervell at 512 and 951 respectively.
10 *Osgood v Nelson* (1872) LR 5 HL 636.
11 [1967] 1 AC 551, [1966] 3 All ER 863, PC.
12 In *R v Derbyshire Police Authority, ex p Wilson* [1990] COD 62 DPA relied on judgment of panel appointed to hear W's case; panel did not give substance of his case; decision quashed. Administrative matters leading up to a decision by chief constable to dismiss probationer could be delegated, not the decision itself: *R v Deputy Chief Constable of Nottinghamshire, ex p Street* (1983) Times, 16 July. And see *Young v Fife Regional Council* 1986 SLT 331.
13 [1986] 2 All ER 257, [1986] 1 WLR 763. And see p 391 below.

A body and its employees

In *A-G, ex rel McWhirter v Independent Broadcasting Authority*[14] it was the duty of the Authority 'to satisfy themselves' that television programmes complied with certain requirements. The Authority consisted of members appointed by the Secretary of State. The court accepted that that duty did not require that the members were themselves to see every programme, that they could leave a great deal to the staff. Only in the most exceptional case ought they to see a programme for themselves in order to be satisfied. (This is realistic. It would be impossible for the members, who were part-time, to do the job.) It followed that there was a duty on the IBA to instruct its senior officials as to the circumstances in which a programme should be referred to it.[15]

A contrasting case is *Allingham v Minister of Agriculture and Fisheries*.[16] A committee had power, lawfully delegated to it by the minister, to give directions concerning the use of land specified in the notice of direction. The committee decided that eight acres of sugar beet should be grown by the occupier of certain land but left it to its officer to select the acres to which the direction should apply. He consulted a sub-committee appointed to make recommendations to the committee; acting on its advice he served a notice on the occupier specifying the acres. The notice was held to be invalid as the committee had left to the officer the duty of deciding something they had to decide for themselves, and a prosecution for breach of the direction failed. Lord Goddard LCJ said:

The real contention of [Allingham] is that [he is] entitled to have the decision of the executive committee and of no one else in this matter ... I think that contention is right.

Government departments

Special reference must be made to these. It is clear that in law functions given to 'the Secretary of State' or the 'the Minister' may subject to any statutory limitation be exercised by his department on his behalf. The constitutional relationship was explained in *Carltona Ltd v Works Comrs*.[17]

In the administration of government in this country the functions which are given to ministers ... are functions so multifarious that no minister could ever personally attend to them ... The powers given to ministers are normally exercised under the authority of the ministers by responsible officers of the department. Public business could not be carried on if that were not the case. Constitutionally, the decision of such an official is, of course the decision of the minister.

In *Lewisham Metropolitan Borough Council v Roberts*[18] a minister was authorised to delegate his power of requisitioning houses. A ministry

14 [1973] QB 629, [1973] 1 All ER 689.
15 It was found to be in breach of that duty in *R v IBA, ex p Whitehouse* (1984) Times, 4 April. See a letter from IBA chairman, Times, 29 October 1987.
16 [1948] 1 All ER 780.
17 [1943] 2 All ER 560.
18 [1949] 2 KB 608, [1949] 1 All ER 815.

official informed Lewisham town clerk of the minister's delegation to him, the clerk, of those powers. A ground on which the validity of the delegation was challenged was that as the official was a delegate of the minister's powers he could not validly effect any further delegation. The court said that this was to misconceive the relationship between the minister and his officials, for:

acts done in the exercise of [the Minister's] functions are equally acts of the Minister, whether they are done by him personally or through his departmental officials, as in practice except in matters of the first importance they almost invariably would be done. No question of agency or delegation as between the Minister and [his official] seems to me to arise at all.

In *R v Skinner*[19] the question was whether the device used to measure the amount of alcohol in the body had as required by statute been 'approved ... by the Secretary of State'. The Court of Appeal stated that the minister's approval could be 'expressed by, and indeed made by, an authorised official of his office'. Notice how the civil servant who in fact approved the device came to be authorised to do so. It was not that the Home Secretary said to him 'Will you look after this for me?' or something to that effect. It was merely that the job of considering the device 'was the part of the Home Office administration with which I was then concerned'.[20] Likewise in *Re Golden Chemical Products Ltd*[1] it was found that the civil servant in question exercised the power given to the Secretary of State because that was the departmental practice, not because it had been delegated to him.

Thus a minister can act through his civil servants. In *Williams v Home Office* (No 2)[2] an attempt was made to show that an admission made by civil servants (that a prison regime was punitive) was the act of the minister, but it was held that in view of the nature of the work they were not expressing the minister's opinion.[3]

Apart from cases where statute so provides, it seems very unlikely that the courts will say that a power given to a minister will have to be exercised by him personally.[4] In *Point of Ayr Collieries Ltd v Lloyd-George*[5] Lord Greene said that it might have been more appropriate for an order taking over a coal mine to have been signed by the minister himself rather than by someone on his staff. But that was not to say that the minister's signature was, as a matter of law, required. He added that different consideration might apply to regulations involving detention without trial. *Liversidge v Anderson*[6] involved such regulations. The report shows that

19 [1968] 2 QB 700, [1968] 3 All ER 124.
20 Ibid at 706 and 126 respectively.
 1 [1976] Ch 300, [1976] 2 All ER 543.
 2 [1981] 1 All ER 1211.
 3 See *Nelms v Roe* [1969] 3 All ER 1379, [1970] 1 WLR 4: *Carltona* principle not applicable to police force, but delegation implied.
 4 ˚or complaints to Parliamentary Commissioner that decision should have been taken by minister see eg HC 170 of 1974, pp 14, 86, 94; HC 178 of 1972–3, para 12; HC 490 of 1971–72 p 132. For commissioner see ch 16 below.
 5 [1943] 2 All ER 546.
 6 [1942] AC 206, [1941] 3 All ER 338.

the detention order was signed by the minister personally, but that may have been because it was thought to be a political rather than a legal necessity. In *Re Golden Chemical Products Ltd*[7] an attempt to distinguish between powers which must (because of their impact on the citizen) and those which need not be exercised by the Secretary of State personally, failed. There remains the possibility that the delegation to a civil servant might be struck down if the official in question was manifestly unfitted for the task on hand (on the ground of irrationality?) or if the task conflicted with any specific statutory function conferred on him.[8]

A statute may require an Act to be done by a minister personally, as for example section 13(5) of the Immigration Act 1971, and section 4 of the Interception of Communications Act 1985.[9] And where a statute said that a certificate 'purporting to be signed by the Secretary of State' was conclusive of certain matters, the prosecution agreed that the certificate had to be signed by him personally.[10]

It seems that certain statutory Treasury functions relating to the management of the home civil service could not be delegated: hence the need for the Civil Service (Management Functions) Act 1992 which authorises the delegation (and sub-delegation) to any other Crown servant.

The relationship between the Secretary of State and a junior minister (not, as in the above cases a civil servant) was raised in *Doody v Secretary of State for the Home Dept*[11] where it was said that the Secretary of State's function of determining the period for which a life sentence prisoner should serve by way of retribution could be exercised by a junior minister. On the other hand the (statutory) advice given by the Lord Chief Justice must be given by him personally. Why the difference? Because just as it is 'obvious' that the realities of departmental administration require delegation, so is it 'obvious' that in the case of the Lord Chief Justice only the office-holder can act. This must be right.[12]

(ii) The cases so far referred to have involved the exercise of discretion by a subordinate part of the body on which the discretion was conferred. We are now concerned with what amounts to improper *transfer of power to another* body. In *Ellis v Dubowski*[13] a local authority committee exercising a statutory power of licensing films granted a licence on

---

7 See fn 1 above.

8 *Oladehinde v Secretary of State for the Home Dept* [1991] AC 254, [1990] 3 All ER 393: delegation to immigration official upheld.

9 Note in s 4(1)(b) the rank of civil servant who can sign (cf authorise) warrant. For safeguards against casual delegation of important powers re police see HC Stdg Cttee D 14 June 1994, col 368.

10 *R v Clerkenwell Metropolitan Stipendiary Magistrate, ex p DPP* [1984] QB 821, [1984] 2 All ER 193.

11 [1994] 1 AC 531, [1993] 3 All ER 92.

12 The issue was raised in *R v Secretary of State for Trade, ex p Anderson Strathclyde plc* [1983] 2 All ER 233 but the court was not called on to decide it. (Secretary of State had personal interest in decision, said decision would be taken by subordinate minister.) For relationship between one Secretary of State and another see *London and Clydeside Estates Ltd v Secretary of State for Scotland* 1987 SLT 459.

13 [1921] 3 KB 621.

condition that no film was to be shown which was not authorised by the British Board of Film Censors. The effect of this, the court said, was to transfer a power which belonged to the committee to a body with no constitutional or statutory authority, but merely an organisation created by the film industry itself. If the arrangements made had reserved to the committee the right to review the Board's decision, they would have been proper, but there was in effect an out and out transfer. In a more recent case it was said that the authority can treat the Board as an advisory body.[14]

The same principle was at stake in *H Lavender & Son Ltd v Minister of Housing and Local Government*[15] where the plaintiff applied for planning permission to extract minerals from an area of high agricultural quality. The local authority refused planning permission, and an appeal to the Minister of Housing was turned down. A reason for turning it down was that it was the minister's policy not to allow mineral working in such an area unless the Minister of Agriculture was not opposed to the working. The court held that the decision 'while purporting to be that of the Minister [of Housing] was in fact and improperly, that of the Minister of Agriculture ... The Minister has by his stated policy delegated to the Minister of Agriculture the effective decision on any appeal ... where the latter objects to the working'. (This case illustrates the point that statutory powers vested in a department are not to be thought of as vested in 'the Government' as a legal entity.)

Contrast *Munasinghe v Secretary of State for the Home Department*[16] where it was held on the facts that there had been no transfer from the defendant to the Department of Employment of the power to give leave to remain in the United Kingdom, but consultation only.[17]

In *Jackson Stansfield & Sons v Butterworth*[18] what was in issue was the transfer of powers from minister to local authority. A regulation concerning the issue of licences authorised a Minister to operate its provisions. The minister could of course choose his own servants for the detailed tasks involved. But what he did was to effectively transfer his functions (by circulars) to local authorities, for a very wide discretion was conferred on them in operating the licensing system, in particular the function of prosecuting for breach of the regulation. Was such a transfer lawful? There was no express power to sub-delegate, nor an express prohibition against doing so. Scott LJ was not prepared to imply such a power. 'The method chosen was convenient and desirable but the power

---

14 *R v Greater London Council, ex p Blackburn* [1976] 3 All ER 184, [1976] 1 WLR 550. See also *Mills v London County Council* [1925] 1 KB 213. (See Video Recordings Act 1984, s 4: Board designated.)

15 [1970] 3 All ER 871, [1970] 1 WLR 1231.

16 [1975] Imm AR 79.

17 Likewise in *Kent County Council v Secretary of State for the Environment* (1976) 33 P & CR 70: no delegation to Energy Secretary. And *R v Secretary of State for the Environment, ex p North Tyneside BC* [1990] COD 195: no delegation of calculation of population figures to Registrar General.

18 [1948] 2 All ER 558.

so to legislate was unfortunately not there'. The court was not, therefore sympathetic to the argument of administrative convenience. One of the arguments in *Blackpool Corpn v Locker*[19] was that there had been no such delegation of the power in question, that the corporation had been acting as a mere agent in that there had been no abdication by the minister of his requisitioning power. The argument was rejected.

(iii) Another aspect of the rule that power is to be exercised only by the person on whom it is conferred is that *to act on the dictation of another*, or to *regard oneself as bound* to act in accordance with the decision, opinion, views or recommendation of another, is in effect to allow that other person to decide. It is to surrender one's discretion to another. Thus where a body is under a duty to perform its functions in such a manner as it considers is in accordance with *guidance* given to it by another, it is not to regard that guidance as though it were a direction.[20] An allegation that guidance was regarded as binding failed in *R v Housing Benefits Review Board of Kensington and Chelsea (Royal) London Borough Council, ex p Robertson*.[1] In giving statutory 'guidance' the Secretary of State said that local authorities were 'not expected' to pay housing benefit in certain circumstances; the respondent Board acted in accordance with that guidance. It was argued that the Board had regarded itself as bound by the guidance. The court said that there was nothing in the wording of the decision or elsewhere beyond the simple fact that the Review Board found as it did (that the applicant was not entitled to benefit) to suggest that it did regard itself as bound. (It might of course: but there was nothing to prove it.)

In *Lonrho plc v Secretary of State for Trade and Industry*,[2] the secretary of State, S, deferred publication of a report saying that he had been advised by the Serious Fraud Office that publication would inhibit inquiries it was making, and might prejudice any later trial. L challenged S's decision. A ground of challenge was that S treated himself as bound to follow SFO's advice, and had thus illegally delegated to it the exercise of the discretion vested in him. The House of Lords rejected this on the facts.

The legality of voting in accordance with the dictates of the party whip has been considered. A member of a local authority who is a member of a party will give weight – very great weight – to the views of the party he belongs to, and to its voting instructions when they apply. He will do this both out of a sense of loyalty and because of the possible invoking of sanctions if he does not (the sanctions being exclusion from party deliberations and benefits and possible de-selection at the next election). Whatever the political realities, the law is that a member of a local authority is under a duty to make up his own mind how to vote on matters

19 [1948] 1 KB 349, [1948] 1 All ER 85; and p 105 above.
20 See *Laker Airways Ltd v Department of Trade* [1977] QB 643, [1977] 2 All ER 182; *R v Police Complaints Board, ex p Madden* [1983] 2 All ER 353, [1983] 1 WLR 447. Likewise guidance must not take the form of a direction: *R v Secretary of State for the Environment, ex p Lancashire County Council* [1994] 4 All ER 165.
 1 (1988) 86 LGR 409.
 2 [1989] 2 All ER 609, [1989] 1 WLR 525, HL.

that come before the council; he must not allow party loyalty to exclude all other considerations from his mind. If in voting for the party line, even against his own inclinations in the matter, he nevertheless regards himself as retaining some discretion in the matter, the legality of his vote cannot be impugned. The facts of the case in which that principle was laid down, *R v Waltham Forest London Borough Council, ex p Baxter*,[3] were that the council resolved to increase the rates significantly. As is common, at a private meeting before the council meeting, the ruling (Labour) group had met to consider its policy and voted in favour of the increase. At the council meeting six members of the Labour group who had voted *against* the increase at the group meeting voted *for* it. Had they done so out of blind obedience to the party line? On the facts the court found not.

Likewise to follow slavishly an electoral mandate by giving effect to it without adequate consideration of its practicality or legality is, it has been said, tantamount to acting on the dictation of another – in this case the party organisation which drafted the manifesto.[4]

There is also the question of the relationship between members and officers of a body. If it could be shown that members slavishly followed the advice of officers, a challenge to their decision could be made.[5] And where a power is exercisable by a council official, it having been lawfully delegated to him, a decision taken by him under pressure from a member of the council which he would not otherwise have taken, is invalid.[6]

The principle in question here is illustrated also by the following cases. Where advice is sought by a body in whom a discretion is vested, the scope of the advice sought must not be such as to pre-empt the body's decision or to make it a foregone conclusion.[7] And where a body has to decide whether to recommend the recognition, for collective bargaining purposes, of a trade union, it can take into account the possibility of industrial strife, but to surrender its judgment in the face of threats of such strife by other unions would be to allow itself to act on their dictation.[8]

(iv) An act may be ultra vires where it consists in the exercise of another's power or an invasion of his function. Thus where a council's rules for the payment of guardians ad litem improperly restricted their discretion it acted unlawfully.[9] And a governor of one prison has no power to order the segregation of a prisoner in another prison; that power belongs to the governor of the prison where he is.[10] Where in an administrative

3 [1988] QB 419, [1987] 3 All ER 671.
4 *Bromley London Borough Council v Greater London Council* [1983] 1 AC 768, [1982] 1 All ER 129.
5 *R v South Somerset DC, ex p DJB (Group) Ltd* (1989) 1 Admin LR 11.
6 *R v Port Talbot Borough Council, ex p Jones* [1988] 2 All ER 207.
7 *Jones v Lee and Guilding* [1980] ICR 310.
8 *United Kingdom Association of Professional Engineers v Advisory, Conciliation and Arbitration Service* [1981] AC 424, [1980] 1 All ER 612.
9 *R v Cornwall County Council, ex p Cornwall ... Guardians ad Litem* [1992] 2 All ER 417.
10 *R v Deputy Governor of Parkhurst Prison, ex p Hague* [1990] 3 All ER 687, aff'd [1991] 3 All ER 733.

scheme decision-making power is distributed amongst various bodies, disputes may arise as to where the boundary between them runs.[11]

(v) The provisions relating to local authorities should be noted. Section 101 of the Local Government Act 1972 gives a wide power to make what are popularly called 'agency arrangements':

(1) ...[A] local authority may arrange for the discharge of any of their functions –
    (a)   by a committee, a sub-committee or an officer of the authority; or
    (b)   by any other local authority.

The section goes on to provide that any arrangements made under it 'shall not prevent the authority or committee by whom the arrangements are made from exercising those functions'. In addition delegation under this or other statutory provisions leaves in the hands of the council a residual responsibility to exercise a degree of control over the committee.[12]

Where a committee is exercising delegated powers all knowledge available in the council is to be imputed to the committee.[13] These provisions show that a committee remains an integral part of the council organisation.

It will be noted that a local authority can delegate functions to *an* (ie one) officer. Can it delegate functions to a committee of one *member*? No, it can not: the usual meaning of committee is of a body of more than one person.[14] (A local authority's standing orders which purport to authorise 'chairman's action' are also ultra vires.) Why should delegation to one officer be proper but not to one member? The judge accepted the view that Parliament might not have thought it safe to entrust decision-making to one person (a member) who has party allegiance whereas it should be possible to rely on an officer to act on behalf of the authority as a whole. And if membership-input into an officer decision is thought desirable, the officer could be authorised to decide in consultation with the committee chairman.[15]

A committee can appoint a sub-committee, but an authorised officer cannot sub-delegate. The arrangement whereby officer A signs for officer B may not however be sub-delegation, but an arrangement whereby A takes decisions in the name of B.[16]

(vi) Where a function is conferred on a person or body, and the quali-fication, composition or method of appointment is provided for, an act done by it when any such requirement is not fulfilled, may be ultra vires.

11 Eg *R v Manchester City Council, ex p Fulford* (1983) 81 LGR 292; *R v North West Thames RHA, ex p Nerva* (1983) Times, 20 October.
12 *City of Birmingham District Council v O* [1983] 1 AC 578, [1983] 1 All ER 497. Contrast committee and working party *R v Eden District Council, ex p Moffat* (1988) Times, 24 November, CA. And see *R v Tower Hamlets LBC, ex p Khalique* (1994) Independent, 7 April for 'grave abuse of power' in setting up 'homelessness board'.
13 *R v Basildon District Council, ex p Martin Grant Homes Ltd* (1987) 53 P & CR 397.
14 *R v Secretary of State for the Environment, ex p Hillingdon LBC* [1986] 1 All ER 810, [1986] 1 WLR 192.
15 *Fraser v Secretary of State for the Environment* (1988) 56 P & CR 386: official decided then got chairman's approval: valid. See M Jones [1987] JPL 612.
16 *R v Southwark LBC, ex p Bannerman* [1990] COD 115.

In *Woollett v Minister of Agriculture and Fisheries*[17] the question was whether the ministry official who convened a tribunal was authorised to do so.

A further fact in *Woollett* was that the statute provided that an act done at a meeting of the tribunal should, notwithstanding that a defect in appointment was afterwards discovered, be as valid as if the defect had not existed. (Such a provision is commonly found in statutes.) The court held that any defect of the kind alleged would be validated by the provision in question. But notice that such a provision will not cure all defects: it appears to be intended to cure procedural defects, so that for example, the appointment by the secretary of a person who was not a panel member would not have been saved.[18]

The presumption of regularity

'Where Parliament has designated a public officer as a decision-maker for a particular class of decisions the High Court ... must proceed on the assumption *omnia praesumuntur rite esse acta* until that presumption can be displaced by the applicant for [judicial] review, on whom the onus lies of doing so'.[19]

This presumption has been applied where the legality of the appointment of a public official was challenged.[20] Where an inspector of taxes served a notice requiring documents to be made available to him (having, as required, first got the consent of a Commissioner of Taxes) the presumption of regularity applied to both.[21] And where the Bank of England issued a notice that certain documents were reasonably required for the performance of its functions, it enjoyed the benefit of the presumption both as to the reasonableness and as to the scope of its functions.[1]

The presumption of regularity has a different application. It is that where there has been a long-term enjoyment of a right which can only have come into existence by virtue of some legal act, the law presumes, in the absence of evidence to the contrary, that there was a lawful origin. The question in one case was whether planning permission had been granted some 40 years previously: a resolution approving the application had been passed, but no document granting permission could be found.[2] The presumption was applied as all concerned had proceeded on the basis

---

17 [1955] 1 QB 103, [1954] 3 All ER 529.

18 See *R v Secretary of State for Education, ex p Prior* (1994) Independent, 6 January. See Lexis.

19 *Inland Revenue Commissioners v Rossminster Ltd* [1980] AC 952, [1980] 1 All ER 80, at 1013, 94 respectively.

20 *Campbell v Wallsend Slipway and Engineering Co Ltd* [1978] ICR 1015; *Ross v Helm* [1913] 3 KB 462.

21 *T C Coombs & Co v Inalnd Revenue Commissioners* [1991] 3 All ER 623, [1991] 2 AC 283.

1 *A & B Bank* [1992] 1 All ER 778.

2 *Calder Gravel Ltd v Kirklees MBC* (1989) 60 P & CR 322.

that it had been granted. But in the *Davey Paxman* case[3] counsel declined to argue that the regulations imposing *charges* must have been made but had been lost.

Fettering discretion by a self-imposed rule

An authority given a statutory discretion is entitled to adopt a policy by which the exercise of the discretion will in future be determined. The policy must of course be one which it is entitled to adopt in that it must not be one which the statute expressly or impliedly prohibits, must not be adopted to achieve an improper purpose, must not be unreasonable etc. These matters are dealt with later. The rule we are concerned with here is that a body given a discretion by statute must not disable itself from exercising that discretion.

In *R v Port of London Authority, ex p Kynoch Ltd*[4] the PLA had statutory power to construct docks, and other persons were empowered to apply to it for a licence to do so. The PLA adopted the policy of not granting a licence to provide something it was its own statutory function to provide. Kynoch was refused a licence. Bankes LJ drew this contrast:

There are on the one hand cases where a tribunal in the honest exercise of its discretion has adopted a *policy*, and without refusing to hear an applicant intimates to him what its policy is, and that after hearing him it will in accordance with its policy decide against him, unless there is something exceptional in his case ... On the other hand, there are cases where the tribunal has passed a *rule* or come to a determination not to hear any application of a particular character by whomsoever made. There is a wide distinction to be drawn between these two classes.[5]

In the first case, the exercise of the discretion is not wholly excluded (even though there is a strong disposition to decide in accordance with the policy); in the second case it is. The decision in the first case is lawful, in the second case it is not. On the facts of *Kynoch* the court found that PLA had given full consideration to the merits of the application.

The dictum of Bankes LJ was considered in the leading case of *British Oxygen Co Ltd v Minister of Technology*.[6] The ministry had power to make grants towards certain capital expenditure and adopted the policy of not paying a grant on any item of plant costing less than £25. The company was refused a grant in pursuance of that policy, and sought a declaration that the ministry was not entitled to refuse a grant on the sole ground of the value of each item. On the basis of *Kynoch* it was argued that the ministry could not make a *rule* for itself as to how it would in future exercise its discretion. The judgments in the House of Lords make it clear that what matters is not whether the decision is called a policy or a rule,

---

3 *Davey Paxman & Co Ltd v Post Office*: see p 103 above.
4 [1919] 1 KB 176.
5 Ibid at 184; emphasis added.
6 [1971] AC 610, [1970] 3 All ER 165. See Rogerson [1971] PL 288, Galligan [1976] PL 332, Kerry (1986) 64 Pub Admin 163 at 170.

but whether the effect of the decision is to exclude the exercise of the discretion in any particular case. The general rule, said Lord Reid, is that any one who has to exercise a statutory discretion must not 'shut his ears' to an application (though that is not to imply that he must give an oral hearing). As the ministry had so many applications to consider, it was, he said, entirely proper for it to have a policy for dealing with them, even one so precise that it could be called a rule, provided it was willing to listen to anyone with something to say and to representations that the policy should be changed. (In this case the minister had in fact considered the company's application, so that it was not necessary to decide whether, if he had refused to consider an application on the ground that it related to an item worth less than £25, he would have acted wrongly. And there was nothing in the Act that prevented the ministry from fixing the figure at £25.)

In *Findlay v Secretary of State for the Home Dept*[7] the legality of rules made by the Home Secretary by which he would in future operate the parole system was challenged. The House of Lords held that the statute in question did not preclude the application of policies in the operation of the system, which is so complex that it was inevitable that there should be policies. If the effect of a policy were to exclude the consideration of individual cases, it would be unlawful, but that was not the case here.

The following cases further illustrate the principle. In *Sagnata Investments Ltd v Norwich Corpn*[8] the court held that the local authority was entitled, within the statute, to have a general policy of refusing applications for licences of amusements arcades – *provided* it was prepared to depart from it when the justice of the particular case required. Likewise a local authority is entitled, under the Education Act 1944, to have a policy of implementing a system of comprehensive education (that is, non-selective at the secondary stage) and to apply it to an individual school – *provided* that it listens to objections and considers in any particular case whether the policy be applied.[9] And it is entitled to have a policy for dealing with the homeless – *provided* that the circumstances of each case are considered.[10] In *R v Secretary of State for the Environment, ex p Reinisch*[11] it was held that the Secretary of State was not entitled in exercising his discretion as to the award of costs of planning appeals, to lay down a single inflexible rule to be applied in all circumstances, but there was no objection to him guiding himself by such a consideration as that costs would in general only be awarded against a party whose behaviour had been unreasonable.

A local planning authority is entitled (is indeed required in some matters) to have policies, and the existence of a policy may raise a presumption against the granting of planning permission (for example a

7 [1984] 3 All ER 801, [1985] AC 318.
8 [1971] 2 QB 614, [1971] 2 All ER 1441.
9 *Smith v Inner London Education Authority* [1978] 1 All ER 411.
10 *Roberts v Dorset County Council* (1977) 75 LGR 462.
11 (1971) 22 P & CR 1022.

policy to maintain a green belt). The refusal of planning permission on the ground of that policy is in order, *provided* that when an application to develop there is made to it the authority considers, at least if requested to do so or if the policy is challenged, whether the policy should be maintained, and if so whether there are any special factors about the application to take it out of the policy.[12] In *Stringer v Minister of Housing and Local Government*[13] the court held that the protection of the Jodrell Bank Telescope against development which would interfere with its use was a policy which the minister could lawfully have within the Town Planning Acts, *provided* that the policy was not pursued to the disregard of all the other relevant considerations which the minister was required to have regard to.

The following cases are examples of decisions being invalidated by the application of a policy fettering a discretion, *as the applicant is thereby deprived of what he is entitled to, the benefit of the exercise of the discretion.*
– The Criminal Injuries Compensation Scheme provides that the Board is to reduce the amount of compensation payable to an applicant or reject the application altogether, if having regard to his conduct it is inappropriate for him to be granted a full award or any at all. The Board implemented that by laying down for itself a rule that 'a member of a gang injured in a gang fight will not receive an award'. By that rule or policy the Board disabled itself from considering on its merits the application of a member of a gang injured in a gang fight whereas the Scheme required every case to be considered on its merits.[14]
– Where a local authority had a discretion to do work on property where the owner had failed to do so, and to charge him for it, an instruction to its officers that they were in every case to do the work, was unlawful (as was the bill sent to an owner for work done in pursuance of that instruction).[15]
– A tribunal which had a power to award 'exceptional circumstances allowances' decided that it would in no case cover costs incurred by an accused person in preparing his case for trial. A decision refusing such costs in pursuance of that policy was referred back to the tribunal.[16]
– Where a local authority byelaw made it an offence to sell articles in the council's parks without permission, and, after granting some permissions, the council resolved to give no future consents, a refusal of consent given in pursuance of that policy amounted to a refusal to exercise the discretion, and mandamus issued to enforce it.[17]

One may fetter discretion not only by policy, but by contract. This is referred to in chapter 13.

12 *Rugby School Governors v Secretary of State for the Environment* (1974) 234 Estates Gazette 371; *Link Homes Ltd v Secretary of State for the Environment* [1976] JPL 430.
13 [1971] 1 All ER 65, [1970] 1 WLR 1281.
14 *R v Criminal Injuries Compensation Board, ex p RJC (an infant)* [1978] Crim LR 220.
15 *Elliot v Brighton Borough Council* (1981) 79 LGR 506.
16 *Dowman v Supplementary Benefits Commission* (1982) Times, 27 January.
17 *R v LCC, ex p Corrie* [1918] 1 KB 68.

Estoppel

The exercise of power may be affected by the operation of an estoppel.[18]

Of the various kinds of estoppel, those that are of relevance here are, first, estoppel by conduct. The rule is that where A has, by words or conduct, made to B a representation of fact with the intention that it should be acted on and B acts on it and thereby alters his position to his detriment, an estoppel is said to arise against A; or, A is estopped or prevented from saying that the fact is otherwise than he represented it to be.

A second kind of estoppel is promissory or equitable estoppel. It differs from the former in that here A makes to B, not a representation of fact, but a promise which is intended to affect legal relations between them and is acted on by B. (A third kind is where a matter has already been determined in earlier judicial proceedings. This is referred to below at p 226.)

Estoppels can bind public authorities.[19] What follows gives some account of their operation and limitations in administrative law.

(i) *There can be no acquisition of power through estoppel.* Estoppel cannot operate so as to enable an authority to do what it has no power to do. It cannot make that which is ultra vires, intra vires. Its powers are fixed by law, and it cannot extend them simply by representing to a third party that they are more extensive than they are. It would, it has been said:

destroy the whole doctrine of ultra vires if it was possible for the donee of a statutory power to extend his power by creating an estoppel.[20]

Thus in *Minister of Agriculture and Fisheries v Matthews*[1] the ministry having acquired possession of land, granted possession of it to the defendant. The defendant claimed that the interest he had thereby acquired was a lease. The ministry said that it was a mere licence. The defendant argued that by virtue of the wording of the grant to him the ministry was estopped from denying that he had been granted a lease, but the court found that the ministry had no statutory power to grant a lease, and therefore the ministry could not be estopped from denying that it was a lease. And where a local authority had power to lease land only with ministerial consent but did so without that consent, it could not be estopped from arguing that the lease was void.[2] A statement by the Secretary of State to an immigrant that he had a right of appeal to a

---

18 The related topic of legitimate expectation is dealt with in ch 9 below.
19 The requirements of estoppel must of course be met. Thus where A told C that a work permit had been issued to B, A was not estopped as against B (*Re Suruk Miah* (1976) Times, 4 February). Where A made a statement to B but B suffered no detriment, there was no estoppel (*Secretary of State for the Home Department v Wedad* [1979–80] Imm AR 27).
20 *Minister of Agriculture and Fisheries v Hulkin* (1948), unreported referred to in *Minister of Agriculture and Fisheries v Matthews* [1950] 1 KB 148, [1949] 2 All ER 724. Relied on unsuccessfully in *R v Secretary of State ex p Ejaz* [1994] 2 All ER 436.
1 Fn 20, above.
2 *Rhyl UDC v Rhyl Amusements Ltd* [1959] 1 All ER 257, [1959] 1 WLR 465. Cf *Janred Properties Ltd v Ente Nazionale Italiano per il Turismo* [1989] 2 All ER 444.

tribunal from his decision did not confer on the *tribunal* a power to hear the appeal which statute did not give it.[3]

(ii) *No estoppel through non- or mis- use of a power.* A public authority is not estopped from exercising a power vested in it simply because it has not used it in the past. *Cambridgeshire and Isle of Ely County Council v Rust*[4] shows that a public authority which has acquiesced in a breach of the law which it has no authority to sanction (in this case relating to the highway) is not thereby estopped from bringing a prosecution for that breach. The public interest in the highway is not to be defeated in that way.[5] In *Customs and Excise Comrs v Hebson Ltd*[6] goods were mistakenly allowed to be imported. That mistake could not fetter the later action of prohibiting their import. In *Yabbicom v King*[7] the local authority had, in error, passed plans for a house submitted by the defendant which were, in one respect, not in accordance with its byelaws. The house was built. The mistaken approval of the plans did not disable the authority from bringing a prosecution for breach of the byelaw: it had no power to dispense with the law.

(iii) *No estoppel to prevent exercise of duty.* A public authority cannot be allowed to be freed by its own acts, through estoppel, from a duty imposed on it by statute.[8] In *Maritime Electric Co Ltd v General Dairies Ltd*[9] ME sold electricity to the public under statutory control. The statute provided that ME was to charge neither more nor less than the price set out in published schedules. By their error they charged GD only one-tenth what they should have charged. When ME sued for the balance GD argued that they were estopped from doing so by the fact that they, GD, had relied on the accuracy of the sums charged in fixing their own prices. The Judicial Committee emphasised that ME were under a public duty, fixed by statute; their mistake could not release them from it any more than an agreement between the parties could have.

The principle of that case is illustrated by *Southend-on-Sea Corpn v Hodgson (Wickford) Ltd.*[10] A senior official of a local authority assured H that certain premises did not need planning permission for use as a builder's yard as there was an existing user right. H thereupon bought the premises. Later the authority told H that there was no such right and served an enforcement notice requiring the use as a builder's yard to cease. H alleged that by reason of the official's assurance the authority was estopped from showing that the premises had not been used long enough to give an existing user right. The court held that if the authority were to be so estopped it would be hindered in the exercise of its statutory

3 *Balbir Singh v Secretary of State for the Home Dept* [1978] Imm AR 204.
4 [1972] 2 QB 426, [1972] 3 All ER 232.
5 See *Epping Forest District Council v Essex Rendering Ltd* [1983] 1 All ER 359, [1983] 1 WLR 158.
6 [1953] 2 Lloyd's Rep 382.
7 [1899] 1 QB 444.
8 See Andrews 'Estoppel against Statutes' (1966) 29 MLR 1.
9 [1937] AC 610, [1937] 1 All ER 748. See Bradley [1981] CLP 1.
10 [1962] 1 QB 416, [1961] 2 All ER 46.

discretion, as it would then be prevented from showing that the enforcement notice was valid. It was not therefore bound by the official's assurance.[11] Though the service of an enforcement notice is a power not a duty, there is a duty to consider the exercise of the power.

Thus an authority cannot be estopped from exercising a duty or a discretion by an employee purporting to determine in advance what the authority itself will have to determine in pursuance of its statutory functions.

Parliament by the [Town and Country Planning] Act of 1971 entrusted the defendant council, acting through their elected members, not their officers, to perform various statutory duties. If their officers were allowed to determine that which Parliament had enacted that the defendant council should determine there would be no need for elected members to consider planning applications. This cannot be.[12]

Where the authority exercises a statutory power to arrange for the discharge of any of its functions by one of its officers (as for example under section 101 of the Local Government Act 1972)[13] and the officer acts within the authority vested in him, a decision taken by him is binding on the authority. This, however, is not to be seen as an exception to the rule stated in the previous paragraph, as the officer is acting within an authority vested in him. 'This kind of estoppel, if it be estoppel at all, is akin to *res judicata*.'[14]

(iv) *Estoppel by holding out.* What if it appears to the third party that the employee has got an authority which (unlike the situation in the previous paragraph) he has not in fact got? Where the appearance of authority arises from some representation *by the employing body* to the third party, then the employer will be bound by the employee's act even though it was outside his actual authority. The employer may properly be said to be estopped by *his* act from denying the employee's authority. For the estoppel to arise there must be some evidence justifying the third person in thinking that what the employee, for example a planning officer, says will bind the planning authority. Holding an office however senior cannot be enough by itself. *Lever Finance Ltd v Westminster (City) London Borough Council*[15] illustrates how an estoppel may arise. L got planning permission for a group of houses. They wanted to vary the plan. The planning officer told them that they did not need fresh planning permission to do so, as the variations seemed to him to be immaterial. L started

---

11 The similarity between this rule and the rule that a public authority cannot by contract fetter the exercise of future executive action (p 429 below), was referred to. See *Rootkin v Kent County Council* [1981] 2 All ER 227, [1981] 1 WLR 1186 p 231 below.

12 Per Megaw LJ in *Western Fish Products Ltd v Penwith District Council* [1981] 2 All ER 204 at 219. And see *Co-operative Retail Services Ltd v Taff-Ely Borough Council* (1979) 39 P & CR 223: local authority not estopped by void grant of planning permission by clerk.

13 See p 215 above.

14 Per Megaw LJ in *Western Fish Products Ltd v Penwith District Council* [1981] 2 All ER 204 at 219. For *res judicata* see p 226 below.

15 [1971] 1 QB 222, [1970] 3 All ER 496.

building the houses in accordance with the varied plan. Neighbours complained. L was advised to apply for permission to validate the variation. When they did so, permission was refused. L brought an action claiming that they were entitled to go on with the work. Now the planning officer had been acting in this way over many years, as had other planning authorities. The Court of Appeal held that in the light of the planning officer's proved practice and of the fact that L had relied on his statement, the authority was to be held to it. There was, in that case, sufficient evidence to justify L thinking that the planning officer had authority to bind the council. 'Whether any one dealing with a planning officer [or any officer in an analogous position] can safely assume that the officer can bind his authority by anything that he says must depend on all the circumstances'.[16]

There is a second case where estoppel may operate. A planning (or other public) authority cannot waive, agree not to enforce, or be estopped from fulfilling a statutory duty but if it waives a *procedural requirement* relating to any application made to it for the exercise of its statutory powers, it may be estopped from relying on a lack of formality. An example is *Wells v Minister of Housing and Local Government*.[17] A person wishing to develop land had to apply for planning permission under section 23 of the relevant Act, or, if he was uncertain whether what he proposed to do involved 'development', he could apply for a determination of that question under section 53. Statutory procedures have to be followed in each case. Wells applied for planning permission. The council's surveyor replied by letter to the effect that permission was not required. When the work was done residents objected to the effect on the neighbourhood. The local authority served an enforcement notice. Wells argued that the surveyor's letter amounted to a determination under section 53 which could not be revoked. The minister (to whom an appeal had been made) argued that for there to be valid determination under that section the correct formalities should have been observed. The Court of Appeal, by a majority, found for Wells: the authority could waive mere technicalities in view particularly of the fact that other authorities had for many years followed that practice.[18] 'I take the law to be that a defect in procedure can be cured, and an irregularity can be waived, even by a public authority, so as to render valid that which would otherwise be invalid'. Russell LJ delivered a persuasive dissenting judgment. He emphasised the importance of the distinction between applying for planning permission and asking whether planning permission is necessary, and said, 'the local planning authority is not a free agent to waive statutory requirements in favour of (so to speak) an adversary; it is the guardian of the planning system'. Indignation that a long practice should be allowed to operate as a trap for the unwary landowner was he said, natural. 'The question is, however, one of law not to be decided by a thoroughly bad administrative practice'.

16 See *London Borough of Camden v Secretary of State for the Environment* (1993) 67 P & CR 59.
17 [1967] 2 All ER 1041, [1967] 1 WLR 1000.
18 See [1983] JPL 493.

The problem can be put this way. On the one hand we have the applicant relying in all honesty on the communication he gets from the authority. To permit estoppel prevents an injustice to the applicant. But there is a wider interest. In the *Lever* and *Wells* cases the public affected had an interest as genuine as that of the applicants. The authority has a duty, in considering planning applications, to take into account all material considerations, which includes the effect on neighbouring properties, amenity etc. If the authority is estopped by an act of its officers it is effectively prohibited from taking those considerations into account. And why should the applicant be released from the requirements of the statutory procedure because of his ignorance of them? In *Brooks and Burton Ltd v Secretary of State for the Environment* Lord Widgery CJ said:

There has been some advance in recent years of this doctrine of estoppel as applied to local authorities through their officers ... [The *Lever* case] no doubt is correct on its facts, but I would deprecate any attempt to expand this doctrine because it seems to me ... extremely important that local government officers should feel free to help applicants who come and ask them questions without all the time having the shadow of estoppel hanging over them and without the possibility of their immobilising their authorities by some careless remark which produces such an estoppel.[19]

In *Western Fish Products Ltd v Penwith District Council*[20] the Court of Appeal agreed with those observations.

(v) *No estoppel against change of policy*. The mere fact that one is the victim of a lawful change of (central or local) government policy does not enable one to raise an estoppel to prevent that change. Thus if government policy is such that one believes that the purchase of certain equipment would be advantageous financially and therefore buys it, one cannot simply because of that purchase, seek to estop a change of policy which will have the effect of making the purchase a waste of money. One is the victim of a change of government policy in arriving at which the government has acted on its view of where the public interest lies.[1]

Robertson's case

A case that raises a number of points and which can be conveniently considered here is *Robertson v Minister of Pensions*.[2] R, an Army officer was injured in December 1939. His entitlement to pension depended on whether his disability was 'attributable to military service'. His inquiry of the War Office brought the reply: 'Your case has been duly considered and your disability has been accepted as attributable to military service'. R, on the faith of that letter, did not take the steps he would otherwise

---

19 (1977) 75 LGR 285 at 296; revsd [1978] 1 All ER 733, [1977] 1 WLR 1294.
20 (1978) 38 P & CR 7, [1981] 2 All ER 204, CA.
 1 *Laker Airways Ltd v Department of Trade* [1977] QB 643, [1977] 2 All ER 182.
 2 [1949] 1 KB 227, [1948] 2 All ER 767.

have taken to get independent medical opinion. Entitlement to pension in respect of injuries suffered after September 1939 should in fact have been dealt with by the Minister of Pensions. That Ministry later decided that R's injury was not attributable to military service. The Pensions Appeal Tribunal upheld that decision and R appealed on the ground that the minister was bound by the War Office Letter.

Denning J said that the letter was on the face of it an authoritative decision intended to be binding and to be acted on. R's forebearing to get medical opinion made it binding. As between subjects, that was enough. But was the Crown, he asked, bound by estoppels? Yes: the doctrine that the Crown is not so bound had long been exploded.[3] But was the Minister of Pensions bound by the War Office letter? Yes: R reasonably thought that his claim would be dealt with by or through the War Office. That department did not refer him to the proper one; they assumed authority over the matter. R was entitled to assume that the War Office had consulted the Minister of Pensions. At this point Denning J said:

In my opinion if a government department in its dealing with a subject takes it upon itself to assume authority upon a matter with which it is concerned, he is entitled to rely upon it having the authority which it assumes. He does not know and cannot be expected to know, the limits of that authority.

He concluded his judgment on another point. The War Office was bound; as it was but an agent for the Crown, the Crown was bound, and as the Crown was bound, so were its other departments. The Minister's job was to administer the Royal Warrant (governing the payment of pensions) issued by the Crown, so he had to administer it so as to honour assurances given by or on behalf of the Crown.

This case has been the subject of a good deal of comment.[4] An important point was that R had no reason for thinking that the proper authority had not taken the decision. Even if he had consulted the document authorising the payment of such pensions he would have found nothing to lead him to suppose that the decision was not authoritative. And it has been pointed out that this was not the case of estoppel operating to supply the lack of legal capacity. The assurance given by the War Office was not relied on as binding that department in a matter in which it had no jurisdiction: the effect of the estoppel was that the legally-competent department (Pensions) was bound by an assurance given by the ostensibly competent department (the War Office).[5]

Particular attention has been paid to the principle enunciated by Denning J quoted above. It is not clear how it can be reconciled with the doctrine that statutory powers cannot be extended by an estoppel. It was

---

3 Nor could the Crown escape by way of the doctrine of executive necessity, see p 444 below.
4 Eg Trietel [1957] PL 321 at 335–339; Hogg *Liability of the Crown*, pp 126–129. As to one department binding another, see *R v Immigration Appeal Tribunal, ex p Venna Ahluwalia* [1979–80] Imm AR 1. And see Wikeley (1986) 15 ILJ 60.
5 Turpin *Government Contracts*, p 32.

authoritatively disapproved in *Howell v Falmouth Boat Construction Co Ltd*.[6] The company agreed to repair Howell's ship. They needed a licence to do so: it was a criminal offence not to have one. The work was started on the basis of an oral licence given by the proper official who later gave a written licence. When the company sued Howell for payment for work done he argued that the work was illegal insofar as it was done on the basis of an oral licence only. The Court of Appeal held, on an interpretation of the relevant Order, that an oral licence was sufficient. Denning LJ said that even if he was wrong about that, the repairer was entitled to rely on the oral licence the official had given him.

> Whenever government officers in their dealings with a subject, take on themselves to assume authority in a matter with which he is concerned, the subject is entitled to rely on their having the authority which they assume.

This, he said, was the principle he applied in *Robertson*.

The House of Lords while agreeing in the result with the Court of Appeal, disapproved of Lord Denning's view of the law. Lord Simonds said:

> I know of no such principle in our law nor was any authority for it cited. The illegality of the act is the same whether or not the actor has been misled by an assumption of authority on the part of a government officer however high or low in the hierarchy.

Lord Normand said:

> It is certain that neither a minister nor any subordinate officer of the Crown can by any conduct or representation bar the Crown from enforcing a statutory prohibition or entitle the subject to maintain that there has been no breach of it.

It will be noted that in the case in question it was a criminal offence to do the work without a licence. Those observations may therefore be limited to saying that the Crown cannot be estopped from bringing criminal proceedings.[7]

Res judicata

A *res judicata* is a final judicial decision pronounced by a judicial tribunal which disposes once and for all of the matter decided. Such matters cannot afterwards be re-litigated by the same parties: they are estopped *per rem judicatam* from doing so. Or we may put it this way: where a decision is binding it may operate (as a *res judicata*) to prevent further litigation of the issues. This is then *issue estoppel*. The doctrine rests on two principles: it is a general rule of public policy that there should be finality in litigation; and, an individual should not be vexed twice for the same cause. These

---

6   [1951] AC 837, [1951] 2 All ER 278.
7   See p 512 below.

principles are so important that they are not confined to private law, but can apply to adjudications in the field of public law.[8]

For *res judicata* to apply there must be a final decision of a *judicial tribunal*. The latter requirement does not limit it to the courts of law: it can apply to tribunals such as the industrial tribunals[9] and, for example, to the Chief Land Registrar[10] though a tribunal of limited jurisdiction cannot, by the operation of this doctrine, be allowed to determine the limits of its own jurisdiction.[1] The decision must be a *judicial decision* in the sense of a decision, determination or adjudication of some question of law or fact.[2] An administrative report made to a department of state solely for its information and guidance without any pretence to a judicial character is not such.[3] And the decision must be *final*, not in the sense that it is not appealable or subject to review by the courts, but that there is a finding on the matters in dispute.[4] Thus where an action was dismissed on the sole ground that the court had no jurisdiction, there was no decision on the matter in dispute, and thus no estoppel.[5]

It seems that *res judicata* is excluded where the situation being dealt with is continuing and not static. Thus it will apply to adjudication by an industrial tribunal on an equal pay claim so as to exclude successive claims, unless it can be shown that there is some appreciable difference in the facts on the two occasions, that is, that the situation was not static.[6] In *Society of Medical Officers of Health v Hope*[7] a local valuation court had ruled that the Society was exempt from rating. The property it occupied was nevertheless included in the next valuation list. The valuation officer did not contend that the Society's status had altered in any way. The House of Lords held that no estoppel arose as an assessment applied for the period of the current list only. Lord Keith's judgment emphasised the duty of the valuation officer to make a fresh valuation list every five years, and the interest of the rate payers. Referring to *Maritime Electric Co Ltd v General Dairies Ltd*[8] he said that a public officer such as this one could not be estopped from carrying out his statutory duties. In the following year this principle was applied to income tax assessments.[9]

Where a statutory scheme provides for or permits successive claims of applications to be made, a decision on a claim is not to be regarded as *res*

---

8 *Thrasyvoulou v Secretary of State for the Environment* [1990] 1 All ER 65, [1990] 2 WLR 1, HL.
9 For industrial tribunals see p 146 above; eg *Green v Hampshire County Council* [1979] ICR 861.
10 *Re Dances Way, West Town, Hayling Island* [1962] Ch 490, [1962] 2 All ER 42, CA.
1 *Crown Estates Comrs v Dorset County Council* [1990] 1 All ER 19, [1990] 2 WLR 89.
2 Spencer-Bower and Turner *The Doctrine of Res Judicata*, p 29.
3 Spencer-Bower and Turner, p 31.
4 Spencer-Bower and Turner, p 132. *Jowett v Earl of Bradford* [1977] 2 All ER 33, *Hanks v Ace High Productions Ltd* [1978] ICR 1155, EAT.
5 *Hines v Birkbeck College* [1991] 4 All ER 450.
6 *McLoughlin v Gordons (Stockport) Ltd* [1978] ICR 561.
7 [1960] AC 551, [1960] 1 All ER 317.
8 [1937] AC 610, [1937] 1 All ER 748. See p 221 above.
9 *Caffoor v Income Tax Comr, Colombo* [1961] AC 584, [1961] 2 All ER 436.

judicata. For example a succession of applications can be made for planning permission. If the first is refused, later ones must nevertheless be considered on their merits, and if a permission is granted but not acted on, a later application for permission for development inconsistent with that for which permission has been given must also be considered on its merits. But where on an appeal against an enforcement notice (in planning law) the inspector (or Secretary of State) decides that a particular use of land is a lawful use within the occupier's established rights, that decision creates an estoppel against a later notice if there is shown to be a sufficient identity of issue between the later and earlier appeals. It is a final decision between the parties.[20]

The doctrine is a product of the adversary system of litigation, so that it will not apply in an inquisitorial or investigatory system[11] nor is the report of a court of inquiry into a shipping accident conclusive of the question of the respective liabilities of the ships involved as the procedure at the inquiry does not provide for a properly contested dispute between the parties.[12] The local audit is such a system, and *res judicata* is inapplicable there.[13] Further it has no place in the field of administrative action on questions of immigration,[14] and it seems that it does not apply in judicial review, except perhaps in planning law enforcement cases.[15]

The administratee estopped

Estoppel may operate against the person dealing with the admini-stration. In *Cohen v Haringey London Borough Council*[16] the court was prepared to accept that C was estopped from arguing (on the basis of the invalidity of a notice served on him) that land in the possession of the authority was his, as he had encouraged the authority to believe that they could remain there subject to the payment to him of compensation. And where a developer gives, at a planning appeal inquiry, an undertaking which is embodied into a condition attached to the planning permission, the undertaking acts as an estoppel to prevent him from later saying that there is no power to require compliance with the undertaking.[17]

But in the following cases estoppel will not operate. Where the citizen has applied for and obtained a licence he is not estopped, by virtue of that application, from later saying that he did not need that licence, with the

10 *Thrasyvoulou v Secretary of State for the Environment* [1990] 1 All ER 65, [1990] 2 WLR 1, HL. But see *R v Wychavon DC, ex p Saunders* (1992) 64 P & CR 120: no estoppel as to merits when earlier decision was on procedure.
11 See Diplock LJ in *Thoday v Thoday* [1964] P 181 at 197, [1964] 1 All ER 341 at 351.
12 *The Speedlink Vanguard and the European Gateway* [1986] 3 All ER 554.
13 *The Local Government Auditor* para 103. For local audit see ch 16 below.
14 *R v Immigration Appeal Tribunal, ex p Cheema* [1982] Imm AR 124.
15 *R v Secretary of State for the Environment, ex p Hackney London Borough Council* [1984] 1 All ER 956, [1984] 1 WLR 592. *R v South Western Hospital Managers, ex p M* [1994] 1 All ER 161 at 171.
16 (1981) 42 P & CR 6.
17 *Augier v Secretary of State for the Environment* (1978) 38 P & CR 219.

effect that any condition attached to the licence is not binding.[18] And where a notice was served and the citizen failed to appeal against it on the merits, he was not estopped from later arguing that the notice was in any case unlawful.[19]

Revocability

The question considered here is whether an administrative authority has power to revoke, modify or change a decision it itself has made.[20] Statute may deal with the matter generally or specifically. The Interpretation Act 1978 provides that a power to make rules, regulations, byelaws or statutory instruments carries with it a power to revoke, amend or re-enact them.[1] The same Act provides[2] that where an Act confers a power or imposes a duty, it is implied, unless the contrary intention appears, that the power may be exercised or the duty performed 'from time to time as occasion requires'. The effect of this provision, it is said,[3] is to rebut the presumption that the power is exhausted by a single exercise.

The *statutory scheme* in question may expressly grant, or withhold, the power to revoke or change a decision. A number of tribunals are given the express power to review their own decisions.[4] The argument that the Crown cannot be estopped from claiming the correct duty payable on imported goods, failed in the face of an examination of the relevant statutes. In the result the decision of the customs officer as to the amount of duty payable could not be reviewed.[5] And a decision of an immigration officer to give indefinite leave to enter the United Kingdom, though based on a mistaken view of the immigrant's status (but not induced by his dishonesty), was irrevocable.[6]

What if there is *no governing statutory rule*? In *Livingstone v Westminster Corpn*,[7] the council abolished the plaintiff's office and resolved on the amount to be paid him as compensation. The district auditor thought this excessive and surcharged the members. The council thereon resolved to reduce the amount of compensation payable. The court held that they could not do this. But notice that this is rather a special case as the payment of the amount resolved by the council to be paid could, by the

---

18 *Newbury District Council v Secretary of State for the Environment* [1981] AC 578, [1980] 1 All ER 731.
19 *Swallow and Pearson v Middlesex County Council* [1953] 1 All ER 580, [1953] 1 WLR 422; *West Ham Corpn v C Benabo & Sons* [1934] 2 KB 253.
20 See Akehurst 'Revocation of Administrative Decisions' [1982] PL 613.
1 See p 101 above.
2 Section 12.
3 *Craies on Statute Law*, p 274. See Bennion *Statutory Interpretation*, p 284.
4 See p 168 above.
5 *Customs and Excise Comrs v Tan* [1977] AC 650, [1977] 1 All ER 432.
6 *R v Secretary of State for the Home Dept, ex p Ram* [1979] 1 All ER 687, [1979] 1 WLR 148.
7 [1904] 2 KB 109. And see *Gould v Bacup Local Board* (1881) 50 LJMC 44.

statute, be enforced as a specialty debt, that is as though the council had entered into an agreement under seal to pay. There can be no doubt that the resolution was unequivocal and irrevocable.

In *Re 56 Denton Road Twickenham*[8] the plaintiff's house was damaged by enemy action. She was told by the War Damage Commission that the house had been preliminarily classified as a 'total loss'. In 1945, after communication between the parties, she was told that classification had been reviewed, and the earlier notification cancelled, and was asked whether she agreed to reclassification as 'not a total loss'. The plaintiff informed the Commission of her agreement. She was entitled to more compensation on classification as 'not a total loss' than as 'total loss'. In 1946 she was told that it had been decided to revert to the 'total loss' classification. She sought a declaration that the 1945 decision was binding on the Commission. The issue, said Vaisey J, was whether that decision was another conditional and preliminary classification and so devoid of finality that no reliance ought to be placed upon it. He accepted the following proposition as representing the law, that where a body has conferred on it the duty of determining a question the determining of which affects the rights of subjects, 'such determination made and communicated in terms which are not expressly preliminary or provisional is final and conclusive, and cannot in the absence of express statutory power or the consent of the person affected be altered or withdrawn by that body'. The 1945 decision was therefore binding.

The defence had argued that they could alter a decision unless it had been acted on so as to create an estoppel. Vaisey J said:

It is, I think, admitted that if she had altered her position in reliance upon it, a case of estoppel would have been raised against the defendants. But I really cannot see that it ought to be denied its proper force and effect, quite apart from such a case.

As to the effect of his judgment, Vaisey J commented, 'This judgment can do no harm to the defendants. Let them mark every intimation of a determination of theirs as "provisional", "subject to alteration", "not to be relied upon" or words to that effect'.

Neither of those cases assisted the applicant in *R v Greater Manchester Police Authority, ex p Cushion*.[9] C, a policeman, had his disability assessed by a medical referee at 30%. This was, by the regulations, 'final', but on being asked to reconsider it on a different basis he re-assessed it at 10%. The first assessment was not, the court said, irrevocable, despite the 'final', as it had been arrived at on a misunderstanding of the regulations. (Did it mean disability for *any* employment, or only for employment as a policeman?) The court pointed out that in both cases referred to the court had said that if the decision which had been held to be irrevocable had been arrived at on the basis of a mistake the outcome might have been different.

8   [1953] Ch 51, [1952] 2 All ER 799: case note by Megarry 60 LQR 13.
9   [1991] COD 327.

Such a mistake was at issue in *Rootkin v Kent County Council*.[10] The council had a statutory *duty* to pay a child's travelling expenses where its home was more than three miles from school; and was *empowered* to pay them when it was under that distance. Mistakenly believing that the plaintiff's house was more than three miles distant the council issued a yearly bus ticket. When the mistake was discovered, the ticket was withdrawn. The plaintiff relied, in part, on *Re 56 Denton Road, Twickenham*: the council had made and communicated to her a determination which could not therefore be revoked. Lawton LJ rejected this. *Livingstone v Westminster Corpn* established, he said, that if a citizen is *entitled* to payment in certain circumstances and a local authority is given the duty of deciding whether the circumstances exist and if they do exist, of making the payment, that is a determination which is irrevocable. But here the plaintiff was, on the correct facts, not entitled to payment, only to the benefit of the exercise by the authority of a discretion.[11]

In *Re 56 Denton Road, Twickenham* the question was whether the 1945 decision was final or merely preliminary or conditional, and Vaisey J suggested how the administration might respond to his ruling. The administration might in some circumstances reasonably adopt procedures for giving what the applicant knows to be an informal ruling in an attempt to avoid the expense of a formal determination.[12] In other circumstances the question may be whether the administration had given merely advice (as to say a person's tax position) or a ruling.[13] Case C 446/K investigated by the Parliamentary Commissioner[14] draws attention to the need for care to be taken by the administration.

Notice that a decision that cannot be re-opened can be re-opened neither for the benefit nor to the detriment of the administratee.

Although in *Re 56 Denton Road, Twickenham* (above) reference is made to the communication of a decision, it would not seem that communication is in all cases necessary to render a decision non-revocable. For example, in *Livingstone v Westminster Corpn* (above) the question of the communication of the content of the council resolution would seem (in the admittedly special circumstances of the case) to be irrelevant. And *R v Criminal Injuries Compensation Board, ex p Tong*[15] shows that an award made by the Board becomes vested on the applicant as soon as the decision to give

10 [1981] 2 All ER 227, [1981] 1 WLR 1186. Case note by DGT Williams [1981] CLJ 198.
11 In *R v Dacorum BC, ex p Walsh* [1992] COD 125 the first decision was vitiated by fraud not mistake.
12 Third Report of the Parliamentary Commissioner, 1977–78, HC 246, p 87.
13 Third Report of the Parliamentary Commissioner 1976–77, HC 223, p 19. The Inland Revenue will in certain cases give an advance assurance to the taxpayer as to the tax repercussion of a proposed transaction. This will be binding. But (i) if it discovers it has made a mistake it can withdraw the assurance before the taxpayer has acted on it. (ii) it will not be bound where the taxpayer does not make full disclosure of the scheme, and (iii) if the taxpayer knows or ought to know (eg from Revenue circulars) that clearance is only given at a certain level within the Revenue, the Revenue will not be bound if it is not given at that level. *Matrix-Securities Ltd v IRC* [1994] 1 All ER 769, HL.
14 Ibid, p 102: see fn 7 at p 233 below.
15 [1977] 1 All ER 171, [1976] 1 WLR 1237, CA.

it is made, so that it is payable to his estate if he dies before the decision is communicated to him. The determination of the moment when a decision becomes effective for the purpose in question requires exami-nation of the particular scheme.[16]

Functus officio

A person is said to be functus officio when he has so acted as to exhaust the power he was exercising. He may not then further exercise that power. Some examples follow, firstly as the rule applies to *judicial* bodies.
– Where a judge finally disposes of the matter before him he is functus officio and neither he nor any other judge of equal jurisdiction may vary that order.[17] Rules of the Supreme Court however, permit mere clerical mistakes to be corrected by the Court at any time; this is the 'slip' rule, to be found in Ord 20, r 11.[18]
– Where under a now repealed provision of income tax law, the annual value of land was in dispute, the Income Tax Commissioners could cause a valuation to be made by a person of skill named by them, 'and the annual value shall be determined in accordance with that val-uation'. When the 'person of skill' completed his valuation he was functus officio, and could not therefore be questioned as to the principles on which he acted in his valuation.[19]
– On a claim for compensation on the revocation of planning permission, the Lands Tribunal assesses the amount necessary to compensate the claimant as at the date of the revocation order: that compensation is limited to the loss arising from the service of the revocation order. Having done that, the Tribunal is functus officio. It follows, it has been held, that the Tribunal cannot further compensate for loss arising from the fact that there has been delay in the payment of compensation.[20]
The functus officio rule may apply to *administrative* bodies.
– A local planning authority is functus officio when it has communicated its decision on a planning application to the applicant. It cannot later change its mind by for example adding conditions to the permission.[1] (It must however consider every application made to it, so that if it rejects an application and later receives a similar application it must consider it afresh on its merits.)

16 See eg *Griffiths v Secretary of State for the Environment* [1983] 2 AC 51, [1983] 1 All ER 439.
17 Re *VGM Holdings Ltd* [1941] 3 All ER 417; *R v British Coal Corpn (No 2), ex p Price* [1993] COD 323.
18 But for inapplicability of slip rule to election court, see *R v Cripps, ex p Muldoon* [1984] QB 686, [1984] 2 All ER 705.
19 *Lyons v Collins (Inspector of Taxes)* [1937] 1 KB 353, [1936] 3 All ER 788.
20 *Hobbs Quarries Ltd v Somerset County Council* [1975] RVR 219.
 1 *Heron Corpn Ltd v Manchester City Council* (1977) 33 P & CR 268. Cf the specific statutory power to revoke a permission.

- Likewise once the Secretary of State has given his decision on a planning application or appeal, he cannot reconsider or review it.[2] Further, it is doubtful whether a 'slip rule' applies in planning law so as to enable him to correct a clerical error as where there is a discrepancy between the formal order and the decision letter which accompanies and explains it.[3]
- Under the Education Act 1944 proposals by a local education authority to close a school require the approval of the Secretary of State. A decision by him on such a proposal cannot be changed except by the submission of a fresh proposal and a decision thereon by the Secretary of State.[4]
- The local government auditor has no power to re-open accounts previously audited and closed, his function as auditor having terminated. The functus officio rule does not however prevent an auditor from considering the legality of an item in accounts currently being audited simply because no action had been taken in relation to such an item in the audited accounts of previous years, for a new audit is a new duty.[5] The *res judicata* rule, we have noted, does not apply: that rule is aimed at parties to litigation, the functus officio is aimed at the deciding official.
- Under the Housing Act 1957 the Secretary of State can give a direction to a local authority to make a payment in respect of a house included in a compulsory purchase order but which is found on inspection by the Department to be well maintained. Where a decision against payment is made by the Department, it cannot on re-examination direct the authority to make a payment, but in the few cases where the Department has found grounds for reversing a decision, it has generally been able to arrange for the local authority to make an exgratia payment.[6]
- X appealed to the Secretary of State against the rejection of his complaint by a Family Practitioner Committee. An official said that under the regulations the appeal could not be entertained. In the light of further information he later said that it could. The Department's legal adviser then observed that the first letter had been so worded that it had to be taken as a formal decision on the appeal, and could not be reconsidered. The Department had inadvertently rendered itself functus officio.[7]

Once the Parliamentary Commissioner has sent the report of his investigation into a complaint to the complainant he is functus, and cannot re-open his investigation except on the basis of a further complaint.[8]

---

2 Third Report of the Parliamentary Commissioner 1974, HC 281, p 42.
3 *Preston Borough Council v Secretary of State for the Environment* [1978] JPL 548. Third Report of the Parliamentary Commissioner, 1988–89, Selected Cases, vol 2, p 8.
4 First Report of the Parliamentary Commissioner, 1974, HC 2, p 14.
5 *The Local Government Auditor*, para 103.
6 Third Report from the Parliamentary Commissioner, 1976–77, HC 223, p 48.
7 Third Report from the Parliamentary Commissioner, 1976–77, HC 223, p 102.
8 *R v Parliamentary Commissioner for Administration, ex p Dyer* [1994] 1 All ER 375. See Clothier, Vol 51, Medico-Legal Journal, 8 at 20.

Finally, for an order of prohibition to issue there must be something to which the prohibition can apply. If the person or body against whom prohibition is sought is functus officio, there will be nothing, and an appropriate alternative remedy might be certiorari.[9]

Retrospectivity

A statute is prospective: it relates to future events. It, or an order made under it, is said to be retrospective if it takes away or impairs any vested right acquired under existing laws or creates any new obligation or imposes a new duty or attaches a new disability in respect of transactions or considerations already past,[10] and 'It would be impossible now to doubt that the court is required to approach questions of statutory interpretation with a disposition, and in some cases a very strong disposition, to assume that a statute is not intended to have retrospective effect.'[11] This is because 'the basis of the rule [against retrospectivity] is simple fairness' so that if for example, it changes the legal character of a person's acts after an event, this may be very unfair and the court 'would look very hard' at a statute which has this effect to make sure that that is what Parliament really intended – which it could of course, by sufficiently clearly expressed words.[12]

In *Secretary of State for Social Security v Tunnicliffe*[13] T received in good faith overpaid benefit. At that time liability to repay was determined by the test of 'due care and diligence' on her part. By the time the department sought repayment a new test had been introduced which turned on misrepresentation or non-disclosure. Was the new test (which might in most cases be stricter) to be applied? It was: to apply it was not unfair to people claiming to retain money to which they were not entitled. However in *Plewa v Chief Adjudication Officer*[14] the House of Lords interpreted the same provisions the opposite way, as it found some unfairness in their operation which had escaped everyone's notice in the earlier case.

Suppose a statute entitles a recipient to a benefit, the amount being calculated by reference to past events. In *Master Ladies Tailors Organisation v Minister of Labour*[15] a statutory order gave employees rights to

---

9 *Estate and Trust Agencies (1927) Ltd v Singapore Improvement Trust* [1937] AC 898, [1937] 3 All ER 324. For prohibition see p 391 below.
10 Maxwell *Interpretation of Statutes*, p 216; *Craies on Statute Law*, ch 16. But see Driedger *Statutes: Retroactive Retrospective Reflections*, 56 Can Bar Reve 264.
11 *L'Office Cherifian ... v Yamashita-Shinnihon Steamship Co Ltd* [1994] 1 All ER 20 at 29, Lord Mustill.
12 Eg War Damage Act 1965. Provision substituting fixed civil penalty for criminal liability retrospective in *Customs and Excise Comrs v Shingleton* [1988] STC 190.
13 [1991] 2 All ER 712.
14 [1994] 3 All ER 323, [1994] 3 WLR 317.
15 [1950] 2 All ER 525. The administration is not infrequently faced with problems of the retrospective application of welfare and social security benefits. Complaints of the refusal to act retrospectively have been investigated by the Parliamentary Commissioner.

holiday pay, the amount to be assessed by reference to periods before the order was made. The employers argued that it was ultra vires for retrospectivity, but a statute 'is not properly called [retrospective] because a part of the requisites for its action is drawn from time antecedent to its passing'. Thus the employer's liability to pay was prospective, the amount being determined by reference to events before that time.

When a statute gives power to investigate certain activities or penalise certain conduct, can events that happened before the Act was passed be taken into account? This depends on the interpretation of the Act.

For the doubtful propriety of retrospective delegated legislation see the reference to the Joint Scrutiny Committee at p93 above, and to Schedule 2 of the European Communities Act 1972 at p 66.

Sabally and N'Jie v HM A-G[16] was a special case. The legality of a statutory order in council retrospectively validating an electoral register (and hence an election) was upheld. The Court of Appeal took the view that the Act in question intended to give the Crown the plenary powers enjoyed by a legislature and it could therefore legislate retrospectively. But it is not clear that the same attitude would be taken towards ministerial powers to legislate. Further the consequences of invalidating the order would in that case have been serious.

Partial validity and severability

Suppose a legislative instrument made under delegated powers is good in part, and bad in part – partly intra, partly ultra, vires: is it possible for the bad to be excised, for the instrument to be 'severed', so that the good remains and is enforceable, or will the bad infect the whole (like the curate's egg),[17] and pull down the good with it? It *is* possible, provided certain tests are met, and always bearing in mind that it is not the court's role to re-write the minister's instrument.

The principles were laid out by the House of Lords in *Director of Public Prosecutions v Hutchinson*.[18] The simplest case is where a statutory instrument contains a number of separate clauses, one of which is ultra vires: 'if the remaining clauses enact free-standing provisions which were intended to operate and are capable of operating independently of the offending clause, there is no reason why those clauses should not be upheld and enforced.'[19] The instrument may in such a case be said to be *textually* severable – the 'blue-pencil' test. In such a case the instrument also passes the test of *substantial* severability, that is, the *substance* of what remains after severance is essentially unchanged in its legislative purpose operation and effect. However, said the House of Lords, to insist always on the test of textual severability may have the unreasonable consequence

16 [1965] 1 QB 273, [1964] 3 All ER 377.
17 (1895) 109 *Punch* 222.
18 [1990] 2 AC 783, [1990] 2 All ER 836.
19 Ibid at 804 and 839 respectively.

of defeating subordinate legislation of which the *substantial purpose* was clearly intra vires, when by some oversight or misunderstanding the instrument goes beyond the scope of the powers given in the Act. In that case the courts may in some measure modify the text (ex hypothesi the mere excision is not possible) in order to achieve severance – but only where it is satisfied that it is effecting no change in the substantial purpose and effect of the instrument.

Take the earlier case of *Dunkley v Evans*.[20] A statutory instrument prohibited fishing in an area defined in the order as within a line drawn between certain map references. The area included a stretch of sea to which the parent Act did not extend. The appellant was convicted of fishing in a part of the prohibited area to which the Act *did* extend. He argued that as the order included an area to which the Act did not extend, the whole order was bad. It would seem that textual severability was not possible; that if the conviction was to stand the court would in effect be redrawing the line defining the prohibited area. However, the High Court held that severability was not confined to cases where 'judicial surgery' was possible (in an action for a declaration the court could have made a declaration that the order did not extend to the excess area in question). The conviction was thus upheld.

In *DPP v Hutchinson* Lord Bridge accepted that the textual severability test could not be applied to the instrument in *Dunkley v Evans*, but thought that to strike down the whole would have been unreasonable: the legislative purpose and effect of the prohibition of fishing in the large area of sea was unaffected by the inadvertent addition of a small area to which the power to prohibit did not extend. (Lord Lowry on the other hand, agreeing that that case produced 'a very sensible result' thought it could be justified by the textual severability test, 'by reference to an imaginary map based on the co-ordinates given in the impugned order.')

In *DPP v Hutchinson* itself an Act authorised the Secretary of State to make byelaws regulating the use of land appropriated for military purposes provided that the byelaws did not 'prejudicially affect any right of common'. The minister made byelaws relating to the Greenham Common (cruise missile) base by which it was an offence to do a number of things set out in twelve paragraphs, including entering the base, damaging the perimeter fence and other related matters, and also to make a false statement to gain entry, obstruct a constable etc. H appealed against her conviction for entering the base on the ground that the byelaws were invalid for prejudicing rights of common. (There were 62 commoners of whom H was not one). The Divisional Court held that though the byelaws were ultra vires for interfering with rights of common, they could be severed *in the sense that* they could be enforced against all except persons entitled to exercise the rights of common. (This, note, could not have been done by wielding a blue pencil, but by writing into the byelaws several exceptions.) The court said that severance was possible in those circum-

20 [1981] 3 All ER 285, [1981] 1 WLR 522.

stances provided the court was satisfied, which it said it was, that the minister, if he had appreciated the limit of his powers, would have gone on to make byelaws which preserved rights of common but affected everyone else.

The House of Lords had no doubt that this was wrong. Textual severance (as explained above) was impossible in that the exercise simply could not be carried out. Nor could the byelaws survive the substantiality test: their substantial purpose was to prohibit access; the prohibitions which achieved this in the byelaw were ultra vires; the paragraphs which may have been valid (eg obstructing a constable) were ancillary to them. Byelaws rewritten to permit free access to commoners would be a wholly different character (contrast *Dunkley v Evans*), nor should one speculate what the minister might have done. The conviction was therefore quashed.

The principles were applied in *Woolwich Equitable Building Society v Inland Revenue Commissioners*.[1] One paragraph of one regulation was ultra vires. Did this invalidate the whole regulation? The House of Lords held that the textual severance of the paragraph would have been possible in the grammatical sense that what was left would not have been altered. But its deletion would have so altered the substance of what was left as to make the regulation in question substantially different from what it was before deletion and it could not be assumed that Parliament would have enacted the regulation in its altered form.

The outcome appears to be as follows. Where textual excision can be done and means no change in substance, severance is possible; where it can be done but means a change in substance, severance is not possible; where excision cannot be done, but the text can be modified without affecting the purpose of the instrument, severance is possible.

It will be recalled that the discussion so far relates to the partial invalidity of a 'legislative instrument'. The problem of partial invalidity may arise in connection with other (non-legislative) documents of a public nature. In *Hutchinson* the House doubted whether the decisions on severability in connection with those other documents were relevant to the question of the severability of legislative documents. Thus in *Thames Water Authority v Elmbridge Borough Council*[2] what was in issue was the validity of a resolution passed by a local authority appropriating land. The land to which the resolution applied included a small area which the authority had no power to appropriate. The resolution was held to be a valid exercise of the power in relation to land which the authority had power to appropriate. In *Hutchinson* the House commented: 'It is one thing to determine the effect of an exercise of statutory power ... which is exercised once and for all [as in the *Thames Water* case]. It is quite another to decide whether an instrument purporting to make a law to which all will be subject so long as the law operated, was a valid exercise of the law-maker's limited power'.[3] The House did not indicate what are the

1 [1991] 4 All ER 92.
2 [1983] QB 570, [1983] 1 All ER 836.
3 [1990] 2 AC 783 at 810, [1990] 2 All ER 836 at 844.

principles in the former case, but noted that all that was involved in *Thames Water* was the interpretation of the resolution.

The following seem to be once-and-for-all cases. In *R v Secretary of State for Transport, ex p Greater London Council*[4] it was held that where the power is to *determine a single sum of money* to be paid, if this is shown to be wrongly calculated, the court cannot, by severing the bad items from the good, in effect recalculate the sum to be paid (that is, rewrite the demand). The whole determination is invalid. Where an authority is *empowered to demand information* the inclusion of an unauthorised demand invalidates the whole where the return is 'one and indivisible' – contrast *Potato Marketing Board v Merricks*.[5] The same principle is at stake – is the whole bad? – when a licence is granted subject to a condition and the condition is ultra vires. Does the licensee get his licence free of the condition, or does the condition infect the licence so that it too is ultra vires? In *Hall & Co Ltd v Shoreham-by-Sea UDC*[6] the condition attached to the planning permission was fundamental to the permission which would not have been granted without it. The unreasonableness of the condition therefore pulled down the permission with it.

A further aspect of this problem is where it is argued, not that an instrument is void as against the whole world, but only as against the complainant. In *Hotel and Catering Industry Training Board v Automobile Proprietary Ltd*.[7] the minister was empowered to establish by order boards for persons employed 'in any activities of industry or commerce'. The order gave the Board jurisdiction over, inter alia, members' clubs. The House of Lords held that such clubs are not engaged in the activities in question and that the order was invalid insofar as it purported to apply to them. Severability was not referred to but in *Hutchinson* Lord Bridge said that the order there was severable. In *Agriculture Horticultural and Forestry Industry Training Board v Aylesbury Mushrooms Ltd*[8] the minister was required, before making the order setting up the board, to consult representative organisations. He failed to consult mushroom growers. This had the consequence that the order did not apply to them, (with the result that the levy imposed on them by the board was not payable). Severability was not raised, nor would it seem possible to have carried out that exercise, though Lord Bridge thought that if the argument had been raised, the outcome might have been different.

---

4 [1985] 3 All ER 300.
5 [1958] 2 QB 316, [1958] 2 All ER 538.
6 [1964] 1 All ER 1, [1964] 1 WLR 240. See also *R v North Hertfordshire District Council, ex p Cobbold* [1985] 3 All ER 486.
7 [1969] 2 All ER 582, [1969] 1 WLR 697 HL.
8 [1972] 1 All ER 280, [1972] 1 WLR 190.

Chapter 8

The misuse of power

All powers, public and private, are liable to be misused. The question here is what constitutes a misuse of public power such that the courts, on application being made to them, will intervene? Institutions other than the courts are also concerned with the misuse of power, and their role is considered in other chapters.

As we have seen, the ultra vires doctrine confines public authorities to those powers granted by statute. But the courts are concerned to see not only whether the power exercised exists, but whether it has been exercised in accordance with certain principles. What those principles are is the subject of this chapter.

Associated Provincial Picture Houses Ltd v Wednesbury Corpn

A convenient place to start is the decision of the Court of Appeal in *Associated Provincial Picture Houses Ltd v Wednesbury Corpn*[1] (hereafter referred to as *Wednesbury*). The case is one of the most frequently referred to in administrative law. Lord Greene's judgment – with which the other members of the court agreed – has been frequently approved of and relied on. It did not purport to create new law but gathered together already established principles. The facts were that the Sunday Entertainments Act 1932 gave local authorities power to allow cinemas to open on Sundays 'subject to such conditions as the authority thinks fit to impose'. Wednesbury Corporation gave the plaintiff permission subject to the condition that no children under fifteen should be allowed in, with or without an adult. The plaintiff brought an action for a declaration that the condition was ultra vires.

In his judgment Lord Greene emphasised two points: first, that the statute had given local authorities a power to impose conditions which was, in its terms, without limitation; second, that the statute did not

1 [1948] 1 KB 223, [1947] 2 All ER 680, CA.

provide an *appeal* from the decision of the local authority on any ground. (If it had provided an appeal, then the court could have reconsidered the *merits* of the authority's decision, and if it disagreed with it replaced it with its own. But it did not.) What then was the court's function? It was to rule on the *legality* of the decision. The courts can, he said, only interfere with an act of executive authority if it be shown that in exercising its discretion the authority has 'contravened the law'. Having established that fundamental point – the court's function – the next question is: What principles are to be applied in deciding whether the authority has acted lawfully? Lord Greene said:

If, in the statute conferring the discretion, there is to be found expressly or by implication matters which the authority exercising the discretion ought to have regard to, then in exercising the discretion it must have regard to those matters. Conversely, if the nature of the subject matter and the general interpretation of the Act make it clear that certain matters would not be germane to the matter in question, the authority must disregard those irrelevant collateral matters. [Let us call these the 'relevancy rules'].

Lord Greene then observed that in the cases various expressions have been used relating to the sort of things authorities must not do, and continued:

I am not sure myself whether the permissible grounds of attack cannot be defined under a single head. It has been perhaps a little bit confusing to find a series of grounds set out. Bad faith, dishonesty – these of course stand by themselves – unreasonableness, attention given to extraneous circumstances, disregard of public policy and things like that have all been referred to, according to the facts of individual cases, and being matters relevant to the question. If they cannot all be confined under one head, they at any rate, I think, overlap to a very great extent. For instance, we have heard in this case a great deal about the meaning of the word 'unreasonable'.

Then Lord Greene goes on at this point to consider how far the possible 'one head' of attack might be said to be 'unreasonableness':

Lawyers familiar with the phraseology commonly used in relation to exercise of statutory discretions often use the word 'unreasonable' in a rather comprehensive sense. It has frequently been used and is frequently used as a general description of the things that must not be done. For instance, a person entrusted with a discretion must, so to speak, direct himself properly in law. He must call his own attention to the matters which he is bound to consider. He cannot exclude from his consideration matters which are irrelevant to what he has to consider. If he does not obey these rules, he may truly be said, and often is said, to be acting 'unreasonably'. Similarly, there may be something so absurd that no sensible person could ever dream that it lay within the powers of the authority. Warrington LJ in *Short v Poole Corpn* gave the example of the red-haired teacher, dismissed because she had red hair. That is unreasonable in one sense [by which Lord Greene may have meant 'absurd']. In another sense it is taking into consideration extraneous matters [viz breaching the relevancy rules]. It is so unreasonable that it might almost be described as being done in bad faith; and in fact all these things run into one another.

Thus 'unreasonable' may be used in more than one sense, including breach of the relevancy rule. Now in this case the plaintiff had not argued that the council had taken an irrelevant matter into account (and Lord Greene said that it had been justified in taking children's physical and moral health into account), so that in that one sense of 'unreasonable' it had not acted unreasonably. But the attack was that the council's decision was 'unreasonable' treating that 'as an independent ground of attack, and Lord Greene indicated that even where an authority has observed the 'relevancy rules', a decision may still be 'unreasonable', when he said:

It may still be possible to say that, although the local authority have kept within the four corners of the matters which they ought to consider they may nevertheless have come to a conclusion so unreasonable that no reasonable authority could ever come to it.

But:

To prove a case of that kind would require something overwhelming, and, in this case the facts do not come anywhere near anything of that kind.

We now consider separately the various 'grounds of attack', not treating them as all falling under the head of 'unreasonableness', but treating that as an independent ground as in *Wednesbury* itself. But before doing so the following is to be noted.

Wednesbury must not be applied indiscriminately. In the first place, it is relevant (obviously) only where the challenge is on the basis of the *Wednesbury* principles. If therefore the challenge is on the ground, say, that the body in question had acted ultra vires in the narrow sense, or had fettered its discretion, or improperly transferred its function to another body, reference to *Wednesbury* (and therefore, for example, to unreasonableness) would be inappropriate.[2] Second, the *Wednesbury* principle is concerned with the extent to which the court in its *supervisory* or *review* capacity can interfere with an administrative discretion. It is not therefore applicable where a court is dealing with an *appeal* from an order by a lower court made in the exercise of a judicial discretion.[3] It is however applicable to the review of a decision by a magistrate's court exercising the *administrative* function of condemning food as unfit for human consumption.[4]

Relevant considerations

Statutory requirements

Before considering the relevancy rule as laid down in *Wednesbury*, first notice that it is common for statute, when granting a discretionary power,

2 See eg *R v Police Complaints Board, ex p Madden* [1983] 2 All ER 353, [1983] 1 WLR 447.

3 *D v M* [1983] Fam 33, [1982] 3 All ER 897. See *Brind v Secretary of State* [1991] 1 All ER 720 at 738c.

4 *R v Archer, ex p Barrow Lane & Ballard Ltd* (1984), 82 LGR 361. The *Wednesbury* principles will also be applicable where the court is exercising a statutory appeal function and the statute in effect so provides: see *Ashbridge Investments Ltd v Minister of Housing and Local Government* [1965] 3 All ER 371, [1965] 1 WLR 1320.

to indicate the limits within which it is to be exercised by stating the matters to which the authority is to have regard in exercising it. For example, when considering an application for planning permission the local authority 'shall have regard to the provisions of the development plan ... and to any other material considerations'.[5] Or an authority may be required to 'have proper regard' to certain matters,[6] or to have certain considerations 'especially in mind',[7] to 'give first consideration' to certain matters;[8] to 'take full account' of advice from a stated source,[9] or have regard to certain matters and 'not to have regard to any other matters'.[10] (The obligation to have regard to a certain matter does not mean that one is to 'slavishly adhere' to it; [11] it means that one must consider it; it does not mean that one cannot consider also other relevant matters, rather that it must be on the list of things one considers. However, in all cases care must be taken to observe the precise wording of the statute in question, as these examples show.)

What considerations are relevant?

To say that relevant factors must be taken into account is easy enough. To know what factors are relevant in any particular case when they are not expressly stated in the Act may not be so easy. In *Findlay v Secretary of State for the Home Department*[12] Lord Scarman, referring to the statutory rules about releasing prisoners on licence, said, 'The statute gives little and at best only indirect guidance as to the factors which the Secretary of State has to consider in the exercise of his power to grant parole or as to the weight to be given to them.'

- A rating authority has discretion to refund overpaid rates. The statute gives no indication of the relevant considerations. In *R v Tower Hamlets London Borough Council, ex p Chetnik Developments Ltd*[13] the House of Lords said that the authority had to have regard to the purpose for which the discretion had been conferred (to enable it to redress an injustice) and that neither the financial circumstances of the over-paying ratepayer nor the financial constraints to which the authority was subject had any relevance to the exercise of the discretion.
- What are the factors a local authority must take into account in deciding whether to evict a tenant? The fact that he has fallen into arrears with his rent is obviously relevant. But this is not the only relevant factor, so that an authority should not automatically evict

5 Town and Country Planning Act 1990, s 70(2).
6 Nurses, Midwives and Health Visitors Act 1979, s 2(6).
7 Ibid, s 5(6).
8 Children Act 1975, s 59.
9 Rent (Agriculture) Act 1976, s 28(7).
10 Price Commission Act, s 2(1).
11 *Simpson v Edinburgh Corpn* 1960 SC 313. For 'shall have regard to but shall not be bound by' see Employment Act 1982, Sch 1, para 7.
12 [1985] AC 318, [1984] 3 All ER 801.
13 [1988] AC 858, sub nom *Tower Hamlets London Borough Council v Chetnik Developments Ltd*, [1988] 1 All ER 961.

such a tenant. Also relevant is the authority's statutory duty to provide temporary accommodation for the homeless (including those evicted for non-payment of rent), and the possibility that the payment of arrears could be secured by an attachment of earnings order (if there are any earnings).[14]

– What factors can a local authority take into account in deciding whether to make a discretionary grant to attend University?[15]
– Can a University take into account potential public disorder in deciding whether to grant permission to hold a meeting in the University?[16]
– What are the relevant considerations in deciding whether to schedule a monument as of national importance?[17]
– Can a local authority take into account its financial situation in deciding the amount of housing benefit to pay to a claimant?[18]
– What matters is a chief constable entitled to take into account in revoking a shotgun certificate?[19]
– And finally, can the Secretary of State take into account a student's inertia in failing to apply for variation of leave to enter the UK?[20]

What constitutes a breach of the relevancy rule?
The requirement is that a relevant factor must, and an irrelevant factor must not, be taken into account. But a factor is not 'not taken into account' unless the decision is affected by it, and to *know* of an irrelevant factor is not the same thing as to be affected by it. Thus it is not enough to prove that an authority knew of an irrelevant factor. If the court is satisfied that the decision was not affected by it, it will not intervene.[1]

If a decision is challenged on the ground that a relevant factor was not taken into account, the factor has to be particularised, the Court of Appeal has indicated.[2] The authority may then respond by showing, by reference to its relevant documents, that it was taken into account. Where a deciding body is required to take a particular factor into account, and its reasoned decision does not specify that factor (so that it appears not to have been taken into account), the court may be prepared to infer that it was taken into account, as where it was in the highest degree improbable that it was not.[3]

14 *Bristol District Council v Clark* [1975] 3 All ER 976, [1975] 1 WLR 1443. Buxton 39 MLR 470.
15 *R v Lancashire County Council, ex p Huddleston* [1986] 2 All ER 941. See Bradley [1986] PL 508.
16 *R v University of Liverpool, ex p Caesar-Gordon* [1990] All ER 821.
17 *R v Secretary of State for the Environment, ex p Rose Theatre Trust Co* [1990] 1 All ER 754.
18 *R v Brent London BC, ex p Connery* [1990] 2 All ER 353.
19 *Chief Constable of Essex v German* [1991] COD 385.
20 *R v Secretary of State for the Home Dept, ex p Animashann* [1990] Imm App R 70.
1 Per the Court of Appeal in the *Wellcome Foundation Ltd v Secretary of State for Social Security* [1988] 2 All ER 684, [1988] 1 WLR 635.
2 *Cannock Chase District Council v Kelly* [1978] 1 All ER 152, [1978] 1 WLR 1.
3 *Davies v London Borough of Hammersmith and Fulham* [1981] JPL 682.

The relevancy test as laid down in *Wednesbury* is that the body in question must take account of relevant factors and ignore irrelevant factors. If it did, that is the end of the case (as Lord Greene expressly said) as far as *that* test is concerned. The body has then acted 'within the four corners of its jurisdiction', and it is not for the court to interfere. If it did, it would be substituting its discretion on the merits for that of the authority, whereas it is properly concerned only with legality.

There is, however, another test of legality and that is unreasonableness. Lord Greene indicated that even where an authority has observed the 'relevancy rule' a decision may still be unreasonable, which in this context means that some error of law was made in the weighing of the various factors. In *West Glamorgan County Council v Rafferty*[4] the council took proceedings to evict gipsies from land it owned which it required for development. In doing so it took relevant factors into account, including its need for the land and its long-standing breach of its duty to provide accommodation for gipsies. It was in weighing those factors that the council went wrong: in doing that the council was not free to discount its breach of the duty Parliament had put on it and thus acted unreasonably.

A local authority's fiduciary duty

In *Prescott v Birmingham Corpn*[5] Jenkins LJ said: 'Local authorities are not, of course, trustees for their ratepayers, but they do, we think, owe an analogous fiduciary duty to their ratepayers in relation to the application of finance contributed by the latter.' It followed that the council could not make a gift of free travel on its buses to old people simply because they thought that that class of persons should on philanthropic grounds be so benefited. In *Roberts v Hopwood*[6] Lord Atkinson had spoken of a local authority as standing somewhat in the position of trustees or managers of the ratepayers' property. In the GLC *Fare's Fair*[7] case the House of Lords approved of the principle stated by Jenkins LJ. One aspect of that case has already been related. A further aspect was that the GLC's power to make grants to the LTE was also subject to its fiduciary duty, as a local authority, to its ratepayers, and to its obligation to balance that duty to transport users when making a grant. The GLC's decision to reduce fares by twenty-five per cent not only transferred the £69m cost of doing so from transport users to ratepayers, but also, because of a consequent loss of support grant, required the ratepayers to find a further £50m without any compensatory improvement in transport services. This was a 'thrift-less' use of ratepayers' money, and a breach of GLC's fiduciary duty.

In *Pickwell v Camden London Borough Council*[8] Ormrod LJ said that both in *Prescott* and the *Fare's Fair* case the existence of the fiduciary

4   [1987] 1 All ER 1005, [1987] 1 WLR 457.
5   [1955] Ch 210, [1954] 3 All ER 698.
6   [1925] AC 678.
7   [1983] 1 AC 768, [1982] 1 All ER 129; see p 200 above. See also p 181 above for 'trust'.
8   [1983] QB 962, [1983] 1 All ER 602.

duty was (no more than) a relevant factor to be taken into account in determining the extent of an authority's power: it did not (as critics had feared) 'open up a route by which the courts can investigate and, if thought appropriate, interfere with any exercise of their discretionary powers by local authorities. This would completely undermine the principle of the *Wednesbury* case ...' Forbes J spoke of the authority's duty to hold the balance between its fiduciary duty to the ratepayers and its duty to provide a wide range of services for its inhabitants; to deliberately tip the balance one way or the other would be wrong, whether this be regarded as taking into account irrelevant factors or as *Wednesbury* unreasonable. 'One way or the other' it will be noted: so that an improper delay in taking action is not legally justified simply because the intent or effect is to benefit the ratepayers.[9] The fiduciary duty to ratepayers is not thus an overriding consideration but one of the relevant considerations to be borne in mind when action affecting their interests is taken. (The courts have not imposed on *central* government a fiduciary duty to taxpayers.)

Improper purpose

Powers are given for achievement of certain ends. Thus a power must be used only for the purpose for which it was given; or, must not be used for a purpose for which it was not given.

How are we to know for what purpose a power is given?

(i) The statute may *expressly state* what that purpose is. In *Sydney Municipal Council v Campbell*[10] the council had statutory power to acquire compulsorily land required for 'carrying out improvements in or re-modelling any portion of the city'. It was restrained from using that power to acquire land for the purpose of benefiting from an anticipated increase in the value of the land.

A body ... authorised to take land compulsorily for specified purposes, will not be permitted to exercise its powers for different purposes ...

and,

where [proceedings] are attacked upon this ground, the party impeaching those proceedings must of course prove that the council, though professing to exercise its powers for the statutory purpose, is in fact employing them in furtherance of some ulterior object.

In this case no plan for improvement or remodelling the land in question was ever considered by the council.

---

9 *Simpsons Motor Sales (London) Ltd v Hendon Corpn* [1962] 3 All ER 75 at 81, per Upjohn LJ, aff'd [1964] AC 1088, [1963] 2 All ER 484. 'Fiduciary' point failed in *R v Inner London Education Authority, ex p Westminster City Council* p 250 below.
10 [1925] AC 338. See *R v Somerset County Council, ex p Fewings* (1995) Independent, 17 March.

In *Sadler v Sheffield Corpn*[11] the corporation had power to dismiss teachers on educational grounds. It was in financial difficulties. It selected teachers for dismissal, not on the ground of their fitness as teachers, but for financial reasons. How was this proved? By reference to what the chairman of the education committee had said at a meeting of the committee; by the fact that the committee never had before it any information about the selected teachers on which they could form any conclusion whether educational grounds existed for their dismissal; and it was left to an official to find educational grounds (to try to justify dismissals taken on unlawful grounds). (Another way of looking at this is that the only relevant considerations were educational, and that financial considerations were irrelevant.)

(ii) The purpose for which a power is given may not be directly expressed in the statute, in which case it will have to be *inferred* from an examination of the statutory scheme. *Padfield v Minister of Agriculture, Fisheries and Food*[12] is an instructive example. Under the milk marketing scheme milk producers had to sell their milk to the Milk Marketing Board, which fixed the price to be paid to them. A different price was paid to producers in each of the regions of England and Wales. One reason for this was that the cost of transporting milk from farm to consumer varied as between regions. The differential between the south-east and the far west regions was 1.19d per gallon. Producers in the south-east region contended that the differential should be increased. As the Board consists of representatives of the regions and acts by a majority of its members, the south-east producers had been unable to get the board to favour their proposals.

However, the Act provided two methods by which persons aggrieved by the board's action could seek a remedy. It was common ground that the first method, arbitration, was inappropriate. The other method was that provided by section 19 of the Act. This gave the minister the power to appoint a committee to report on a complaint to him; on the basis of that report the minister could amend or revoke the scheme. Padfield (one of the members of the south-east regional committee) made a complaint on the question of differentials to the minister and asked him to refer it to the committee for investigation. This the minister refused to do. Padfield applied for a mandamus.

A reason the minister gave for not referring the complaint was that it seemed to him to be a kind which properly fell to be dealt with through the normal democratic machinery of the scheme. In this the minister was mistaken the House of Lords said. The very existence of section 19 showed an intention to provide some protection against the normal working of the scheme. (Padfield, as we have seen, had been outvoted on the Board.) This reason showed, the House said, that the minister had misunderstood the duties imposed on him, and had failed to exercise his discretion in a manner consistent with the intention implicit in the Act. He had not

11 [1924] 1 Ch 483.
12 [1968] AC 997, [1968] 1 All ER 694.

understood the purpose for which the power had been given to him. By misunderstanding what was required, the minister had in effect thwarted or run counter to (as Lord Reid put it), the policy and objects of the Act, and a power can be used only to further the purposes of the Act. The minister was therefore required (by mandamus) to 'consider the complaint according to law'. (He then referred the complaint to the committee which supported Padfield. But the minister rejected its recommendations in the interests of milk producers as a whole.)

(iii) It may be impossible to discover the purpose. In *R v Secretary of State for the Environment, ex p Newprop*[13] the respondent rejected a request to exercise his power to 'call-in' a planning application. It was argued that this decision thwarted the purpose of the Act, but the court found that no purpose could be gleaned from the Act which could be said to be thwarted by the defendant's decision.

It should be said that the *Padfield* argument fails more often than not.[14]

An (earlier) leading (and notorious) case on improper motive is *Roberts v Hopwood*.[15] The Poplar Borough Council acting under the power to pay its employees 'such wages as [the council] think fit' decided on a minimum wage of £4 a week. This was substantially in excess of the national average wage for similar workers, especially women. The district auditor acting under his statutory duty to 'disallow every item of account contrary to law' surcharged the councillors the sum of £5,000. The House of Lords held that the council had indeed acted 'contrary to law'. It had in effect used its power to pay wages for an improper purpose, namely, to make gifts. It will be noted that as it had used its power for an improper purpose it had inevitably not allowed itself to be guided by the relevant considerations (it seems that this must always be the case, as in *Sadler v Sheffield Corpn*), which included the cost of living, wages paid by national and other local authorities and awards of joint industrial councils.[16] In the *Wednesbury* case Lord Greene said that *Roberts v Hopwood*, which was relied on, was a quite different class of case. The sum agreed to be paid was fixed, he said, by reference to irrelevant and in disregard of relevant considerations – whereas in *Wednesbury* regard had not been had to irrelevant considerations.

13 [1983] JPL 386.
14 As for example *Brind v Secretary of State* [1991] 1 All ER 720, *Freight Transport Association Ltd v London Boroughs Transport Cttee* [1991] 3 All ER 915, *R v Secretary of State for Health, ex p US Tobacco International Inc* [1992] 1 All ER 212, *R v Secretary of State for Trade, ex p Chris International Foods* (1983) Times 22 July: banana imports prohibited under 'war-time' legislation. *Re Kay* [1991] COD 63.
15 [1925] AC 578. For background see Keith-Lucas 'Poplarism' [1962] PL 52; Jones 'Herbert Morrison and Polarism' [1973] PL 11.
16 This was the emphasis given to *Roberts v Hopwood* by the court in *Pickwell v Camden London Borough Council* (above) where it was alleged by the auditor that the authority had acted 'contrary to law' by virtue of the wage agreement it made with its striking employees to get them back to work. Applying *Wednesbury* principles the court ruled that it had not so acted.

A charge of improper motive might arise when an authority has an interest in the matter over which it is exercising a power as in *Westminster City Council v British Waterways Board*.[17] The Council was a tenant of a piece of land rented from the Board. The refusal by the Council to give planning permission to the Board in order to protect the Council's occupation as tenant would be wrongful as being improperly motivated (or for taking into account an irrelevant consideration).

Power to punish?

In some cases the courts have shown that the use of power in order to punish, penalise or coerce is unlawful where the power is not granted for that purpose.[18] In *Wheeler v Leicester City Council*[19] three members of Leicester Rugby Football Club were invited by the English Rugby Union to participate in a rugby tour of South Africa. The club had for many years used a recreation ground owned by the Council. The council had a strong anti-apartheid policy and disapproved of members of a well-known club associated with the town participating in the tour. It raised the matter with the club, and being dissatisfied with the Club's failure to condemn the tour and to discourage its members from taking part in it, withdrew the use of the ground for a year. The club challenged the legality of that action. A majority of the Court of Appeal found for the council, ruling that it could not be said that it had acted *Wednesbury unreasonably*, but was reversed by the House of Lords. Lord Templeman was clear that the council had acted wrongly in using its statutory power for the purpose of punishing the club when it had done no wrong. Lord Roskill saw the council's conduct as an attempt to force acceptance by the club of their own policy on their own terms, and considered that it had acted *Wednesbury unreasonably* and also procedurally improperly. The other members of the House of Lords agreed with the two judgments.

In *R v Liverpool City Council, ex p Secretary of State for Employment*[20] the council resolved to reject all use of and support for the government's Employment Training Scheme on the grounds that it did not pay the rate for the job, did not give participants the protection of full employment, etc. In pursuance of that it decided not to give financial assistance to organisations who took part in the scheme. Those organisations would be acting lawfully in participating in the scheme, and the court had no doubt that the purpose was, as in *Wheeler*, to punish or coerce those who would not toe the council's line; it could not be compelled to support the scheme, but it acted unlawfully in seeking to deter in the way it did.

17 [1985] AC 676, [1984] 3 All ER 737.
18 *R v Secretary of State for Health, ex p Hickey* (1992) 10 BMLR 126 'withholding' for breach of terms of service by doctor could be punitive, not merely compensatory; and it was not unreasonable.
19 [1985] AC 1054, [1985] 2 All ER 1106.
20 (1988) Times, 12 November.

In *R v Ealing London Borough Council, ex p Times Newspapers Ltd*[1] the publishers of certain newspapers were involved in an industrial dispute with former employees. In response to a call by the unions involved, three councils banned from their libraries all copies of the newspapers published by the employers. These publications had been part of the library service up to the ban. The court held that the reason for the ban was so that it could be used as a weapon in the industrial dispute. It was therefore imposed for an ulterior object and was not within the council's statutory powers relating to libraries. The references in the *Wheeler* case to punishment and coercion were also relied on.

It was sought to apply *Wheeler* in *R v Newham London Borough Council, ex p Haggerty*.[2] The council adopted a standing order which required council members seeking appointment to committees to complete a declaration of pecuniary interests and to disclose certain personal details. The applicant thought this was an invasion of privacy and sought to have the standing order declared unlawful. It was, he said, wrong to punish a person who has done no wrong; it was, as in *Wheeler*, an attempt to coerce him to adopt a particular view (there, as to South Africa, here as to the requirements of open government). The argument was rejected. The authority was entitled in law to lay down criteria determining membership of its committees, and the applicant did not meet those criteria. Of course, if it could have been shown that the criteria were unreasonable or otherwise unlawful that would have been different, but that was not argued.

Mixed motives

An authority may act for mixed motives, some good, some bad. If there can be said to be a dominant motive and if the *dominant motive is a proper one*, the act will be valid. In such a case, the fact that an incidental benefit is conferred or a subsidiary purpose is achieved will not invalidate the exercise of the power. For example in *Westminster Corpn v London and North Western Rly Co*[3] the corporation had power to build subterranean public lavatories. They built some in such a way that it was possible by means of the subway to pass from one side of the street to the other. The corporation had no power to construct a subway and the railway company argued that the lavatories were built in order to make the subway. While agreeing that 'if the power to make one kind of building was fraudulently used for the purpose of making another kind of building', the exercise of the power would be invalid, the House of Lords found that the corporation

---

1 (1986) 85 LGR 316.
2 (1986) LGR 48. *R v Greenwich London Borough Council, ex p Lovelace* [1990] 1 All ER 353, [1990] 1 WLR 18: councillor removed from committee to ensure policy followed – no simple desire to punish shown. *R v Hendon Justices, ex p DPP* [1993] 1 All ER 411: did JPs dismiss information to punish prosecution inefficiency?
3 [1905] AC 426. The company was claiming damages and an injunction for trespass. And see *R v Merseyside County Council, ex p Great Universal Stores* (1982) 80 LGR 639.

had not so acted. The subway was therefore an added bonus. The only evidence to support the contention of improper purpose seems to have been the width of the access tunnels which it was alleged, were wider than would be necessary for lavatories.[4] Contrast *Lynch v Sewers Comrs of London*[5] where the authority had no power to acquire land for the purpose of changing the level of a street, but had power to acquire it for street widening. The actual widening proposed was of a strip of maximum width of 12 inches, but the level of the entire street was to be changed.

But if *any* of the purposes is an unauthorised purpose and can be said to have *materially affected* the authority's decision, the act will be ultra vires, as where a body could lawfully spend money on the publication of information, but a major purpose in doing so was political persuasion. (This also meant taking irrelevant considerations into account.)[6]

If the good and bad purposes are *inextricably mixed*, the action will be unlawful. If, in *Sadler v Sheffield Corpn*[7] the educational and financial purposes could be said to be mixed, the corporation's decision would have been bad on that ground. In *R v Lewisham London Borough Council, ex p Shell UK Ltd*[8] the council's purpose in boycotting Shell products (because of a South African connection) was not simply to promote good race relations in the borough (which was its duty) but to exert pressure on the company to sever links with South Africa (the maintenance of which was not unlawful). This latter purpose had exerted a very substantial influence on the decision and was inextricably mixed up with the lawful purpose. The boycott was therefore unlawful.

Politics – pre-eminently extraneous?

Politicians' main concern is not for the law, it is for politics, and in particular for getting elected, and when elected, using the power achieved with the hope that it will have the happy result for them of advantaging the party to which they belong, thus prolonging its and their retention of power. The effect of their actions on public opinion is very much in their minds – that is after all why we have elections, to help to ensure that those who hold certain (elective) offices will feel accountable to the public for what they do. (The accountability of those who are appointed, is another matter.) We vote for the candidate of our choice so that he will take decisions in accordance with policies of which we broadly approve. But when he comes to take a decision he does so within the framework of the law. Having reached a view of what is politically desirable – his first

4   *R v Exeter City Council, ex p JL Thomas & Co Ltd* [1991] 1 All ER 413: dominant motive to see site developed, not to force out existing adjoining users.
5   (1886) 32 ChD 72: acquisition prohibited pending trial of issue.
6   *R v Inner London Education Authority, ex p Westminster City Council* [1986] 1 All ER 19.
7   [1924] 1 Ch 483; see p 246 above.
8   [1988] 1 All ER 938.

concern – he may find that the law inhibits him, in which case he may seek to get it changed. If on the other hand he legally has a choice or discretion he will exercise it in accordance with his political stance. In *Cardiff Corpn v Secretary of State for Wales*[8a] the Welsh Office asked Cardiff why it had given planning permission when its planning officer had recommended refusal. The court commented thus on this 'rather odd question':

Apparently these officers sometimes forget that local planning authorities consist of democratically elected members, and the members are, in my view, in practice constantly considering what their voters may want and may, on dealing with any question, deal with it in accordance with what they think will be satisfactory to those whose votes they have solicited in the past and intend to solicit in the future.

The reference to soliciting votes is not to be taken as meaning that it would be proper for a bargain to be struck between a member and a voter. The point is rather that in deciding on an application for planning permission, the widest considerations can be taken into account, including in particular the impact of the proposed development on the environment. In those circumstances it is proper and necessary for members to try to assess and to take into account what the public generally, that is, the voters, want. In taking his decision, whether or not it has political implications, he must of course act within the law. He must not for example fail to take into account a relevant factor because to do so may lead to a conclusion that is for him politically unacceptable or embarrassing. He cannot decline to carry out a legal duty because it is politically inexpedient, or because of fear of political criticism.

In *R v Board of Education*[9] Swansea Corporation paid teachers in non-provided (church) schools less than those in provided schools. The question was referred for decision to the Board of Education (a government department), and the Board's refusal to intervene was challenged in the courts. In the Court of Appeal Farwell LJ said:

[I]f the Board did know the law to be as it now admitted to be, they must have acted upon a consideration of something extraneous and extra-judicial which ought not to have affected their decision, and this was suggested by the Attorney General when he said that the Board were in a difficulty and that questions of policy were involved. If this means that the Board were hampered by political considerations, I can only say that such considerations are pre-eminently extraneous, and that no political consequences can justify the Board in allowing their judgments and discretion to be influenced thereby.[10]

In *Padfield*, in addition to the reasons referred to above for not referring the complaint to the committee, a letter from the ministry to Padfield had said, 'In considering how to exercise his discretion the Minister would, amongst other things address his mind to the possibility that if a complaint were so referred and the committee were to uphold it, he in turn would be

8a (1971) 22 P & CR 718.
 9 [1910] 2 KB 165 aff'd [1911] AC 179.
10 [1910] 2 KB 165 at 181.

expected to make a statutory order to give effect to the committee's recommendations.' Lord Reid commented, 'If this means that he is entitled to refuse to refer a complaint because if he did so he might later find himself in an embarrassing situation, that would plainly be a bad reason.'[11] Lord Upjohn said, 'This fear of parliamentary trouble ... is alone sufficient to vitiate the Minister's decision which ... can never validly turn on purely political considerations, he must be prepared to face the music in parliament.'[12] He referred to the dictum of Farwell LJ above.

In some cases where council decisions have been struck down for eg taking into account irrelevant factors or acting from an improper motive we can see that the council was motivated by political considerations (which we ourselves might or might not approve of) for example the *Ealing* and *Lewisham* cases above. They were struck down not because of the political motivation but for the defects mentioned. In *Roberts v Hopwood* (p 247 above) Lord Atkinson thought that the Poplar Council had been motivated by 'misguided principles of socialistic philanthropy'. We can presume, can we not, that he would have taken the same view of the Council's equal pay policy if it had been motivated by principles of philanthropy?

To act under the significant influence of an improper motive is, we have seen, to act unlawfully. Thus, where a decision is primarily or significantly motivated by consideration of party political advantage then, if this could be proved, it would be open to challenge. This might be the case when, with the intent of getting such advantage, homeless persons' accommodation is moved by a Conservative council from a marginal Conservative to a Labour ward.

Where a local authority was empowered to spend money on giving public information on local government matters and did so also for the purpose of persuading the public to its view on the question of the government financing of local authorities, that additional (political) purpose was improper and invalidated the expenditure.[13] (The expenditure was by a Labour council; the challenge to it was by a Conservative council – its political motivation in doing so was not considered.)

In *R v Secretary of State for the Home Department, ex p Ruddock*[14] it was argued that it could be inferred that a warrant to tap telephones had been issued for the improper purpose of gaining party advantage. On the facts the court was unable to draw that inference, in the light, for example, of the timing of the issue of the warrant in relation to a general election. And in any case, 'I do not think what is done by government for purposes of national security and what may assist it against a party in opposition are necessarily mutually exclusive or severable'. And if the purpose of a course of action by a local authority is to make it impossible for a change

11 [1968] AC 997 at 1032, [1968] 1 All ER 694 at 701.
12 Ibid, at 1061 and 719 respectively.
13 *R v Inner London Education Authority, ex p Westminster City Council* [1986] 1 All ER 19; [1986] 1 WLR 28.
14 [1987] 2 All ER 518, [1987] 1 WLR 1482.

of policy to be initiated in the event of a change of political control of the authority, such course of action may be unlawful.[15]

In the context of the considerations that can properly be taken into account by the Attorney General in deciding whether or not to institute criminal proceedings, it has been suggested that 'partisan politics' refers to 'actions designed to protect and advance the retention of constitutional power by the incumbent government and its political supporters'.[16]

A local ombudsman has considered allegations of the improper intrusion of party politics into local authority decisions.[17]

Attempts have been made to justify the propriety of decisions challenged in the courts of reference to statements made in election manifestos. The courts appear to have been ambivalent about this. In one case the importance of the mandate created by the electorate's approval of a manifesto policy of the winning (Conservative) party in a local election was stressed;[18] in another (where Labour won) it was denied;[19] and in a third[20] a judge relied on the views of the Conservative minority to justify the reasonableness of the Conservative minister's action in intervening in the decisions of the Labour-controlled council.

Some decisions are manifestly based, and accepted to be properly based, on political judgment. 'The formulation and the implementation of national economic policy are matters depending essentially on political judgment. The decisions which shape them are for politicians to take and it is in the political forum of the House of Commons that they are properly to be debated and approved or disapproved on their merits.'[1] How far they are therefore beyond the reach of judicial review is considered later.

One area where political considerations are thought to dominate is in the appointment by ministers to a range of public offices. Where statute lists the criteria for appointment, they will have to be observed. Legal objections to appointments on the ground of the political affiliation of the appointee are not likely to succeed. Objection is more suitably made in the political forum. Statute may expressly provide for political balance in appointment.[2]

---

15 See Kerr LJ diss in *R v Hammersmith and Fulham London Borough Council, ex p Beddowes* [1987] QB 1050, [1987] 1 All ER 369.

16 Edwards in Glazebrook (ed) *Reshaping the Criminal Law* p 375.

17 Foulkes 'The Work of the Local Commissioner for Wales' [1978] PL 264 at 282 for one example. It can safely be assumed that there are others.

18 *Secretary of State for Education v Tameside Metropolitan Borough* [1977] AC 1014, [1976] 3 All ER 665, p 267 below.

19 The *Fare's Fair* case, p 200 above.

20 *Norwich City Council v Secretary of State for the Environment* [1982] QB 808, [1982] 1 All ER 737. See McAuslan [1983] MLR 1.

1 Per Lord Bridge in *Hammersmith LBC v Secretary of State* [1990] 3 All ER 589 at 637. See *R v Secretary of State for Foreign Affairs, ex p World Development Movement Ltd* [1995] 1 All ER 611.

2 Local Government and Housing Act 1989, s 15. See HL Debs vol 518 col 112. *R v Warwickshire County Council, ex p Dill-Russell* [1991] COD 375.

Unreasonableness

It will be recalled that in *Wednesbury* Lord Greene distinguished between the 'rather comprehensive sense' in which the word 'unreasonable' may be used – failing to take into account relevant considerations for example – and the stronger sense of acting in a way in which no reasonable person would act. The use of the word 'unreasonable' in the *Wednesbury* context now means unreasonable in that latter, stronger, sense. (The phrase *'Wednesbury unreasonable'* will be found in the cases, and here.) One may express this stronger test as: has the authority come to a conclusion so unreasonable that no reasonable authority could have come to it? Another formulation, from Lord Greene's judgment, is whether what was done was so absurd that no sensible person could ever dream that it lay within the authority's power to act as it had. Lord Diplock has referred to the test as being whether, looked at objectively, the decision is 'so devoid of any plausible justification that no reasonable body of persons could have reached it'.[3]

In the *GCHQ* case Lord Diplock classified the grounds on which administrative action can be challenged as illegality, procedural irregularity – and irrationality. By 'irrationality' I mean what can by now be succinctly referred to as 'Wednesbury unreasonableness'. Having thus equated the two he defined what he meant by irrationality – a decision which is 'so outrageous in its defiance of logic or of accepted moral standards that no sensible person who had applied his mind to the question to be decided could have arrived at it'.[4] Clearly few decisions are going to be so bizarre as to fail this test, and a challenge on this 'unreasonable' ground is an argument of last resort, almost perhaps of desperation.

A judge is on dangerous ground in striking down as unreasonable the decision of a statutory authority, taken on a matter given to it for decision by Act of Parliament. To do so would seem to be getting perilously close to the judge substituting his view of what the decision should be on the merits, for that of the authority in question. Lord Greene himself sounded a warning note against doing that.[5] The emphatic language in which the unreasonableness test is expressed underlines the point that the court is exercising a supervisory, not an appellate function.[6]

The court's willingness to intervene on this ground is likely to be affected by the matter in issue or the status and function of the authority in question. Thus in *British Airways Board v Laker Airways Ltd*[7] it was said that where the subject matter of the decision challenged concerned

3   *Bromley London Borough Council v Greater London Council* [1983] 1 AC 768, [1982] 1 All ER 129 at 821 and 159 respectively.
4   *Council of Civil Service Unions v Minister for the Civil Service* [1985] AC 374 at 410, [1984] 3 All ER 935 at 951.
5   See reference to Divisional Court's judgment in *Lonrho plc v Secretary of State for Trade and Industry* [1989] 2 All ER 609, [1989] 1 WLR 525, HL.
6   See Lord Ackner in *Brind v Secretary of State for the Home Dept* [1991] 1 AC 696, [1991] 1 All ER 720.
7   [1985] AC 58, [1984] 3 All ER 39.

international relations between the UK and a foreign state, a very strong case would have to be made out to justify intervention on this ground. Local authorities and ministers are of course elected, and it is a strong thing for a court to say that they have moved beyond the bounds of reasonableness. The courts acknowledge that they should for that reason be hesitant in arriving at such a judgment. Lord Greene made the point in *Wednesbury,* and in *West Glamorgan County Council v Rafferty*[8] the court said that in a case involving the weighing of social factors by an elected council, where a lawful procedure had been followed, the facts would have to be exceptional and extreme for the court to say that the decision was one no reasonable council could take. In *Kruse v Johnson*[9] the validity of a local authority byelaw was challenged on the ground of unreasonableness. Lord Russell CJ said that in matters which directly and mainly concern the people of the country, their representatives may be trusted to understand their own requirements better than judges.

A reluctance to intervene may also be seen where a body though not elected is 'most representative and responsible'[10] or 'independent and expert'.[11]

In *Nottinghamshire County Council v Secretary of State for the Environment*[12] the ministerial order challenged related to *public expenditure* and had been *approved by the Commons.* The House of Lords was not prepared to intervene at all on the grounds of *Wednesbury* unreasonableness. It would have to be shown, it said, that the absurdity of the order was so great that the minister's order could not have been framed by a bona fide exercise of political judgment – in other words that it had been made in bad faith, as to which see p 262 below. (It could however be challenged on other grounds eg the narrow ultra vires point, or for procedural defect.)

There has been a good deal of litigation in recent years animated by party political controversy. Litigation may be seen as a continuation of that controversy by other means. In such cases the judge is likely to be found insisting that the court has no concern with politics (that is, the merits of the dispute). In *R v North West Thames Regional Health Authority, ex p Nerva*[13] for example the RHA had threatened to exercise a power to remove members of the District Health Authority who voted against what the RHA regarded as necessary spending cuts in the NHS. This was challenged as *Wednesbury unreasonable.* The court indicated that it did not wish to be asked to deal with that 'unreasonableness' 'in cases where the dispute arises between parties who hold genuine but

---

8 [1987] 1 All ER 1005, [1987] 1 WLR 457. See p 244 above.
9 [1898] 2 QB 91.
10 The Independent Broadcasting Authority (see p 38 above), per Lord Denning in *A-G, ex rel McWhirter v IBA* [1973] QB 629 at 651, [1973] 1 All ER 689 at 701.
11 The Advisory, Conciliation and Arbitration Service (see p 39 above), per Lord Scarman in *United Kingdom Association of Professional Engineers v Advisory Conciliation and Arbitration Service* [1980] 1 All ER 612 at 619.
12 [1986] AC 240, [1986] 1 All ER 199. See *R v Secretary of State for Health, ex p Cormack* (1990) 6 BMLR 81.
13 (1983) Times, 20 October.

diametrically opposed [political] convictions'. It would be otherwise, though, if the challenge were, say, simply on the relevancy test.

Local authority byelaws may be invalidated on the ground of unreasonableness. In *Kruse v Johnson*[14] Lord Russell CJ said that the following might constitute unreasonableness:

If for instance they were found to be partial and unequal in their operation as between classes; if they were manifestly unjust; if they disclosed bad faith; if they involved such oppressive or gratuitous interference with the rights of those subject to them as could find no justification in the minds of reasonable men, the court might well say, 'Parliament never intended to give authority to make such rules; they are unreasonable and ultra vires'.

In *Anderson v Alnwick DC* the court said with reference to that: 'The more modern doctrine of *Wednesbury* unreasonableness is in our judgment closely allied to those principles'.[15]

An example of an unreasonable byelaw is found in *Arlidge v Islington Corpn*.[16] It required landlords of lodging houses to cause the premises to be cleansed. It was held to be unreasonable in that it applied to a landlord who had no right of entry to leased premises and would therefore be trespassing if he complied with the byelaw. (The court was, however, sympathetic to the aim of the defendants in making such a byelaw, and suggested how it might be achieved.)

In *Sparks v Edward Ash Ltd*[17] it was argued that the Pedestrian Crossing Regulations made by a minister were void for unreasonableness. Scott LJ referring to the views of Lord Russell, just quoted, said:

If it is the duty of the courts to recognise and trust the discretion of local authorities, much more must it be so in the case of a minister directly responsible to Parliament, and entrusted by the constitution with the function of administering the department.

The unreasonableness of the regulations was said to consist in the requirements they exacted from drivers and in causing motor traffic to slow down to an extent injurious to the commercial community. Scott LJ concluded that the court had no power to declare the regulations invalid for unreasonableness 'certainly not on any ground submitted in argument before us'. In *Maynard v Osmond*[18] where a challenge to the reasonableness of the Police (Discipline) Regulations was made, the court did not suggest that the regulations could not be invalidated on that ground (but did not find them unreasonable).

We now consider some cases where unreasonableness or irrationality was found. It will be noted that in some cases the decision could have

14 [1898] 2 QB 91.
15 [1993] 3 All ER 613 at 625.
16 [1909] 2 KB 127.
17 [1943] 1 KB 223, [1943] 1 All ER 1. He continued: '[There] is a further consideration that these regulations have to be laid on the table of both Houses – and can be annulled in the usual way.' See cases at fn 12 above.
18 [1977] QB 240, [1977] 1 All ER 64, CA.

been struck down on another, narrower, ground. In *Backhouse v Lambeth London Borough Council*[19] the council increased the rent of one of its houses from £8 per week to £18,000 a year. It did so under an Act which authorised it to make 'such reasonable charges for the tenancy' of the houses as it determined. The object was to evade duties put on it by another Act to raise rents generally. The court ruled that the decision was one which no reasonable council could have arrived at; but note that it was also held not to be a valid exercise of the power to make a 'reasonable charge'.

In *R v Tunbridge Wells Health Authority, ex p Goodridge*[20] the Authority had a duty to consult about any proposal to make a 'substantial variation' in its services. It resolved on the temporary closure of a 'cottage hospital' and referred to plans to reopen it as a rehabilitation unit for the mentally infirm. The court said that no reasonable authority could have taken the view that the 'temporary closure' was not a 'substantial variation'; after that closure the hospital would never again open as a 'cottage hospital' (one staffed by general practitioners who are entitled to admit patients to it).

A local authority may, in granting planning permission impose 'such conditions as it thinks fit'. In *Hall & Co Ltd v Shoreham-By-Sea UDC* [1] the defendant granted the plaintiff planning permission subject to conditions which required them to construct a road on their land and dedicate its use to the public. No compensation was payable to them for the loss of the land to be used for the road. The court could not find 'clear and unambiguous words in the Town and Country Planning Act authorising the defendants in effect to take away the plaintiffs' right of property without compensation by the imposition of conditions such as those sought to be imposed'. The conditions were therefore ultra vires in pursuance of the principle that a statute is not to be construed as taking away rights of property without compensation unless the intent to do so is clearly expressed. They were also said to be unreasonable, but that was unnecessary. In *Bernard Wheatcroft Ltd v Secretary of State for the Environment*[2] it was said that to give planning permission for a development substantially different from that applied for, would be *Wednesbury unreasonable*. But as the authority is not then giving a decision on the application made to it, which is the extent of its power, it would be ultra vires on that narrower ground.

In *R v Ealing London Borough Council, ex p Times Newspapers Ltd*[3] the court said that no rational local authority would for a moment have thought that it was open to it to impose the ban in the discharge of its duty to provide a library service. (About 30 authorities had thought it. Notice the multiplicity of defects: an ulterior object; irrelevant consideration; frustrating the policy of the Act.)

19 (1972) Times, 14 October.
20 (1988) Times, 21 May.
 1 [1964] 1 All ER 1, [1964] 1 WLR 240.
 2 (1980) 43 P & CR 233.
 3 (1986) 85 LGR 316; and p249 above.

In *R v Secretary of State for the Environment, ex p Fielder Estates (Canvey) Ltd*[4] F's planning application had been refused and an inquiry held. It had been arranged for one of the objectors to give evidence on the second day of the inquiry. When he turned up to do so he found that the inspector had by oversight closed the inquiry at the end of the first day. In response to his complaint the Secretary of State decided that a new inquiry should be held before a new inspector. F applied for judicial review of that decision. The court pointed out that three other courses had been open to the Secretary of State which were simpler and less expensive and inconvenient than the decision taken. The decision was thus irrational and verged on absurdity.

There are many cases where unreasonableness has been alleged but not found by the court. Some examples follow. In *R v Greenwich London Borough Council, ex p Cedar Holdings Ltd*[5] the applicants sought to quash the general rate set by the Council. It was shown that the members had been fully advised as to the relevant considerations they should take into account. The applicants were thus reduced to arguing that despite that advice they had arrived at a decision so unreasonable that the court should infer that they must have ignored or misunderstood it. The court rejected the 'dangerous and seductive' argument. In *R v City of Birmingham Metropolitan District Council, ex p Sale*[6] the council could properly postpone temporarily the demolition of certain houses. It was argued that no reasonable authority could, as this one did, regard 24 years as temporary. The court felt unable, in the absence of evidence, to say whether or not it was unreasonable – it might be, it might not be. (It was not therefore obviously absurd, as in *Backhouse*, above.) And in *Lonrho plc v Secretary of State for Trade and Industry*[7] the argument that the minister had acted perversely in failing to publish a report was said to be unsustainable: he was entitled to take the view that publication might prejudice a fair trial.

In *R v Rushmoor Borough Council, ex p Crawford*[8] the majority party on the council suspended the main minority party from membership of all committees. Was this unreasonable? The court said that to take that action on party-political grounds was not unreasonable – but to take it on other grounds could be. (The decision was however unlawful as contrary to standing orders: which could presumably be altered by the council for future action.)

An allegation of irrationality failed in *R v Secretary of State for the Home Department, ex p Ruddock*[9] It was said to consist in the signing by the Home Secretary of a warrant for tapping the telephones of members of the Campaign for Nuclear Disarmament, when the criteria for doing so

4   (1989) 57 P & CR 424.
5   [1983] RA 173.
6   (1984) 48 P & CR 270.
7   [1989] 2 All ER 609, [1989] 1 WLR 525, HL.
8   (1981) Times, 28 November. See Gregory [1983] PL 20.
9   [1987] 2 All ER 518, [1987] 1 WLR 1482.

did not apply. There was evidence from a former intelligence officer that the criteria did not apply. But, the court asked, was the contrary view one which was 'so outrageous in its defiance of logic' that no sensible Secretary of State could have arrived at it? It was not.

The test applied was, of course, that of Lord Diplock. He also suggested, it will be recalled, that outrageous defiance of 'accepted moral standards' could also constitute irrationality. There appears to be no case where the breach of such standards has been overtly relied on, and it is not perhaps clear what are the accepted moral standards in public administration as distinct from legal requirements (and, in another context, the standards of good administration). Perhaps it means no more than this, that it is wrong, and immoral, to use a power for a purpose and in a way that the law does not countenance.[10]

Statute and reasonableness

It is not uncommon for statute, when empowering an authority to, say, make a charge, to require that the charge shall be 'reasonable'. It is not clear that the addition of the word 'reasonable' adds, in law, anything, as the authority must in any case act reasonably. Why then was the word added? Out of an abundance of caution? Or as a reminder to the authority?

Another situation is whether statute says that if A is thought to be acting 'unreasonably' B may do something about it. For example under section 68 of the Education Act 1944 where the Secretary of State is satisfied that a local education authority is acting unreasonably he may give it such directions as appear to him to be expedient. In *Secretary of State for Education v Tameside Metropolitan Borough Council*[11] he gave such a direction to the council, as he thought it was acting unreasonably in the arrangements it was making for the selection of children for admission to grammar schools. Was the direction lawful? The Secretary of State had relied on the administrative disruption the new method would cause in saying that the council was acting unreasonably. He was entitled, the House said, to ensure that the disruption was not unreasonable – in the sense of being greater than a body elected to carry out a new programme ought to impose on those affected. But, the House said, this *was* an elected body: indeed the change in the method of allocation had come about precisely because the Conservatives had gained control of the council at an election at which selection for secondary education had been an issue between the parties. An election, the House noted, may well lead to an abrupt reversal of policy necessitating administrative change. And the electorate, in voting for that change, must be taken to have accepted

---

10 'A government ... is limited by the purposes it serves. It has no moral authority to act ultra vires those purposes', H J Laski *A Grammar of Politics*, p 134.
11 [1977] AC 1014, [1976] 3 All ER 665. See Bradley, *The Listener*, 5 May 1977; Foulkes [1976] 126 NLJ 649 (appointment of teacher by pulling name out of tea-cosy). Debate at 922 H o C Report (5th series) col 590.

the degree of disruption to the arrangements already made for selection of their children. In the outcome the House said that it was impossible to say that no reasonable authority could have taken the view that a satisfactory selection of pupils could not have taken place within the time – ten weeks – available.

It will have been noted that the *Wednesbury* unreasonableness test was applied – 'no reasonable authority etc'. This is the test the courts apply to administrative authorities. Now it is the case that the Secretary of State has important administrative responsibilities for the provision of an education system. Is it right therefore that a body with *administrative* oversight over another should have to apply the same test of unreasonableness to that other as the *courts* apply to administrative bodies?

Proportionality

The concept of proportionality is well established in Community law and that of other European institutions. It says that the means used by authorities must be appropriate to achieve the objective sought, and must not go beyond what is necessary to attain that objective. Brief references to some cases will illustrate this. In *Commission v United Kingdom*[12] the UK introduced restrictions on the import of certain poultry products as a means of combating a particular disease. The European Court of Justice held that where imports came from a country where the disease had not been detected over a number of years, a total prohibition on imports from there was out of proportion to the aim pursued. In *R v Intervention Board for Agricultural Produce, ex p E D & F Man Ltd*[13] a regulation which prescribed a forfeiture of a £1.6m security for failure to comply with a time limit for applying for a licence was struck down on the same ground: the same penalty was imposed for much more serious defaults. The concept is also applied by the European Court of Human Rights. Article 8 of the Convention on Human Rights provides that there is to be no interference with the exercise of the right to a home except such as is necessary in the light of certain interests, including the economic well-being of the country. In *Gillow v United Kingdom*[14] G, who owned a house in Guernsey, was refused a licence to live in it. The court held that the licensing legislation itself was not disproportionate to the economic well-being of the island, but the refusal of a licence to G was: insufficient weight had been given to G's particular circumstances. The Committee of Ministers of the Council of Europe have recommended to member countries certain principles to guide them in their law and administrative practice.[15] One of them is that when exercising a discretionary power an authority should maintain

12 [1982] ECR 2793, [1982] 3 CMLR 497.
13 [1986] 2 All ER 115; *Milk Marketing Board v Cricket St Thomas Estate* (1990) Times, 20 March.
14 (1986) 109 ECHR 6.
15 R (80) 2.

a proper balance between any adverse effects which its decisions may have on the interests of persons, and the purpose it seeks to achieve.

What of English law? In the *GCHQ* case[16] Lord Diplock, after classifying the various grounds of challenge as illegality, irrationality and procedural impropriety, referred to the possible acceptance of proportionality into English law. To what extent has it already been accepted? *Statute* may expressly rely on it. The Data Protection Act 1984 lays down certain principles which have to be applied by data users (which includes public authorities). One of them is that personal data held for any purpose 'shall be adequate, relevant and *not excessive*' in relation to that purpose. Under the Prevention of Oil Pollution Act 1971, where an oil spillage from a ship may cause pollution the Secretary of State may take certain preventive action. If it turns out that that action was such that the good it did was disproportionately less than the damage suffered as a result of that action, a person who suffers loss as a result of that action (eg by an order that the ship is or is not to be moved) is entitled to compensation. Third, the Road Traffic Act 1991, s 66(3)(d) requires a penalty charge to be reduced proportionately.

The *government* relies on the idea when justifying a refusal to give information sought by a parliamentary question on the ground that the cost of obtaining the information would be 'disproportionate'[17] (presumably to the usefulness of the information, as seen by itself). (Adam Smith stated that the subjects of the State 'ought to contribute towards the support of the government as nearly as possible in proportion to their respective abilities'.)

In the *legislature*, membership of House of Commons committees has regard to the balance of the parties in the House, ie in some degree proportionate to their relative strengths.[18] It would be agreed that in devising an electoral system, special regard must be paid to the requirement of proportionality – that is to the relationship between the number of votes cast and the number of seats gained.

What of the *courts*? It is a general principle that a penalty, criminal or otherwise, should be proportionate to the wrong.[19] In *R v Barnsley Metropolitan Borough Council, ex p Hook*[20] the revocation of a licence was quashed as disproportionate to the licence holder's wrong doing. In *R v Brent London Borough Council, ex p Assegai*[1] the banning of a school governor from visiting all council premises was wholly out of proportion to what was alleged against him.

---

16 *Council of Civil Service Unions v Minister for the Civil Service* [1985] AC 374 at 410, [1984] 3 All ER 935 at 950.
17 HC Official Report, 6th series, vol 121, col 358w. And see *Legal Entitlements and Administrative Practices* (HMSO): para 25 – de minimis practices in not paying or claiming amounts due to be proportionate to amount involved.
18 For local authorities see now Local Government and Housing Act 1989, ss 15 to 17.
19 Eg *Director of Public Prosecutions v Channel Four TV Co Ltd* [1993] 2 All ER 517.
20 [1976] 3 All ER 452, [1976] 1 WLR 1052.
1 (1987) Times, 18 June.

Proportionality may be relevant in considering the remedy for a tortious wrong.[2]

What then, to return to Lord Diplock's dictum, of proportionality in judicial review? Earlier cases could be said to have been decided on the basis of proportionality. For example in *Roberts v Hopwood*[3] Lord Atkinson said there did not appear to be 'any rational proportion' between the wages actually and reasonably paid. One could say that the rent in *Backhouse v Lambeth London Borough Council*[4] was wildly disproportionate to the value of the house. Cases where decisions have been struck down for procedural errors might also be explained on the grounds of proportionality, as for example *Lee v Department of Education and Science*.[5]

But the question is whether proportionality is a separate ground of review, separate, that is, from illegality, procedural impropriety and irrationality/unreasonableness. Or is it but an aspect of the last-mentioned? According to the House of Lords in *Brind v Secretary of State for the Home Dept*[6] it is not a separate ground. In that case the legality of the minister's direction to the Independent Broadcasting Authority and the BBC was challenged. One of the grounds of challenge was that the direction (requiring the IBA and the BBC not to broadcast direct statements by rep-resentatives of certain organisations) was disproportionate. This was advanced as a separate ground from *Wednesbury unreasonableness*. Counsel emphasised that he was not seeking to blur the distinction between an appeal on the merits and the review of legality, but the House thought that proportionality as a separate ground inevitably involved the court in re-weighing the merits – and this amounts to an appeal, which is not the court's function. The House acknowledged that unreasonableness may be achieved through the gross disproportion of a measure – but this does not make it a separate ground. Nevertheless Lord Templeman thought that proportionality was a correct test in this case, and Lord Roskill thought that, with reference to Lord Diplock's dictum, this was not an appropriate case in which to take the first step towards proportionality as a separate ground of review.

Bad faith

The courts have in the past referred to acts motivated by an improper purpose as not having been done 'in good faith', or as having been done mala fide. But bad faith should be limited. Thus Megaw LJ:

---

2   *Burton v Winters* [1993] 3 All ER 847: self-help not available where disproportionate to damage; *Rantzen v Mirror Group Newspapers (1986) Ltd* [1993] 4 All ER 975 (damages for libel).
3   [1925] AC 578. See p 247 above.
4   (1972) Times 14 October, p 257 above.
5   (1968) 66 LGR 211, p 280 below.
6   [1991] 1 AC 696, [1991] 1 All ER 720. *R v Secretary of State for the Home Dept, ex p Adams* (1995) Independent, 28 April.

I would stress, for it seems to me that an unfortunate tendency has developed of looseness of language in this respect, that bad faith, or as it sometimes put, 'lack of good faith', means dishonesty: not necessarily a financial motive but still dishonesty. It always involves a grave charge.[7]

It is not, he said, to be taken as synonymous with an honest though mistaken view as to the extent of one's powers or with the taking into account of irrelevant considerations.

Dishonesty, as Megaw LJ added, 'always involves a grave charge'. The person or body against whom the charge is made is entitled to have it particularised. The burden of proof is a heavy one. In *Potato Marketing Board v Merricks*,[8] Devlin J held that while the Board had been unnecessarily heavy handed, there was no sign of bad faith. In *Barber v Manchester Regional Hospital Board*,[9] Barber alleged that his dismissal was done mala fide. The court held that while he had been treated unfairly the officials of the Board had acted in the honest if mistaken belief that it would be in the best interest of the health service if Barber's services were dispensed with: honesty negatives bad faith. In *Mustafa v Secretary of State for the Home Department*[10] the minister gave directions for M's removal to Cyprus, but acknowledged that it was not reasonable to return M there until social disturbances were over – the date of this could not of course be known. M argued that as there could be no good purpose in giving an unenforceable direction there must have been some other motive, so that the minister had not been acting bona fide. The court held this was not enough to establish bad faith. The direction was not a cloak for an ulterior purpose. There was good cause for it – a criminal conviction; and its non-implementation was done for humanitarian reasons.

Some indication of how malice could manifest itself in decision-making in a local authority can be found in *Jones v Swansea City Council*.[11] Suppose the leader of the controlling group is actuated by malice in his vote; that the members of his group support him in the vote (so that the decision is then that of the council) but the vote was not whipped. In the absence of explanation from those members it would be open to the court to infer that they too had voted whilst affected by malice – the malice of the leader.

A choice of powers

Where an authority has at its disposal more than one way of achieving a desired end, can its choice ever be invalidated? A leading case is

---

7 *Cannock Chase District Council v Kelly* [1978] 1 All ER 152 at 156, [1978] 1 WLR at 6. Reiterated at [1981] 2 All ER 204 and 215.
8 [1958] 2 QB 316, [1958] 2 All ER 538.
9 [1958] 1 All ER 322, [1958] 1 WLR 181.
10 [1979–80] Imm AR 33.
11 [1990] 3 All ER 737, [1990] 1 WLR 1453. And *R v Derbyshire County Council, ex p Times Supplements* [1991] COD 129.

Westminster Bank Ltd v Minister of Housing and Local Government.[12] The bank's application for planning permission was refused on the ground that the land in question was needed for road widening. An alternative method of restricting development open to the local authority was by prescribing an improvement line under the Highways Act. If that procedure had been used, compensation would have been payable to the bank: none is payable on refusal of planning permission. For that reason the legality of the refusal was challenged. The House of Lords upheld the refusal. Lord Reid said, 'No doubt there might be special circumstances which make it unreasonable or an abuse of power to use one of these methods, but here was non.' Even if the only reason why the local authority proceeded by way of refusing planning permission was to avoid paying compensation, there was, he said, nothing wrong with that. Thus the use of a power which can validly be chosen cannot be upset simply because it means greater loss or inconvenience to those affected than if another available power had been used.[13] But in *Hall & Co Ltd v Shoreham-by-Sea UDC*[14] the Court of Appeal in holding the condition attached to the planning permission to be unreasonable, was influenced by the fact that if the local authority had used powers available under the Highways Act 1959, compensation would have been payable to the plaintiff.

A choice of powers was in issue in *Asher v Secretary of State for the Environment.*[15] Councillors refused to increase council house rents as required by law. The minister had four courses open to him: applying for a mandamus, appointing a Housing Commissioner, reducing the authority's housing subsidy, directing the district auditor to hold an audit. He chose the last course of action. This resulted in the councillors being surcharged and disqualified. They said that the minister's direction to hold the audit was ultra vires, as the minister was motivated by an ulterior purpose, to see them punished. (*Sydney Municipal Corpn v Campbell*[16] was relied on.) Or at least, they said, he was influenced by irrelevant considerations. (*Associated Provincial Picture Houses Ltd v Wednesbury Corpn*[17] was referred to.) The court found no abuse of power. Balancing the advantages and disadvantages of one course of action against another is what ministers have to do. In the absence of bad faith the decision could not be questioned. Even if the minister thought that the result of his decision might be that the councillors would be disqualified, there was nothing wrong with that, the court said. Contrast *R v Secretary of State for the Environment, ex p Fielder Estates (Canvey) Ltd*[18] where the choice made from four possible courses of action was held to be irrational.

12 [1971] AC 508, [1970] 1 All ER 734.
13 See *R v Immigration Appeal Tribunal, ex p Cheema* [1982] Imm AR 124; *R v Exeter City Council, ex p J L Thomas* [1990] 1 All ER 413.
14 [1964] 1 All ER 1, [1964] 1 WLR 240; p 238 above.
15 [1974] Ch 208, [1974] 2 All ER 156.
16 See p 245 above.
17 See p 239 above.
18 (1988) 57 P & CR 424, p 258 above. See *R v Chief Constable of West Midlands, ex p Carroll* (1994) Times, 20 May unfair to dispense with services rather than bring disciplinary charges.

In 1975 a road construction company faced liquidation with a motorway contract unfinished. Having decided that the least expensive way of ensuring that the motorway would be finished was by giving the company financial assistance, the government had to examine the statutory powers available. There was power to give assistance under the Highways Act to finance road construction companies, and under the Industry Act to rescue particular firms for employment reasons, etc. The department had no doubt that the former was the more appropriate. The Public Accounts Committee noted that under the latter, specific parliamentary approval would have been necessary, whereas it was not under the former.[19]

Where a choice of powers is available, to fail to consider the use of one of them may invalidate the use of the one chosen.[20]

The use, to a citizen's disadvantage, of an alternative procedure, though lawful, may justify criticism by an Ombudsman.[1]

Subjectively worded pre-conditions for exercise of power

It is common for statute to provide that A may exercise a power 'if he is satisfied' as to B, or 'if he thinks that' a certain state of affairs, (B), exists, or some similar formulation. The donee of the power, A, appears to be the sole judge of whether the conditions exist which justify his exercise of the power. Is that the case? On what grounds can his judgment be upset?

In *Liversidge v Anderson*[2] the Home Secretary could under a Defence Regulation make an order directing a person to be detained 'if he has reasonable cause to believe [him] to be of hostile origin or associations'. Liversidge was detained by such an order and sued the Home Secretary for false imprisonment. The majority of the House of Lords held that it *could not inquire* whether in fact the Home Secretary had reasonable grounds for his belief. The order was not challengeable except for bad faith. In effect the House decided that the words 'if the Secretary of State has reasonable cause to believe' meant 'if the Secretary of State thinks he has reasonable cause to believe'. Lord Atkin, in his celebrated dissent, said that the words gave the minister only a conditional authority to detain without trial, the condition being that he had reasonable cause for the belief which led to the detention order.

The factual background in *Nakkuda Ali v Jayaratne*[3] was very different: it was to do with the regulation of a licence to trade. The regulation in question provided 'where the Controller had reasonable grounds to believe that any dealer is unfit to be allowed to continue as dealer, the Controller may cancel the textile licence ...'. Lord Radcliffe, delivering the judgment of the Privy Council referred to *Liversidge v Anderson* and said:

19 Sixth Report from the Committee of Public Accounts, 1975–6, HC 584.
20 *R v Stroud District Council, ex p Goodenough* (1980) 43 P & CR 59.
 1 Eg Annual Report of the Parliamentary Commissioner for 1976, HC 116, paras 35, 36.
 2 [1942] AC 206.
 3 [1951] AC 66. See Simpson *In the highest degree odious*.

Their Lordships do not accept a similar construction of the words of [this] regulation ... Indeed it would be a very unfortunate thing if the decision of *Liversidge's* case came to be regarded as laying down any general rule of law as to the construction of such phrases when they appear in statutory enactments ... After all, words such as these are commonly found when a ... law making authority confers powers on a minister or official. However read, they must be intended to serve in some sense as a condition limiting the exercise of an otherwise arbitrary power. But if the question whether the condition has been satisfied is to be conclusively reached by the man who wields the power, the value of the intended restraint is in effect nothing ... Their Lordships therefore treat the words in [this] regulation ... as imposing a condition that there must in fact exist such reasonable grounds known to the Controller, before he can validly exercise the power of cancellation.

In *Liversidge's* case Lord Atkin was prepared to accept that a different form of wording from that in issue could have imposed a purely subjective test and suggested 'A-B may if he is satisfied that there is reasonable cause to believe ...' In *Ross-Clunis v Papadopoullos*[4] a colonial governor had power to impose a collective fine if he 'satisfied himself' as to certain matters. The Privy Council said that while the test whether the governor had satisfied himself was a subjective test (namely whether he believed himself to be satisfied), if it could be shown that there were no grounds on which he could be satisfied, a court might infer either that he did not honestly form that view or that, in forming it, he could not have applied his mind to the relevant facts.

The Secretary of State sought to rely on Lord Atkin's example, quoted above, as justifying a subjective test, in *Secretary of State for Employment v Associated Society of Locomotive Engineers and Firemen (No 2)*.[5] The statutory provision in question was that where it appeared to the Secretary of State that there were reasons for doubting whether workers taking part in a strike were doing so in accordance with their wishes, he could apply to the Industrial Court for an order for a ballot to be held amongst them. The Court of Appeal was not prepared to say that the test here was wholly subjective. The question was not therefore whether the court *could* inquire into the minister's reasons, but whether in the present case it *should*, and the court would intervene where in the nature of things there could be no evidence on which a reasonable minister could have formed the reasons for the doubts in question; or if it could be shown that on the facts of the particular case no reasonable man in the position of the Secretary of State could have reached his conclusion without misdirecting himself, it would be open to the court to act on the basis that the statutory requirements were not satisfied. Lord Denning's opinion was that the words 'if it appears to the Secretary of State' do not put the decision beyond challenge. 'The scope available to the challenger depends very much on the subject matter with which the minister is dealing.' In this case the court would intervene if the minister did not act in good faith, or acted on

---

4   [1958] 2 All ER 23, [1958] 1 WLR 546, PC.
5   [1972] 2 QB 455, [1972] 2 All ER 949.

extraneous considerations, or misdirected himself. But if he honestly took a view of the facts or the law which could reasonably be entertained, his decision was not, in this emergency procedure intended to deal with strikes affecting the national economy, to be set aside simply because someone thereafter thought his view was wrong.[6]

There was a quite different factual situation again in *Secretary of State for Education and Science v Tameside Metropolitan Borough Council*.[7] The question was whether section 68 to the Education Act 1944 gave an absolute discretion to the Secretary of State. The section provides that 'if the Secretary of State is satisfied' that any local education authority have acted unreasonably he may give such directions as appear to him expedient. The House of Lords was clear that the words 'if the Secretary of State is satisfied' did not confer absolute discretion on him and that it could decide whether grounds existed which were capable of supporting his decision, and whether he had misdirected himself in law in arriving at his decision. Lord Wilberforce commented:

This form of section is quite well known, and at first sight might seem to exclude judicial review. Sections in this form may, no doubt, exclude judicial review on what is or has become a matter of pure judgment. But I do not think that they go further than that. If a judgment requires, before it can be made, the existence of some facts, then although the evaluation of those facts is for the Secretary of State alone, the court must inquire whether those facts exist, and have been taken into account, whether the judgment has been made on a proper self-direction as to those facts, whether the judgment has not been made on other facts which ought not to have been taken into account. If these requirements are not met, then the exercise of judgment, however bona fide it may be, becomes capable of challenge.

This line of authority was confirmed in *IRC v Rossminster Ltd*.[8] Acting under a warrant an Inland Revenue official could remove from premises 'any things whatsoever found there which he has reasonable cause to believe may be required as evidence'. When the legality of a seizure was challenged the Revenue conceded that the officer must in fact have reasonable cause for his belief, and that it was not enough that he honestly believed that he had such cause. The existence of that reasonable cause is a matter of fact to be tried on evidence. Lord Scarman commented: 'The ghost of *Liversidge v Anderson* therefore casts no shadow upon this statute. And I would think it need no longer haunt the law. It was laid to rest by Lord Radcliffe in *Nakkuda Ali v Jayaratne* and no one in this case had sought to revive it. It is now beyond recall.' Lord Wilberforce said '[P]arliament by using phrases such as "is satisfied", "has reasonable cause to believe" must be taken to accept the restraints which the courts in many cases have held to be inherent in them.'

---

6 In the ballot the workers indicated their support for the strike. See also p 329 below.
7 [1977] AC 1014, [1976] 3 All ER 665. See p259 above. Applied in *Norwich City Council v Secretary of State for the Environment* [1982] 1 All ER 737.
8 [1980] AC 952, [1980] 1 All ER 80.

Uncertainty

Where an administrative decision or rule is expressed in ambiguous language – capable of bearing more than one meaning – the court will have to decide in the light of all the relevant circumstances what meaning is to be given to it. Where a penal liability is involved, it is to be interpreted strictly, for, 'A man is not to be put in peril upon an ambiguity'.[9] Where it is impossible to resolve an ambiguity or where the decision is capable of no sensible meaning, it will be void for uncertainty.

Uncertainty is, however, most likely to be invoked in administrative law where a decision or rule lacks *that precision which the circumstances require*.[10] In particular where a prohibition supported by criminal penalties is enforced on the citizen, he is entitled to know with some precision what he must not do. In *Kruse v Johnson*[11] Matthew J said that a byelaw must be certain 'in that it must contain adequate information as to the duties of those who are to obey'. In *Nash v Finlay*[12] several byelaws pronounced certain acts to be annoyances, for example, using threatening, abusive or insulting behaviour, or a squirt. Nash was prosecuted under another byelaw which made it an offence 'wilfully to annoy passengers in the street'. The court ruled that in the light of the other byelaws, it was difficult to understand what activities that byelaw was intended to cover. It was void for uncertainty. And in *Staden v Tarjanyi*[13] a byelaw forbidding hang-gliding was bad for uncertainty (but not unreasonableness) as it did not indicate sufficiently clearly what was prohibited. In *R v Barnet London Borough Council, ex p Johnson*[14] the (Conservative) council granted permission for the use of land for a festival subject to conditions intended to discourage controversial discussion, eg the land was not to be used in connection with any political activity, and no organisation which sought to oppose a political party could attend. These absurd conditions were struck down for uncertainty, meaningless and unreasonableness, as well as for improper purpose (and for having been imposed by reason of a blanket policy).

An enforcement notice served under the Planning Acts has to specify the matters alleged to constitute a breach of planning control, and the steps required to remedy the breach: it must do this not with total precision, but so as to make clear what is alleged and what is to be done.[15] The same principle applies to a notice served under the Housing Act requiring repairs to be done.[16]

9 Per Lord Simonds in *London and North Eastern Rly Co Ltd v Berriman* [1946] AC 278, [1946] 1 All ER 255.
10 Eg *Alderson v Secretary of State for the Environment* (1985) 49 P & CR 307 ('locally'); *United Bill Posting Co Ltd v Somerset County Council* (1926) 42 TLR 537 ('natural beauty').
11 [1898] 2 QB 91.
12 (1901) 85 LT 682.
13 (1980) 78 LGR 614.
14 (1989) Times, 26 April.
15 Eg *Newport v Secretary of State for the Environment* (1980) 40 P & CR 261.
16 Eg *Our Lady of Hal Church v Camden London Borough Council* (1980) 40 P & CR 472.

Where a permission is given to do something but subject to a condition then, especially if breach of the condition may lead to criminal proceedings, the condition must be expressed with sufficient precision. Thus a condition attached to a planning permission requiring a site to be 'kept in a tidy state', or that 'no nuisance is to be caused' by the operations permitted, would be void.[17] But a condition (imposed in the interest of preserving a green belt) limiting the occupation of a cottage to persons whose employment is in agriculture or in an industry mainly dependent on agriculture was valid. It could, the House of Lords said, be sensibly applied to such cases as might arise and therefore had sufficient precision for meeting the purpose for which it was imposed.[18]

Inconsistency

Consistency in decision-making is a major administrative virtue, and one of the purposes of bureaucratic procedures. Administrators must, within the statutory framework provided evolve policies and procedures which will ensure its achievement. The Chief Adjudication Officer has referred to the difficulties of Adjudication Officers in achieving consistency.

AOs ... must impose a period [of disqualification for benefit] ranging from one day to 26 weeks with no assistance by way of statutory guidelines. This is asking a good deal of them. They understandably feel the need for more detailed guidance ... in the interests of consistency and fair treatment, but legal advice confirms that I am unable to do more than guide them on their general approach.[19]

The Home Office has sent a circular to police authorities to try to reduce inconsistencies in the use by police of the cautioning of offenders.

In general the provision of an appeal system should help to ensure consistency among those whose decisions are subject to appeal, particularly where reasons have to be given by the appellate body: the insistence by the courts on adequate and clear reasons will be significant in achieving that consistency.

The Board of Inland Revenue has said that where different bodies of Appeal Commissioners are taking inconsistent views of the law on some point, it is up to it to try to achieve consistency by taking the matter before the court.[20]

When it was proposed to delegate the Secretary of State for Health's power of deciding certain appeals, the first idea was that it should be delegated to the 14 Regional Health Authorities, but this was rejected on the ground that consistency would be difficult to achieve. The power was therefore delegated to one RHA which acts on behalf of all the others.[1]

17 Circular 1/85 of the Department of the Environment. A condition to a licence to deal in milk was invalid for uncertainty in *R v Milk Marketing Board, ex p North* (1934) 50 TLR 559.
18 *Fawcett Properties Ltd v Buckingham County Council* [1961] AC 636, [1960] 3 All ER 503.
19 Annual Report for 1987–88, para 4.15. For AOs see p 141 above.
20 125th Report Cmnd 8947 (1983) Ch VI.
 1 See the First Report of the FHSA Appeal Unit, pub Dept of Health 1994.

The Chief Planning Officer, referring to the system whereby planning appeals are decided by individual inspectors has said that close and continuing attention is paid within the Inspectorate to ensuring a consistent approach on the part of inspectors.[2] And in the same field, the court has ruled that where an appeal is being considered by an inspector, a previous appeal decision in respect of the same land materially indistinguishable from the present must be taken into account. He is free to depart from the previous decision, but before doing so ought to have regard to the importance of ensuring consistency, and must give reasons for departing from it.[3]

In order to achieve consistency in, for example, handling a large number of applications for grants, an administrative authority may adopt a policy or general rule. The propriety of doing so is acknowledged by the courts, provided of course the policy is within any statutory limits and does not deprive the authority of the ability to exercise its discretion in respect of the merits of each case.[4]

A policy may then be necessary to ensure consistency: but a policy may be incompatible with a consistency being argued for. Thus if a prosecuting authority, for example the Revenue, can lawfully have a policy of selective prosecution, this may mean that it is discriminating between one dishonest taxpayer and another. But what consistency (and fairness) requires in such a situation is that each case is considered fully on its merits to see whether the criteria for prosecution are satisfied.[5]

Inconsistency in decision making is an aspect of unfairness and in its desire to see fair administration the court may be influenced by any proved inconsistency. In *HTV Ltd v Price Commission*[6] the inconsistency of the Commission's decision was powerful support for the argument that it must have misunderstood its powers.

There is no doubt that inconsistency could justify a finding of maladministration by an Ombudsman. The Parliamentary Commissioner has referred to the need on his part to promote consistency by departments in their use of the Code of Practice on Access to Government Information.[7]

Delay

All decisions and procedures take some time: delay means taking an inappropriate, unnecessary or unreasonable amount of it. What is

2   Chief Planning Inspector's Report for 1981.
3   *North Wiltshire DC v Secretary of State for the Environment* (1993) 65 P & CR 137.
4   See p 217 above.
5   *R v Inland Revenue Comrs, ex p Mead* [1993] 1 All ER 772. Counsel for M relied on a statement in the IR's 'Taxpayer's Charter' – 'You will be treated in the same way as other taxpayers in similar circumstances'. This has now been replaced by : 'You are entitled to expect the IR to be fair by treating everyone with equal fairness'. What, if anything, does this mean?
6   [1976] 1 CR 170.
7   Annual Report for 1993.

appropriate etc will differ from case to case. For example: a report on the exercise by local authorities of their development control functions said:

The need to process [planning] applications speedily must be balanced with other factors such as the requirement to act fairly and professionally ... It must be recognised also that there is a minimum period of time in which it is reasonable to expect applications to be determined. This time includes the basic administrative and professional work as well as the consultation processes.[8]

It may be important for a decision-maker to resist pressure for a quick decision.[9] It is clear that institutional arrangements may affect the time taken to arrive at decisions. We noted in an earlier chapter the administrative changes made over a period of years to the decision-making process in respect of planning appeals. These appear to have been made largely because of concern over delayed appeal decisions.[10]

Although delay in itself does not found a cause of action, a court may be prepared to imply some limit to the life of a statutory power granted without express limit of time, and to quash a decision taken beyond what it regards as its reasonable life[11] and it may imply a duty to consider a claim timeously.[12] Delay in the use of power will be a significant element in deciding whether it has been abandoned;[13] and delay may throw doubt on the motive of the decision-maker in exercising a power, or on its reasonableness.[14] Where delay in dealing with a matter is shown to be due to the allocation of inadequate resources by government, legal action will be successful only if it can be shown that there was a duty to make specific resources available – which is not likely.[15]

Delay is one of the matters that institutions other than the courts will concern themselves with, for example the Council on Tribunals[16], and Parliamentary Committees.[17] Allegations of delay do of course fall within the concerns of the Ombudsmen[18] and the National Audit Office.[19]

Where a member of the public delays in submitting a claim, the authority must, in relying on it, give proper consideration to the reasons for it.[20]

---

8 Audit Inspectorate *Local Planning: the Development Control Function* (HMSO).
9 *Matrix-Securities Ltd v IRC* [1994] 1 All ER 769.
10 See p 123 above.
11 *R v Governor of Durham Prison, ex p Singh* [1984] 1 All ER 983, [1984] 1 WLR 704.
12 *R v HM Treasury, ex p Petch* [1990] COD 19.
13 *Grice v Dudley Corpn* [1958] Ch 329, [1957] 2 All ER 673.
14 *R v Birmingham District Council, ex p Sale* (1984) 48 P & CR 270. *Preston v IRC* [1985] 2 All ER 327.
15 See eg the *Hincks* case p 185 above; cf Ombudsman's attitude, p 543 below.
16 See p 170 above.
17 See ch 16 below.
18 In case 217/V the complaint was of *delay*; in the preceding case in the report – C168/V – the complaint was that the decision had been taken so *quickly* that it could not have been properly considered: First Report from the Parliamentary Commissioner, 1975–76, HC 37, p 78. For the Parliamentary Commissioner, see ch 16 below.
19 See ch 16 below.
20 *R v Criminal Injuries Compensation Board, ex p S* (1995) Independent, 28 March.

Chapter 9

Procedure and the law

Procedure is important. It acknowledges the value of and the need to protect certain interests, or fails to do so: it can hinder or assist efficient administration. It must always observe the requirements of statute and the common law. There is no statute of general application laying down principles of good procedure to be observed by public authorities: the statute establishing the administrative scheme in question has to be looked at to see what procedure, if any, is to be followed. It is in fact very common for a statute conferring a power on a public authority to require it to follow a specified procedure. There may, for example, be a duty to consult, to ascertain the views of those affected, to give notice to the public or to the individuals concerned of proposed action, to hold a public inquiry, to pass a resolution in specified terms, to lay a document before Parliament, etc.

A common ground for attacking in the courts an administrative decision is that the authority has not followed the procedure required by statute. This will involve the court in interpreting the statutory requirement. In addition to this interpretive role the courts have come to impose their own procedural requirements on administrative authorities under the rubric of 'the rules of natural justice' or, nowadays 'fairness', but the role of ministers, administrators, parliamentary draftsmen and members of the legislature and others in evolving and providing in statute, sometimes in great detail, procedural safeguards should not be overlooked and should indeed be seen as the primary source of such safeguards. This is not to say that such safeguards are always provided, or that they are adequate.

A further introductory point to be noted is that an attack on the legality of the *procedure* followed is generally made because of disagreement with the *merits* of the decision taken following the procedure in question. Clearly if one is advantaged by a decision one is not likely to query the procedure by which it was arrived at. On the other hand if one is disadvantaged by a decision but an attack on the merits is not thought likely to succeed, an attack on the procedure may be contemplated.

It might be possible and thought profitable to attack both the merits and the procedure.

272

The effect of successfully showing that the procedure was defective is considered below. But even if the decision is struck down because of the defective procedure (which may not be the case), the victory may prove to be hollow, for it may be possible for the authority to go back to the beginning, this time following the correct procedure, and arrive quite lawfully at the same decision.

Statutory requirements

The effect of the failure to observe statutory requirements

A statute which imposes a procedural obligation may state what the effect is of a failure to observe that obligation. But it does not generally do so. That means that it is up to the courts to say what the effect of such a failure is to be. Important though procedure is, it is not the case that failure to observe a procedural requirement will necessarily invalidate the act to which it relates. Those who hope to trip up the administration by proving a procedural error may well be disappointed. What then is the test to apply in order to determine the effect of a failure to observe a procedural requirement? It is sometimes said that the test is to classify the requirement as either mandatory or directory. If it is mandatory the effect of not following the required procedure is to invalidate or nullify the decision in question, whereas if it is only directory the failure does not have that effect: the decision stands. It was put this way in 1877:

You cannot safely go further than that in each case you must look to the subject matter; consider the importance of the provision that has been disregarded and the relation of that provision to the general object intended to be secured by the Act; and upon a review of the case in that aspect decide whether the matter is what is called imperative or only directory.[1]

But this does not mean, as it used to be taken to mean, that the test is, 'Is the procedural requirement mandatory or directory?' The test is rather, 'What is the statutory requirement? Has it been complied with? If not, is non-compliance so *important* that its effect is to invalidate the decision or act in question?' To say, therefore, that a procedure is mandatory or directory, is to express the *conclusion* that (in the first case) failure is so important that it must invalidate the act, or (in the second case) that it is not so important. Woolf LJ put it this way in *R v London Borough of Lambeth, ex p Sharp*:

When the provisions of [procedural] regulations are contravened, almost invariably it is unhelpful to consider what are the consequences of non-compliance with the regulations by classifying them as containing mandatory or directory provisions, or as containing a condition precedent, or as containing a provision which renders a decision void or voidable, or by considering whether they contain a provision which goes to jurisdiction. What has to be considered is: what is the particular provision designed to achieve?[2]

1   By Lord Penzance in *Howard v Bodington* (1877) 2 PD 203.
2   (1988) 55 P & CR 232.

But, he added, and as some of the cases referred to below show, one has to look not merely at the nature of the failure in question but at all the relevant circumstances such as the interest of the party applying for relief, the lapse of time, the effect on the public etc.

A difficulty with the *importance* test is that in view of the uncertainty of the relevant factors and the weight to be given to them, it may be difficult to say what the effect is of a failure to observe a procedural requirement. It might then be thought that the former test (is it mandatory or directory?) provided a higher degree of certainty and was therefore of greater utility. However, it never was the case that that test provided any greater degree of certainty: as explained, the test itself depended on a judgment as to the importance of the procedure in question.

What guidance can we get from the cases?

(i) It is likely to be the case that if the administration is imposing a financial burden or other restriction on the citizen, procedural require-ments must be strictly observed. In *Vale of Glamorgan Borough Council v Palmer and Bowles*[3] a prosecution was brought for breach of a tree preservation order. The legislation required the order to refer to a map 'deposited for inspection' at a place convenient to where the trees are. The map is to enable the public to find out what trees are affected by the order: failure to deposit the map in the required place rendered the order invalid. And where an improvement notice failed, as required by the Housing Act, to specify the works to be done and to give the authority's estimate of the cost of carrying them out, it had no statutory force.[4] Contrast the following. An enforcement notice, seeking to prohibit unauthorised development of land, must, among other things, specify the matters alleged to constitute a breach of planning control. The notice must make it clear what the authority is alleging: if that is done, the notice has not got to 'slavishly adhere to the magic words used in the Act itself'.[5] There was substantial compliance with the requirement.

(ii) Failure to comply with a statutory requirement to hold an inquiry, or make an investigation or consult before taking action affecting others' interests is likely to invalidate the action. Thus where a recognition issue was referred to ACAS, it was required to ascertain the opinion of the workers to whom the issue related. Failure by ACAS to ascertain the opinion of a section of the workers (who had an important interest in the validity of any recommendation ACAS might make) invalidated ACAS's report.[6]

R v Brent London Borough Council, ex p Gunning[7] concerned the obligation of a local authority to 'consider a report' from its education committee before exercising its educational functions. What was the effect

3   (1982) 81 LGR 678.
4   *Canterbury City Council v Bern* [1981] JPL 749.
5   *Eldon Garages Ltd v Kingston-upon-Hull County Borough Council* [1974] 1 All ER 358, [1974] 1 WLR 276.
6   *Grunwick Processing Laboratories Ltd v Advisory, Conciliation and Arbitration Service* [1978] AC 655, [1978] 1 All ER 338. For ACAS see p 39 above.
7   (1985) 84 LGR 168.

of the failure (as in this case) to consider such a report? The court was clear that the legislature had indicated that it was important that the authority should have the evidence of its expert education committee before exercising its education functions. The exercise of any such function without first considering such a report was ultra vires.

(iii) A common procedural requirement is that the public or a particular section of it is to be informed of proposed action so that those informed can object, make representations etc. The requirement may be no more than to 'give public notice', or it may be spelled out in some detail. In the first case, the notice must do what is fairly and reasonably necessary to enable members of the public to appreciate that their interests are affected. Thus a public notice concerning common land was legally ineffective where it did not adequately identify the land, and members of the public were substantially prejudiced by being deprived of the opportunity of making objections.[8] In *Coney v Choyce*,[9] the requirements to give public notice were detailed: notices had to be given in three places. They were not given in one of these places. The court found that there was substantial compliance with the requirements. Furthermore the plaintiffs were very well aware of the proposals, so in contrast with the previous case had suffered no prejudice by the failure in question. The fact was that they had lost the battle (over the reorganisation of schools) on the merits, and were looking for some procedural defect to have the decision invalidated. But, as stated, the court found that the purpose of the legislation had been achieved. (Even if it had found for the plaintiffs, the court would have refused a remedy because of the prejudice[10] that the invalidation of the decision would cause to many other people.)

It is clear then that it is not enough to look at the procedural defect in isolation. This is brought out in another 'public notice' case, *R v London Borough of Lambeth, ex p Sharp*.[11] The local authority proposed to build an athletic track within a conservation area. They failed to comply with planning law regulations insofar as the notice published in the local newspaper did not specify the period during which objections should be made. The Court of Appeal noted that the local authority was using the special form of procedure whereby in effect the authority seeks to grant planning permission to itself. In that context the breach was fundamental 'bearing in mind that it is a provision which requires notification of proposed development to members of the public. This was in a conservation area and is obviously a matter of general local public interest. Public notification of the proposed grant of planning permission must accordingly

---

8 *Wilson v Secretary of State for the Environment* [1974] 1 All ER 428, [1973] 1 WLR 1983; *Smith v East Essex County Council* (1977) 76 LGR 332.

9 [1975] 1 All ER 979, [1975] 1 WLR 422.

10 On the question of prejudice note that a number of important statutes provide that defects of form or procedure are not to be a ground for setting aside an order (such as a ministerial decision on a planning appeal) unless the applicant has been 'substantially prejudiced' thereby. This is an acknowledgement that in the correct circumstances procedural errors can properly be overlooked. See eg Acquisition of Land Act 1981, s 24.

11 (1988) 55 P & CR 232.

be of fundamental public importance.' Now the applicant did not see or know about the defective notice for many months after it had been published – how, then, could he have been misled by it? Woolf LJ said:

While this is a factor to which the court should have regard, the position of the applicant is that he is making the application not only on his behalf but, in effect, on behalf of the public. In considering whether or not relief should be granted, the court, in my view, must have very well in mind the fact that regulations such as the one under consideration are designed to give to the public generally notice of proposals of this sort.[12]

(iv) A failure to adhere to a statutory requirement to inform the other party of his right of appeal (as of a right to object) may be fatal. In *London and Clydeside Estates Ltd v Aberdeen District Council*[13] the defendant proposed to acquire the plaintiff's land compulsorily. As required by the plaintiff it provided them with a certificate stating its opinion as to the possibility of future development of the land being permitted. This governed the amount of compensation payable. Statute required the certificate to include a statement of the plaintiff's right of appeal to the Secretary of State against the certificate. It contained no such statement. The plaintiff's appeal to the Secretary of State was out of time. The House of Lords held that the certificate was invalid. To the defendant's argument that the plaintiff had not been misled by the omission, the House of Lords replied that that was irrelevant to the question of the certificate's validity. In *Agricultural, Horticultural and Forestry Industry Training Board v Kent*[14] an assessment notice failed clearly to state the Board's address to which appeals could be sent: that was, the Court of Appeal thought, enough to invalidate the notice.

(v) Time-limits play an important part in the law. They may be specified or unspecified. In either case the effect of failure to comply will, as with other procedural requirements, depend on the circumstances. Under planning legislation, a local authority is to give notice of its decision on a planning application with eight weeks; if it does not, it is deemed to have refused permission.[15] However, a grant of permission outside that period is valid so that if the grantee appeals to the Secretary of State against a condition attached to the out-of-time grant, the local authority cannot argue that it was not valid and cannot be appealed against.[16] Likewise a refusal outside that period is valid and can be appealed against. In *Secretary of State for Trade and Industry v Langridge*[17] the minister was required to ('shall') give ten days' notice to L of his intention to apply to the court for an order disqualifying him from being a director. He gave nine. What was the effect of the shortfall? The Court of Appeal noted that

---

12 See *R v Swansea City Council, ex p Elitestone Ltd* (1993) 66 P & CR 422: non-availability of public document constituted prejudice though no specified individual affected.
13 [1979] 3 All ER 876, [1980] 1 WLR 182.
14 [1970] 2 QB 19, [1970] 1 All ER 304.
15 SI 1988/1813, art 23.
16 *James v Secretary of State for Wales* [1968] AC 409, [1966] 3 All ER 964.
17 [1991] 3 All ER 592; *Simpson v A-G* [1955] NZLR 271: time limit for issuing General Election writs not adhered to, Election not invalidated.

the object of the Act in question was to protect the public, that the protection given to L by the ten day notice was slight, that even if the application to the court was to be held void because of the shortfall the minister could immediately serve another notice. On the facts L was not prejudiced, and the shortfall was due to a genuine mistake by the ministry. The majority concluded that the procedural irregularity did not affect the validity of the application to the court.

As to unspecified time-limits, 'immediately' has been interpreted to mean that the act must be done with all reasonable speed according to the circumstances of the case.[18] Where a disciplinary charge had to be laid 'as soon as possible', it was held that this meant as soon as possible in the circumstances of the case: but this, it was said, should not lead to the requirement being treated as less stringent than on its terms it was meant to be – and the phrase was not to be equated to 'as soon as reasonably practicable'. The outcome, on the facts, was that the charge was nullified.[19]

(vi) We have seen in chapter 3 that various orders and regulations are statutorily required to undergo some form of parliamentary process. Clearly the necessity or possibility of Parliamentary involvement must be given high value but it is necessary to consider separately the significance of the various forms of parliamentary involvement. One such form is that an order or regulation is not to be made unless a draft has been laid before Parliament and been there approved. Notice that this is a prohibition on the *making* of the order: the requirement of laying and approval goes to the power of making the order at all. It has been indicated that a failure to observe that requirement would have the effect of nullifying the consequent order.[20] This is clearly right. The need to obtain a consent to the making of an order is in the nature of a condition precedent, and a failure to obtain it fatal to the order's vires: all the more so when the consent required is that of the body which empowered the making of the order in the first place: and even more so when the consent required is that of Parliament. A different requirement is that where regulations have been made, they are not to have effect unless affirmatively approved. Here again 'are not to have effect' surely cannot be evaded. On a descending scale of importance is the requirement that a regulation which has been made shall be laid before Parliament and there be subject to annulment ie be subjected to the possibility of being annulled. What effect is to be given to the failure to give Parliament the opportunity of annulling an instrument? What if the requirement was a bare laying requirement? Where a statutory instrument has by inadvertence not been laid, the official practice is to lay a new instrument before Parliament

---

18 *R v Inspector of Taxes, ex p Clarke* [1974] QB 220, [1972] 1 All ER 545; *Cullimore v Lyme Regis Corpn* [1962] 1 QB 718, [1961] 3 All ER 1008.
19 *R v Chief Constable of the Merseyside Police, ex p Calveley* [1986] QB 424, [1986] 1 All ER 257. For 'as soon as practicable' see *Merrill v Chief Constable of Merseyside Police* [1990] COD 61.
20 *R v Department of Health and Social Security, ex p Camden London Borough Council* (1986) Times, 5 March.

and to say that failure to lay the original instrument did not prevent it having full legal effect from the date it purported to do so, but it is possible to argue the contrary, hence the laying of the new instrument.[1] An Indemnity Act is sometimes required as in the case of the Town and Country Planning Regulations (London) (Indemnity) Act 1970. It was explained that the Act was needed as private rights were affected and planning permissions granted over a five-year period by the Greater London Council would be otherwise invalid.

Ministerial orders and regulations, and other decisions, are commonly required to be published in various specified ways. Those which are statutory instruments are subject to requirements as to numbering, printing, and availability for sale. It may follow from *R v Sheer Metalcraft Ltd*[2] (which concerned a statutory instrument) that failure to observe those requirements will not invalidate an instrument.

Notice that statute may well impose some procedural obligation on the administratee as well as on the administrator. An example is *Howard v Secretary of State for the Environment*.[3] A person on whom an enforcement notice is served may appeal to the Secretary of State. The Act provides that the appeal 'shall be made by notice in writing ... which shall indicate the grounds of the appeal and state the facts on which it is based'. The appeal has to be submitted within 42 days. The plaintiff gave notice of appeal within that time, but the notice did not give the grounds or facts required. Those were notified outside the 42-day period. The court held that nevertheless the appeal had been validly made. How is the distinction to be explained? The effect of submitting an appeal is to suspend the enforcement notice: no steps can be taken to enforce it until the appeal is disposed of. There has to be therefore some fixed time by which the appeal is to be notified. The purpose of the other requirement on the other hand, is merely to inform the minister of the grounds and facts: that can be done later, and in any case, even if the grounds etc were given, they might well have to be amended after submitting the notice.

Statutory consultation

Consultation is an important part of public administration, and aspects of it and of related procedures have been considered (see p 128 above). The requirements of a statutory duty to consult are not infrequently considered by the courts and the outcome may be explained as follows. (The imposition by the courts of a duty to consult, give a hearing etc, is considered at p 282 below.)

---

1 Eg H of C Official Report (5th series) vol 718, col 1339. For failure to consult Council on Tribunals, and re-making of regulations, see its Annual Report for 1967, para 43.
2 [1954] 1 QB 586, [1954] 1 All ER 542. See p 84 above.
3 [1975] QB 235, [1974] 1 All ER 644, CA.

First, a dispute may arise as to what matters are to be the subject of consultation, as in *Sinfield v London Transport Executive*[4] where the question was whether, in view of the proposed alteration of bus routes, consultation had to take place on traffic congestion only, or also on inconvenience to bus passengers.

Second, consultation involves communication with the person consulted. So it has been held that where there is an obligation to consult a particular body 'the mere sending of a letter constitutes but an attempt to consult and this does not suffice'.[5] If the letter is received, but no reply sent, the obligation is satisfied. What if the failure to receive a reply is due to the non-receipt of the letter seeking consultation? Does it follow that where no reply is received, a further letter must be sent inquiring whether the first letter had been received? It is arguable that the test ought to be whether reasonable steps had been taken to contact those entitled to be consulted.

Third, on matters the subject of consultation, there is a duty not merely passively to receive and consider the views expressed but to volunteer[6] sufficient information to enable those consulted to consider properly their response to the proposals. In *Rollo v Minister of Town and Country Planning*[7] the validity of an order designating Crawley as a new town was challenged for lack of consultation (there being such a duty). The challenge failed on the facts, but Lord Greene indicated what consultation requires:

The minister in fulfilling the duty of consultation, would naturally and indeed ought to put to the authorities any point on which in his honest opinion he considered they could assist him in the task which he had in hand ... he must allow any authority who has a point it considers will help him to put it forward.

Bucknell LJ approved of the way Morris J had put in the court below:

The Minister, with receptive mind, must by such consultation seek and welcome the aid and advice which those with local knowledge may be in a position to proffer.[8]

In *Fletcher v Minister of Town and Country Planning*[9] Morris J said that the minister had satisfied the obligation to consult by clearly informing the local authorities that he had under consideration the development of a new town, and by giving them the opportunity of saying anything they wanted to say. Nevertheless the information volunteered by the authority must include the reasons for what is proposed: how else can they be intelligibly considered?

4　[1970] Ch 550, [1970] 2 All ER 264; *R v Devon CC, ex p Baker* [1995] 1 All ER 73: was consultation about closure or relocation on closure? And see *R v Tunbridge Wells Health Authority, ex p Goodridge* (1988) Times, 21 May.
5　*Agricultural, Horticultural and Forestry Industry Training Board v Aylesbury Mushrooms Ltd* [1972] 1 All ER 280 at 284, [1972] 1 WLR 190 at 194. Case note by Foulkes 35 MLR 647.
6　See Lord Bridge in *Westminster City Council v Greater London Council* [1986] AC 668, at 693, [1986] 2 All ER 278 at 289.
7　[1948] 1 All ER 13.
8　Ibid at 16 and 17.
9　[1947] 2 All ER 496.

The fact is that the precise requirements of consultation will differ from case to case. In *Port Louis Corpn v A-G of Mauritius*[10] Lord Morris said that 'the nature and effect of consultation must be related to the circumstances which call for it'. For example consultation may in certain circumstances be a continuous or iterative, not a one-off, process.[11] (Where there is a succession of meetings they should not be looked at in isolation.[12]) And in *R v Secretary of State for Health, ex p US Tobacco International Inc*[13] consultation was said to require a high degree of fairness and candour. This was because the regulations being challenged, though general, applied almost exclusively to the applicant, and their effect was catastrophic. This obliged the minister to give them a full opportunity to know and respond to the scientific material and its evaluation which led to the change of policy to which the regulations gave effect.

Fourth, consultation must be started at the appropriate time, that is, before the point at which the proposals on which consultation is required have become so inflexible that consultation can serve no useful purpose.

Fifth, the person consulted must, subject to any statutory time-table, be allowed a reasonable time to put his case. In *Lee v Secretary of State for Education and Science*[14] the Minister was by law bound to give school governors 'an opportunity of making representations to him' on a certain matter. He gave them four days! The Department conceded that there was a duty to give a real and not an illusory opportunity to make representations. The court held that four days was wholly unreasonable and extended the time by four weeks. In the *Port Louis* case the authority was given only eleven days to submit their comments, a time which seemed to the Board to be 'remarkably short and particularly so in the absence of stated reasons which pointed to a measure of urgency'.

Concerning the effect of urgency, in *R v Secretary of State for the Environment, ex p Association of Municipal Authorities* the Secretary of State,[15] S, consulted, as he was obliged to, with AMA and others before making regulations. AMA argued that the consultation was wholly inadequate. S sought to justify the inadequate consultation on the ground of urgency. The court said that urgency could not absolve from the duty to consult at all. The question was, given the urgency, was the consultation adequate? On the facts it was not. (Note that statute may absolve from the duty to consult in the case of urgency.)

Finally, consultation in all cases clearly requires that the opinions and views expressed be considered with, as Morris J put it, a 'receptive' mind. If

---

10 [1965] AC 1111, [1965] 3 WLR 67.
11 *R v Shropshire Health Authority, ex p Duffus* (1989) Times, 16 August: where there is a duty to consult X on 'proposals' and they are altered as a result of consultation with others, is there a duty to consult X again? In *R v Lord Chancellor, ex p Law Society* (1993) Time,s 5 May, counter-proposals by Society did not justify further consultation.
12 See fn 9 above.
13 [1992] 1 All ER 213.
14 (1968) 66 LGR 211. See Crossman, *The Diaries of a Cabinet Minister*, Vol 2, pp 479, 485, for 'political insanity' and Prime Minister's rebuke.
15 [1986] 1 All ER 164, [1986] 1 WLR 1.

it could be shown, as in *Wood v Ealing London Borough*[16] that those consulted were presented with a *fait accompli*, there would be a failure to consult.

Failure to consult may be a matter for criticism by administrative law institutions other than the courts. The Parliamentary and Local Commissioners may find such failure to constitute maladministration. In one case of interest the Parliamentary Commissioner ruled the general practice of consulting traders through a trade association to be satisfactory, but that the department had a responsibility to ensure that any information the association disseminated was accurate.[17] A parliamentary committee may also take an interest in the extent of consultation. The Joint Committee on Statutory Instruments in considering regulations on the contentious issue of the weight limits of lorries asked the department for a list of organisations consulted and for the result of the consultations.[18]

Fairness in administration

We have considered various procedural requirements imposed on public authorities by statute, and the courts' attitude towards a failure to observe them. In addition the courts may impose procedural requirements on public authorities, either where there are no statutory procedural requirements[19] or by adding to them. It may be easier for the courts to imply procedural safeguards where Parliament has provided none, than where it had laid down a procedure, for where it has provided a procedure, particularly where it is detailed, the courts may be reluctant to add to it, a reluctance which, however, they will overcome where they have found it necessary to ensure that fairness is achieved. Lord Reid warned that 'before this unusual kind of power is exercised it must be clear that the statutory procedure is insufficient to achieve justice and that to require additional steps would not frustrate the apparent purpose of the legislation.'[20] Lord Bridge put it this way, '[I]t is well established that when a statute has conferred on any body the power to make decisions affecting individuals the courts will not only require the procedure prescribed by statute to be followed, but will readily imply *so much and no more* to be introduced by way of additional procedural safeguards as will ensure the attainment of fairness.'[1] Great weight must thus be given to the statutory procedure and to the purpose it is intended to achieve.

16 [1967] Ch 364, [1966] 3 All ER 514.
17 Third Report, 1977–8 HC 246, p 238. For the Commissioner, see ch 16 below.
18 Third Report from the Joint Committee on Statutory Instruments, 1982–3, HC 29–iv. For the Committee see p 92 above.
19 Procedural requirements may be added to the exercise of prerogative as of statutory powers, see the *GCHQ* case, p 290 below.
20 *Wiseman v Borneman* [1969] 3 All ER 275 at 277.
 1 *Lloyd v McMahon* [1987] AC 625 at 703, [1987] 1 All ER 1118 at 1161. Italics mine. 'So much and no more': *R v Birmingham City Council, ex p Ferrero Ltd* [1993] 1 All ER 530: sufficient – more would frustrate statute. *R v Secretary of State for the Home Dept, ex p Abdi* (1994) Independent, 21 April: procedure for asylum seeker not so unfair as to require additional obligation, which might frustrate statute, cf *R v Secretary of State for the Home Dept, ex p Pegg* (1994) Independent, 9 Sept: mandatory life system unfair, duty to give reasons added.

From natural justice to fairness

Historically, the principles on which the court acted were expressed in terms of natural justice. What is 'natural' justice? Is it to be distinguished from some other kind of justice? It has been suggested that the distinction is rather between a basic part of justice which may be called 'natural', and its super-structure (though it may be that justice itself is 'far from being a "natural" concept').[2] Or it is 'justice that is simple or elementary as distinct from justice that is complex, sophisticated and technical'.[3] Or we may say that it represents the basic irreducible procedural standard with which administrators are required to comply. Or perhaps the 'romantic' word 'natural'[4] could with advantage be dropped.

If administrators were required to comply with justice that is 'complex, sophisticated and technical' what would be required of them? We may identify as features of the full judicial process: notice of the specific issue to be tried; of the place and time of the hearing which will be in public; legal representation; the submission of evidence by each party, including the calling of witnesses subject to cross-examination, and the making of the decision on the basis only of the evidence produced, its announcement and the reasons therefor and a right of appeal. By way of contrast, at the opposite end of a spectrum, we may think of the administrative process thus: the authority is of opinion that certain action is necessary; it gathers information and opinions from whatever source it pleases, gives such weight to such part of it as seems to it to be relevant, arrives at a decision in private, announces it when and to whom it thinks fit without disclosing the evidence on which it is based or the reasons for the decision.

The 'basic' content of the judicial model is expressed in terms of 'rules' of natural justice which are, first, that a person affected by a decision has a right to be heard, second, that the person taking the decision must not be biased.[5] (There seems no reason why they should not be expressed as one rule, that there is a right to a fair hearing, or that there is a duty to give a fair hearing.)

To what kinds of decisions or, in what situations, are these rules applicable? There was a time when they were said to be applicable only when the act in question was classified as judicial, rather than executive or administrative. This meant that in deciding whether natural justice had to be observed in any particular case and what it required, one asked, first, was the act in question judicial in its nature. If the answer was no, natural justice did not have to be observed. If yes, the next question was, what did natural justice require in this particular case. This approach is illustrated by the following cases.

2 Per Megarry VC in *McInnes v Onslow-Fane* [1978] 3 All ER 211 at 219, [1978] 1 WLR 1520 at 1530.
3 Per Megarry J in *John v Rees* [1970] Ch 345 at 399, [1969] 2 All ER 274 at 306.
4 Ormrod LJ in *Norwest Holst Ltd v Secretary of State for Trade* [1978] Ch 201 at 226, [1978] 3 All ER 280 at 294. For a statutory use of the phrase see Foreign Compensation Act 1969, s 3(10). For duty to have regard to need to observe 'justice and fairness' see Education Reform Act 1988, s 202(2)(c).
5 Or *audi alteram partem* and *nemo judex in sua causa*, but to what advantage?

In *Nakkuda Ali v Jayaratne*[6] the controller of textiles in Ceylon had power to cancel the licence of a dealer in textiles where he had 'reasonable grounds to believe' that the dealer was unfit to continue in business. The Privy Council held that the controller, in withdrawing the dealer's licence, was not acting judicially, in that he was not 'determining a question', but was taking executive action so that he was not bound to give the dealer a hearing. In *R v Metropolitan Police Comr, ex p Parker*,[7] a cab driver's licence was revoked by the Commissioner. The court held that the Commissioner's function was administrative and that neither he nor a committee set up to advise him was bound to hear any evidence from the cab driver. A leading case is *Franklin v Minister of Town and Country Planning*.[8] The minister had made a draft order under the New Towns Act 1946 designating Stevenage as a 'new town'. Objections were lodged and a public local inquiry was held. The minister confirmed the order. Before these events, and even before the Act became law, the minister had spoken at a public meeting called to explain why Stevenage had been selected. In reply to the heckling the minister said, 'It is no good your jeering: it is going to be done.' The legality of the minister's order was challenged on the ground inter alia that this remark and others showed that he was biased in that he did not approach the public inquiry and the confirmation of the order with a mind open to conviction. The House of Lords held that the minister's statutory duties were 'purely administrative' and that any reference to judicial duty or bias on the part of the minister was irrelevant.

In *Ridge v Baldwin*,[9] one of the seminal cases in modern administrative law, Ridge, the Chief Constable of Brighton, was tried for conspiring to corrupt the course of justice but acquitted. Nevertheless, the trial judge severely criticised his conduct; his position was clearly untenable. The Watch Committee then dismissed him using a statutory power which empowered them to dismiss any constable 'whom they think negligent in the discharge of his duty'. Ridge was not present at their meeting nor was he given notice of the proposal to dismiss him, particulars of the ground on which it was based, or an opportunity of putting his case. The Court of Appeal, relying on *Nakkuda Ali* (above) (and upholding the High Court) held that the committee was acting only in an administrative capacity, but the House of Lords disagreed. As the committee had not, as they found, observed the rules of natural justice, its decision was void.

Cooper v Wandsworth Board of Works[10] was one hundred years before *Ridge v Baldwin*. The Board was empowered by statute in some circumstances to demolish houses. It pulled down Cooper's without giving him a hearing. Cooper argued that no man is to be deprived of his property without being given an opportunity to put his case. But was this principle

6 [1951] AC 66.
7 [1953] 2 All ER 717, [1953] 1 WLR 1150, DC.
8 [1948] AC 87, [1947] 2 All ER 289.
9 [1964] AC 40, [1963] 2 All ER 66.
10 (1863) 14 CBNS 180.

not limited to judicial hearings? The judgments proceeded on the basis that Cooper's right to a hearing depended on the answer to that question, spoke of the Board's 'jurisdiction' over the matter, emphasised the significance of the fact that an appeal from the Board's decision would itself be judicial, and concluded that he was entitled to a hearing. Now if we remove that conceptual approach the question to ask would be, not, is this a judicial or administrative activity but, what was the case for and against imposing an obligation to give a hearing – and the court did look at the issue in that way. It emphasised the severity of the power granted to the Board.[11] And the desirability of a hearing was explained this way by Erle CJ:

I cannot conceive any harm that could happen to the district board from hearing the party before they subjected him to a loss so serious as the demolition of his house; but I can conceive a great many advantages which might arise in the way of public order, in the way of doing substantial justice, and in the way of fulfilling the purposes of the statute, by the restriction which we put upon them, that they should hear the party before they inflict upon him such a heavy loss ... I have not heard a word to show that it would not be salutary that they should hear the man who is to suffer from their judgment before they proceed to make the order.[12]

Procedures cannot in fact be easily classified into the judicial on the one hand and the administrative on the other. They vary even within the judicial, running 'from the borders of pure administration to the full hearing of a criminal cause or matter in the Crown Court'.[13] This difficulty of applying the judicial/administrative dichotomy led to the use at one time of the concept of the quasi-judicial, that is, of the administrator having in some way to behave like a judge in respect of some part of his administrative function (that is quasi-judicially). This was an added complication – in what way, and in respect of what part? (The use of 'quasi-judicial' survives in some quarters.)

These points must raise doubts as to whether the correct approach is to test the validity of administrative procedure by reference to those used in the courts of law – that is, whether it accords to what is judicial. In *Local Government Board v Arlidge*[14] a local authority made a closing order in respect of an unfit house. After an inquiry, held in connection with an appeal against the order, the order was confirmed by the Board (a government department). The legality of the order was challenged on grounds relating to the procedure followed by the Board in arriving at its decision. The House of Lords was unanimously and strongly of the opinion that as the function in question had been given to a department and not

---

11 The Act, of 1855, provided that if seven days' notice was not given before laying the foundation of a house or making any drain, the Board could demolish the house, alter the drain etc. There had been severe outbreaks of cholera in the preceding decades.
12 Byles J memorably said that a long line of decisions established that 'although there are no positive words in a statute requiring that a party shall be heard, yet the justice of the common law will supply the omission of the legislature'.
13 Per Lord Lane CJ in *R v Commission for Racial Equality, ex p Cottrell and Rothon* [1980] 3 All ER 265 at 271, [1980] 1 WLR 1580 at 1587.
14 [1915] AC 120.

to a court of law, it was proper for the department to follow its own procedure in the matter, subject of course to any statutory requirements. It was a fallacy, it said, to assume that the procedures of a court of law were appropriate, and to test the Board's procedures by reference to them.

Taking stock at that point, the first four cases referred to – *Nakkuda Ali, ex p Parker, Franklin* and *Ridge v Baldwin* show both the importance then made of the distinction between the judicial and the administrative, and the difficulty of making it. If, however, we look at the older case of *Cooper v Wandsworth Board of Works* we see a different approach being suggested (never mind the classification of the act, what is the case for and against a hearing?) leading to the conclusion that the party affected was entitled to a hearing. In *Local Government Board v Arlidge* again, the testing of an *administrative* decision by what was done in a court of law, ie in a *judicial* context, was rejected. Of course, the House of Lords said, the decision-maker had to give both sides a fair hearing. This could be said to be acting judicially in that that is what a court does, but it is not the case that one had to do this – act fairly – only if one was acting judicially, for the obligation to act in that way – to 'act in good faith and fairly listen to both sides' – lies on 'anyone who has to decide anything', as Lord Loreburn put it.[15]

There were thus conflicting lines of authority, but the narrower view (requiring the 'rules of natural justice' to be applied only when the administrator was acting 'judicially', and exemplified particularly by *ex p Parker* – p 283 above) prevailed at least until *Ridge v Baldwin* which is regarded as changing the atmosphere of this part of administrative law.

An important case leading towards the recognition of a general duty to act fairly was *Re K (H) an infant.*[16] K was entitled to enter the UK if he satisfied the immigration officer that he was under 16. The officer took the view on the evidence that K was at least 16. K sought to quash the order refusing him admission. He argued that in deciding whether or not he was 'satisfied', the immigration officer was acting in a judicial or quasi-judicial capacity and had to conform with the rules of natural justice (which, it was alleged, he had not done). Lord Parker CJ said that he doubted whether immigration officers could be said to be acting in the sense contended for but that even if the officer was not, he must at any rate give the immigrant an opportunity of satisfying him as to his age, and for that purpose let the immigrant know what his impression was so that he could disabuse him of it. 'That is not, as I see it, a question of acting or being required to act judicially but of being required to act fairly.' He added: 'I appreciate that in saying that, it may be said that one is going further than is permitted on the decided cases because heretofore at any rate the decisions of the courts do seem to have drawn a strict line in these matters according to whether there is or is not a duty to act judicially or quasi-judicially.' (And referring to *Nakkuda Ali*, he said that it was not there said that if there was no duty to act judicially then there

15 In *Board of Education v Rice* [1911] AC 179 at 182. See Dicey (1915) 31 LQR 148.
16 [1967] 2 QB 617, 1 All ER 226.

was no duty even to be fair.) Salmon LJ agreed that judicial procedures were not required of the immigration officer; he had to act 'fairly in accordance with the ordinary principles of natural justice'. Blain J said that whether the officer's function was administrative, executive or quasi-judicial he had to act fairly, by which he meant applying his mind dispassionately to a fair analysis of the particular problem and the information available to him in analysing it. (The court was agreed that the officer had acted fairly.)

We find in that bold decision both a refusal to be strait-jacketed in the judicial-administrative dichotomy and the introduction of (or reintro-duction or emphasis on) the idea of fairness. In *Schmidt v Secretary of State for Home Affairs*[17] S, a US citizen, had been allowed into the UK for a limited period. His application to the Home Secretary for an extension of leave was rejected without giving him a hearing. Lord Denning said that the former distinction between acting administratively and acting judicially was no longer valid. And in *R v Gaming Board for Great Britain, ex p Benaim and Kahdia*[18] he categorised as heresy the view that the principles of natural justice apply only to judicial and not to administrative proceedings.

This trend was further reinforced by the Court of Appeal in *Re Pergamon Press Ltd*.[19] The Board of Trade ordered an investigation into the affairs of P Ltd. The directors of that company said that the inspectors appointed by the Board should conduct the investigation as if it were a judicial inquiry in a court of law. The opposing view was that the inspectors were not bound by the rules of natural justice. Neither extreme view was correct. The inspectors had to act fairly even though they were only acting administratively.

In *R v Commission for Racial Equality, ex p Cottrell & Rothon*[20] Lord Lane CJ said 'It does not profit one to try to pigeon-hole the particular set of circumstances either into the administrative pigeon-hole or into the judicial pigeon-hole. Each case will inevitably differ, and one must ask oneself what is the basic nature of the proceeding which was going on here?' In *Bushell v Secretary of State for the Environment*[1] Lord Diplock said:

[R]ather than use such phrases as 'natural justice', which may suggest that the prototype is only to be found in procedures followed by English courts of law, I prefer to put it that in the absence of any [detailed statutory rules] the only requirement ... as to the procedure to be followed at a local inquiry ... is that it must be fair to all those who have an interest in the decision that will follow it.

In *Council of Civil Service Unions v Minister for the Civil Service*[2] Lord Roskill said that natural justice might now be laid to rest and be 'replaced

---

17 [1969] 2 Ch 149, [1969] 1 All ER 904.
18 [1970] 2 QB 417, [1970] 2 All ER 528.
19 [1971] Ch 388, [1970] 3 All ER 535.
20 [1980] 3 All ER 265, [1980] 1 WLR 1580.
 1 [1981] AC 75, [1980] 2 All ER 608.
 2 [1985] AC 374, [1984] 3 All ER 935.

by speaking of a duty to act fairly'. Lord Scarman spoke of 'the requirement of natural justice namely the duty to act fairly', observing that it is required of purely administrative acts, and in *Lloyd v McMahon*[3] Lord Bridge said that the phrase 'the requirement of fairness' better expresses the concept underlying the 'so-called rules of natural justice'.

We have therefore arrived at the position that in seeking to impose some procedural requirement on the administration it is not now necessary to show that the body in question was in the circumstances acting judicially (or quasi-judicially), or to refer to rules of natural justice. It is enough to ask whether in all the circumstances of the case, it was acting fairly. There is no doubt however that reference is still being made to the requirements of the rules of natural justice, particularly, but not exclusively, when referring to bodies, such as tribunals, which have a high judicial content.

One point needs clearing up. Reference to the 'rules' of natural justice suggests that they provide a more certain answer to the questions that arise than the seemingly rather vague 'fairness'. But the 'rules' never did provide that certainty. Lord Morris said:

We often speak of the rules of natural justice. But there is nothing rigid or mechanical about them ... [A]ny analysis must bring into relief rather their spirit and their inspiration than any precision of definition or precision as to application ... The principles and procedures are to be applied which in any particular situation are right and just and fair. Natural justice, it has been said, is only 'fair play in action'.[4]

Tucker LJ said:

The requirements of natural justice must depend on the circumstances of the case, the nature of the inquiry, the rules under which the tribunal is acting, the subject matter that is being dealt with and so forth.[5]

Referring to that dictum and speaking of fairness, Sachs LJ said:

In the application of fair play there must be real flexibility, so that very different situations may be met without producing procedures unsuitable to the object in hand ... In each case careful regard must be had to the scope of the proceeding, the source of its jurisdiction (statutory in the present case), the way in which it normally falls to be conducted and its objective.[6]

A caveat against the use of fairness as a substitute for natural justice must be entered; first, fairness can be achieved other than through (the equivalent of) the rules of natural justice (for example through estoppel or the rule against retrospectivity); and second, 'fairness' may suggest that the courts are concerned with the fairness of the *merits* of a decision rather than with the *procedure* by which it is arrived at.

3 [1987] AC 625, [1987] 1 All ER 1118.
4 *Wiseman v Borneman* [1969] 3 All ER 275 at 278.
5 *Russell v Duke of Norfolk* [1949] 1 All ER 109 at 118.
6 *Re Pergamon Press Ltd* [1970] 3 All ER 535 at 542, [1970] 3 WLR 792 at 801. See now the restatement by Lord Mustill of the application of fairness – 'essentially an intuitive judgment' – in *Doody v Secretary of State for the Home Dept* [1994] 1 AC 531, [1993] 1 All ER 92. See Mullen (1975) UT LJ 281, Loughlin (1978) UT LJ 215.

The right to a hearing

A person who is adversely affected by administrative action may argue that that action was unlawful because he was not given an opportunity to put his case against it. He may say that he should have been *consulted* or been allowed to make *representations* or to submit *objections* or *observations*, or be given an *interview*, or in some other way to have been 'heard'. (It is of course common for statute to provide some procedural protection, perhaps of the kind just specified and the court may be asked to say whether it has been provided. Note, too that the concept of the 'hearing' is a broad one: it does not necessarily imply an oral procedure and may be taken to include the other procedures referred to.) The gravamen of the complaint is that he was denied an adequate opportunity to put to the administration in the appropriate way facts, opinions, arguments, etc which he thinks it necessary for the protection of his interest to put. If the terminology of natural justice is used he will argue that the rules of natural justice applied and that they required him to be given the opportunity he desired to influence the decision-maker. If the terminology of fairness is used, the only question will be, what did fairness require in the circumstances of his particular case. In either case (natural justice or fairness) what is required is an analysis of the interests involved and of the protection needed against the action being taken.

An attempt to state some general principles determining the right to be heard was made in *Durayappah v Fernando*.[7] A statute empowered a minister to dissolve a municipal council when it appeared to him that it was not competent to perform its duties. The minister had failed to give the council a hearing before dissolving it, but was he bound to do so? Lord Upjohn, delivering the judgment of the Judicial Committee of the Privy Council, said that it was not possible or desirable to give an exhaustive classification of the cases in which a hearing is required. The correct approach, he suggested, is to bear in mind three matters: (a) the nature of the property or office held or status enjoyed by the complainant, (b) the circumstances in which the other, deciding, party is entitled to intervene, and (c) when the latter's right to intervene is proved, the sanctions he can impose on the complainant.

Let us apply these three criteria. As to (a), in the case itself, in which the Judicial Committee held that the council was entitled to a hearing, the council was entrusted with the administration of a large area and the discharge of important duties, so that its activities should not be lightly interfered with. In *Ridge v Baldwin*[8] the plaintiff held the office of chief constable. In *Cooper v Wandsworth Board of Works*[9] the plaintiff's house was demolished. In *Schmidt v Secretary of State for Home Affairs*[10] the applicant was an alien applying for an extension of leave to stay here. As an alien he had, the court ruled, no rights that were capable of being

7 [1967] 2 AC 337, [1967] 2 All ER 152.
8 [1964] AC 40, [1963] 2 All ER 66. See p 283 above.
9 (1863) 14 CBNS 180; see p 283 above.
10 [1969] 2 Ch 149, [1969] 1 All ER 904.

interfered with or, therefore, being protected.[11] though Lord Denning added, 'If his permit is revoked *before* the time limit expires, he ought, I think, to be given an opportunity of making representations: for he would have a legitimate expectation of being allowed to stay for the permitted time.'[12]

As to criterion (b) suggested in *Durayappah* it was, in that case, most serious to allege that a body of its nature was not competent. And in *Ridge v Baldwin* the authority had to be of the opinion that the chief constable was negligent in the performance of his duties.

As to the third criterion, the sanction available, in *Durayappah* the sanction was dissolution, in *Ridge v Baldwin*, dismissal; in *Cooper v Wandsworth Board of Works* the house was demolished. In *Re Pergamon Press Ltd*[13] the outcome of the inspector's investigation would only have been a report to the Department of Trade. Even so, the consequences of the report might have been serious for the applicant. In *R v Commission of Racial Equality, ex p Cottrell and Rothon*[14] on the other hand the court, acknowledging the relevance of a penalty, took into account but discounted the possibility of one being applied.

As in *Durayappah* the following cases involved more than one criterion. In *R v Secretary of State for the Environment, ex p Norwich City Council*,[15] Lord Denning observed that in exercising his default power, the Minister had dismissed the local authority, replaced it by his own civil servants, and made it pay the costs. The rules of natural justice or simple fairness required that this should not be done unless the authority was told what was alleged, and given an opportunity of answering. (This had in fact been done.) In *R v Secretary of State for the Environment, ex p Brent London Borough Council*,[16] the minister had made a rate support grant order. This entitled Brent to receive the amount provided by the order. The Minister then acquired statutory power to reduce it. He did so without hearing any representations from Brent. His decision was quashed.

Notice that the above cases show that public bodies as well as citizens are entitled to fairness. But in *Hammersmith and Fulham London Borough Council v Secretary of State for the Environment*[17] the House of Lords declined to say that a local authority was entitled to a hearing when its interest was essentially political only; those affected by the minister's decision 'capping' the authority's expenditure were community charge-payers and users of local services. Following from that, note that the duty to give a hearing may be found to be owed only to the person *directly* affected. Thus where L decided that X was not fit to trade with Y, Y was not entitled to be heard.[18]

11 But see now Immigration Appeals Act 1969, at that time before Parliament (p 139 above).
12 'Legitimate expectation' is referred to at p 290 below.
13 [1971] Ch 388, [1970] 3 All ER 535, CA.
14 [1980] 3 All ER 265, [1980] 1 WLR 1580.
15 [1982] QB 808, [1982] 1 All ER 737.
16 [1982] QB 593, [1983] 3 All ER 321.
17 [1991] 1 AC 52, [1990] 3 All ER 589.
18 *R v Life Assurance and Unit Trust Regulatory Organisation Ltd, ex p Ross* [1993] QB 17, [1993] 1 All ER 545.

Legitimate expectation

The right to a hearing, or to be consulted, or generally to put one's case, may also arise out of the action of the authority itself. This action may take one of two, or both, forms: a *promise* (or a statement or undertaking) or a regular *procedure*. Both the promise and the procedure are capable of giving rise to what is called a legitimate expectation, that is, an expectation of the kind which the courts will enforce. The analogy with estoppel will be apparent.

Consider first how an enforceable legitimate expectation can arise from a statement or undertaking. In *A-G of Hong Kong v Ng Tuen Shiu*[19] Ng was an illegal immigrant. The government announced a policy of repatriating such persons and stated that each would be interviewed and each case treated 'on its merits'. Ng was interviewed, and his removal ordered. His complaint was that at the interview he had not been allowed to explain the humanitarian grounds on which he might be allowed to stay, but only to answer the questions put to him; that though he was given a hearing, it was not the hearing in effect promised, as the promise was to give one at which 'mercy' could be argued. The Judicial Committee agreed that, on that narrow point, the government's promise had not been implemented; his case had not been considered on its merits, and the removal order was quashed. Ng succeeded on the basis that he had a legitimate expectation that he would be allowed to put his case, arising out of the government's promise that everyone affected would be allowed to do so.

In *Council of Civil Service Unions v Minister for the Civil Service*[20] Prime Minister Thatcher issued an instruction that civil servants engaged on certain work would no longer be permitted to be members of trade unions. The House of Lords held that those civil servants had a legitimate expectation that they would be consulted before such action was taken, as it was well-established practice for government to consult civil servants before making significant changes to their terms and conditions of service. In this case, it will be noted, legitimate expectation arose not (as in *Ng*) out of a *promise*, but out of the existence of a regular *practice* which could reasonably be expected to continue.

Some rules about the circumstances in which such promises or practices will be binding must be noticed.

(i) The statement or practice must be sufficiently clear and unambiguous, and expressed or carried out in such a way as to show that it was intended to be binding. Thus a statement will not be binding if it is tentative,[1] or if there was uncertainty as to what was said.[2] Where it was

---

19 [1983] 2 AC 629, [1983] 2 All ER 346.
20 [1985] AC 374, [1984] 3 All ER 935. See p 53 above. See Craig (1992) 108 LQR 79. For unions' entitlement to be consulted see *Re NUPE and COHSE's application* [1989] IRLR 202; *R v Devon County Council, ex p Baker* [1995] 1 All ER 73.
1 *R v Board of Inland Revenue, ex p MFK Underwriting Agencies Ltd* [1990] 1 All ER 91. *R v Jockey Club, ex p RAM Racecourses* [1993] 2 All ER 225.
2 *R v Shropshire Health Authority, ex p Duffus* (1989) Times, 16 August. See Lexis.

said that a recommendation from X was 'almost invariably' accepted there was no legitimate expectation that it would be accepted.[3]

(ii) The statement or practice must be shown to be applicable and relevant to the present case, and stand four-square with it. Thus where an offer of an interview had been made in 1986, but action was taken in 1988 without an interview, there was no legitimate expectation of an interview in 1988 as the circumstances then were quite different.[4] In *North East Thames Regional Health Authority, ex p de Groot*[5] it was held that a legitimate expectation to be re-appointed to the Authority on the nomination of the TUC on the expiry of a term of office could not arise from the practice of acting on such nomination. There might be many reasons for non re-appointment, and to allow the argument would fetter the Authority's discretion. It followed that there was (what was sought) no right to be heard before the decision not to re-appoint was taken. And an attempt to show that a legitimate expectation that a Lord Mayor would vote in a non-partisan way arose out of (not a practice but) an agreement to that effect, failed when it was shown that the agreement did not cover that point.[6]

(iii) Legitimate expectations are enforced in order to achieve fairness. Thus where it was argued that a previous practice of giving an oral hearing gave rise to a legitimate expectation of a hearing, the House of Lords said that the question was whether the official in question (the district auditor) had acted unfairly: he had not – in the circumstances a decision on the papers was fair.[7]

(iv) If the statement said to be binding was given in response to information from the citizen, it will not be binding if that information is less than frank, and if it is not indicated that a binding statement is being sought.[8]

(v) He who seeks to enforce must be a person to whom (or a member of the class to which) the statement was made or the practice applied. Where a department told all health authorities including B that C was amongst those who should be consulted, it was accepted that this gave rise to a legitimate expectation on the part of C that they would be consulted by B.[9] But where a particular practice had operated in relation to one class of taxpayer so that a legitimate expectation arose from it, the benefit of it could not be claimed by taxpayers not in that class.[10]

It is necessary to refer here to a case which, though not based on legitimate expectation, has been brought into later discussions on it.

3 *R v Secretary of State for the Home Dept, ex p Sakala* (1994) Times, 26 January.
4 *R v Secretary of State for the Home Dept, ex p Malhi* [1990] 2 All ER 357 (1986: application to stay. 1988: resistance to deportation order.)
5 (1988) Times, 16 April.
6 [1989] 3 All ER 149, [1990] 2 WLR 255. Approved at [1989] 3 All ER 156.
7 *Lloyd v McMahon* [1987] AC 625, [1987] 1 All ER 1118.
8 *R v Board of Inland Revenue*, fn 1 above.
9 *R v Shropshire Health Authority, ex p Duffus* fn 2 above.
10 *R v Inland Revenue Comrs* [1990] 1 All ER 173 at 182. In the *Ng* case (above) note the persons to whom the undertaking was intended to apply and how and where Ng heard of it.

In *R v Liverpool Corpn, ex p Liverpool Taxi Fleet Operators' Association*,[11] Liverpool City Council had the duty of licensing the number of taxis it thought appropriate, and had fixed the number at 300 for some years. It was considering increasing that number. The Association was interested in the number not being increased (because of the increased competition that would follow), and they were invited to make their view known to the council, which they did. The council decided to increase the number by stages, but accompanied this with an *undertaking* that this would not be put into effect until a private Bill promoted by it and aimed at controlling the number of private hire vehicles operating in the city, was in force. (The Association had argued for such control.) The council was later advised that this undertaking was not binding on it, so decided, without telling the Association, to implement the increase in the number of licences forthwith. The Court of Appeal said that while the undertaking might not be binding on it, the council could not resile from it without first giving the Association an opportunity to make representations.

The concept of expectation, legitimate or otherwise, was not referred to. Lord Denning MR relied on the authority of *Robertson v Minister of Pensions*[12] and *Lever Finance Ltd v Westminster City Council*,[13] that is, to cases on estoppel and referred to the need to honour an undertaking. The authority could not divest itself of its statutory power or duty (*Birkdale District Electric Supply Co Ltd v Southport Corpn*[14] was referred to), but the carrying out of this undertaking was entirely compatible with them. Indeed, said Lord Denning, the public interest was better served by their honouring rather than breaking the undertaking. The court was clear that it was *not* the case that the authority could not depart from its undertaking – but they could do so only after hearing what the Association had to say. (The remedy granted was an order of prohibition to prevent the council from increasing the number of licenses without first hearing the Association.)

Though the concept of expectation was not referred to one could say that the Association had a legitimate expectation that it would be further consulted before the timing of the introduction of the policy was altered to its detriment, both because of the previous consultation with it, which acknowledged its interest in the matter; and because of the undertaking as to when the policy would be effected. (The undertaking, note, was not an undertaking to give a hearing.)

It is important to emphasise that in none of the cases referred to was there any question of the authority *not being able to change its policy* on this ground: the court expressly said so in a number of them.

Consider two examples. In *Findlay v Secretary of State for the Home Department*[15] the effect of a change to the parole policy was that certain

11 [1972] 2 QB 299, [1972] 2 All ER 589.
12 [1949] 1 KB 227, [1948] 2 All ER 767. See p 224 above.
13 [1971] 1 QB 222, [1970] 3 All ER 496. See p 222 above.
14 [1926] AC 355. See p 444 below.
15 [1985] AC 318, [1984] 3 All ER 801.

prisoners would have to stay in prison longer than under the previous policy. Certainly they expected to be released on the earlier date, but, said Lord Scarman, that was not the kind of expectation that was enforceable. The only legitimate (and enforceable) expectation Findlay had was that his case would be individually examined: he had no right not to have the policy changed to his detriment. In *R v Secretary of State for Health, ex p US Tobacco International Inc*,[16] UST had built a factory with government encouragement and grant to manufacture X which had a health risk. The government later changed its mind about the magnitude of that risk and made regulations forbidding the manufacture of X. There could be no legitimate expectation inhibiting such a change of policy (though the regulations were struck down on other grounds). However certain legitimate expectations may arise in connection with policies and their application, and changes to them.

(i) Where a policy has been published, *it must be applied to cases falling within it*. In *R v Secretary of State for the Home Dept, ex p Khan*[17] K wished to adopt a child living abroad. A standard Home Office letter given him (at a citizen's advice bureau) stated the four criteria on which the Home Office had to be satisfied before giving permission. In considering the application, which was refused, a fifth criterion was taken into account. The refusal was quashed. Parker LJ said that the Secretary of State had a duty to exercise his power (which was, in this case, non-statutory) fairly. And just as in the *Liverpool Taxis* case the authority was held not to be entitled to resile from an undertaking and change its policy without giving a hearing, so here, if the Home Secretary undertook to allow in persons if certain conditions were satisfied, he too should not be allowed to resile from the undertaking without giving those affected a hearing. *Ng*, too, was relevant, he said. The terms of the Home Office letter were just as certain, in his view, as the question and answer in *Ng*'s case. The letter afforded K a 'reasonable expectation' that if the Home Secretary was satisfied as to the four specified matters an entry certificate 'would be granted'. The criteria having been published, there was a legitimate expectation that they would be applied: it would be unfair not to do so.[18] (Note also that Parker LJ said that K could not say, and had not said, that he had spent money on the faith of the letter. This, on those terms, excluded the operation of estoppel.) Dunn LJ agreed that the Secretary of State had acted unfairly, but he arrived at the conclusion via a different route, relying instead on the *Wednesbury*[19] formulation: the letter in effect indicated what matters the Secretary of State regarded as relevant; in

16 [1992] 1 All ER 212, [1992] QB 353.
17 [1985] 1 All ER 40, [1984] 1 WLR 1337.
18 Where criteria on which licences will be issued have been notified, the criteria can be changed, provided it is done fairly – see *R v Independent Television Commission, ex p TSW Broadcasting Ltd* (1992) Times, 30 March, HL. See Lexis. Student embarking on long course cannot expect criteria applying at beginning will not change during it provided fairness observed – *R v Joint Committee on Higher Medical Training, ex p Goldstein* (1992) 11 BMLR 10.
19 See p 239 above.

taking into account the natural parents' inability to care for the child he had taken into account an irrelevant consideration and had acted unfairly and unreasonably. He agreed that the letter did not create an estoppel. (Watkins LJ dissented.) The decision having been quashed, it was open to the Home Office to reconsider K's application on the basis of the letter ie the four criteria, or, if they operated the new policy ie including the fifth criterion, to give K an opportunity to say why it should not be applied in his case.

(ii) Where it has been the practice to publish a policy, there may be a legitimate expectation that *changes to it will be published*. In *R v Secretary of State for the Home Dept, ex p Ruddock*[20] R asserted that her telephone had been unlawfully 'tapped'. The criteria on which calls are intercepted by the government were published six times by Home Secretaries between 1952 and 1982. There was here an expectation, not of a hearing, but that as it had been the practice to publish the current policy, any change to it would be published. (The complaint was not that that had not been done but that the decision to tap had not been taken in accordance with published criteria. Not surprisingly, R could not prove that.)

It might be unfair to make a change in policy in such circumstances unless the body announces in advance *its intention to do so* so as to allow an affected person to make representations before any change is carried out.[1]

Bias

One of the rules of natural justice is that a party affected by a decision must be heard, and we have seen how far fairness requires it. The other rule is the rule against bias. And clearly to be biased – that is, to be disabled from taking a balanced view of what has to be decided – is unfair. So we are now concerned with this rule of natural justice, or, with the extent to which the duty to be fair excludes bias.

But what is bias? How is it proved? Until the recent House of Lords decision of *R v Gough*[2] there was a good deal of confusion as to the test to apply to determine bias. There seemed to be at least two, and in the light of the wide range of situations where bias might be alleged, it was uncertain which test applied where; another view was that there was hardly any difference between them. An unsatisfactory state of affairs, recounted in the judgment of Lord Goff.

The law can now be summarised thus:

(i) Where a person sitting in a judicial capacity has a pecuniary interest in the outcome of the proceedings, he must not sit: if he does, the decision will be struck down. In such a case it is irrelevant that there is in fact no

20 [1987] 2 All ER 518.
1 By Laws J in *R v Secretary of State for Transport, ex p Richmond on Thames LBC* [1994] 1 All ER 577.
2 [1993] AC 646, [1992] 4 All ER 481.

bias; the court will not even inquire whether there was; the 'judge' is conclusively presumed to be biased. (As is well known, even a decision of a Lord Chancellor has been struck down on this ground.[3])

This rule, as laid down in *Gough*, is expressed as applying to one sitting in a judicial capacity. 'Judicial' is of course ambiguous, but it is clear that the rule is not confined to those sitting in the law courts.

In *R v Hendon RDC, ex p Chorley*,[4] X agreed to buy land from Y subject to the condition that the council's consent was first obtained to X's proposal to erect buildings thereon. The council resolution granting him permission was quashed by order of certiorari on the ground that one of the councillors who voted for it was acting as Y's estate agent in the transaction.[5]

It will be noticed that the financial interest of one member was enough. In *Gough* bias of one member was assumed to be enough.

(ii) If actual bias (even of one member) is proved, the decision cannot stand.

(iii) But *actual* bias does not have to be proved. The question is whether there is such a degree of possibility of bias that the court will not allow the decision to stand, as where a member of the body has an interest in the proceeding which falls short of a direct pecuniary interest – see (i) above. The factual situations are so varied that the possession of such an interest will not necessarily disqualify. Each case depends on its merits (and it behoves anyone who thinks that his interest might disqualify, to disqualify himself). The facts having been established, what test will the court apply to determine whether the interest does disqualify? Before *Gough*, the test might have been whether there was a 'reasonable suspicion of bias' or a 'real likelihood' of it; with the added complication of saying whether the court should ask whether the 'reasonable man' (with knowledge of all the facts as laid before the court) would find bias, or whether the court itself should find bias. However, that is behind us. The test now, according to *Gough*, is whether the court thinks there is *a real danger of bias*, in the sense that the person in question might have unfairly regarded with favour or disfavour the case of a party to the issue under consideration. The word 'danger' – as opposed to 'likelihood' – indicates that the court is to consider the *possibility*, rather than the probability, of bias.

(iv) But is the 'real danger of bias' test always appropriate? In *Gough* the court was concerned with jurors, magistrates, courts and other tribunals, bodies with a strong judicial element. Consider *R v Sevenoaks District Council, ex p Terry*[6], a pre-*Gough* case. The council owned a site suitable for development. It agreed with its officers' recommendation that proposals put forward by developers, including taking a lease of the site, should be accepted. Some months later the council granted the developers the planning permission necessary for the proposals to be given effect.

3 *Grand National Canal v Dimes* (1852) 3 HL Cas 759.
4 [1933] 2 KB 696.
5 Members of many public authorities are now required, under pain of prosecution, to disclose any pecuniary interest in any matter coming before the authority: see p 454 below.
6 [1985] 3 All ER 226.

This was challenged on the ground of bias. The court said that of course the council had to act fairly, but it was not uncommon for a local authority to be obliged to make a decision relating to land in which it had an interest. In such a situation, it said, the application of a rule designed to ensure that a person acting *judicially* does not appear to be biased would often produce an administrative impasse. (*Chorley* was also distinguished as there an individual councillor – not as here the council as a whole – had a financial interest in the matter.) The correct test, the court said, was whether before deciding to grant permission the council had acted in such a way that it could not exercise proper discretion. It had not so acted on the facts: the decision to grant planning permission was not a foregone conclusion.[7]

In *R v City of Wakefield, ex p Warmfield Co Ltd*[8] it was said that *Gough* was not to be regarded as overriding *ex p Terry* (not itself cited in *Gough*), but that whether *Gough* or *ex p Terry* applied there was no hint of bias: it was not enough to show a pre-existing policy, or that commercial arrangements were already in place.

The rest of this section explains the situations in which bias might be found to exist. It will be noted that the cases are pre-*Gough*, and were decided on tests other than that laid down in *Gough*.

(v) Participation in, or even mere presence at a hearing by a person extraneous to the deciding body and whose presence may influence or inhibit the discussion in some way, may invalidate the decision, particularly of course when that person is in some way a party to the proceedings.

In *Cooper v Wilson*,[9] Cooper, a police sergeant, had been disciplined by his chief constable. He appealed to the Watch Committee. The chief constable was in effect a party to the appeal, as respondent. At the meeting of the Committee which heard the appeal, the chief constable sat next to the chairman. When the evidence had been heard the appellant withdrew, but the chief constable remained with the Committee while they deliberated. A majority of the Court of Appeal held that this invalidated the decision even accepting that the chief constable had taken no part in its deliberations. The risk of bias was enough.[10] (Notice that at an ordinary meeting of the Committee the chief constable, as the chief officer, would quite properly be sat next to the chairman. But when exercising this appellate function the arrangements should have reflected the nature of the proceedings.)

In *R v Barnsley Metropolitan Borough Council, ex p Hook*,[11] Hook had a licence to trade in Barnsley market. A complaint about his behaviour

---

7 This approach was followed in *R v St Edmundsbury Borough Council, ex p Investors in Industry Commercial Properties Ltd* [1985] 3 All ER 234, [1985] 1 WLR 1168. And see *R v Secretary of State for Trade, ex p Perestrello* [1981] QB 19, [1980] 3 All ER 28.
8 (1994) 67 P & CR 199.
9 [1937] 2 KB 309, [1937] 2 All ER 726.
10 See *Rees v Crane* [1994] 2 AC 173, [1994] 1 All ER 833: No assumption of undue influence through presence of third party assuming no personal malice on his part.
11 [1976] 3 All ER 452, [1976] 1 WLR 1052.

was made to the market manager who reported it to the appropriate committee. Hook's licence was revoked. At the appeal the manager, who was of course in the position of complainant or prosecutor, was (at the least) present while the committee was considering what its decision should be. Its decision was quashed.

In *R v Leicestershire Fire Authority, ex p Thompson*[12] disciplinary proceedings against a fire officer were heard by the authority rather than by the chief fire officer, as the former had made serious allegations against the latter. The case was found proved. Some minutes after the committee had begun to deliberate on the sentence the chief fire officer was called in. After a significant time the committee announced its decision. In response to protests that the chief fire officer had been present when the committee were deliberating on sentence the chairman stated that that officer had merely been asked for advice on the implication for the officer of various penalties the committee could impose, and that the sentence had been decided by the committee. The court ruled that it must have appeared to the accused that the chief fire officer had been taking part in the deliberations on sentence. In view of his hostility to the fire officer this was a clear breach of the rules of natural justice. In other cases, the court said, such a statement as that made by the chairman might put matters right, but not here.

Strong reliance was placed on that case in *R v Chief Constable of South Wales, ex p Thornhill*.[13] Thornhill, T, was charged with a disciplinary offence by a senior officer, D. When, after a hearing before the Chief Constable, C (at which D was not present), C was in his office considering his decision, D (and others) entered his office. C offered no explanation for this but when litigation was indicated, said that it was necessary for him to consult these officers on a completely different matter on which the Home Office wanted an urgent report. T claimed (only) that D's action might have given the impression that injustice might have been done. The court found that there was no 'real likelihood of bias'; and if T had a 'reasonable suspicion' of it, it was laid to rest by C's explanation.

In *Ward v Bradford Corpn*[14] a disciplinary committee of a local authority's college of education considered allegations against a student and expelled her. The authority's assistant education officer stayed with the committee whilst it deliberated, took part in the discussion and made comments adverse to her. It was argued that this invalidated the committee's decision. The Court of Appeal was clearly not happy about it. Phillimore LJ said it was 'dangerous to allow any outsider to attend meetings of the disciplinary committee'. Lord Denning said that the official could give advice on policy but it would be wrong for him to give evidence

12 (1978) 77 LGR 373. And see Council on Tribunals Annual Report for 1981–82, para 3.41.
13 [1987] IRLR 313.
14 (1972) 70 LGR 27: p 323 below. And see *Middlesex County Valuation Committee v West Middlesex Assessment Area Committee* [1937] Ch 361, [1937] 1 All ER 403; *Haddow v Inner London Education Authority* [1979] ICR 202.

as to the facts or to give an opinion on innocence or guilt. The official came very near the line but did not in the circumstances go over it.

In *Palmer v Inverness Hospitals Board*[15] the Board's solicitor 'deployed many arguments legitimate or otherwise to persuade the Board' to reject the report of a committee which recommended that P should not be dismissed. This was contrary to natural justice. The correct way for a legal adviser to act in disciplinary proceedings was considered in *Re Chien Sing-Shou*[16] where however the legal adviser was a member of the disciplinary body. For the role of a legal assessor, see the Professions Supplementary to Medicine Act 1960, 2nd Sch, para 4(3) and SI 1964/ 951.

(vi) Bias may arise where a deciding party had some previous involvement with the matter in issue. If he has already formed a concluded view of the matter, this disables him from considering it fairly. In *R v Kent Police Authority, ex p Godden*[17] B certified that G was unfit for duty. When the question of the termination of G's employment came up later B was debarred from certifying as to G's condition, as he had already formed a view on the matter.

However, we must distinguish between the case where the decision-making has formed a concluded view from that where only a provisional view has been formed. In *R v Secretary of State for the Environment, ex p London Borough of Southwark*[18] the minister decided that the council's local plan should not take effect unless approved by him (the 'call-in' procedure). His rejection of the local plan was challenged on the ground that his reasons for doing so showed that he had already made up his mind about the merits of the plan before calling it in. The ministry admitted that it had formed a view of the merits of the plan before doing so, but had reconsidered them. The court was satisfied that there was no evidence to the contrary.

A person holding an inquiry or acting as a tribunal will, quite properly, read the documents submitted by the parties relating to the hearing. As a result of doing so he will begin to form a tentative or preliminary view of the matter. There is nothing wrong in that: it does not constitute bias and he may form a view as the hearing proceeds.[19] But what he must not do, as a result of forming that view, is to shut his ears to the evidence or to give the impression that he is doing so. Where 'at least a degree of hostility and a degree of refusal to pay attention to the evidence' was shown so as to give the impression to reasonable people attending the inquiry that justice was not being done, the decision was quashed.[20]

---

15 1963 SC 311.
16 [1967] 2 All ER 1228, [1967] 1 WLR 1155.
17 [1971] 2 QB 662, [1971] 3 All ER 20, CA. See Industrial Injuries case RI/42/59: tribunal chairman knew of case as coroner. Council on Tribunals Annual Report for 1965, para 58.
18 (1987) 54 P & CR 226.
19 *Bolton Metropolitan BC v Secretary of State for the Environment* (1994) 67 P & CR 337.
20 *Halifax Building Society v Secretary of State for the Environment* (1983) Estates Gazette 679.

In *London and Clydeside Estates v Secretary of State for Scotland*[1] it was sought to upset the minister's decision on a planning appeal as he had, before he was a minister and as an MP, expressed active support for an objector to the proposed development. The court agreed that if a minister had expressed support with a degree of intransigence or intemperance so as to betray a mind not only closed to reasoned argument but unable to weigh proved facts in a fair way, then there would be a strong case for saying that he had disqualified himself from acting. What the Secretary of State had said as MP was far removed from that.

Also to be distinguished from forming a concluded view of the particular issue in question is the expression of general policy support.

In *R v Reading Borough Council, ex p Quietlyn Ltd*[2] Q's application for a sex shop licence was considered by a panel of three councillors and refused. Two of them were members of the majority group on the council which had earlier said it was not in favour of sex shops, and one of these, B, had publicly agreed that sex shops should be banned. The court said it was not wrong to appoint to the panel persons who had expressed views about whether *in general* licences ought to be granted. It might have been better if B had not been appointed, but an 'informed observer' would not have found his appointment wrong.[3]

Questions of bias might arise where a person is involved in considering repeated applications or appeals. The statutory scheme and problems of practical administration would have to be considered.

(vii) Questions of some practical importance and difficulty involving bias may arise where a number of bodies is involved in an administrative scheme and one or more persons are members of more than one of those bodies. In *Hannam v Bradford City Council*[4] H was a teacher at a school maintained by the defendant. His contract was terminated by the school governors. The defendant has power to prohibit H's dismissal. The appropriate committee of the defendant council decided not to exercise that power (this was later confirmed by the council). Three of the ten members of that committee, including its chairman, were also governors of the school in question. None of them had attended the governors' meeting at which it was decided to end H's employment. The Court of Appeal held that H had nevertheless made out a case of bias. Sachs LJ said:

The governors did not, on donning their committee hats, cease to be an integral part of the body whose action was being impugned and it made no difference that they did not personally attend the governors' meeting.

In *Hamlet v General Municipal Boilermakers and Allied Trades Union*[5] it was said that there is no rule of natural justice that a member of a body

1 1987 SLT 459.
2 (1986) 85 LGR 385.
3 In *R v Secretary of State for Health, ex p Prison Officers Association* [1992] COD 177 the appointment of members of a statutory inquiry was challenged for their bias.
4 [1970] 2 All ER 690, [1970] 1 WLR 937, CA. And *Herring v Templeman* [1973] 3 All ER 569 re-expulsion of student from college.
5 [1987] 1 All ER 631, [1987] 1 WLR 449.

who has sat at first instance is thereby disabled from sitting on an appeal. This is surely unacceptable. However, in that case the relationships were wholly governed by contract, and the terms of the contract had been complied with.[6]

(viii) We have seen that the existence or extent of the right to a hearing is affected by relevant statutory provisions. Likewise there may be statutory rules relating to bias. Statute may ensure that a person does *not* act in a situation where he might be thought to be biased.[7] On the other hand, it might *require* or empower him to act in a matter in which he has an interest and might be thought to be biased: the rule against bias may have to give way to the rule of necessity. In *Wilkinson v Barking Corpn*[8] a statute gave employees of a local authority pension rights. Any question as to an employee's entitlement was, by the statute, to be determined initially by the authority and, on appeal, by the minister. Both bodies were required to pay contributions to the fund out of which any pension was payable. It was argued that the decision of both was void as they were interested in the outcome and, in effect, judges in their own cause. It was held that as the statute provided for this method of adjudication, the courts could do nothing. In *Jeffs v New Zealand Dairy Production and Marketing Board*[9] the Privy Council found that though the Board had a duty to act judicially in the matter in question, the statute clearly contemplated that it should decide the matter even though its pecuniary interests might be affected.

In *R v Frankland Prison Board of Visitors, ex p Lewis*[10] Lewis was found guilty by the Board of a disciplinary offence. The chairman of the Board had been chairman of the local review committee who had interviewed him for the purpose of the Parole Board's consideration of his case. Did this disqualify the chairman? The Board had administrative functions in relation to the running of the prison in addition to its judicial, disciplinary function. Woolf J said that as statute gave it both those functions the Board should not be too ready to regard its general background knowledge of a particular prisoner as disqualifying it, and a reasonable man would have to take into account the functions of the Board in deciding whether it could properly act in any particular case.

An important aspect of this problem is that of bias arising from ministerial or other policy. In *Franklin v Minister of Town and Country Planning*[11] the House of Lords, it will be recalled, (see p 283 above) said the minister's function in deciding whether to confirm the draft order

6 And see the special case of *R v Crown Court at Bristol, ex p Cooper* [1990] 2 All ER 193: licensing justices exercise partly judicial, partly administrative function.

7 Eg Local Government Act 1974, Sch 4, para 1(2); SI 1985/1066.

8 [1948] 1 KB 721, [1948] 1 All ER 564.

9 [1967] 1 AC 551, [1966] 3 All ER 863. And see *R v Whyalla City Corpn, ex p Kittle* (1979) 20 SASR 386; *H Tolputt & Co Ltd v Mole* [1911] 1 KB 836; *Tito v Waddell* (No 2) [1977] Ch 106 at 239, [1977] 3 All ER 129 at 239.

10 [1986] 1 All ER 272, [1986] 1 WLR 130.

11 [1948] AC 87, [1947] 2 All ER 289.

previously made by him was 'purely administrative', and that reference to judicial duty was irrelevant. The only question therefore was whether he had properly carried out the statutory duties imposed on him. These were to appoint a person to hold the public inquiry and to consider his report. There was, said Lord Thankerton (in whose judgment all other members of the House concurred), no suggestion that the inquiry was not properly conducted, nor was there any criticism of the inspector's report. This being so, the only ground of challenge must be either that the minister did not consider the report and the objections – and of this there was no evidence – or that 'his mind was so foreclosed that he gave no genuine consideration to them, which is the case made by the appellants'. After examining what the minister had said Lord Thankerton concluded that it had not been established that the minister had forejudged any genuine consideration of the objections or that he had not genuinely considered the objections at the later stage when they were submitted to him.

Thus the statutory duty to consider the objections required their genuine consideration. The 'purely administrative' functions had to be exercised in an unbiased way. We may take Lord Thankerton's statement that reference to judicial duty was irrelevant as meaning that even though his function could not be classified as judicial, the minister had to act without bias, fairly. That interpretation is wholly in accordance with the present law.

True, to have a policy – as, in the *Franklin* case, about the building of new towns – means, or may mean, a predisposition to decide particular cases falling within it in a particular way, and if this is 'bias' then to have a policy is to be biased. But this cannot be a disqualifying interest: the statute places it on the minister. This is not to say that a minister could not be held to be biased because of some personal relationship between himself and the matter in issue – a financial benefit for example[12] or actual malice, but the 'interest' inherent in advancing a policy cannot of itself connote bias. In *R v Amber Valley District Council, ex p Jackson*[13] the members of the majority party on the council were politically predisposed, as a matter of policy, in favour of a proposed development for which planning permission was being sought by a company. This predisposition did not disqualify them or the council from adjudicating on the planning application. They were of course under a duty to act fairly and to take all material considerations, including objections, into account. There was no evidence that they would not do so.

This is a convenient place to mention parenthetically the following point. Where a person is charged before a disciplinary body of an organisation with bringing that organisation into disrepute,[14] or with breaching its

---

12 Should a town be developed towards or away from the minister's farm, where his department's decision was required?: see Crossman *The Diaries of a Cabinet Minister* vol 1, p 380.
13 [1984] 3 All ER 501, [1985] 1 WLR 298.
14 *Roebuck v National Union of Mineworkers (Yorkshire Area)* (No 2) [1978] ICR 676.

code of professional conduct,[15] the interest of the members of that organisation in its repute cannot be a disqualifying interest.[16]

What fairness requires in particular administrative contexts

Three preliminary points are to be made. First, the requirements of fairness depend on the context. This has been said too often to require authority. Second, it is not enough to show that some procedure other than the one followed by the decision-maker would be better or more fair. What must be shown is that the procedure followed was unfair. (Likewise with reasonableness: it is not enough to show that another decision would be equally or more reasonable: it must be shown that the decision taken was unreasonable.)

And third, the issue is whether the decision-maker was unfair, not whether his advisers were. In *R v Independent Television Commission, ex p TSW Broadcasting Ltd*[17] TSW submitted a bid to ITC for a licence to transmit commercial television programmes. To assist the members of the ITC, its staff put in a paper assessing that bid, which failed. A ground for challenging that decision was that the paper was slanted against TSW and did not provide a fair picture of the pros and cons of its bid; that since the paper formed part of ITC's decision, that decision should be quashed on the ground of procedural irregularity. The House of Lords rejected this. Lord Goff said that the argument confused the role of the ITC itself with that of its staff. 'Those who draft advisory papers are not decision-makers, nor are they performing a judicial or quasi-judicial role. The duty to act fairly is laid not upon the staff but upon the decision-maker himself, here the Commission.' Even if there had been errors in the paper there was no reason to assume that they would have infected the reasoning of the ITC which formed its independent judgment and did not simply follow the paper's recommendation. (It is possible to envisage circumstances – for example where the body in question accepted a recommendation as a matter of course or without discussion – where the court's decision might be otherwise.)

Making subordinate legislation
In *Bates v Lord Hailsham of St Marylebone*[18] it was argued that an order regulating solicitors' remuneration would be ultra vires and void for want of natural justice if an opportunity was not given to make representations on it. Megarry J took the view that the function of making the order was

---

15 *Re S (a barrister)* [1981] QB 683, [1981] 2 All ER 952.
16 But those charged with the regulation of a profession should be careful in framing the constitution of the governing body and of its disciplinary tribunals to ensure that the task of investigating and presenting a complaint and the task of adjudication on it are in different hands: per the tribunal in *Re S* (above). For example of separation of investigative and disciplinary functions see Professions Supplementary to Medicine Act 1960, s 8.
17 (1992) Times, 30 March. HL. See Lexis.
18 [1972] 3 All ER 1019, [1972] 1 WLR 1373.

legislative, rather than executive or administrative, and that neither natural justice nor fairness affected the process of legislation whether primary or delegated.

Is this satisfactory? First, was the making of this order part of 'the legislative process'? This particular order, affecting the remuneration of 26,000 solicitors is of sufficient generality to be regarded as legislative in nature. But was the making of it a part of the legislative process? One could of course say that the legislative process is that process which results in a legislative rule. But this order was made by the administration and what we are concerned with is the procedure to be followed by the administration no matter how many people are affected. Now it will be agreed that when a decision adversely affects an individual it is right that that individual should be given the right to comment, make representations, etc. Why should a decision affecting more than one person not involve the same right? Are the requirements of fairness less when one is dealing with a number greater than one? Would it not be in accordance with established values and with good administration for the courts to impose a duty to consult in the making of general rules? However, in this particular case, there was a statutory duty to consult A. The plaintiff was arguing that there was also a duty to consult him, B. It is easy to see that since statute dealt with the matter of consultation, a court might be reluctant to impose an additional duty to consult, a line of argument which the judge took. It follows that if there were no such statutory provisions for consultation at all, it would be less difficult for the court to impose a duty. The common law could, as elsewhere, remedy the omission of the legislature.[19] In *R v Secretary of State for Health, ex p US Tobacco International Inc*[20] the court did not shrink from talking of fairness in the context of making regulations, but there was a statutory duty to consult, and in the circumstances the court said that a high degree of fairness had to be achieved in the carrying out of that duty.

Initiating a procedure

Where the administration is merely initiating a procedure or seeking to establish whether a prima facie case against the citizen exists, the question is whether the courts will be likely to extend the statutory procedure at least where it gives a full opportunity to be heard later in the proceedings. In *Wiseman v Borneman*[1] a tribunal's function was to decide whether, on the basis of documents submitted to it by the taxpayer and by the Inland Revenue, there was a prima facie case for the Revenue to recover unpaid tax. The House of Lords held that the taxpayer was not entitled to see and answer the statements in the Revenue's documents to the tribunal.

19 For judicial review of Lord Chancellor's failure to consult with Bar over legal aid fees despite legitimate expectation see *R v Lord Chancellor, ex p Alexander* (1986) Times, 21, 22, 24, 27 March.
20 [1992] 1 All ER 212, [1992] QB 353.
1 [1971] AC 297, [1969] 3 All ER 275.

But some of the judgments suggest that that procedure would not have been adequate if the tribunal had been entitled to pronounce a final judgment: in that case the courts could supplement it as in *Cooper v Wandsworth Board of Works*[2] Lord Reid said:

Every public officer who has to decide whether to prosecute or raise proceedings ought first to decide whether there is a prima facie case but no one supposes that justice requires that he should first seek the comments of the accused or the defendant on the material before him. So there is nothing inherently unjust in reaching such a decision in the absence of the other party.

This dictum was applied in *Norwest Holst Ltd v Secretary of State for Trade*[3] The Secretary of State appointed inspectors to investigate the company's affairs. The company contended that he had not acted in accordance with the rules of natural justice in refusing to give them an opportunity to answer complaints against them before appointing the inspectors. The Court of Appeal held that the Secretary of State's decision was no more than an administrative decision the effect of which was to set in train an investigation at which those involved would have an opportunity of stating their case.[4]

Where an authority is empowered to 'suspend' a person or his licence, must it give him a hearing before imposing the suspension? In *R v Secretary of State for Transport, ex p Pegasus Holidays (London) Ltd*[5] the Secretary of State granted T a permit to operate charter flights subject to a condition as to the competence of T's aircrew. On receiving information that there were serious grounds for concern as to the aircrew's competence the Secretary of State provisionally suspended T's permit pending an inquiry into the matter. Unfairness was alleged in that no opportunity had been given to T to make representations to the Secretary of State prior to the suspension. Schiemann J held that the requirement that a person should have such opportunity could be waived where the action contemplated was merely the provisional suspension of a permit in an emergency situation which might result in the loss of many lives if action was not taken. On the facts the Secretary of State had good cause for alarm and was justified in taking swift action. (Would he not have been open to criticism for giving more weight to T's claim to a hearing than to the public's right to be protected against incompetent aircrew?)

Two earlier cases involved suspension from the Labour Party. In *John v Rees*[6] Megarry J took the view that suspension was penal, and that the rules of natural justice applied as much as to expulsion. In *Lewis v Heffer*[7] Lord Denning said that those words did apply to a suspension inflicted by way of punishment, for example suspension from practice as a lawyer for

2   (1863) 14 CBNS 180: see p 283 above. And see *Pearlberg v Varty* [1972] 2 All ER 6, [1972] 1 WLR 534, HL.
3   [1978] Ch 201, [1978] 3 All ER 280, CA.
4   And see *Moran v Lloyd's* [1981] 1 Lloyd's Rep 423, CA.
5   [1989] 2 All ER 481, [1988] 1 WLR 990.
6   [1970] Ch 345, [1969] 2 All ER 274.
7   [1978] 3 All ER 354, [1978] 1 WLR 1061.

a period, but they did not apply when the suspension was made as a holding operations, pending inquiries, (which was the case here) as when a man is suspended on full pay. In *ex p Pegasus*, above, the judge preferred to proceed on the basis that natural justice did apply, but that in an emergency situation, where only a provisional suspension was in issue, 'one is at the low end of the duty of fairness'.

These and other cases show that there are many situations in which fairness does not require that a person must be told of complaints against him. This is likely to be the case where the investigation is preliminary only, where there is a full chance to deal with the allegations later, where urgency justifies not giving a hearing etc.

But there is no absolute rule that no opportunity to put one's case need be given, provided a later opportunity is given to do so. What is necessary to achieve fairness always depends on the circumstances. Thus where[8] there was a three-stage procedure for removing a judge, with a right to a hearing at stages two and three, fairness required a hearing at the first stage also given the seriousness of the charges, the publicity given to the matter and the damage to the judge's reputation (but it was emphasised that the ruling was not limited to those holding judicial office. It was noted also that there was no question of urgency.)

Licensing applications

Licensing procedures are legion. Some are laid out in statute in great detail; but whether or not that is the case the courts are not infrequently involved in questions concerning the legality of the procedure followed. In *R v Liverpool Corpn, ex p Liverpool Tax Fleet Operators' Association*[9] Lord Denning said that it was 'putting it a little high' to say that in exercising a licensing function a local authority was acting judicially. 'They may be said to be exercising an administrative function. But even so in our modern approach they must act fairly, and the courts will see that they do.'

Is an applicant for a licence entitled to support his application with *oral* arguments where the statute is silent on the matter? It seems not. It is within the licensing authority's discretion, and in deciding whether the discretion has been properly exercised, the court will take into account among other things the practicalities of the situation.

Is an applicant entitled to deal with objections made to his application by third parties? In *R v Huntingdon District Council, ex p Cowan*[10] C applied to H for a licence for public entertainment. H received observations on the application from a fire authority and objections from the police (C had been required by the statute to notify these bodies), and an objecting petition from the public. C was not told that objections had been received; the application was refused. Glidewell J said that the exercise of a licensing

8 *Rees v Crane* [1994] 2 AC 173, [1994] 1 All ER 833.
9 [1972] 2 QB 299, [1972] 2 All ER 589.
10 [1984] 1 All ER 58, [1984] 1 WLR 501.

function is one to which the rules of natural justice (or, we may say, fairness) normally apply, including the giving of notice of the substance, at least, of objections, and giving some opportunity to respond to those objections. Nothing in the relevant Act excluded that requirement. He added that it did not necessarily follow that an oral hearing should take place: written representations might in many cases suffice.

The following case shows that if an applicant is given a hearing an objector may be entitled to one. In *R v Great Yarmouth Borough Council, ex p Bottom Bros Arcades Ltd*[11] M applied for planning permission for an amusement arcade. Objectors understood that it would be refused in line with the council's established policy. Unusually the planning committee gave M an oral hearing, and recommended approval. The objectors' request to be heard was denied. The court held that they should have been. (The argument that they had a legitimate expectation of being heard was rejected.)

In *R v Bristol City Council, ex p Pearce*[12] P's application for a street trader's licence was refused. The committee had had before it an objection from another trader. The court held that the committee (though not bound to give an oral hearing or to give reasons: it had done neither) had to tell applicants of the substance of objections, and to allow them to comment on them, which it had not done. (But it refused a remedy, as the objector had merely said that if P were granted a licence, he would suffer increased competition – which was obvious.)

It seems from these cases that it is the substance of or a sufficient indication of the objections that has to be notified. One asks, why not the actual objection? There may be a significant difference between the actual terms of the objection and the terms as paraphrased for the applicant by the authority. It may be said that if there was such 'significant difference' there would be a failure to give the 'substance' as a 'sufficient indication' of the objections. But how is the applicant to know whether the 'substance' does accurately reflect the actual terms? The development of the law on this point has been affected by the leading case of *R v Gaming Board for Great Britain, ex p Benaim and Khaida*.[12a] B applied for a certificate of consent from the Board. He gave all the information required but it was clear to him, at a meeting at the Board, that it had acquired much further information about him. B sought to quash the Board's refusal of consent because it refused to give him details of the objections the Board had to his application based on that further information. The Court of Appeal held, contrary to the Board's assertion, that the Board was bound to observe the rules of natural justice. But what did they require here? – that the Board had to give the applicant an opportunity of satisfying them of the matters the Board was required to take into account such as character and reputation, and had to let him know what their impressions were so that he could disabuse them: without necessarily disclosing every detail or who their informants were they had to give the applicant sufficient

11 (1987) 56 P & CR 99.
12 (1985) 83 LGR 711.
12a[1970] 2 QB 417, [1970] 2 All ER 528.

indication of the objections raised against him so as to enable him to answer them. All this the Board had done. Lord Denning contrasted this situation with that in *Ridge v Baldwin*[13] where a man was dismissed from an office and *Cooper v Wandsworth Board of Works*,[14] where a man was deprived of his property. In such cases 'chapter and verse' had to be quoted against him. But here the Board did not *charge* B with doing anything wrong: their job was rather to inquire into the applicant's character etc and to protect the public interest. Notice the circumstances of the case. The Board was set up to ensure that gaming was not allowed to get into the hands of disreputable and criminal elements, a policy aim with which the court naturally had sympathy.

In *McInnes v Onslow-Fane*[15] the plaintiff made his sixth application for a boxing manager's licence. His request for an oral hearing and for notification of anything that might prevent him getting a licence was refused. Megarry VC said that in a *forfeiture* case notification of charges was plainly apt; but in an *application* case there was no charge, so no need to be heard in answer, only the question of general suitability. There was an *intermediate* category, where the applicant had some legitimate expectation from what had happened, that his application would be granted, as where he applied for *renewal* of his licence: this should be treated as akin to forfeiture. This was not such a case. Being an application case, what did fairness require? The licensing authority accepted that it had to act without bias and not in pursuance of a capricious policy. It was not argued that it had not so acted. The court was unwilling to add a duty to give an oral hearing (or to give reasons).

Central Council for Education and Training in Social Work v Edwards[16] concerned not an application for a licence but for admission to a college. It was held that an applicant was not entitled to a hearing or to be given reasons for refusing to admit him. If, however, he was interviewed, it had to be (and had not been) done fairly: it was proper for the court to intervene in the present case as the institution, a polytechnic, was publicly funded, and as the applicant was deprived of the opportunity to get a professional qualification.

Investigative procedures

Investigative procedures are of considerable importance in public administration and have not surprisingly been considered by the courts at the instance of those who feel hard done by them. The contrast between such procedures and the judicial process has been referred to.[17]

Investigative procedures are, as the following cases will show, used in many different contexts, but there is no doubt that, whatever the context,

13 [1964] AC 40, [1963] 2 All ER 66; p 283 above.
14 (1863) 14 CBNS 180; p 283 above.
15 [1978] 3 All ER 211, [1978] 1 WLR 1520.
16 (1978) Times, 5 May.
17 See p 158 above.

they must be fair. The precise requirements of fairness will, as is often said, differ from case to case. An understanding of what fairness demands can therefore only be hoped for by examining particular cases. In *R v Deputy Industrial Injuries Comr, ex p Moore*[18] Diplock LJ referred to the investigative nature of insurance tribunals. This was relevant to the question of the kind of evidence they could rely on. He said that in a case such as this there were two relevant rules of natural justice (or two relevant aspects of fairness). The *first* was that the tribunal must base its decision on the evidence, that is, 'on material which tends logically to show the existence or non-existence of facts relevant to the issue to be determined ... He may take in to account any material which, as a matter of reason has some probative value'. The *second* rule is that the tribunal must listen fairly to the contentions of all persons who are entitled to be represented at the hearing, it must inform every person represented of any evidence it proposes to take into account whether found by a party or discovered by the tribunal itself; it must allow each party to comment on that evidence, and to address argument to it on the whole of the case.

An investigative procedure of a very different kind was in issue in *Mahon v Air New Zealand Ltd*.[19] Following an air disaster in which an aircraft owned by the defendant crashed in Antarctica killing 257 people, a judge of the New Zealand High Court was appointed to be a Royal Commission to inquire into the disaster. The judge, the appellant M, found that the cause of the disaster was the act of the airline in changing the computer flight track of the aircraft without telling the aircrew, and that this mistake was due to the airline's incompetence. He also found that there had been a deliberate destruction of documents. Accordingly, exercising a statutory power, the judge ordered the airline to pay a large sum towards the cost of the report. The airline applied for judicial review of the order as to costs (not of the report itself). Lord Diplock delivering the judgment of the Privy Council, said that the requirements of natural justice that applied to this case were the two indicated (by Diplock LJ) in *ex p Moore* (above), and concluded, very reluctantly, that the judge's findings (that there had been a deliberate destruction of documents and concealment in the change of flight path) had been made in the absence of any probative evidence and without giving the persons affected an opportunity to rebut them. Those findings were the basis of the costs order, which therefore had to be quashed.

Insurance tribunals (referred to in *ex p Moore*) and their successors are, despite the reference to their investigative function, much more towards the judicial end of the spectrum than the procedural in the case just mentioned, and than in that now to be considered.

The companies' legislation has long contained provisions providing for the appointment by a government department in certain circumstances of inspectors to investigate the affairs of companies. The inspector's function is to establish the facts, and to report. In *Re Pergamon Press*

18 [1965] 1 QB 456, [1965] All ER 81.
19 [1984] AC 808, [1984] 3 All ER 201.

Ltd[20] the inspectors wished to take evidence from the directors of the company, but the directors asked for assurances that if allegations were made against them by other witnesses they would be given an opportunity to read the transcripts of evidence and of meeting allegations. This the inspectors refused to do. Were they right?

The Court of Appeal, after examining the statutory context and purpose of the procedure in issue, concluded that the directors were not entitled to the assurances they sought. They were in effect arguing that the inspectors should act like a court of law, which they were not. The procedure could be left to the inspectors subject to this, that, in Lord Denning's words, 'Before they could condemn or criticise a man, they must give him a fair opportunity for correcting or contradicting what is said against him. They need not quote chapter and verse. An outline of the charge will usually suffice.'[1]

In *Selvarajan v Race Relations Board*[2] Lord Denning, referring to the many types of bodies which have to investigate and form an opinion, said that what fairness required depended on the nature of the investigation and the consequences it might have.

The fundamental rule is that, if a person may be subjected to pains or penalties or be exposed to prosecution proceedings, or be deprived of remedies or redress, or in some such way adversely affected by the investigation and report then he should be told the case made against him and afforded a fair opportunity of answering it ... It need not put every detail of the case against a man. Suffice it if the broad grounds are given.

In the case in question S alleged that the Board's procedure in investigating – and rejecting – his complaint was unlawful in various respects. Scarman LJ observed that S's allegation was based on a complete misconception of the Act – that in creating the Board and its network of investigating committees an administrative agency whose procedures were not adversarial: its functions were to investigate, form an opinion, conciliate and as a last resort to bring civil proceedings.

Lord Denning's dictum was relied on in a case involving an investigation of quite a different nature in *Public Disclosure Commission v Isaacs*.[3] The Bahamas Public Disclosure Act 1976 requires members of Parliament of the Bahamas to disclose their financial affairs to the Commission. The Commission examines every declaration made to it and if satisfied with it, publishes a summary of the declaration. Any person may make a written complaint to the Commission in relation to such summary. The Leader of the Opposition, KI, complained that the financial reports made by the Prime Minister, P, had been incomplete. The Commission investigated the complaint and concluded that it was not substantiated. KI sought a certiorari on the ground that once the Commission had formed the opinion

20 [1971] Ch 388, [1970] 3 All ER 535.
 1 For sequel see *Maxwell v Department of Trade and Industry* [1974] QB 523, [1974] 2 All ER 122: An unsuccessful challenge to the inspectors' procedure, their report being very critical of the plaintiff.
 2 [1976] 1 All ER 12, [1975] 1 WLR 1686.
 3 [1989] 1 All ER 137, [1988] 1 WLR 1043.

that a complaint should be investigated it was obliged to give the complainant an opportunity to meet the case made by the declarant, in this case, in answer to the complaint. Lord Bridge, delivering the judgment of the Privy Council, said that once the complaint had been put to the Commission, the procedure could take one of two possible courses of action. The first was that the procedure should take on a fully adversarial course of action, the parties putting their cases, and the Commission adjudicating between them. The second was that the Commission should act as a purely inquisitorial body making whatever further inquiries it thought necessary, and reaching its conclusion on them. Lord Denning's dictum in the *Salvarajan* case, above, was relied on as showing that there was on the Commission the duty KI contended for. However, that dictum did not apply here. KI was not liable to be 'subjected to penalties' or 'deprived of any remedies or redress'. He was merely assisting the Commission in the performance of its duties. He could not be told 'the case made against him' as no case was made against him; it was he who was making the case. True, the Commissioner's decision showed that KI's complaint was not substantiated so that he was 'adversely affected' by it; but this was not enough to outweigh the other considerations. (Any political disadvantage he might suffer was irrelevant.)

In *R v Secretary of State for Health, ex p Prison Officers Association*[4] an inquiry was held into allegations of ill-treatment of mental patients. The court, emphasising the inquisitorial rather than the adversarial function of the inquiry said, 'No one is on trial ... So decisions such as which documents are seen, which witnesses are called and how the witnesses are handled in terms of how much evidence is led, what cross-examination is allowed and to what extent attention is paid to rules governing the admissibility of evidence are all matters for the [inquiry] subject only to the overriding requirement that the proceedings shall be fair ... [W]hat cannot be done is to say that the proceedings of any inquiry are fundamentally flawed just because, for example, formal discovery or cross-examination has not been permitted to go as far as it would normally go in a trial.'

Ombudsmen's investigations

Ever since the office of Parliamentary Commissioner was created it has been the Commissioner's practice, when he has carried out his investigation into the complaint submitted to him, to send a draft of his report to the department complained of – but not to the complainant. A challenge to the legality of this practice failed in *R v Parliamentary Commissioner, ex p Dyer*.[5] The court found that there were good reasons for sending it to the department which did not apply in relation to the complainant.

---

4   (1991) Independent, 16 October. See Lexis.
5   [1994] 1 All ER 375. See Marsh [1994] PL 347. For Parliamentary Commissioner see ch 16 below.

Employment

Where the relationship is of master and servant, we are normally in the field of the common law of contract so that the principles of administrative law, including the right to a hearing, may have a limited or no application.[6] Where, however, the employment is in the public sector, statutory procedural safeguards may have to be observed. A related consideration is the remedy available. At common law the most that can be obtained in an ordinary master servant relationship is damages where the dismissal is wrongful: no order for reinstatement will be made. In the field of public employment, however, questions of vires and therefore of the nullity of official action, can arise. Associated with that is the question whether proceedings must be brought under RSC Ord 53.[7]

Ridge v Baldwin[8] concerned the dismissal of a chief constable. The Watch Committee acted under section 191(4) of the Municipal Corporations Act 1882 which empowered them to dismiss any constable 'whom they think negligent in the exercise of his duty'. In his judgment Lord Reid, referring to the right to be heard before being dismissed, distinguished three cases: (i) dismissal of a servant by his master, (ii) dismissal from an office held during pleasure, (iii) dismissal from an office where there must be something against a man to warrant his dismissal. Concerning (i) Lord Reid said, a master can terminate the contract at any time for any reason or none; though to do so may constitute a breach of contract for which damages may be awarded. 'So the question in a pure case of master and servant does not at all depend on whether the master has heard the servant in his own defence: it depends on whether the facts emerging at the trial prove breach of contract.' In case (ii) to say that an office is held during pleasure means that the person having the power of dismissal need not have anything against the officer, so he need not give any reason. But *Ridge*'s case, he said, did not fall within (i) as a chief constable is not the servant of anyone, nor within (ii), as the statute permitted the Watch Committee to remove him only on the grounds of negligence or unfitness. He thus fell within (iii), and in such cases 'I find an unbroken line of authority to the effect that an officer cannot lawfully be dismissed without first telling him what is alleged against him and hearing his defence or explanation'. (If, said Lord Reid, this case had arisen thirty or forty years previously, there would have been no difficulty in deciding the issue in favour of Ridge in view of principles established by cases going back to 1615, including *Cooper v Wandsworth Board of Works*.[9] How then had it come about that the Court of Appeal had held that Ridge was not entitled to a hearing? Because, said Lord Reid, limitations on the principles of natural justice had been introduced in various cases concerning ministers'

---

6   See Lord Wilberforce in *Malloch v Aberdeen Corpn* [1971] 2 All ER 1278, [1971] 1 WLR 1578: applied in *McClory v Post Office* [1993] 1 All ER 457.
7   See p 368 below.
8   [1964] AC 40, [1963] 2 All ER 66. And see p 283 above.
9   (1863) 14 CBNS 180; see p 283 above.

duties when they might have been justifiable,[10] but those limitations had wrongly tended to be reflected in cases dealing with a different subject matter, such as this.)

The following cases refer to Lord Reid's classification. In *Chief Constable of North Wales v Evans*[11] it was agreed that a probationary constable, who can, under the relevant statutory regulations, be dismissed by the chief constable when he considers that he is not fit to perform his duties, etc falls into Lord Reid's third class.

In *Tucker v British Museum Trustees*[12] the court said that the statute under which T was employed clearly empowered the trustees to appoint him during their pleasure and this they had expressly done. T therefore fell within the second of Lord Reid's categories. The Director of the Museum on the other hand holds office under the statute 'during such times as he shall behave well therein': so he could not be dismissed except for misconduct and after due inquiry in accordance with the requirements of natural justice.

In *Malloch v Aberdeen Corpn*[13] M was dismissed from his job as school teacher without a hearing. The House of Lords held that if M's status had been governed solely by common law then as one holding a public office during pleasure (Lord Reid's second class), he would not have been entitled to a hearing. However, a statute of 1882 provided that no resolution for the dismissal of such a teacher was to be valid unless notice of the motion for his dismissal was sent to the teacher not less than three weeks before the meeting, and unless the resolution to dismiss was agreed to by a majority of all the members of the body in question. M's common law position was thus 'fortified by statute' and it was implicit in the provision referred to, that he was entitled to be heard. Lord Reid observed that an elected public body is in a very different position from a private employer. True, many of its servants in the lower grades are in the same position as servants of a private employer, that is, in the first category:

But many in higher grades or 'offices' are given special statutory status or protection. The right of a man to be heard in his own defence is the most elementary protection of all and where a statutory form of protection would be less effective if it did not carry with it the right to be heard, I would not find it difficult to imply this right.

Lord Wilberforce, while acknowledging that it was right not to weaken the principle that a person holding office at pleasure has no right to be heard (a principle which 'for reasons of public policy applies at least as a starting point to so wide a range of the public service') said that the right to be heard is so important that that principle should not prevent the

---

10 He presumably had in mind cases such as *Franklin v Minister of Town and Country Planning*, p 283 above.
11 [1982] 3 All ER 141, [1982] 1 WLR 1155.
12 (1967) 112 Sol Jo 70. 'Dr Tucker maintained that the real reason for his dismissal was his interest in the Loch Ness monster ...' (1976) Times, 15 March.
13 [1971] 2 All ER 1278, [1971] 1 WLR 1578.

courts from examining the framework of the employment to see whether that right existed.[14]

One of the concepts used in this discussion is that of 'office' and 'office-holder'.[15] It is not entirely clear what an office-holder is, but it seems safe to make the following points: (i) A distinction may be made between public and other offices. The former includes (but is not limited to) the case where a person exercises his rights independent of contract as for example a police officer. (ii) The question whether a person holds an office or is an employee, may arise in a number of contexts including the law of taxation and of redundancy. (iii) A person may be an officer for one purpose but not another. (iv) An office-holder may or may not have a contract of employment. An example of the situation where he has not is where he is elected to a position eg a local authority councillor. (v) As regards the right to a hearing, the crucial question seems to be not whether a person is or is not an office-holder, but whether a statutory or other requirement provides or is to be interpreted as providing the elementary safeguard of a right to a hearing.[16]

A further consideration in the question of the right to a hearing under the rules of natural justice or fairness is now to be found in the law of unfair dismissal. By the Employment Protection (Consolidation) Act 1978 an employee within the scope of the Act who is dismissed may submit a claim to the industrial tribunal that he was unfairly dismissed. It is up to the employer to prove that the dismissal was in all the circumstances reasonable. This matter is better pursued elsewhere.[17]

What a fair hearing consists of

Must there be an oral hearing?
No: it depends on the circumstances – which did not require one in *Lloyd v McMahon*.[18] If substantial issues of fact cannot be resolved on the written evidence then an oral hearing may be required, though the mere fact of a conflict of evidence would not be enough. The subject-matter of the dispute (eg sex discrimination) and its character (as judicial or administrative) may be relevant. Administrative convenience is not wholly irrelevant in deciding on hearing or no-hearing, but must not override the exigencies

---

14 The sequel to *Malloch* should be noted: see Harlow [1976] PL at 120. Lord Wilberforce doubted *Tucker* (above) and *Vidyodaya University of Ceylon v de Silva* [1964] 3 All ER 865, [1965] 1 WLR 77 (dismissal of professor). For a trade union case and contrast between contract and public power see *Stevenson v United Road Transport Union* [1977] 2 All ER 941, [1977] ICR 893. For court's role where employing body has 'Visitor' see *Page v Hull University Visitor* [1993] AC 682, [1993] 1 All ER 97.
15 See eg Freedland *The Contract of Employment*, p 285.
16 *Yates v Lancashire County Council* (1974) 10 ITR 20, EAT (police); *Breen v Amalgamated Engineering Union* [1971] 2 QB 175, [1971] 1 All ER 1148 (trade union office-holder); *Social Club and Institute Ltd v Bickerton* [1977] ICR 911, EAT (club).
17 See eg Hepple and O'Higgins *Employment Law*.
18 [1987] AC 625, [1987] 1 All ER 1118.

of the particular case.[19] (It would not be lawful to have an inflexible policy of no-hearing.) Likewise where a minister had a discretion to dispense with an oral hearing on an appeal to him the same considerations would apply.[20]

Must a multi-member body meet?

There are many circumstances in which statute requires a decision to be taken at a meeting, and specifies a quorum.[1] If there is no such provision, must the members of a multi-member body meet, or can they arrive at their decision by written and/or electronic communication? There can be no absolute rule. In *R v Army Board of the Defence Council, ex p Anderson*[2] the matter in question was determined by the (two) Board members who considered the papers separately, and reached individual conclusions. Dealing as it did with a fundamental statutory right – not to be discriminated against – the Board had to reach, the court said, a high standard of fairness: one of the many flaws was that the members should have met together.

Adequate notice, adjournment

The notice given of a hearing must be of sufficient length to enable the case to be prepared. In *R v Thames Magistrates' Court, ex p Polemis*[3] a conviction was quashed as the defendant had clearly not had sufficient time to prepare his defence: this was more important than the fact that he might leave the jurisdiction. But where in *Ostreicher v Secretary of State for the Environment*,[4] adequate notice of a public local inquiry was given, it was not improper for a last minute application for a deferment to be refused and for the inquiry to proceed in the applicant's absence.

To fail to accede to a request for an adjournment may amount to a failure to give a hearing and thus to a failure of natural justice as in *R v South West London Supplementary Benefit Appeal Tribunal, ex p Bullen*.[5] The applicant was given 48 hours' notice to attend a hearing. He immediately told the tribunal that the time of the hearing coincided with an interview for employment and asked for an adjournment. The refusal of an adjournment was unlawful.[6]

In *R v Panel on Take-overs and Mergers, ex p Guinness plc*[7] the Panel declined G's request to adjourn an inquiry. The Court of Appeal concluded

---

19 *R v Army Board of the Defence Council, ex p Anderson* [1991] 3 All ER 375.
20 *R v Department of Health, ex p Gandhi* [1991] 4 All ER 547.
 1 *R v Camden Education Appeal Committee, ex p X* [1991] COD 195.
 2 As fn 19 above. See *Ex p Ladbroke Group Ltd* (1969) Times, 28 February: chairman sat too far from members.
 3 [1974] 2 All ER 1219, [1974] 1 WLR 1371.
 4 [1978] 3 All ER 82, [1978] 1 WLR 810. And see *R v North, ex p Oakey* [1927] 1 KB 491.
 5 (1976) 120 Sol Jo 437.
 6 And *Priddle v Fisher & Sons* [1968] 3 All ER 506, [1968] 1 WLR 1478; *Performance Cars Ltd v Secretary of State for the Environment* (1977) 34 P & CR 92.
 7 [1989] 1 All ER 509, [1989] 2 WLR 863, CA.

that though the decision was open to criticism, the procedure as a whole was not unfair to G – that, note, being the test.

Evidence

We have seen in some of the above cases that the person affected was entitled to know the substance of the case against him or the substance of objections to his proposals. He is not therefore necessarily entitled in such circumstances to know and challenge the specific evidence against him.

In a situation in which the judicial model applies more completely, the evidence on which the authority acts is known and is challengeable. In *R v Army Board of the Defence Council, ex p Anderson*[8] the question was whether, when the Board was considering a complaint of racial discrimination, it had to disclose to the complainant all the material seen by it, or only the gist of it. The court held that as the Board was not taking an administrative decision (requiring it merely to consult) but had a duty to adjudicate on a specific complaint of breach of a statutory right, it had to disclose all the material. This was in contrast with cases towards the administrative end of the spectrum. In *R v Department of Health, ex p Gandhi*[9] the appeal to the minister (in the matter of the distribution of medical services) was nearer the administrative end. Nevertheless the procedure had to be fair, and in this case required the disclosure to the appellant of all material necessary to enable him to present his appeal and to answer any points made against him.[10]

A different question is that of hearsay evidence. Where there are statutory rules governing the procedure in question (and it is always with those that one starts), they may expressly relax the strict rules of evidence, as for example, by permitting hearsay evidence as in *R v Deputy Industrial Injuries Comr, ex p Moore*[11] (where there was no such express relaxation) but in *R v Hull Prison Board of Visitors, ex p St Germain (No 2)*[12] it was emphasised that the Board's right to admit hearsay evidence was subject to the overriding obligation to provide the accused prisoner with a fair hearing; this, depending on the circumstances, might require the Board to permit cross-examination of witnesses whose evidence was initially before the Board in the form of hearsay.

Witnesses

Natural justice may be infringed where a person is *not allowed to call witnesses* in support of his case. In *R v Hull Prison Board of Visitors, ex p St Germain (No 2)*,[13] the High Court stated that a person charged with a

8 As fn 19 above.
9 As fn 20 above.
10 For breach of natural justice on this ground by university examiners see *R v Aston University Senate, ex p Roffey* [1969] 2 QB 538, [1969] 2 All ER 964.
11 [1965] 1 QB 456, [1965] 1 All ER 81. See p 308 above.
12 [1979] 3 All ER 545, [1979] 1 WLR 1401.
13 [1979] 3 All ER 545, [1979] 1 WLR 1401.

serious disciplinary offence under the (statutory) Prison Rules has a right to be heard himself, and to call any evidence likely to assist in establishing facts in issue. No objection could be made to the chairman of the disciplinary tribunal having a discretion to refuse to allow a witness to be called, but it had to be exercised on proper grounds. Thus he could, for example, limit the number of witnesses where he had good reason to believe that the prisoner was trying to render the hearing virtually impracticable by calling a large number of witnesses. (On the facts some of the Board's findings were quashed.)

There are cases on the *right to cross-examine witnesses*. In *University of Ceylon v Fernando*[14] an inquiry had been held into an allegation by one student, B, that another, F, had cheated in an examination. B gave evidence when F was not present. The allegation was found proved. F alleged that the decision was contrary to natural justice in that the inquiry had not told him that he could have cross-examined B. The Privy Council said that this was not in itself a breach of natural justice, but it 'might have been a more formidable objection' if F's request to question B had been refused. In *R v Army Board of the Defence Council, ex p Anderson*[15] Taylor LJ said that the object of an oral hearing 'will usually be to enable witnesses to be tested in cross-examination although it would be possible to have an oral hearing simply to hear submissions'. One could imagine a court deciding that in some circumstances a party should be told of his right to cross-examine.

A request to cross-examine was refused in *Nicholson v Secretary of State for Energy*.[16] The National Coal Board applied for a permit to carry out open-cast mining. Objections having been made, an inquiry was held. The plaintiff was allowed to cross-examine NCB witnesses, but not those who gave evidence for local authorities, as the inspector feared they would be repetitious and irrelevant. In fact the local authority's evidence was very relevant to the plaintiff's case. The Secretary of State's permit was quashed. (The court acknowledging the administrative inconvenience caused by its decision, suggested that the reconvened inquiry could be limited to the evidence in question.)

In *R v Commission for Racial Equality, ex p Cottrell and Rothon*[17] the Commission decided, on investigation, that a firm had contravened the Race Relations Act, notified the firm of that fact, and told them of their intention to issue a 'non-discrimination notice' under the Act. The firm accepted the opportunity of making oral representations, but the witnesses on whose evidence the Commission relied were not present and could not therefore be cross-examined. The firm sought to quash the decision for that inability to cross-examine. Lord Lane CJ, emphasising the administrative, as opposed to the judicial, nature of the investigation, was clear that it did not require the formalities of cross-examination. The firm sought

14 [1960] 1 All ER 631, [1960] 1 WLR 223.
15 As fn 19 above.
16 (1978) 76 LGR 693.
17 [1980] 3 All ER 265, [1980] 1 WLR 1580.

to rely on *R v Hull Prison Board of Visitors, ex p St Germain (No 2)*[18] but the facts of that case were very different: that was 'truly a judicial proceeding' and there had been an inability to cross-examine on hotly-disputed questions of identity.

In *Bushell v Secretary of State for the Environment*[19] the purpose of the inquiry (p 119 above) was to enable objections to be heard to two motorway schemes. The policy decision to build the roads was in part based on estimates of future traffic along them, and the methods used by the Department to arrive at those estimates were set out in a manual published by it, 'the Red Book'. The objectors were challenging not the routes proposed for the roads, but the need for them at all, and were critical of the traffic prediction methods contained in the Book. They were allowed to make their objections to it and to call witnesses in support but were not allowed to cross-examine the Department's witness on the subject. They alleged a breach of the rules of natural justice. The House of Lords emphasised the object of the inquiry: unlike civil litigation its purpose is to ensure to citizens affected, the opportunity to be heard in support of their objection, and that the minister is thereby better informed of the facts. To achieve that object the inspector had a discretion to disallow cross-examination which was not likely to serve any useful purpose. As all the objectors' objections had been placed before the minister, it could not be said that the inspector's refusal to allow cross-examination was unfair. And in any case the methodology used in the Red Book, which was applied *nationally*, was not suitable for investigation at individual *local* inquiries.

Legal representation

Do the rules of natural justice, or does fairness, entitle one to insist on the right to legal representation at the hearing? In *Pett v Greyhound Racing Association*[20] P was a greyhound trainer. The defendants proposed to hold an inquiry into the withdrawal of P's dog from a race on a suspicion of it having been drugged. The rules of the inquiry did not exclude legal representation. P's request to be represented by solicitor and counsel was refused. He sought a declaration that the defendants were acting ultra vires in refusing to allow him to be represented and also an interlocutory injunction restraining the holding of the proposed inquiry unless he was allowed legal representation. On the application for the injunction the Court of Appeal took the view that prima facie the trainer was entitled to an oral hearing, and as the case concerned his reputation and livelihood, to appoint agents – in this case lawyers – to speak for him. The application for an injunction was therefore granted. P's action for the declaration then came on. Lyell J relying on *University of Ceylon v Fernando*[1] held

18 Fn 13, above.
19 [1981] AC 75, [1980] 2 All ER 608.
20 [1969] 1 QB 125, [1968] 2 All ER 545.
 1 [1960] 1 All ER 631, [1960] 1 WLR 223; p 316 above. But that case was not about legal representation. For representation before tribunals see p 162 above.

that P did not have a right to be legally represented: 'I find it difficult to say that legal representation before a tribunal is an elementary feature of the fair dispensation of justice. It seems to me that it arises only in a society which has reached some degree of sophistication in its affairs.'[2]

In *Enderby Town Football Club Ltd v Football Association Ltd*[3] the plaintiff club had been fined by the FA county organisation and appealed to the FA. A rule of the FA excluded legal representation, and the FA refused the club's request to be legally represented at the appeal. The club sought an injunction to restrain the hearing of the appeal unless it was allowed legal representation. This case differs from *Pett* therefore in that there was a rule excluding representation. The Court of Appeal did not grant the injunction. The reason why legal representation was sought was because difficult points of law were involved in the appeal. That being so, said the court, the best way to proceed was for these points to be brought before the courts themselves for decision (in an action for a declaration) rather than before the FA. If the club chose to put them before the FA, they should abide by FA rules. The court also saw some advantages in some circumstances in there not being legal representation. Lord Denning's approach to the general question of the right to be legally represented was that when the rules say nothing there is no absolute right to representation – it had to be open to it to permit legal representation in the exceptional case. (His Lordship referred here to *British Oxygen v Ministry of Technology*.)[4] And that was, in his view, why the court had intervened in *Pett*, for there the tribunal had refused legal representation because it never allowed it. Lyell J was, he thought, wrong.

The above case concerned non-statutory bodies and 'domestic' tribunals. Contrast the following. In *Fraser v Mudge*[5] a prisoner was charged with an offence against prison discipline. The (statutory) Prison Rules say that at any inquiry into a charge against a prisoner he is to be given a full opportunity of hearing what is alleged against him and of presenting his case. He claimed to be *entitled* to be represented by lawyers. The Court of Appeal (on his *ex parte* application for an injunction) said that he was not. (Cases must be decided quickly, and legal representation means delay.) In *Maynard v Osmond*[6] disciplinary proceedings were brought against a police constable. The relevant statutory regulations provide that the case against the accused '*shall* be presented by a member of a police force ...' that the accused '*may* conduct his defence either in person or by a member of a police force ...'. The Court of Appeal was not prepared to interpret the latter rule as entitling the accused to be represented by a lawyer, or even as giving the chief constable any discretion in the matter. In principle, said Lord Denning, a man charged with a serious offence is entitled to

2   *Pett v Greyhound Racing Association (No 2)* [1970] 1 QB 46, [1969] 2 All ER 221. See [1970] 1 QB 67n, [1970] 1 All ER 243n. GRA made new rules allowing legal representation.
3   [1971] Ch 591, [1971] 1 All ER 215.
4   [1971] AC 610, [1970] 3 All ER 165, p 217 above.
5   [1975] 3 All ER 78, [1975] 1 WLR 1132.
6   [1977] QB 240, [1977] 1 All ER 64.

legal representation. But statute can decree otherwise, and had done so here. Other considerations were that a police officer could do as good a job as a lawyer at the hearing and that on appeal to the Secretary of State legal representation is allowed.

The above cases (and many others) were referred to in *R v Secretary of State for the Home Department, ex p Tarrant*.[7] T and four others, prisoners, were charged with assaulting prison officers, or mutiny. Their requests for legal representations or the assistance of a friend or adviser at the hearing before the prison board of visitors were rejected. The High Court ruled, in this application to quash the board's adjudications, that, following *Fraser v Mudge*, a prisoner is not *entitled* as of right to legal representation. But effect had to be given to the principle[8] that a prisoner retains all his civil rights which are not taken away expressly or by implication. It followed from this that a prisoner was entitled *to the exercise of the board's discretion* in the question of representation. In none of the five cases did the board exercise its discretion as it took the view that it had no power to grant what was asked. The court could therefore quash the adjudications. But should it? With regard to those charged with mutiny, no reasonable board could have refused legal representation, because of the complexity and seriousness of the matter. With regard to those charged with assault, their request for assistance should have been considered. Certiorari was ordered.

In *Hone v Maze Prison Board of Visitors*[9] the question of the right to legal representation was considered by the House of Lords on appeal from Northern Ireland. Hone (H) was charged before the Board with an offence against Prison Rules which was also a criminal offence (assault). The single question for the House was whether H was entitled as of right to legal representation before the Board. In seeking to show that *Fraser v Mudge* (above) was wrong, it was argued that a hearing before a Board is 'sophisticated';[10] there is an oral hearing, a formal plea is entered, cross-examination is allowed, punishments are imposed, free legal aid is available etc, and any person charged with a crime (or its equivalent) is entitled as a matter of natural justice to legal representation. The argument was rejected. It did not follow that, because a charge before a tribunal relates to facts that also constitute a crime, the tribunal is *required* to grant legal representation. If that were so, Lord Goff said (with whose judgment the others of the Committee concurred) the same argument would apply to hearings before a prison governor, and H accepted that there was no such right there where the facts might also indicate a crime. Both governor and Board have to observe the rules of natural justice: it was difficult, Lord Goff said, to imagine any circumstances where the rules would require legal representation before the governor; before the Board there was no right in every case but it might be required as in the

7 [1985] QB 251, [1984] 1 All ER 799.
8 See *Raymond v Honey*, p 203 above.
9 [1988] AC 379, [1988] 1 All ER 321.
10 For 'sophistication' see p 318 above, fn 2.

facts in the *Tarrant* case. The difference between the two was not legal but practical.

Appeal

Natural justice does not require the provision of a right of appeal.[11] But the existence or use of a right of appeal within an organisation raises some questions. In *Annamunthodo*'s[12] case A had appealed from the decision to expel him to the union's annual conference. The Privy Council held that by appealing against the decision he had not thereby forfeited his right of redress in respect of that decision in the courts.

The next question is this: if there is a defect at the hearing but none at the appeal, can the unsuccessful appellant overturn the decision by reference to the defective hearing, or is the defect cured by fairness at the appeal? In *Leary v National Union of Vehicle Builders*[13] Megarry J said that 'it was a general rule that a failure of natural justice in the trial body cannot be cured by a sufficiency of natural justice in an appellate body'. The correct thing to do, he suggested, was for the trial body to re-hear the case, rather than to treat any further hearing as an appeal. (It might not be possible for the tribunal, under its rules, to do that.) The principles were considered in *Calvin v Carr*[14] which concerned the disqualification of a racehorse owner by a Jockey Club. The Judicial Committee said that 'no clear and absolute rule can be laid down on the question' whether defects at a hearing can be cured by a fair appeals procedure. There are however, it said, a number of typical situations as to which some general principles ca be stated. *First*, there are cases where the rules provide for a re-hearing by the original body or some fuller form of it. This may be found in relation to social clubs. In such a case one can readily conclude that the first hearing is superseded by the second (or putting it in terms of contract, the parties agree to accept the decision, original or adjourned). *Second*, at and the other extreme, are those cases where one has to conclude that the complainant is entitled to a fair hearing at both stages. Whether or not a case falls within this class depends on an examination of the whole hearing structure in the context of the activity in question. Thus it might well be the case in trade union affairs where it might be difficult for *appeals* to be conducted impartially, so that a fair *trial* was essential. Planning and employment were also instanced. There is however, *thirdly* an intermediate category, where on the rules and in the contractual context, the parties are to be taken to have agreed to accept what in the end is a fair decision, though a flagrant defect at the hearing or a biased appellate body would not be countenanced by the court. This category would seem to consist principally of domestic disputes, that is one arising in an organisation a person joins and whose rules he therefore

11 Per Lord Denning in *Ward v Bradford Corpn* (1972) 70 LGR 27 at 37.
12 *Annamunthodo v Oilfields Workers Union* [1961] AC 945, [1961] 3 All ER 621.
13 [1971] Ch 34, [1970] 2 All ER 713.
14 [1980] AC 674, [1979] 2 All ER 440. Case note by Elliott 43 MLR 66.

accepts. This case fell into this class: and the plaintiff had received, overall, full and fair consideration. Megarry J, the Judicial Committee said, had stated the matter too broadly in *Leary v National Union of Vehicle Builders* (above). The problem was further referred to in *Lloyd v McMahon*[15] where the district auditor certified that members of a local authority had caused loss to the authority by their wilful default. From such a certificate, appeal lies to the High Court. If there is a lack of fairness in the procedure followed by the auditor, is this cured by a fair hearing on the merits before the Court? The House of Lords declined to review the general principles considered in *Calvin v Carr* (noting that they were confined to 'domestic' tribunals) emphasising that it was a question of interpreting the statute in question. The speeches on this strictly obiter point may be summarised by saying that, where the court concludes after a full examination of the propriety of the certificate that its issue was justified, it should not quash the certificate on the grounds that there had been some error in the procedure followed by the auditor unless the error had caused extreme prejudice.

And in *Johnson v Secretary of State for Health*[16] it was held that certain procedural defects by a committee dealing with a complaint (by a patient against a dentist) were curable by an appeal hearing by the minister which was a full hearing before a lawyer and with legal representation – neither of which obtained at the committee hearing. In *R v Bradford Justices, ex p Wilkinson*,[17] on the other hand, it was said that in *judicial* (in this case criminal) proceedings the defendant was entitled to a proper trial and a proper appeal. The decision at the trial stage was therefore quashed despite the availability of an appeal. 'Domestic or administrative proceedings are a long way from judicial proceedings.'

A useless formality?

When a person affected by a decision claims that it is bad because he was not given a hearing, it is sometimes replied that there was no point in giving him a hearing, that it would have been a useless formality as the decision would have been the same even if a hearing had been given. This is an argument which, it is hoped, the courts will look at critically. In *General Medical Council v Spackman*[18] Lord Wright said, 'If the principles of natural justice are violated in respect of any decision, it is immaterial whether the same decision would have been arrived at in the absence of the departure from the essential principles of justice.' In *Ridge v Baldwin*[19] it was argued that the case against Ridge was so clear that nothing he could have said would have made any difference: that what he did warranted dismissal. That, said Lord Reid, was a very doubtful excuse,

15 [1987] AC 625, [1987] 1 All ER 1118.
16 (1992) 16 BMLR 1.
17 [1990] 2 All ER 833.
18 [1943] AC 627, [1943] 2 All ER 337.
19 [1964] AC 40, [1963] 2 All ER 66. See p 283 above.

but in any case failed on the facts, as Ridge might have been able to persuade the committee to allow him to resign and thereby preserve his pension rights. In *Malloch v Aberdeen Corpn*[20] the defendants argued that the hearing would have been a useless formality as they were in any case bound to dismiss M as he did not have qualifications required by law. But the House of Lords held that that was arguable. In *R v Secretary of State for the Environment, ex p Brent London Borough Council*[1] the court held that the Minister had acted wrongly in reducing Brent's entitlement to a grant without giving them a hearing. The court was asked to say that if the Minister's decision was quashed and the Minister listened to what Brent had to say, he would inevitably come to the same conclusion as before, and that therefore the decision should not be quashed. The court declined. It was not satisfied that the same decision was inevitable, but even if the ultimate outcome was the same decision as before, 'we are not prepared to hold that it would have been a useless formality for the Secretary of State to have listened to the representations. The importance of the principles to which we have referred to above far transcend the significance of this case. If our decision is inconvenient, it cannot be helped. Convenience and justice are often not on speaking terms.'

Unfortunately, there are some cases where the 'useless formality' argument has prevailed. In *Glynn v Keele University*,[2] where a student was disciplined, the court ruled that the failure to give a hearing was a breach of natural justice, but refused a remedy on the ground that nothing the student could have said could have affected the disciplinary decision which was, the court thought, 'intrinsically a perfectly proper one' in the light of the student's behaviour. In *Cinnamond v British Airports Authority*[3] the plaintiff minicab driver (and five others) had been prosecuted many times by the Authority and convicted and fined, for touting at Heathrow Airport. They were then prohibited by the Authority from entering the airport for any purpose other than as bona fide passengers until further notice. They applied for a declaration that the ban was invalid for (amongst other reasons) breach of natural justice as they had not been given an opportunity of making representations. Lord Denning said that the argument, that if a hearing had been given a less severe decision might have been arrived at, applied only when there was a 'legitimate expectation' of being heard. Here there was none; if the plaintiffs were of good character they would have had such an expectation, and been entitled to a hearing.[4] (Lord Denning thought that the suspension of a police officer for misconduct without a hearing, on full pay, was an apt analogy.) Shaw LJ thought that the plaintiffs so far put themselves outside the limits of tolerable conduct as to disentitle themselves to expect that anything they

20 [1971] 2 All ER 1278, [1971] 1 WLR 1578. See p 312 above.
 1 [1982] QB 593, [1983] 3 All ER 321.
 2 [1971] 2 All ER 89, [1971] 1 WLR 487.
 3 [1980] 2 All ER 368, [1980] 1 WLR 582, CA. Case note by Ward at (1981) 44 MLR 103.
 4 'It is the mark of a noble nature to be more shocked by the unjust condemnation of a bad man than of a virtuous one.' – Coleridge.

said could have any influence. In *Ward v Bradford Corpn*,[5] where a student was expelled from college, Lord Denning seemed to say that, as 'she would never make a teacher' the undoubted defects in the hearing leading to her expulsion could be overlooked.[6]

The 'useless formality' approach devalues the obligations of natural justice,[7] involves the court in forming a view of the merits of the decision challenged, rather than its legality, and means that the greater the (apparent) misbehaviour the less the entitlement to procedural protection.

5 (1972) 70 LGR 27. See p 297 above.
6 Lord Denning has acknowledged that he allowed his personal view of the student's conduct to override his knowledge that the tribunal had acted improperly (interview in *The Guardian* newspaper 20 December 1978) and has observed, 'The Law Reports wisely took no notice of the case. It was solely on its facts' (foreword to Lasok (ed) *Fundamental Duties*). It was a unanimous judgment.
7 See Clark 'Natural Justice: Substance and Shadow' [1975] PL 27.

Chapter 10

The duty to give reasons

Should reasons be given?

'I regard the giving of satisfactory reasons for a decision as being the hallmark of good administration and if I were asked to identify the most beneficial improvement which could be made to English administrative law I would unhesitatingly reply that it would be the introduction of a general requirement that reasons should normally be available, at least on request, for all administrative actions.'[1]

Why is the giving of reasons so important? To be acting lawfully, the administrator must *have* reasons for his decision. To have to *give* them is some assurance that those reasons will be good in law, for, having made them known, his decision must be open to scrutiny. To give reasons is to invite accountability and to expose oneself to criticism; it helps to ensure that power is not arbitrarily exercised. The Franks Report of 1957, referring to ministerial decisions taken after the holding of an inquiry gave reasons why reasons should be given.

It is a fundamental requirement of fair play that the parties concerned in one of these procedures should know at the end of the day why the particular decision has been taken. Where no reasons are given the individual may be forgiven for concluding that he has been the victim of arbitrary decision. The giving of full reasons is also important to enable those concerned to satisfy themselves that the prescribed procedure has been followed and to decide whether they wish to challenge the minister's decision in the courts or elsewhere. Moreover as we have already said in relation to tribunal decisions a decision is apt to be better if the reasons for it have to be set out in writing because the reasons are then more likely to have been properly thought out.[2]

An obligation to state the reasons for a decision together with a right of appeal against the decision is likely to concentrate the mind rather carefully on the decision. The Chief Inspector of Audit, referring to the electors' right to require the district auditor to give written reasons for

1 Woolf *Protection of the Public*, p 92.
2 The Franks Report, 1957 (Cmnd 218), para 98.

rejecting an objection to the accounts said, 'These statements of reasons, which recite in detail the facts and law relating to the decision, need to be prepared with great care since they will come before the courts in the event of an appeal.'[3]

The obligation to give reasons will help the administrator to keep to the legally straight-and-narrow, thus ensuring no legal challenge is possible. Such a reasoned decision will persuade those affected by it that it is a correct decision. Unstated reasons may be good ones; as reports from the ombudsmen show it not infrequently happens that when the reason for a decision is given, dissatisfaction and suspicion are removed which would not have existed had reasons been given in the first place. To give reasons may well reduce the number of unsustainable appeals.

If reasons for a decision are given, they may disclose grounds on which the decision can be challenged. Thus where the Chief Registrar of Friendly Societies was not required to give reasons for a decision (only the 'considerations' he had in mind in making it), but did so he thereby 'volunteered a large number of hostages to fortune'.[4] And contrariwise, as the Boundary Commission had not given reasons for a decision, this made it difficult for the court to decide whether it had acted wrongfully.[5] This consideration may of course persuade the administrator to refrain from giving reasons, where he is not bound to, as in the following case. The Parliamentary Commissioner investigated a complaint about a decision on a claim for exemption from estate duty. His report contains this paragraph:

After the Army Board had given their decision, the Army Department considered the form in which the Board's decision should be communicated to the complainants. The Ministry's file shows that at first the intention was to send a reasoned rejection; but the Permanent Under-Secretary eventually accepted advice that a decision letter without reasons was preferable, because a letter that entered into detail of the reasons leading to the decision might provide an opportunity for a charge that the discretion had been exercised on the wrong principles and, on those grounds, a Court might entertain an enquiry.[6]

In *R v Civil Service Appeal Board, ex p Cunningham*[7] the Board explained why it never gave reasons for its decisions. Leggatt LJ commented that despite the Board's assertions that in doing so it served the parties better, the inadequacy of the explanation 'prompts the cynical suspicion that the Board may be more affected by the fact that it is less trouble for the Board if reasons do not have to be given, that reasons render the inner workings of the Board open to public scrutiny, and that reasons may constitute hostages to fortune in cases such as this'.

Given that reasons should be given, further questions are: are they to be given only if requested, and if so, when must the request be made? Are

3 Report of the Chief Inspector of Audit for year ending 31 March 1978, para 55.
4 *R v Chief Registrar of Friendly Societies, ex p New Cross Building Society* [1984] 2 All ER 27 at 55.
5 *R v Boundary Commission for England, ex p Foot* [1983] QB 600, [1983] 1 All ER 1099.
6 Annual Report of the Parliamentary Commissioner for Administration for 1971, p 34.
7 [1991] 4 All ER 310.

the reasons to be put in writing, or is oral delivery adequate? Are they to be given at the same time as the decision is announced, or may they be given later?

In what situations, if any, might an exemption from giving reasons be justified? Both statute and judicial decisions provide examples. A Social Security Commissioner is expressly exempt from a duty to give reasons when refusing leave to appeal to him from the decision of an attendance allowance board on a point of law. The Court of Appeal has suggested[8] why this exemption was granted – that to have to give reasons would slow up the work in a field where expedition is required and there is already a heavy work load; and the great majority of cases are unlikely to raise substantial points of law. Reasons will not be insisted on by the courts where national security might be jeopardised,[9] and statute expressly exempts certain bodies operating in this field from giving reasons.[10]

Where a person is an applicant for a licence, appointment or admission to an organisation, and the decision has to be taken on broad grounds of suitability,[11] or where the decision turns on questions of opinion or even perhaps instinct,[12] reasons, or at any rate detailed reasons, cannot, it is said, be expected. An exceptional case is where the giving of reasons might cause distress to the recipient.[13]

It is sometimes suggested that reasons cannot practically be expected where the deciding body consists of a number of persons (say five); and that in such a case there is a danger that the reasons would tend to become short and stereotyped rather than full and informative (that is, not really 'reasons' at all, or not worth having).[14] But local authority committees, to take one example, are required to give their reasons for refusing planning permission and in other cases.[15]

8 *R v Secretary of State for Social Security, ex p Connolly* [1986] 1 All ER 998, [1986] 1 WLR 421.
9 *R v Secretary of State for the Home Dept, ex p Hosenball* [1977] 3 All ER 452, [1977] 1 WLR 766. And now *Ex p Adams* (1995) Independent, 28 April.
10 Eg Interception of Communications Act 1985, Sch 1, para 4(2).
11 *McInnes v Onslow-Fane* [1978] 3 All ER 211, [1978] 1 WLR 1520. Section 44(2) of the British Nationality Act 1981 provides that the Secretary of State 'shall not be required' to give any reasons for eg a decision on an application for naturalisation. Defending this, it was explained that the Secretary of State is not prohibited from giving reasons, that they are sometimes given, but that in any case it is generally possible for the applicant to know the reason for the refusal as where he has been 'sailing rather too close to the wind financially ... or whatever' – H of C Official Report, SCF, (1980–81) col 1961.
12 *Guppys (Bridport) Ltd v Sandoe* (1975) 30 P & CR 69.
13 Mental Health Review Tribunal (Procedure) Rules 1983, SI 1983/942. The Committee advising on the bona fides of applicants from the forces for release in order to stand for Parliament is to give no reasons for their decision 'so as to avoid impugning in any way the character of the applicant or indeed laying themselves open to the possibility of legal action for defamation': First Report from the Select Committee on Parliamentary Elections, 1962–3, HC 111.
14 Lord Denning in *Payne v Lord Harris of Greenwich* [1981] 1 WLR 754 at 758.
15 For dismissal of suggestion of impossibility of disaggregating the 'collective view' of a committee of academics assessing the quality of a research institute see *R v Higher Education Funding Council, ex p Institute of Dental Surgery* [1994] 1 All ER 651.

The Speaker is required *not* to give reasons for his decision on an application for an emergency debate under Public Business Standing Order No 20.

Is there a duty to give reasons?

By statute?
There is no general statutory duty to give reasons for all administrative decisions, but a duty to do so will be found to be imposed in many particular cases. As we have seen[16] section 10 of the Tribunals and Inquiries Act 1992 imposes such a duty on *tribunals* listed in the First Schedule to the Act; and requires that where a minister notifies any decision taken by him after the holding of a statutory *inquiry*, he must furnish a statement of the reasons for the decision. (But the section also provides that that duty does not apply to ministerial decisions in connection with the preparation, making, approval, confirmation or concurrence in regulations etc of a legislative and not executive character.) In addition many examples could be listed of a statutory duty to give reasons for specific adverse decisions.

The precise wording of the statute must be considered. Thus where a local planning authority refuses to give planning permission, it must 'state clearly and precisely their full reasons' for the refusal.[17] In another planning context the minister must give 'such statement as he considers appropriate of the reasons governing his decision'.[18] There is then no general statutory duty to give reasons, but there are many specific statutory requirements, and the courts are called on to interpret them.

At common law?
There being no general statutory duty to give reasons, what of the common law? Has it in this matter 'supplied the omission of the legislature'? It has not. 'I accept without hesitation ... that the law does not at present recognise a general duty to give reasons for an administrative decision'.[19] But – in the next sentence – 'it is equally beyond question that such a duty may in appropriate circumstances be implied'.

What are those circumstances?

(i) Where there is a right of appeal

In *R v Crown Court at Harrow, ex p Dave*[20] the Crown Court gave a decision without reasons. There was an appeal, by way of case stated, against that decision. An application to that court to 'state a case' (for the consideration of the appeal court) must state the ground on which the

---

16 See p 166 above.
17 SI 1988/1813, Reg 25.
18 Town and Country Planning Act 1971, s 9(8).
19 Lord Mustill in *Doody v Secretary of State for the Home Dept* [1994] 1 AC 531 at 564, [1993] 3 All ER 92 at 110. See Craig (1994) 53 CLJ 282.
20 [1994] 1 All ER 315.

court's decision is questioned. But if reasons are not given, how can one know what ground to rely on? The decision was quashed for absence of reasons: that absence made it impossible to exercise the right of appeal. Now the Crown Court was exercising a judicial function and there is a strong tradition that reasons should be given when that function is exercised (though there are exceptions). Nevertheless the general point remains: where a person has a right of appeal against a decision he must be given sufficient reasons to enable him to decide whether to exercise that right.

(ii) Where judicial review is available

The grounds on which judicial review may be had have been considered, for example, reliance on irrelevant considerations. But, unless it is very obvious that such considerations have been relied on, how can the applicant for judicial review know this unless reasons are given? In *Doody v Secretary of State for the Home Department*[1] D had been sentenced to a mandatory life sentence on conviction for murder. In such a case the trial judge makes a recommendation to the minister as to what the penal (as opposed to the 'public risk') element of the sentence should be. He argued, inter alia, that he was entitled to know the reasons why the minister departed from that recommendation by lengthening the penal element (as he was entitled to do). Noting that the minister's decision was susceptible to judicial review, Lord Mustill delivering the judgment of the House of Lords said, 'To mount an effective attack on the decision, given no more material than the facts of the offence and the length of the penal element, the prisoner has virtually no means of ascertaining whether this is an instance where the decision-making process has gone astray. I think it important that there should be an effective means of detecting the kind of error which would entitle the court to intervene, and in practice I regard it as necessary for this purpose that the reasoning of the Home Secretary should be disclosed'.[2]

If it is a general principle that there should be 'an effective means of detecting the kind of error which would entitle the court to intervene', and if the absence of reasons disables one from detecting that kind of error, then it would seem to be a general principle that reasons should be given for decisions which are potentially subject to judicial review, though the House has denied, as we have seen, that there is a general duty to give reasons. Nevertheless this is a major exception to the rule of no-reasons.

It is the case, in contrast to a (statutory) right of appeal, that leave is necessary in order to apply for judicial review. Is that a good reason for saying that reasons must be given where a *right* of appeal is otherwise foiled, but need not be given in the case of judicial review, as there is *no right* to that procedure? Surely not. Access to the court is regarded by the courts themselves as a basic right; to make the distinction referred to is an important inroad into its exercise. Further, there is a right to *apply* for

1   Footnote 19 above.
2   Ibid at 565 and 111.

judicial review, that is, to set in motion the machinery for challenging the decision in question and 'that right is nugatory unless the award [of compensation – the decision being challenged] is so aberrant as to compel the inference that it must have been wrong, or unless the board explains how the figure was arrived at ...'[3] Lord Donaldson MR has stressed the obligation of the decision-maker to the *court*: 'if leave is granted, the court is entitled to expect that the respondent will give the court sufficient information to enable it to do justice, and this in some cases will mean giving reasons or fuller reasons for a decision than the complainant himself would be entitled to'.[4]

(iii) Inferring misuse of power from absence of reasons

In *Padfield v Minister of Agriculture, Fisheries and Food*[5] the minister was under no statutory duty to give reasons for refusing to refer a complaint to a committee but did so; when the legality of the refusal to refer was challenged, he argued that if he had given no reason, his decision could not have been challenged, and that he should be in no worse position for having done so. The House of Lords disagreed but also rejected the premise – it was not the case that a decision could not be challenged because reasons for it were not given. Illegality may be established without reasons. Thus to relate that principle to the facts of the case, a public officer has a duty not to frustrate the policy and objects of the statute under which he is acting. If the Act appeared to favour his taking a certain course, and he took a contrary course without giving reasons, the court might infer that he had no good reason for doing so and was thus not using his power for the purpose intended by the Act; his action would be unlawful on that ground, not for not giving reasons. Lord Upjohn said that if a minister did not give any reason for a decision 'it may be, if circumstances warrant it, that a court may be at liberty to come to the conclusion that he had no good reason for reaching that conclusion and directing a prerogative order to be issued accordingly'.

These observations held out some hope that a general duty to give reasons was evolving from the court's willingness to infer, where reasons were not given, that there were none (or that they were bad in law?) and that therefore the decision could not stand. The hope was not fulfilled. In *Secretary of State for Employment v Associated Society of Locomotive Engineers and Firemen (No 2)*[6] the minister could apply to a tribunal for an order that a ballot be held amongst striking workers, where it appeared to him that there were reasons for doubting whether they really wanted to strike. He did not give his reasons for his doubts, and when the legality of his action was challenged, did not tell the court what his reasons were but merely suggested the grounds on which a reasonable minister might have formed the view that there were reasons for such doubts.[7] That was

3   Leggatt LJ in *R v Civil Service Appeal Board, ex p Cunningham* [1991] 4 All ER 310 at 325.
4   Ibid at 315.
5   [1968] AC 997, [1968] 1 All ER 694.
6   [1972] 2 QB 455, [1972] 2 All ER 949.
7   Nor was he willing to disclose his reasons to the House of Commons 838 H of C Official Report (5th series) col 218 (G Howe). See also p 266 above.

enough for the Court of Appeal. However, if when a decision is challenged for 'no-reasons' the court is prepared to accept the respondent's statement as to what reasons he might have had, no such challenge is likely to succeed. (The real reason might or might not be amongst those given as those the authority might have had.) And unfortunately the giving ex post facto of reasons one might have had is apt to encourage cynical thoughts.

The *Padfield* 'hope' (that if no reason was given, the court might infer no good reason existed) was largely extinguished in *Lonrho plc v Secretary of State for Trade & Industry*[8] The minister's decision not to refer a take-over bid was attacked for irrationality. It was argued, on the basis of what was said obiter in *Padfield*, that the fact that he gave no reason for his decision led to the conclusion that no rational ground existed for his decision. The House said:

> The absence of reasons for a decision where there is no duty to give them cannot of itself provide any support for the suggested irrationality of the decision. The only significance of the absence of reasons is that if *all* the other known facts and circumstances point *overwhelmingly* in favour of a different conclusion, the decision-maker who has given no reasons cannot complain if the court draws the inference that he had no rational reason for his decision.[9]

(iv) Reasons required in imposed procedural contexts

A duty to consult may be imposed by statute, or as an additional requirement, by the court. Consultation, to be effective, may well require reasons for the proposed action to be given. Likewise the duty to give a hearing etc may arise from a legitimate expectation and here too reasons for the action or proposed action (eg a change of policy or the application of a new policy) may be required. And a promise to give reasons, or a practice of giving them, may found a legitimate expectation of having them.

(v) Reasons as a requirement of fairness

Is it not possible to base the duty to give reasons on fairness (or natural justice)? The Committee on Ministers' Powers, in 1932, thought that there were some circumstances when the refusal to give reasons for a (judicial or quasi-judicial) decision 'may be plainly unfair'.[10] The Franks Committee said that if tribunals' or ministers' decisions were to be fair, they should give reasons. What of the law? In *R v Civil Service Appeal Board, ex p Cunningham*[11] C, a prison officer, was dismissed. On appeal to it the Board found his dismissal to be unfair and recommended compensation of £x. Being a prison officer, he was excluded from going to an industrial tribunal about his dismissal. If he had been able to do so a tribunal would have awarded him not less than £2x. The Board refused, as we have seen, to give reasons. Applying Lord Bridge's dictum in *Lloyd v McMahon*,[12] Lord

8 [1989] 2 All ER 609, [1989] 1 WLR 525.
9 Emphasis added. In *ex p Cunningham* below, the meagre award was, in the absence of reasons, irrational.
10 Cmd 4060, p 80.
11 [1991] 4 All ER 310.
12 See p 281 above.

Donaldson MR, noting the character of the Board – a fully judicial body – and the framework in which it operated – asked what procedural safeguards were required to ensure *fairness*, and concluded that the giving of reasons was necessary. McCowan LJ said that the court was not required to tolerate the unfairness of reasons not being given, and Leggatt LJ said that the duty to act fairly extended to the duty to give reasons. In *Doody*[13] the House of Lords arrived at the conclusion that reasons were required, by two routes. One of these has been noted: the other was what fairness required '... I simply ask, is it fair that the mandatory life prisoner should be wholly deprived of the information which all other prisoners receive as a matter of course ... It is not.' (Notice that in both cases the unfairness was by comparison with analogous cases: what an applicant to an industrial tribunal, or what other categories of prisoners, would get.) Lord Mustill noted, as general background to his task of finding what fairness required, 'a perceptible trend towards an insistence on greater openness, or if one prefers the contemporary jargon 'transparency', in the making of administrative decisions'.

However, in *R v Higher Education Funding Council, ex p Institute of Dental Surgery*[14] the court was unable to find grounds for imposing a duty to give reasons. The Institute challenged the research assessment grading given it by the Council, on the grounds of unfairness due to lack of reasons. Sedley J found that there being no general duty to give reasons, there will be some decisions which cry out for reasons, but others where fairness does not demand them. The subject-matter of some decisions is so highly regarded by the law – for example, personal freedom (see *Doody*) – that reasons must be given as of right; likewise where the decision appears aberrant (as in *ex p Cunningham*) so that the recipient may know whether it is challengeable. In this case neither intrinsically nor on the evidence was there sufficient basis to hold the decision aberrant. (Unlike in *ex p Cunningham* the court could not compare the decision with another.) Among other points made by Sedley J were: (i) there was not a duty to give reasons simply to enable grounds of challenge to be exposed, though there was a case for that in *Doody;* (ii) the distinction between this case on the one hand and *Doody* and *ex p Cunningham* on the other was not that reasons were required in the latter two on the ground that the procedure in those cases was judicial or quasi-judicial (therefore requiring reasons), but was not here.

Reasons given ex post facto
Where reasons are not given for a decision, but given at a later stage in response to a challenge, there might be a suspicion that they have been tailored to meet the challenge. In *R v Independent Television Commission, ex p TSW Broadcasting Ltd* the Master of the Rolls asserted that the respondent's affidavit recollections 'might conceivably have been in-

13 [1994] 1 AC 531, [1993] 3 All ER 92.
14 [1994] 1 All ER 651.

fluenced by an ex post facto belief that TSW's application was weaker that it may or should have seemed at the time of decision.' In the House of Lords[15] Lord Templeman found that observation 'unjust and inaccurate' (by reference to contemporaneous documents). But in *R v Home Secretary, ex p Nelson*[16] Pill J said that while there might be occasions when an affidavit could be admissible, relevant or even helpful, in the particular circumstances that the applicant 'could be concerned with the likelihood of subsequent rationalisation of a decision that had not been properly considered at the time'.

An affidavit by an official of the deciding body expressing his own views of why the authority decided as it did, will not assist the authority.[17] It seems that where a tribunal has given a decision the court will not accept affidavit evidence to say that the tribunal meant something different from what is said in its judgment. In *R v Deputy Chief Constable of the North Wales Police, ex p Hughes*[18] it was said that assuming that that principle could be applied to an administrative decision (which was doubted) there was no reason to exclude the respondent's affidavit seeking to explain his decision suspending a police officer from membership of the force.

What the duty requires

Where there is a duty to give reasons, what is required? In *Re Poyser and Mill's Arbitration*[19] a landlord sought possession of an agricultural holding on the ground that the tenant had broken covenants in the lease. The arbitrator – a tribunal listed in the First Schedule to the Tribunals and Inquiries Act, and therefore bound by that Act to give reasons – found that breaches of covenant had been committed but he did not specify which covenants had been broken.

Megaw J said:

Parliament provided that reasons shall be given, and in my view that must be read as meaning that proper, adequate reasons must be given. The reasons that are set out must be reasons which will not only be intelligible, but will deal with the substantial points that have been raised.

This statement had the express approval of the House of Lords in *Westminster City Council v Great Portland Estates plc*.[20] A very similar indication of the scope of the duty, referring to an inspector's planning decision, was suggested by Phillips J:

15 (1992) Times, 30 March. See Lexis. For discovery to challenge accuracy of reasons in judicial review proceedings see *R v Secretary of State for the Environment, ex p Islington LBC* (1991) Independent, 6 September.
16 (1994) Independent, 2 June.
17 *R v Tunbridge Wells Health Authority, ex p Goodridge* (1988) Times, 21 May.
18 [1991] 3 All ER 414. *R v Secretary of State for Education, ex p Standish* (1993) Times, 15 November: no reasons given for disbarring teacher: affidavit of no assistance: decision quashed.
19 [1964] 2 QB 467, [1963] 1 All ER 612.
20 [1985] AC 661, [1984] 3 All ER 744.

It seems to me that the decision must be such that it enables the appellant to understand on what grounds the appeal has been decided and be in sufficient detail to enable him to know what conclusions the inspector has reached on the principal important controversial issues.[1]

In *Save Britain's Heritage v Secretary of State for the Environment*[2] Lord Bridge commented on the criteria suggested by Megaw J: (emphasis added)

The application of the first two of these presents no problem. If the reasons given are *improper* they will reveal some flaw in the decision-making process which will be open to challenge on some ground other than the failure to give reasons. If the reasons given are *unintelligible*, this will be equivalent to giving no reasons at all. The difficulty arises in determining whether the reasons given are *adequate*, whether, in the words of Megaw J they deal with the substantial points that have been raised or, in the words of Phillips J enable the reader to know what conclusion the decision-maker has reached on the principal controversial issues. What degree of particularity is required? ... I do not think one can safely say more in general terms than that the degree of particularity required will depend entirely on the nature of the issues falling for discussion.

The following cases illustrate. In *Doody* (above) it was said that the prisoner needed to know the substance or gist of the judge's advice and of the reasons. This might or might not involve verbatim quotation from that advice. In *ex p Cunningham* (above) Leggatt LJ said 'Nothing more onerous is demanded of the Board than a concise statement of the means by which they arrived at the figure awarded.' In *ex p Dave* (above) the court said that when deciding an appeal against conviction by justices the Crown Court had to give sufficient reasons to show that it had identified the main contentious issues and how it had resolved them. *Evans v Secretary of State for Social Security*[3] concerned the duty of medical appeal tribunals to give reasons for their decisions, including their finding on all questions of fact material to the decision. Four appeals were dealt with in this case which is interesting as showing how the precise requirements of the duty depends on the particular facts: had there been a medical examination? Were there questions of causation of injury? What if the claimant is renewing a claim for an allowance already enjoyed for ten years? An order made by the Home Secretary excluding a person from the UK under the Prevention of Terrorism Act 1989 does not have to recite specific reasons for doing so. It is enough to say that it is made on grounds of national security.[4] And where the Home Secretary decides to deport a person on the grounds that his deportation was deemed to be conducive to the public good 'for reasons of national security' a statement to that effect was a sufficient 'statement of the reasons for the decision' required to be given to the deportee.[5]

1 *Hope v Secretary of State for the Environment* (1976) 31 P & CR 120, 123.
2 [1991] 1 WLR 153, [1991] 2 All ER 10.
3 (1993) 16 BMLR 100.
4 *R v Secretary of State for the Home Dept, ex p Gallaher* (1994) Times, 16 February.
5 *R v Secretary of State for the Home Dept, ex p Cheblak* [1991] 2 All ER 319.

In *R v Secretary of State for the Home Department, ex p Swati*[6] S had to satisfy the immigration officer of three matters, one of which was that he was genuinely seeking entry for the period requested. The IO's reason for refusal was 'I am not satisfied that you are genuinely seeking entry only for this limited period' (which was one week). The reason, the Court of Appeal held, was a *proper* one (it was one the IO could in law rely on) and it was *adequate* (it indicated why entry was refused). It did not set out *how* the IO arrived at the view she did, which might have been to do with the answers S and his host gave to her, or to do with his possession or otherwise of a return ticket. Of these matters the Court, it pointed out, was ignorant. These, as one judge put it, were 'the reasons for the reason', which S was not entitled to. Furthermore – an important point as this was an application for leave to apply for judicial review – S could have appealed against the IO's decision to an adjudicator: on giving notice of appeal he would have been entitled not only to the reason, but to a statement of the facts relating to the decision, and on the appeal the facts could have been reconsidered. (He would have had to leave the UK in order to appeal.)

In testing the quality of the reasons given will the court take into account the constitution or status of the body in question?

'The court should not approach decisions and reasons given by committees of laymen expecting the same accuracy in the use of language which a lawyer might be expected to adopt. This was a lay committee [of school governors] with a lay clerk.'[7] Contrast this with planning law. 'I emphatically reject the proposition that in planning decisions the ... "quality' of the reasons required to satisfy the statutory requirement varies according to who is making the decision, how much time he has to reflect on it, and whether or not he had legal assistance, or depends upon the degree of importance which attaches to the matter falling to be decided. The obligation, being imposed on the Secretary of State and his inspectors in identical terms, must be construed in the same sense.'[8]

Failure to give any, or adequate, reasons

(i) If statute requires reasons to be given and none is given, the court may order them to be given.[9]

(ii) A decision may be struck down in the following cases: if reasons are 'improper' (eg show that improper matters were taken into account and

6 [1986] 1 All ER 717, [1986] 1 WLR 477.
7 *Choudhury v Governors of Bishop Challenor ... School* [1992] 3 All ER 277. And see *Metropolitan Properties (FGC) Ltd v Lannon* [1969] 1 QB 577, [1968] 3 All ER 304.
8 *Save Britain's Heritage v Secretary of State for the Environment* [1991] 2 All ER 10. *Ex p Swati* applied in *R v Secretary of State for the Home Dept, ex p K Mohammed* [1990] Imm AR 439: reason (not satisfied applicant was a genuine student) adequate: planning law requirements contrasted.
9 *Iveagh (Earl) v Minister of Housing and Local Government* [1962] 2 QB 147, [1961] 3 All ER 98.

thus disclose an error of law); if reasons are 'inadequate' (ie do not deal adequately with the principal issues, though it is possible that though inadequate, no disadvantage is shown, perhaps because it is obvious to the complainant what the reasons were); if reasons are unintelligible or obscure as where they are contradictory or leave substantial doubt as to what matters were taken into account.

(iii) Where the adequacy of the reasons themselves is not attacked, a failure to give them may not invalidate the decision to which they relate. For example, on attaching conditions to the grant of planning permission, the local authority must give its reasons. In *Brayhead (Ascot) Ltd v Berkshire County Council*[10] it was said that failure to do so did not mean that an appeal could not be brought against the decision on the ground that there was, in the absence of reasons for it, no decision to appeal against; nor did it mean that the condition could not be later enforced by the authority on the ground that it was invalid for lack of reasons.

(iv) Where a decision is arrived at for a reason that is a wrong reason, but the same decision must as a matter of law have been arrived at if the right reason had been relied on, the decision will not be quashed. Thus when the Secretary of State wrongly took the view that planning permission was not in law necessary, but it was not in law necessary for a quite different reason from that relied on by him, his decision stood.[11]

(v) What if a number of reasons are given, and some are good, but one or more is bad? If the reasons are impossible to disentangle, the decision will be bad. But if it is possible to disentangle them and one is bad, the decision will not be upset if the court is satisfied that the decision-maker would have reached precisely the same decision on the valid reasons.[12]

(vi) The absence or inadequacy of reasons may have consequences other than in litigation. For example, where a local planning authority refuses planning permission, it must give its reasons. Where an appeal to the Secretary of State from a refusal is successful, and the Secretary of State finds that the authority's reasons were wholly inadequate, he may award costs against the authority. The inadequacy of reasons may also be a matter for criticism by an Ombudsman or by the Council on Tribunals.

(vii) Where there is a power to remit a decision to the deciding tribunal or administrative authority, the inadequacy of reasons would be a good ground for doing so. There is, it is said, ample precedent for the use of the power by the Employment Appeal Tribunal in relation to industrial tribunals.[13]

---

10 [1964] 2 QB 303, [1964] 1 All ER 149.
11 *Glasgow District Council v Secretary of State for Scotland* 1980 SC 150.
12 *R v Broadcasting Complaints Commission ex, p Owen* [1985] QB 1153, [1985] 2 All ER 522; *Westminster Renslade Ltd v Secretary of State for the Environment* (1984) 48 P & CR 255.
13 *Yusuf v Aberplace Ltd* [1984] LS Gaz R 2381.

Reasons and grounds

Finally, the distinction between reasons and grounds should be noticed, as where statute provides that reasons have to be given for refusing a licence, but grounds for appealing against the refusal have to be given.

Assume that a licence may be refused where an applicant has not proved his suitability to hold one; to say that a licence is refused because the applicant has not proved his suitability could be said to be the reason. But if the authority is required to give its reasons for refusing a licence, would it be enough simply to say that the applicant was not fit, simply to assert the existence of the circumstances which justify the refusal? We could say that only the ground for the decision is given, not the reason. Or we could say, as in *ex p Swati*[14] that the reason for the refusal is the applicant's unfitness, and that the reasoning leading to that conclusion is 'the reason for the reasons' – which in *Swati* did not have to be given. But it by no means follows, as many of the cases quoted above show, that *Swati* is of general application.

The distinction between ground and reason was relevant in the following cases. In *Tambimutta v Secretary of State for the Home Department*[15] the ground of refusal was that the appellant had not satisfied the requirements of the immigration rules. Everything else, it was said, was reasons or particulars; the distinction was important as the grounds could not be amended by the defendant, but the reasons could. In *R v Immigration Appeal Tribunal, ex p Mehra*[16] it was held that the Tribunal could take into account reasons not given in the notice of refusal but not grounds other than those given in the notice.

Section 1(1) of the Vaccine Damage Payments Act 1979 says that in giving a decision as to whether a person is entitled to compensation the Secretary of State is required to give the grounds for his decision. (Where an applicant appeals from a Secretary of State decision to a tribunal, the tribunal must give its reasons.) In *R v Secretary of State for Social Services, ex p Loveday*[17] the court declined to interpret 'grounds' in those provisions as meaning 'reasons'.

14 See p 334 above.
15 [1979–80] Imm AR 91.
16 [1983] Imm AR 156.
17 (1983) Times, 18 February.

Chapter 11

Judicial review

Historically the courts exercised control over the legality of the acts of the administration by means of the writs (now orders) of certiorari, prohibition and mandamus which (together with habeas corpus) are known as the prerogative orders. (Briefly, certiorari will quash an unlawful decision, prohibition is to prevent a body from acting unlawfully, mandamus compels the performance of a duty.)

It is essential to note:

– these three orders were and are available only in respect of the exercise of public power;
– the procedure to be followed to get these orders – now 'the application for judicial review' – has been and is different from that to be followed in an ordinary action for say breach of contract or tort. The main points to bear in mind are that the court's *leave* is required in order to apply for judicial review, and there is a very short *time-limit* within which that leave must be sought.

The other remedies which are available in respect of public (as well as of private) power are the declaration and the injunction, the former declaring what the law on a disputed point is, the latter enjoining the performance of a particular act. The grounds on which these five remedies are available in respect of a public law act have been considered in earlier chapters. (A characteristic of these remedies is that their grant is in the court's discretion.) Another remedy to be considered in association with these five remedies is that of damages.

Judicial review – the public law element

Possibly the only essential elements [required to attract the High Court's supervisory review] are what can be described as a public element, which can take many different forms, and the exclusion from the jurisdiction of bodies whose sole source of power is a consensual submission to its jurisdiction.

Thus Donaldson MR in *R v Panel on Take-overs and Mergers, ex p Datafin plc*.[1]

The public element note, 'can take many different forms' which, considered later, we list here as having its origin in statute, in the prerogative or by virtue of the nature of the function in question. We consider first however the exclusion referred to in the quotation, noting that this cannot be considered in isolation from the other criteria referred to.

Agreement

Where the decision challenged is taken in pursuance solely of an agreement and there is no statutory involvement, the decision is not subject to judicial review and thus the criteria of unlawfulness applied in judicial review proceedings are irrelevant – there may or may not be a remedy in the law of contract. In *R v National Joint Council for Dental Technicians, ex p Neate*[2] N's contract of apprenticeship provided that any dispute between the parties to the contract should be submitted to the Council (NJC) in question. A dispute was so referred. N sought to have its decision quashed by certiorari. The court was very clear, despite the possible implications of NJC's name, that the NJC was in no sense a public body. Its authority did not depend on any statute but on the agreement in question. By contrast, if, for example a statute gave power to compulsorily acquire land, and an arbitrator was set up by Parliament to assess the compensation payable, then of course the courts would be concerned to control the legality of the exercise of the arbitrator's jurisdiction within the limits conferred by Parliament. But to allow a certiorari to go, as here, to a private arbitrator would be 'a great departure from the law' and 'revolutionary'.

Then consider *Law v National Greyhound Racing Club Ltd*.[3] The NGRC is a company formed under the Companies Act and limited by guarantee. It licences trainers etc, promulgates 'rules of racing' and appoints stewards to enforce them. Everyone who participates in racing at licensed courses is by the rules deemed to have submitted himself to the rules and to the NGRC. Law was suspended by stewards for breach of the rules, and challenged the decision in the courts not by judicial review, but by an ordinary action. NGRC argued that he should have done so by judicial review. This would have been the case if NGRC was operating in the field of public law. The Court of Appeal held that the stewards' authority derived wholly from a contract between Law and the NGRC. Thus NGRC's argument was rejected. The court acknowledged that a large section of the public is interested in the proper management of dog racing and thus in the work of the NGRC – but this was not the criterion to be applied. (It

1   [1987] QB 815, [1987] 1 All ER 564.
2   [1953] 1 QB 704, [1953] 1 All ER 327.
3   [1983] 3 All ER 300, [1983] 1 WLR 1302.

will be noted that the fact that the NGRC was formed under machinery provided by statute – the Companies Act – was not enough to give it the necessary public law element. On the other hand, as we shall see, if a power is a public law power, it is nonetheless so because it is exercised by a registered company.)

A number of cases have concerned the Jockey Club, which governs horse racing. A decision to remove a man's name from the panel of chairmen of race stewards was said[4] to have its source in consensual submission to the Club's jurisdiction, as did a decision to disqualify a horse which failed a drug test.[5] But in another case it was said that a decision of the Club on the allocation of fixtures at racecourses, being akin to a statutory licensing scheme, would be subject to judicial review if it were not for authority to the contrary.[6] Notice therefore that regard must be had to the nature of the particular decision being challenged. And the fact that the Club is (now) the creation of a (Royal) charter made no difference: compare the status of the NGRC in *Law*.

Statute

Prisons: governors and visitors

The powers and duties of the prison authorities, in particular those of the Home Secretary and of prison governors, are statutory. Rules for the maintenance of discipline in prisons are made under statute. Statute also provides for the appointment of prison Boards of Visitors. Boards are to satisfy themselves as to the state of the prison premises, the administration of the prison and the treatment of the prisoners; they are also to inquire into any matter into which the Secretary of State asks them to inquire; and are to direct the attention of the governor to matters calling for his attention. In addition (and importantly) the Board has an adjudicatory role. If a prisoner is charged with a breach of prison rules he may be dealt with and punished by the governor, or, in more serious matters, by the Board.

In *R v Hull Prison Board of Visitors, ex p St Germain (No 2)*[7] the question was whether a decision of the Board in the exercise of its adjudicatory function was subject to judicial review (on the grounds of breach of the rules of natural justice). The High Court held not. The order being challenged was 'made in private disciplinary proceedings ...'. The Court of Appeal, in a judgment which had important consequences,[8] reversed that decision.

The court also referred to the position of the governor who has both management and disciplinary, adjudicatory, functions. It doubted whether

---

4 *R v Disciplinary Committee of the Jockey Club, ex p Massingberd-Mundy* (1989) [1993] 2 All ER 207.
5 *R v Disciplinary Committee of the Jockey Club, ex p Aga Khan* [1993] 2 All ER 853.
6 *R v Jockey Club, ex p RAMM Racecourses Ltd* (1990) [1993] 2 All ER 225.
7 [1979] 3 All ER 545, [1979] 1 WLR 1401.
8 See p 419 below.

the latter were subject to judicial review, referring to the governor's private law disciplinary machinery. In a later case the same court held that such decisions were not subject to review, though the governor would be reviewable if the question of the legality of detention was in issue. But in *Leeds v Parkhurst Prison Deputy Governor*[9] the House of Lords rejected the argument that as the prisoner could petition the Home Secretary against the governor's decision, and as the minister's decision would be subject to review, the governor's decision was not. The governor, it was pointed out, is not the mere servant of the Secretary of State. To see him as nothing more than a manager appointed by and accountable to him was wrong. His office is created by statute and his functions are conferred directly on him and on him alone by statutory rules – that is, it is not the case that the functions are conferred on the Secretary of State and delegated by him to the governor. Many of those functions are purely administrative and involve no adjudication. Lord Oliver said:

> But the function of adjudicating on charges of infraction of prison discipline is not one which involves merely the performance of duty concerning some private right, as for instance in the case of the governing body of a social club or a trade union. It is a public function which affects the liberty and to a degree the status of the party affected by it.

Lord Bridge concluded:

> Thus a governor adjudicating on a charge of an offence against prison discipline bears on his face all the classic hallmarks of an authority subject to judicial review.

The nationalised industries

The National Coal Board (now British Coal) was created by the Coal Industry Nationalisation Act 1946. By section 46 of that Act the Board has a duty to consult with organisations appearing to it to represent a sub-stantial proportion of its employees with a view to establishing consultative machinery. In *R v British Coal Corpn, ex p Union of Democratic Mine-workers*[10] the UDM challenged the Board's interpretation of the obligation imposed on it by that section. This challenge was properly brought by way of judicial review, that is, the Board's decision was an exercise of public power. Contrast *R v National Coal Board, ex p National Union of Mineworkers.*[11] The Board's decision to close a colliery was challenged by judicial review. The substance of the challenge was that the Board had not acted fairly in rejecting the recommendation of an Independent Review Board set up by agreement between trade unions and the Board. It was argued that in taking its decision the Board was exercising a duty arising from statute and in particular section 46 above. The court rejected this. Section 46 conferred a duty as to the establishing of machinery for settlement of terms and conditions of employment. It

---

9 [1988] AC 533, [1988] 1 All ER 485.
10 [1988] ICR 36.
11 [1986] ICR 791.

did not go beyond that to the product of such consultation. The Board has statutory functions, and for some purposes is a public body, but it could not be said to be:

empowered by statute to make the decision which is attacked here nor is that decision in any way part of its activities as a public body which can be reviewed. The decision by the NCB in respect of [this] colliery is, in my judgment, an executive, or business or a management decision in exactly the same category as a decision in similar circumstances made by a public company.

In *R v Midlands Electricity Board, ex p Busby*,[12] B agreed to be supplied by a pre-payment (ie money-in-the-slot) meter. The agreement provided that coins put in the meter became the property of the Board, but that even if the money was stolen from the meter, the customer remained indebted to the Board for the sum in question. Sixty-two pounds was stolen from the meter. It was argued that the agreement was ultra vires the Board; or if not, to enter into it or to enforce it was, in B's circumstances, unreasonable. The court rejected both arguments, but our concern with the case in this context is with the appropriateness of judicial review. Schiemann J said, 'Parliament intended Electricity Boards to be run in general on commercial lines' and then added, 'but has to a degree regulated by statute the rights and duties of both of the Board and its customers.' It was the extent of those statutorily-regulated rights and duties which was in issue here, and which was therefore properly challengeable by judicial review. (It may also be noted that an agreement between Board and customer did not constitute a contract.[13] Thus in the *NCB* case the cutting off of the employee's work was not an exercise of public power, whereas here, the cutting off of the customer's electricity supply was.)

The National Health Service
The NHS authorities are of course statutory, and there is no question but that in the exercise of their statutory functions they may be subject to judicial review. In *R v Ethical Committee of St Mary's Hospital, Manchester, ex p Harriott*[14] H challenged the decision to refuse her in vitro fertilisation. The hospital had set up the Ethical Committee, its membership consisting of doctors, nurses, scientists, officers and members of the Health Authority. It provided a forum for the discussion of issues of concern to its members, and was a mechanism for assuring the Authority that satisfactory standards were being maintained in this field. It does not seem to have been argued that the Committee was not subject to judicial review. There was no statutory duty to set up the Committee, and no such duty on the Committee to advise or decide. Even so, the statutory basis of the Authority's function, and the public interest in the principles on which the facilities in question were provided, gave the Committee, it is suggested, a strong public law element. What *was* argued was that judicial

12 (1987) Times, 28 October.
13 See p 461 below. Note also the status of the Board as an 'organ of the state': see *Foster v British Gas*, p 36 above.
14 [1988] 1 FLR 512, [1988] Fam Law 165.

review did not lie to review mere advice given by the Committee. The court doubted whether that was right but ruled that in any case the advice given was unobjectionable. (Health Authorities are now required by government to set up Local Research Ethics Committees.)

Broadcasting

The Independent Broadcasting Authority (IBA) (now superseded by the Independent Television Commission) was a statutory corporation. Its job was to provide certain broadcasting services. Television programmes broadcast by it were provided by 'programme contractors' who entered into contracts with it. Section 20(5) of the Broadcasting Act 1981 provides that every such contract was to contain provisions to ensure that if certain changes took place in the persons having control of the programme contractor, the IBA was to determine the contract. Granada was a programme contractor. In addition to its contract with IBA, its articles of association provided that no shareholder was entitled to vote in respect of more than five per cent of the total number of voting shares unless he was 'approved' by the IBA. Rank sought to acquire control of Granada. To effect this they needed IBA's permission to exercise voting rights in excess of the five per cent. The IBA's refusal was challenged by an application for judicial review. If the IBA, in so refusing, was exercising a section 20(5) power, its decision was reviewable. But it was not. It was exercising a power given it by Granada's articles of association. True, the IBA's power to act in the approving capacity under the articles was statutory, but to attract judicial review it is not enough merely to show a statutory power to act: the action must be in pursuance of public law, which this decision was not.[15] (It appears that a policy consideration urged on the court, unsuccessfully, was that judicial review should be available as it was difficult to see what alternative remedy a dissatisfied shareholder had.)

Local authorities: markets

The question of the relationship of public law and contract has been raised in connection with the operation of markets by local authorities. In *R v Barnsley Metropolitan Borough Council, ex p Hook*[16] the local authority's right to hold a market was confirmed by Act of Parliament which gave the authority power to regulate the conduct of the market and to make byelaws. By those byelaws one could not erect a stall in the market without being allocated a space by the superintendent. H had been allocated a space by a licence. He challenged the legality of the revocation of his licence. The licence itself was contractual, but it was held that the authority's action in *revoking* it was a question of public law, and was therefore reviewable by the court. In *R v Basildon District Council, ex p Brown*[17] the local authority opened a market under statutory powers. B was granted

15 *R v Independent Broadcasting Authority, ex p Rank Organisation plc* (1986) Times, 14 March, CA.
16 [1976] 3 All ER 452, [1976] 1 WLR 1052.
17 (1981) 79 LGR 655.

a licence to trade there, subject to the council's regulations. It was argued by the council that their relationship was governed by the ordinary (private) law of contract so that the authority's reasons for terminating the arrangement was irrelevant and could not be reviewed by the court. The court agreed that as the market was carried on under statutory powers the decision in question was reviewable.[18]

In *R v Wear Valley District Council, ex p Binks*[19] the applicant B, by agreement was allowed by the council to station her caravan in a town's market-place in the evenings and there sell hot food. The public had a right of access to the market-place at all times. Without giving B notice of their intention, the council revoked the agreement on one month's notice. The court ruled that whether or not the council could be said to be regulating a public market in giving and revoking a licence to trade, there was a public law element in their decision in that matter.

Local authorities: schools
The actions of local authorities in relation to their schools are susceptible to judicial review, as are the decisions of grant-maintained (re central government funded) schools[20] and city technology schools.[1] Independent schools ie those that charge fees, operate within a statutory framework of control, but the relationship there between pupil and school is that of a contract in which there is no statutory involvement, so that an expelled pupil could have no recourse to judicial review, only to the law of contract.[2]

Local authorities: planning
In *R v Elmbridge Borough Council, ex p Health Care Corporation*[3] E told H that the planning permission they had been granted had not been validly implemented. There is no express statutory authority to say that, but E was nevertheless exercising a statutory power when doing so because of the terms of section 111 of the Local Government Act 1972.[4]

Prerogative

The nature of the 'prerogative' has been referred to.[5]

The Criminal Injuries Compensation Scheme was set up not by Act, but by administrative decision; not by Parliament, but by government. The Scheme provides for the payment of compensation to persons suffering

---

18 Likewise in *R v Birmingham City Council, ex p Dredger* 91 LGR 532 the exercise of the council's monopoly power to regulate the holding of markets (specifically to fix rents) was a public law question. See ch 16 below for Local Ombudsman's jurisdiction.
19 [1985] Ch 52, [1985] 2 All ER 699.
20 *R v Secretary of State for Education ex p Prior* (1994) Independent 6 January.
 1 *R v Governors of Haberdashers' Aske's Hatcham College Trust, ex p Tyrell* (1994) Independent, 12 October.
 2 *R v Fernhill Manor School, ex p Brown* [1992] COD 446.
 3 (1992) 63 P&CR 260.
 4 See p 206 above.
 5 See p 52 above.

personal injury attributable to a criminal offence. Application for compensation is made to the Criminal Injuries Compensation Board, the members of which are appointed by government. In deciding whether compen-sation is payable, and if so how much, the Board applies the rules set out in the Scheme. In *R v Criminal Injuries Compensation Board, ex p Lain*,[6] Lain sought judicial review, by way of certiorari, to quash a decision of the Board for error of law. The important and novel question for the court was whether such a decision, taken in the context of a prerogative and not a statutory scheme, was subject to judicial review. Diplock LJ observed that the Board's authority did not derive from any agreement between the Crown and applicants for compensation but rather from instructions by the executive government. The Board, the court said, was to be regarded as equivalent to a tribunal, and the court had no difficulty in showing that historically certiorari was available to quash decisions of *courts* whose authority derived from the prerogative: why not therefore decisions of a *tribunal* akin to a court whose authority was also so derived? On the facts, certiorari did not ensue as no error of law was shown, but the very important point was established that a decision, the authority for which was based in the prerogative, was not for that reason only immune from judicial review.

In the *GCHQ*[7] case the court's jurisdiction over other acts and decisions (ie other than decisions of tribunals) deriving authority from the common law (or prerogative) was unequivocally established. The facts will be found at p 53 above.

Lord Fraser said:

There is no doubt that if the 1982 Order in Council had been made under the authority of a statute the power delegated to the minister by Art 4 would have been construed as being subject to an obligation to act fairly. I am unable to see why the words conferring the same powers should be construed differently merely because their source was an Order in Council made under the prerogative.

Lord Diplock put it this way:

For a decision to be susceptible to judicial review the decision-maker must be empowered by public law (and not merely, as in arbitration, by agreement between parties) to make decisions that, if validly made, will lead to administrative action or abstention from action ... The ultimate source of the decision-making power is nearly always nowadays a statute or subordinate legislation made under the statute; but in the absence of any statute regulating the subject matter of the decision the source of the decision-making power may still be the common law itself ie that part of the common law that is given by lawyers the label of 'the prerogative'.

Since the *GCHQ* case the reviewability of the exercise of prerogative powers has been established or accepted in other cases.

Ex gratia payments   The Home Office had a policy of paying compensation to persons who, having been convicted, are imprisoned and later

6   [1967] 2 QB 864, [1967] 2 All ER 770.
7   [1985] AC 374, [1984] 3 All ER 935.

have their conviction quashed. Those payments were made under the prerogative. In *R v Secretary of State, ex p Weeks*,[8] though the application for judicial review of the Home Secretary's refusal of compensation was unsuccessful, counsel for the Home Office accepted that the matter was justiciable, while wishing to reserve the point.

Prerogative of mercy In *R v Home Secretary, ex p Bentley*[9] it was said that the formulation of policy for the grant of a pardon was probably not justiciable, but the minister's failure in this case (concerning a 19-year-old, the applicant's brother, hanged 40 years before) to recognise that the prerogative of mercy could be exercised in many different circumstances was reviewable.

Immigration Where a person has a notice served on him that his deportation is 'conducive to the public good for reasons of national security' he can have his case considered by a panel appointed by the Home Secretary to advise him. This replaced a statutory right of appeal. Decisions of the panel are susceptible of judicial review (but there would be little chance of success).[10]

Contract In *R v Lord Chancellor, ex p Hibbitt and Saunders*[11] the exercise by the minister of the common law (or prerogative) power to enter into a contract (in particular the tendering conditions laid down) was held not to be subject to judicial review (despite the unfairness acknowledged by the court to have been done to the applicants). The contract was for the employment of court shorthand writers. Their importance is acknowledged by statute, but that is not enough.

Passports There is no statute law concerning the issue etc of those identity documents called passports, and the matter therefore falls under the prerogative. In *R v Secretary of State for Foreign Affairs, ex p Everett*[12] the Court of Appeal held that it was 'common sense' and 'obvious' that a refusal or withdrawal of a passport fell into that area of the prerogative power that was reviewable, though on the facts a remedy was not granted.

The nature of the function

The public law element in or 'publicness of' a decision or action which has to be present for it to be subject to judicial review may therefore have its source in statute or the common law. However, the publicness may be shown to be present by considerations other than its *source*. This was shown in *R v Panel on Take-Overs and Mergers, ex p Datafin plc*[13] (the

---

8 (1988) Times, 15 March. And *R v Secretary of State for the Home Department, ex p Harrison* [1988] 3 All ER 86. See Criminal Justice Act 1988, s 133 for statutory provision for payment of compensation.
9 [1993] 4 All ER 442.
10 *R v Secretary of State for the Home Dept, ex p Cheblak* [1991] 2 All ER 319, [1991] 1 WLR 890.
11 (1993) Times, 12 March.
12 [1989] QB 811, [1989] 1 All ER 655.
13 [1987] QB 815, [1987] 1 All ER 564.

Datafin case).

The case concerned a contested take-over, and a complaint to the Panel by one of the contestants that the other had acted contrary to the rules of the Panel. The Panel rejected the complaint. The complainant sought leave to apply for judicial review of the Panel's decision.

What is the Panel? It is an unincorporated body of some 15 members appointed by various City and professional bodies such as the Stock Exchange, the banks, etc. The chairman and deputy chairman are appointed by the Bank of England, as is the Panel's chief officer. *What does it do?* It devises and promulgates the City Code on Take-Overs and Mergers; it investigates and reports on alleged breaches of the Code and applies sanctions.

The Panel argued that it was not subject to judicial review as the court's jurisdiction was confined to bodies whose power derived solely from statute or the prerogative, and the Panel's power did not so derive. The Court of Appeal ruled that in determining whether the decisions of a particular body are subject to judicial review, a court is not confined to considering the *source* of that body's powers and duties but can also look at their *nature* (not, that is, at where it formally *gets its functions from*, but at what it *does*). In this case the Court of Appeal was unanimous that if a body is *performing a public duty*, then it is subject to public law. *What of the panel?* The following reasons led the court to conclude that it was performing a public duty. (i) The leading part played by the Bank of England in setting up the panel was significant. (ii) Most of the important take-overs will be of companies whose shares are listed on the Stock Exchange. In exercising its listing function the Stock Exchange exercises a statutory public law power which is subject to judicial review. A company seeking a listing for its shares must observe the Take-Over Code. Thus the Panel, the Code, the Stock Exchange and the listing requirements are closely inter-meshed. (iii) The Code does not have the force of law but seeks to ensure that those who enjoy the facilities of the securities markets in the UK observe good standards of commercial behaviour. The Panel's decisions in applying the Code may affect persons who are not members of bodies represented on the Panel. (iv) If the panel finds a person to be in breach of the Code it may deprive him of his ability to enjoy the relevant facilities. It may refer the case to the Department of Trade, etc. (v) The Department of Trade has refrained from including in the statutory Licensed Dealers' Rules detailed provisions about take-overs because it considers it better to rely on the effectiveness and flexibility of the Code.

Lloyd LJ, agreed that one could infer the necessary public element from the nature of the duty. 'But', he asked himself 'suppose I am wrong; suppose that the courts are indeed confined to looking at the source of power ...'. If that were so, the source of the power here was 'indeed governmental, at least in part'. One could say that the panel was established 'under the authority of [the] government ...'. It was not right to say that the government had deliberately refrained from exercising power. There was an implied devolution of power. Nicholls LJ, referring to the listing requirements, said that the system was undistinguishable in its effect from a delegation by the Stock Exchange of its public law function to a group of people, the Panel, which includes its representatives, and Donaldson MR, said that the Panel's source of power was 'only partly based on moral persuasion and the assent of institutions and their members, the bottom line being the statutory powers exercised by the Department of Trade and the Bank of England'. He continued, 'In this context I should be very disappointed if the courts could not recognise the realities of executive power and allowed their vision to be clouded by the subtlety and sometimes complexity of the way in which it can be executed.'

How has *Datafin* been applied?[14]

The Advertising Standards Association is responsible for supervising the advertising industry's system of self-regulation which includes investigating complaints made to it that an advertisement is in breach of the industry's code of conduct. In *R v Advertising Standards Authority Ltd, ex p Insurance Services plc*[15] a decision of the Association was held subject to review, and quashed.

In *R v Code of Practice Committee of the Association of the British Pharmaceutical Industry, ex p Professional Counselling Aids Ltd* [16] the Committee was (reluctantly) said to be subject to review as it performed a public duty in controlling the advertising etc of medicines. (The Code had been agreed with the Department of Health). 'Reluctantly' because the effect of *Datafin* could be to swamp the courts with 'domestic' issues, and the imposition on such bodies of standards of conduct never intended (here the allegation was of irrelevancy, unreasonableness and failure to give an oral hearing).

The decisions of governing bodies of religious organisations have been challenged. In *R v Chief Rabbi of the United Hebrew Congregations, ex p Wachmann*[17] the Chief Rabbi ruled that W was not fit to hold office as a rabbi. The court held that public interest in the matter was not enough: there had to be a potentially governmental interest in the decision, and here there could clearly be none. And in *R v Imam of Bury Park Mosque, ex p Ali*[18] the Imam refused 204 people membership of the mosque etc. The only possible public element was that the Imam was carrying out a function ordered by the court (in earlier proceedings), and that was not enough. As in *Wachmann* the issue raised question of religious law in which the court would not interfere.

The non-subjection of governing bodies in sport has been referred to.[19] The predominant element of agreement in such cases was held to outweigh any public element of their activities. It was said of the Jockey Club that though not a public body it had public powers – but they were not

14 Susceptibility to review following *Datafin* conceded in *R v Lautro, ex p Ross* [1992] 1 All ER 422.

15 (1989) 9 Tr LR 169. And see *R v Advertising Standards Authority Ltd, ex p Vernons Organisation Ltd* [1993] 2 All ER 202.

16 (1990) 10 BMLR 21.

17 [1993] 2 All ER 249, [1992] 1 WLR 1306.

18 [1992] COD 132.

19 See p 339 above.

governmental. To the argument that if the Club did not regulate the industry the government would have to, the court replied that it had not. The cases were reviewed in *R v Football Association Ltd, ex p Football League Ltd*.[20] The judge said that the ratio of *Datafin* is that a body may be subject to judicial review if it regulates an important aspect of national life and does so with the support of the state in that, but for its existence, the state would create a public body to perform its functions. The FA was not such a body; its virtually monopolistic powers arose from private law only.

It must be right for the court not to allow its 'vision to be clouded' by the complex ways in which executive power can be exercised. However, as long as judicial review is confined to public power, and as long as public and private are enmeshed, so will there be an area of uncertainty as to the activities subject to judicial review. And to introduce into the equation the speculation that if the arrangements were not as they are the government (any government?) would itself take action must enlarge that area. The effect of *Datafin* appears to have been limited.[1]

Applying for judicial review

Recent developments

The procedure that has to be followed to get the prerogative orders has long been different from that followed in ordinary actions for breach of contract or tort. In 1969 the Law Commission recommended that a wide ranging inquiry should be undertaken into administrative law.

The government's response was that the time for such an inquiry was not right; instead it asked for the Law Commission:

to review the existing remedies for the judicial control of administrative acts and omissions with a view to evolving a simpler and more effective procedure.

In 1976 the Commission published its Report on Remedies in Administrative law.[2] The Report emphasised its narrow scope, and confined itself to an examination of the procedure for judicial control exercised through the five remedies being discussed here and made recommendations. Concerning the procedure for getting the prerogative orders, which is governed by the Rules of the Supreme Court, Order 53 the Report noted that the applicant first applied ex parte (that is, only the applicant himself is heard, not the other side) for *leave to apply* for the order, this application being accompanied by a statement of the grounds on which the relief was sought supported by affidavits. Leave being granted, the application for the order itself was made by 'originating motion'. A second very important

20 [1993] 2 All ER 833. And see *R v Insurance Ombudsman Bureau, ex p Aegon Life Assurance* (1994) Independent, 11 January: not reviewable; see p 556 below.

1 See *R v Corporation of Lloyds, ex p Briggs* [1993] 1 LL.R. 176: even if Lloyds performs public function, rights relied on in this case related exclusively to contractual relationship. *B v Royal Life Saving Society, ex p Howe* [1990] COD 499; Society's useful functions not enough; incorporation by charter of no weight.

2 Cmnd 6407: hereafter, Law Commission – Remedies.

feature of the procedure under Order 53 was that an application for a prerogative order *could not be made in conjunction with an application for any other remedy*, the relevant ones for our purpose being injunction, declaration and damages. If therefore, for example, an application was made for certiorari to quash an order by which a public authority took possession of one's property, one could not join with that a claim to damages or an injunction in respect of the trespass in the case where the order was quashed.

An important difference between the procedure for prerogative orders and an ordinary action that the Report noted concerned *discovery of documents*. This is available in the latter case but in the former, though available, was rarely if ever ordered. And the *time-limits* for bringing proceedings for the prerogative orders were shorter, in the case of certiorari, six months.

One possibility for reform considered by the Law Commission was that the procedure applicable to the prerogative orders should be assimilated to that of ordinary civil actions begun (as for injunction and declaration) by writ or originating summons. Proceedings in the public law field would be on the same footing as those in private law. The Commission's conclusion was that the proceedings applicable in the private law field have their own difficulties (in particular opportunities for delay); and that the procedure for obtaining a prerogative order was relatively simple, inexpensive and speedy. It therefore rejected that possibility.

On the question of the need to get leave to bring proceedings for a prerogative order, the Law Commission thought worthy of retention 'a procedure which provides an expeditious method whereby the court can sift out the cases with no chance of success at relatively little cost to the applicant and no cost to any prospective respondent'.[3] (Notice that while leave is not required to bring an ordinary action, the defendant can apply to have the proceedings struck out on the ground, inter alia, that no reasonable cause of action is disclosed.)[4]

Having then satisfied itself that there should continue to be a distinctive procedure for the application for the prerogative orders the Law Commission recommended that there should be a form of procedure to be entitled an 'application for judicial review'. By means of this an applicant would be able to obtain not only any of the prerogative orders but also, where appropriate, a declaration or injunction. The essential characteristics of those remedies would not be affected, and the declaration or injunction would be available by *this* procedure only when a public law issue was involved. Why that limitation? The prerogative orders are in respect of public law. A special procedure applies in respect of them, and if the declaration and injunction were to be available by that procedure, it could only be in respect of a public law issue.

We have noted that a claim to damages could not be joined to an application for a prerogative order. The Law Commission thought that

3 Law Commission – Remedies, para 38.
4 RSC Ord 18, r 19.

there might be cases where the court, having decided on an application for judicial review that an illegality had occurred, might be able to make an award of damages. The difficulty would be that the form of the proceedings for a prerogative order, with reliance on affidavit evidence, (that is, on documents only) would not normally be suitable for the proof and assessment of damages. The power to make an award of damages on an application for judicial review could only be used therefore where there was no remaining dispute that the damage did result from the illegality or as to the fact or extent of damage or as to the quantum of damages. Notice that this was not a proposal for a new remedy of damages for loss arising from illegal administrative acts, but only that damages for loss under the existing law of contract and tort might be awarded in judicial review proceedings.

The Law Commission recommendations were concerned with the procedural disadvantage in seeking a remedy through the prerogative orders, which are available only in respect of public law issues. However, public law issues do not arise only in applications for prerogative orders. They could arise collaterally in ordinary actions in contract or tort or in criminal proceedings, or directly in ordinary actions for a declaration or an injunction. The Commission was clear that the new procedure they recommended, the 'application for judicial review', was *not to be exclusive* in the sense that it would become the only way by which issues relating to the legality of the actions of public authorities could come before the courts.

Action taken to implement the Law Commission's recommendations in its 1976 Report is explained below. The Commission gave further consideration to this and related questions in the early 1990s and published a report in 1994.[5] This is also referred to in the following pages.

The application: the present position
The position now is this. Significant changes were made to Order 53 in 1977 in order to implement some of the Report's recommendations, by SI 1977/1955. It was amended by SI 1980/2000 and SI 1982/1111. (The title of the Order was changed from 'Application for Certiorari Prohibition and Mandamus' to 'Application for Judicial Review'.) And now section 31 of the Supreme Court Act 1981 enacts some of but not all the provisions of Order 53, with power to set out the details in rules of court. Section 31 (1) of the Supreme Court Act 1981 now provides:

An application to the High Court for one or more of the following forms of relief, namely—
(a)   an order of mandamus, prohibition or certiorari;
(b)   a declaration or an injunction under subsection (2); ...
shall be made in accordance with rules of court by a procedure to be known as an application for judicial review.

---

5   *Administrative Law: Judicial Review and Statutory Appeals.* Hereafter Law Com No 226.

Thus, as recommended by the Law Commission's 1976 Report, it is now possible to apply for any of the three prerogative orders and a declaration and an injunction in the same proceedings. The court will, in its discretion, award whichever of the remedies (if any), or combination thereof is appropriate.

In addition, on an application for judicial review *damages* may be awarded; and application may be made for *discovery* of documents. However, no change has been made to the requirement of *leave*. These matters are dealt with later.

Capacity to apply
One who is a person in the eyes of the law – a human or a body corporate – has capacity to apply for judicial review. It has been held that an unincorporated association, not being a 'person' has no such capacity.[6] The Law Commission has recommended that they should, by one or more of the members applying in a representative capacity.[7]

Making the application

The ex parte application
Section 31(3) of the Supreme Court Act 1981 provides:

No application for judicial review shall be made unless the leave of the High Court has been obtained in accordance with rules of court ...

The rules of court provide that application for leave is to be made ex parte to a single judge (not as before to the Divisional Court). Notice of the application is given by filing in the Crown Office,[8] a notice in Form 86A containing a statement of the relief sought, the grounds on which it is sought etc, and an affidavit which verifies the facts relied on. The judge may determine the application without a hearing unless a hearing is requested in the notice of the application. (Many hearings are requested). This procedure enables the court to deal with applications more expeditiously and at less expense than was formerly the case. Where the application is refused it may be renewed by applying within ten days to a single judge in which case there is an oral hearing. (Where the initial refusal of leave is from an oral hearing, the application can only be renewed to the Court of Appeal.) If the court grants leave to apply, the application is made by 'originating motion' to a single judge sitting in open court unless the court directs that it is to be made to a Divisional Court.

As stated, application for leave to apply is made ex parte, and no provision is made for the proposed respondent to be informed of the application in order to be heard in relation to it. There is, however, jurisdiction for the court, on application, to set aside any ex parte order.

6 *R v Darlington BC, ex p Association of Darlington Taxi Drivers* (1994) Times, 21 January. *R v London Borough of Tower Hamlets, ex p Tower Hamlets CTA* [1994] COD 325.
7 Law Com No 226, para 5.38.
8 See p 361 below.

The Law Commission has recommended amendments to Form 86A so as to provide more information in order to help the judge in deciding whether to allow the application to proceed. It has also recommended a 'request for information' procedure by which the judge could ask the respondent for information.[9]

The need for leave

It is surely remarkable that permission, even of a High Court judge, is necessary in order to challenge the legality of administrative action by way of judicial review. Leave is not necessary where the challenge is by way of the standard 'six weeks' procedure,[10] nor of course if one is suing a public authority in contract or tort. In that last case the defendant can apply to have the proceedings struck out on the ground, inter alia, that no reasonable cause of action is disclosed.

Is the need for leave justified? The Law Commission's view in its 1976 Report was that it was. The argument there relied on could be, but has not been, applied to litigation generally. However, in public law cases there are additional considerations. The view of the Law Commission in its 1994 Report, is that it is essential to filter out hopeless applications for judicial review; and that that is the purpose of the leave requirement. Why is it essential? Because ill-founded applications delay finality in decision-making; they exacerbate delays within the judicial system; and hold up the progress of well-founded claims. All these are important policy considerations underlying Order 53.[11]

The Commission suggests that the filter stage should be known as the 'preliminary consideration' rather than the leave stage. This, it says, is not a mere cosmetic: it is important to remove the perception that a citizen seeking a prerogative order is at a substantial disadvantage as compared with one asserting a private right – as that is not the case. Finally, it could be said that a filtering requirement is beneficial to an applicant, and relatively cheaply, if he hears from the court itself whether he has no or some prospect of success. Not everyone agrees with the paternalistic attitude implicit in that.

The Commission goes on to suggest that, as in too many cases applications for leave are determined for the first time at oral hearings, the application for preliminary consideration (ie leave) should be determined entirely on paper unless the application includes a claim for immediate interim relief or where it appears that a hearing is desirable in the interests of justice.

The next question is, what test the court applies in deciding whether to grant leave. Judicial statements suggest that the test is whether the applicant has, or might turn out to have, an arguable case; he must show a real as opposed to a theoretical possibility of such a case. It seems that there is a wide disparity in the rate of granting leave as between different

9 Law Com No 226, Part IV.
10 See p 425 below.
11 Law Com No 226, para 5.1.

subject-matters and as between different judges. The Law Commission thinks that it should be stated in the Rules that 'unless the application discloses a serious issue which ought to be determined it should not be allowed to proceed to a substantive hearing'.[12]

It had been judicially suggested that it should be possible for a judge to give leave on some grounds but refuse it on others; the Law Commission so recommends.[13]

Time-limits for applying

The grant of the prerogative orders being in the court's discretion, delay in applying could be taken into account in deciding whether or not to grant leave or relief. The rule used to be that for a certiorari, application for leave had to be made within six months of the decision challenged, but even if application was made within that time, the court still could refuse relief.

The Law Commission's view in its 1976 Report was that any period is inevitably arbitrary as a general rule. A more satisfactory way of dealing with the problem was, in its view, to give the court more precise guidance as to the circumstances in which the discretion should be exercised, and they had this to say.

We would wish to emphasise that when an individual makes an application for judicial review what will be in issue will be not only the vindication of his personal right but also the assertion of the rule of law in the public sphere. We do not think therefore that delay on the part of the applicant should of itself be the deciding consideration.[14]

The rules are now as follow. Section 31(6) of the Supreme Court Act 1981, provides:

Where the High Court considers that there has been undue delay in making an application of judicial review, the court may refuse to grant
(a)   leave for the making of the application, or
(b)   any relief sought on the application
if it considers that the granting of the relief sought would be likely to cause substantial hardship to, or substantially prejudice the rights of any person, or would be detrimental to good administration.

Section 31 (7) provides that subsection (6) is without prejudice to any enactment or rule of court which has the effect of limiting the time within which an application for judicial review may be made. Order 53, r 4 (1), a rule of court, provides:

An application for leave to apply for judicial review shall be made promptly and in any event within three months from the date when grounds for the application first arise unless the Court considers that there is good reason for extending the period within which the application shall be made.

---

12 Ibid, para 5.14.
13 *R v Secretary of State for Transport, ex p Richmond upon Thames LBC* [1994] 1 All ER 577 at 600; Law Com No 226.
14 Law Commission – Remedies, para 50.

In a number of cases the difficulty of reading these two provisions together was commented on. For example s. 31 (6) does not define undue delay whereas rule 4 (1) does; and that rule deals only with an application for leave to apply, whereas section 36 (6) deals with both granting of leave and granting of relief. The law was clarified in *Caswell v Dairy Produce Quota Tribunal*.[15] C applied to the tribunal for a milk quota. The tribunal fixed it in 1984 on the basis of the expected 1985 production. More than two years later C applied for and was granted leave to apply for judicial review of that decision (on the basis that the question of delay would be dealt with at the hearing). At the hearing the judge concluded that the tribunal had erred in law. There was no appeal from that decision. But what of the delay?

The outcome of the House of Lords decision is this: (noting that the phrase in section 36 (6) 'an application for judicial review' must be read as referring, where appropriate, to an application for leave to apply for judicial review).

– When an application for leave to apply is not made promptly and in any event within three months, the court may refuse leave on the ground of delay unless it considers that there is good reason for extending the period.
– Even if it considers that there is such good reason, it may still refuse leave on the ground of undue delay (or, where leave has been granted, substantive relief) if in its opinion the granting of the relief sought would be likely to cause hardship or prejudice or would be detrimental to good administration.

Thus in this case the fact that the judge had granted leave long after the three-month period had run out did not preclude the court from subsequently refusing substantive relief on the ground of undue delay under section 31 (6).[16]

The Law Commission's view is that there should be special time limits, but also flexibility and discretion in their operation. It recommends that section 31 (6) be replaced by a provision empowering time limits to be specified by rule, and that the rule should provide (i) that application 'shall be made within three months ...'; (ii) that the courts may refuse an application made *within* three months if satisfied: (a) that the application is not sufficiently prompt; and (b) that if the relief sought were granted it would be likely to cause substantial hardship etc or be detrimental to good administration; (iii) that an application may be made *after* three

15 [1990] 2 AC 738, [1990] 2 All ER 434.
16 That there was undue delay in this case was undoubted, and it was not suggested that hardship or prejudice were likely to be caused by the grant of the relief sought (certiorari). But was the judge right to say that the grant of relief would be detrimental to good administration? He was. There was a finite amount of quota available. If relief was granted in this case there would probably be a significant number of further applications and these might lead to all allocations back to 1984 having to be reopened – a very clear case of detriment to good administration. In the outcome, C was left with the declaration the judge had granted that the tribunal's decision was unlawful. Note that the fact that there is a good reason for the undue delay does not mean that there was not undue delay. See also *R v Secretary of State for Health, ex p Furneaux* [1994] 2 All ER 652: delay; relief would prejudice third party; refused. Also *R v Department of Health, ex p Gandhi* [1991] 4 All ER 547.

months if the court is satisfied: (a) that there is good reason for the application not having been made within that period; and (b) if relief were granted it would not be likely to cause hardship, etc.[17]

Locus standi

A person who brings legal proceedings must have some interest in the subject-matter of the litigation. Where he alleges an interference with a private right, for example an incursion on to his property constituting trespass, his interest is obvious. He has locus standi, or standing. But the prerogative orders are available only in respect of the exercise of public power, and it may be more difficult for a litigant to show an interest in the exercise of that power which is sufficient to permit him to challenge its exercise: he must be in some way affected by it. He must have locus standi.

One of the problems the Law Commission's 1976 Report drew attention to was whether the test for locus standi is the same for all three prerogative orders. It noted that the trend of the most recent decisions was towards the development of a single concept applicable to them all; that the underlying purpose of the three orders is the same insofar as they aim not at the assertion of a private right but at the upholding of the law in the public interest; and that the law concerning the standing required for the declaration and injunction had also been developing. What was needed was a formula which 'allows for further development of the requirement of standing by the courts having regard to the relief which is sought'. Its recommendation was that the court should not grant any relief sought on an application for judicial review 'unless it considers that the applicant has a sufficient interest in the matter to which the application relates'.

The amended Order 53, having continued the requirement of leave, provided that the court was not to grant leave 'unless it considers that the applicant has a sufficient interest in the matter to which the application relates'. And section 31 (3) of the Supreme Court Act 1981 puts the same words into statutory form.

Important guidance on the meaning of the new statutory formula was given by the House of Lords in *IRC v National Federation of Self-employed and Small Business Ltd*.[18] The facts were these. There had been a practice for casual employees[19] working for national newspapers to receive their wages without deduction of tax, and for them to supply fictitious names and addresses (eg Mickey Mouse) when drawing wages so as to avoid paying tax. Their true name and addresses were only known to the unions (which operated a closed shop). When the Inland Revenue found out about this they made an arrangement with the unions, employers and employees whereby the employees were required to register with the Inland Revenue, and submit tax returns for the previous two years, and the Revenue agreed not to investigate tax evaded prior to that period. The Federation, claiming

17 Law ComNo 226, para 5.23.
18 [1982] AC 617, [1981] 2 All ER 93, HL. See Cane [1981] PL 322.
19 The case is sometimes referred to as the *Fleet St Casuals* case.

to represent some 5,000 taxpayers applied for judicial review under Order 53, seeking (i) a declaration that the Revenue had acted unlawfully in making the arrangement, and (ii) a mandamus directing the Revenue to assess and collect tax on the employees as required by law. Had it 'sufficient interest'?

Lord Wilberforce stated that the fact that the same formula – 'sufficient interest' – is used to cover all the forms of remedy allowed by the rule does not mean that the test is the same in all cases. Thus, for example one must have a 'sufficient interest' to apply for both certiorari and mandamus, but the 'interest' of a person seeking to compel (by mandamus) an authority to carry out its duty, is likely to be different from and more stringent than the 'interest' a person has to have in order to quash (by certiorari) a decision which an authority in exceeding its powers has taken to his detriment.

A point of great importance is this. Leave to apply for judicial review has to be obtained. If the court taking the view that the applicant has got standing, grants leave to apply on the (possibly one-sided) evidence before it, when the application comes in due course before the court it is open to the court then to say that the applicant has not got a sufficient interest. A reading of section 31 (3) of the Supreme Court Act 1981 may suggest that the question of sufficient interest arises only when leave to apply is sought ('The court shall not grant leave …') but in the *Fleet St Casuals* case the House of Lords laid it down very clearly that that is not so. The reason is that the sufficiency of the interest can be determined adequately only in the knowledge of 'the matter to which the application relates' and that information is not likely to be before the court on the application for leave to apply. The applicant must have '*a sufficient interest in the matter to which the application relates*'. Except in simple cases where it is obvious that the applicant has no sufficient interest, the question whether he has 'sufficient interest' cannot be treated as a jurisdictional or preliminary issue in isolation at the stage of applying for leave to apply. It is instead to be treated as a possible reason for the exercise of the court's discretion to refuse the application for judicial review when that comes before the court on the notice of motion and the evidence of both parties is before it. In the *Fleet St Casuals* case itself, for example, how could one say whether the Federation had a 'sufficient interest' in the arrangement made by the Inland Revenue without examining the legislation governing the work of the Revenue and its relationship to taxpayers? The House concluded that the Federation had not got a 'sufficient interest' but said that, on the basis of the affidavit evidence before it, the High Court had not been wrong to grant leave.

The 'sufficient interest' necessary for the various remedies is referred to in the discussion below of each of them separately, but the treatment of this and other aspects of the remedies cannot be kept in water-tight compartments. A general point is that the court is entitled in appropriate cases to consider of its own motion whether the applicant has a sufficient interest, if the respondent does not himself raise the issue.[20]

The Law Commission's 1994 recommendations are mentioned later.

---

20 *R v Oxford, ex p Levey* (1986) Times, 1 November.

Discovery etc

Order 53 provides that in proceedings for judicial review, application may be made for various interlocutory orders – for discovery of documents, for discovery by interrogatories (that is the submission of questions to be answered by the other side), and that the court should order the deponent of an affidavit to attend for cross-examination on his affidavit. The grant of these orders is of course in the court's discretion.

Discovery of documents is considered in chapter 15, and judicial review referred to there. In this context the case of *R v Secretary of State for the Home Department, ex p Herbage No 2*[1] (where an order for discovery was made, but an order for interrogatories was refused) can be usefully looked at. As for cross-examination: it is probably the case that in most applications for judicial review the facts are agreed: only the law is in issue. But if the facts as disclosed by the documents are in dispute, it will not be possible for the court to resolve them unless some further inquiry can be made into them. *R v Waltham Forest London Borough Council, ex p Baxter,*[2] was a case where cross-examination took place. See also *R v A-G, ex p Imperial Chemical Industries plc*[3] (where discovery is also referred to), and *R v Secretary of State for Transport, ex p Sheriff Ltd*[4] for further examples.

Damages and judicial review

As we have seen, it used to be the case that damages could not be had in connection with an application for judicial review, but that is not now so. Section 31 (4) of the Supreme Court Act 1981 provides:

(4)   On an application for judicial review the High Court may award damages to the applicant if—
(a)   he had joined with his application a claim for damages arising from any matter to which the application relates; and
(b)   the court is satisfied that, if the claim had been made in an action begun by the applicant at the time of making his application, he would have been awarded damages.

The limitations of the section will be carefully noted. A paraphrase might be helpful. Where judicial review is applied for (that is, one of the five remedies referred to in section 31 (1)) there may be joined to that application a claim for damages arising from any matter to which the application relates. The court may then award damages if satisfied that if the claim for damages had been made in an ordinary action begun by the applicant at the time of making his application for judicial review, he *would* have been awarded damages.

1   [1987] QB 1077, [1987] 1 All ER 324.
2   [1988] QB 419, [1987] 3 All ER 671; see p 214 above.
3   [1987] 1 CMLR 72.
4   [1987] PL 141; and p 456 below. (Dispute over whether meeting with civil servant had taken place.)

Cases illustrating the availability of damages.   In *R v Liverpool City Council, ex p Coade*[5] L did not deny that they had delayed by some months in paying C (and others) their salaries, the amount of which had been fixed by statutory instrument under the Remuneration of Teachers Act 1965. (The delay had been caused by other employees' strikes). C sought a mandamus – and damages. The court accepted that the claim for outstanding unpaid arrears of statutory remuneration due constituted a claim for damages which could have been brought by action (and could therefore be awarded on the application for judicial review). However, a claim was also made for damages for the 'distress and inconvenience' caused by the delay in payment. The court ruled that even if damages were payable under that head it would be 'wholly inappropriate to advance such a claim in the context of judicial review'. Why? Because (as noted elsewhere), judicial review is normally by way of documentary evidence. If this particular claim was made in an action, the plaintiff would have to give oral evidence to substantiate his distress. To assess the loss on the basis of a bald claim made on the application for judicial review was impossible.

In *R v Board of Visitors of Gartree Prison, ex p Sears*[6] the Board awarded S eight days' cellular confinement. The Board conceded in those proceedings that they had acted without jurisdiction, so certiorari issued on S's application to quash the decision. S had presumably suffered the punishment, so much good the quashing did him personally. But he added to the application to quash a claim for damages. This raised the question: is it the tort of false imprisonment (the only one relevant here) to detain a lawfully detained prisoner in a particular way? Mann J thought not. However, if it had been tortious to do so (or if some other tort such as assault was alleged), there is no doubt that damages could have been obtained on the application to quash.[7]

An ordinary claim for damages is not to be made under Order 53.   Under section 31 (4) damages are claimed in connection with an application for judicial review or as additional or subsidiary to that application. An ordinary claim for damages, without more, cannot be made on an application for judicial review. Or, to put it the other way round, if, on analysis, the claim is essentially for damages and an ordinary action has been brought, a defence application to have it struck out on the ground that the plaintiff should have taken Order 53 proceedings will not succeed.

The claim for damages being ancillary to the application for judicial review, falls with it. As stated above, a claim for damages under section 31 (4) is subordinate to and dependent on an application for judicial review. It seems to be the case that if that application fails because no element of public law is shown to be present, then there can be no award of damages.

---

5   (1986) Times, 10 October.
6   (1985) Times, 20 March.
7   As to the position in tort see *Hague v Deputy Governor of Parkhurst Prison* [1992] 1 AC 58, [1991] 3 All ER 733.

This was indicated in *R v Secretary of State for the Home Department, ex p Dew*.[8] D, while in prison, required, but was not given, medical treatment. He sought an order of mandamus to compel the provision of such treatment, the damages for the pain and suffering caused by the delay in treatment. Prior to the hearing of the application, treatment was provided so that a mandamus was not needed. However, D pursued his claim for damages. To establish this he had to show that he would have had an arguable case for judicial review before the treatment to his arm. The Court ruled that he had no such case. His claim was at best a claim in common law for damages. As the application for judicial review had for that reason to be struck out, there was nothing to which the claim for damages could connect, and it too fell. (It remained open to D to bring ordinary tort proceedings, as he was still within the limitation period.)

Declaration and injunction

As we have seen it is now possible for a declaration and/or an injunction to be obtained by way of judicial review. Section 31 (2) of the Supreme Court Act 1981 provides:

A declaration may be made or an injunction granted under this subsection in any case where an application for judicial review, seeking that relief, has been made and the High Court considers that, having regard to –

(a) the nature of the matters in respect of which relief may be granted by orders of mandamus, prohibition or certiorari;
(b) the nature of the persons and bodies against whom relief may be granted by such orders; and
(c) all the circumstances of the case,

it would be just and convenient for the declaration to be made or the injunction to be granted, as the case may be.

Thus where an application is made (by judicial review) for a declaration or an injunction the court may grant it where it is 'just and convenient' to do so. In deciding whether it is just and convenient the court must have regard to the matters specified in paragraphs (a), (b) and (c). Our concern is particularly with (a) and (b) which can be explained thus. The declaration and injunction are obtainable by an ordinary action in a private law matter as well as in public law matters. The prerogative orders are available only where there is a substantial public law element. As declarations or injunctions may now be awarded by the procedure (application for judicial review) that has historically been the one to follow where a prerogative order is desired, the court, in deciding whether to award a declaration or an injunction must bear in mind the kinds of matters for which and kinds of bodies against whom the prerogative orders lie. In other words the declaration or injunction applied for in judicial review proceedings must be in respect of a public law matter. This is referred to further in the section on the declaration.

8 [1987] 2 All ER 1049, [1987] 1 WLR 881.

Switching

A 'switching procedure' is to be found in Order 53 rule 9 (5) as follows:

Where the relief sought is a declaration, an injunction or damages and the Court considers that it should not be granted on an application for judicial review but might have been granted if it had been sought in an action begun by writ by the applicant at the time of making his application, the Court may, instead of refusing the application, order the proceedings to continue as if they had been begun by writ ...

As we have seen, before the new Order 53 was made it was not possible to combine the declaration, an injunction or damages with an application for judicial review, but it is now possible. This 'switching procedure' is intended to safeguard the position of an applicant who, on applying for either declaration or an injunction by way of or (with regard to damages) in connection with any application for judicial review is found not to be entitled to those remedies by that procedure. The 'switch', if permitted, ensures that the claim for any of those remedies, if it is obtainable in an action, can proceed as if it has been begun by action. If it is obtainable by action, it could have been so brought in the first place and the applicant is not to be penalised by having sought it by way of or in connection with an application for judicial review.

The following cases indicate the operation of the procedure. Notice, first, that the procedure is available only where a declaration or injunction is sought by way of application for judicial review (or damages sought in connection with it). In *R v East Berkshire Area Health Authority, ex p Walsh*[9] Walsh sought certiorari to quash his dismissal. This was refused as the relationship between himself and his employer did not have sufficient public element to subject it to a prerogative order. His application to 'switch' was refused: he had applied for a certiorari only. Contrast *R v South Glamorgan Health Authority, ex p Phillips.*[10] Here the certiorari and declaration sought on an application for judicial review were refused on the same ground as in *ex p Walsh*. But the 'switch' to an ordinary action was allowed and in the result a declaration was made (that a decision of a disciplinary tribunal could not stand because of procedural defects).

In *Davy v Spelthorne Borough Council*[11] it was shown that where the only claim is for damages (in that case for negligence) the remedy is properly sought by an ordinary action. Where an application for judicial review is properly made (ie where there is sufficient public law element) a claim for damages (arising from any matter to which the application relates) may be joined if the claim could have been made in a private law (ordinary) action begun at the time of making the application. But if it is shown that the application for judicial review was not properly brought (because there is no sufficient public law element), the claim for damages

9 [1985] QB 152, [1984] 3 All ER 425; see p 369 below.
10 (1986) Times, 21 November; (1986) Independent, 25 November, Lexis, p 370 below.
11 [1984] AC 262, [1983] 3 All ER 278.

(being ancillary to it) will fail; and the applicant will not be allowed to switch: by definition his claim was only ever in private law. One might have thought that the fact that it only ever was in private law was a good reason for allowing the applicant to switch thus safeguarding his position. However, the rule as stated here seems to flow from *R v Secretary of State, ex p Dew* (the facts of which are at p 359 above).

The Law Commission supports the logic of this, but recommends that the rule should be amended so as, in effect, to allow a claim for a declaration to proceed in the *Ex p Walsh* situation.[12]

The 'switching' or 'transfer' proceeding is out of Order 53 into an ordinary action, not the other way round. In *Roy*[13] for example, there could have been no switch if the courts had said he should have gone by judicial review. The Law Commission recommends[14] that it should be possible to transfer in to order 53 provided the plaintiff satisfies the criteria for granting leave (or, in accordance with its recommendation, for an application being allowed to proceed to full judicial review).

Additional remedies?

The Law Commission has recommended[15] that the court should be empowered to order restitution and to award a liquidated sum (the payment of a debt) in judicial review proceedings provided that, in both cases, that remedy would have been granted in an action begun by writ, as in the case of damages.

Crown Office List

Important changes have taken place in the court's arrangements for dealing with administrative law cases. A special list, known as the Crown Office List has been created to which are allocated, amongst other matters, Order 53 cases.[16] This was modelled on the former Commercial List, now Commercial Court.[17] The handling of the cases on the list is undertaken by judges nominated for that purpose. The Crown Office List is in effect a specialist administrative law court, created by delegated legislation and administrative arrangement.[18]

There have in the past been advocates of an Administrative Court or an Administrative Division of the High Court.[19] It has little or no support now.

---

12 Law Com No 226, para 3.18.
13 See p 367 below.
14 Law Com No 226, para 3.21.
15 Ibid, para 8.5.
16 *Practice Direction* [1981] 3 All ER 61, [1981] 1 WLR 1296.
17 Supreme Court Act 1981, s 6 (1) (b).
18 See Blom-Cooper 'The new face of judicial review' [1982] PL 250 and 353.
19 For summary see Foulkes *Introduction to Administrative Law* (4th edn) p 302.

The Law Commission has pointed to the large increase in recent years in applications for leave for judicial review, and consequent delays in hearing cases. Its 1994 Report is concerned principally with the procedure for applying for review, which could address case-load problems only to a limited extent. However, Appendix C to its Report gives an interesting account of 'case-load management issues' – for example, is there the right number of nominated judges? Is their time put to the best use? Should certain cases be heard outside London, by certain QCs acting as deputy High Court judges, or by the county court?

Procedural Exclusivity

O'Reilly v Mackman

Section 31 of the Supreme Court Act 1981 and the new Order 53 recast the rules for obtaining the prerogative orders and the remedies of declaration and injunction, the availability of damages, etc. Before these changes were made it was open to a person aggrieved by administrative action to challenge it by way of a prerogative order (in which case he would be subject to the limitations which applied – referred to above) or, alternatively, he could bring an ordinary action for a declaration (where such a remedy was helpful and appropriate) in which case he would be free of those limitations. It was indeed the existence of those limitations which some years before had led to the increased use of declaration, and the view of it as something of an all-purpose remedy.

It was the use after the introduction, by section 31 and the new Order 53, of the new procedure, of that alternative procedure – seeking a declaration by way of an ordinary action – that was challenged in *O'Reilly v Mackman*.[20] O'Reilly commenced such proceedings in order to establish that a decision of Hull Prison Board of Visitors was void for having failed to observe the rules of natural justice. The Board applied to the High Court for the action to be struck out *as an abuse of the process of the court*. In the outcome it was. In the House of Lords, Lord Diplock's speech was concurred with by his colleagues.

Lord Diplock observed that if O'Reilly's allegations were true he would have had a remedy by proceeding under Order 53 which, whether he had sought a certiorari or a declaration, would have required him to obtain the leave of the court. The question for the court was simply whether the plaintiff, now that the new Order 53 was in operation, could be allowed to apply for a declaration by means of an ordinary action. The parties agreed that O'Reilly had no such private right of action against the Board on the ground of its breach of natural justice: one cannot sue for damages for breach of contract or in tort for that defect. Thus, the Board's decision had not, Lord Diplock said, infringed or threatened to infringe any right (common law or statutory) the plaintiff had derived from *private* law. Now the Board's power was conferred on it under statute; and in deciding

20 [1983] 2 AC 237, [1982] 3 All ER 1124.

whether a charge against O'Reilly was proved, it was acting as a statutory tribunal (in contrast with a domestic tribunal whose powers are conferred on it by contract), and had to act fairly. If O'Reilly could make good his allegation, he was entitled to a public law remedy which would have the effect of preventing the Board's decision from having an adverse effect on him. (As the effect of the Board's decision was that O'Reilly would be incarcerated for longer than would otherwise have been the case, O'Reilly had *locus standi* to challenge the decision.)

Could he seek to have the legality of the decision reviewed, by an ordinary action, not for breach of contract or tort, but for a declaration of the illegality?

Reviewing developments in administrative law over the previous thirty years Lord Diplock observed that although the availability of certiorari had been widely extended,[1] an applicant had suffered from certain procedural disadvantages (referred to above). It was for this reason that actions for declarations affecting public law rights had been entertained by the courts. Having regard to the disadvantages *then* obtaining it could not *then* have been an abuse of the court's process to proceed by way of an action for a declaration instead of applying for a certiorari. But those procedural disadvantages were, said Lord Diplock, removed by the new Order 53. The procedural limitations that remained, such as the need for leave, were a necessary protection to public authorities against 'claims which it was not in the public interest for the courts to entertain'. They were 'safeguards imposed in the public interest in respect of groundless, unmeritorious or tardy attacks on the validity of decisions made by public authorities in the field of public law'.

O'Reilly conceded that by bringing the action for a declaration he had been able to evade the protection given by Order 53 to public authorities, but argued that this could be taken into account by the judge in deciding, at the conclusion of the trial, whether in the exercise of his discretion to grant the declaration. Lord Diplock replied that so to delay the judge's decision would defeat the public policy that underlies the grant of those protections, namely 'the need, in the interests of good administration and of third parties who may be indirectly affected by the decision, for speedy certainty as to whether it has the effect of a decision that is valid in public law ... Unless such an action can be struck out summarily at the outset as an abuse of the process of the court the whole purpose of the public policy to which the change in Order 53 was directed would be defeated'.

Lord Diplock acknowledged that neither section 31 nor Order 53 expressly provides that application for judicial review is to be the *exclusive* procedure by which the declaration or injunction may be obtained for infringing rights protected by public law. The great variation between cases made it proper to rely on the inherent power of the court, exercised on a case-by-case basis, to prevent abuse of its process, whatever form it might take. It was not therefore wise to lay down categories of cases in which it would necessarily always be such an abuse to seek a remedy

1   This is referred to at p 376 et seq, below.

against infringement of public rights by way of one ordinary action. But, now that the old procedural disadvantages had been removed:

It would in my view as a general rule be contrary to public policy and as such an abuse of the process of the court, to permit a person seeking to establish that a decision of a public authority infringed rights to which he was entitled to protection under public law, to proceed by way of an ordinary action and by this means evade the provisions of Order 53 for the protection of such authorities.[2]

While it would normally be appropriate to apply this general rule, there may, said Lord Diplock, be exceptions to it which should be developed on a case-by-case basis. He gave as examples the cases where the invalidity of the decision is a collateral issue, and where the parties agree to the 'writ' procedure.

The instant case, where the only relief sought was a declaration of nullity, was a 'blatant attempt' to evade the protection of Order 53. The action was therefore struck out. The decision introduced what became known as the principle of 'procedural exclusivity'.

Before considering how Lord Diplock's general rule has been applied in later cases, the following points can be made.

Before the new Order 53 the alternatives of seeking a declaration by way of an ordinary action and of proceeding under Order 53 for a prerogative order were available. The Law Commission's recommendation would have continued that dichotomy, which was exacerbated by the provision of the new Order 53 that a declaration may be obtained under that Order. The House of Lords reacted to that situation by making Order 53 the exclusive procedure for challenging public power.

It was generally thought that the object of the reform of the Order 53 procedure was to smooth out the difficulties in the way of those challenging the exercise of administrative power. A result of *O'Reilly* was to increase the difficulties in those cases where proceedings for a declaration could previously have been brought by action, and to raise in an acute form the distinction between public and private. Inevitably there was a number of cases working out the implication of the decision, not a few of which went to the House of Lords.

O'Reilly v Mackman applied

Lord Diplock acknowledged that the principle in *O'Reilly v Mackman* would have to be worked out on a case-by-case basis. The judgment in *Cocks v Thanet District Council*[3] was delivered on the same day as that in *O'Reilly*. Cocks brought an ordinary action claiming a declaration that the council was in breach of the statutory duty it owed him to provide him, as a homeless person, with housing accommodation. The House of Lords analysed the statutory scheme thus. Where a person claims accommodation on the ground of homelessness, the local authority has certain public law functions, to make inquiries and decide whether there

2   [1983] 2 AC 237 at 285, [1982] 3 All ER 1124 at 1134.
3   [1983] 2 AC 286, [1982] 3 All ER.

is a duty to house. If, as a result, a duty to house does exist, the local authority has what the House of Lords called the 'executive function' of carrying out that duty. This duty is enforceable by an ordinary private law action for damages. It follows that before such a private right can come into existence there must be the appropriate public law decision.[4] In order to establish this (private) right, Cocks had to call in question the precedent public law decision – and thus to proceed with Order 53. This, like *O'Reilly*, he had not done.[5]

The rather complex case of *Davy v Spelthorne Borough Council*[6] resolved itself, by the time it reached the House of Lords, into a claim by D against S in tort, alleging negligent advice by S resulting in his inability to appeal against an enforcement notice served by S on him and to which he alleged he had a good defence. S said that D's allegation meant that he was asserting a right to which he was entitled to protection under public law, and therefore should have used Order 53. Lord Fraser with whom three other members of the House agreed, rejected the argument.

The present proceedings so far as they consist of a claim for damages for negligence, appear to me to be simply an ordinary action for tort. They do not raise any issue of public law as a live issue.

In *Cocks*, Cocks was seeking to overturn the decision of the local authority; in this case, far from wishing to impugn the order, D's case was that he had lost his chance to do so. Lord Wilberforce, concurring in the result, put it this way. What was alleged? That S owed D a duty of care and was in breach of it, causing him damage. How could such an action be an abuse of the process of court (the basis of decision in *O'Reilly's* case)? Before an action could be so classified it had at least to be shown that the claim *could* and *should* be brought by way of application for judicial review. Both those requirements were met in *O'Reilly v Mackman*: in this case neither. The claim for damages *could not be pursued under Order 53*, as under that the right to damages is linked to an application for judicial review – unless judicial review lies, damages cannot be given.[7] And if the claim could be brought under Order 53, it could not be said that it *should* be. Unlike in *O'Reilly v Mackman* it could not be shown here that the plaintiff was improperly seeking to evade the protection which the Order confers on public authorities.[8]

Wandsworth London Borough Council v Winder[9] dealt with a different situation as here the public authority was the plaintiff, not the defendant.

4 This includes deciding on the suitability of accommodation, a challenge to which must be by way of judicial review, not an action in tort *Ali v Hamlets LBC* [1992] 3 All ER 512 CA.

5 See *Ettridge v Morrell* 85 LGR 100. Declaration sought of entitlement to use premises for election meeting. Held: no public law decision to be taken, there being a duty to make premises available on application being made cf *Cocks*: duty to decide whether C entitled to housing.

6 [1984] AC 262, [1983] 3 All ER 278.

7 See p 357 above.

8 Cf *G v Hounslow LBC* 86 LGR 186: tort action raised ultra vires question; *O'Reilly v Mackman* rule not deflected by private law rights intermingling with public law.

9 [1985] AC 461, [1984] 3 All ER 83. See Forsyth [1985] PL 355.

The defendant W was a tenant of one of the authority's flats. He had a contractual right to occupy the flat provided he paid the rent etc. This was an ordinary private contractual right. Acting under its statutory powers the authority increased the rent. W refused to pay the full increase. The authority took proceedings in the county court for arrears of rent and possessions of the premises. W defended the action on the grounds that the increases were ultra vires, and *counter-claimed for a declaration* that the increases were of no legal effect. The authority argued that the only procedure by which their decision could be challenged was by Order 53. Lord Fraser, with whom three other members of the House agreed, pointed to two differences between this case and *O'Reilly*. In that case the plaintiff had not suffered any infringement of private law rights whereas here the tenant complained of this; and in that case the action had been initiated by those affected by the exercise of public power, unlike here. Did Lord Diplock's general rule apply?

First the principle behind *O'Reilly* and *Cocks* was the need for 'speedy certainty' in the interests of good administration and of third parties who might be affected. In this case other tenants and the ratepayers might also be affected, and the Order 53 procedure might well be suitable. But there were other ways of getting speedy decisions, and in any case the arguments for protecting public authorities had to be set against the arguments for preserving the right of a citizen to defend himself against unmeritorious claims. Second, it was a very strange use of language to describe W's behaviour as an abuse or misuse of the court's process: he had not selected the procedure but was merely exercising his right to deny that he owed what it was said he owed. Third, a central aspect of the judicial review procedure was that success there required an exercise of the court's discretion in the applicant's favour, whereas the defence was put forward here as a matter of right. Thus it was impossible to accept that the right to challenge the authority's decision in the course of defending an action could have been swept away by Order 53. Fourth, section 31 of the Supreme Court Act referred to an 'application': this could not have the effect of limiting a defendant's rights sub silentio.[10]

In *Doyle v Northumbria Probation Committee*[11] probation officers issued a writ for breach of contract (in the withdrawal of allowances). The Committee, a statutory body, claimed that the payment of the allowances was ultra vires itself; (it was *this* that raised the public law issue). The court said this was a genuine private law claim which did not depend on the plaintiff's asserting any public law infringement of their rights. The action was not an abuse of the court's process.

The impact of *O'Reilly v Mackman* could arise in other circumstances. Where a person is prosecuted for contravening a byelaw, other subordinate legislation or a statutory order of some kind, and argues in defence that

10 For criticism of the decision see Woolf [1986] PL 220; for reply, and generally, see Beatson (1987) 103 LQR 34: For matters not to be questioned except by an application for judicial review (thus not by way of defence) see Local Government Finance Act 1988, ss 138, 142.
11 [1991] 4 All ER 294.

the byelaw etc is for some reason invalid, it has long been the practice for the Magistrates' Court before whom he is prosecuted (or, on appeal, the Crown Court) to rule on the validity of the byelaw etc. Was it a consequence of *O'Reilly v Mackman* that the defendant would in future have to challenge the validity of the byelaw etc by way of judicial review? Was it contrary to public policy for a defendant to challenge its validity except by that procedure? In *R v Crown Court at Reading, ex p Hutchinson*[12] the High Court was clear that it was not. 'Neither section 31 of the 1981 Act nor RSC Order 53 has taken away the right of the defendant in criminal proceedings to challenge the validity of a byelaw under which he is charged.'[13]

The impact of *O'Reilly* has recently been considered, yet again by the House of Lords, in *Roy v Kensington and Chelsea and Westminster Family Practitioner Committee*.[14] It concerned the relationship between a general medical practitioner and his FPC (now FHSA), the relationship being governed by statute and ministerial regulations. A doctor is eligible for the 'full rate' of allowance if the FPC is of opinion that he is devoting a substantial amount of time to his practice. The FPC thought R was not, and withheld some remuneration. R sued for money owed. The FPC applied to strike out R's claim as an abuse of the process of the court: he should have applied for judicial review, they said. There *was* a public law element in that the FPC had to exercise a public law function when forming an opinion on the matter in issue, as required by the regulations, so it could be said that, even if R had a private right to the remuneration he first had to challenge the exercise of a public law function (as in *Cocks*). A further strand in the case was whether the relationship between R and FPC was contractual, for if it was he could of course proceed by ordinary action. The House of Lords ruled that R's action could proceed for these reasons: (i) it did not matter whether or not the relationship was contractual; R had a private law right to his remuneration arising either from the statutory scheme or from a contract; (ii) although he was seeking to enforce a public law duty (as mentioned) his private law right dominated; (iii) the order he sought could not be granted on judicial review (he was not seeking damages); (iv) where an individual right is claimed, as here, questions of leave and the short time-limit should not intrude, nor should the relief be discretionary (cf Order 53); (v) the action should be allowed to proceed unless it was plainly an abuse of process, which it was not, and more generally, (vi) unless the procedure followed was ill-suited to dispose of the question in issue, it was better to hear a case than have a debate about the form of the proceedings. All these, and other, grounds, favoured R's action proceeding.

To recapitulate: Lord Diplock in *O'Reilly* suggested the general rule that it was an abuse of the process of the court for a person seeking to establish that a decision of a public authority infringed rights to which he

---

12 [1988] QB 384, [1988] 1 All ER 333.
13 But see *Bugg v DPP* [1993] 2 All ER 815 for ground of challenge.
14 [1992] 1 AC 624, [1992] 1 All ER 705.

was entitled to protection under public law action to proceed by way of an action: you must use Order 53. There might, he said, be exceptions, and the above cases show that where there is an infringement of an individual right which gives rise to a cause of action in private law there is no requirement to use Order 53 – even though public law issues are raised which require decision.[15] (In *O'Reilly* itself, as explained, there was no cause of action in private law.)

In its 1994 Report the Law Commission noted the public interest factors underlying the use of Order 53 in purely public law cases: the need to ensure that public authorities observe the law, that individuals are able to get a remedy for substantiated grievances; the need for speed and certainty in administrative decision-making, particularly where a large section of the community will be affected: this justifies a short time limit. On the other hand the Law Commission acknowledged that where a case involves a properly constituted private law cause of action (or when it is necessary to decide whether a person should be prevented from raising a defence to such an action on the ground that it raises an issue of public law) 'a more flexible procedural approach is needed to ensure that private law rights are not 'trumped' by public law justifications'.

The Commission's conclusion is that:

We accordingly believe that the present position whereby a litigant is required to proceed by way of Order 53 only when–
(a) the challenge is on public law and no other grounds ie where the challenge is solely to the validity or legality of a public authority's acts or omissions and
(b) the litigant does not seek either to enforce or defend a completely constituted private law right
is satisfactory.[16]

O'Reilly v Mackman : the 'obverse'

In certain circumstances therefore a litigant is required to use Order 53. Now there is what is said to be the 'obverse' to the rule in *O'Reilly*: not that in some cases you *must* use Order 53, but that in some cases you *cannot* use Order 53. It will be recalled (p 388 above) that where the basis of jurisdiction, the exercise of which is challenged, is agreement, the rights in question are enforceable in private law only. The cases referred to above relating to sporting and religious bodies, and others, illustrate this. Employment by a public body in particular is likely to raise the question of public versus private law, as in the following. In *R v Post Office, ex p Byrne*[17] a Post Office manager took disciplinary action against a subordinate, the applicant B, who applied for certiorari to quash the decision

15 See *Mercury Communications Ltd v DG Telecommunications* (1995) Times, 10 February, HL; *Vince v Chief Constable of Dorset Police* [1992] 3 All ER 98: questions of public law affected private rights.
16 Law Com No 225, para 3.15. See *Fredman v Morris* 'The Costs of Exclusivity' [1994] PL 69; Alder, 'Hunting the Chimera: the end of *O'Reilly v Mackman*' (1993) 13 LS 183.
17 [1975] 1 CR 221.

on the ground that the procedure used broke Post Office disciplinary rules. The Post Office is a statutory body and B argued that its disciplinary procedure derived from a statutory obligation imposed on the Post Office to enter into negotiations with representatives of employees, and that therefore a manager exercising those powers came within the category of persons to whom certiorari lies. The argument was rejected. The legal authority exercised by the manager derived exclusively from the contract of employment B had with the Post Office; this was a private law rather than a public law relationship. The Post Office was dealing with him as an employee, not as a 'subject'.[18]

In *R v East Berkshire Health Authority, ex p Walsh*,[19] W was employed by the Authority. Ministerial regulations provided that 'where conditions of service ... of any class of officers have been the subject of negotiations by a negotiating body and have been approved by the Secretary of State ... the conditions of service of any officer belonging to the class shall include the conditions so approved'. W belonged to a class whose conditions had been so approved, and his conditions of service therefore included the conditions in question. His employment was terminated by a senior employee. He sought judicial review of his dismissal on the ground that there had been breaches of natural justice in the procedure. Had he chosen the correct procedure? Hodgson J, accepting that there is no public law element in the 'ordinary' master-servant relationship, thought that where the servant 'holds office in a great public service', the public was properly concerned that he should be treated lawfully and fairly by his employer, and this justified judicial review. The Court of Appeal disagreed. Mere employment by a public authority does not inject any element of public law, nor the fact that the employee is an 'officer' or is in a 'higher grade'. Was there anything here that took W's status out of 'mere employment'? No. The effect of the ministerial regulations was that the authority's contracts with certain employees, including W's, were required to be on certain terms. This did not take the relationship out of the ordinary master-servant relationship. Hodgson J had relied on *Vine v National Dock Labour Board*,[20] *Ridge v Baldwin*[1] and *Malloch v Aberdeen Corpn*[2] in coming to his conclusion, but in those cases statute directly restricted the authority's freedom to dismiss, and in such a case the employee could acquire public law rights in respect of the dismissal. W's complaint had merely been that he had been dismissed without being heard. If his complaint had been of the legality of the delegation by the Authority of its powers of dismissal; or if his conditions of service had differed from those approved by the Secretary of State, judicial review proceedings might have been appropriate. (The rules of natural justice can be imported into a private contractual relationship, but their import will not of itself bring with it a

18 See *R v BBC ex p Lavelle* [1983] 1 All ER 241, [1983] 1 WLR 23. No certiorari to quash disciplinary proceedings; for status of BBC see p 37 above.
19 [1985] QB 152, [1984] 3 All ER 425.
20 See p207 above.
 1 See p 283 above.
 2 See p 312 below.

public law element into the relationship. Whether the employer is in breach of the rules of natural justice is one thing; whether the employee is entitled to a public law remedy is another.)

In *R v South Glamorgan Health Authority, ex p Phillips*[3] P was a State Registered Nurse. She sought judicial review of a finding of professional misconduct made against her by a disciplinary tribunal of the Authority. An attempt was made to distinguish *Walsh* by arguing that the disciplining of P necessarily involved consideration of the extent of her (and of any other SRN's) obligation to her profession (in which the public would have an interest); and that the Authority was not only the private employer of P but exercised its functions in the health service in relation to the public at large. This attempt to inject a public law element was unsurprisingly unsuccessful.

R v Trent Regional Health Authority, ex p Jones[4] concerned yet another aspect of employment in the NHS. The Authority advertised a post of consultant grade. J applied. The authority re-advertised. This implied a decision not to appoint J, who applied for the decision to re-advertise to be quashed. Was the decision subject to judicial review? Regulations have been made by way of statutory instrument detailing the procedure for the appointment of consultants, involving the consideration of applications by an Advisory Committee whose constitution is prescribed by the regulations. The Authority is not to appoint except from persons whose names are submitted to it by the Committee. The court stated that once the Authority had those names before it, no statutory provision bore on *the process of appointment by it*. Its decision in the matter complained of was not therefore subject to judicial review.

In *R v Derbyshire County Council, ex p Noble*[5] a doctor, N, employed by a police authority, D, sought judicial review of his dismissal (on notice as his contract provided). What possible public law element was there in that? D had a statutory duty to provide a police force for its area, and a statutory power to employ civilians for police purposes – here, N. This was not enough: there had to be some statutory involvement in the matter complained of, that is the termination of the contract. Here there was none. (Any remedy N had, if any, would be by way for breach of contract or by application to an industrial tribunal.)

Is the relationship between a civil servant and his employer (the Crown) contractual, with the result that the employer's decisions on matters affecting that relationship are not subject to judicial review? In *R v Civil Service Appeal Board, ex p Bruce*[6] B was dismissed and appealed to the Board, which dismissed his appeal. He sought judicial review of the Board's decisions (for failure to give reasons). May LJ concluded that it had not been shown that there was a contract of service between B and the Crown. That being so, there was a sufficient public law element to entitle B to

3   (1986) Times, 21 November.
4   (1986) Times, 19 June.
5   [1990] ICR 808, CA.
6   [1988] 3 All ER 686, aff'd [1989] 2 All ER 907.

apply for judicial review. (However, the court declined to grant a remedy as B could take the matter to an Industrial Tribunal and had indeed commenced proceedings there.)

Soon after the *Bruce* case came *R v Lord Chancellor's Dept, ex p Nangle*.[7] Allegations against N of sexual harassment had been upheld. His appeal to the department's permanent secretary was dismissed. He sought judicial review of both decisions (alleging procedural errors). The court was quite clear, not following *Bruce*, that all the incidents of a contract of employment *were* present in a civil servant's relationship with the Crown, which was thus governed by private law, and any possible remedy was to be sought in an action for breach of contract. Notice, however, a difference between *Bruce* and *Nangle*. In the former, the challenge was to a decision of the Board, which was seen to be an independent body, a tribunal, set up (under the prerogative) to exercise a judicial function; in the latter the challenge was to the outcome of the internal disciplinary procedure of the department which arose out of the employee's contract with his employer.

In *McLaren v Home Office*[8] M was a prison officer, and thus a civil servant, though appointed under statutory powers, not the prerogative. He sought by way of an ordinary action (not judicial review) a declaration as to the terms of his employment (specifically whether the terms of a collective bargain between his trade union and the Home Office had become terms of his contract of employment), and claimed moneys due. The Court of Appeal had no doubt that this was a question of private law.

We have previously noted that in deciding whether it is appropriate to proceed by judicial review or by action, the precise nature of the matter in dispute must be considered. It is not the case that even if the relationship is contractual the dispute may not raise a public law issue. Thus in *R v Secretary of State for the Home Dept, ex p Attard*[9] the question was whether the statutory Code of Discipline for prison officers could be supplemented by the Home Office invoking a power of suspension available for civil servants generally. This was clearly a public law issue concerning the extent of Home Office and prison governors' powers. Likewise in *Bruce* (above) judicial review as noted, was appropriate as the power of an independent tribunal was in issue. In the earlier case of *R v Secretary of State for the Home Dept, ex p Benwell*[10] the applicant, a prison officer, was dismissed for breach of the statutory Code of Discipline. Hodgson J said that in dismissing Benwell the Home Office was 'performing duties imposed upon it' by statute and was therefore subject to judicial review. The court was influenced by the consideration that Benwell not being an employee, had no recourse to the industrial tribunals, so that if the court could not exercise its power of review he would have nowhere else to go. The courts have since said that it is not the case that if one does not have a private law remedy one necessarily has a public law remedy.

---

7 [1992] 1 All ER 897.
8 [1990] ICR 824, CA.
9 [1990] COD 261.
10 [1984] 3 All ER 854, [1985] QB 554.

Certiorari

Before considering in detail the remedies available in judicial review it is necessary to say that for judicial review to be available, and assuming the necessary public element, there must be something that is reviewable. That 'something' will be different according to the remedy sought. Thus if certiorari is sought (to quash) there must be something that is quashable: if a declaration as to legal rights is sought, legal rights must be in issue, and the 'something' here may be by no means something that is quashable.

These remedies are discretionary, and whether one or (as may be the case) more than one is sought the court may grant whichever is appropriate, or none, as the following pages show. They also show that there may be nothing to which any of the remedies is applicable, so that the question of the exercise of discretion does not arise.

What it is and does

Historically certiorari was a royal demand for information.[11] The theory was that the sovereign is appealed to by one of his subjects who complains of an injustice done to him, whereupon the sovereign, saying that he wishes to be certified (certiorari) of the matter, orders the records of the matter to be transmitted to him, so that if necessary the proceedings could be transferred to his court. In the seventeenth century there developed from this the certiorari to quash. The Crown's interest in the prerogative orders is indicated by the way the cases are referred to. It shows that the proceedings are brought in the name of the Crown against the body whose activity the Crown wishes to inquire into followed by the name of the person who is activating the Crown to take the proceedings. (These proceedings may be brought by a government department.) The word 'certiorari' does not appear on the order itself, the effective wording of which is that 'the said [order/decision etc] be quashed'.[12]

In considering the availability of certiorari, these questions will be seen to arise: what kinds of decision by what kinds of body are liable to be quashed; what interest must the applicant for the order have in the matter complained of; and what is the effect of the order?

It is convenient to take the last question first. The effect of the quashing of a decision is illustrated by the following. *R v Immigration Appeal Tribunal, ex p Mehemet*[13] was a deportation case. The deportation procedure is in two stages: there is the *decision* to make an order, followed by the *making* of the order. A deportation *order* made against M was quashed by the High Court. M contended that the quashing of the order meant

---

11 See de Smith 'The Prerogative Writs' (1951) 11 CLJ 40; E G Henderson *Foundations of English Administrative Law*.

12 The Law Commission proposes that 'a quashing order' be substituted for certiorari (a mandatory order for mandamus, and a prohibiting order for prohibition). Law Com No 226, para 8.3.

13 [1978] Imm AR 46,

that the *decision to make* the order fell with it. The argument was rejected, 'One can well imagine the case in which, after a perfectly lawful decision to make an order, some small technical defect appeared in the reasoning and procedure following the making of the decision. It would be absurd if such a technical defect in the making of the order itself brought down the decision to make the order'.[14] However, after the deportation order had been made against M a decision was taken to deport his wife and child as being members of a family of a person (M) who 'is or has been ordered to be deported'. When the deportation order against M was quashed, it could be no longer said that M was a person who 'is or has been ordered to be deported'. The mere survival of the *decision* to make a deportation order against M was not enough to satisfy that requirement.

It is to be noted that, on quashing a decision, the court does not substitute its own decision, nor does it direct the body as to the decision it is to come to on reconsidering the matter. Suppose X is refused a grant, and the court quashes the refusal. This does not mean that X gets the grant, but at the most that the application has to be re-considered. Of course the decision will be reached in the light of the court's ruling so that if a decision is quashed for a procedural error, the correct procedure as indicated by the court, must be followed when the matter is considered afresh. The decision to refuse a grant might be quite properly arrived at again. The amended Order 53, and now section 31 (5) of the Supreme Court Act 1981, makes provision for a decision to be remitted.

If, on an application for judicial review seeking an order of certiorari, the High Court quashes the decision to which the application relates, the High Court may remit the matter to the court, tribunal or authority concerned, with a direction to reconsider it and reach a decision in accordance with the findings of the High Court.

(Certiorari may in any event be combined with mandamus, for example where a decision is quashed for bias, mandamus may go to require a new hearing before a differently constituted body.)

What acts and decisions are subject to certiorari

To be subject to certiorari an act, decision etc must have the necessary public law element. This has been considered.

Given that the decision has the necessary public law quality, is there any limitation within that category? Earlier this century some confusion was introduced into this area. In *R v Electricity Comrs, ex p London Electricity Joint Committee Co (1920) Ltd*[15] the Commissioners had statutory power to make schemes for setting up joint electricity authorities. The applicants argued that a proposed scheme was ultra vires the Commissioners and sought certiorari and prohibition. The Commissioners

14 Ibid at 48.
15 [1924] 1 KB 171, CA.

argued that the orders (then called writs) were not available against them for a number of reasons, one of which was that the decision in question was not of the kind subject to the writs.

Bankes LJ said:

Originally no doubt the writ [of prohibition] was issued only to inferior courts using that expression in the ordinary meaning of the word 'court'. As statutory bodies were brought into existence exercising legal jurisdiction, so the issue of the writ came to be extended to such bodies. There are numerous instances of this in the books, commencing in quite early times.[16]

Atkin LJ said:

Doubtless in their origin [both writs] dealt almost exclusively with the jurisdiction of what is described in ordinary parlance as a court of justice. But the operation of the writs has extended to control the proceedings of bodies which do not claim to be, and would not be recognised as, courts of justice. *Wherever any body of persons having legal authority to determine questions affecting the rights of subjects, and having the duty to act judicially, act in excess of their legal authority they are subject to the controlling jurisdiction of the King's Bench Division exercised in these writs.*[17]

On the facts the Commissioners had to decide whether to constitute a joint authority, and with what powers they would invest it. That question necessarily involved the withdrawal from existing bodies of some of their rights, and imposed on them new duties, including subjection to the control of the new body. The Commissioners were therefore 'determining questions affecting the rights of subjects', and as they were proposing to act ultra vires, prohibition issued.

We must now consider the last sentence of Atkin LJ's dictum, quoted above (hereafter 'the Atkin dictum') which, it will be noted, applies to both certiorari and prohibition. Notice the 'and' in the Atkin dictum. Does it mean that for the writs to go two requirements must be met: the body must have legal authority to determine questions affecting the rights of subjects, *and*, as an additional requirement, must have the duty to act judicially: In *R v Legislative Committee of the Church Assembly, ex p Haynes-Smith*[18] certiorari and prohibition were applied for in respect of action taken by the Committee and the Assembly towards altering the Prayer Book by the Prayer Book Measure 1927. Were those bodies acting in the matter amenable to those writs? Lord Hewart CJ, referring to the Atkin dictum, said that it was not enough that the body had legal authority etc: there must be superadded to that characteristic the further characteristic that the body has 'the duty to act judicially'. Whether or not the bodies in question had the first characteristic, he was certain they did not have the second.

---

16 Ibid at 193.
17 Ibid at 204 He instanced the Board of Education, the Light Railway Commissioners, the Comptroller General of Patents etc. Emphasis added.
18 [1928] 1 KB 411, DC.

This need to find that the body had a duty to act judicially meant that if the court found a decision to be so defective that it had to be quashed, it had to find that it was engaged in a judicial function even if it was not obvious that that was the case. Thus in *R v Postmaster General, ex p Carmichael*[19] (decided just before the *Legislative Committee* case) a Post Office employee was entitled to compensation if he obtained a certificate from a doctor appointed for that purpose that he was suffering from telegraphists' cramp. A doctor certified that the applicant was not so suffering. The certificate was described by Lord Hewart CJ as 'so much waste paper' as the doctor in question had not been appointed to act. It had to be quashed. But could one say that a doctor issuing a medical certificate acts judicially? The Lord Chief Justice said that looking at the part a certificate of this nature played in the making of any claim for compensation, it was 'of the nature of a judicial act', and amenable to certiorari. Thus he found that that quality was not in the procedures followed but in the importance of the document to the applicant's claim. In *R v Boycott, ex p Keasley*[20] also a medical certificate, that a boy was ineducable, was quashed by certiorari. Lord Hewart said that the certificate purported to be and to look like a decision of a quasi-judicial authority so as to come within the range of certiorari. He had to engage in these contortions in order to quash what had to be quashed as it was done without authority.

In *R v Manchester Legal Aid Committee, ex p R A Brand & Co Ltd*,[1] X started an action against Brand and became bankrupt, whereon X's trustee in bankruptcy, intending to continue the action, sought legal aid. The legal aid committee in deciding whether he was, from a financial point of view, entitled to aid, took into account the financial circumstances of the bankrupt only, and not of his trustee, and granted a legal aid certificate. Brand sought certiorari to quash the granting of the certificate, alleging that the committee should have taken the trustee's circumstances into account, in which case a certificate should not have been granted. Is a decision of a legal aid committee subject to certiorari? Why not, one might say, given that it is a statutory scheme? However, the committee contended that its proceedings were not subject to certiorari as, referring to the Atkin dictum, it had no duty to act judicially. Such a duty arose, the committee said, only where there is a duty to hear both sides to a conflict and here there was no question of 'both sides' but only of the application by one party to the committee, and the latter's duty to apply the relevant rules to the application. The court said that that interpretation of words 'duty to act judicially', was in conflict with a long line of cases (including the last two cases referred to here). Certiorari issued.

Later in *Ridge v Baldwin*[2] Lord Reid showed that the view expressed by Lord Hewart, (that the duty to act judicially was an additional requirement) was irreconcilable with earlier authorities, and that one

19 [1928] 1 KB 291.
20 [1939] 2 KB 651, [1939] 2 All ER 626.
 1 [1952] 2 QB 413, [1952] 1 All ER 480.
 2 [1964] AC 40, [1963] 2 All ER 66.

may infer the judicial element required for certiorari to go, from the nature of the power. The need for the 'superadded characteristic' had resulted, for a time, in a limitation being placed on the availability of certiorari, but Lord Reid's judgment removed it.[3] Indeed Salter J in his judgment in *R v Legislative Committee of the Church Assembly* had taken a different view from Lord Hewart: the power to determine and decide, which made a body amenable to certiorari, carried with it of necessity, he said, the duty to act judicially.

The following cases illustrate the immediate post-*Ridge v Baldwin* approach. In *R v Paddington Valuation Officer, ex p Peachey Property Corpn Ltd*[4] the court, referring to the Atkin dictum, spoke of a valuation officer as a public officer entrusted with a public duty. He had legal power to determine questions affecting the rights of subjects, namely, to assess the value of hereditaments. 'This power *carries with it* the duty to act judicially ... the [valuation] list is liable to be quashed on certiorari.'

In *R v Barnsley Metropolitan Borough Council, ex p Hook*[5] Scarman LJ observed that in exercising a statutory power to licence market trading the council was a body having legal authority to determine questions affecting rights of subjects; and that it followed that it was under a duty to act judicially.

We have now, however, moved on to the more satisfactory position that it is not necessary, in order to show that a decision is liable to be quashed by certiorari, to make *any* reference to a duty to act judicially. In *O'Reilly v Mackman*[6] Lord Diplock said that it is enough to show that the body or person in question has 'legal authority to determine questions affecting the common law or statutory rights or obligations of other persons as individuals',[7] and in *Leech v Parkhurst Prison Deputy Governor*[8] Lord Oliver said that the susceptibility of a decision to the supervisory jurisdiction of the court 'does not rest on some fancied distinction between decisions which are administrative and decisions which are judicial or quasi-judicial'.

'Having legal authority ...'

Another aspect of the phrase in the Atkin (and Diplock) dictum, 'having *legal* authority to determine questions affecting the *rights* of others', has

---

3   Note that the Atkin dictum refers to the circumstances in which certiorari (and prohibition) is available. In *Ridge v Baldwin* what was directly in issue was not whether certiorari was available, as the plaintiff was seeking a declaration, but whether natural justice should have been observed. Lord Reid was seeking to undermine the authority of a few cases in which it was held that the acts in question were not 'judicial', and that the rules of natural justice did not apply. To do this he showed that Lord Hewart's dictum, which was about the availability of certiorari and had influenced those cases, was itself not to be relied on. See *R v Hillingdon LBC, ex p Royco Homes Ltd* [1974] QB 720, [1974] 2 All ER 643.
4   [1966] 1 QB 380, [1965] 2 All ER 836.
5   [1976] 3 All ER 452, [1976] 1 WLR 1052 CA.
6   [1983] 2 AC 237, [1982] 3 All ER 1124.
7   Ibid at 279 and 1129.
8   [1988] 1 All ER 485 at 505.

to be considered. The scheme administered by the Criminal Injuries Compensation Board was, as we have seen, not set up by statute but under the prerogative. In *R v Criminal Injuries Compensation Board, ex p Lain*,[9] Lain applied for a certiorari to quash a decision of the Board for error of law. The Board did not deny that it had a duty to act judicially – that is, that it fell within the second leg of the Atkin dictum – but argued that it had no 'legal authority' in the sense of having *statutory* authority. The court held the Board was no less 'lawful' for having been set up under the prerogative than under statute; and though not set up by Act, Parliament had provided money to satisfy the Board's awards. But did the Board have authority 'to determine questions affecting the *rights* of others'? The Board said not, in that a determination of the Board gave rise to no enforceable rights, but only gave the applicant an opportunity to receive the bounty of the Crown. As to that, the court said that the Atkin dictum did not expressly refer to enforceable rights (in the very case in which it was uttered the scheme in question created no immediately enforceable rights); certiorari is available even though the decision is *merely a step* towards the creation of legally enforceable rights, and the fact that payment was ex gratia (that is, that a determination by the Board that a particular sum be offered to an applicant gave him no right to sue for that sum) did not mean that the determination was without legal effect, as it would render lawful and irrevocable a payment to a subject which would otherwise be unlawful and recoverable. There was in fact no error of law found in the Board's decision, but since then few of the Board's decisions have been struck down for error of law.

R v Boycott, ex p Keasley[10] also shows that a 'mere step' may be subject to certiorari. The medical certificate which was successfully impugned did not itself enable the local authority to send the boy to an institution; it was but 'an early stage in a chain of circumstances' which could result in that happening. But statute provided for it, it was the crucial foundation for what followed, and it was of the highest importance for the boy the court said.

In *R v Hull Prison Board of Visitors, ex p St Germain (No 2)*[11] the Board argued that its decisions did not 'affect the rights' of prisoners, as the prison rules merely refer to the power to grant remission for good behaviour. This was rejected: the Board's decisions were realistically to be seen as punishments.

A case where there was 'legal authority' but not 'to determine questions affecting legal rights' was *R v Legislative Committee of the Church Assembly, ex p Haynes-Smith*.[12] The court explained that the powers conferred by Parliament on the Assembly, were powers to initiate legislation. Measures prepared by the Assembly if eventually approved by Parliament would, as statutes, affect the rights of subjects. But the Assembly itself had no power to determine questions affecting the rights

9 [1967] 2 QB 864, [1967] 2 All ER 770. See p 343 above.
10 [1939] 2 KB 651, [1939] 2 All ER 626. See p 375 above.
11 [1979] 3 All ER 545, [1979] 1 WLR 1401.
12 [1920] 1 KB 411.

of subjects. What if the decision sought to be challenged consists merely of advice or recommendation? In *R v Electricity Comrs*[13] the Commissioners argued that they were merely *advisers*, and came to no decision at all. This was rejected. The fact that their order was not to be operative until confirmed by both Houses did not mean that they did not have to keep within the limits of their statutory jurisdiction. And in *R v Boundary Commission for England, ex p Foot*,[14] the court, while acknowledging that the Commission's role was limited to making *recommendations* had no doubt that it was quite proper for it to consider whether the Commission had misconstrued its statutory remit.

Where a person is served with a deportation order in circumstances in which he has no appeal to the immigration tribunals, he may make representations to a non-statutory panel appointed by the Home Secretary to *advise* him. The panel is susceptible of judicial review.[15]

In *R v Norfolk County Council, ex p M*[16] it was argued that what had been done had had *no effect on the applicant* and could not therefore be reviewed. Following complaints by a girl against M of indecent assault, the council's case conference decided that M had sexually abused the girl, and that his name be put on their child abuse register. This was done. M was told – as was his employer, who suspended him. M's application for judicial review was resisted on the ground that the decision and registration were merely an internal part of the council's administrative procedure; that no consequence flows from the mere fact of entry on the register until access is sought to it by those entitled to such access. The court agreed that access is limited, but it includes certain potential employers; the register's security could not be guaranteed; and M had suffered considerable distress. The register was a blacklist and had dangerous potential: it could not be immune from judicial control (on the merits the council had acted unfairly and unreasonably). Certiorari issued to quash the decision and the register entry.

Orders and regulations subject to parliamentary procedure

There is no doubt that 'subordinate legislation is subject to some degree of judicial control in the sense that it is within the province and authority of the courts to hold that particular examples are not authorised by statute, or as the case may be by the common law, and so are without legal force and effect'.[17] Where, however, there is some Parliamentary involvement in the legislation, consideration of the relationship between the judiciary

13 [1924] 1 KB 171. See p373 above.
14 [1983] QB 600, [1983] 1 All ER 1099.
15 *R v Secretary of State for the Home Dept, ex p Cheblak* [1991] 2 All ER 319, [1991] WLR 890, CA.
16 [1989] QB 619, [1989] 2 All ER 619, in *R v Harrow London Borough Council, ex p D* [1990] 3 All ER 319, CA.
17 *R v Her majesty's Treasury, ex p Smedley* [1985] QB 657, [1985] 1 All ER 589, at 666 and 593.

and the legislature may affect the willingness or ability of the court to intervene. The precise extent of parliamentary involvement has to be considered in each case.[18] In *R v Hastings Local Board of Health*[19] the Secretary of State could by provisional order[20] empower the Board to purchase land compulsorily. The order was of no validity unless confirmed by Act of Parliament. Certiorari was sought to quash an order on the grounds of both procedural and substantive defects, but was refused. The court expressed a reluctance to step between the order and the confirmatory Bill, noting that if the order was made without jurisdiction Parliament could throw out the Bill (so that to that extent there was a remedy). Further the provisional order procedure was provided in order to remove the need, in many cases, for a private bill: Parliament had put the Secretary of State in the position a Select Committee would have been in relation to such a bill.[1]

The decision was relied on, but unsuccessfully, in *R v Electricity Comrs, ex p London Electricity Joint Committee Co (1920) Ltd*,[2] where the vires of a statutory scheme proposed by the respondents was challenged. It was argued that as the Commissioners' function was to make an order which required the approval of the Minister of Transport, who in turn submitted it for the approval of both Houses, the court would be interfering with the parliamentary process. The argument was rejected. Parliament, it was said, had by an Act laid down the limits of the Commissioners' jurisdiction: why should it object to a court keeping them within it? Atkin LJ observed that in *Hastings* the provisional order was of no validity unless confirmed by Act of Parliament, so that there was there no order in respect of which certiorari could issue; and that the issue of prohibition in the *Electricity Commissioners* case would not in any way affect the power of the legislature to carry out the scheme by Act of Parliament.

One technique in connection with the making of administrative orders or subordinate legislation is that a *draft* of a proposed order etc is to be submitted for parliamentary approval. Can the legality of a draft be challenged? In *R v Her Majesty's Treasury, ex p Smedley*,[3] member states of the EEC had given undertakings that the expenditure contemplated by the EEC budget would be met out of funds provided by them. To implement its undertaking the Treasury laid before both Houses of Parliament a *draft* Order in Council made under the European Communities Act 1972. If the draft were to be approved by both Houses, the Order would then be made. (The order would specify the undertaking as a community treaty and its effect would be that the British Government would pay £120 m to the EEC budget.) At the point in time with which we

18 See ch 3 above.
19 (1865) 6 B&S 401.
20 See p 58 above.
 1 In *R v Ecclesiastical Committee of the House of Commons, ex p The Church Society* (1993) Times, 4 November: the Committee is statutory.
 2 [1924] 1 KB 171; p 373 above.
 3 [1985] QB 657, [1985] 1 All ER 589.

are concerned, there was as yet therefore no order in existence. Smedley applied for a certiorari to quash the Treasury's determination that the undertaking was a treaty, or a declaration that the determination was ultra vires. The Treasury argued, inter alia, that to grant relief at that stage would be an improper interference in Parliamentary proceedings. The Court of Appeal said not. What was Parliament's function in respect of the draft Order? Essentially one of veto. An expression by the court of the legality of the determination could not interfere with that. It might even (as in the *Electricity Comrs* case) be of assistance to Parliament to give a ruling at that stage.

In none of these cases mentioned above had the stage been reached where Parliament had actually *approved* the order. It is clear that even where Parliament has positively approved an order the order retains its subordinate quality and is subject to judicial review. Now there are, as we have seen, different grounds on which review may be sought. The significance of this is brought out in this context in *Nottinghamshire County Council v Secretary of State for the Environment*.[4] The relevance of the case here is that the House of Lords accepted the possibility of declaring to be illegal, *guidance* issued by a minister and approved by the House of Commons, but said that the circumstances would have to be extreme that would lead a court to intervene on the grounds of unreasonableness; and that as the approval of the Commons had been obtained 'it would be necessary to find as a fact that the House of Commons had been misled ...'. Compare *R v Secretary of State for Health, ex p Cormack*[5] where regulations (not guidance) subject to annulment (not requiring approval) were challenged on grounds of irrationality in proceedings for a declaration (not certiorari). Leave to apply for judicial review was refused.

The vulnerability of regulations is illustrated by *R v Secretary of State for Health, ex p US Tobacco International Inc*[6] where regulations subject to annulment were quashed for procedural defects by the department.

Locus standi

In a preceding section we examined the new formula for standing: that the applicant must have a 'sufficient interest in the matter to which the application [for judicial review] relates'. While the courts do not regard themselves as confined by any earlier formulation of the standing required, (for example 'person aggrieved') it is necessary to consider earlier decisions if only to illustrate the problem. In one of the leading cases, *R v Surrey Justices*[7] an inhabitant of a parish obtained certiorari to quash orders of the justices certifying that certain roads in the parish were no longer

4 [1986] AC 240, [1986] 1 All ER 199. See p 255 above.
5 (1990) 6 BMLR 81.
6 [1992] 1 All ER 212, [1992] QB 353.
7 (1870) LR 5 QB 466.

liable to be repaired at its expense. Blackburn J distinguished between a 'party aggrieved' (that is one who could show that he had suffered some private wrong); and one who came forward as one of the general public having no particular interest in the matter – a 'stranger'. In the first case the person was entitled to the writ *ex debito justitiae* (he was owed it by justice) so that it would issue on his application unless there were special factors, such as his own conduct, which in its discretion the court thought disentitled him to it. In the second case it was entirely within the court's discretion whether to grant relief. This distinction was relied on in, *R v Thames Magistrates' Court, ex p Greenbaum*[8] where Denning LJ said:

When application is made to [the court] by a party or person aggrieved, it will intervene (it is said) *ex debito justitiae*, in justice to the applicant. When application is made by a stranger it considers whether the public interest demands its intervention. In either case it is a matter which rests ultimately in the discretion of the court.

But what made a person 'aggrieved'? How was a 'stranger' to be recognised? The facts of that case were that the applicant, Greenbaum (G) and another, H, had applied to a local authority for a licence to trade at a certain site in a street. G was granted the licence. H appealed to the magistrates' court; the other party to the appeal was the local authority. The magistrate said that H should have the site. G applied for a certiorari to quash that decision on the ground that the magistrate had no jurisdiction in the matter. But had he standing? He had not, after all, been a party to the proceeding he was seeking to quash. The Court of Appeal was clear that G had standing. Parker LJ said G was a person 'with a particular grievance of his own'. Denning LJ said that he was 'certainly a person aggrieved; and not a stranger. He was affected by the magistrate's orders because the magistrate ordered another person to be put on his pitch'.

In *R v Liverpool Corpn, ex p Liverpool Taxi Fleet Operators' Association*[9] Lord Denning said:

The writs of prohibition and certiorari lie on behalf of any person who is a 'person aggrieved' and that includes any person whose interests may be prejudicially affected by what is taking place. It does not include a mere busybody who is interfering in things which do not concern him: but it does include any person who has a genuine grievance because something has been done or may be done which affects him.

The last phrase ('but ...') is perhaps another way of expressing the 'sufficient interest' which a person must now have. To take another pre-new Order 53 case. In *R v Manchester Legal Aid Committee, ex p R A Brand & Co Ltd*[10] certiorari to quash the committee's decision to grant legal aid to X was granted on the application, it will be noted, of the prospective defendant. What affected him was the grant of legal aid to

---

8 (1957) 55 LGR 129.
9 [1972] 2 QB 299, [1972] 2 All ER 589.
10 [1952] 2 QB 413, [1952] 1 All ER 480 – p 375 above.

the plaintiff – a 'sufficient interest' no doubt. But in *R v Legal Aid Board, ex p Bateman*[11] it was held that (though a sufficient interest need not be financial) a solicitor's client had no standing to challenge a decision of the Board affecting the solicitor's remuneration. (The fact that B had been granted legal aid to bring the proceedings was irrelevant.)

In *R v International Stock Exchange, ex p Else*[12] a company did not challenge the cancellation of the listing of its shares, but its shareholders did. Their interest was sufficient. In *R v London Borough of Haringey, ex p Secretary of State for the Environment*[13] the applicant, though not directly affected by a tax set by H had sufficient interest in its level to ask the court to require H to perform its tax-setting function lawfully. In *R v Immigration Officer, ex p Shah*[14] a person about to be deported had sufficient interest to seek to quash a direction to remove him, even though the direction was addressed not to him, but to an airline.

The problem of locus standi is illustrated well in *taxation* cases. In the *Fleet St Casuals* case,[15] it will be recalled, the applicants (for a declaration and a mandamus) – a group of taxpayers – had no locus standi. In the *Smedley* case (p 379 above) the Master of the Rolls said that it was not necessary to decide Smedley's standing, but he would be 'extremely surprised' to find himself taking the view that Smedley, a taxpayer and elector, had not got standing. Slade LJ had little doubt that Smedley had standing, if only as a taxpayer, in view of the serious question raised by him. In the *Fleet St Casuals* case one group of taxpayers was seeking to involve itself in the legality of an arrangement made by the Revenue with another group: in *Smedley's* case a general constitutional question of prime importance was raised by him. In *R v A-G, ex p Imperial Chemical Industries plc*[16] ICI sought declarations that the government was acting unlawfully in the way it was arriving at the valuation of certain products. The effect it was claimed, was to disadvantage ICI as against its (oil company) competitors. Had it standing? It had. ICI, the court said, was complaining of the Revenue's ultra vires act not as a taxpayer but as a competitor – but as one whose interest in the matter had been recognised by the Revenue from the outset; and the need for confidentiality as to the other (the oil companies) taxpayers' affairs had not been in issue in this case.

Another general issue is *censorship*. Shortly before the new Order 53 came *R v Greater London Council, ex p Blackburn*.[17] Blackburn sought prohibition to prevent the GLC from acting unlawfully in the matter of film censorship. Who was Blackburn? What was his interest? Lord Denning's answer: 'Mr Blackburn is a citizen of London. His wife is a ratepayer. He has children who may be harmed by the exhibition of

11 [1992] 3 All ER 490.
12 [1993] 1 All ER 420.
13 [1991] COD 135.
14 [1982] 2 All ER 264, [1982] 1 WLR 544.
15 See p 355 above.
16 [1987] 1 CMLR 72.
17 [1976] 3 All ER 184, [1976] 1 WLR 550, CA.

cinematograph films. If he has no sufficient interest, no other citizen has'. Stephenson LJ said 'They live in the GLC's jurisdiction and have locus standi. Mrs Blackburn is a ratepayer'. Bridge LJ agreed that Mrs Blackburn had locus standi as a ratepayer. In the *Fleet St Casuals* case where Order 53 was considered for the first time, Lord Diplock regarded the distinction made between the two applicants in the *Blackburn* case as 'carrying technicality to the limits of absurdity having regard to the subject matter of the application' in that case, in view of the fact that local government franchise is not limited to ratepayers. To revert to technical restrictions on locus standi, in order to prevent serious breaches of the law by those exercising governmental functions, would be, he said 'to reverse that progress towards a comprehensive system of administrative law that I regard as having been the greatest achievement of the English courts in my judicial lifetime.'[18]

A prominent feature of the last two decades has been the growth in the number of *interest groups* and *pressure groups* such as residents' associations, environmentalist societies. They raise very clearly the problem of standing. In *Covent Garden Community Association Ltd v Greater London Council*,[19] the Association was formed to safeguard the interests of Covent Garden residents, and eighty per cent of its members were residents. The Council granted planning permission[20] for the change of use of premises it owned in the area to office use. The Association sought to quash that decision by certiorari (for procedural ultra vires and breach of natural justice).[1] Had it locus standi? Woolf J said it would be quite out of accord with the general approach to questions of locus standi in prerogative proceedings to say that the applicants did not have standing. On the merits certiorari did not issue, but on the question of standing the case has been described as 'an important concession to the ideology of public participation'.[2]

In *R v Chief Adjudication Officer, ex p Bland*,[3] B, a miner, applied for judicial review to quash a decision whereby a deduction was made from his supplementary benefit because he was on strike. B's standing was not in issue, but the National Union of Mineworkers, to which B belonged, and the Trades Union Congress, to which the NUM was affiliated, were applicants with B for the relief in question. The court refused B leave on grounds other than standing but said that it would have held that the NUM had standing (one of its main objects is the protection of its members' interests, and it had called the strike); but not the TUC (which has as a main object the protection of the interests of unions affiliated to it) – the nexus there was too remote.

In *R v Secretary of State for Social Services, ex p Child Poverty Action Group*[4] Woolf J held that CPAG had standing to challenge a ministerial

18 Lord Diplock was appointed a judge of the High Court in 1956.
19 [1981] JPL 183.
20 This was permitted under planning law.
 1 For availability of certiorari to quash planning permission, see p 386 below.
 2 [1981] JPL 183.
 3 (1985) Times, 6 February; and p 385 below.
 4 (1985) Times, 8 August.

decision affecting social security claimants generally, as it had been designed to serve the interests of such claimants. However, the Court of Appeal found against CPAG on the merits, so that the question of standing did not require an answer. But the Greater London Council was a joint applicant with CPAG. Woolf J said that it has no express or implied status to represent claimants for benefit; nor as a local authority had it any right to adopt the role of guardian of the public interest. The Court of Appeal agreed.

In *R v Secretary of State for the Environment, ex p Rose Theatre Trust Ltd*[5] the company challenged the decision not to 'schedule' (and thus give special protection to) the remains of an Elizabethan theatre. The company had been formed by those, including archaeologists, who thought it should be used as a vehicle for their campaign. They agreed that the company had no greater interest than those who formed it. The court declined to give it standing, acknowledging that this meant that an unlawful ministerial act could go unchallenged in the courts.

Fortunately this attitude was not followed in *R v HM Inspectorate of Pollution, ex p Greenpeace Ltd (No 2)* [6] in which G challenged a decision concerning discharge of radioactive waste at Sellafield granted to a third party. G was, the court said, an expert, respected body, and the issues it raised were serious; it had many supporters in the area effected; and the inadequacy of possible alternative legal challenges was relevant. It had standing.

Interest groups are interested in specific issues. *Political parties* are interested in all matters concerning the public interest. In *R v Boundary Commission, ex p Foot*[7] the Commission had, as required by statute, prepared for submission to the Secretary of State a report containing its recommendations for the revision of parliamentary constituency boundaries. The legality of this report was challenged not technically by the Labour Party but by four members including the leader and chief whip, and all of course electors. The Court of Appeal found that they came nowhere near proving illegality. That being so, it found it 'unnecessary to express any opinion' on the question of the applicants' locus standi – which was not fully argued anyway. We can say that there is a very great public interest in the principles on which constituency boundaries are drawn, and in the Commission adhering to the statutory rules prescribed for it. Who has *not* got an interest in this? A political party may of course think itself particularly disadvantaged by proposed boundary changes. (It was a prohibitory order, not certiorari that was applied for, but that would make no difference.) On the question of standing, the Law Commission has recommended that an application should not proceed to a substantive hearing unless the court is satisfied that the applicant has been or would be adversely affected, or the court considers that it is in the public interest for an applicant to make the application. The issue of standing would, as

5 [1990] 1 All ER 754. See Schiemann [1990] PL 342.
6 [1994] 4 All ER 329: note relevance that certiorari not mandamus was sought.
7 [1983] QB 600, [1983] 1 All ER 1099.

now, be a relevant factor when considering the grant of a remedy at the substantive hearing.

The court's discretion

The discretionary nature of the prerogative orders has already been emphasised, and we now consider the factors that may affect the grant of the remedy.[9]

Alternative remedy
The availability to the applicant of another remedy which is equally or more convenient, beneficial and effective will be a very relevant factor. This may take several forms.

(a) A right of appeal. In *R v Peterkin, ex p Soni*[10] certiorari was applied for to quash the decision of an immigration adjudicator, as an alternative to appealing to the Immigration Appeal Tribunal. Lord Widgery CJ said that although the error of law on the face of the record constituted a prima facie case for interference, certiorari would be refused as the Tribunal could deal with the injustice.

[W]here Parliament has provided a form of appeal which is equally convenient in the sense that the appellate tribunal can deal with the injustice of which the applicant complains this court should in my judgment as a rule allow the appellate machinery to take its course. The prerogative orders form the general residual jurisdiction of this Court whereby the court supervises the work of inferior tribunals and seeks to correct injustice where no other adequate remedy exists, but both authority and common sense seem to me to demand that the court should not allow its jurisdiction under the prerogative orders to be used merely as an alternative form of appeal when other and adequate jurisdiction exists elsewhere.

In *R v Chief Adjudication Officer, ex p Bland*,[11] B applied for a certiorari to quash a decision affecting the amount of social security benefit he could get. The decision could have been appealed against through the social security tribunals. The court said that it should be chary of by-passing such specialised appeals machinery. A suitable test case could be brought through the tribunals. The argument that judicial review would be speedier was rejected.

In *R v Chief Immigration Officer, Gatwick Airport, ex p Kharrazi*[12] an Iranian boy of 16 was refused entry. His right of an appeal to an adjudicator could be exercised only from outside the UK. This, in Lord Denning's view, rendered the right of appeal useless, and the decision was quashed. But in *R v Secretary of State for the Home Department, ex p Swati*[13] the Court of Appeal said that that case was exceptional in that the Iranian

8 Law Com No 226 para 5.16 et seq.
9 See Bingham 'Should public law remedies be discretionary?' [1991] PL 64.
10 [1972] Imm AR 253.
11 (1985) Times, 6 February.
12 [1980] 3 All ER 373, [1980] 1 WLR 1396.
13 [1986] 1 All ER 717, [1986] 1 WLR 477.

authorities would not let people of his age leave the country, and the principle in *ex p Soni* was reiterated. It also pointed out that the statutory appeal has a *wider range* than judicial review.

In *R v Birmingham City Council, ex p Ferrero Ltd*[14] B issued a notice requiring the withdrawal of F's product. F had a right of appeal to the magistrates, but applied for a certiorari. The court held that the appeal was 'geared exactly' to deciding the real issue – the safety of the goods: judicial review denied.

Where the passing of a resolution to purchase property compulsorily was said to be unfair, judicial review was denied: the statutory procedure for appealing against the compulsory purchase order was suitable.[15]

In the following cases judicial review was allowed despite the availability of an appeal.

In *R v Hillingdon London Borough Council ex p Royco Homes Ltd*[16] certiorari was applied for to quash the grant of conditions attached to a planning permission. In such a case there is an appeal to the Secretary of State and a further appeal on a point of law to the High Court. Generally, said Lord Widgery, that system of appeals is more effective and more convenient than an application for certiorari. This is because on an appeal to the Secretary of State, *all the issues* between the parties whether of law, fact or policy can be disposed of at one hearing whereas certiorari is limited to questions of law.

Lord Widgery also observed that certiorari is *speedier* and *cheaper* and it might well be proper to allow it to be used. However, he said:

I would define a proper case as being a case where the decision in question is liable to be upset as a matter of law because on its face it is clearly made without jurisdiction, or made in consequence of an error of law. [This was such a case which involved an *important point of law*.][17]

In *R v Huntingdon District Council, ex p Cowan*[18] an appeal lay from a decision of the council to the magistrates' court; but the court exercised its discretion in favour of the applicant on the ground that the point on which the decision was being challenged was one which *applied to all local authorities* (in contrast with another case there referred to), and had *not been previously considered* by the courts.

In *R v Chief Constable of the Merseyside Police, ex p Calveley*[19] a disciplinary hearing was convened by the Chief Constable to hear charges against C based on complaints made against him some three years before. C protested that the delay made the hearing unfair, but it was held, and it found against C. C gave notice of appeal to a tribunal, but before it sat applied to have the Chief Constable's decision quashed. The Court of

14 [1993] 1 All ER 530.
15 *R v Central Manchester Development Corpn ex p Merlin ... Ltd* (1992) 64 P&CR 392. For CPO procedure see p 119 above.
16 [1974] QB 720, [1974] 2 All ER 643.
17 Cf *R v Epping Forest DC, ex p Green* [1993] COD 81.
18 [1984] 1 All ER 58, [1984] 1 WLR 501.
19 [1986] QB 424, [1986] 1 All ER 257.

Appeal, reversing the court below, said that despite the appeal procedure, judicial review was available in the exceptional circumstances of the lengthy delay before the hearing.

In *R v Paddington Valuation Officer, ex p Peachey Property Corpn*[20] the applicants had a statutory right of appeal to the local valuation court and thence to the Lands Tribunal. The Court of Appeal agreed that if the dispute were about the valuation of particular properties that procedure should be followed, but certiorari was appropriate in this case as the applicants were impugning the whole of the list. An appeal may be made to the county court against a control order made under the Housing Act. Such an order may, nevertheless, be subject to certiorari where the challenge is to the power to make the order at all, rather than to procedural or technical matters.[1]

The available alternative may be an appeal *by way of case stated*. It has been said that judicial review is preferable to a case stated in respect of decisions of a Mental Health Review Tribunal as it allows a broader consideration of the issues, and a more comprehensive range of reliefs.[2] In *R v Margate JJ, ex p Haddow*[3] there was no appeal against the sentence of imprisonment except by case stated, which was not helpful in the circumstances. Judicial review was available. Another alternative is an appeal *on a point of law*. The advantages of challenging decisions of rent assessment committees by way of judicial review rather than by such an appeal have been explained.[4]

(b) Action in tort. In *R v Patents Appeal Tribunal, ex p J R Geigy SA*,[5] the tribunal in granting a patent had refused G's request to exercise its power to insert in the patent a notice of G's patent which was likely to be infringed by the users of X's patent. On G's application for certiorari it was held that the possibility of legal proceedings by G against the users of X's patent for infringement of his (G's) patent, was not a suitable alternative remedy to the grant of a certiorari to him.

(c) Ministerial action. We have noted the relevance of a right of appeal to a minister. Another possible ministerial involvement is by way of *default action* perhaps at the instance of a person affected. This is taken account of. In *R v Ealing London Borough Council, ex p Times Newspapers Ltd*[6] the court said that the statutory remedy in that case was cumbersome, and swift action was necessary. Furthermore, there had been a clear abuse of power.

In *R v Hull Prison Board of Visitors, ex p St Germain*[7] the Court of Appeal was quite clear that a prisoner's right to *petition* the Home

---

20 [1966] 1 QB 380, [1965] 2 All ER 836.
1 *R v London Borough of Southwark, ex p Lewis Levy Ltd* [1984] JPL 105.
2 *Bone v Mental Health Tribunal* [1985] 3 All ER 330.
3 (1992) Times, 30 July.
4 *Ellis & Sons Fourth Amalgamated Properties v Southern Rent Assessment Panel* (1984) 270 EG 39.
5 [1963] 2 QB 728, [1963] 1 All ER 850.
6 (1986) 85 LGR 316; and see p 249 above.
7 [1979] QB 425, [1979] 1 All ER 701.

Secretary against a disciplinary award by a Board was not to be equated to a formal appeal. In *R v Camphill Prison Deputy Governor, ex p King*[8] that court held that the prisoner's only remedy was to petition the Home Office, whose decision alone would be subject to judicial review. But in *Leech v Parkhurst Prison Deputy Governor*[9] Lord Bridge pointed out the inadequacy of the petition as a remedy, and the adjudication was quashed.

(d) Ombudsmen. In *R v Monmouth District Council, ex p Jones*[10] the court rejected the suggestion that judicial review should be denied as the applicant could have complained to the Local Ombudsman.

(e) No alternative remedy. Thus if some other procedure is available to an applicant and it is equally valuable to him in the particular circumstances as judicial review, he may be denied judicial review. If in the circumstances it is not equally valuable, the court is likely to exercise its discretion in his favour. Even more so, if there is no alternative procedure available to him. Thus in *R v Secretary of State for the Home Department, ex p Benwell*[11] the court was very much influenced in granting a remedy by the fact that the applicant prison officer, unlike an ordinary employee, had no other remedy. In the Datafin[12] case the Master of the Rolls, observing that it was 'unthinkable' that the Panel should go on its way cocooned from the attention of the courts, said:

We sought to investigate whether it could conveniently be controlled by established forms of private law eg torts such as actionable combinations in restraint of trade, and to this end, pressed counsel for the applicants to draft a writ. Suffice it to say that the result was wholly unconvincing, and not surprisingly, counsel for the Panel did not admit that it would be in the least effective.

If no remedy of any kind is provided by statute, only judicial review is available – as in the case of 'homelessness' decisions by local authorities. This has led to a large number of applications for judicial review in such cases, and this in turn has led to the suggestion that a right of appeal to court or tribunal should be provided in such cases.

The applicant's behaviour

In the exercise of its discretion the court will take into account the *behaviour of the applicant*, as in *R v South Holland Drainage Committee Men*[13] where the applicant could not complain, it was held, of defects in a decision as to the amount of compensation he was entitled to; one of the defects he had caused, the other he had waived. In *R v Secretary of State for Education and Science, ex p Birmingham District Council*[14] the council had made proposals for closing a school. These received the necessary ministerial approval. The council later changed its mind about the merits

  8 [1985] QB 735, [1984] 3 All ER 897.
  9 [1988] AC 533, [1988] 1 All ER 485. *R v Devon County Council, ex p Baker* [1995] 1 All ER 73: review not precluded by default power.
 10 (1985) 53 P & CR 108.
 11 [1985] QB 554, [1984], 3 All ER 854.
 12 [1987] QB 815, [1987] 1 All ER 564. See p 345 above.
 13 (1838) 8 Ad & El 429.
 14 (1984) Times, 18 July.

of its proposal (following a change of political control) and sought to quash the approval on the ground of its *own* procedural error when formulating its proposals. Certiorari was refused. An applicant's economy with the truth in his affidavit supporting his application will tell against him.[15] And where the payment of rates had been withheld for some years without excuse a remedy for the improper denial of a refund was refused.[16]

The status of the tribunal In deciding whether to exercise its discretion to grant certiorari the court may be influenced by *the status of the tribunal* or other authority and its desire to interfere with the work it does. In the early 1950s the courts were very ready to upset the decisions of rent tribunals as they were dissatisfied with their general standard of competence. In due course the government appointed lawyers as their chairmen, with beneficial results. *R v National Insurance Comrs, ex p Michael*[17] shows the court taking the view that they should intervene in the work of the Commissioners very sparingly because of the calibre of those appointed. Contrast *R v Preston Supplementary Benefit Appeal Tribunal, ex p Moore*[18] where the court took (on the application of a student) a non-interventionist line with the Tribunal (even though it had probably made an error of law) on the ground that the legislation should be administered with as little technicality as possible and should not become a happy hunting-ground for lawyers.

The range of complainants In *R v Secretary of State for Social Services, ex p Association of Metropolitan Authorities*[19] the court held that the Secretary of State had failed to fulfil his obligation to consult before making regulations. One of the reasons the court gave for not quashing the regulations was that although six organisations were, and were habitually, consulted on these matters, only one of them applied for the regulations to be struck down, and that one only on the ground that it (not others) had not been consulted.

Compare *R v Tunbridge Wells Health Authority, ex p Goodridge*[20] where it was argued that the court should not quash the decision to close a facility as no objection had been made to it by the Community Health Council, that other doctors had proposed only modifications to the scheme, not rejection (and that reconsideration would cause delay). The court rejected this: the flaw in the decision was no mere technicality. On the other hand widespread support did not help the doctor-applicant in *R v Secretary of State for Health, ex p Cormack*.[1]

---

15 *Johnson v Secretary of State for Health* (1992) 16 BMLR 1.
16 *R v Brent London Borough Council, ex p Dovot Properties* (1990) Times, 7 March. A comparison may be made with the maxim 'He who comes to equity must come with clean hands'.
17 [1977] 2 All ER 420. [1977] 1 WLR 109.
18 [1975] 2 All ER 807, [1975] 1 WLR 624.
19 [1986] 1 All ER 164, [1986] 1 WLR 1; see p 280 above.
20 (1988) Times, 21 May.
 1 (1990) 6 BMLR 81.

The effect of quashing
A relevant consideration in deciding whether or not to grant certiorari (and the other orders) is *the effect of doing so*. In *R v Brent Health Authority, ex p Francis*[2] the BHA had excluded the public from a meeting. The legality of that decision and therefore of the resolutions passed at the meeting was challenged. The court found that the authority had acted lawfully. But even if it had not, it would not have quashed the (important financial) resolutions passed there. Why not? The complaint had not been about the legality of the resolutions (their substance – cuts in NHS expenditure – was what the applicant was concerned about) but that the public had not been admitted to hear the discussion preceding them. The effect of certiorari would have been to give the applicant an opportunity to hear the discussion at a re-held meeting; but also it would have brought about a 'completely irregular situation' in the financing of the NHS in Brent. It was not worth causing the latter by granting the former. (Earlier meetings had been broken up by protesters.) In *R v Hillingdon Health Authority, ex p Goodwin*,[3] by contrast, certiorari to quash a decision to close a hospital temporarily was resisted on the ground that this would cause delay in a financial situation that did not permit it. The court held however that, in view of the failure to take an important matter into account in arriving at the decision, and that delay would be minimal, the decision should be quashed.

In *R v Greater London Council, ex p Royal Borough of Kensington and Chelsea*[4] the applicant sought to quash a precept issued by GLC on the ground that it wrongly took certain items of expenditure into account. McNeill J said that even if GLC had acted unlawfully, to quash the precept would be 'outrageous'. The GLC ('knee-deep in counsel's opinions' before it acted – a relevant consideration) would have been deprived of funds necessary to provide for the needs of the community; and the proportion of disputed items to the total precept was slight.

In the *AMA* case (p 389 above) another reason the court gave for declining to quash the regulations (which were to do with housing benefit) was that if it did so all applicants who had been refused benefits on the basis of those regulations would be entitled to make fresh claims, and all auth-orities would be required, to their inconvenience, to consider each such claim. (While not quashing the regulations, the court granted a declaration that the minister had failed to comply with his statutory duty.)

In cases in which judicial review of prison governors' decisions was sought, review was denied on the ground that to grant it would make the governor's job even more difficult than it is, but in *Leech v Parkhurst Prison Deputy Governor*[5] the House of Lords, while acknowledging that no one can predict with certainty what the outcome of making judicial review available might be, thought the balance of advantage was in favour of judicial review.

2   [1985] 1 All ER 74, [1984] 3 WLR 1317.
3   [1984] ICR 800.
4   (1982) Times, 7 April, Lexis.
5   [1988] AC 533, [1988] 1 All ER 485.

In the above cases the issues were administrative and financial difficulties. In the *Datafin*[6] case the Court of Appeal was concerned about the effect on the market of judicial review of the Panel's decisions and thought that a declaration, operating prospectively only, rather than a certiorari to quash, would normally be the most appropriate remedy.

A reason for declining to quash is where there is *no point in it*. Amongst the reasons given in *R v Monopolies and Mergers Commission, ex p Argyll Group plc*[7] for not quashing were that the Commission would have reached the same decision as the chairman. A court can consider whether the same decision would be reached again. But this can be speculative, and the court must be cautious.[8]

In *R v North West Thames RHA, ex p Daniels*[9] the closure of a medical unit was unlawful for failure to consult. The court declined to quash the decision to close, as the unit had already closed and the certiorari would serve no purpose. (A declaration was refused for the same reason.)

Johnson v Secretary of State for Health[10] concerns the effect *on a third party*. Disciplinary proceedings against J, a dentist, on the basis of a complaint by his patient M, resulted in J being fined the sum of £250, £200 of which was to go to M. If (because of procedural errors) the penalty on J was quashed M would not get his £200 – a reason for not quashing, as was the point that if it were, the obligation to investigate the complaint would stand and six years had now passed since the events in question.[11]

Prohibition

As we have seen, the only difference between certiorari and prohibition is that the former quashes what has been done in abuse or excess of power, and the latter restrains such action.

R v Liverpool Corpn, ex p Liverpool Taxi Fleet Operators' Association[12] usefully raised the question of the appropriate remedy. The facts will be found at p 292 above. The Association applied for certiorari, mandamus and prohibition. Roskill LJ said:

For my part I see no ground for allowing an order of certiorari to go. The resolution of 22 December [increasing the number of licences] is not suggested to have been ultra vires. Moreover, now to quash it, as Lord Denning MR has pointed out, causes difficulties in relation to the earlier resolution of 4 August, [increasing the number but giving an undertaking not to increase it further] which was rescinded by the resolution complained of. Nor can I see any ground for an order of mandamus, for I see no failure by Liverpool Corporation to exercise a power which it is required by Parliament to exercise. It seems to me that if any redress

6 [1987] QB 815, [1987] 1 All ER 564. See p 345 above.
7 [1986] 2 All ER 257, [1986] 1 WLR 763. See p 208 above.
8 *R v Wiltshire County Council, ex p Bryden* [1991] COD 31.
9 (1993) 19 BMLR 67.
10 (1992) 16 BMLR 1.
11 For various public policy grounds unsuccessfully suggested for not quashing decision see *R v General Council of the Bar, ex p Percival* [1990] 3 All ER 137.
12 [1972] 2 QB 299, [1972] 2 All ER 509, CA.

can be given, it must be redress by way of an order of prohibition. The applicants have not sought relief, as perhaps they might have done, by way of injunction or declaration.

In this case therefore prohibition issued to prevent an authority continuing an unfair procedure and to enable it to tackle the problem afresh and to arrive at a conclusion after hearing the interested parties.

In the following cases prohibition was, for the reasons given, inappropriate. In *A-G of Hong Kong v Ng Yuen Shiu*[13] prohibition had issued from the Hong Kong court to the Director of Immigration to prevent Ng's removal until an opportunity had been given to him to put his case. The Judicial Committee thought certiorari to quash the decision to remove was more appropriate. (This was without prejudice to a fresh removal order after a proper inquiry into Ng's case.)

In *R v Boundary Commission for England, ex p Foot*,[14] if relief had been necessary, prohibition would not have been issued, as the effect would have been to preclude Parliament from considering the Commission's proposals. The appropriate remedy would have been a declaration, which would have been of assistance to the Commission and Parliament.

In *R v Greater London Council, ex p Blackburn*,[15] Blackburn showed that the GLC was applying the wrong test for censorship of films. However, it was not compelled to censor films for adults, so that it could cease doing so or could amend its rules so as to accord with the law. In those circumstances the Court of Appeal decided that it was not necessary for prohibition to issue there and then: the GLC should be given an opportunity to adopt one of those courses. Blackburn was given leave to apply later if necessary for prohibition.

Mandamus

What it does

Mandamus is a court order which commands a person or body to perform a public duty. Failure to obey it may lead to proceedings for contempt of court.[16] In addition or in lieu the court may direct that the act be done by someone else at the cost of the defaulter. It is thus a powerful weapon in the hands of the court.

Mandamus is a public law remedy and will not therefore lie in respect of duties of a private nature, even if the body in question is created by statute and could in respect of other of its functions be compelled by mandamus, as for example where the Industrial Court was acting as private arbitrator.[17] In principle it would seem that a common law, as

13 [1983] 2 AC 629, [1983] 2 All ER 346. See p 290 above.
14 [1983] QB 600, [1983] 1 All ER 1099. See p384 above.
15 [1976] 3 All ER 184, [1976] 1 WLR 550. See p382 above.
16 *R v Poplar Borough Council, ex p LCC* (No 2) [1922] 1 KB 95.
17 *R v Industrial Court, ex p ASSET* [1965] 1 QB 377, [1964] 3 All ER 130. *Imperial Metal Industries (Kynoch) Ltd v Amalgamated Union of Engineering Workers* [1979] 1 All ER 847; [1979] ICR 23.

well as statutory, duty may be enforced by mandamus.

Mandamus enforces duties not powers, but in some cases a power may be coupled with a duty so that the donee of the power would be obliged to exercise it. These and other aspects of duties, have been referred to in chapter 6.

What appears to be a duty may be rather a statement of objectives, or a programme of action. For example, under the Gas Act 1972 it was the duty of the British Gas Corporation 'to develop and maintain an efficient and coordinated and economical system of gas supply for Great Britain'. Is that a duty to be enforced by mandamus? What would the court's order be? 'Be efficient and economical'? Because an obligation is not so enforceable does not mean that it is meaningless; perhaps it should be seen as enforceable principally through the political rather than the legal process. But this does not mean that the legal implications of such a 'target' duty may not be considered by the court.[18]

If a duty is to be enforceable by mandamus, it must be such that the court's direction can have specificity. A request to a court to issue an order 'as imprecise as Nelson's Trafalgar signal' would be unlikely, for that reason, to be granted.[19]

Mandamus is available to enforce a wide range of duties. Here are some examples. It will issue at the instance of a ratepayer to enforce a local authority's duty to allow examination of its accounts,[20] to restore a person to public office of which he has been wrongly deprived,[1] to a recorder to issue a bench warrant,[2] to the Registrar of Joint Stock Companies to register a company,[3] to an immigration officer to give an immigrant proper opportunity to satisfy him of his qualification to enter the UK,[4] to a minister to require him to exercise a power in accordance with correct legal principles,[5] to a local authority to make byelaws[6] and to register a common lodging house,[7] to an inferior tribunal to hear a case where it mistakenly thought it had no jurisdiction to do so or refused to do so[8] and to magistrates who wrongfully dismissed informations.[9] It has also been used to overcome a delay in administrative procedure which amounted to an interference with the applicant's rights.[10]

18 Eg *R v Secretary of State for Health ex, p Keen* (1990) 10 BMLR 13.
19 *Re Guyer's Application* [1980] 2 All ER 520, [1980] 1 WLR 1024. See *R v Stroud District Council, ex p Goodenough, Usborne and Tomlin* (1980) 43 p & CR 59.
20 *R v Bedwellty UDC, ex p Price* [1934] 1 KB 333.
1 *Bagg's Case* (1615) 11 Co Rep 93b.
2 *R v Lloyd-Jones, ex p Thomas* [1958] 3 All ER 425, [1958] 1 WLR 1110.
3 *R v Registrar of Joint Stock Companies, ex p More* [1931] 2 KB 197.
4 *Re H K (infant)* [1967] 2 QB 617, [1967] 1 All ER 226.
5 *Padfield v Minister of Agriculture, Fisheries and Food* [1968] AC 997, [1968] 1 All ER 694.
6 *R v Manchester Corpn* [1911] 1 KB 560.
7 *R v London Borough of Hounslow, ex p Pizzey* [1977] 1 All ER 305, [1977] 1 WLR 58.
8 Eg *R v West Norfolk Valuation Panel, ex p H Prins Ltd* (1975) 73 LGR 206.
9 *R v Hendon JJ, ex p DPP* [1993] 1 All ER 411: also certiorari to quash a nullity (how can you quash what does not exist?).
10 Eg *R v Secretary of State for the Home Dept, ex p Phansopkar* [1976] QB 606, [1975] 3 All ER 497.

Mandamus will not lie to enforce an award of the Criminal Injuries Compensation Board or similar ex gratia payments,[11] but will lie to the Board to require it to act in accordance with correct procedure and with the terms of the Scheme.[12]

The possibility of the reviewability (whether by mandamus or otherwise) of a prosecution *policy* was established in *R v Metropolitan Police Comr, ex p Blackburn*.[13] The discretion whether or not to prosecute in a *particular* case is also reviewable.[14]

The court's discretion

The grant of a mandamus is in the court's discretion. What considerations will influence the court? The availability of an equally convenient beneficial and effectual remedy is relevant.[15] A leading case is *Pasmore v Oswaldwistle UDC*.[16] The council had a duty to provide sewerage for effectually draining their district. The applicant said that the sewers were not adequate for effectually draining their premises and sought an order of mandamus. However, the Act imposing the duty on the council provided for complaints to be made to the Local Government Board, that is, the minister, when the council was in default. The Board could then require the council to fulfil its duty; if it failed to do so the duty could be enforced by a mandamus on the application of the Board. The court said that accordingly it was not open to a particular individual to apply for mandamus.[17]

But where the remedy is not equally convenient, beneficial and effectual, it will not disentitle the applicant to a mandamus. Thus where there is a remedy by way of *criminal proceedings*, mandamus will not be withheld if the punishment will not ensure that the duty is carried out. For example in *R v Bedwellty UDC, ex p Price*[18] it was argued that mandamus should not issue to enforce the authority's duty to allow inspection of its accounts as officials of the local authority could be prosecuted for not allowing the accounts to be inspected, but the court pointed out that a prosecution would not necessarily result in the accounts being made available:

11 *R v Criminal Injuries Compensation Board, ex p Lain* [1967] 2 QB 864, [1967] 2 All ER 770.
12 *R v Criminal Injuries Compensation Board, ex p Clowes* [1977] 3 All ER 854, [1977] 1 WLR 1353.
13 [1968] 2 QB 118, [1968] 1 All ER 763, CA. And *(No 3)* [1973] QB 241, [1973] 1 All ER 324.
14 *R v General Council of the Bar, ex p Percival* [1990] 3 All ER 137.
15 Cf the rules for certiorari, p 385 above.
16 [1898] AC 387, applied *R v Kensington and Chelsea (Royal) London Borough Council, ex p Birdwood* (1976) 74 LGR 424; *Southwark London Borough Council v Williams* [1971] Ch 734, [1971] 2 All ER 175, CA.
17 And see *Watt v Kesteven County Council* [1955] 1 QB 408, [1955] 1 All ER 473, CA – duty to provide sufficient schools; minister may give directions; no mandamus to individual.
18 [1934] 1 KB 333.

mandamus issued. In *R v Metropolitan Police Comr, ex p Blackburn*[19] it was said that the fact that Blackburn could have instituted criminal proceedings would not disentitle him to mandamus.

There have been cases where the relevance of the availability of an *appeal* has been considered. In *R v Paddington Valuation Officer, ex p Peachey Property Corpn Ltd*[20] mandamus to make a new valuation list was resisted on the ground that statute provided for an appeal to the valuation court. The Court of Appeal agreed that that procedure should be followed where the objection was to the valuation of a particular hereditament, but here the validity of the whole list was being challenged. In that case the appeal was nowhere near as convenient etc. In *R v Stepney Corpn*[1] the council had a duty to pay compensation for loss of office. In calculating the amount payable, it (improperly) followed Treasury practice. An appeal lay against the decision – to the Treasury. This was clearly not satisfactory and no bar to a mandamus to the Council to exercise its discretion properly. The cases listed below are examples of decisions where an appeal was held to be a satisfactory remedy.[2]

In *R v Poplar Borough Council (No 1), ex p LCC*[3] the statutory remedy of distress was said to be ludicrously inadequate.

A further consideration that may arise is the *financial ability* of the authority to comply with the court order. In *R v Poplar Borough Council, ex p LCC* the applicants had issued precepts to the Borough Council, which refused to pay. It did not dispute the validity of the demand or its obligation to pay, but resisted mandamus on the ground of the poverty of the area compared with other areas within the LCC. The court said that it had no concern with such matters; the council's remedy was to seek a change in the relevant legislation. Mandamus issued to pay the precept, if necessary by levying a rate for that purpose. In *R v Secretary of State for Social Services, ex p Hincks*[4] the problem was different. The *extent* of the duty – which was not in issue in this *Poplar* case – was said there to depend on the availability of resources.

In *R v Kerrier District Council, ex p Guppys (Bridport) Ltd*[5] the *'floodgates'* argument was used. Mandamus to make the authority take certain action in respect of unfit houses was resisted on the grounds that if it was granted, there would be a great flood of applications (there being over one million unfit houses in the country). The court was not satisfied that that was likely to happen in view of the consideration, amongst others, that mandamus is discretionary.

As in the case of specific performance the court will not grant mandamus if the form of the order requires day-to-day supervision. In *R v Peak Park*

---

19 [1968] 2 QB 118, [1968] 1 All ER 763. See p 392 above.
20 [1966] 1 QB 380, [1965] 2 All ER 836. See p 387 above.
1 [1902] 1 KB 317.
2 *R v Port of London Authority, ex p Kynoch Ltd* [1919] 1 KB 176; *R v City of London Assessment Committee* [1907] 2 KB 764.
3 [1922] 1 KB 72.
4 See p185 above.
5 (1976) 32 P & CR 411.

Joint Planning Board, ex p Jackson[6] J, an elected member of a Council, had been appointed by it as one of the members of the Board. His appointment was rescinded by the Council. J sought mandamus, as against the Board to treat him as a member, and as against the Council to rescind the appointment of his successor on the Board and to treat him, J, as a member of the Board. The court ruled that in law J could not be replaced as the Council thought fit. But what was the appropriate order? Not mandamus, as an order to treat J as a member of the Board would require continual examination of the circumstances. The court therefore allowed the addition of an application for a certiorari, and issued it, so as to quash the purported removal of J from the Board.

In *R v Ealing District Health Authority, ex p Fox*[7] the DHA was in breach of its duty to provide services for F. Certiorari issued to quash its decision not to provide the relevant service for him. Mandamus was refused as it would in effect compel a doctor to provide a service which he thought was not in F's best interest; but a declaration as to the DHA's legal error and the extent of its duty was granted.

As noted above (p 372) to have judicial review there must be something to review. In *R v Devon County Council, ex p L*,[8] L asked DCC to instruct its employees on a certain matter affecting him. Following their reply L applied for a mandamus. It was rejected as the reply had done no more than set out the history of events: it had not declined to give the assurance asked for – there was nothing to review.

Locus standi

A strict view of the standing necessary for a mandamus was taken in *R v Lewisham Union*.[9] The court insisted that an applicant had to have a 'legal specific right' to the performance of the duties in question. The facts were that the guardians of the poor of the Lewisham Union were by statute required to take measures to secure the vaccination of persons within their area. They had no other public health functions. The Lewisham Board of Works was under a duty to exercise certain public health functions including the prevention of infectious diseases. As the guardians had never carried out the duties referred to, the Board applied for a mandamus. The court briefly rejected the application applying the test referred to (but also on the ground that the Local Government Board could have taken steps to ensure that the guardians carried out their duty). That test was applied in *R v Customs and Excise Comrs, ex p Cooke and Stevenson*.[10] A Finance Act provided that the annual duty payable on the grant of a licence for betting premises could be collected by the Commissioners in two half-yearly instalments. As a result of representations by

6 (1976) 74 LGR 376.
7 [1993] 3 All ER 174.
8 [1991] COD 205. And see *R v Leicestershire Education Authority, ex p Cannon* [1991] COD 120.
9 [1897] 1 QB 498.
10 [1970] 1 All ER 1068, [1970] 1 WLR 450.

bookmakers the Commissioners were authorised by the Treasury to accept payment by monthly instalments. Two bookmakers applied for a mandamus to compel the Commissioners to act as the Act required, but did they have sufficient interest? Lord Parker CJ delivering the judgment of the court said:

Quite clearly the applicants have no such [legal] specific right as individuals. They are not complaining that a licence was not issued to them; they are not complaining that they were not offered the same terms as other bookmakers with regard to monthly payments. They are not seeking to enforce any specific right or, put another way, any specific duty owed to them.

Even so, he continued, it might be enough if they could show some interest over and above that of the community as a whole, and they had sought to do that by arguing that the statute was intended to curtail the activities of bookmakers, and that the requirement of half-yearly payments contemplated that some betting premises would have to close, whereas the arrangements sanctioned by the Treasury meant that the applicants' competitors were more numerous than they would otherwise have been. The court rejected this argument: the Finance Act was concerned with the collection of tax; the regulation of bookmakers was dealt with by the Betting Acts. And in any case, the court said, (and this may have been its main objection) the applicant's motive was to put people out of business and nothing more.[11] In *R v Metropolitan Police Comr, ex p Blackburn*[12] the Court of Appeal doubted whether the applicant had a sufficient interest in the policy decision he was challenging to entitle him to a mandamus, though Salmon LJ had no doubt that if the chief officer of police gave instructions that no house-breaker was to be prosecuted, any householder in the district would have standing to get the order withdrawn.[13]

In *R v Manchester Corpn*[14] the Corporation had promoted a private bill to run a tramway. As a result of a petition by an insurance company a clause was added to the bill requiring the Corporation to make byelaws prescribing the minimum distance to be maintained between trams. (The shorter the distance, the greater the number of accidents and of insurance claims.) The Corporation made a byelaw but the company showed that it did not comply with the requirements of the Act. The company had standing to obtain a mandamus requiring a proper byelaw to be passed, as they were seeking to enforce a clause obtained on their own petition.

That a ratepayer has a sufficient interest in the financial affairs of his local authority to obtain a mandamus in a matter affecting the authority's finances is suggested by *R v Hereford Corpn, ex p Harrower*.[15] The Corporation placed a contract for the central heating of council flats without inviting tenders, and thus in disregard of its own standing orders. Electrical contractors on the Corporation's approved list applied for a

11 For sequel see Finance Act 1970, s 1(5)(6)(7).
12 [1968] 2 QB 118, [1968] 1 All ER 763. See p 394 above.
13 See *R v Oxford, ex p Levey* (1986) Times, 1 November.
14 [1911] 1 KB 560.
15 [1970] 3 All ER 460, [1970] 1 WLR 1424.

mandamus to make the Corporation comply with its own standing orders. It was held that this was not a sufficient interest but 'if they or some of them are ratepayers as well then ... there would be sufficient right to enable them to apply for a mandamus'.

The test today is of course that of 'sufficient interest in the matter to which the application relates'. In *IRC v National Federation of Self-Employed and Small Businesses Ltd*[16] (the facts of which are at p 355 above) the question was whether the Federation had a 'sufficient interest' to apply for or obtain a mandamus (or a declaration). The complaint was the failure of the Inland Revenue to collect tax due from other people. The House of Lords said that examination of the legislation, far from conferring on the taxpayer the right to inquire about other people's tax, indicated the reverse by reason of the confidentiality of the relationship between the taxpayer and the Inland Revenue. The applicant did not therefore have a sufficient interest in the matter.[17] *R v Lewisham Union*[18] came in for particular criticism. Lord Diplock had 'no hesitation in saying that it is inconceivable that mandamus would have been refused in the circum-stances of that case if it had come before a Divisional Court at any time during the last twenty years' – a period which he said, has 'witnessed a dramatic liberalisation of access to the courts'. Two cases illustrate this. A High Street shopkeeper represented, with two others, the High Street Action Group. They had sufficient interest to require the observance by the local authority of the law concerning the demolition of buildings in the High Street.[19] And the standing of a Chamber of Commerce, representing local shopkeepers, to require the proper enforcement by the local authority of the law on Sunday trading, was not challenged.[20]

Mandamus and the Crown

Mandamus being a coercive order does not lie against the Crown directly. It is also said that mandamus cannot be directed 'to any servant of the Crown simply acting in his capacity of servant'.[1] This is based on the general principle that where an obligation is cast on a principal it cannot be enforced as against the servant as long as he is merely acting as a servant. Thus where in *R v Treasury Lords Comr*[2] the Treasury refused to reimburse certain local authorities' costs, mandamus against the Treasury was refused (even though it had acted quite wrongly) as the duty in question lay in law on Her Majesty. The Treasury's only constitutional duty was to advise the Crown: it owed no duty to third parties. Likewise,

16 [1982] AC 617, [1981] 2 All ER 93.
17 Compare the council tax system where the taxable value of properties is in a public document.
18 [1897] 1 QB 498; p 396 above. Contrast with that case *R v Cotham* [1898] 1 QB 802.
19 *R v Stroud District Council, ex p Goodenough* (1980) 43 P & CR 59.
20 *R v Braintree District Council, ex p Willingham* (1982) 81 LGR 70.
 1 *R v Secretary of State for War* [1891] 2 QB 326 at 334, CA.
 2 (1872) LR 7 QB 387.

the Secretary of State for War in carrying out the terms of a Royal Warrant regulating Army pay was responsible only to the Crown.[3] And in any case the warrant gave no legal right to pay.

On the other hand, if a statutory duty is directly imposed upon a designated Crown servant and it is owed to another person, mandamus will lie against him even though he is a Crown servant and is in that matter exercising a Crown function. It has accordingly lain against the Special Commissioners of Income Tax to issue orders for the repayment of overpaid tax. The duty in such a case is laid directly on the servant.[4] There are plenty of examples of mandamus issuing to ministers to carry out their statutory duties.[5] Indeed that has always been the case, as can be seen as long ago as 1850 in *R v Woods, Forests (etc) Comrs, ex p Budge*, where Sir Freserick Thesiger expressed the proposition in argument in this form: 'Whenever a person, whether filling an office under the Crown or not, has a statutory duty towards another person a mandamus will lie to compel him to perform it'.[6] (This now presumably applies to a common law duty also.)

The availability of mandamus depends therefore on whether the duty is cast on the Crown or on a named Crown servant and in the latter case, whether the duty is owed to the Crown or not. To say that mandamus does not lie against the Crown is not therefore the same thing as saying that it does not lie in respect of Crown activities.

Injunction

Its scope

The injunction is in origin an equitable remedy. It is a court order requiring the party to whom it is addressed to refrain from doing, or occasionally, as a mandatory injunction to do,[7] a particular act. Its principal use as a private law remedy is to restrain a wrongful act such as the commission of a tort or a breach of contract. It may be used against public bodies also for that purpose. It is also available against them to prevent an unlawful act as in *A-G v Fulham Corpn* (p 199 above) and in an *Bradbury v Enfield London Borough*.[8] Local ratepayers obtained an injunction to prevent the authority from making the changeover from selective to comprehensive secondary education until the prescribed statutory procedure was followed.

---

3   *R v Secretary of State for War* [1891] 2 QB 326.
4   *R v Income Tax Special Purposes Comrs* (1888) 21 QBS 313.
5   *Padfield*, p 246 above was such a case.
6   Per Lord Parker CJ in *R v Customs and Excise Comrs, ex p Cooke and Stevenson* [1970] 1 All ER 1068 at 1072, [1970] 1 WLR 450 at 455.
7   See *Harold Stephen & Co Ltd v Post Office* [1978] 1 All ER 939, [1977] 1 WLR 1172, CA (postal service); *Gravesham Borough Council v British Railways Branch* [1978] Ch 379, [1978] 3 All ER 853 (ferry service); *De Falco v Crawley Borough Council* [1980] QB 460, [1980] 1 All ER 913 (housing). Remedy refused in all cases.
8   [1967] 3 All ER 434, [1967] 1 WLR 1311.

Statute may provide for its compliance to be enforced by an injunction as for example the right of a council tenant to buy his dwelling under the Housing Act 1985.[9]

Further, the High Court has an inherent power to secure by injunction obedience to the law even if statute provides some other remedy. In *A-G v Harris*[10] Harris had been convicted 142 times of selling flowers on the footpath outside a Manchester cemetery, and his wife 95 times. The maximum fine was £2. The fines imposed were paid. The Court of Appeal held that though each offence was trivial, it was right that the harasses should be stopped from deliberately flouting the law, and an injunction was granted. And in *A-G v Chandry*[11] the use of a building without a fire certificate was prevented by injunction pending trial of the criminal offence of doing so.

Injunctions have also been used to remedy the inefficacy of planning law, including that of criminal law.[12] However, the House of Lords has since indicated[13] that the procedure of involving the assistance of the civil courts in aid of the criminal law is to be used only in the most exceptional cases.[14] This is because an injunction may expose the defendant, in the event of its breach, to a more severe penalty than Parliament prescribed for the criminal offence; and of course the standard of proof is lower in civil than in criminal proceedings.

As for the availability of the injunction in judicial review proceedings, we have noted, p 359 above, the terms of section 31(2) of the Supreme Court Act 1981.

Injunctions and the Crown

The availability of one coercive order – the mandamus – against Crown functionaries has been referred to. As to another coercive order – the injunction – the issue was complicated by section 21 (1) (a) of the Crown Proceedings Act 1947:

> Where in any proceedings against the Crown any such relief is sought as might in proceedings between subjects be granted by way of injunction or specific performance, the court shall not grant an injunction or make an order for specific performance, but may in lieu thereof make an order declamatory of the rights of the parties.

This was taken to mean what it appears to mean: no injunctions.

In *R v Secretary of State for Transport, ex p Factortame Ltd*[15] the European Court of Justice stated that Community law required the

9 *Taylor v Newham* LBC [1993] 2 All ER 649, CA.
10 [1961] 1 QB 74, [1962] 3 All ER 207.
11 [1971] 3 All ER 938, [1971] 1 WLR 1614.
12 Eg *A-G v Bastow* [1957] 1 All ER 497, [1957] 1 QB 514; *A-G (Egham UDC) v Smith* [1958] 2 QB 173, [1958] 2 All ER 557.
13 *Gouriet v Union of Post Office Workers* [1978] AC 435, [1977] 3 All ER 70.
14 Eg *City of London Corpn v Bovis Construction Ltd* [1992] 3 All ER 697: Noise notice served, criminal proceedings adjourned several times, notice ignored: injunction.
15 [1990] 3 CMLR 867.

national court to set aside any rule of national law which prevented it from granting interim relief which ought otherwise to be available. The House of Lords then held[16] that where European Community rights are involved, the courts have jurisdiction to grant an interim injunction against ministers, (and also to disapply an Act of Parliament).

As far as *domestic* law was concerned, it was thought that the effect of section 31 (2) of the Supreme Court Act 1981 and the new Order 53, rule 3 (10)[17] was to give the court power to grant injunctions against Crown servants. The House of Lords rejected this in another *Factortame* case.[18] But in *M v Home Office*[19] it held that there *is* jurisdiction to make coercive orders, including injunctions, against ministers. (One argument was that section 21, above, applies to 'civil proceedings' and, by section 38 (2) of the same Act civil proceedings do not include proceedings by way of judicial review.)

Interim injunctions

In proceedings for an injunction the plaintiff may as part of the inter-locutory process apply for an interim injunction the purpose of which is to maintain the status quo until the trial of the action, to give protection to the plaintiff. In *American Cyanamid Co v Ethicon Ltd*[20] Lord Diplock, delivering the judgment of the House of Lords, explained the guidelines to be applied. If it is to grant such an injunction the court must be satisfied that the claim is not frivolous or vexatious, in other words, that there is a serious case to be tried. If it is so satisfied the court then has to ask itself whether it is 'just or convenient' to grant the injunction. The availability of damages has to be considered. Their availability to the plaintiff, should he win the trial, will normally preclude the grant of an interim injunction. If that is not so, the court has to consider whether, if an injunction is granted, the defendant, should he win, will be adequately compensated by the payment of damages to him by the plaintiff, (which the plaintiff will normally be required to undertake to pay as a condition of the grant of the interim order). If there is doubt as to the adequacy of the remedy of damages, the court has to consider where the 'balance of convenience' lies, and for that purpose all the relevant factors have to be considered.

The *American Cynamid* case did not involve a public authority. Are the principles any different in such a case? The question was considered in

16 [1990] 2 AC 85, [1989] 2 All ER 692.
17 'Where leave to apply for judicial review is granted then (a) if the relief sought is an order of prohibition or certiorari, the grant shall operate as a stay of the proceedings to which the application relates until the determination of the application or until the court otherwise orders; (b) if any other relief is sought, the court may at any time grant in the proceedings such interim relief as could be granted in an action begun by writ.'
18 [1991] 1 All ER 70.
19 [1993] 3 All ER 547.
20 [1975] AC 396, [1975] 1 All ER 504.

Factortame Case No. 2.[1] Lord Goff said that the question of the availability
of damages is in general irrelevant in cases involving public bodies. (This
is because, on the one hand, there is no general right to indemnity by
reason of damages suffered by an invalid administrative action; and on
the other, an authority acting in the public interest will itself have suffered
no loss remediable by damages.) It thus becomes a question of the 'balance
of convenience' and here the fact that the public authority had duties to
the public is a relevant factor. Thus if what the authority has done is on
the face of it lawful there is a strong case for upholding, at the interlocutory
stage, what it has done and thus refusing to grant an interim injunction.
But facts can be infinitely various, so there can be no *rule* to that effect.
Lord Goff concluded 'Even so, the court should not restrain a public
authority by interim injunction from enforcing an apparently authentic
law unless it is satisfied, having regard to all the circumstances, that the
challenge to the validity of the law is, prima facie, so firmly based as to
justify so exceptional a course being taken'.[2]

When the Crown brings a law enforcement action, in which an injunction is sought to restrain the subject from breaking a law where the
breach would be harmful to the public or a section of it, the court has a
discretion not to require an undertaking in damages from it. Furthermore
that privilege applies to other public authorities, including a local
authority, when exercising a law enforcement function in the public
interest.[3]

The Law Commission has recommended that primary legislation is
desirable to ensure the availability of interim relief against the Crown ie
against ministers in their official capacity and against government
departments in judicial review proceedings. It has also pointed out that
Order 53, rule 3 (10) states that interim relief may be granted where
leave to apply is *granted*. It recommends that it should be made clear
that such relief can be granted before it has been decided whether or not
to grant leave to apply. This would be done only in cases of urgency, for
example homelessness (where a person is about to be evicted) or
immigration (where a person is about to be deported) where any delay
would render any relief pointless.[4]

Locus standi

An action for an injunction may be brought by the Attorney-General for
the protection of the public rights or interests or to restrain a public body
from exceeding its power. The Attorney-General as an officer of the Crown
represents the public, and it is a principle of English law that public rights
can be asserted in a civil action only by him. It follows that a private

1   [1991] 1 All ER 70.
2   Ibid at 120. See *R v Inspectorate of Pollution, ex p Greenpeace Ltd* [1994] 4 All ER 321.
3   *Kirklees Metropolitan Borough Council v Wickes Building Supplies Ltd* [1993] AC 227,
    [1992] 3 All ER 717.
4   Law Com No 226, para 6.13, 6.17.

individual (including a public authority) cannot, in principle, sue for an injunction to restrain a breach of public law.[5] However, that individual will have locus standi where the interference with a public right involves interference with some right of his own (e g where an obstruction is so placed on a highway that the owner of premises abutting on the highway is specially affected by the obstruction interfering with his private right of access from his premises) or where by interference with a public right he suffers some special damage peculiar to himself. In either case he will have suffered an actionable tort. If he cannot bring himself within either of those classes he can go to the Attorney-General and ask him to intervene either *ex officio* – by taking proceedings himself – or by giving him permission to use his name. The latter is known as a relator action. The relator must satisfy the Attorney-General that the action is one which should be brought. The Attorney-General's refusal of consent cannot be reviewed by the court, and if consent is refused the individual will not be able to bring those proceedings in his own name.[6]

The authority principally relied on for the above statements, it will have been noted, is *Gouriet v Union of Post Office Workers*. Notice that the case concerned relator actions, and was not to do with the exercise of governmental powers by a public authority defendant. It follows that the case is of no relevance when an injunction (or a declaration) is sought by way of application for judicial review.[7] The test for locus standi for injunction or declaration sought by that procedure is now 'that the applicant has a sufficient interest in the matter to which the application relates'.[8]

The special position of local authorities must be considered. Section 276 of the Local Government Act 1933 provided that where a local authority deemed it expedient for the promotion or protection of the interests of the inhabitants of the area they might prosecute or defend any legal proceedings. It was held[9] that this did not authorise the institution by a local authority of proceedings for the suppression or prevention of a public nuisance in its own name and without obtaining the concurrence of the Attorney-General, the reason being that the section did not say that a local authority could take proceedings which no private person could take and which were unknown to the law. Section 222 of the Local Government Act 1972 now provides:

5 *Gouriet v Union of Post Office Workers* [1978] AC 435, [1977] 3 All ER 70. For proposal for a Director of Civil Proceedings see Woolf (1986) 130 SJ 762 and [1986] PL, 220 at 236.
6 Ibid. But in the light of the *GCHQ* case, p 53 above, could the court now review the exercise by the Attorney-General of this prerogative power? See Hough (1988) 8 JLS 189.
7 Per Lord Diplock in *IRC v National Federation of Self-Employed and Small Businesses Ltd* [1982] AC 617 at 639, [1981] 2 All ER 93 at 102. See *Barrs v Bethell* [1982] Ch 294, [1982] 1 All ER 106.
8 Supreme Court Act 1981, s 31 (3); p 355 above.
9 *Prestatyn UDC v Prestatyn Raceway Ltd* [1969] 3 All ER 1573, [1970] 1 WLR 33. And see *Hampshire County Council v Shonleigh Nominees Ltd* [1970] 2 All ER 144, [1970] 1 WLR 865.

(1) Where a local authority considers it expedient for the promotion or protection of the interests of the inhabitants of their area—

(a) they may prosecute or defend or appear in any legal proceedings and, in the case of civil proceedings, may institute them in their own name, and

(b) they may, in their own name, make representations in the interests of the inhabitants at any public inquiry held by or on behalf of any Minister or public body under any enactment.

This section, unlike that of the 1933 Act, confers on local authorities a power additional to that of the Attorney-General to enforce obedience to public law. It is therefore open to such an authority[10] to bring civil proceedings to restrain by injunction anticipated criminal offences[11] without resort to the Attorney-General. (The exercise of that power is subject to the control of the courts applying the principles of the *Wednesbury*[12] case.)

In *Gravesham Borough Council v British Railways Board*[13] two local authorities acting under section 222 sought a mandatory injunction ordering the Board to maintain ferry services across the Thames between their two districts. There was no challenge to their locus standi. The Port of London Authority brought a separate action in respect of the same matter. Its locus standi was challenged. Like a private individual seeking to sue in respect of a public nuisance (the ferry being an extension of the highway) it had to show some special damage suffered beyond the general inconvenience suffered by the public. This it was able to show, as the withdrawal of certain ferry sailings would have affected its labour force and involved it in extra costs.

The court's discretion

The grant of an injunction is in the court's discretion,[14] and may be refused on a number of well-established grounds, which the following cases illustrate.

The conduct of the applicant may debar him, as in *Glynn v Keele University*.[15]

An injunction to continue an activity may be refused where the activity can only be carried on at a loss;[16] or where though hardship may be caused by that activity not being carried out, it would be outweighed by the hardship caused to the public authority by being required to carry it out.[17]

10 Cf *London Docklands Development Corpn v Rank Hovis Ltd* (1985) 84 LGR 101. See Hough 'Local authorities as guardians of the public interest' [1992] PL 130.

11 Eg *City of London Corpn v Bovis Construction Ltd* [1992] 3 All ER 717 (interim injunction to restrain Sunday trading); *Westminster City Council v Jones* 80 LGR 24 (planning law 'stop' notice); *Kent County Council v Batchelor* [1978] 3 All ER 980 (tree preservation order).

12 See p 239 above.

13 [1978] Ch 379, [1978] 3 All ER 853.

14 But see *Taylor v Newham LBC* [1993] 2 All ER 649.

15 [1971] 2 All ER 89, [1971] 1 WLR 487. See p 322 above.

16 *A-G v Colchester Corpn* [1955] 2 QB 207, [1955] 2 All ER 124.

17 *Gravesham Borough Council v British Railways Board* [1978] Ch 379, [1978] 3 All ER 853.

In *Pride of Derby and Derbyshire Angling Association Ltd v British Celanese Ltd*[18] an injunction restraining the pollution of rivers was granted against a commercial undertaking, a public corporation and a local authority, Derby Corporation. On appeal Derby argued that the injunction should not apply to them as compliance by them would be dependent in the grant of a loan by central government to improve their sewerage system. The argument was rejected, but the injunction against them was suspended for two years. (This power to suspend is an aspect of the flexibility of this remedy.)

In *Bradbury v Enfield London Borough*[19] it was argued that the grant of an injunction would cause administrative chaos as children had already been allocated to schools. The court doubted this, but said that in any case the bureaucrats had to be kept in order.

As the injunction is in origin an equitable remedy, the applicant may be left to his common law remedy of damages where that is thought to be adequate.[20] It may in general be refused where there is some other alternative remedy. One of the grounds for refusing an injunction in *Gravesham Borough Council v British Railways Board*[1] was that the Board would be liable to an indictment if it failed in its public obligation. We have noted a number of cases where an injunction was granted despite the availability of criminal penalties, where they had proved ineffectual.[2] In *Kent County Council v Batchelor*[3] the council had made tree preservation orders in respect of B's land. It is a criminal offence to contravene such orders. An injunction to prevent breaches of the orders was resisted but Talbot J said that it was not correct to look at the matter as if the council was seeking only to prevent further breaches of the order. It had duties under the legislation to protect areas of natural beauty, and those duties were not fulfilled merely by making tree preservation orders. In any case the council disclaimed any intention to prosecute.

As we have noticed,[4] a statute imposing a duty may provide an administrative procedure for its enforcement. What will the effect of that be on the availability of an injunction? In *Bradbury v Enfield London Borough*[5] one of the grounds for seeking an injunction to prevent a reorganisation of the schools was that they would not come up to the physical standard prescribed by statutory regulations. Section 99 of the Education Act 1944 provides that if the minister is satisfied that any local education authority 'have failed to discharge any duty imposed upon them by ... this Act' he may make an order declaring them to be in default,

---

18 [1953] Ch 149, [1953] 1 All ER 179.
19 [1967] 3 All ER 434, [1967] 1 WLR 1311.
20 This was one of the grounds for refusing an injunction on the application of the Port of London Authority in *Gravesham Borough Council v British Railways Board* [1978] Ch 379, [1978] 3 All ER 853; p 404 above.
1 [1978] Ch 379, [1978] 3 All ER 853.
2 See p 400 above.
3 [1978] 3 All ER 980, [1979] 1 WLR 213; case note by Feldman (1979) 95 LQR 174.
4 See p 108 above.
5 [1967] 3 All ER 434, [1967] 1 WLR 1311.

and give directions which are enforceable by mandamus. This section deprived the complainant of a remedy via the courts, as it also did in *Watt v Kesteven County Council*[6] where the alleged breach was of the duty under section 8 of the Act to make available sufficient schools for their area. However, in *Meade v Haringey London Borough*[7] it was held that the remedy of a complaint under section 99 would not exclude an application to the courts for an injunction (or a declaration) by parents where the failure to perform the section 8 duty is caused by a decision taken ultra vires or by an act of malfeasance, as in that case where sufficient schools were 'available' but the authority closed them because of a dispute with school caretakers. This was not a simple 'failure', said Eveleigh LJ, but positive conduct bringing the system to a halt. (The Secretary of State had in fact been asked to intervene under section 99 but thought the authority was not in breach of its section 8 duty.)

An injunction will not be granted where there is no need for it in the sense that the authority is thought likely to observe the court's ruling without the threat of enforcement.[8]

Declaration

Declaring legal rights

A declaration or declaratory judgment is an order of the court which merely declares what the legal rights of the parties to the proceedings are, and which has no coercive force – it does not require anyone to do anything. It is available in both private and public law situations. It may seem curious that a plaintiff should seek an order which does not carry with it any threat of force should it be disobeyed. However: (a) in many cases in administrative law (and elsewhere) there is no question of the defendant not being prepared to observe the law; the problem is discovering what the law is, rather than securing its observance; (b) though a declaration has no coercive force it may effectively undermine the enforceability of an administrative act. If a decision is declared to be in law a nullity, no legal consequences can flow from it. If for example a contract entered into by a public authority were declared ultra vires it could not be sued on, and an ultra vires condition attached to a licence would not have to be complied with as there would be no legal means of enforcing it; (c) a declaration can be combined with other remedies.

At common law there was no such thing as a judgment which merely declared rights: the action had to be to recover land, damages etc. In Chancery a binding declaration of right could be made but only if some right to relief which the court could grant was established. In 1883 a Rule of the Supreme Court was introduced which empowered the court to make a binding declaration of rights. It was described as 'an innovation of a

6   [1955] 1 QB 408, [1955] 1 All ER 473.
7   [1979] 2 All ER 1016, [1979] 1 WLR 637.
8   Eg *R v Hereford and Worcester Local Education Authority, ex p Jones* [1981] 1 WLR 768.

very important kind'.[9] It is now Order 15, rule 16 of the Rules of the Supreme Court. It provides:

No action or other proceeding shall be open to objection on the ground that a merely declaratory judgment or order is sought thereby, and the Court may make binding declarations of right whether or not any consequential relief is or could be claimed.

The effect of the rule is to give a general power to make a declaration whether or not there is a cause of action at the instance of a party interested in its subject matter.

A leading case is *Dyson v A-G*.[10] The Inland Revenue Commissioners sent Dyson a form requiring him to send them certain information, and a notice of a penalty for failure to do so. He sued the Attorney-General for a declaration that the form was ultra vires. This was held to be the correct procedure, even through Dyson had no cause of action that would have entitled him to any other form of judicial relief; and even though he could have waited until the penalty was imposed and set up by way of defence the invalidity of the notice. The procedure was indeed welcomed. Farwell LJ said,[11] '[T]he convenience in the public interest is all in favour of providing a speedy and easy access to the courts for any of His Majesty's subjects who have any real cause of complaint against the exercise of statutory powers'. Notice that a declaration is available against the Crown.

We have noticed the circumstances in which a declaration is available in judicial review proceedings.[12] A question that has arisen is whether, in the light of the wording of section 31 of the Supreme Court Act 1981 a declaration is available in judicial review even though none of the three prerogative orders is available in the circumstances of the case. It seems that it is. Such a declaration was granted in the *Gillick Case*[13] and in the *Equal Opportunities*[14] case.

When a declaration will be available

The declaration, it is clear, is a wide-ranging remedy. Denning LJ went so far as to say[15] that there is no limit to the power to award a declaration except such limit as the court may impose upon itself. We consider now some cases where a declaration has been made or, if not made, refused on the merits of the claim.

Persons aggrieved by statutory instruments or byelaws and other subordinate legislative instruments have obtained declarations that the

9 By Lindley MR in *Ellis v Duke of Bedford* [1899] 1 Ch 494 at 515.
10 [1911] 1 KB 410; subsequent proceedings [1912] 1 Ch 158; *Guaranty Trust Co of New York v Hannay & Co* [1915] 2 KB 536.
11 At 423.
12 See p 359 above.
13 See p 409 below.
14 See p 409 below.
15 *Barnard v National Dock Labour Board* [1953] 2 QB 18 at 41, [1953] 1 All ER 1113 at 1119.

instruments were ultra vires or at least not binding on them.[16] The illegality of statutory 'guidance' given by a minister has been declared.[17]

The legality of forms issued by public authorities demanding information of the recipient has been challenged.[18] Reports by an official body recommending that a union should be, or should not be, recognised have been challenged by declaration.[19] A declaration has been obtained that the Bank of England was not entitled to deduct tax from dividends payable to the plaintiff[20] and that the revocation of a television licence was unlawful.[21]

The reasonableness of conditions imposed by a planning authority when granting planning permission,[22] or a caravan site licence,[23] or on approving the opening of Sunday cinemas[1] has been questioned by an action for a declaration, as has the validity of an appeal lodged against refusal of planning permission.[2]

A public authority may, by a declaration, get a court ruling on the extent of its disputed powers, as whether it is entitled to place electricity transmission lines over another person's land;[3] and whether its housing policy infringed the race relations legislation.[4] Disputes between public authorities may be usefully resolved by the declaration, for example the legality of electoral arraignments proposed by the Boundaries Commission[5] or of a public inquiry held in connection with local government reorganisation.[6]

The declaration has been used by public employees to determine the legality of action taken towards them by their employers; by schoolteachers to determine whether they are bound to collect money for,[7] or supervise,[8] school meals and by police officers as to the duty of the chief constable to

---

16 Eg *Agricultural, Horticultural and Forestry Industry Training Board v Aylesbury Mushrooms Ltd* [1972] 1 All ER 280, [1972] 1 WLR 190.

17 *Laker Airways Ltd v Department of Trade* [1977] QB 643, [1977] 2 All ER 182, CA.

18 *Dyson v A-G* [1911] 1 KB 410; *Powley v Advisory, Conciliation and Arbitration Service* [1978] ICR 123.

19 *Grunwick Processing Laboratories Ltd v Advisory, Conciliation and Arbitration Service* [1978] AC 655, [1978] 1 All ER 338; *United Kingdom Association of Professional Engineers v Advisory, Conciliation and Arbitration Service* [1981] AC 424, [1980] 1 All ER 612.

20 *Bowles v Bank of England* [1913] 1 Ch 57.

21 *Congreve v Home Office* [1976] QB 629, [1976] 1 All ER 697, CA.

22 *Fawcett Properties Ltd v Buckingham County Council* [1961] AC 636, [1960] 3 All ER 503.

23 *Chertsey UDC v Mixnam's Properties Ltd* [1965] AC 735, [1964] 2 All ER 627,

1 *Associated Provincial Picture House Ltd v Wednesbury Corpn* [1948] 1 KB 223, [1947] 2 All ER 680, CA.

2 *Howard v Secretary of State for the Environment* [1975] QB 235, [1974] 1 All ER 644, CA.

3 *Central Electricity Generating Board v Jennaway* [1959] 3 All ER 409, [1959] 1 WLR 937.

4 *Ealing London Borough v Race Relations Board* [1972] AC 342, [1972] 1 All ER 105.

5 *London Borough of Enfield v Local Government Boundary Commission for England* [1979] 3 All ER 747, HL.

6 *Wednesbury Corpn v Ministry of Housing and Local Government (No 2)* [1966] 2 QB 275, [1965] 3 All ER 571, CA.

7 *Price v Sunderland Corpn* [1956] 3 All ER 153, [1956] 1 WLR 1253.

8 *Gorse v Durham County Council* [1971] 2 All ER 666, [1971] 1 WLR 775.

appoint 'custody officers' at police stations;[9] by police officers,[10] health service employees[11] and dock workers[12] as to whether their dismissal was valid.

In *Gillick v West Norfolk and Wisbech Area Health Authority*[13] the Department of Health and Social Security issued a circular to Authorities containing *advice* to the effect that the law was that a doctor consulted by a girl under 16 would not be acting unlawfully if he prescribed contraceptives for her. The plaintiff sought a declaration that the advice was unlawful. Lord Bridge was concerned with the question whether mere advice such as this was, which bound no one, and was non-statutory, could be subject to judicial review. But he accepted that the effect of an earlier case[14] was that:

if a government department, in a field of administration in which it exercises responsibility, promulgates in a public document, albeit non-statutory in form, advice which is erroneous in law, then the court ... has jurisdiction to correct the error of law by an appropriate declaration.

(The House of Lords did declare the advice to be legal.)[15]

The legality of a leaflet issued by the government explaining the law about a tax was liable to judicial review (but not declared to be unlawful).[16]

In *Equal Opportunities Commission v Secretary of State for Employment*[17] the EOC considered the UK to be in breach of EC law. The minister replied that it was not. EOC sought judicial review of what it called the minister's 'decision' to that effect. The House of Lords did not think the minister's letter was a 'decision'; it merely conveyed his 'view'. However, that did not matter: the question was whether review was available for securing a declaration that UK law was incompatible with EC law; it was available, and it was in breach.

Where a declaration will not be made

Despite the width and flexibility of the declaration, there are some circumstances where it will not be made. In the *first* place the courts are courts of law, so that a declaration will not be available in respect of a matter that is not within the realm of law and legal rights. In *Malone v Metropolitan Police Comr*[18] the plaintiff sought a declaration that the

---

9 *Vince v Chief Constable of the Dorset Police* [1993] 2 All ER 321.
10 *Ridge v Baldwin* [1964] AC 40, [1963] 2 All ER 66.
11 *McClelland v Northern Ireland General Health Services Board* [1957] 2 All ER 129, [1957] 1 WLR 594, HL.
12 *Barnard v National Dock Labour Board* [1953] 2 QB 18, [1953] 1 All ER 1113.
13 [1986] AC 122, [1985] 3 All ER 402.
14 *Royal College of Nursing v Department of Health* [1981] AC 800, [1981] 1 All ER 545.
15 Cf *R v London Waste Regulation Authority, ex p Specialist Waste Management Ltd* – officials advice that licence was needed not amenable to judicial review (1988) Times, 1 November.
16 *R v Secretary of State for the Environment, ex p Greenwich LBC* (1989) Times, 17 May.
17 [1994] 1 All ER 910.
18 [1979] Ch 344, [1979] 2 All ER 620.

tapping of his telephone violated the European Convention for the Protection of Human Rights. The Convention has the status of a treaty and does not have the force of law in England.[19] After analysing Order 15, rule 16 Megarry VC said:

if the proceedings are brought in respect of moral, social or political matters in which no legal or equitable rights arise, the objection to the court deciding such matters remains.

Likewise a declaration cannot be made to prevent the Crown from entering into an international treaty.[20]

In *Cox v Green*[1] it was held that a dispute over professional medical ethics, not involving legal rights, is not a fit subject for inquiry in an action for a declaration.

In *R v Secretary of State for Defence, ex p Sancto*[2] parents of a deceased soldier sought judicial review of the refusal to let them see the report of an inquiry into his death. But they had no legal right to see it, nor had the minister a duty in the matter. The court's assistance was not therefore available in respect of the 'outrageous' decision.

Second, the court will not grant a declaration on a matter which by statute is within the exclusive jurisdiction of another tribunal or other body. In *Barraclough v Brown*[3] the plaintiff had a statutory right to recover in a court of summary jurisdiction certain expenses. The House of Lords said that as the plaintiff's claim arose only under a statute he was confined to the procedure there laid down, and could not seek a declaration from the High Court that, in the particular circumstances which had arisen, he had a right to recover his expenses in the court of summary jurisdiction. That court had by the statute exclusive jurisdiction in the latter. Likewise, where income tax legislation gave the taxpayer the right to apply to tax Commissioners for an adjustment of his liability to tax, that right could not be enforced by any other method: it had no existence apart from the statute which created it.[4] And where an employee could take her claim of discrimination to an industrial tribunal her judicial review proceedings were struck out. (It was in any case a private law claim.)[5]

Contrast *Pyx Granite Co Ltd v Ministry of Housing and Local Government*.[6] Pyx sought a declaration that it was entitled to carry out certain work without planning permission. The minister argued that, in accordance with *Barraclough v Brown*, the court had no jurisdiction to grant a

19 See now Interception of Communications Act 1985.
20 *Blackburn v A-G* [1971] 2 All ER 1380, [1971] 1 WLR 1037, CA.
1 [1966] Ch 216, [1966] 1 All ER 268.
2 (1992) Times, 9 September. Discovery not possible as there was no litigation between the parties.
3 [1897] AC 615.
4 See *Argosam Finance Co Ltd v Oxby* [1965] Ch 390, [1964] 3 All ER 561, CA; and *Jensen v Trinity House of Deptford Corpn* [1982] 2 Lloyd's Rep 14: statutory remedy for complaint of failure to consider applications for pilotage to be pursued.
5 *Equal Opportunities Commission v Secretary of State for Employment* [1994] 1 All ER 910.
6 [1960] AC 260, [1959] 3 All ER 1.

declaration as section 17 of an Act laid it down that if anyone wished it to be determined whether planning permission was necessary for proposed work, he could apply to the local planning authority. But a vital distinction between those two cases, the court said, was that in the earlier the plaintiff's right to recover arose only under the statute, and for that reason he was confined to its procedure. In the *Pyx* case on the other hand the Act restricted the landowner's common law right to deal with his land as he pleased: section 17 was a method that could be used to determine his rights if he chose to do so. 'In its absence (section 17) the right now claimed by the company of going to the court for declaratory relief could hardly have been doubted'. The section provided an alternative but not an exclusive remedy. Viscount Simonds said, 'It is a principle not by any means to be whittled down that the subject's recourse to Her Majesty's courts for the determination of his rights is not to be excluded except by clear words'. No such words were found in *Ealing London Borough Council v Race Relations Board*,[7] where the Board's contention, that the court had no jurisdiction to grant the plaintiff a declaration that it was not unlawfully discriminating against an applicant for housing accommodation, was rejected.

Third, a declaration will not be granted if the effect is to usurp the authority of the body in question. In *Shah v Barnet London Borough Council*[8] B refused S a grant to attend University on the ground that he was not 'ordinarily resident' here. The House of Lords held that B had applied the wrong test for determining that question, and that S was ordinarily resident. What was the appropriate remedy? Certiorari to quash the decision and mandamus to require its reconsideration – not a declaration of S's right to a grant, as that would usurp S's function. It was *its* job to decide, applying the right test, whether S was entitled to a grant.[9]

Fourth, although the person seeking a declaration need have no cause of action, he must be claiming relief. So that if what he is seeking will not relieve him from any real liability, disadvantage or difficulty, a declaration will not be granted.[10] In the following three cases the events had not yet happened: the question raised was hypothetical. In *Re Barnato*[11] a declaration to determine whether, if an advance were to be made from a trust fund, estate duty might in certain circumstances be payable, was refused. The court said that no doubt it would be convenient to the trustee to get such a determination but, if people could go to the court merely because they wanted guidance as to the ordering of their affairs, there would be no end to the litigation that would follow. In *Re Carnarvon Harbour Acts, 1793 to 1903, Thomas v A-G*[12] a Harbour Board wished to

7 [1972] AC 342, [1972] 1 All ER 105.
8 [1983] 2 AC 309, [1983] 1 All ER 226.
9 But see *Barty-King v Ministry of Defence* [1979] 2 All ER 80 where the court granted a declaration not merely that a tribunal's decision was a nullity, but what the decision should have been.
10 *Thorne RDC v Bunting* [1972] Ch 470, [1972] 1 All ER 439.
11 [1949] Ch 258, [1949] 1 All ER 515; *R v Hillingdon London Borough Council, ex p Tinn* [1988] Fam Law 388.
12 [1937] Ch 72.

know what the effect was on certain of its powers under its private Act, of the Settled Land Act 1925. Convenient though it might be to have the question answered the point at issue was not a practical one at that moment: the Board had not purported to exercise the powers in question. In *British Oxygen Co Ltd v Board of Trade*[13] the plaintiff sought a declaration whether in any case where the Board had already approved capital expenditure for grant purposes, it could later change its mind. The High Court granted a declaration that it could not. The Court of Appeal struck out the declaration as being on a hypothetical point.

There are, however, cases where a declaration has been granted in respect of events that have not yet happened, but here the questions needed to be answered for real practical purposes. In *Airedale NHS Trust v Bland*[14] a declaration was granted as to the lawfulness of action which doctors wished to take. The court's ruling would have, and had, immediate practical effect – the patient's death.[15] In *R v British Coal, ex p Price*[16] BC sought a declaration that it would not be in breach of a previous court order if it closed ten mines: this was a live issue – the real fear of contempt proceedings by the union.

Fifth, a declaration may be refused where it is of no practical value.

In *Williams v Home Office (No 2)*[17] the plaintiff sought a declaration that the Home Office had acted ultra vires in setting up a special control unit in which he had been detained. A ground for refusing a declaration was that the unit had been closed and there was no evidence that the Home Office intended to reopen it. In *R v Bromley Licensing Justices, ex p Bromley Licensed Victuallers Association*[18] the court, having clarified the law as to the grant of liquor licenses refused a declaration that the grant in question was unlawful as 'quite pointless': the event in question had already taken place.[19]

Contrast *R v Secretary of State for the Home Department, ex p Ruddock*[20] The applicants sought a declaration that the tapping of their telephones was unlawful. By the time the case came to be heard an Act had made new arrangements under which the courts would have no supervisory role over the interception of communications. But this, said Taylor J, did not make the proceedings merely academic. The acts alleged were subject to judicial scrutiny at the time they were done, and if wrongdoing were proved the court should not refrain from saying so simply because inquiry into any such future allegations could not be dealt with by the court.[1]

13 [1969] 2 Ch 174, [1969] 2 All ER 18; affd [1971] AC 610, [1970] 3 All ER 165.
14 [1993] 1 All ER 821.
15 Note too the *Gillick* and *RCN* cases (p 409 above) where there was a general public interest in having the law clarified.
16 (1993) Times, 28 May.
17 [1981] 1 All ER 1211.
18 [1984] 1 All ER 794, [1984] 1 WLR 585.
19 See to *A-G v Colchester Corpn.* [1955] 2 QB 207, [1955] 2 All ER 124 (ferry had ceased operating: declarations of no value. Likewise *R v North Thames RHA, ex p Daniels* (1993) 19 BMLR 67 medical unit closed.
20 [1987] 2 All ER 518, [1987] 1 WLR 1482.
1　See Laws (1994) 57 MLR 213 for 'hypothetical' and 'academic' questions.

Sixth, what of the declaration in the context of the criminal law? In *Imperial Tobacco Ltd v A-G*[2] criminal proceedings were instituted against the company for breach of the Lotteries Act. Before the charges were tried the company sought a declaration that was lawful. Had the court jurisdiction to grant one, in view of the fact that the case was already before another court? The House of Lords held that while in the light of the *Pyx Granite*[3] case there was jurisdiction to do so, where criminal proceedings were properly instituted and were not vexatious or an abuse of the process of the court, it was not a proper exercise of judicial discretion for a judge in a civil court to grant the defendant in the criminal proceedings a declaration that the facts to be alleged by the prosecution do not prove the offence charged. To make such a declaration would usurp the function of the criminal court; it would not bind that court; and its only practical effect would be to prejudice the criminal trial one way or the other. The question was relevant in *Airdale NHS Trust v Bland*[4] where, however, it was the legality of proposed action that might have been a criminal (or civil) wrong that was in issue. The court granted a declaration that the disconnection of life-sustaining treatment for the defendant was lawful.

Locus standi

Generally the requirement of standing is the same as for injunction. The principles set out in *Gouriet*[5] apply to declarations as to injunctions, but the proceedings in that case were not by way of judicial review. The House of Lords there reversed the Court of Appeal's ruling that the plaintiff could claim a declaration that the trade union would be in breach of the criminal law in embargoing mail to South Africa. A case much relied on by Gouriet was *Dyson v A-G*[6] where (see p 407 above), the plaintiff sought a declaration that the form he was required to complete and the threatened penalty were ultra vires. Now it is true that a large number of people were in the same circumstances as Dyson, but this did not disentitle him to sue for a declaration, for he was not asserting a public right or the existence of public wrong. He was seeking to protect himself. This private right (not to be penalised) was none the less private because the private rights of others were likewise affected. Gouriet, on the other hand, did not claim that any private right of his was affected.

In *Royal College of Nursing of the United Kingdom v Department of Health and Social Security*[7] the DHSS issued a circular advising that nurses committed no offence when participating in the termination of pregnancy by a certain procedure. The RCN sought a declaration that the

2 [1981] AC 718, [1980] 1 All ER 866.
3 See p 411 above.
4 [1993] 1 All ER 821. See Lord Mustill's consideration of the three possible consequences of a declaration.
5 *Gouriet v Union of Post Office Workers* [1978] AC 435, [1977] 3 All ER 70; p403 above.
6 [1911] 1 KB 410.
7 [1981] AC 800, [1981] 1 All ER 545.

advice was wrong. Its main objects are to further nursing as a profession, to raise standards of nursing, and to represent its members' interests. It advises members of the relevant law. The case went to the House of Lords. In the High Court neither party wished to take a point as to the court's jurisdiction but, said Woolf J, questions of locus standi cannot be overcome by consent of the parties. Were not the plaintiffs, as in *Gouriet*, asking the court to declare public rights? This case, said Woolf J, was exceptional 'because of the special responsibilities that the college has in providing not only advice but also insurance for its members, and the relationship between the department and the nurses, many of whom are employed by bodies acting under the supervision of the department' (that is, NHS authorities).[8]

The *RCN* case was referred to in the *Gillick* case (p 409 above). What was Gillick's standing? She had five daughters under 16 (and five other children). She failed to get an assurance from the Authority that they would not act in accordance with the advice in the circular (about contraception) towards her daughters (though it was observed that no one suggested that her daughters would then be likely to seek such advice). Apart from that, there was no reference to the possible difficulty of locus standing in the way of what some of the Law Lords called her 'crusade' (which was unsuccessful).

In *Equal Opportunities Commission v Secretary of State for Employment*[9] a question was whether the EOC had standing. One of its statutory functions is to work towards the elimination of sex discrimination; the matter to which its application related was the compatibility of UK legislation on that topic with EC law. It therefore had 'a sufficient interest'.

In *R v Secretary of State for Foreign Affairs ex p Rees-Mogg*[10] R-M sought a declaration that the UK could not lawfully ratify a Treaty on European Union. There was no dispute as to his standing but the court, referring to the *Smedley* case (p 379 above), accepted the concern of R-M (a former editor of The Times) for constitutional issues.

With regard to local government, the adequacy of standing was not raised in *Prescott v Birmingham Corpn*[11] but the plaintiff was a ratepayer and this seems to give standing on the issue of ultra vires expenditure. As for an authority's own locus, the terms of section 222 of the Local Government Act 1972 should be noted.

There are some cases concerning the standing of competitors. In *Charles Roberts & Co Ltd v British Railways Board*[12] the plaintiff sought a declaration that the Board had no legal authority to make railway tank wagons. Who was the plaintiff? A manufacturer of such wagons. The question of standing was not raised by the parties or the court. In *Wilson,*

---

8 *Imperial Tobacco Ltd v A-G* p 413 above was said to be 'clearly distinguishable'.
9 [1994] 1 All ER 910.
10 [1994] 1 All ER 457. See *R v Foreign Secretary, ex p WDM Ltd* [1995] 1 All ER 611.
11 [1955] Ch 210, [1954] 3 All ER 698; p 244 above. See *R v Hereford Corpn, ex p Harrower*, p 397 above; *R v Greater London Council, ex p Blackburn* p 382 above; *Adams v Metropolitan Police Comr* [1980] RTR 289.
12 [1964] 3 All ER 651, [1965] 1 WLR 396.

Walton International (Offshore Services Ltd) v Tees and Hartlepool Port Authority[13] the defendants sold their dock to the lowest of three bidders. The plaintiff had made a higher bid and sought a declaration that the contract between the defendants and the purchaser was void as contrary to public policy and the defendant's constituent statute. Buckley J found against the plaintiff on the merits but added that even if he had not he would have ruled that it had no locus standi. Its interest as a would-be purchaser was not enough, and the statute in question had not been passed for the protection of the plaintiff or of people buying property from the Authority. The reluctance to intervene at the instance of a would-be purchaser is also illustrated by *Honeywell Information Systems Ltd v Anglian Water Authority*.[14] In *Booth & Co (International) Ltd v National Enterprise Board*[15] the plaintiff thought it was adversely affected by action taken by the NEB in relation to its competitors. It was held that it had no locus standi for a declaration that the Board was in breach of ministerial directions.

Declaration and dismissal from public employment

The courts will not grant a decree of specific performance for breach of a contract of employment. If an employer wrongly dismisses an employee, the employee's remedy is to sue for damages (or to claim statutory compensation): the court will not order the employer to reinstate him.[16] A declaration that a dismissal was wrongful will not normally be given: damages is an adequate remedy, and insofar as a declaration is tantamount to reinstatement, to grant it might be equivalent to specific performance. But in the field of public employment there is an additional factor: public authorities must keep within the limits of their statutory powers. The leading case is *Vine v National Dock Labour Board*.[17] Vine was wrongly removed from the register of dock workers. The Court of Appeal awarded damages but refused a declaration (the practical effect of which would be that the Board would be required to reinstate him) for reasons given above. However, the House of Lords granted the declaration as well as damages. This was not an ordinary master and servant case. Vine was employed under a statutory scheme. The defendant, a statutory body, acted ultra vires (see p 207 above). In the ordinary master and servant situation a dismissal, though wrongful, is effective, whereas Vine's name had never, in law, been removed from the register. A further consideration was that

---

13 [1969] 1 Lloyd's Rep 120. See also *A-G v Crayford UDC* [1962] Ch 575, [1962] 2 All ER 147 (p201 above) where the bringing of the action was now described as 'curious' and 'odd'.
14 (1976) Times, 30 June. The plaintiff's locus standi was as a water-rate payer.
15 [1978] 3 All ER 624.
16 Statutes giving power to order reinstatement included the Checkweighing in Various Industries Act 1919, now repealed, the Reserve Forces (Safeguard of Employment) Act 1985.
17 [1957] AC 488, [1956] 3 All ER 939.

if a declaration was not granted Vine would have been disabled from getting work on the docks as only those on the register could get work.[18] Damages was not an adequate remedy.

In *McClelland v Northern Ireland General Health Services Board*[19] the plaintiff was employed as a senior clerk by the defendant statutory board on the terms of a scheme contained in a statutory instrument. She was dismissed for reasons which the instrument did not countenance (redundancy). The House of Lords declared that her service had not been validly terminated. The question of damages as an adequate remedy was not referred to. *Vine* was not referred to. The description of the post as 'permanent' was another factor in the decision.

A declaration of the invalidity of a dismissal has been made where a local authority empowered by statute to dismiss for educational reasons only, was found to have dismissed for reasons of economy: it had used its power for an improper purpose.[20]

A declaration of the invalidity of a dismissal may be made where the authority has failed to observe the rules of natural justice, where it can be shown that they apply. *Ridge v Baldwin*[1] was such a case, as was *Cooper v Wilson*.[2] In *Palmer v Inverness Hospitals Board*[3] P, a doctor, was dismissed. The ministry had issued a circular to hospital authorities setting out the procedure they should follow in such cases. The court held that this was incorporated into P's contract of employment. The procedure had not been followed and P's dismissal was annulled. In *Malloch v Aberdeen Corpn*[4] a teacher's dismissal was quashed. (In *Vidyodaya University of Ceylon v Silva*[5] the court did not intervene in the dismissal of a professor, but the question there was complicated by the fact that it was a certiorari that was applied for.)

Cases inconsistent with the above must be noticed. In *Barber v Manchester Regional Hospital Board*[6] B was employed as a doctor by the Board. He was entitled, before being dismissed, to the protection of a procedure which involved putting his case before the minister. This was not done. B was granted a declaration that the *minister* had been in breach of his duty. But the court held that B's relationship with his employer – the Board – was that of an ordinary master-servant contract despite what it called its 'strong statutory flavour'. B was not therefore granted a declaration as against them that his contract had never been validly terminated, but he was awarded damages. (Contrast the treatment accorded to the clerk in *McClelland*, above.)

---

18 The dockworkers did not, note, work for the Board, but for individual employers: the Board kept the register. The dock labour scheme has now been abolished.
19 [1957] 2 All ER 129, [1957] 1 WLR 594, HL.
20 *Sadler v Sheffield Corpn* [1924] 1 Ch 483.
1   [1964] AC 40, [1963] 2 All ER 66; p 283 above.
2   [1937] 2 KB 309, [1937] 2 All ER 726; p 296 above.
3   1963 SC 311.
4   [1971] 2 All ER 1278, [1971] 1 WLR 1578, HL; p 312 above.
5   [1964] 3 All ER 865, [1965] 1 WLR 77.
6   [1958] 1 All ER 322, [1958] 1 WLR 181.

In *Francis v Municipal Councillors of Kuala Lumpur*[7] Francis was employed as a clerk by the local authority. He was dismissed by a body not empowered by statute to do so. He sought a declaration that his dismissal was ultra vires and that he therefore continued in their employment. *Vine* was relied on. But the very special circumstances of that case did not apply here, an ordinary master-servant relationship. Even if it was possible to say that Francis' service was 'statutory' it was not the case that in the absence of a declaration he would be disabled from getting work as a clerk. Damages were adequate: if a declaration were granted he would have a claim to compensation far in excess of the amount by way of damages.[8]

The problem of the appropriate remedy in case of unlawful dismissal is well illustrated in *Chief Constable of the North Wales Police v Evans*.[9] The Chief Constable, C, told Evans, E, a probationary constable, that he could resign or be dismissed. He resigned. C's action was grossly unfair and unlawful. E sought certiorari to quash the decision which induced his resignation, mandamus to require reinstatement, and a declaration that C's decision was unlawful and void. The High Court declined to grant any remedy except costs. The Court of Appeal granted a declaration that the decision was a nullity. But, said the House of Lords, where did that leave the parties? Did it mean that E was to be treated as if he had for the four years since the void decision been in the employ of the police force, as if he had successfully completed his probationary period and was now an established constable with rights to pension and pay etc? From E's point of view, mandamus was the only satisfactory remedy. But it was unusual to grant it in an employment case, since to do so might 'border on usurping' C's power (which, be it noted, he had abused). The outcome was a declaration that by reason of the unlawfully induced resignation, E became entitled to the same rights and remedies, not including reinstatement, as he would have had if his services had been unlawfully dispensed with. This would clarify E's position, and leave him free to pursue appropriate remedies – in particular, of course, money. E could have, but had not, claimed damages in his Order 53 application. It might, it seems, have been open to him to apply to amend his statement by adding such a claim. C's counsel told the House of Lords that if the case went in E's favour, it would offer him monetary compensation. Their Lordships hoped it would be on a generous scale; and that if E applied to re-join the North Wales police his application would be given very serious consideration.

---

7 [1962] 3 All ER 633, [1962] 1 WLR 1411.
8 For an unsuccessful attempt to extend administrative law principles to an ordinary contractual relationship see *Gunion v London Borough of Richmond-upon-Thames* [1981] Ch 448, [1980] 3 All ER 577.
9 [1982] 3 All ER 141, [1982] 1 WLR 1155.

Judicial review and administration

In 1949 a total of 34 applications were made for orders of certiorari, mandamus and prohibition of which 11 were granted. In 1969, there were 184 applications, of which 55 were granted. As we have noted, the procedure for obtaining a judicial review was amended in 1977, and again in 1980. In 1980, 356 applications were received; in 1988 over a thousand in 1993, 2886 and in 1994 slightly more.[10] (An average 30 per cent are refused.) The increase is obvious. Even so, it may be said that the number of cases is very small compared with the literally countless decisions taken by public authorities that might be susceptible to judicial review but this is true of other areas of law – how many contracts are made daily, and how many actions for breach of contract are there? In any event the importance of judicial decisions cannot be measured by the number of cases alone.

The *respondents* to the applications for leave cover a wide range of public bodies but are principally from central government. Of these a high proportion concern immigration. In 1993 there were 668 applications in that area. Another major area, involving local government, is homelessness – 447 cases in that year.

The following have been suggested as the causes of the *general* increase in applications – more intensive state control, increased awareness of practitioners of the potential of judicial review, the availability of legal aid and law centres, and of suitable textbooks. Alongside these also the judicial strategy which resulted in the old prerogative writs growing into a system of law for controlling the administration.[11]

Why is it that a *particular* area of public administration attracts, at any one time, a significant amount of judicial review? Relevant considerations may be: (a) the quality of the decision-making, where perhaps the challengeable decisions are taken at a fairly low level in the administration; (b) that the stakes are high for the applicant; (c) the existence of an organisation which provides advice or financial assistance for applicants; (d) that the legislation is complex and/or controversial; and (e) where one case shows that decisions previously thought to be beyond the reach of judicial review are not, leading to a spurt of applications. As for homelessness, a very relevant factor is that there is no appeal from an adverse decision – judicial review is the only remedy. Leave is granted in 40% of such cases. The Law Commission agrees that the figures 'raise serious questions about the standard of decision-making in that area'. It recommends a right of appeal to a court or tribunal.

What is the effect of judicial review? In a particular case the mere application may produce a result favourable to the applicant. There is a high rate of settlement or withdrawal between the grant of leave and the substantive hearing; this may be due to the fact that grant of leave and service of notice of motion prompts many respondents to reconsider the decision. If the case proceeds the respondent may concede its error and

10 These figures and those given below are taken from Law Com No 226.
11 Sedley 'Where Next?' in *Public Interest Law* ed Cooper & Dhavan, at p 415.

submit to judgment. The quashing of a decision, or a direction that it be reconsidered, may or may not result in the applicant obtaining what he wants.

A court decision may have important implications, for good or ill, in a particular area of administration. The Report of the Committee on the Prison Disciplinary System said:[12]

We would observe there that the *St Germain* case[13] can be seen as a major turning point, not only in that it brought board of visitors' proceedings under judicial review, but also in the radical change which took place in the view taken of the place of boards of visitors within the disciplinary process and in their relationship to prison management.

In its evidence to the Committee the Home Office observed that the 'court's continuing intervention is having a cumulative impact both on the hearings themselves and on the confidence of board members ... [It has] imported a previously unfamiliar degree of formality and legalism into adjudications'. The evidence went on to say that the introduction of legal representation 'represents potentially the most significant and far reaching of the decisions which the court has yet made in this field ... There is no doubt that many boards have viewed the introduction of lawyers with considerable misgiving'.[14]

The impact of the House of Lords' decision in the *Fare's Fair* case[15] has been particularly studied. The interpretation of the statutory provisions adopted by the House of Lords in that case was, it appears, so contrary to the understanding of those working under the Act that the decision had the effect of creating caution and uncertainty about all the powers on which the GLC relied (and of course affected other authorities as well). More generally, the climate of litigation in central/local government relations during the last decade has influenced the organisation and process of decision-making in local authorities.[16]

Planning is an area that has long been subject to judicial scrutiny at the instance primarily of disappointed would-be developers. One administrator working in this field reported:

The Department is swift to act on court decisions. A law student who worked with me for a time said he was amazed to find how conscious we were of the powers of the courts when so few of our cases were actually challenged. This is true, for we must behave as though every decision is going to be challenged even though only a handful of cases are.[17]

The Framework Document of the Planning Inspectorate Agency[18] states that one of the main performance measures of the Agency is the number of cases lost in the High Court.

12 Cmnd 9461–II Appendix 14, para 15.
13 See p 339 above.
14 Cmnd 9641-II Appendix 5, para 4.
15 See p 200 above.
16 L Bridge et al *Legality and Local Politics*.
17 Payne, 'Planning Appeals' (1971) 57 JTPI 114.
18 See p 125 above.

A significant number of judicial review cases in a particular area may cause the government to realise that there are defects there and to change the arrangements, as in the case of Special Educational Needs Tribunals.[19]

In some areas, the effect of court rulings can be conveniently made known to the relevant decision-makers. In the case of prison administration the Home Office circulated to Prison Boards of Visitors' chairmen in 1982 a summary of the *Tarrant* judgment. In the Immigration Department of the Home Office there is, we are told,[20] an appreciation of the need to amend staff instructions whenever changes in the law make existing instructions obsolete, and of the need to make case workers more aware of the significance for their work of the principles of judicial review. In planning, considerable resources are spent on the continuing training of inspectors: this will doubtless include information about the effect of judicial decisions.

In these areas there is a direct structural administrative link with the decision-making bodies and persons. This may not always be so, as in the case of education appeal committees. The procedure to be followed by them was indicated by the court in *R v South Glamorgan Appeals Committee, ex p Evans*, but the case has not been reported. The Council on Tribunals has sought to ensure that its effect is observed.[1]

It should be appreciated that ministers and those who serve them see government as a political process, and are primarily concerned with the political consequences of what they do. Judicial review of administrative action is 'sporadic and peripheral'[2] or 'casual and almost accidental'.[3] Administrators doubtless see it in that light, as peripheral or marginal to their main concern. Within the limits of their policies (which may or may not be fair) they are concerned with the fairness of the system of administration (because it is not politically wise to be thought to be unfair), and insofar as the courts are likewise concerned with fairness in administration (and insofar as they both mean the same thing by fairness) they may be thought to agree with the Master of the Rolls[4] that the courts and the administration are partners with a common aim, namely the maintenance of the highest standards of public administration.

A potential disadvantage of judicial review is that the fear of it may stultify the administration. There is a balance to be struck here. On the one hand the administrator should be aware or made aware of the possible legal consequences of what he is doing (as by making a statement that could later be construed by a court as raising a legitimate expectation in the mind of the recipient, to the disadvantage of the administration) but he should not on the other hand be encouraged always to seek legal advice before taking decisions, as this would make administration slower and more costly. A fear of judicial intervention is perhaps suggested by the

19 See p 152 above.
20 D Seymour, in a paper to the Administrative Law Bar Association, October 1987.
1   See Annual Report for 1987–88 para 2.38. For those Committees see p 152 above.
2   De Smith *Judicial Review of Administrative Action*, p 1.
3   W I Jennings *Principles of Local Government Law* (4th edn) p 237.
4   In *R v Lancashire County Council, ex p Huddlestone* [1986] 2 All ER 941.

title of a pamphlet prepared by the Treasury Solicitor and made available to departments – 'The judge over your shoulder' – with its implication that he is 'breathing down your neck'.[5]

A former Treasury Solicitor said in 1986[6] that changes in the scope and rules of administrative law over the previous 25 years had 'less effect than might have been expected on the course of administration', though he notes two changes: the degree of certainty in the rightness of advice and decision-taking is less than it was; and there is a more general feeling that law will apply to many unexpected aspects of decision-taking, and that at any time it may trip up the unwary. A result has been 'an acceptance that law has a pervasive role to play in administration even if that role is generally seen as rather uncertain in its impact and aimed particularly at blatant error and anomaly'. It seems that lately greater attention is being paid in the training of civil servants to the impact of judicial review.[7]

What is said in the above paragraphs is relevant to the question of the control of government by administrative law, of which judicial review is seen by some as the primary mechanism. Some take the view that the purpose of administrative law is to 'control' government. Griffith and Street noted the ambiguity of the word. 'Banks control a river; a driver controls a car.'[8] Clearly quite different ideas; the car will not go at all unless the driver takes some action, whereas the water will go somewhere, the question being whether it can be contained within certain limits, natural or man-made. Dunsite[9] has suggested that control 'means limitation of excess, or correction of deviation, or the capacity to change the world-as-it-is, in some particular manner, into the world-as-you-would-have-it-to-be'. So therefore one body is 'in control of' another if it has sufficient understanding of the latter's principles of action, and sufficient power, to achieve that limitation, that correction or that change.

'Limitation of excess' immediately suggests the role of the ultra vires doctrine and in this sense the courts can 'control' the administration in that after the act has been done the court says whether or not it was lawful. If by 'control' we mean causing the act not to be taken in the first place, the courts will 'control' action only if the principles and rules they apply are known to (and observed by) the administration and provide adequate guidance in the particular case.[10] Furthermore the courts' 'control', whether *pre* or *post* that event, does not stop the government acquiring through statute what might be regarded as an excess of power,

---

5 One of the arguments used against the introduction of an Ombudsman also – ch 16 below.
6 Kerry, 'Administrative Law and Judicial Review' (1986) 64 Pub. Admin 163.
7 See *Review of Governmental Legal Services*, 1989, Cabinet Office, para 9.6.
8 *Principles of Administrative Law* (1st edn) p 24. See also Rawlings 'Judicial Review and the "control of government" ' (1986) 64 Pub Admin 135. And Gregory 'Parliamentary Control and the Use of English' (1990) 43 Parly Affairs 59. Vickers contrasted instruments for *altering* the car's behaviour with those for telling us *how it is* behaving: both are needed – in administrative law terms reports, accounts, statistics etc, information and assessment: vol 30 Pub Admin 71 at 79.
9 'Administrative law and control over government' (1984) 26 Mal LR.
10 See unpublished Ph D (Wales) thesis by D A Obadina.

or retrospectively validating that which was held to be invalid. As to whether or not the courts 'control' the administration in the sense of changing the world-as-it-is, the above paragraphs can again be referred to.

Administrative law does not consist only of judicial review. The totality of its devices and of its institutions – the Ombudsmen, the various state auditors, the Council on Tribunals, etc – must be considered in asking whether there is that proper balance between the necessary grant of public power and checks on its exercise that each of us may individually desire. And finally, administrative law exists in its constitutional and political setting. We may take the view that our greatest concerns – as of ministers and administrators – are in the broad sense political, not legal.[11]

11 Sunkin & Le Sueur 'Can government control judicial review' (1991) 44 CLP 161 is of interest.

Chapter 12

Statutory appeals and applications

In the previous chapter we considered judicial review of administrative action by way of certiorari etc, which is achieved by way of an application for judicial review which is of course concerned with the legality of the decision challenged.

In contrast with judicial review, statute not infrequently provides for an *appeal* to a court from specified decisions; or permits an *application* to be made to the court to *quash* specified decisions.

Statutory appeals

There is a large number of cases where statute provides for an appeal to be made from an administrative authority (particularly a local authority) to a court, just as there are appeals to tribunals. And as in the case of tribunals, we must know against precisely what the appeal lies, the ground on which it can be brought, and the role and power of the court in determining it. Here are two examples from the many that could be chosen.

If a local authority refuses the licence necessary for erecting scaffolding on a highway or issues a licence containing terms to which the applicant objects, the applicant may appeal to a *magistrates' court* against the refusal or the terms. In the case of appeal against refusal, the court may direct the authority to issue the licence. In an appeal against the terms, the court may alter the terms.[1]

A local authority may serve a notice on a person requiring him to provide sanitary appliances at a place of entertainment.[2] The person on whom a notice is served may appeal to the *county court* against the notice on one or both of these grounds: (i) that a requirement of the notice is unreasonable; (ii) that it would have been fairer to serve the notice on another person who is an owner or occupier of the relevant place in question (in which case the other person is to be made a respondent to the appeal). On

1 Highways Act 1980, s 169.
2 Local Government (Miscellaneous Provisions) Act 1976, s 20.

an appeal the court shall either quash the notice or dismiss the appeal or, where a ground of appeal is (ii) above, may modify the notice so that its requirements are imposed on another person or order that the appellant be entitled to recover from such other person part of the expenses incurred by the appellant in complying with the notice.

Further examples, raising the questions of the *nature* of the appeal, the *role* of the court, and the *suitability* of the appeal being heard by a court are as follows. In *Sagnata Investments Ltd v Norwich Corpn*[3] the plaintiffs' application for a permit to provide an amusement arcade was refused by the local authority on the ground (inter alia) that it would be likely to have undesirable effects on young people, and they appealed to Quarter Sessions (now the Crown Court). The Recorder allowed the appeal (although the elected local authority had decided by 41 votes to one that they did not want amusement arcades in Norwich). The Court of Appeal held (Lord Denning dissenting) that the Recorder had been right to regard the appeal as a complete rehearing, to reconsider all the evidence, hear fresh evidence, and on that basis come to his own conclusion. If it were otherwise, said the court, the provision for appeal would be illusory since the Recorder, being confined to the bare knowledge that the local authority had refused the application and their written grounds for refusal, would be powerless to make an effective examination of those reasons. However, although the appeal was by way of rehearing, the court in considering that appeal had to pay proper regard to the decision of the authority and could not exercise its discretion uninfluenced by the local authority's opinion. It may seem inappropriate that a decision of this nature, given to an elected body, should be overridden by a court of law. However, there is a long history of control of local government bodies by such appeals, inappropriate though they may now seem to be.

Under the General Rate Act, a person who 'is aggrieved by any neglect, act or thing done or omitted by the rating authority may appeal ... to the Crown Court'. The ratepayers applied unsuccessfully for remission of their rates and appealed to the Crown Court, which said it had no jurisdiction to hear an appeal against the non-exercise of the authority's discretion. On appeal[4] it was argued (in an attempt to limit the wide effect of the section in question) that the Crown Court was an inappropriate body for hearing appeals on matters essentially of administrative discretion; that the rating authority was the only body which had the necessary knowledge to make informed decisions, and that in any event any decision that is capricious etc can be challenged by judicial review. In the House of Lords Lord Oliver, with whom the other judges agreed, said;

I can readily see that a rehearing in a Crown Court by a judge and two or more magistrates ... of the rating authority's decision, taken in the light of all the local factors which the rating authority is likely to be in the best position to assess, is something which may be attended by a good deal of delay and administrative

---

3 [1971] 2 QB 614, [1971] 2 All ER 1441, CA. Case note by Prophet [1971] PL 162.
4 *Investors in Industry Commercial Properties Ltd v Norwich City Council* [1986] AC 822, [1986] 2 All ER 193.

inconvenience if such appeals come to be regularly pursued. Nevertheless, from the earliest times, the legislation has conferred on ratepayers the very widest right to appeal which Parliament, in enacting the consolidating legislation, has not thought fit to confine or restrict except to the extent expressly mentioned. The imposition of further restriction is a matter for Parliament.

Where the local government auditor finds that a loss has been incurred by the wilful misconduct of any person, he is to certify that the amount of the loss is due from that person. A person aggrieved by that decision may 'appeal against the decision to the court' and the court may 'confirm, vary or quash the decision or give any certificate that the auditor could have given'. In *Lloyd v McMahon*[5] the question arose as to the court's role. Lord Bridge said:

The language describing the court's powers could not possibly be any wider. Procedurally there is nothing ... to limit in any way the evidence which may be put before the court on either side.

Lord Keith:

It would be quite unreasonable and not in accordance with the intendment of the enactment, to hold that the court, where [as here] an issue is raised as to the fairness of the procedure adopted by the auditor, is confined to a judicial review species of jurisdiction so as to have power to quash or affirm the auditor's certificate without entering on its own examination of the merits of the case.

Thus it was, in this case, entirely proper, the House of Lords said, for the court to reconsider the councillor's behaviour and decide for itself whether it amounted to wilful misconduct: it was not confined merely to considering whether the auditor had made an error law, and if he had, quashing his decision.

Applications to quash

An important and widely used statutory provision is that which permits a decision, order etc to be challenged in the courts within a specified *time* on specified *grounds* and by specific *procedure*. Such a procedure is found for example in the important Acquisition of Land Act 1981 consolidating earlier legislation. That Act provides that if a person aggrieved by a compulsory purchase order made under the Act desires to question its validity on the ground: (i) that its authorisation is not empowered to be granted under the Act,[6] or (ii) that any relevant requirement of the Act has not been complied with,[7] he may apply to the High Court within six weeks for it to be quashed. The six weeks runs from the date on which notice of the making or confirmation of the order is first published. The

---

5 [1987] AC 625, [1987] 1 All ER 1118.
6 Eg *Hazeldine v Minister of Housing and Local Government* [1959] 3 All ER 693, [1959] 1 WLR 1155.
7 Eg *Brown v Minister of Housing and Local Government* [1953] 2 All ER 1385, [1953] 1 WLR 1370.

court may quash the order if satisfied that –

(a) the authorisation granted by the compulsory purchase order is not empowered to be granted ... or (b) the interests of the applicant have been substantially prejudiced by any relevant requirement of the [Act] not having been complied with ...

In addition, when an application to quash is made to the court, the court may suspend the operation of the order until the final determination of the application.

The Act goes on to say that apart from the procedure referred to – application to the High Court within six weeks – a compulsory purchase order made under its provisions 'shall not ... be questioned in any legal proceedings whatsoever'.[8]

The meaning of that provision was considered by the House of Lords in *Smith v East Elloe RDC*.[9] The council made a compulsory purchase order of Smith's land. More than five years later Smith sued the council (and others) claiming (amongst other things) that the order was made and confirmed in bad faith, and was therefore invalid. As the six weeks' limit had long expired, application to quash could not be made under the 1946 Act. Smith therefore sought a declaration. The defendants applied to have the writ set aside on the ground that under the 1946 Act it was now too late to question the order. In face of the apparently impregnable provision that the order could 'not be questioned in any legal proceedings whatsoever' Smith argued that an order made in bad faith is not a valid order at all, and that there was no need for Parliament to refer in the Act to bad faith as a ground of invalidity as it is always assumed that statutory powers must be exercised in good faith. A majority of the House of Lords held that the wording in question was a plain prohibition against the court exercising any jurisdiction in the matter, and that therefore the writ should be set aside. Some of their Lordships thought that an order could not be set aside on the ground of bad faith even if an application was made within the six weeks' period, as that is not a specified ground of challenge.[10]

Statutory exclusion of the court

In *Smith v East Elloe RDC*, and analagous provisions, the oversight of the court is not excluded – provided the short time limit for invoking its jurisdiction is observed.

There are other devices by which the government, through Parliament, can seek to limit or exclude the court's oversight of administrative decisions.

8 Sections 23–25. Similar provisions will be found in other statutes, eg Housing Act 1985, Sch 22, para 7. See *R v Cornwall County Council, ex p Huntington* [1994] 1 All ER 694: no judicial review before order made. Transport and Works Act 1992, s 22 (3) – order not to be questioned before or after made. For the origin of this '6-weeks procedure', dating from 1930, see Robson *Justice and Administrative Law*, p 485, and Willis, *Parliamentary Powers of English Government Departments*, p 138. Current legislation prefers '42 days'.
9 [1956] AC 736, [1956] 1 All ER 855.
10 Smith later unsuccessfully sued the clerk to the council; see p 494 below.

– An Act may provide that a regulation or order made under it 'shall have effect as if enacted in this Act'. This might appear to elevate the regulation or order to the status of an Act. The effect of such a clause was considered in *Minister of Health v R, ex p Yaffe.*[11] The Committee on Ministers' Powers said of the decision: 'The House [of Lords] laid it down that while the provision makes the order speak as if it were contained in the Act, the Act in which it is contained is the Act which empowers the making of the order, and that therefore if the order as made conflicts with the Act it will have to give way to the Act'.[12]

– A clause may provide that confirmation of an order by a minister 'shall be conclusive evidence'[13] that the requirements of the Act under which the order is made have been complied with. The Committee on Ministers' Powers thought it 'plain that the protection afforded by this clause is not limitless ...'[14]

– Another exclusionary clause is one which says that the decision of a minister, tribunal or other body is 'final'. It means that the decision is final in that there is no appeal, is final on the facts, but it does not exclude *review.*[15]

– An Act may provide that a decision 'shall not be questioned in any legal proceedings whatsoever', or 'shall not be called in question in any court of law' without the benefit, be it noted, of a six-week, (or any other) period (as in *Smith v East Elloe RDC*) in which to do so. Such an exclusionary clause was in issue in *Anisminic Ltd v Foreign Compensation Comm-ission.*[16] The Egyptian government paid a sum of money to the UK government to meet claims in respect of loss caused by its sequestration of British property. It was the Commission's job to determine claims made against that sum. An Order in Council required the Commission to treat a claim as established if a claimant satisfied it of certain matters. The matters in issue in this case related to Anisminic's nationality. The Commission took the view that Anisminic had not made out its case. Its reason was that the Order in Council required Anisminic to satisfy it not only that it was British (which it was) but also that its 'successor in title' was (which it was not). Anisminic sought a number of declarations concerning its claim.

---

11 [1931] AC 494.
12 Cmd 4060, p 40. For the contrary case see National Insurance Act 1965, s 116(2) providing that regulations reproduced in the Act were to be reviewable as though they were only regulations.
13 *Ex p Ringer* (1909) 25 TLR 718.
14 Cmd 4060, pp 40, 41. See *R v Registrar of Companies, ex p Central Bank of India* [1986] QB 1114, [1986] 1 All ER 105 for such a clause. (For matters as to which the certificate in question is now conclusive see Companies Act 1989, s 94.) Many exclusionary provisions have recently been repealed, for example an 'as if enacted' clause in s 2(4) of the Emergency Powers Act 1920 and in s 10 of the Light Railways Act 1896, but the 'conclusive evidence' clause in that latter section remains. An 'and have effect as an Act of Parliament' clause in the Fishery Harbours Act 1915 (see 2(3)(i)) was also repealed – Statute Law (Repeals) Act 1986, Sch 1, Pt XII.
15 *R v Medical Appeal Tribunal, ex p Gilmore* [1957] 1 QB 574, [1957] 1 All ER 796.
16 [1969] 2 AC 147, [1969] 1 All ER 208. For the Commission see p 138 above.

The House of Lords held, by a majority, that the Commission had misinterpreted the Order in Council, in that Anisminic did not have to satisfy it that its successor in title was British, that therefore when the Commission rejected Anisminic's claim it based its decision on a matter which it had no right to take into account , or, made an inquiry which the order did not empower it to make, and that the Commission's decision was therefore a nullity.

But what of section 4 (4) of the Foreign Compensation Act, which provides that a determination by the Commission 'shall not be called in question' in any court of law (the reason for this was the need to avoid delay in the distribution of compensation). Did not this debar the courts from considering Anisminic's claim? Lord Reid summed up the arguments this way:

The Commission maintain that these are plain words [of section 4 (4))] only capable of having one meaning. Here is a determination which is apparently valid; there is nothing on the face of the document to cast any doubt on its validity. If it is a nullity that could only be established by raising some kind of proceedings in court. But that would be calling the determination in question, and that is expressly prohibited by the statute. [Anisminic] maintain that that is not the meaning of the words in this provision. They say that 'determination' means a real determination and does not include an apparent or purported determination which in the eyes of the law has no existence because it is a nullity. Or, putting it another way, if one seeks to show that the determination is a nullity one is not questioning the purported determination – one is maintaining that it does not exist as a determination.

The House of Lords accepted Anisminic's argument (which has the look of 'a conjuring trick to please a lawyer').[17] Now there was no doubt that the Commission had jurisdiction to hear the claim made to it by Anisminic: it was entitled to enter on the inquiry in question. And it is certainly the case that a decision on a matter one is not entitled to inquire into is a nullity as having been arrived at without jurisdiction. How then could it be said in this case that the Commission's decision was a nullity, as it could enter on the inquiry in question and thus had jurisdiction? For the very important reason that there are other matters which will deprive a body of jurisdiction and render its decision a nullity. Thus Lord Reid said:

There are many cases where although the tribunal had jurisdiction to enter on the inquiry, it has done or failed to do something in the course of the inquiry which is of such a nature that its decision is a nullity. It may have given its decision in bad faith. It may have made a decision which it had no power to make. It may have failed in the course of the inquiry to comply with the requirements of natural justice. It may in perfect good faith have misconstrued the provisions giving it power to act so that it failed to deal with the question remitted to it. It may have refused to take into account something which it was required to take into account. Or it may have based its decision on some matter which, under the provisions setting it up, it had no right to take into account. I do

17 The phrase, though not with reference to this case, is in C H Sisson, *The Spirit of British Administration*, p 54.

not intend this to be exhaustive. But if it decides a question remitted to it without committing any of those errors, it is as much entitled to decide that question wrongly as it is to decide it rightly.

Thus a very expansive view is taken of errors which deprive of jurisdiction and make the decision ultra vires and void. In *Re Racal Communications Ltd*[18] Lord Diplock said that the 'breakthrough' made by *Anisminic* was that:

as respects administrative tribunals and authorities, the old distinction between errors of law that went to jurisdiction and errors of law that did not was for practical purposes abolished. Any error of law that could be shown to have been made by them in the course of reaching their decision on matters of fact or of administrative policy would result in their having asked themselves the wrong question with the result that the decision they reached would be a nullity.

Notice the opening phrase of that quotation – 'as respects administrative tribunals and authorities.' Now in *Pearlman v Keepers and Governors of Harrow School*[19] statute said that the decision of a county *court* (that the installation of a central heating system was a 'structural alteration') was 'final and conclusive'. The majority of the Court of Appeal held that the county court judge had misconstrued the meaning of 'structural alteration', that this constituted an error of law which deprived the court of jurisdiction. Geoffrey Lane LJ dissented, saying, with reference to what Lord Reid said in *Anisminic*, that while the ambit of excess of jurisdiction is very wide, he could see no way in which the judge had contravened any of the precepts laid down by Lord Reid, or in any way gone outside his terms of reference: he considered the matter he was required to consider, and did not embark on any unauthorised extraneous or irrelevant exercise. In *Re Racal Communications Ltd* the House of Lords approved the dissenting judgment of Geoffrey Lane LJ. In the case of 'administrative tribunals and authorities' it was, said Lord Diplock, to be presumed that Parliament did not intend to give them power to determine questions of law conclusively but no such presumption was to be made in the case of an inferior court of law whose decision was made 'final and conclusive' by statute (as was the case in *Pearlman*). Likewise in *Re Racal* statute said that the High Court judge's decision 'shall not be appealable'. Statute clearly prohibited an appeal, the House of Lords said, reversing the unanimous view of the court below that the judge made an error of law which made him refuse jurisdiction (to make an order) when he ought to have exercised it.

Where *Anisminic* applies it looks as though Parliament's intention is subverted by the judges. Is it then possible for Parliament, by suitable wording, wholly to exclude the courts from considering a challenge to the legality of a decision of a public body? Consider the following: 'The decisions of the Tribunal (including any decisions as to their jurisdiction) shall not

18 [1981] AC 374, [1980] 2 All ER 634.
19 [1979] QB 56, [1979] 1 All ER 365.

be subject to appeal or liable to be questioned in any court.'[20] This seems judge-proof: not that the judges would wish to intervene in the decisions of the body in question.

Ouster clauses and time-limit clauses

We must now follow up another aspect of *Anisminic* and that is its relationship to the *East Elloe* case and time-limit clauses generally. There were some critical observations about *East Elloe* in *Anisminic* from which it seemed that it might be possible to challenge the many kinds of orders in planning, housing, compulsory purchase, etc after the prescribed six week period. There were a number of cases in which it was sought to apply *Anisminic* to such orders, arguing that on the basis of that case the orders were nullities. For various reasons the argument did not succeed.[1]

The relationship between *East Elloe* and *Anisminic* was raised directly in *R v Secretary of State for the Environment, ex p Ostler*.[2] The facts concerned a scheme to build an inner ring road in Boston, Lincolnshire. In 1972 the local authority took steps to acquire the necessary land compulsorily. There were to be two separate local inquiries, the first to consider objections to the road itself, the second to consider objections to the side roads giving access to that road. At the first inquiry, held in September 1973, a trader withdrew an objection after the Department of the Environment had given him a secret assurance that an access road, C Lane, would be widened. Following the inquiry the compulsory purchase order was made in May 1974. At the second inquiry the widening of C Lane was in issue. Ostler, whose premises would be affected by the widening, wanted to explain that he would have objected to the road at the first inquiry if he had known of the plan to widen C Lane. His evidence was disallowed. An order for widening the lane was made. Ostler later heard of the secret assurance given about C Lane and applied for certiorari to quash the compulsory purchase order of May 1974. Some eighteen months had now passed. Had the court jurisdiction to question the order in view of the six week clause? The Court of Appeal unanimously held that it had not. *East Elloe* was conclusive, and was to be readily distinguished from the *Anisminic* case on the following grounds. *First*, the relevant clause in *Anisminic* acted as a complete ouster, whereas in *East Elloe* the clause allowed a period of six weeks for lodging a challenge to the order. Goff LJ however did not regard this as a satisfactory distinction between the case as the majority in *Anisminic* had in effect denied the significance of that distinction. The argument for the distinction is that

20 Interception of Communications Act 1985, s 7(8).

1 *Hamilton v Secretary of State for Scotland* 1972 SLT 233; *Routh v Reading Corpn*, (1970) 217 Estates Gazette 1337; *Jeary v Chailey RDC* (1973) 226 Estates Gazette 1199.

2 [1977] QB 122, [1976] 3 All ER 90. Gravells 'Time Limit Clauses and Judicial Review: the Relevance of Context' (1978) 41 MLR 383. Alder 'Time Limit Clauses and Conceptualism – a Reply' (1980) 43 MLR 670.

where there is a complete ouster clause the courts are justified in intervening on the *Anisminic* principle, whereas the six weeks clause does give the citizen an opportunity to challenge the decision. In *Ostler* itself of course, where he did not know of the defect until long after the six weeks had passed, the right to challenge given by statute was of no use to him.

A *second* reason given by the Court of Appeal for distinguishing *Anisminic* and *East Elloe* was that in the former case the House of Lords was considering a determination 'by a truly judicial body', (that is, the Foreign Compensation Commission) whereas in *East Elloe* it was considering an order 'very much in the nature of an administrative decision', (that is, a compulsory purchase order) the distinction being that in the former the tribunal considers the rights of the parties without regard to the public interest, whereas in the latter the public interest plays an important part. The *third* reason given by the Court of Appeal relates to the question of jurisdiction. Thus Goff LJ said that in *Anisminic* the House was dealing simply with a determination that was a purported determination only, as the tribunal, having misconceived the effect of the statute, acted outside its jurisdiction, whereas in *East Elloe* and *Ostler* the court was dealing with an actual decision made within jurisdiction though sought to be challenged. Shaw LJ spoke of the decision in *Anisminic* as one that could not in any circumstances have been valid, whereas that in *East Elloe* and in this case was one which could be arrived at as a proper order. However, it seems fairly clear that the grounds of challenge in both *East Elloe* and *Ostler* raise questions of jurisdiction according to the *Anisminic* principle. In sum therefore the reasons given by the Court of Appeal for distinguishing *Anisminic* are unsatisfactory. Indeed Lord Denning has, extra-judicially, withdrawn the reason he gave for deciding as he did in *Ostler* and said[3] that he would wish his decision to rest on the last paragraph of his judgment, which reads thus:

Looking at it broadly, it seems to me that the policy under-laying the statute is that when a compulsory purchase order has been made, then if it has been wrongly obtained or made, a person aggrieved should have a remedy. But he must come promptly. He must come within six weeks. If he does so, the court can and will entertain his complaint. But if the six weeks expire without any application being made, the court cannot entertain it afterwards. The reason is because, as soon as that time has elapsed, the authority will take steps to acquire property, demolish it and so forth. The public interest demands that they should be safe in doing so. Take this very case. The inquiry was held in 1973. The orders made early in 1974. Much work has already been done under them. It would be contrary to the public interest that the demolition should be held up or delayed by further evidence or inquiries.

It is indeed the case that the time limit clauses were invented so as to enable public authorities to proceed with their road-building or slum-clearance programme or whatever it may be, free, once the six weeks is over, from the possibility of litigation which might delay their work for

3 *The Discipline of Law*, p 108.

many years. The need for some such limitation is evident, as Lord Denning indicates, though whether six weeks is in every case the right period might be arguable. Nor does it follow that Ostler should have been without remedy. Perhaps in such a situation a remedy in damages is or ought to be available. And finally, there is the Ombudsman. Ostler's case was in fact referred to the Parliamentary Commissioner for Administration who concluded that there were 'serious shortcomings' in the way the Department had handled the proposals relating to the road scheme; and that although there was no evidence of bad faith on the part of the Department, there had been a departure from the maxim that justice must not only be done but be seen to be done.[4] In the result the Department agreed to make an ex gratia payment in respect of Ostler's reasonable costs incurred in going to the Court of Appeal. Further, the Department subsequently included Ostler's premises (which had been affected by the road-widening) in a compulsory purchase order subject to the normal compensation.[5]

Locus standi

Just as there is the question of locus standi in the context of judicial review, so there is in the context of statutory appeals and applications to quash. In the latter cases, as in the former, the wording of the statute will have to be considered. The statute may indicate specifically and narrowly who can appeal or apply. It may for example be 'the person on whom the order was served'; or 'the parent of the child in respect of whom the order was made'. The phrase commonly used to indicate the standing required when seeking to quash by means of a statutory application is 'a person aggrieved.' This phrase is used in a variety of administrative contexts and has been given a variety of interpretations. In *Cook v Southend District Council*[6] the Court of Appeal took advantage of the opportunity to clarify the law. The particular issue in that case was that S had revoked C's licence as a taxi-driver. C successfully appealed to the magistrates court which awarded costs against S. A 'person aggrieved' could appeal from that decision to the Crown Court. Was S a 'person aggrieved'? (It was a 'person') The High Court held that it was – because an order for costs was made against it. The Court of Appeal said that to be 'aggrieved' it was enough that an adverse decision had been made against it, so that S could appeal even if no order for costs had been made. The phrase in question was to be given its ordinary natural meaning. As Lord Denning had said 'The words do not include, of course, a mere busybody who is interfering

---

4   This is the dictum of Lord Hewart CJ in *R v Sussex JJ, ex p McCarthy* [1924] 1 KB 256 at 259. Henston, *Lives of the Lord Chancellors*, p 804 says that Lord Hewart was incapable of observing it in his own court.

5   *Ostler* was followed in *R v Secretary of State for the Environment, ex p Kent* (1989) 57 P&CR 431.

6   [1990] 1 All ER 243.

in things which do not concern him: but they do include a person who has a genuine grievance because an order has been made which prejudicially affects his interests'.[7] In another case[8] it was said that 'to be 'aggrieved' a person must be affected by the matter of which he complains.'

With particular reference to the 'six weeks' procedure discussed above, the court had once taken a narrow view of 'person aggrieved' in planning law so that only a person who had a *right* to appear at a planning inquiry could apply to quash the consequent decision, but a later decision[9] extended this to one who had been permitted to appear.

7   *A-G of the Gambia v N'Jie* [1961] AC 617 at 634, [1961] 2 All ER 504 at 511.
8   *Arsenal Football Club Ltd v Smith* [1979] AC 1 at 27, [1977] 2 All ER 267 at 280.
9   *Turner v Secretary of State for the Environment* (1973) 28 P&CR 123.

Chapter 13

The contracts of public authorities

There can be no doubt of the importance of the contract in public law. Very large sums of public money, raised by taxation, are used in the acquisition, through contracts, of goods and services, and the legality of such expenditure and the efficiency of contracting procedures are of concern.

Many services formerly provided by public bodies are now 'contracted-out'; the responsibility for the provision of the services remains with the public body but it carries out that responsibility not through contracts with its own employees – and thus by itself – but by ensuring, through the terms of the contract, that the service is provided by another party, the contractor, who himself contracts with his employees. In contrast with that arrangement, we may find services previously the responsibility of, and provided by, a public sector body now the responsibility of, and provided by, a private sector body in accordance with an agreement with a regulatory body. Many services previously provided by public bodies – the boards of nationalised industries – are now provided by companies subject to the terms of licences which may have a contractual element; and the relation-ship between the provider and user of their services has moved in the direction of contract.

There are also 'near contracts' as for example the Framework Document which determines the relationship between a government and its Agency.[1] The word 'contract' is used in connection with internal arrangements in the National Health Service.[2] More generally, the concept of the contract is more widely used than in the legal sense of an agreement enforceable in the courts. It is used in political theory to explain the origin of the state and the basis of, and limits to, civil obligations.[3] The questions then are: who are the parties to the 'contract', what does the contract create (the community or the government, or both) what are its terms, and what are

1 See p 19 above. See generally Freedland 'Government by Contract and Public Law' [1994] PL 86.
2 See p 459 below.
3 See G H Sabine *A History of Political Theory.*

the consequences of its breach? The concept is also used, again by way of analogy, in the context of social work,[4] not because the relationships are intended to be governed by an action for breach of contract, but in order to *clarify* relationships, to provide some *precision* as to who is to do what and thus acknowledge *responsibility*. The relationship between University and State has been referred to as a 'contract'.[5] In these and other such cases the elements of agreement and mutuality of obligations are being drawn on from the legal concept of contract. The use of the concept of the trust in a similar way has been referred to.[6] The obligations of one generation to the next in the matter of, say, environmental pollution have been spoken of as arising from a contract or trust in the matter.

Contracts and contracting

An account of the law of the contracts of public authorities starts from the proposition that the ordinary rules of the private law of contract apply.[7] However, the fact that one or both of the contracting parties is a public authority may involve some departure from those rules, or the application of special rules.

Capacity to contract

The Crown has an unlimited common law power to contract. An express statutory restriction on doing so in any particular case will of course override the common law power. A minister of the Crown is sometimes given a statutory power to contract. If he purports to act under that power, but exceeds it, will he be caught by the ultra vires rule or can he rely on his common law power? The principle in *A-G v De Keyser's Royal Hotel Ltd*[8] suggests that he cannot rely on it. It has been suggested that the reason for conferring such statutory powers is to strengthen parliamentary political and financial control over the minister's exercise of those powers.[9]

Public authorities whose powers are defined by statute are subject to the ultra vires rule. A contract made in excess of the authority's power will be ultra vires and void, and neither party will be able to sue on it; this includes the third party who honestly and reasonably believes the authority had power to do so.[10]

---

4 Nelken, 'The use of "contracts" as a social work technique' [1987] CLP 207.

5 *Review of the University Grants Committee*, Cm 81, 1987, para 2.21.

6 See p 181 above.

7 See generally, Turpin *Government Procurement and Contracts*; J D B Mitchell *The Contracts of Public Authorities*.

8 [1920]AC 508.

9 See Daintith, 'Regulation by Contract: the New Prerogative' [1979] CLP 41 and 'The Techniques of Government' in *The Changing Constitution*, 3rd edn Jowell and Oliver.

10 Section 9 of the European Communities Act 1972 does not apply to statutory authorities.

Crown contracts and public finance

(i)   Crown contracts involve the expenditure of public money; this raises wider constitutional questions of the control of national finances, which can only be briefly mentioned here.[11] Parliament's control over finance is fundamental to our constitutional arrangements. Its approval is necessary for the *raising* of money and this is given, apart from taxes raised on a permanent basis, through the annual Finance Act which gives effect to the Budget proposals. Prior statutory authority is also necessary for *expenditure*.[12] Money granted by Parliament in any session for the service of the Crown must during that session be appropriated by Act of Parliament to some distinct use to take effect in that financial year. This is done by the annual Appropriation Act. The Appropriation Acts appropriate money by Votes specifying only their general purpose under broad heads eg social services, agriculture. Sums are not therefore provided by reference to specific contracts.

(ii)   Specific statutory sanction is not normally required by a department for the making of a contract which involves the expenditure of public money. A contract entered into within the scope of his authority by a Crown servant on behalf of the Crown and in pursuance of its functions will bind the Crown. A department may even enter into a contract which involves the future payment of sums not yet voted by Parliament. The legislature's control over the executive is nominally maintained in that actual payment under the contract depends on parliamentary sanction being given in due course in an Appropriation Act. It is even possible for contractual liabilities to be incurred in respect of activities which have not yet received statutory approval. Again, parliamentary approval will normally be obtained subsequently. Legally, therefore, departments enjoy a wide freedom to contract within the framework of funds voted or to be voted by Parliament.

(iii)   The question now to be considered is the effect on the contract of the failure by Parliament to provide the necessary funds. This will not normally arise as sums sufficient to carry on government, including those necessary for the performance of contracts, are usually voted. But what if this is not the case? The leading though rather exceptional case is *Churchward v R*.[13] C contracted with the Admiralty to convey such mails as he should from time to time be required to convey from Dover to the continent over a period of years. The Admiralty agreed to pay him £18,000 pa 'out of moneys to be provided by Parliament'. When the contract still had seven years to run the Admiralty discontinued employing C, and the Appropriation Act for that year expressly provided that no part of the sum appropriated for the carriage of mails was to be paid to C after a certain date.[14] C brought a petition of right claiming £126,000 damages

11 See Beer *Treasury Control* and Normanton *The Accountability and Audit of Governments*.
12 Adherence to this requirement is monitored by the Comptroller and Auditor General (see p 528, below). See Daintith in Friedmann (ed) *Public and Private Enterprise*, pp 209–213.
13 (1865) LR 1 QB 173.
14 See Wilson *Cases and Materials on Constitutional Law* (1st edn) p 496 for the reason for this.

for breach of contract. There was clearly no money available out of which the annual payments could legally be made. C therefore put his claim for damages on the basis that the Admiralty had failed to employ him to carry the mails. He argued that he was entitled to carry all the mails required to be carried. There was no such express obligation – could it be implied? The relevance of the fact that remuneration was to be paid out of funds provided by Parliament was that C argued that if he had been allowed to do the work Parliament would have voted the funds, and therefore there was an implied obligation to allow him to do the work so that he could go before Parliament and claim the funds out of which he could be remunerated.

Cockburn CJ said that the obligation could not be implied, as the Crown would not then, for example, be free to use vessels other than C's for postal communication with the Continent in time of war. Taking into consider-ation the point that remuneration was stated in the contract to be 'out of moneys provided by Parliament', the contract clearly envisaged that Parliament might not find the money and if the obligation argued for were to be implied, the position would then be that the department would have entered into a contractual obligation of which Parliament dis-approved and for which it refused to find the money. If, in fact, the department did this, it could not enforce the contract, for a court would say that the provision of funds was a condition which had to be fulfilled if the contract was to be sued on. The obligation to employ C could not therefore be implied. But Cockburn CJ thought that if no express reference had been made in the contract to the provision of funds by Parliament the contract would have been binding even in the absence of appropriation. Shee J expressed the view, obiter, that a condition as to the provision of funds by Parliament is to be implied into all government contracts. If this is interpreted to mean that the provision of funds is a condition precedent to the *validity* of government contracts, then it has been shown that in the context of Parliament's role in the budgetary system, such a rule would be 'wholly impracticable'.[15]

Consideration has been given to this problem in few other cases. In *New South Wales v Bardolph*[16] the government entered into a contract with B for the insertion of a weekly advertisement in B's newspaper for a period of more than a year. The contract was not authorised by the legislature or by an executive order, but sums included in the relevant Appropriation Act for government advertising were more than enough to meet the sums payable under the contract. Shortly after the contract was made, there was a change of government and the new government refused to go on with the contract.[17] B sued for damages: the court found for him. Dixon J said that the contract had been entered into by the appropriate officer acting with authority and in pursuance of a regular and recognised

15 See Turpin op cit p 92.
16 (1934) 52 CLR 455.
17 The contract had been entered into by a Labour Government for the advertisement of a Government Tourist Bureau in the journal *Labour Weekly*.

activity of the government. It was therefore a Crown contract. No statutory power was necessary to make the contract binding on the Crown. He said further that a contract made conditionally on appropriations by Parliament and even before funds have been made legally available, is binding. The law on this matter seems to be as follows:

–   The prior provision of funds is not a condition precedent to the validity of a Crown contract, which is binding even before money has been appropriated to it. Thus, if at the time when the contract is sued on (by either party) funds have not yet been provided, the action can be sustained.
–   But *payment* by the Crown under a contract is dependent on the voting of funds by Parliament. Until therefore appropriation is made, the Crown's obligation to pay under the contract cannot be enforced. But, as noted above, money is not appropriated to specific contracts but to services of a very general nature. What matters is that funds should be available to be applied to the contract in question.
–   It is always open to the Crown to stipulate in a contract that payment is only to be 'out of moneys provided by Parliament'.
–   If adequate funds are provided whether generally or for the specific contract, an action will lie for failure to pay. If, however, funds are expressly refused, payment cannot be made or successfully demanded.

The problem here discussed arises only in relation to the Crown contracts, not to those of local authorities or public corporations, as it exists because of the relationship between government and Parliament.[18]

The confirmation of contracts by Parliament

Where an agreement is later 'confirmed' by Act of Parliament, do rights and duties arise from the contract or from the Act? In *R v Midland Rly Co*[19] two railway companies agreed to amalgamate. The agreement provided that any differences should be submitted to arbitration. The amalgamation was later effected by a private Act of Parliament, of 1863. By that Act the agreement was 'confirmed and made binding upon' the companies. A later general Act of 1873 said that differences which were under the provisions of any *statute* required or authorised to be referred to arbitration were to be referred to the Railway Commissioners. Differences arose between the companies. Should they be referred to arbitration or to the commissioners? This turned on whether the requirement to refer to arbitration arose under a statute, (the Act of 1863 which 'confirmed'; and made binding the agreement), or under the agreement. It was held that it was made under the agreement. The parties had entered into a

18 For government contracts subject to a condition that they shall not be binding until approved by a resolution of the House of Commons, see House of Commons Standing Orders (Public Business) 1988, HC 1, SO 55–57.
19 (1887) 19 QBD 540.

binding agreement for amalgamation and arbitration before the Act was passed: the Act merely confirmed an already binding agreement.

Contrast *Pyx Granite Co Ltd v Ministry of Housing and Local Government*.[20] If certain development had been 'authorised by' a local Act it could be carried out without planning permission. In 1924 the Conservators of the Malvern Hills intended to promote a private Bill to extend their powers of control over the Hills. Pyx, a quarrying company, objected. The outcome was an agreement between Pyx and the Conservators by which Pyx gave up certain rights to quarry but acquired others. The resulting Act of 1924 which the Conservators obtained said that 'for the protection of the company' the heads of agreement drawn up between the parties 'are hereby confirmed and made binding upon' the parties. Was the development which the agreement permitted 'authorised by' the Act of 1924 or merely by the agreement? Unlike in *R v Midland Railway Co* just considered, there was here no binding agreement between the parties before the Act. The heads of agreement, Lord Jenkins said, could have no validity independently of the Act. The authorisation was therefore given by the Act, and planning permission was not necessary. The fact that the provision was inserted in the Act expressly for the protection of Pyx was also relevant.

Fettering freedom of action by contract

In *Rederiaktiebolaget Amphitrite v R*[1] the Swedish owners of the ship *The Amphitrite* wished to trade with the UK. This was during the 1914–18 war, and the British Government had a policy by which neutral ships in British ports were allowed to leave only if their place was taken by ships of the same tonnage. The owners got a guarantee from the relevant British authority that if the ship carried approved goods to the UK, it would be allowed to leave. The arrangement was honoured. Being minded to trade again with the UK the owners were given a similar guarantee, but this time the ship was detained and eventually sold. The owners sued the government on a petition of right for damages for breach of contract. Rowlatt J held that the arrangement did not constitute an enforceable contract.

No doubt the government can bind itself through its officers by a commercial contract, and if it does so it must perform it like anybody else or pay damages for the breach. But this was not a commercial contract; it was an arrangement whereby the government purported to give an assurance as to what its executive action would be in future. And that to my mind is not a contract for the breach of which damages can be sued for in a court of law. It was merely an expression of intention to act in a particular way in a certain event.[2]

20 [1960] AC 260, [1959] 3 All ER 1.
  1 [1921] 3 KB 500.
  2 At 503. In *Paet v Secretary of State for the Home Department* [1979–80] Imm AR 185 an assurance that an application would be favourably considered was said to fall within this principle and to be no more than an expression of intention.

On the face of it there might seem to be no reason why the arrangement could not be construed as contractual. But as the above extract shows the arrangement was demoted to a mere 'expression of intention to act in a particular way in a certain event'. Rowlatt J went on to say that 'his main reason for so thinking' was that

it is not competent for the government to fetter its future executive action which must necessarily be determined by the needs of the community when the question arises. It cannot by contract hamper its freedom of action in matters which concern the welfare of the state.

It will be noted that Rowlatt J accepted the possibility of the Crown being bound by 'commercial' contracts. He did not define that category. He seems to be saying that some agreements do not, and some do, affect the welfare of the state, that the former, being therefore merely commercial, will be enforced by the courts, while the latter will not be, for to permit their enforceability would be to allow the 'needs of the community' to be overridden by the right of the private contractor. They fall within the area of executive discretion, and a mere statement as to how that will in the future be exercised cannot be allowed to bind the executive, and cannot therefore be construed as a contract. If there is such a distinction in law, one would have to agree that the availability of shipping to the government during the 1914–18 war did concern the welfare of the state. But there was no question in these proceedings of the court ordering the Crown to let the ship go, only whether it should compensate the shipowner for the loss of his ship: did any reason of public policy prevent that?

This *doctrine of executive necessity* propounded in *The Amphitrite* has not been extensively considered in the courts. In *The Steaua Romana*[3] wireless apparatus had been hired out and installed by a Belgian company in two Rumanian ships in 1940. The ships were requisitioned by the Crown which agreed to hire the apparatus at the agreed rates. After the outbreak of war with Rumania in 1941 the ships were seized as prize, and the question was whether the apparatus was also to be regarded as seized. The court declined to take the view that the Crown, 'having been pleased through one officer to hire the apparatus would be capable of ordering another officer to seize these ships without implicitly excluding the apparatus so hired', and the court was indeed prepared to regard any deliberate inclusion of the apparatus in the seizure as 'inconsistent with the Crown's own contract', but it seems that the *Amphitrite* doctrine was not raised in argument.

Denning J sought to limit the application of the *Amphitrite* doctrine in *Robertson v Minister of Pensions*.[4] R, an Army officer, was told by the War Office that his disability was accepted as attributable to military service. The Ministry of Pensions later decided that the applicant's disability was not so attributable. Was the War Office letter binding on the Crown? (This, it will be noted, was not concerned with contract, but with the revocability

3 [1944] P 43.
4 [1949] 1 KB 227, [1948] 2 All ER 767. And see p 224 above.

of an administrative act.) Referring to one of the points raised by the Crown, Denning J said, 'Nor can the Crown escape by praying in aid the doctrine of executive necessity, that is, the doctrine that the Crown cannot bind itself so as to fetter its executive action. That doctrine was propounded in the *Amphitrite* but it was unnecessary for the decision because the statement there was not a promise which was intended to be binding, but only an expression of intention.'[5] However Rowlatt J's reason for excluding the government's undertaking from the class of contractual promises was the inability of the Crown to fetter its future executive action, though we could say that the rest of the sentence from his judgment from which that phrase is taken indicates that this applies only when 'the needs of the community' are at stake which they were in *Amphitrite* but not *Robertson*. Denning J added that 'The defence of executive necessity is of limited scope. It only avails the Crown where there is an implied term to that effect or that is the true meaning of the contract.' In *Board of Trade v Temperley Steam Shipping Co Ltd*[6] a ship was chartered by the Crown from the company. The charterparty contained a provision under which if, from breakdown of machinery, the work of the ship was suspended for a period of more than twelve hours, no hire was to be paid by the Crown for the whole of that period. The ship broke down. Surveyors thought extensive repairs were necessary. An Act of Parliament (the purpose of which was to safeguard the manufacture of munitions of war) provided that only such repairs could be carried out as a government official thought necessary. The lesser repairs he thought adequate, were done. As a result of the inadequacy of those lesser repairs the ship broke down again and was out of use for sixteen days. The Crown claimed that hire was not payable for that period. The company argued that by refusing to authorise the necessary repairs the Crown was in breach of an implied term in the charterparty that it would do nothing to prevent them from keeping the ship seaworthy and from earning their hire (that is to say, that it would agree to whatever repairs were necessary to ensure that the ship's work was not suspended for more than twelve hours so that it could earn its hire). The court was not prepared to accept that a government would agree not to exercise a power given by an Act intended to safeguard the public interest in the manufacture of munitions, merely because the exercise of the power would interfere with the performance of the contract in question by the shipowner. In the result therefore, the company's argument failed, and no hire was payable.

There was no reference in the judgments to the *Amphitrite* case. However both cases were referred to in *Crown Lands Comrs v Page.*[7] The Crown had, through the Commissioners, granted a lease of premises to Page. The question was whether it could later, through the Minister of Works, requisition those premises under statutory powers. Now where a private person grants a lease, a term will be implied into the lease that

5 At 231 and 770 respectively.
6 (1926) 26 Ll L Rep 76.
7 [1960] 2 QB 274, [1960] 2 All ER 726.

he must not act inconsistently with that lease so as to deprive the tenant of his 'quiet enjoyment' of the premises. Was such a term to be implied into Page's lease so as to render the questioning invalid? The Court of Appeal said not. Devlin LJ said:

When the Crown, or any other person, is entrusted, whether by virtue of the prerogative or by statute with discretionary powers to be exercised for the public good, it does not, when making a private contract in general terms undertake (and it may be that it could not even with the use of specific language validly undertake) to fetter itself in the use of those powers and in the exercise of its discretion.

What if there had been an express and not an implied covenant for quiet enjoyment? Devlin LJ said:

When the Crown, in dealing with one of its subjects, is dealing as if it too were a private person, and is granting leases or buying and selling as ordinary persons do, it is absurd to suppose that it is making any promise about the way in which it will conduct the affairs of the nation ... Even if, therefore, there was an express promise by the Crown that it would not do any act which might hinder the other party to the contract in the performance of his obligations, the covenant or promise must by necessary implication be read to exclude those measures affecting the nation as a whole which the Crown takes for the public good.[8]

But what are the limits on this doctrine? Does it not enable the Crown to evade all its contractual obligations? Devlin LJ thought not.

[It] does not mean that the Crown can escape from any contract that it finds disadvantageous by saying that it never promised to act otherwise than for the public good ... [It is not the case that] the Crown can never bind itself in its dealings with the subject in case it might turn out that the fulfilment of the contract was not advantageous.[9]

The doctrine of executive necessity is, it would seem, of limited application. It will be noted that the cases related to Crown contracts only.

A rule analogous to that in *The Amphitrite* – or it may be the same rule – is that *an authority on which a power is conferred by statute or the common law cannot disable itself by contract from exercising that power.* (The cases will be seen to relate to bodies other than the Crown.) In *Ayr Harbour Trustees v Oswald*[10] the trustees had statutory powers to compulsorily acquire land to be used as need might arise for the construction of harbour works. They agreed with a person whose land they had so acquired, not to construct works on that land in such a way as to affect injuriously the use of other land retained by him. The House of Lords held that the agreement was ultra vires the trustees. Lord Blackburn said:

Where the legislation confers powers on any body to take land compulsorily for a particular purpose, it is on the ground that the using of that land for that purpose

8 Ibid at 291 and 735 respectively.
9 [1960] 2 QB 274 at 293, [1960] 2 All ER 726 at 736.
10 (1883) 8 App Cas 623.

will be for the public good. Whether the body be one which is seeking to make a profit for shareholders, or, as in the present case, a body of trustees acting solely for the public good ... a contract purporting to bind them and their successors not to use those powers, is void.[11]

In this case the trustees had been created for the very purpose of managing and improving the harbour. To that end they had been given powers to compulsorily purchase land and use it for their purposes. By this contract they had put it out of their power to use some of the land so acquired for the purpose for which the statute authorised them to acquire it. They were thus renouncing a part of their statutory birthright; or, they could not release the power which the statute had attached to the land.[12]

In *York Corpn v Henry Leetham & Sons Ltd*[13] the corporation had statutory duties with regard to the management of the navigation of two rivers, and power to charge such tolls for navigation as it deemed necessary. The corporation agreed to allow the company to use the rivers for a fixed annual sum. This arrangement could be continued for as long as the company wished. The agreement was ultra vires: by it the corporation had disabled itself possibly for ever from exercising its statutory powers in respect of the tolls, no matter what emergency might arise. *Ayr Harbour Trustees v Oswald* was applied.

In *Re Staines UDC's Agreement, Triggs v Staines UDC*[14] T owned land which he leased to X for use as a private sports ground. As long as the land was used for that purpose the UDC, a local authority, was willing not to carry out its intention to acquire the land compulsorily as a public open space. On the other hand it wished to have the opportunity of buying the land for that purpose if at any time it was no longer used as a sports ground. It therefore acquired from T an option to buy the land. A clause in the contract said that if the UDC did not exercise the option within a specified period the land should be for ever free from the Council's power of acquisition. A further clause stated that so long as the land was occupied by X the Council would not acquire it, and a third said that the Council would not make any claim for betterment. These clauses were unenforceable against the council as it 'could not effectively contract not to exercise its statutory powers or to abdicate its statutory duties'.

In *Stringer v Minister of Housing and Local Government*[15] Cheshire County Council agreed with Manchester University to use its planning powers in such a way as to discourage development in the vicinity of the Jodrell Bank telescope. It thereby disabled itself from taking into account all the matters it was required by statute to take into account when considering planning applications. The agreement was therefore ultra vires the Council.

11 Ibid at 634.
12 The two ways of looking at the decision stated in this sentence were expressed in the *Birkdale* and *Stourcliffe* cases, below.
13 [1924] 1 Ch 557.
14 [1969] 1 Ch 10, [1968] 2 All ER 1.
15 [1971] 1 All ER 65, [1970] 1 WLR 1281.

The power to make public health byelaws is given to a local authority to be exercised by it for the public good as it sees it. The authority cannot therefore fetter the exercise of that power by reason of an arrangement with a private individual. This is shown by *William Cory & Son Ltd v London Corpn*.[16] The city corporation had a contract with Cory by which Cory agreed to remove refuse in barges provided with specified fittings. When the contract still had twenty years to run the corporation made a byelaw under its public health powers which required any vessel hired for removing rubbish to be provided with certain fittings. These were of a more rigorous standard than those required by the contract with Cory. It was held that a term was not to be implied into the contract that the corporation would not make any byelaw inconsistent with their contract. Such a term would, it was said, be ultra vires the corporation. To imply it would be to impose an unwarranted fetter on the corporation in the exercise of its public health powers vested in it for the public good. The contract was, however, frustrated from the day the byelaw came into force.

Now every contract to some extent limits or fetters the future actions of the parties to it, but the law cannot be that every contract entered into by a public authority is ultra vires as fettering its powers. Some contracts must be valid as an exercise of those powers. As will be seen, the *Ayr Harbour* principle is of limited application.

In *Birkdale District Electric Supply Co Ltd v Southport Corpn*[17] the company, operating under statutory powers took over from Birkdale local authority its electricity undertaking and agreed not to charge private consumers in Birkdale more than was charged to such consumers in neighbouring Southport by the Southport Corporation, which operated an electricity supply undertaking for its area. Later, the area of the Birkdale authority was merged with that of Southport, and later still the company (which continued to supply Birkdale) increased its charges to Birkdale private consumers over those made to Southport consumers. The corporation sought an injunction to prevent them doing so. The company argued, relying on the *Ayr Harbour* case, that the agreement was ultra vires as being incompatible with its statutory powers to determine the rates at which it would supply electricity. The House of Lords held that the agreement was enforceable.[18] There was, Lord Sumner said, a wide difference between this contract and that in the *Ayr Harbour* case. This was a mere contract entered into with regard to trading profits which might or might not be beneficial to the company. In the *Ayr Harbour* case, the trustees agreed never to use part of the land they had acquired for the statutory purpose for which they had acquired it. Here the

16 [1951] 2 KB 476, [1951] 2 All ER 85.
17 [1926] AC 355.
18 The *Birkdale* case was sought to be relied on in *R v Greater London Council, ex p Burgess* [1978] ICR 991 in a challenge to a closed shop: it was unsuccessfully argued that by adopting a closed shop the local authority denied itself the powers inherent in it as a local authority. See also *Meade v Haringey London Borough* [1979] 2 All ER 1016 at 1025.

electricity supply company could, if it chose, terminate its existence by going into liquidation. The Harbour trustees were constituted by statute which conferred their powers and defined their purposes. By contrast, the object of the statutory order under which the company operated was, said Lord Sumner, to get a supply of electricity to the area in question, and the order achieved this by getting a trading company to undertake the business. Its object was not to ensure a certain level of profit to the company. If the argument was that the agreement might lead to financial disaster for the company, and its ultimate liquidation, the order itself imposed a maximum price that could be charged by the company. How then could it be said to be part of the legal objects of the grant of these powers that they should never have that result? The company's profit and loss account was its own affair. Doubt was also cast on the *York* case.

Reliance on the *Ayr Harbour* case failed also in *Stourcliffe Estates Co Ltd v Bournemouth Corpn*.[19] The Corporation bought some land from the company to be used as a public park and covenanted not to erect any buildings on it except 'such structures as summer houses, a bandstand or shelters'. The company applied for an injunction to stop the corporation building lavatories there. The Corporation argued that the covenant was ultra vires, as it had statutory power to build lavatories in any public park. The Court of Appeal had no doubt that the covenant was perfectly valid and the *Ayr Harbour* case had no application. In that case the trustees contracted never to use land for the purpose for which they had been given statutory powers compulsorily to acquire it. In this case there was no dedication by Parliament of this particular land to any particular purpose. It was a voluntary bargain, and it was a startling thing for the authority to say that they were not bound by the restrictive covenant.

In *Dowty Boulton Paul Ltd v Wolverhampton Corpn*[20] Wolverhampton Corporation owned an airfield. In 1935 it conveyed land adjoining it to D and also granted to D the right to use the airfield for 99 years. By 1970 the airfield was rarely used and the Corporation made known their intention of using it as a housing estate. D having issued a writ, moved for an interlocutory injunction that the Corporation should do nothing which would prevent them from using the airfield. The Corporation argued that the grant was subject to an implied condition enabling it to determine it, should it see fit to put the property to some other use in the exercise of any of its statutory powers. The court rejected 'this startling proposition'. The grant was a valid exercise of its powers, even though it *pro tanto* excluded the exercise of other statutory powers. However the remedy sought was refused: the only possible remedy lay in damages, the court said.[1]

In *R v Hammersmith and Fulham London Borough Council, ex p Beddowes*[2] the council owned a housing estate consisting of nine blocks of

19 [1910] 2 Ch 12.
20 [1971] 2 All ER 277, [1971] 1 WLR 204.
 1 For sequel see [1976] Ch 13, [1973] 2 All ER 491. The case was followed in *ABC Containerline NV v New Zealand Wool Board* [1989] 1 NZLR 372.
 2 [1987] QB 1050, [1987] 1 All ER 369.

flats which needed modernisation. Acting under a power to dispose of land held for housing purposes, it resolved to sell one block to X, and to enter into a series of negative covenants which would effectively prevent it from creating any new lettings on the remainder of the estate, that is, from exercising its statutory power to provide housing accommodation in respect of the remainder of the estate. Was this an *Ayr Harbour* case? No, said a majority of the Court of Appeal. In that case the contract was incompatible with the trustees' statutory purpose; in this case the contract was a valid exercise of a power which merely limited the exercise of another statutory power, as in the *Dowty* case.[3]

Compulsory contracts?

A contract entered into out of fear that, if it is not, the government might use administrative or seek legislative powers to bring about the result it desires, is nonetheless a contract. Is it correct to say that such a contract is entered into compulsorily? A realistic view is that the 'threat' of or indication of the intent to resort to other legitimate measures if the contract is not entered into is a not uncommon state of affairs. Such an express or implied threat does not of course justify in law setting the contract aside. Some examples of contracts entered into in the knowledge of such possibility follow. There is statutory power to regulate the price of drugs. The Pharmacy Price Regulation Scheme, first negotiated between the Department of Health and drug companies in 1957 and most recently in 1993, controls the price of drugs not directly but indirectly through regulating the profitability of companies from their sales to the National Health Service.[4] The same Department enters into agreements with tobacco companies whereby the latter give public warning of the damage caused by their products. So far governments have refrained from legislating, but the companies' actions are presumably affected by their perception of a government's willingness to introduce legislation. A third example is to be found in the Ministry of Supply Act 1939, section 7(3). This provided that where the minister was satisfied that any person who produced any articles required for the public service had been requested to enter into a contract for the delivery of such articles (on terms which the minister thought fair) and refused or failed to do so, the minister could direct him to deliver those articles.[5]

There is a category of what we may properly call compulsory contracts. The procedure for the compulsory purchase of land is firmly based on an analogy with free market sales, virtually the only cause of difference being the element of compulsion. Whereas a sale by agreement is based on a contract freely entered into, a compulsory purchase is based on a notice

---

3   See also *British Transport Commission v Westmorland County Council* [1958] AC 126, [1957] 2 All ER 353.
4   See HC 80, 1993–94.
5   See W Ashworth *Contracts and Finance* (HMSO) p 42.

to treat. This specifies the land in question, expresses willingness to treat for its purchase etc. The notice to treat, together with the agreed compensation, constitutes an enforceable contract.[6] Such a contract is sometimes found referred to as a parliamentary contract.[7]

The duration and termination of a public contract

A question of general contract law concerns the duration of a contract for the supply of goods or services where the contract does not provide for its duration, and, where it is terminable by notice, the length of notice required. This question has a particular public law significance where the parties contract against a statutory background. In *Tower Hamlets London Borough Council v British Gas Corpn*[8] the parties entered into a contract in 1970 for the supply and purchase of gas at an agreed price. The contract made no provision for its duration or terminability. At the end of 1977 (by which time the price of gas had very markedly increased) the defendant gave the plaintiff twelve months' notice of the termination of the contract. It was *agreed* by the parties that a contract such as this could not be treated as having been intended to remain in force for ever. It was, the Court of Appeal said, a commercial agreement determinable by reasonable notice. That being agreed, the *first* question was: how long had the contract to run for before notice of termination could be given – was 1977 too soon? The test, the court said, was not whether a 'reasonable time' had elapsed, but whether the giving of the notice could be shown to have involved a breach of any express or implied term of the contract. On the facts no such breach was involved. The *second* question was whether adequate notice had been given. The rest was whether the period had been shown by the plaintiff to be unreasonable. On the facts it was not.[9] (The court observed that the local authority were not at the mercy of the corporation as far as their capital expenditure – the central heating equipment – was concerned as the corporation was under a statutory duty 'to satisfy, so far as it is economical to do so, all reasonable demands for gas'.[10])

In other cases the question has been whether the contract *was terminable by notice*. In *Spenborough UDC's Agreement*[11] it was agreed between C, the owner of a carpet factory, and a local authority S, that C could discharge effluent into S's sewers for an agreed charge. The agreement did not limit the amount of effluent that could be discharged. This

---

6 See K Davies *Law of Compulsory Purchase and Compensation*.
7 Eg in *Grice v Dudley Corpn* [1958] Ch 329, [1957] 2 All ER 673.
8 [1984] CLY 393.
9 In *Birkenhead School Ltd v Birkenhead County Borough* (1973) Times, 16 March, three years' notice required to end agreement by defendant to take up and pay for places at school.
10 And see *Staffordshire Area Health Authority v South Staffordshire Water Co* [1978] 3 All ER 769, [1978] 1 WLR 1387.
11 [1968] Ch 139, [1967] 1 All ER 959.

increased considerably and S's sewage plant could not cope with it. Could S determine the agreement? The court noted that C could have relied on a statutory right to discharge into the sewer but chose instead to negotiate for rights of a different kind. This indicated that the agreement was negotiated for commercial reasons and on a commercial basis. That being so, was it commercially sensible to suppose that either party thought S was taking on obligations that it could not put an end to? It was not. The contract was therefore terminable by notice.

Contrast *Watford Borough Council v Watford Rural District Council.*[12] The two councils had jointly administered two cemeteries. In 1963 they agreed that the former would in future be solely responsible for them, but the latter would make an annual contribution to their upkeep. In 1984 the latter gave twelve months' notice to terminate the agreement. The agreement had no term providing for its termination. Was such a term to be implied? In the above two cases the commercial nature of the agreement was emphasised. In this case the court held it was not a commercial contract. 'It was an arrangement reached between two local authorities the better to discharge a public duty and to provide a public service under the Burial Acts without any profit motive present at all.' In view parti-cularly of the fact that the parties were seeking to discharge a continuing (and not terminable) public duty, and also other factors such as the language of the agreement, the agreement was intended to bind each in perpetuity.[13]

Selecting the contractor

If there is only one supplier then the question of the selection of a contractor does not arise. Apart from this the purchasing authority will have to decide, subject to any statutory restraints, on the method of placing the contract. With regard to government contracts it has long been the policy that contracts should be placed only after inviting competitive tenders, unless there are good reasons for doing otherwise.

The European Community has, since 1971, issued a number of Directives co-ordinating procedures for the award of public works and public supply contracts. They have been wholly implemented in the UK by regulations made by the Treasury by way of statutory instrument under section 2(2) of the European Community Act 1972. The two sets of regulations (for supply ie goods, and works, respectively)[14] are essentially the same, and the main points can be summarised thus. They apply to certain public bodies (including government departments and local authorities) when they are seeking offers in relation to certain goods and building and engineering works. They deal in particular with the treat-ment to be accorded to suppliers who are nationals of, and established in, a member State. Certain contracts are excluded from the application of

---

12 (1987) 86 LGR 524.
13 In *Islwyn Borough Council v Newport Borough Council* (1993) Independent, 19 August: contract to operate jointly a leisure centre not terminable by notice (and later statute did not frustrate agreement).
14 SIs 1991/2679 and 1991/2680.

the regulations (eg transport, defence material); and those where the value of the contract is below the threshold specified.

The principal requirement of the Regulations is that, in seeking offers, a contracting authority must use one of three procedures: the open procedure whereby any person who is interested may submit a tender; the restricted procedure whereby only those persons selected by the contracting authority may submit tenders; and the negotiated procedure whereby the contracting authority negotiates the terms of the contract with one or more persons selected by it. The Regulations lay down provisions for making the choice of procedure. The negotiated procedure may only be used in certain limited circumstances.

The contracting authority is required to publicise its intention to seek offers in relation to such contracts in the Official Journal of the European Communities although this requirement is dispensed with in most circumstances when the negotiated procedure is used. The form of the advertisement and the information which it has to contain in relation to the proposed contract is specified. The various procedures also lay down the time to be allowed for the response by potential suppliers to the invitations and for obtaining relevant documents. The Regulations also specify the matters to which the contracting authority may have regard in treating suppliers as ineligible or in selecting suppliers to tender for or to negotiate the contract. The detailed rules for the selection of suppliers are laid down and relate to their business and professional status, their economic and financial standing and their technical capacity.

The contracting authority is required to award a public supply contract on the basis either of the offer (including in-house bids) which offers the lowest price or the one which is the most economically advantageous.

Finally, the Regulations provide that the obligation on a contracting authority to comply with the Regulations, and with any enforceable Community obligation in relation to the award of a public supply contract, is a duty owed to suppliers. A breach of the duty is not a criminal offence but is actionable by a supplier.

When a contract falls within the terms of the Regulations, then of course the choice of contractor is made in accordance with those terms.[15] As for contracts beyond the reach of the Regulations, it seems that as far as the Crown is concerned its choice of contractor can be determined by considerations collateral to the main object (buying goods etc) such as the desire to give preference to small firms or to UK industry generally.

The question achieved some prominence in 1977–78. The government took the view that in order to combat inflation, pay increases should not exceed 10 per cent. These 'guidelines' had no statutory force. The government sought to give effect to its policy by *refusing to enter into contracts* with firms who were in breach of the guidelines in agreeing to pay their employees increases greater than those thought desirable by the government. The Attorney-General asserted[16] the government's right 'subject to

15 *General Building Maintenance v Greenwich LBC* 92 LGR 21.
16 In a statement to the court in *Holiday Hall & Co Ltd v Chapple* (1978) Times, 7 February.

any relevant statutory provisions, to place its contracts in the manner which in its view will best serve the national interest, and hence to take into account, among other relevant factors, whether an employer is or is not observing the White Paper guidelines for the purpose of controlling inflation'. An opposing view was that the government's action was unconstitutional and that a court might declare its action to be unlawful in a particular case on the ground that any alleged breach of pay guidelines would not be relevant to the proper exercise of its discretion in choosing whom to contract with.[17] The issue was not litigated.[18]

A different technique available to the government was to seek to insist on the *insertion in government contracts of conditions* obliging the contractor to comply with current pay policy (as published from time to time in a White Paper) and to report to the government the details of any pay agreement with his employees, and giving the government the right, after giving the contractor the opportunity to make representations, to terminate the contract on notice.

(The government sought to enforce its anti-inflation policy not only through its contracting power, but also through its various grant-giving powers. A constraint here however was that grant-giving powers are normally statutory, and therefore the considerations that could be taken into account in giving or withholding grants might be limited by the statute. The grant-giving powers would have to be individually examined.[19])

The exercise by statutory bodies of their contracting powers is limited by any procedural or substantive limitations that may be imposed by statute. As for procedure, a local authority is required to have standing orders with respect to the making by it of contracts for the supply of goods or materials or for the execution of works.[20] Those standing orders are to 'include provision for securing competition for such contracts and for regulating the manner in which tenders are invited' but may also exempt compliance with them in certain circumstances. (A person entering into a contract with a local authority is not bound to enquire whether the standing orders have been complied with, and non-compliance does not invalidate a contract.) Although under the rules tenders may have to be obtained,[1] there is no legal obligation to accept the lowest tender, though failure to do so might be a ground for criticism by the local government auditor.

---

17 (1978) Times, 18 February, reporting counsel's opinion obtained by John Lewis Partnership. The House of Commons rejected a motion approving the government's policy: the government thereupon discontinued the use of the powers referred to: 960 H of C Official Report (5th series); cols 676, 692, 920.

18 Following the *GCHQ* case (p 53 above) Crown contracting procedures are not beyond judicial review on the ground that they are in exercise of the prerogative power. But see *R v Lord Chancellor, ex p Hibbitt and Saunders*, p 345 above.

19 See Ferguson and Page (1978) 128 NLJ 515; Elliott (1978) 7 ILJ 120; Ganz [1978] PL 333; Daintith [1979] CLP 41.

20 Local Government Act 1972, s 135.

1 For obligation to get tenders for 'works contracts' see Local Government, Planning and Land Act 1980, s 7 as amended by Local Government Act 1988, s 32. For tendering procedure for waste disposal contracts see Environmental Protection Act 1990, Sch 2; *R v Avon County Council, ex p Terry Adams Ltd* (1994) Times 20 January, CA.

Some years ago some local authorities resolved not to contract with companies whose activities the ruling group disapproved of, for example companies which had contracted for work at USA nuclear weapons bases in the UK. Was that lawful? The (consequent) Local Government Act 1988 provided that certain contracting functions (such as drawing up lists of tenderers) must be exercised without reference to 'non-commercial' matters. These include the political or industrial interests of the contractor, and any involvement he may have with irrelevant fields of government policy, as where he has defence contracts.

The price

Traditionally it had been assumed that the process of competitive tendering, of itself, ensures that the prices bid by potential suppliers represent the best value for money for departments. This is not necessarily the case.[2] In *non-competitive contracts* (the distinguishing feature of which is that there is often only one potential supplier as well as a single buyer – this is especially the case with defence equipment) special arrangements have been found necessary to try to ensure prices which are fair to both supplier and government. In 1968 an agreement was reached between government and industry. This provided for a new profits formula in pricing non-competitive contracts, post-costing procedures and a *Review Board for Government Contracts*.

The object of the *profit formula* is to give contractors a fair return on the capital employed, on the basis of comparability with industry, but because capital employed cannot in practice usually be identified, the formula works by paying a return on costs. The principle of comparability is approved by the Public Accounts Committee, but the profit formula operates artificially as a substitute for competition, and it wishes to see a reduction in the use of non-competitive contracts, and hence reliance on the formula. Further, it finds that the formula returns too high a level of profit to contractors.

Under *post-costing* the Ministry is entitled to post-cost non-competitive contracts selectively on completion of the contract. This will be done only for certain purposes, eg pricing follow-on contracts. It may lead to a claim by the department for a refund.

The *Review Board for Government Contracts* has five members, two nominated by the Treasury, two by the CBI, and an independent chairman. Its function is (a) periodically to review the operation of the profit formula and (b) where either party complains to it that the price negotiated was not 'fair and reasonable', to determine what adjustment in the price should be made. As to (a), four reports have been produced,[3] as to (b) less than one case a year is submitted to the Board. The Board has commented that

2　See *Government Purchasing: A Review of Government Contract and Procurement Procedures* (HMSO, 1984).
3　The Board also publishes an Annual Report.

they are by no means a full measure of the extent to which disputes have arisen as to whether contract prices negotiated were 'fair and reasonable'. In the great majority of cases, disputes are resolved without the need for reference to the Board. The Board thinks that reference should be made to it only when the parties disagree on a question of principle. In such cases the Board seeks to elucidate the principle so as to strengthen the guidelines available for amicable resolution of future differences. Contracts provide for the parties to be bound by the Board's decision.

This system of control of profits and losses is, as Turpin says, of exceptional interest, (but probably largely ignored in courses in administrative law). Turpin continues, 'The whole structure rests, not upon statute or regulations, but upon an agreement between the Government and the representatives of its contractors. The operation of the system depends upon the inclusion in individual contracts of an appropriate condition. The arrangements are a striking demonstration of the informal and consensual character of the British system of procurement.'[4]

Terms and conditions

The law applicable to public authorities' contracts is, in principle, the ordinary law of contract (subject to the *Amphitrite* and related rules referred to above). Their contracts are thus, for example, subject to the Sale of Goods Act 1979 and the Supply of Goods and Services Act 1982 which state, amongst other things, the terms to be implied into such contracts.

It is now very common for business organisations to draw up standard form contracts. These contracts, generally drawn up so as to favour the organisation, are presented to the other and no deviations from the terms will be allowed. The government also uses standard form contracts: their use ensures uniformity between departments, and saves time. It has drawn up standard conditions for two types of contracts entered into by departments, those for stores purchases and those for building and civil engineering works. The conditions seek to ensure fairness to the contractor and also to safeguard the interests of the State. For example the standard conditions for stores purchases prohibit the transfer or sub-letting of the contract without permission, and provide for the testing of material used. The department is empowered to determine the contract at any time by giving the contractor written notice of the agreed length. The department is then liable to pay for the work done, will take over at a fair price all unused materials, and will indemnify the contractor against any liabilities caused by the determination of the contract which would otherwise involve the contractor in an unavoidable loss. The contractor must take all reasonable steps to see that secret or confidential information is at all times strictly safeguarded, and he must put the same duty on his employees.

4   Op cit p 179.

It will be seen that as far as the contractor is concerned the government's standard terms are little different in effect from legislative rules. Thus when arrangements for reference to the Contracts Review Board was established, a new condition was added to government contracts. It has been suggested that standard terms should be legislative in form as they are in effect.[5]

Turpin has observed that it is extremely unusual for government contracts to be the subject of litigation: disputes are generally settled by informal negotiation between government and contractor.

Thus while in theory government contracts are subject to the ordinary rules of contract law, such rules have in practice only a residuary or contingent application to the relations established by the contract. These relations are indeed mainly regulated by the standard conditions normally included in government contracts, which have usually acquired a settled interpretation in the practice of those engaged in government contracting.[6]

The Unfair Contract Terms Act 1977 imposes limits on the extent to which civil liability for breach of contract or for negligence can be avoided by means of contract terms or otherwise. Sections 2 to 7 of the Act apply only to business liability, that is, liability arising from things done in the course of a business or from the occupation of premises used for the business purposes of the occupier. 'Business' is defined in section 14 as including 'the activities of any government department or local or public authority'. By the Act exclusion of liability for certain matters is permissible only if the exclusion is reasonable. A contract term is, by section 29(2) to be taken as meeting the test of reasonableness 'if it is incorporated or approved by or incorporated pursuant to a decision or ruling of a competent authority acting in the exercise of any statutory jurisdiction or function and is not a term in a contract to which the competent authority is itself a party'.[7] However nothing in the Act removes or restricts the effect of, or prevents reliance on, any contractual provision which is authorised or required by the express terms or necessary implication of an enactment.[8]

We have noted how far the *selection* of contractors can be made with considerations of various public policies in mind. Likewise the *terms* of a public authority's contract can be devised for purposes collateral to the main purpose of the contract – the acquisition by the authority of goods and services. Thus the standard conditions referred to above forbid the

---

5   Street *Government Liability*, pp 104–105.
6   *International Encyclopaedia of Comparative Law*, vol vii, ch 4, *Public Contracts*, p 33.
7   It has been suggested that the terms which the Civil Aviation Authority requires to be included in contracts of carriage by air as a condition of a grant of an air transport licence under s 65 of the Civil Aviation Act fall within that provision: Rogers and Clarke *Unfair Contract Terms Act 1977*. And see Telecommunications Act 1984, Sch 5, para 12(7).
8   Section 29(1). See now EC Directive 93/13, OJL 21 April 1993, pp 29–34, intended to approximate laws of member states; terms reflecting mandatory statutory or regulatory provisions outside its scope.

contractor from practising racial discrimination.[9] Second, it is possible for government contracts to stipulate particular methods of production in order to encourage advanced manufacturing techniques. Third, conditions can be inserted to require contractors to pay their sub-contractors within thirty days of invoice – this in an attempt to deal with cash-flow problems caused by the late payment of bills. And finally, as a major consumer, the government can often exert a powerful influence over its suppliers, as it did by encouraging mergers in the road construction industry. As an illustration of the power a government can exert through its contractual function, it is said that the United States government 'has achieved a greater degree of de facto management control over the aerospace industry through the contract device than the British government has achieved by nationalising certain industries'.[10]

The disclosure of interests

The Royal Commission on Standards of Conduct in Public Life, which reported in 1976, said that 'the main safeguard [against conflicts of personal interest with official duties] is for the public servant to declare his private interests whenever they have a bearing on his official duties'.[11]

All parts of the public sector have rules to deal with conflicts of interest, but the detailed arrangements vary. Only an outline is called for here. (It will be noted that the rules are not necessarily confined to interests in contracts, but this is a convenient place to consider them.)

In local government the Local Government Act 1972 provides that a member of a local authority who has a direct or indirect pecuniary interest in any contract, proposed contract or any other matter must, if he is present at a meeting of the authority when that matter is discussed, disclose his interest. It is a criminal offence to fail to do so. The consequence of disclosure is that he is disabled from taking part in the discussion of the matter or voting on any question in relation to it. A public record of disclosures must be kept by the authority. A local authority employee who knows that he has a pecuniary interest in a contract entered into by his authority must notify them of it.[12]

The provisions are applied by statute to certain bodies associated with local authorities, including police authorities. As for national health service authorities, statutory regulations impose on members virtually the same obligations as are imposed on members of local authorities.[13] The conduct of those authorities' employees is governed by the standing orders of the authorities themselves.

9 For former Fair Wages Resolution of the House of Commons see Kahn Freund's *Labour and the Law* (3rd edn) p 196. Resolution rescinded in 1983: 34 H of C Official Report (6th series) col 499.
10 Smith and Hague *The Dilemma of Accountability in Modern Government*, p 19.
11 Cmnd 6524, para 124. See now the report of the (Nolan) Committee on Standards in Public Life, Cm 2850, May 1995.
12 See Local Government Act 1972, ss 94–98, 105 and 117.
13 Eg SI 1990/1331 reg 20; SI 1990/2024, reg 20.

The members of the nationalised industries' boards are, either by the statute creating the board or by regulations made thereunder, required to disclose pecuniary interests, normally only as they arise in relation to contracts made by the boards. Disclosure of interests by these boards' employees is a matter for each board to decide upon.

There are no statutory rules about disclosure of interests by civil servants, but each department prepares its own rules, breach of which is dealt with under disciplinary procedures. The general principles which apply state, amongst other things, that an officer who comes into official contact with any matter concerning a business organisation in which he has an interest must disclose his interest and ask that some other official deal with the matter. There are also rules about ministers' interests.

Administrative arrangements or contracts

Schemes, grants and licences

So far in this chapter we have considered various aspects of public authorities' contracts. In this part we consider how far administrative arrangements of various kinds are contractual in nature.

Relations within an organisation are not contractual; one does not contract with oneself. Central government, though acting through different branches, does not contract with itself, any more than one department of a company or a local authority contracts with another. When the Post Office was a Crown body, and acted as agent for the Home Office in the collection of television licence fees (which are to pay for the BBC), the agreement between them was not a contract. When, in 1969, the Post Office ceased to be a Crown body, the agreement became contractual, and in that guise was found unsatisfactory.[14] Relations between different governmental organisations – say local authority agency arrangements – are of course capable of being contractual.[15]

A statute providing for the creation of a *scheme* may provide whether or not it is to be enforceable as a contract.[16] If it does, not the scheme will have to be examined to see whether it is contractual in nature. One of the necessary components of a contract is consideration, and its presence or otherwise in the following case was the key issue. The Apple and Pear Development Council is a statutory body whose activities include promoting the production and marketing of the eponymous fruits. The Council is funded by the imposition on growers of a compulsory levy. The question (which was relevant to tax liability under EC law) was whether the Council's services funded by the levy were done for 'consideration'. The

14 HC 401, 1984–85.
15 An agreement between local authorities for dealing with questions arising under the Housing (Homeless Persons) Act 1977 was not a legally binding code but merely a policy document: *Eastleigh Borough Council v Betts* [1983] 2 AC 613, [1983] 2 All ER 1111.
16 See for example the now repealed s 16 of the Community Land Act 1975, and s 21 of the Industry Act 1975.

court held not. There was no direct link between the service provided and the consideration received. The service was for the benefit of the whole industry; any individual benefit was indirect. The charges were imposed by statute not contract.[17]

By a *grant* is meant here the giving of financial assistance by a government to a non-government body.[18] A grant is normally paid only on the proof, to the satisfaction of the paying authority, of the existence of a specified state of affairs, and subject to appropriate conditions. As there is no developed legal concept of government grant the transaction must, it would seem, be classified as either a contract or a conditional gift, depending on the circumstances of each case,[19] though from the point of view of the recipient it may not appear to make much difference, and certainly the onerousness of the terms on which the money is paid out will not depend on the classification. It has been suggested that although the category of contract may not be suitable to meet the needs of the great variety of assistance arrangements,[20] it does emphasise the consensuality of the relationship between grantor and grantee: it is freely entered into by the grantee.[1]

However, it must be emphasised that where a grant is paid under statute, then whether or not the relationship between grantor and grantee is contractual will depend on an examination of the statute in question. In *R v Secretary of State for Transport, ex p Sherriff & Sons Ltd*[2] Sherriff, S, applied to the Department for a grant. The Department told him he would get one, but before paying it changed their mind. S successfully applied for a certiorari to quash the revocation of the grant, and the Department later paid it. The grant was thus paid later – over three years later – than it should have been. This in turn meant that S had incurred over £100,000 in interest charges on money which they had had to borrow because of not getting the grant. In these judicial review proceedings S sought to recover that sum. Has the court jurisdiction to grant interest in such proceedings? S relied firstly on section 35A of the Supreme Court Act 1981 which says that in any proceedings in the High Court for the recovery of a *debt*, interest may be ordered to be paid: was the grant a debt for this purpose? The court said not. The Act under which the grant was paid merely empowered the Secretary of State to pay a grant, it did not vest any right to a grant in an applicant: it would have been different

---

17 *Apple and Pear Development Council v Customs and Excise Comrs* [1988] 2 All ER 922.
18 We are not therefore concerned with grants from central to other governmental bodies.
19 For grant regulations using the language of offer and acceptance, see SI 1975/1763, reg 8.
20 A 'subsidy' or 'contribution' may be a grant: see *Wood v South Western Co-operative Housing Society Ltd* (1982) 44 P & CR 198 CA. For grant as reward not compensation see *Palatine Graphic Arts Co Ltd v Liverpool City Council* [1986] QB 335, [1986] 1 All ER 366.
1 Daintith 'Recent Trends in the Implementation of Economic Policy', IALS Workshop, 1979; Sharpe 'Unfair Competition by Public Support of Private Enterprises' (1979) 95 LQR 205. See Steinberg, 'Federal Grant Dispute Resolution' in *Drafting Federal Grant Statutes*, Administrative Conference of the United States, pp 192–212.
2 (1988) Independent, 12 January. See Bradley [1989] PL 197.

if the statute itself created an entitlement to the money. Furthermore the words of the section showed that it was intended to operate only in the field of private, not public, law (yet another example to be noticed of this distinction): it speaks of 'plaintiff', 'cause of action', etc. S argued secondly that a contractual relationship existed between S and the Department: a letter constituted an offer, and the carrying out of the works in question was the acceptance. The court rejected

this superficially attractive argument ... There was no intention to create contractual relations. The respondent was simply exercising a statutory power to grant money out of public funds on conditions over which he had discretionary control ... The indicia of contract simply do not apply. The respondent's exercise of his discretion can no doubt be reviewed as a matter of public law ... But if for example he should decide to add a condition or term or to change his mind in some aspect of the offer after receiving further information, he cannot in my judgment be sued for breach of contract in an action for damages.

The judge regretted having to find as he did, and suggested that legislation to remedy the situation might be appropriate.[3]

If the grantor-grantee relationship is contractual, then a complaint to an Ombudsman about the action of the grantor authority is excluded by the provision in the relevant legislation which prohibits investigation by him of a complaint of any action taken 'in matters relating to any contractual or other commercial transactions'.[4] For example an educational institution which ran a course for overseas students with financial support from the Foreign Office complained to the Parliamentary Commissioner of the department's decision to discontinue the scheme in breach of guarantee and 'in disregard of its contractual obligation' arising therefrom. The Commissioner was able to investigate the complaint only on being assured by the institute that it had no intention to regard the matter as contractual in the strict sense of the term.[5]

Two Australian cases are worth noting. In *Australian Woollen Mills Ltd v Commonwealth of Australia*[6] the government introduced a scheme for subsidising wool purchases; the details were in letters sent to all manufacturers. The company's claims that contracts were thereby constituted (the letter being offers, the purchases acceptances) was rejected. In *Administration of the Territory of Papua and New Guinea v Leahy*[7] the Administration's policy was to eradicate cattle tick. After the unsuccessful use of materials supplied free by the Administration the parties agreed on further steps to be taken. These too failed and Leahy alleged the existence of a contract under which the Administration agreed to do the job properly. The argument was rejected. The Administration was merely giving effect to its policy of dispensing aid to deal with the problem and

3   And see *Cato v Minister of Agriculture, Fisheries and Food* [1989] 3 CMLR 513.
4   See ch 16 below.
5   Fifth Report of the Parliamentary Commissioner, Session 1972–3, HC 406, p 81. See *Walters (Inspector of Taxes) v Tickner* [1992] STC 343: sponsorship by government department of student held to constitute contract – see case stated.
6   [1955] 3 All ER 711, [1956] 1 WLR 11.
7   (1961) 105 CLR 6.

Leahy was a person seeking that assistance.[8] Likewise in *R v Knowsley Metropolitan Borough Council, ex p Maguire*.[9] A letter saying that taxi-cab licences would be given to applicants was held not to be an offer so as to ripen into a contract when M bought a taxi, and thus entitle him to damages when he was refused a licence. Neither policy documents nor letter setting out the policy were to be construed as offers to the world at large.

Like a grant, a *licence* may or may not be contractual. Some clearly are not and are purely regulatory, such as the driving licence and planning permission. The relationship between the Independent Broadcasting Authority and the programme contractors was clearly expressed in the language of contract.[10] It has been suggested that if, in the granting of franchises, a failure to act fairly had been alleged, the classification of the relationship as either licence or contract might have been important.[11] The statutory language of the relationship between the Secretary of State and oil companies franchised to get oil from the North Sea is, on the other hand, that of licensing. The Act[12] empowers the minister to grant licences, and the model clauses[13] speak of the licensee, and of his being given licence (or exclusive licence) and liberty to do certain things.

Contract and regulation

A public authority may have both contractual power and a regulatory function in respect of the same area of activity. What if they overlap? A good example is from planning law. On the grant of planning permission the planning authority can impose conditions relevant to the development for which permission is granted. In addition, the legislation provided that an authority could enter an agreement for regulating the development of land. Development could thus be controlled through regulation (by the condition) or through agreement, and not necessarily as alternatives in any particular case, but jointly. The relationship between these two functions was considered in *Good v Epping Forest District Council*.[14] It was argued that the terms of an agreement were void if they could not lawfully have been imposed as conditions; that the authority could not achieve by agreement what it could not achieve by condition (eg requiring work to be undertaken on land other than that for which permission to develop was granted). The Court of Appeal disagreed. The statutory functions were distinct; they involved different procedures and had different consequences. The validity of the agreement depended, not on

8 Also held, applying *East Suffolk Rivers Catchment Board v Kent*, no liability in tort: see p 486 below.
9 (1992) Independent, 19 June.
10 See p 38 above.
11 Lewis, 'IBA Programme Contracts Awards' [1975] PL 317 at 325.
12 Petroleum (Production) Act 1934.
13 SI 1976/1129.
14 [1994] 2 All ER 156.

what could be achieved by condition, but on whether it was made, as statute required, for the purpose of regulating the development of the land.

The legislative provision for such agreements has since been replaced by provision for the 'planning obligation'.[15] A person interested in land may 'by agreement or otherwise' enter into an obligation restricting its use, requiring operations to be carried out, requiring money to be paid etc. A restriction is enforceable by injunction, and a sum due may be sued for. The obligation must be by an instrument executed as a deed.

The distinction between the two functions of contract and regulation is further illustrated by *R v Newcastle-upon-Tyne City Council, ex p Dixon*.[16] N was the registration authority under the Registered Homes Act 1984. It also had responsibilities to provide residential care for the old, sick etc, under an Act of 1948, and in pursuance of that Act contracted with operators of homes where it wished to provide for the care in question. The contract required the homes to be registered under the 1984 Act, and imposed on the operators obligations additional to those imposed by that Act. It was argued that the mixing of the statutory standards and contract requirements produced conflict with the statutory rights under the Act, and created uncertainty. The court held that there was no reason in law why N should not impose a stricter contractual regime than that imposed by statute in order to fulfil its duties under the 1984 Act; and there was not the confusion or uncertainty alleged, and though the statutory rights and duties were incorporated into the contract, the contractual provisions neither could nor did affect them.

'NHS contracts'

The structure of the National Health Service and the 'buying' and 'selling' of facilities within the 'internal market' by means of 'NHS contracts' has been referred to.[17] An 'NHS contract' is a term of legal art. It is defined[18] as 'an arrangement under which one health service body ('the acquirer') arranges for the provision to it by another health service body ('the provider') of goods or services which it reasonably required for the purposes of its functions.' Is an 'NHS contract' a contract? It is not. The Act goes on to provide:

Whether or not an arrangement which constitutes an NHS contract would, apart from this subsection, be a contract in law, it shall not be regarded for any purpose as giving rise to contractual rights or liabilities ...

What if a dispute arises? How is it to be resolved? The subsection continues:

15 Planning and Compensation Act 1991, s 12.
16 (1993) 17 BMLR 82.
17 See p 29 above.
18 National Health Service and Community Care Act 1990, s 4.

but if any dispute arises with respect to such an arrangement, either party may refer the matter to the Secretary of State for determination under the following provisions of this section.

Furthermore, if during negotiations intending to lead to what will be an 'NHS contract', one party thinks that the terms proposed by the other are unfair (by reason of unequal bargaining position between the parties), the proposed terms can be referred to the Secretary of State for determination. A reference to the Secretary of State may be determined by him or by a person appointed by him. On such determination the terms to be included in the 'NHS contract' may be specified, and a party may be directed to enter into the arrangement; further the terms of the arrangement may be varied or it may be brought to an end. (The variation or termination is deemed to have been agreed by the parties). Very clearly 'NHS contracts' are not contracts, but administrative arrangements.

An example of a 'NHS contract' is an arrangement between a health authority and a hospital it had previously managed but is now an NHS Trust whereby the latter agrees to provide certain services for the former. An arrangement between the health authority and one of its hospitals which had not become an NHS Trust (and thus remained a 'directly managed unit') would not be an NHS contract; it might be put in the form of a contract proper, but it would not be one: it would be an arrangement internal to the health authority and enforced by the usual management process. But an agreement between say a health authority or a NHS Trust on the one hand, and a private sector hospital (or other facility) on the other would, of course, be capable of being a contract in the full sense.

The non-contractual services of certain utilities

The relationship between a person who acquires by agreement goods or services provided by a public authority is prima facie contractual.[19] For example the relationship between a passenger and the British Railways Board is contractual, as is that between a local authority and a tenant of a house owned by it. Any statutory intervention that there might be in the terms of those or similar cases does not take the relationship out of the category of contract any more than it would were the relationship between private individuals.

However certain services provided by certain public authorities even though the language of agreement may be used, are not contractual, with the result of course that in the event of breach, contractual remedies will not be available to either party, though other remedies, common law or statutory, may be.[20]

---

19 An agreement to pay for services over and above those a public authority is bound to provide without charge is neither illegal nor void for want of consideration: *Glasbrook Bros Ltd v Glamorgan County Council* [1925] AC 270 (police). *China Navigation Co v A-G* [1932] 2 KB 197 (armed forces).
20 An unusual case was *Evans v BBC and IBA* (1974) Times, 27 February. The All Party Committee on Broadcasting (which had on it representatives of the three main parties

Electricity boards (and, before nationalisation, the various companies and local authorities which supplied electricity) were by the Electric Lighting (Clauses) Act 1899 under a duty to supply those persons stated in the Act to be entitled. The Act laid down a complete code, dealing with such matters as the method of charging, the provision and testing of meters, security for payment of an account etc., and also imposed penalties on a board for failure to give and continue a supply of electricity. In *Willmore and Willmore v South Eastern Electricity Board*[1] the court accepted the Board's argument that it 'ought to treat the supply of electricity by the Board not as the acceptance of an offer by the plaintiffs to take and pay for a supply, so as to create contract, but as given in pursuance of the Board's statutory duty to give a supply to a consumer who, being entitled, demands it'. (The plaintiff's only remedy was therefore to sue for the statutory penalty imposed by the 1899 Act of £2 a day). Post-privatisation, the relationship between a 'tariff customer' of a 'public electricity supplier' remains non-contractual[2] unless he enters into a 'special agreement' with the supplier.

Gas also has long been supplied in accordance with a statutory code under which there is an obligation to give a supply of pure gas at the prescribed pressure to those entitled to demand it.[3] Here again the relationship was not contractual. That remains the position as regards a supply by a 'public gas supplier'.[4]

Likewise with regard to the supply of water by a public authority – the relationship was not contractual.[5] The duties of 'water undertakers' under the Water Industry Act 1991 are statutory.

In *Triefus Co Ltd v Post Office*[6] the plaintiff sent overseas two postal packets containing diamonds worth £20,000. They were stolen by an employee of the Post Office. It was held in this action that there is no contractual relationship between the sender of the mails and the Post Office. Section 28 of the Post Office Act 1969 now provides that the Post Office may make schemes as respects any of its services for determining

as well as of the defendants) allocated times for party political broadcasts in the period before the General Election 1974. The Welsh Nationalist Party was told of the time allocated to it. The Committee changed the times, and the Party was dissatisfied with the alternative offered. In interlocutory proceedings it argued that the arrangement between it and the defendants constituted a contract; the defendants argued that it was mere invitation by them to use their broadcasting facilities. The Court of Appeal was prepared to say that, on the ex parte evidence before it, there was a legally binding contract. Damages would be an inadequate remedy. The defendants were ordered to see that the broadcast went out as first agreed.

1 [1957] 2 Lloyd's Rep 375. And now *Norweb plc v Dixon* [1995] 1 WLR 636.
2 Electricity Act 1989, ss 16 to 24. Standards of Service are agreed with the Director General of Electricity Supply; failure to meet them involves payment of a penalty as fixed by DGES.
3 *Clegg, Parkinson & Co v Earby Gas Co* [1896] 1 QB 592. Gas Act 1972, Sch 4, replacing Gas Act 1948, Sch 3 which itself replaced earlier codes.
4 Gas Act 1986, ss 9 to 15.
5 *Read v Croydon Corpn* [1896] 1 QB 592. Domestic user contracted typhoid; no liability in contract, but in tort for negligence and breach of statutory duty.
6 [1957] 2 QB 352, [1957] 2 All ER 387. See Foulkes (1980) 11 Camb LR 11.

the charges and other terms and conditions applicable 'save insofar as they are subject to an agreement between it and a person availing himself of those services'. The possibility of services being provided by contract is thus not excluded. (The Post Office enters into contracts for the carriage of mails by British Railways Board and air transport companies. It also has statutory powers to require the carriage of mails.)[7]

In *Pfizer Corpn v Ministry of Health*[8] the question was whether the supply of drugs on prescription to hospital out-patients was by way of contract of sale. The drugs were supplied, on payment of a fee, under arrangements laid down in ministerial regulations. The House of Lords held that the supply was not by sale. The considerations that weighed with their Lordships were that there was no need for any agreement: there was a statutory right to demand the drug on payment and a statutory obligation to supply; and that the fee required to be paid (10p) was in no sense the price as it was not related to the cost of the drug.[9] (There was not as in the gas, electricity and water cases a complaint of a failure to supply or of a defective supply.)

Telecommunication services used to be provided by the Post Office, then by British Telecommunications (both public corporations), but now by British Telecommunications plc. Nothing done under schemes made by the first two for providing their services led to a contract with the customer. Significantly, now that British Telecommunications has been privatised, services provided by it under its schemes *are* by way of contract.[10]

Agency

In general the ordinary rules of agency apply to contracts made by public authorities.

An agent is a person who is authorised to act for the principal and who has power to affect the legal relations of the principal with a third party usually by contracting on his behalf. (A servant may be an agent.) Where the agent acts within the scope of the authority expressly conferred on him his act will bind the principal. The agent is then acting within his *actual* authority.

The authority of an employee of a public body – the Crown, local authority, public corporation etc – to contract on behalf of his employer is normally laid down in that body's internal rules. For example, in a particular case, authority may be subject to a financial limit. It is very

7 Post Office Act 1953, ss 33–42.
8 [1965] AC 512, [1965] 1 All ER 450.
9 It was not argued that there could be a sale to a hospital *in*-patient to whom an inclusive charge is made. What if the drugs are supplied free (to a person exempt from this tax)? This is not a gift as there is a duty to supply; the transaction is sui generis. The provision of blood to the NHS by members of the public is by way of gift – see R M Titmuss *The Gift Relationship*.
10 Telecommunications Act 1984, Sch 5, para 12. For privatisation see p 46 above.

unlikely that the contractor will know what is the extent of the authority of the civil or other public servant he is dealing with. If, in fact, the contract is within his authority, it will bind the employing body. And of course if the contractor knows that the contract is not within the servants' authority, it will not bind it.

What if it appears to the contractor that the employee has got an authority which he has in fact not got? Here a principle of the law of agency may help him. It is that where the appearance of authority arises as a result of some representation whether by words or conduct, made *by the principal* to the third party, the principal will be bound by the agent's act even though it was outside his actual authority. This is known as *apparent* or *ostensible* authority, or as *agency by estoppel*.[11] In a Privy Council case, *A-G for Ceylon v Silva*,[12] the Principal Collector of Customs was empowered by an ordinance (a piece of delegated legislation) to sell unclaimed goods. He sold steel plates to S. In fact he had no authority to do so (as they were Crown property and the ordinance did not bind the Crown), and refused to deliver them to S who sued the Crown for breach of contract. S argued that even if the Collector had no actual authority to sell the goods, the Crown was bound as the Collector acted within an apparent authority. The argument was rejected. The Judicial Committee held that there had been no representation or holding out by the principal – the Crown – so that the case was not one of apparent authority. No representation by an *agent* constitutes a holding by the principal: thus 'no public officer, unless he possesses some special power, can hold out on behalf of the Crown that he or some other public officer has the right to enter into a contract in respect of the property of the Crown when in fact no such right exists'.[13]

What of the fact that he held an office the holder of which was empowered by the Ordinance to sell, and that he represented that the goods were saleable – could he not be regarded as having ostensible authority to make that representation? The Judicial Committee said not: the Collector's authority was limited by the Ordinance, a legislative document. (They acknowledged that it caused hardship to the purchaser to put on him the burden of finding out from that document the extent of the Collector's authority, but to hold otherwise, they said, would be to hold that a public officer could by unauthorised acts modify or extend the provisions of a legislative document.)

It does not follow from the decision – which turned on the fact that the Collector purported to act beyond the limits put on his authority by a legislative document – that the Crown can in no circumstances be bound by the operation of agency by estoppel.

In addition to his actual or apparent authority, an agent is impliedly authorised to do what is *usual*, in the trade or profession in which he is employed by his principal, for carrying out his authority. This does not

11 For estoppel see also p 220 above.
12 [1953] AC 461.
13 Ibid at 479. See *In re Selectmove Ltd* [1995] 1 WLR 474.

depend on a holding out by the principal. But no usual authority can exceed a limit put on the agent's authority by a legislative document.

An agent who enters into a contract on behalf of a principal will incur no personal liability on the contract, unless he expressly or impliedly undertakes such liability. It is very unlikely that a Crown servant would be held to have given such an implied undertaking.

But we must now consider the doctrine of *warranty of authority*. If a servant or agent expressly purporting to act on behalf of his employer enters into a contract which he has no authority to make, he will not bind his employer by it, so that the third party will not be able to sue the employer. Nor will he be able to sue the servant on the contract, for he did not purport to contract with him, but with the employer. However, the third party may in such circumstances sue the servant for breach of warranty of authority – he who professedly contracts as an agent is deemed to warrant that he had authority to do so. Can a Crown servant be sued on that ground? In *Dunn v Macdonald*[14] M was Crown Commissioner for an area in what is now Nigeria. He engaged D as a consular agent for a three year period. D was dismissed by the Crown before that period had expired. Having unsuccessfully sued the Crown for damages,[15] he sued M. His first argument, that his contract was with M, was rejected as he had in the earlier case treated himself as a servant of the Crown, and could not now argue that he was a servant of M. He then argued that M was liable to him for breach of warranty of authority – he had, D argued, warranted that he was authorised to engage D for the fixed period, and he was not so authorised. The Court of Appeal was unanimously of the view that the action was not maintainable. The doctrine that an agent who makes a contract on behalf of his principal is liable for a breach of an implied warranty of authority is not applicable, the court said, to a contract made by a public servant acting on behalf of the Crown. To accept that proposition, said Chitty LJ, would have the effect of practically abolishing the personal immunity of a Crown servant on a contract entered into by him on behalf of the Crown, and that could not be permitted. The case may, however, not be authority for the general proposition that a Crown servant can never be sued for breach of warranty of authority, only where the warranty relates to contracts of employment with the Crown, for special rules apply there, as we shall see.

Such exemption from liability as applies to a Crown servant does not, however, apply to any other public servant who is not a Crown servant.

Employment in the public sector

This is a large topic in itself; this section touches on some points of interest.

Just as there is not one institution called 'the administration' but rather a number of institutions which may be so called, so 'employment in the

14 [1897] 1 QB 555.
15 *Dunn v R* [1896] 1 QB 116.

public sector' embraces a number of institutions and differing legal relationships. There is firstly Crown employment, aspects of which are referred to below. A number of distinctions can be made here. There is employment in the office of a minister of the Crown, that is as a political director of one of the various government departments. With this must be contrasted employment in the civil or military service of the Crown, that is within the departments (including executive agencies) headed by ministers. A further category of Crown appointment is to the judiciary; as is well known, some of these appointments are given a measure of statutory protection. Other public appointments equally requiring and given such protection include the Data Protection Registrar, the Parliamentary Commissioner for Administration and the Comptroller and Auditor General.

Significant aspects of employment relationships in the National Health Service have been referred to above, and some reference will be found to employment by various public corporations.[17]

Concerning local authorities, the duties of some of their employees are imposed directly on them by statute, in contrast, that is, with the situation where the duty is put on the authority which it then carries out through its employees. Reasons for this could be that it is easier to enforce a duty put on one individual than on a body corporate, that there may be good reason to doubt the eagerness of the authority to carry out the duty, and in order to act as a check on the activities of the authority itself. The remuneration of its employees is determined by the authority following the usual industrial relations procedures. However, in the case of school teachers, remuneration is determined, subject to certain consultations and possibly parliamentary involvement, by the Secretary of State.[18] The Education Reform Act 1988 has also had some impact on employment relationships in education. The Act requires local education authorities to draw up schemes for delegating the management of schools to schools' governors and for allocating them appropriate finances. There are in the Act rules relating to the appointment and dismissal of school staff by the governors, distinctions being made between head teachers and other teachers, and between teaching and non-teaching staff. The Act also enables schools to 'opt-out' of the (frying-pan) control of the local authority into the (fire of the) control of the government. Schools which do this are known as grant maintained schools; the teachers at such schools are employees of the school, not the local authority.

The arrangements for the registration of births, deaths and marriages set out in the Registration Service Act 1953, are of interest in this context. The Registrar General is a Crown appointment. At the local level there are also superintendent registrars and registrars (hereafter registrars) for the appropriate local authority area. The registrars are appointed by the local authority in question; on a vacancy occurring, if the authority

16 See S Fredman and G S Morris *The State as Employer*.
17 See ch 2 above.
18 Teachers' Pay and Conditions Act 1987.

fails to appoint, the Registrar General may do so. There has to be for the area of each authority a scheme drawn up by the authority and approved by the minister. This scheme provides for fixing the salary to be attached to the office, and confers on an official of the authority power to fix the hours of attendance of the registrar and generally to supervise the administration of the scheme. However, though appointed by, paid by and in some degree supervised by, and working in premises provided by the local authority, the registrar holds his office at the pleasure of the Registrar General. In *Miles v Wakefield Metropolitan District Council*[19] registrars had declined, in breach of their obligations, to conduct weddings on Saturday mornings and the local authority withheld part of their remuneration for which a registrar sued. It was accepted for the purpose of the appeal that there was no contractual nexus between the registrar and the authority. But the nature of his remuneration and the terms of his tenure of office were so closely analogous to those of a contract of employment that his claim to remuneration had to be approached in the same way as a claim under a contract of employment. (The question of a local authority's vicarious liability for an officer in somewhat the same position as the registrar was considered in *Stanbury v Exeter Corpn.*)[20]

The Crown

The position of the Crown in contract has necessarily been referred to frequently in this chapter. In this penultimate section of the chapter we consider some rules relating specifically to it.

Suing the Crown

Before the Crown Proceedings Act 1947 there was no legal right to sue the Crown. The historical reason for this lay in the feudal rule that the king could not be sued in his own courts. The injustice of this Crown immunity was somewhat mitigated in that the Crown might permit itself to be sued by granting a petition of right. A petition of right was however only available for breach of contract and certain related matters but not for torts. A further mitigation was that statutes provided directly or indirectly that certain departments could be sued.

The Crown Proceedings Act[1] made the Crown suable in contract.[2] However it does not say that the Crown is now as liable on its contracts as if it were a private person of full age and capacity. It expresses its liability by saying in section 1 that where a claim might before the Act have been enforced on the grant of a petition of right or under certain

19 [1985] 1 All ER 905, [1985] 1 WLR 822.
20 [1905] 2 KB 838.
 1 See G L Williams *The Crown Proceedings Act 1947*. Hogg, *Liability of the Crown*.
 2 For position in tort, see ch 14, below.

statutes, the claim may now, subject to exceptions, be enforced as of right. The statutory provisions in force before the Act, providing that certain departments could be sued (referred to in the previous paragraph), were superseded by the Act.

The parties[3]

Civil proceedings against the Crown are instituted against the appropriate 'authorised government department'. The Minister for the Civil Service publishes a list specifying these departments. If none of them is appropriate or if the person bringing the proceedings has any reasonable doubt which of those departments is appropriate, the Attorney-General should be sued. Civil proceedings by the Crown may be instituted either by an authorised department or by the Attorney-General.

Civil proceedings may be brought against the Crown in the county court where the matter is within the jurisdiction of that court. On certain grounds the Crown can have such proceedings transferred to the High Court. The trial of proceedings in the High Court by or against the Crown is held in London only, unless the court with the consent of the Crown otherwise directs.

Remedies

We have seen that as against the Crown the court cannot grant an injunction. Nor can it make an order of specific performance or for the recovery of land or delivery of property. In lieu thereof it can grant a declaration. No proceedings can be brought against the Crown for the arrest of a ship or other property belonging to the Crown.

When a court order is made against the Crown for the payment of money by way of damages or otherwise, the appropriate department 'shall pay to the person entitled the amount ... due'. But the payment of the money cannot be enforced against the Crown by the normal processes of execution or attachment (e g by seizing and selling goods of the judgment debtor). On the other hand any order in favour of the Crown 'may be enforced in the same manner as an order made in an action between subjects'. All these rules will be found in the Crown Proceedings Act 1947.[4]

In general the periods of limitation in actions by or against the Crown or other public authorities are the same as in actions between subjects. But special periods apply to certain proceedings by the Crown, for example, for the recovery of tax.

3 This applies also to tort liability.
4 Crown Proceedings Act 1947, ss 15, 17, 19, 20.

Crown employment

Dismissability at will
An ordinary contract of employment can be terminated by either party giving the other the proper amount of notice unless the contract is for a definite agreed period of time, in which case it must run its full course though in either case the contract may be ended summarily by one party on the ground that the other has failed in his obligations towards him. By contrast:

It is now well established in British constitutional theory ... that any appointment as a Crown servant, however subordinate, is terminable at will unless it is expressly otherwise provided by legislation.[5]

In *Riordan v War Office*[6] R, a civilian War Office employee, was, by the relevant regulations (made under the *prerogative*) entitled to fourteen days' notice of termination of employment. Nevertheless the court held that in so far as the regulations purported to take away the Crown's right to dismiss summarily they could be ignored by the Crown.

What is the legal basis of the rule of dismissability at will? Is it that there is an implied term to that effect in the contract of employment? Now an implied term will be ineffective where there is an express term to the contrary. In *Riordan's* case there was such an express term: nevertheless he was liable to instant dismissal. Therefore the basis of the rule cannot be that it is an implied term. But is the relationship contractual at all? Certainly contractual remedies are, or may be, available in respect of other aspects of Crown employment than dismissal. There seems no doubt that the Crown can sue the servant for breach of his obligations to it for example for failure to give faithful service and to take reasonable care of property entrusted to him. In *Riordan's* case the regulations also said that Riordan was bound to give one week's notice: if he did not, one week's pay could be recovered from him by way of damages. Presumably the courts would enforce this. Furthermore it seems to be established law that a civil servant can sue for arrears of pay (this is referred to below). Does all this add up to saying that there is a contractual relationship between the Crown and its servant? Even if it is, it might be subject to the Crown's right to dismiss at will. As Lord Atkin once said, 'A power to determine a contract at will is not inconsistent with the existence of a contract until it is so determined'.[7] The question of the relationship between civil servant and Crown has been considered in the context of the availability to the civil servant of judicial review.[8]

The justification for the rule of dismissability at will is perhaps to be found in the requirements of public policy so that the Crown cannot by contract exclude the operation of the rule. The rule can thus be seen as another aspect of the rule, previously considered, concerning the freedom

5   *Kodeeswaran v A-G of Ceylon* [1970] AC 1111 at 1118.
6   [1959] 3 All ER 552, [1959] 1 WLR 1046.
7   *Reilly v R* [1934] AC 176 at 179.
8   See p 370 above.

of executive action.[9] The element of public policy is presumably that the continuance in office of a Crown servant may be detrimental to the public interest on the ground, for example, of inefficiency, engaging in political activity, or of security. But any employer can dismiss summarily any employee whose conduct constitutes a serious breach of his obligations to his employer.

Now it is a tort for A to induce B to break his contract with C. Where B is a civil servant and C is the Crown, is their relationship contractual so as to involve A in tortious liability where he so induces B? Section 30(1) of the Employment Act 1988 provides that 'where any person holds any office or employment under the Crown on terms which do not constitute a contract of employment between that person and the Crown, those terms shall nevertheless be deemed to constitute such a contract' for the purpose of the rule, and related rules, referred to.

Salary

It is clear that a military servant cannot sue for arrears of pay owing to him.[10] What of the civil servant? In *Lucas v Lucas and High Comr for India*[11] it was held that he cannot sue for it, but that case is of doubtful authority on that point,[12] and in *Terrell v Secretary of State for the Colonies*[13] Lord Goddard LCJ said, obiter, that he could sue for it. In 1926 in *Mulvenna v Admiralty*[14] Lord Blackburn had said that there was an implied condition in every contract between the Crown and a public servant that the servant has no legal right to be remunerated. In *Kodeeswaran v A-G of Ceylon*[15] it was pointed out that the only cases cited in support of that were those which established that the Crown can dismiss at will, and that Lord Blackburn treated it as a consequence of this that a Crown servant could not sue for this pay. This reasoning, said the Privy Council, was defective, the conclusion was contrary to authority and wrong. Indeed the current of authority for one hundred years before 1926, though sparse, was to the effect that a civil servant's arrears of salary constituted a debt recoverable by petition of right. It is reasonable to conclude from this that a civil servant can today sue for arrears of pay.

The Crown can dismiss and at the same time offer re-employment at a reduced salary.[16] In this event the servant is free to treat the contract as ended, and to leave, or to accept re-employment by continuing to serve the Crown. In either case he has a legal right to the salary already earned under the previous contract.

9 See p 439 above.
10 *Mitchell v R (1890)* [1896] 1 QB 121.
11 [1943] P 68, [1943] 2 All ER 110.
12 Logan 'A Civil Servant and his Pay' (1945) 61 LQR 240.
13 [1953] 2 QB 482, [1953] 2 All ER 490.
14 1926 SC 842.
15 [1970] AC 1111.
16 *A-G for Guyana v Nobrega* [1969] 3 All ER 1604.

There are special rules about the attachment of Crown servants' wages.[17]

Terms and conditions

The terms and conditions of service in the civil service are in general arrived at after consultation with representatives of civil servants and then laid down in regulations made under the prerogative by the Department for the Civil Service, formerly by the Treasury.[18] In *Rodwell v Thomas*[19] R alleged that the procedure whereby he had been dismissed was not in accordance with that laid down in a Treasury circular, and sought a declaration to that effect. R first had to show, as would a private employee suing on a collective agreement entered into between his union and the employer, that the terms of the regulations had been incorporated into his contract. The court could not accept that this had happened. The court added, that even if the terms had been incorporated into R's contract, it would disregard any terms as to the manner of dismissal as a clog on the Crown's right of dismissal at pleasure at any time. In *Dudfield v Ministry of Works*[20] the plaintiff, a lift attendant, sued for a 2s (10p) a week wage increase agreed by the relevant joint council but withheld by the government during a 'pay pause'. The plaintiff fell at the hurdle which defeated Rodwell, for the court held that even assuming that a civil servant could sue for his pay (and it offered no opinion on the point) the function of the council was purely consultative, and its agreements were not intended to be contractual terms as between plaintiff and defendant. However, in *Sutton v A-G*,[1] S, a post office telegraphist, enlisted on the strength of a Post Office circular which offered full civil pay in addition to military pay to those who joined a specified branch of the Army. The circular was held by the House of Lords to be part of his contract of service with and enforceable against the Crown.

Crown servants, like other public servants, are not prevented by statute from joining the appropriate trade union.[2] Civil servants' trade unions may affiliate to the Trades Union Congress and most do so, including the Association of First Division civil servants.

Civil servants of Under Secretary rank and above are required to obtain the government's assent before accepting, within two years of leaving the service, offers of employment in business and other bodies with close financial links with government. But there is no legal sanction for breach of the requirement.[3]

17 Attachment of Earnings Act 1971, ss 22 and 24(2)(b). For payment of bankrupt Crown servants' wages, see Bankruptcy Act 1914, s 54 now repealed by Insolvency Act 1985.
18 See *Council of Civil Service Unions v Minister for the Civil Service* [1985] AC 374, [1984] 3 All ER 935; *Cresswell v Board of Inland Revenue* [1984] 2 All ER 713.
19 [1944] KB 596, [1944] 1 All ER 700.
20 (1964) 108 Sol Jo 118.
 1 (1923) 39 TLR 294. For fuller report see Blair 'The Civil Servant – Political Reality and Legal Myth' [1958] PL 32.
 2 But see *Council of Civil Service Unions v Minister for the Civil Service* [1985] AC 374, [1984] 3 All ER 935; for special position of police, see Police Act 1964, s 47.
 3 See [1981] PL 310. For exclusion of civil service and other public employment from Ombudsman investigation see ch 16, below.

Employment legislation and the Crown

As is well known, there is a great deal of legislation affecting the individual contract of employment. An important question is how far Crown employment is affected by that legislation. The Employment Protection (Consolidation) Act 1978 consolidates most of the modern legislation on individual employment. Part I of the Act concerns the right of the employee to certain information about his terms of employment. Part II deals with certain rights arising in the course of employment such as the 'guaranteed week' and the right to time off to carry out certain public duties, and Part III deals with maternity rights. Part IV concerns the right of the employee to a minimum period of notice, and section 53 to a written statement of reasons for dismissal. Part V is to do with the right not to be unfairly dismissed, Part VI with the right of an employee who is dismissed for redundancy to a redundancy payment, and Part VII with the situation that arises when an employer becomes insolvent. Part VIII is to do with industrial tribunals.

Section 138 of the Act states how much of all that applies to Crown employment. Of Part I only the section relating to the right to itemised pay statements applies. Parts II, III and V apply, and section 53 (only) of Part IV. Part VIII also applies. The fact that, for example, Part VI dealing with redundancy pay does not apply does not mean that civil servants made redundant do not get redundancy pay. Alternative and parallel arrangements are made administratively. For the purpose of these rules Crown employment is defined as 'employment under or for the purposes of a government department or any officer or body exercising on behalf of the Crown functions conferred by any enactment'.[4] But service in the armed forces is excluded;[5] and employment by a National Health Service Authority is stated not to be Crown employment for this purpose.[6] Also excluded is any employment in respect of which there is in force a certificate issued by or on behalf of a minister of the Crown certifying that employment of a description specified in the certificate, or the employment of a particular person so specified is required to be excepted from the meaning of Crown employment (for the purpose of this section), for the purpose of safeguarding national security. And where a complaint is made by an employee to an industrial tribunal of unfair dismissal or discriminatory action short of dismissal because of trade union activities, then if it is shown that the action complained of was taken for the purpose of safeguarding national security, the tribunal shall dismiss the complaint. A ministerial certificate that the action was taken for that purpose is conclusive.[7]

4 Section 138(2).
5 Section 138(3).
6 Section 138(5). For NHS authorities see p 25 above.
7 Sch 9, para 2. Such a certificate was issued in *Council of Civil Service Unions v Minister the Civil Service* [1985] AC 374, [1984] 3 All ER 935. Formal arrangements have been established within the civil service for dealing with security risks: see HL Debs vol 177 col 159–161. For provision for termination of employment on security grounds of certain non-Crown servants only with ministerial consent see eg Atomic Energy Authority Act 1954, Sch 1, para 4; Post Office Act 1969, Sch 1, para 12(1).

The applicability of the laws of unfair dismissal to Crown employment will be particularly noted. The Employment Protection (Consolidation) Act 1978 provides that every employee has the right not to be unfairly dismissed. Claims of unfair dismissal are determined by an industrial tribunal. It is for the employer to show what was the reason for dismissal, and that the dismissal related to the employee's conduct, qualifications etc. Whether the dismissal was fair or not will depend on whether the employer can satisfy the tribunal that he acted reasonably in treating the reason for dismissing the employee as a sufficient reason for doing so.

The Sex Discrimination Act 1975 and the Equal Pay Act 1970 apply to Crown employees.[8]

The definition given above of Crown employment shows that for the purpose of these rules, employees of the legislature are not in Crown employment.[9]

Restitution

The law of restitution is the law relating to all claims which are founded on the principle of unjust enrichment.[10] That is the principle that lies behind the right, for example, of a plaintiff to recover money paid to the defendant under mistake or compulsion; or where there was a total failure of consideration; or where the defendant received from a third party money for which he was accountable to the plaintiff. (These are examples of claims in quasi-contract, an important part of the law of restitution.)

The law of restitution is highly developed and complex. Its application in public law was recently clarified by the House of Lords. The Board of Inland Revenue made (by statutory instrument) regulations concerning the payment of tax by building societies. The Woolwich Building Society (W) challenged, by way of judicial review, the validity of the regulations, and they were held to be ultra vires.[11] In the meantime W had paid the £57m in tax claimed by the Revenue under the regulations. (In doing so W said that payment was subject to any right to recover it as a result of the review it had initiated.) The Revenue repaid the £57m, plus interest – from the date of the judge's order. W then claimed interest from the date they had made the payment (£6.7m). The House of Lords held[12] (by three to two) that money paid by a subject to a public authority in the form of taxes or other levies (charges and fees) pursuant to an ultra vires demand by the authority is prima facie recoverable forthwith as of right together with interest. (There are a number of statutory provisions for the repayment of tax: none applied here. This right thus exists at common

---

8 See *Department of the Environment v Fox* [1980] 1 All ER 58, [1979] ICR 736.

9 See Lock 'Labour Law, Parliamentary Staff and Parliamentary Privilege' 12 ILJ 28.

10 See Goff and Jones *The law of Restitution*.

11 *Woolwich Equitable Building Society v Inland Revenue Commissioners* [1991] 4 All ER 92, [1990] 1 WLR 1400.

12 *Woolwich Equitable Building Society v Inland Revenue Comrs (No 2)* [1993]AC 70, [1992] 3 All ER 737.

law.) The Bill of Rights required this result, as did 'the simple call for justice': any other decision was quite unacceptable. The Revenue's convenient view was that repayment was a matter for its own discretion.

The case involved an ultra vires regulation, but the majority observed that the principle of recoverability applies where there is an erroneous interpretation of an intra vires regulation: in neither case is the demand lawful.

Two other aspects of the law of restitution must be mentioned. First: money is recoverable where it is paid under *duress* or compulsion. Say an official demands the payment of a fee and the citizen pays relying for the validity of the demand on the fact that the person making the demand holds a public office, which creates in his mind a virtual compulsion.[13] It then transpires that there was no authority to make the demand. Before *Woolwich* this question would have been determined by the application of the concept of duress, but it can now be seen that it would be disposed of on the principle laid down in that case. In some cases it was argued that duress had been applied not by reason, as in the case just mentioned of office-holding, but of a power to withhold supplies (as of water, for non-payment) or a threat to bring legal proceedings to enforce the claim for non-payment.[14] In neither such case did the court regard this as constituting duress: the payments were made to settle a claim. In *Woolwich* W also made the point that when the Revenue makes a demand for tax the demand is 'implicitly backed by the coercive power of the state and may well entail (as in the present case) unpleasant economic and social consequences ...' as Lord Goff put it. He went on to say that in this case 'the concept of compulsion would have to be stretched to the utmost'[15] and was difficult to sustain. There was, of course, no need to rely on it, given the principle which the House laid down. In *William Whiteley Ltd v R*[16] the plaintiff carried on an activity which the Inland Revenue said required a licence on which duty was payable. The plaintiffs contended that no licence was required, but in the face of threatened proceedings, paid up. They then established in litigation that a licence was not required, and sued to recover back the duty paid, but failed. The money had been paid under a view of the law which could have been, and eventually was (successfully) challenged. The plaintiff had given way simply to settle the claim. And there was no evidence of duress, only a threat to use legal proceedings to enforce the claim. This looks like the position in *Woolwich* so that doubt has been cast on the decision. If however the decision is interpreted as a voluntary payment made to settle a claim, it can, it seems, stand.

The second aspect of the law of restitution to be mentioned is that money paid under a *mistake of law* is (with exceptions) not recoverable. Suppose that W had originally paid under mistake of law, that is, they at

13 *Morgan v Palmer* (1824) 2 B&C 729.
14 *Slater v Burnley Corpn* (1888) 59 LT 636.
15 As fn 12, at p 172.
16 (1909) 101 LT 741.

that time thought or assumed that the regulations in question were good in law. Having been paid under mistake of law the money would not be recoverable, it seems. But this could not, surely, prevent them later claiming repayment on the ground that the regulations were ultra vires. This point is quite separate from and, it might be thought, more fundamental than, that of mistake of law.

As stated, the decision in *Woolwich* was by a bare majority. The minority took the view that the state of the law did not justify the line the majority took, and that the resolution of this question required action by the legislature not the judiciary, in view of practical difficulties left in the wake of the majority decision.

Chapter 14

The torts of public authorities

It is convenient to start from the proposition that the ordinary law of tort applies to public authorities as it does to private individuals, so that when an administrative act involves a tort, such as trespass, negligence or nuisance, the usual tests will be applied to determine its liability, and the usual remedies will be available to persons affected. However, the fact that the defendant is acting under a statutory power or duty or exercising functions which have no parallel to those exercised by private individuals requires some modification of the ordinary law of tort in its application to them. In earlier chapters we have considered the circumstances in which an act of the administration may be held to be null and void. An important consideration is this: it is not the case that the fact that an administrative act is null entitles a person affected by the nullity to an action in tort, and damages. Proof of ultra vires or of a breach of natural justice means that the act was done without power or jurisdiction, not that damages are payable. For damages to be payable it must be shown that the act in question constituted a tort or some other wrong sounding in damages.[1] It will however be noted that where a claim lies in damages it is now possible to join it to an application for judicial review.[2]

The defence of statutory authority

When it is alleged that a body has committed a tort it may, by way of defence, seek to show that the act complained of was authorised by Parliament (by way of Act or statutory order) to be done (and that therefore

---

1   See per Lord Wilberforce in *Hoffman-La Roche v Secretary of State for Trade* [1975] AC 295 at 358, [1974] 2 All ER 1128 at 1148. *Dunlop v Woollahra Municipal Council* [1982] AC 158, 1981] 1 All ER 1202, PC. In *Cooper v Wandsworth Board of Works* for example, p 283 above, there was a failure to give a hearing; damages were awarded not because of that failure but because the failure rendered the decision to enter the land unlawful so that the entry constituted trespass.
2   See p 357 above.

the plaintiff is entitled only to such compensation, or other remedy if any as the Act provides for). Whether or not, and if so to what extent, the statute provides a defence to the particular claim will depend on the precise provision of the statute as interpreted by the court.

The very reason why statutory powers are needed may be to authorise the commission of acts that would otherwise be tortious – normally a *nuisance* – at common law. If an act clearly falls within the authority given no action lies, as for example in *Dormer v Newcastle upon Tyne Corpn*.[3] The defendant was empowered by a (private) Act to place in any street 'any posts ... or other fence ... for the protection of passengers and traffic and for the prevention of accidents'. Acting under that power the defendant set up a barrier along the edge of the pavement in front of the plaintiff's premises to prevent people crossing the road at that point. This allegedly caused a diminution in the plaintiff's trade amounting to a *nuisance*. The action was dismissed. Slesser LJ said that the effect of the exercise of the relevant statutory powers was necessarily to create what would otherwise constitute a nuisance.

Likewise in *Goldberg & Son Ltd v Liverpool Corpn*.[4] The *nuisance* alleged was the erection outside the plaintiff's premises of a pole and fusebox needed to supply electricity to the defendant's tramway system. The relevant Act empowered the defendant to provide that system and to put in the plaintiff's street all such works as were necessary for that purpose. Lord Lindley MR said, 'That is an express power to do acts which but for that power would be unquestionably common law nuisances'. Judgment for the defendant.

Notice that both in this case and in *Dormer v Newcastle upon Tyne Corpn* the court emphasised that the corporation being empowered to do what it did, and having acted bona fide, the exact position of the 'obstacles' in question was not a matter for the court and could not be questioned by it.

Contrast the earlier, important case of *Metropolitan Asylum District v Hill*.[5] The board had a general statutory power to buy land and build hospitals on it. Residents of Hampstead alleged that a hospital built there for the treatment of infectious diseases constituted a *nuisance*, and a jury agreed. On appeal the board argued that what had been done was done under statutory authority and was not therefore subject to an action at the suit of an individual affected, who had to submit to any inconvenience caused in view of the public benefit resulting from the hospital. The argument was rejected by the House of Lords. The Act merely empowered the board to acquire land by agreement, it gave no compulsory powers nor provided for compensation for persons affected. Therefore, although the hospital could not be provided at all without statutory powers, those powers were not to be interpreted as empowering the board to act regardless of others' interests. Lord Blackburn acknowledged that this

3   [1940] 2 KB 204, [1940] 2 All ER 521.
4   (1900) 82 LT 362.
5   (1881) 6 App Cas 193.

view of the law might create great difficulties in finding sites for this kind of hospital at all, but agreed that this site could not be used in the way proposed. In the two cases previously mentioned, the authorities were empowered to place objects in the street: they necessarily created nuisances. A hospital is not necessarily a nuisance: the power to build it could be exercised only where a nuisance was not created.

Compare *Manchester Corpn v Farnworth*.[6] The Corporation was authorised by private Act to build an electricity generating station on a specified area of land. A neighbouring farmer's land was grossly polluted by fumes from the station's chimneys. The Corporation admitted nuisance, but argued that the building of the power station having been authorised by statute, the emission of fumes necessarily followed, and that they were therefore not liable. The House of Lords rejected that as the test for liability. Lord Dunedin said:

When parliament has authorised a certain thing to be made or done in a certain place, *there can be no action for nuisance caused by the making or doing of that thing if the nuisance is the inevitable result of the making or doing so authorised.* The onus of proving that the result is inevitable is on those who wish to escape liability for nuisance, but the criterion of inevitability is not what is theoretically possible but what is possible according to the state of scientific knowledge at the time, having also in view a certain common sense appreciation, which cannot be rigidly defined, of practical feasibility in view of situation and expense.[7]

On the evidence, the pollution that was caused was not shown by the defendants to be the inevitable result of the building of the power station; there would necessarily be some fumes, but not necessarily those emitted. The defendants were not able to show (the burden being on them in both matters) that they had used all reasonable diligence to prevent it. (The remedies granted were an injunction, suspended for one year, and such damages as were sustained by the plaintiff up to the date when the injunction ceased to be suspended or should be dissolved, whichever happened first. The defendant could apply to discharge the injunction (a) on establishing that they had exhausted all reasonable modes of preventing mischief to the plaintiff or (b) on submitting in the future to use the most effective of those modes until replaced by more effective modes of prevention which might thereafter be discovered, and use them.)

Notice that in this case the land on which the power station was to be built was specified, whereas in *Metropolitan Asylum District v Hill*[8] the defendant board could choose where to put its hospitals. There was liability in nuisance in both cases; in the hospital case, the works authorised to be done could only be done where they did not cause a nuisance, in the power station case the injuries suffered from the works authorised to be done on the land specified were not the inevitable result of what was authorised.

6 [1930] AAC 171.
7 At 183. Emphasis added.
8 (1881) 6 App Cas 193.

These principles were applied in *Allen v Gulf Oil Refinery Ltd*.[9] The company was authorised (by private Act) to construct (and therefore impliedly to operate) a refinery on a particular site. The House of Lords held, on a preliminary issue, that the company was therefore entitled to statutory immunity in respect of any nuisance which was an *inevitable* result of operating on the site *a* refinery (not necessarily the one actually built). It was for the defendant to show that the nuisance created (the proof of the existence of which was on the plaintiff) was an inevitable result of *a* refinery on the particular site. To the extent that the actual nuisance caused by the refinery actually constructed exceeded the nuisance which inevitably resulted from any refinery on that site, the statutory immunity would not apply.[10]

Clearly the immunity from an action in nuisance provided by statutory authority can mean that those living in the neighbourhood may be considerably disadvantaged. It seems that we must say that Parliament is presumed to have considered the interests of those affected by the works in question, and has decided that the benefits to the community at large must have precedence over these interests.

It is sometimes the case that compensation for injury suffered by works is provided for. The effect was considered in *Marriage v East Norfolk Rivers Catchment Board*.[11] The defendant acting under statutory powers dredged a river and placed the spoil on the plaintiff's bank with the result that when the river flooded, the flood water was not able to escape by its usual channels, and damaged the plaintiff's property. The plaintiff sued in nuisance. The Act in question provided that where injury was sustained by any person by reason of the execution by the Board of its powers, the Board was liable to make full compensation. The plaintiff's action was dismissed. Tucker LJ said:

Where there is no such [compensation] clause and where the legislature has authorised the execution of specific works, the court will be vigilant to see that an injured party is not deprived of his remedy unless the language of the statute and the nature of the works authorised necessitate such a conclusion. In my view, quite different considerations arise in cases like the present, where the statute to be construed is not concerned with specific works but is conferring a wide discretion on a statutory authority, necessarily involving interference with the legal rights of riparian owners and expressly providing a remedy by way of compensation for such interference.[12]

---

9 [1981] AC 1001, [1981] 1 All ER 353, HL; case note by Murdoch 97 LQR 203.

10 Likewise in *Tate & Lyle Industries Ltd v Greater London Council* [1983] 2 AC 509, [1983] 1 All ER 1159, statutory authority to build jetties in the Thames conferred immunity in respect of inevitable siltation and not in respect of additional siltation caused by the particular design chosen. See *Gillingham Borough Council v Medway (Chatham) Dock Co Ltd* [1992] 3 All ER 923 applying the Gulf Oil case: whether planning permission, not Act, give immunity. *Hunter v Canary Wharf Ltd* (1994) Independent, 20 December, interference with TV reception by defendant's tower erected with planning permission.

11 [1950] 1 KB 284, [1949] 2 All ER 1021.

12 Ibid at 294 and 1026.

Where a nuisance is attributable to the exercise by a body of a statutory duty it will not be liable for the nuisance in the absence of negligence. This is so even if the statute expressly states that the body is not exonerated from an action in nuisance.[13]

Negligent exercise of statutory powers

Can the negligent exercise of a statutory power give rise to liability in tort? In *Mersey Docks and Harbour Board v Gibbs*[14] the plaintiff's ship was stranded on a mud-bank negligently left at the entrance of a harbour vested by statute in the Board. The Board sought to evade liability on the ground that they were not a trading company but a public body of trustees constituted by the legislature for the purpose of maintaining the docks, and for using the tolls collected from dock users for that purpose, not for private profit. The House of Lords said it was clear law that a body providing such facilities for profit and collecting tolls from users could be liable in negligence for failing to take care to prevent injury. And there was no reason for distinguishing the position of the Board, whose liability for the negligence of its servant was affirmed. Thus a public body exercising a statutory power can incur liability for the negligent exercise of that power.

In the leading case of *Geddis v Bann Reservoir Proprietors*[15] the defendant had statutory powers to construct a reservoir and send its waters through the channel of the river Muddock to supply the river Bann. The Muddock overflowed, flooding the plaintiff's land. The cause of the overflowing was the defendant's failure to cleanse the channel. The plaintiff alleged *negligence*; the defence was that 'all that has been done was done under the authority and in pursuance of an Act of Parliament. The consequence of what has been done must be borne by the [plaintiff].' The House of Lords found for the plaintiff. Lord Blackburn said:

The channel of the Muddock as it exists at present is not able to carry off the water they [the defendants] have put into it, and if they have no power to cleanse the channel of the Muddock ... then they are not liable to damage for doing that which the Act of Parliament authorised, namely pouring part of the water of the reservoir into the Muddock that it may go into the Bann. For I take it without citing cases, that *it is now thoroughly well established that no action will lie for doing that which the legislature has authorised if it be done without negligence,* although it does occasion damage to anyone; but an action does lie for doing that which the legislature has authorised, if it be done negligently. And I think that if by a reasonable exercise of the powers, either given by statute to the promoters,

---

13 *Dunne v North Western Gas Board* [1964] 2 QB 806, [1963] 3 All ER 916. *Department of Transport v North West Water Authority* [1984] AC 336, [1983] 3 All ER 293. See Law Com No 32, p 20–21. For inadequacy of common law to deal with liability for nuclear energy and statutory imposition of strict liability and compulsory insurance see Street and Frame *Law relating to Nuclear Energy.*
14 (1866) LR 1 HL, 93.
15 (1878) 3 App Cas 430.

or which they have at common law, the damage could be prevented, it is, within this rule, 'negligence' not to make such reasonable exercise of their powers.[16]

The outcome of the case therefore turned on whether the defendants had the power in question to cleanse the Muddock. The Act was far from clear on it, but the House held that a more just result would be achieved if such a power was found, as otherwise the defendants could carry on their undertaking without regard to the damage they caused other people and without paying compensation. There being a power, an action lay for its negligent exercise.

Thus an action may lie for that which the legislature has authorised, if it be done negligently. It is well known that to establish liability in negligence the plaintiff must prove (a) that the defendant owed a duty of care towards him, (b) that he was in breach of that duty, and (c) that the loss he, the plaintiff, suffered was caused by that breach of duty.

The duty of care

The celebrated dictum of Lord Atkin in *Donoghue v Stevenson*[17] will be familiar, that a duty of care is owed to persons who are 'so closely and directly affected by my act that I ought reasonably to have them in contemplation as being so affected when I am directing my mind to the acts or omissions which are called in question', and he added that there would no doubt be cases 'where it will be difficult to determine whether the contemplated relationship is so close that the duty arises'. That is to say, there must be not only *foreseeability of harm*, but the requisite *proximity* of relationship. When it is alleged that the negligence was in the exercise of a statutory power, then the requirements of the statutory scheme must be considered in deciding whether the relationship gives rise to that duty.

In *Home Office v Dorset Yacht Co Ltd*[18] youths sentenced to Borstal training were camping on an island under the supervision of prison officers who were acting under statutory powers. They escaped one night while the officers slept, boarded a yacht moored at the island, and in man-oeuvring it damaged the plaintiff's yacht. The plaintiff argued that the Home Office was vicariously liable for the officers' careless supervision of the youths (not for the action of the youths themselves). The House of Lords held that the necessary relationship existed between the prison officers and the boys, and between the officers and the yacht owners, to put on the officers a duty of care. There was foreseeability of damage, and the necessary proximity of relationship because the officers had brought the youths near to where the yachts were and created a potential situation of danger for the plaintiff. But the class of persons to whom the duty of care to prevent a trainee from escaping was owed was limited: the duty was owed only to those whom the officer could reasonably foresee had property in the vicinity of the place of detention which the detainee was

16 (1878) 3 All Cas 430 at 455.
17 [1932] AC 562.
18 [1970] AC 1004, [1970] 2 All ER 294.

likely to steal or damage in the course of evading recapture. The risk of sustaining damage from the tortious acts of criminals is shared by the public at large. Of course members of the public have a right of action in tort against the criminal himself (for what it is worth) but against those who supervise him only where, as in this case, a 'close and direct' relationship between the supervisor and the plaintiff can be shown.

To turn to another, related area of public administration, what are the obligations in tort of the police to individual members of the public? In *Hill v Chief Constable of West Yorkshire*,[19] S had murdered a number of young women. His last victim was the plaintiff's daughter. She alleged negligence on the part of the police in failing to use reasonable skill in apprehending S, and that by their breach of duty they failed to detect S before he murdered Miss Hill. But was that duty of care owed to individual members of the public? It is quite clear that an individual police officer may be liable in tort to a person who is injured as a direct result of his acts so that he may be liable in negligence, for example, in driving a police vehicle. And police officers owe a common law duty to the general public to enforce the criminal law. This duty may be enforced by mandamus but, as we have seen,[20] the chief officer of police has a wide discretion as to the way that duty is discharged; it is for him to decide how his resources are to be deployed etc. The courts would not interfere with the exercise of that discretion except in extreme cases. Thus the law on judicial review shows that the common law imposes no specific requirements as to the way the duty is to be discharged. 'This is not a situation where there can readily be inferred an intention of the common law to create a duty towards individual members of the public.' The plaintiff argued that that duty arose from the reasonable foreseeability of harm to potential victims if S was not detected. There could indeed be said to be such foreseeability: but that was not enough: there must also be the 'requisite proximity of relationship' between plaintiff and defendant. The *Dorset Yacht* case, like this, concerned the possibility of civil liability for failure to control another man to prevent his doing harm to a third. But this case lacked the characteristics which in *Dorset Yacht* gave rise to a duty of care – for example S, unlike the Borstal trainees, never was in police custody; and Miss Hill was not at any special distinctive risk, unlike the owners of the yachts in relation to the foreseeable conduct of the boys. In *Dorset Yacht* there was the necessary proximity: here there was not. Accordingly the plaintiff's claim was struck out for disclosing no reasonable cause of action.

There was, however, the courts say a separate ground why an action for damages in negligence should not lie against the police in circumstances such as these – public policy. As is well known, this is a dangerously imprecise concept. It is important to consider what the justification is said to be. The possibility of being sued in negligence (as of other liability) will often be in the public interest, as it will tend to encourage the observance of a proper degree of care. However, in the view of the House

---

19 [1989] AC 53, [1982] 2 All ER 238.
20 See p 394 above.

of Lords, this would not be the case in respect of police activities. Why? Because 'the general sense of public duty which motivates police forces is unlikely to be appreciably reinforced' by the possibility of being sued in negligence in respect of the investigation of crime. Further the contemplation of that possibility may lead them to adopt a 'detrimentally defensive frame of mind'. Again, the trial of some claims in negligence of this kind might involve close examination of matters which the courts would regard as inappropriate for them to form a view on, such as the best way to deploy available resources. Such actions would take up a lot of police time better spent on trying to catch criminals. In his judgment Lord Templeman asked whether an action for damages is 'an appropriate vehicle for investigating the efficiency of a police force', and firmly concluded that it was not. This action could only investigate whether an individual police officer was negligent in say, overlooking important information. The efficiency of the police force, which was essentially what the plaintiff was concerned about, raised many other questions which could only be investigated 'by an inquiry instituted by the national and local authorities which are responsible to the electorate for that efficiency'.

In *Alexandrou v Oxford*[1] there was held on the facts (concerning an activated burglar alarm) to be no such special relationship between the police and the owner of the burgled property as gave rise to a duty of care. Public policy was also invoked. Thus *Hill* was applied, as it was in *Osman v Ferguson*[2] on the public policy point (though it was arguable that on the facts there was a 'close proximity'), and in *Ancell v McDermott*[3] on the public policy point. In *Hughes v National Union of Mineworkers*[4] the public policy ground for striking out a claim in negligence by a policeman against his chief constable for injuries suffered in the course of his employment was that to hold that a duty of care was owed in the circumstances (the control of public disorder) would be significantly detrimental to that control. Nor does a police officer investigating a crime suspected to have been committed owe to the *suspect* a duty of care as to the way he carries out the investigation. It would be contrary to public policy to prejudice, by fear of a potential action in negligence, a discharge of the important duty of investigating crime.[5] (There was in addition the difficulty of showing that the injury reasonably foreseeable was such as to establish the proximity of relationship between the parties necessary to create a duty of care.)

In *Anns v London Borough of Merton*[6] the council made regulations about the foundations required for buildings and had power to inspect such foundations. It was held that there was sufficient proximity of relationship between the council and the owners of a building whose

1 [1993] 4 All ER 328.
2 [1993] 4 All ER 344.
3 [1993] 4 All ER 355.
4 [1991] 4 All ER 278.
5 *Calveley v Chief Constable of the Merseyside Police* [1989] AC 1228, [1989] 1 All ER 1025.
6 [1978] AC 728, [1977] 2 All ER 792.

foundations had been inspected to give rise to a duty of care. (But in *Murphy v Brentwood District Council*[7] *Anns* was overruled on the ground that there was no liability for the cost of remedying a defect to a building resulting from a negligent failure to ensure that the building was erected in accordance with building regulations, as this was pure economic loss: to allow this would lead to an unacceptably wide category of claims. Personal injury was not in issue.)

In *Yuen Kun Yeu v A-G of Hong Kong*[8] Lord Keith said, 'The issues in this appeal raise important issues of principle, having far reaching implications as regards the potential liability in negligence of a wide variety of regulatory agencies ... Such agencies are in modern times becoming an increasingly familiar feature of the financial, commercial, industrial and social scene.' The facts were that the Commissioner of Deposit-taking Companies in Hong Kong had various statutory regulatory functions in respect of deposit-taking companies. Such companies had to be registered, and the Commissioner had wide discretion to refuse registration, or suspend or revoke it. The plaintiff, YK and others, made substantial deposits with a registered company. Within a few months the company went into liquidation and YK lost his money. YK sued in negligence, alleging that the Commissioner knew or ought to have known, had he taken reasonable care, that the company's affairs were being conducted speculatively; that he failed to exercise his powers so as to ensure the company complied with its statutory obligations, and that he should either never have registered the company or have revoked its registration before YK made the deposit.

The question then was: did the Commissioner owe to members of the public who might be minded to deposit their money with deposit-taking companies a duty, in the discharge of his supervisory functions, to exercise reasonable care to see that such members did not suffer loss through the affairs of the company being carried on in a fraudulent or improvident fashion? What test was to be applied in deciding that question? Lord Keith emphasised the two necessary elements, foreseeability of harm, and a close and direct relationship of proximity between the parties. In deciding whether the necessary relationship exists, all the relevant circumstances must be examined.

What were those circumstances here? They were that one (only) of the purposes of the statute was to provide for the protection of the depositors. The obligations placed on the companies by the statute, supported by criminal sanctions, went a long way to secure that object. Also important was the discretion given to the Commissioner. Doubtless it was reasonably foreseeable by him that if an uncreditworthy company were to be registered, would-be depositors might lose their money – but that was not enough to create a duty of care. Furthermore the Commissioner was not only concerned with would-be, but with present depositors. And he had no power to control the day-to-day activities of a company – only to decide whether or not it could trade. Knowledge by a company of the

7 [1990] 2 All ER 908.
8 [1988] AC 175, [1987] 2 All ER 705.

Commissioner's powers might influence it, but would not prevent a determined fraud. For these reasons the court could not find any intention in the scheme that the Commissioner, in deciding whether to register or de-register a company, should owe any statutory duty to potential depositors, and 'it would be strange that a common law duty of care should be superimposed on such a statutory framework'. Before YK deposited money with the company there was no relationship of any kind between them and the Commissioner. But, if it were the case that there was available to the Commissioner information not available to the public which raised doubts about the company, would this give rise to a duty of care to prevent the company causing loss to those who had deposited money with it? The Privy Council said not. As noted above, and in contrast with *Dorset Yacht*, the Commissioner had no power to control the day-to-day acts of the company, only to stop the company from trading, and the decision whether or not to do so 'was clearly well within the discretionary sphere of his functions' (i e it was not an operational act for which there could be liability in negligence). 'The circumstance that the Commissioner had ... cogent reason to suspect that the company's business was being carried on fraudulently and improvidently did not create' the necessary relationship – which is that it must be 'close and direct' if it is to give rise to a duty of care.[9]

In *Curran v Northern Ireland Co-ownership Housing Association Ltd*[10] there was an allegation of negligence by a grant-giving body in permitting work done with the grant to be done defectively. But here too there was no control, in this case of the building operations.

In *Ryeford Homes Ltd v Sevenoaks District Council*[11] the plaintiff alleged negligence by the council in deciding whether to grant planning permission which had the effect of injuriously affecting his property. Noting that the council's function was regulatory, the court held that there was no sufficient proximity in law between the parties; and in any case it would be contrary to public policy to allow the action to proceed: the duty was to the public as a whole; further, breach of the duty would result in economic loss only, which, in the circumstances, was irrecoverable in negligence.

In *Jones v Department of Employment*[12] the absence of a duty of care was explained on grounds other than proximity and foreseeability of harm. J had applied for unemployment benefit. The adjudication officer, AO, decided against him but the appeal tribunal held in J's favour. J then sued the Department, claiming negligence in the AO. Did the AO owe a duty of care to J? He did not. Statute provided a right of appeal from the AO to the tribunal and eventually to the Court of Appeal; and there was the possibility of judicial review, and of an action in tort for misfeasance. It was not just and reasonable to add to this a duty of care to a claimant at common law.[13]

9   For Bank of England's supervisory role over banks see *Minories Finance Ltd v Arthur Young* [1989] 2 All ER 105. And see *Davis v Radcliffe* [1990] 2 All ER 536, [1990] 1 WLR.
10 [1987] AC 718, [1987] 2 All ER 13.
11 [1990] JPL 36.
12 [1989] QB 1, [1988] 1 All ER 725. For AOs see p 141 above.
13 Followed in *Mills v Winchester Diocesan Board of Finance* [1989] ch 428, [1989] 2 All ER 317.

In *Martine v South East Kent Health Authority*[14] it was held that when applying to a JP for an 'urgent' order for closing a nursing home, the defendant had no duty of care in negligence fully to investigate the case. This was not on the grounds referred to above (eg proximity), rather that the check to its action was that it was not it but the JP who had to be satisfied of the relevant matters; this was by analogy with the rule that the litigant does not owe a duty of care to another as to the manner in which the litigation is conducted. Further, to expose the defendant to the possibility of an action in negligence might cause delay in invoking the procedure in question, which might affect the well-being of the patients. But in *Welsh v Chief Constable of Merseyside Police*[15] (which concerned criminal proceedings) it was held that an action could lie against the Crown Prosecution Service which in exercising its administrative (as opposed to its judicial) functions failed to keep a court informed of the state of an adjourned case, causing the plaintiff to be arrested. There was there a sufficient proximity between the CPS and the plaintiff to raise a duty of care; it was fair, just and reasonable for an action to lie, and there were no public policy grounds why it should not. There were no safeguards as in the *Martine* case.

Breach of duty of care

There must be not only a duty of care, but also *a breach of that duty*. In *Rowling v Takaro Properties Ltd*[16] the decision of the minister, R, to refuse consent to a proposed share issue (intended to rescue Takaro, T) had been quashed by the New Zealand courts on the ground that R had taken an irrelevant matter into account. The minister then had to reconsider his decision. All this meant delay, and because of that T's main backers pulled out. In these proceedings T claimed that its loss was due to R's mistake in taking the irrelevant matter into account, and sued in negligence, arguing that R owed it a duty not to make a mistake in interpreting his statutory powers. Did R owe T a duty of care? As the question was not fully argued the Board were not, Lord Keith said, to be taken as expressing any opinion on the point. But, observing that the question was 'intensely pragmatic', they did say that though it could not be said that to make an error of the kind in question could never be 'negligent', there were a number of indications which militated against the imposition of liability in such a case, eg possible harmful effects in delaying administration through the seeking of legal advice, and the difficulty of identifying the circumstances in which a minister is under a duty to seek such advice. However the more important question here was, assuming such a duty, whether there had been a breach of it; on the facts the Board concluded that there had not.

Plaintiff's loss must be caused by breach of duty

In an action for negligence the plaintiff must show that the loss he suffered was *caused* by the defendant's acts. In *East Suffolk Rivers Catchment*

---

14 (1993) 20 BMLR 51.
15 [1993] 1 All ER 692.
16 [1988] AC 473, [1988] 1 All ER 163.

Board v Kent[17] a high sea made a breach in a sea wall, as a result of which Kent's land was flooded. The Board acting under its statutory *powers* repaired the wall, but did it so inefficiently that the land was flooded for much longer than it would have been had the job been done properly. The House of Lords held that the Board was not liable in damages to Kent. The original flooding was not caused by the Board and if, in the exercise of its discretion, the Board had decided *to do nothing* about the breach, the land would have been flooded for as long as it was in fact flooded. The Board had not by the inexpert exercise of its powers *added* to the damage Kent would have suffered had it done nothing. If such additional damage had been caused, it would have been liable, as it would have been if it had been under a *duty* rather than a power to act. Applying Lord Blackburn's dictum in *Geddis*, (p 479 above) the Board had acted negligently, but escaped liability on *causation* grounds as its negligence had not caused the damage suffered which was caused by nature. The earlier case of *Sheppard v Glossop Corpn*[18] was referred to. There the defendant had statutory power to light the whole or part of their district, that is, it had a discretion not a duty. They placed a lamp on a certain wall, but extinguished it (and others) at 9pm: this was done from motives of economy. The plaintiff suffered injuries at 11.30pm which he would not have suffered had the lamp not been extinguished. He sued for negligence for breach of an alleged duty to light the streets sufficiently. The Court of Appeal's judgment may be paraphrased thus. The Act gave a discretion whether or not to light. If in lighting the district the defendant acted negligently by for example allowing the gas to escape, or leaving a lamp post unprotected in the middle of the highway, they would be liable. Lord Blackburn's words in *Geddis* were, as Scrutton LJ put it 'addressed to negligence in the direct operation of the powers conferred'. They did not apply to the exercise of the discretionary decision whether or not to light the lamps, how long to keep them lit, etc.

Applying that approach in the *East Suffolk* case, if, the House of Lords said, the Board had in its discretion done nothing, or if, having started the work it had abandoned it, it would have incurred no liability, on the analogy of the local authority deciding whether or not to light, and if so when to turn off the lights. It was not therefore liable for taking longer over the job than it ought to have. Lord Atkin dissented, arguing that a public authority, whether acting under a duty or a power, must act without negligence, or, not improperly. This included a duty to act with reasonable dispatch. His was the only judgment to refer to *Donoghue v Stevenson*.

The operational/policy (discretion) distinction

In *Anns v London Borough of Merton*[19] there emerged the distinction between operational and discretionary (or policy) decisions. Its significance

17 [1941] AC 74, [1940] 4 All ER 527.
18 [1921] 3 KB 132.
19 [1978] AC 728, [1977] 2 All ER 492.

was that there could be liability in negligence for the former but not the latter. The reason why there could be no liability for the latter was that discretionary decisions were given by statute to the public authority for it to take, and the taking of such decisions involved considerations which it was inappropriate for a court of law to concern itself with. An early example is *Sheppard v Glossop Corpn*, above. Why did the defendant turn the lights off at 9pm? In the interests of economy; that is, in the financial situation it found itself in, it decided to allocate its resources in that particular way, a matter to be left to the authority. The distinction underlay what Lord Diplock said in *Home Office v Dorset Yacht Co*.[20] For example, the adoption of an open Borstal system, or of a system of releasing trainees on parole were both policy decisions for which the civil law concept of negligence was inapplicable: only the public law doctrine of ultra vires was relevant, though the distinction was, said Lord Wilberforce in *Anns*, one of degree: the more operational the decision, the easier it might be to impose a duty of care. In that case the decision in *East Suffolk Rivers Catchment Board v Kent*[1] (486 above) was reinterpreted in the light of the operation/discretion dichotomy. Lord Wilberforce thought that the case was a good example where the operational activity (repairing a breach in the wall) was 'still well within the discretionary area', so that it was difficult to prove a duty of care.

A distinction which cannot classify the repair of a hole in a wall as policy or operational is not very helpful, and it has now largely been discarded. Thus in *Rowling v Takaro Properties Ltd*.[2]

> Their Lordships ... incline to the opinion ... that this distinction does not provide a touchstone of liability but rather is expressive of the need to exclude altogether those cases in which the decision under attack is of such a kind that the question whether it has been made negligently is unsuitable for judicial resolution, of which notable examples are discretionary decisions on the allocation of scarce resources ... If this is right, classification of the relevant decision as a policy or planning decision in this sense may exclude liability; but a conclusion that it does not fall within that category does not ... mean that a duty of care will necessarily exist.

The minister's decision in this case – whether to give consent to a proposed share issue – could be said to be of a policy rather than an operational character; but in view of the function of that distinction (as just set out), it could not be said that the allegation of negligence in that case was of itself of such a character as to make the case unsuitable for judicial decisions – though as we have seen it was suggested that it was not.

20 [1970] AC 1004, [1970] 2 All ER 294. See p 482 above.
 1 See *Rigby v Chief Constable of Northamptonshire* [1985] 2 All ER 985, [1985] 1 WLR 1242: decision not to buy latest piece of equipment, policy; but liability in negligence for not having fire-fighting equipment available when using present equipment which had fire risk.
 2 [1988] AC 473, [1988] 1 All ER 163. See p 485 above.

In *Lonrho v Tebbitt*[3] L had acquired a percentage of the share capital of a company and made a bid for it. Its bid was referred by T, the Secretary of State for Trade, to the Monopolies and Mergers Commission which reported that the merger might operate against the public interest. T then required L to give an undertaking that it would not acquire more of the company's capital. The target company was then acquired by another company, so that the undertaking was no longer required but (it was alleged) T delayed in releasing it, causing L loss. L claimed that that delay was in breach of a duty of care which T owed it. T applied to strike out the claim, as disclosing no reasonable cause of action. The court ruled that the imposition of the undertaking was a matter of public law, that L had a private interest in having it released as soon as possible, that this arguably gave rise to a duty of care. T relied on the policy/operations dichotomy, but the court referred to the difficulties of that distinction that had been noted in *Rowling*, and that it was there suggested that whether a duty of care should be imposed was an intensely pragmatic question, well suited to a case-by-case development, but requiring careful analysis. Thus, while L's claim should not be struck out, much would turn on the facts as disclosed in the action. It might be difficult, the court thought, to prove both the duty and its breach.

Action for breach of statutory duty

Where a statutory duty is placed on one person, and another is injuriously affected by his failure to perform that duty, the person affected may be able to sue for that failure in an action for breach of statutory duty. Such an action is an action in tort, may be joined with a claim in negligence, and is to be distinguished from proceedings brought to claim a statutory benefit. Failure to carry out a statutory duty may also lead to an application for judicial review. There may also be default powers; or proceedings may lie for civil or criminal penalties. The relevance of these is referred to.

It might seem that this action is of considerable potential in administrative law insofar as public authorities operate in obedience to statutory duties. In what circumstances will the imposition of a duty be construed as giving a right of action for breach of the duty? The Act imposing the duty may itself expressly state whether or not such an action is to lie.[4]

If the Act contains no such clear indication then whether or not an action lies in tort 'is often a difficult question ... The only rule which in all circumstances is valid is that the answer must depend on a consideration of the whole Act and the circumstances including the pre-existing law, in which it was enacted'.[5] Consider industrial safety legislation where duties

---

3   [1992] 4 All ER 280.
4   Eg: no action, Civic Amenities Act 1967, s 18(5); action, Rent (Agriculture) Act 1976, s 28(8). See *Merlin v British Nuclear Fuels* (1990) Independent, 3 April.
5   Per Lord Simonds in *Cutler v Wandsworth Stadium Ltd* [1949] AC 398 at 407.

are put on employers to, for example, fence dangerous machinery. Bearing in mind that the statute imposes criminal penalties for breach of such duties, will such breach also give rise to a cause of action in tort at the suit of an employee? The courts have in such cases said 'Yes': the very purpose of the rule requiring fencing is to protect those exposed to the risk.

The test for deciding whether an action for breach of statutory duty lay used to be whether the plaintiff belonged to the *class* of persons intended to be protected – the employees working at dangerous machinery could certainly be said to belong to such a class, but the conclusion that they have such a right is today to be arrived at not by the 'class' test, but by asking whether Parliament could be said to have intended to confer on the plaintiff a private law cause of action, leading to a claim for damages. In the case just put – fencing machinery – it could be said to have done that, as that was the reason why the duty was imposed.

In *Hague v Deputy Governor of Parkhurst Prison*[6] the question was whether breach of a Prison Rule gave rise to a cause of action at the suit of a prisoner. Rule 43 had been activated by the prison authorities thereby removing H from 'association' with other prisoners. But they had acted in breach of that Rule – hence this action. In the House of Lords H's counsel approached the case through the 'class' test – H belonged to a class intended to be protected. But this was held not to be the correct test, which is as stated above. Applying the correct test, the purpose of the Rule was to give an obviously necessary power to segregate prisoners liable to disturb the running of the prison: its purpose was preventive or regulatory, not to protect prisoners against loss or injury. But if a prison rule could be said to be for that purpose, an action might lie – for example an industrial safety rule applying to employment in a prison workshop.

In *Calveley v Chief Constable of the Merseyside Police*[7] a tribunal failed in its duty to give a police officer notice of matters alleged against him. This obligation was clearly for his *benefit*, but its *purpose* was not to protect him from injury or loss of the kind attracting compensation – any remedy would have been by way of judicial review.

In *West Wiltshire District Council v Garland*[8] it was held that the statutory duty of a district auditor who had audited the council's accounts was enforceable by an action for damages by the council, as the primary purpose of the Act imposing the duty was to protect the council. (Local taxpayers are also protected, but this does not exclude the duty owed to the council. Nor is a duty owed to the council's employees.) Where the duty is interpreted as being owed to the *public at large*, it follows that no action will lie at the suit of an individual. In *Cutler v Wandsworth Stadium Ltd*[9] the breach of duty was the defendant's failure to provide space where bookmakers could carry on their activities at race-tracks. The House of

6 [1992] 1 AC 58, [1991] 3 All ER 734.
7 [1989] AC 1228, [1989] 1 All ER 1025.
8 [1995] 2 All ER 17, CA.
9 [1949] AC 398.

Lords held that while bookmakers might benefit from the operation of the Act, its main purpose was rather the interest of the public who resorted there, or that of the community as a whole. In *R v Inner London Education Authority, ex p Ali*[10] the court held that the duty of an education authority to provide sufficient schools for its area, being of a general nature, is intended for the benefit of the public in general, and not to give an individual a cause of action. And in *M v Newham London Borough Council*[11] M, a minor, alleged breach of duty imposed by statute concerning the care of children. The Court of Appeal held that protection of children was indeed a prime object of the legislation, but the duties were framed in terms too general to permit the action.

A statute that imposes a duty may also provide a remedy for its breach, such as a default power or criminal sanctions. The availability of such remedies may lead the court to conclude that, as Parliament has conferred other rights to secure observance of the duty, no action should lie in tort for that purpose. It does not so conclude in the case of industrial safety legislation, for example. But in *Cutler v Wandsworth Stadium Ltd* (above) there was a criminal penalty for breach, it was not inadequate and might even lead to revocation of the licence to run the track. In some social welfare cases (housing, and the home-help service) the court has ruled that the default procedure was the appropriate remedy, as it did in *E v Dorset County Council*[12] concerning the duty to assess a child's special educational needs. In *Atkinson v Newcastle and Gateshead Waterworks Co*[13] the defendant was in breach of its duty to keep water in the mains at a certain pressure with the result that it could not deal with a fire. Breach involved a criminal penalty. The court ruled that no action lay. It weighed with Lord Cairns LC that the court was here dealing not with a public general statute but with a private Act which was 'rather in the nature of a private legislative bargain with a body of undertakers as to the manner in which they will keep up certain public works'.[14] Such an Act had to be much more strictly interpreted, he said, than a public general statute: it could not be part of that 'contract' that the company should be turned in effect into gratuitous insurers against fire. Contrast *Read Croydon Corpn*[15] The defendant was under a statutory obligation to provide a supply of pure and wholesome water: a penalty was imposed for breach. The duty was said by the court to be owed only to that class of persons entitled to demand a water supply, and the plaintiff ratepayer was, but his daughter living with him was not, within that class. He could therefore sue for breach of the statutory duty; she could not, though she could sue in negligence (They both contracted typhoid through drinking impure water.) In view of the demise of the 'class' test, would the decision be the same today? Stable J said that it was difficult to think of a duty more particularly

10 (1990) 2 Admin LR 822.
11 (1994) 19 BMLR 107.
12 [1994] 4 All ER 640 – now on appeal to the House of Lords.
13 (1877) 2 Ex D 441, CA.
14 Ibid at 448.
15 [1938] 4 All ER 631.

concerning the individual as such than the supply of pure domestic water, as opposed, that is, to a duty owed primarily to the community the performance of which incidentally benefits individuals. And it may be suggested that in contrast with the previous case, 'You can insure against it' would hardly be an acceptable answer to a person who contracts typhoid.

McCall v Abelesz[16] suggests that in no case where an Act merely creates a criminal offence and imposes no duty will an action for breach of statutory duty lie, though in that case another remedy (for breach of covenant of quiet enjoyment) was available in respect of the action complained of.

Having established that action lies for breach of statutory duty at his suit, the plaintiff will have to show that the defendant was in fact in breach of that duty (which may be absolute or a duty to take reasonable care) and that the damage he suffered was caused by that breach.[17]

Negligent misstatements

In *Hedley Bryne & Co Ltd v Heller and Partners Ltd*[18] the House of Lords held that a negligent misrepresentation about a customer's credit-worthiness, given in answer to an inquiry, might give rise to a claim for damages at the instance of the party making the inquiry who had foreseeably relied[19] on the representation and suffered financial loss thereby. For such a liability to arise there must be a voluntary assumption of responsibility towards a particular party, giving rise to a special relationship. It would seem that if the work of a public authority involved giving advice of a kind which called for special competence, the authority could be regarded as having held itself out as having that special competence and be liable on that ground. For example, the Export Credit Guarantees Department, a government department, was empowered to give guarantees to manufacturers and others in the UK for the purpose of encouraging trade with other countries. Credit insurance was made available by it to insure the exporter against the risk of not being paid by the foreign buyer. ECGD publicise its activities and in particular state that it exists to assist the exporter and asserts its expertise in this field. In *Culford Metal Industries Ltd v Export Credit Guarantees Department*[20] the plaintiff alleged that the advice it had sought and obtained from the Department was negligent. The Department accepted that the *Hedley Byrne* principle could apply but argued that it had not been negligent. On the facts the court found for the plaintiff.

16 [1976] QB 585, [1976] 1 All ER 727, CA.
17 See Cane 'Ultra Vires Breach of Statutory Duty' [1981] PL 11.
18 [1964] AC 465, [1963] 2 All ER 575.
19 No reliance in *Mills v Winchester Diocesan Board of Finance* [1989] 2 All ER 317 at 332.
20 [1981] Com LR 127.

In *Yuen Kun Yeu v A-G of Hong Kong*[1] referred to at p 483 above, the plaintiff also argued that by registering the company the Commission made a representation that the company was creditworthy, and that when he deposited money with it he was relying on the representation, which was made negligently. The court's answer was that the statute's effect was to place a duty on the Commission to supervise companies in the general public interest, but no special responsibility towards individual members of the public. The statute gave the public some protection but did not institute such a stringent system of supervision as to warrant an assumption by a depositor that all companies were sound. To treat registration as a guarantee of the soundness of a company was not reasonable.

The need to exercise care when issuing a statutory certificate is shown by the somewhat special case of *Ministry of Housing and Local Government v Sharp*.[2] The Ministry had paid to N compensation to which he was entitled on being refused planning permission to develop land. The Ministry then served a compensation notice on the local authority, who registered it in the local land charges register. This had the effect of charging the land with the sum in question so that if permission was later granted the compensation paid would be returnable to the Ministry. Permission was later granted to N who sold the land. The prospective purchaser requested a search to be made of the register. The search was made by an employee of the local authority. He negligently failed to record the compensation notice so that the purchaser took the land without an obligation to repay the compensation. The Ministry then sued for loss of entitlement to repayment of the compensation. One of the points in issue was the liability of the authority's employee (for whom the authority was vicariously liable). Lord Denning MR had 'no doubt' that he was liable. He was under a common law duty to use due care. This arose not from any voluntary assumption of responsibility but from the fact the person making the statement knows or ought to know that others would act on the faith of the statement being accurate. Salmon LJ said that the facts showed as close a degree of proximity between the parties as existed in *Donoghue v Stevenson*.[3] It was not in his view the case that the obligation to take care necessarily depended on the voluntary assumption of responsibility and in any case he was far from satisfied that the council did not voluntarily undertake responsibility. He further pointed out that this was not a case where the plaintiff had been misled by a careless statement made to it by the defendant, or made by the defendant to someone else who the defendant knew would be likely to pass it on to a third party such as the plaintiff, 'but the categories of negligence are never closed'.

The Parliamentary Commissioner[4] has investigated a number of complaints of negligent advice by civil servants. In one[5] the complainant,

---

1   [1988] AC 175, [1987] 2 All ER 705. See *T v Surrey County Council* [1994] 4 All ER 577 for circumstances in which action for negligent misstatement lay.
2   [1970] 2 QB 223, [1970] 1 All ER 1009.
3   [1932] AC 562.
4   See ch 16 below.
5   Case C 414/L, Annual Report for 1969, p 28.

a director of a company, having been made redundant, inquired at the local employment exchange about redundancy payment. The manager expressed the opinion that he was self-employed and so not entitled to the payment: though information in his office would have shown that the complainant paid national insurance contributions at the employed persons rate. When later the complainant applied to an industrial tribunal for a redundancy payment the claim was rejected as being out of time. The complaint to the Commissioner was therefore of the loss of the redundancy payment because of the misleading advice. The complaint was upheld and the complainant was paid by the department what he would have received by way of redundancy payment.

Exemplary damages

The purpose of an award of damages is to compensate the plaintiff for loss or injury suffered, not to punish the defendant. However in some circumstances exemplary damages may be awarded, the purpose then being to punish or deter the defendant. One of the few categories of cases in which such damages are awarded, and which is of relevance in administrative law, is in respect of 'arbitrary and outrageous use of executive powers' or 'oppressive, arbitrary or unconstitutional action by servants of the government', as Lord Devlin put it.[6] 'Government' in this context is not confined to central government: it can include servants of local government,[7] and the police,[8] or more generally persons exercising governmental functions. This would not include a nationalised body set up for commercial purposes though it might apply to such a body which had and had misused a power of entry.[9] A further limitation is the torts in respect of which such damages are payable. There is some uncertainty about this, but they seem to include nuisance, trespass and false imprisonment, but not negligence or public nuisance.

Public authorities as plaintiffs

In principle public authorities are not only subject to the law, but can also take advantage of it, as by suing in tort and contract (and by applying for judicial review). But there are some rights available to private citizens which government institutions are not in a position to exercise unless they can show it is in the public interest to do so.[10] The House of Lords ruled in *Derbyshire County Council v Times Newspapers Ltd*[11] that not

6 *Rookes v Barnard* [1964] AC 1129, [1964] 1 All ER 367. *Cassell & Co Ltd v Broome* [1972] AC 1027, [1972] 1 All ER 801.
7 *Bradford Metropolitan BC v Arora* [1991] 2 QB 507, [1991] 3 All ER 545.
8 *Treadaway v Chief Constable of West Midlands* (1994) Independent, 23 September.
9 *AB v South Western Water Services Ltd* [1993] 1 All ER 609.
10 *A-G v Guardian Newspapers Ltd* (No 2) [1990] 1 AC 109, [1988] 3 All ER 545.
11 [1993] AC 534, [1993] 1 All ER 1011.

only is there no public interest favouring the rights of organs of government to sue for libel, but that it is contrary to the public interest that they should have it. 'It is of the highest public importance that a democratically elected governmental body, or indeed any governmental body should be open to uninhibited public criticism.' Note: (i) What constitutes a governmental body for this purpose may arise in the future. (ii) The authority might be able to sue in malicious prosecution or resort to the law of criminal libel. (iii) An action in defamation could be brought by an individual who was defamed by a publication attacking the actions of a body of which he was a member or an employee. Should special rules apply to them? (iv) Should the rule apply only to governmental bodies: what about powerful non-governmental bodies?

Misfeasance in a public office

This tort has come into some prominence fairly recently, and would seem to have considerable potential. It could be said to have been acknowledged in *Smith v East Elloe RDC*.[12] In that case proceedings were brought against the Council, the relevant Ministry and the Council's clerk, alleging, as against the first two that a compulsory purchase order was made and confirmed in bad faith, and as against the clerk that he knowingly acted wrongfully and in bad faith in procuring the order. The House of Lords struck out the proceedings against the first two defendants, but not against the clerk. Lord Simonds said that the injustice of excluding the courts from inquiring into the validity of the compulsory purchase order was not as great as it seemed 'for the bad faith or fraud is of individuals and ... even if the validity of the order cannot be questioned, an aggrieved person may have a remedy in damages against those individuals'. Their Lordships did not refer by name to a tort of misfeasance in a public office. (In the event the clerk's bad faith was not proved: his purpose was not to damage the plaintiff but to advance the interests of the Council.)[13]

In *David v Abdul Cader*,[14] on appeal to the Privy Council from Ceylon, the Board said that *malicious* misuse of a statutory power to grant a licence could give rise to this action, though much, they said, would turn on what the 'malice' was found to consist of. (The judgment noted that the law had developed in the fifty years since *David v Bromley Corpn*[15] where the plaintiff's claim in tort for the rejection, through ill-will, of plans submitted by him, was struck out: the alternative possible remedy of a mandamus was noted by that court).

---

12 [1956] AC 736, [1956] 1 All ER 855. See p 426 above.
13 *Smith v Pywell and Spicer* (1959) 173 Estates Gazette 1009, [1959] CLY 321. See Hall 'Smith v East Elloe RDC and Legal Liability in respect of Fraud' (1957) 21 Conv (NS) 455.
14 [1963] 3 All ER 579, [1963] 1 WLR 834.
15 [1908] 1 KB 170.

In *Dunlop v Woollhara Municipal Council*[16] the Privy Council agreed that for a public authority to pass *without knowledge* of its invalidity and without *malice*, a resolution which is of no legal effect does not amount to misfeasance for the purpose of this tort. (Note the possibility of judicial review).

For this tort to be committed there must be (as well as damage to the plaintiff caused by the defendant's act) (i) misfeasance (or misconduct) (ii) in a public office.

Misfeasance

The cases referred to indicate that the relevant concepts are malice, and knowledge of the invalidity of the act. The position now appears to be as follows. Misfeasance can be committed in one of two ways, the first being where there is *malice*, that is, an intent to injure. It is possible for malice to infect the decision of a body corporate. A question that arises is whether in a multi-member body such as a local authority the personal malice of one member – in the case in question the leader of the ruling group – followed by the voting by the group for the resolution moved by the leader, is enough to render the authority itself liable.[17]

The second way misfeasance can be committed is where the official *knew that* he had no power to do what he did and that his action would injure the plaintiff (even if his intention was to confer the benefit on another but the act had the foreseeable and actual consequence of injuring the plaintiff).

A Canadian case illustrates, *Roncarelli v Duplessis*.[18] The plaintiff held a licence from the Quebec Liquor Commission. He provided bail for fellow-members of a religious sect when they were charged with offences relating to the distribution of pamphlets etc. The activities of the sect were offensive to the Quebec government. Acting on the instructions of the Premier of Quebec the Commission revoked the licence. The premier had acted so as to punish the plaintiff because of his assistance to the sect, and to warn others. The Supreme Court of Canada awarded damages to the plaintiff in this action against the Premier personally. The fact that the Premier believed that he was acting in the best interests of Quebec was, the court said, irrelevant to the issue of his responsibility for acts done in excess of his legal authority; and he had acted in the knowledge that he did not have authority to do so.

In *Bourgoin SA v Ministry of Agriculture, Fisheries and Food*[19] the minister revoked a licence to import turkeys. His purpose was to protect English producers. But he knew this was not a purpose for which the power could be used, and that revocation would damage the plaintiff, French producers. An action lay for misfeasance.

16 [1982] AC 158, [1981] 1 All ER 1202.
17 *Jones v Swansea City Council* [1989] 3 All ER 162, [1990] 1 WLR 54.
18 {1959] 16 DLR (2d) 689.
19 [1986] QB 716, [1985] 3 All ER 585.

Public office

There being a tort of misfeasance in a public office, the question may arise as to whether the defendant held a public office. There can be no doubt that the defendants in the cases referred to did hold public offices. A holder of a public office (which can include a body corporate) may be liable in this tort in respect of the exercise of any of its functions, including contractual functions.[20]

Finally, note the question of *vicarious liability*. Where an employee is alleged to have committed this tort, the plaintiff will wish to hold his employer liable. In *Racz v Home Office*[21] the House of Lords held that the Home Office could be liable vicariously for misfeasance by prison officers, provided their acts fell within the limits of those for which, in accordance with ordinary principles, an employer would be liable vicariously.

Statutory compensation

The relevance of the statutory availability of compensation to a claim in tort has been referred to. That is an important topic in its own right and justifies this brief account of some of the rules.

We consider *first*, compensation for the compulsory purchase of land. The Franks Report had this to say:

One final point of great importance needs to be made. The evidence which we have received shows that much of the dissatisfaction with the procedures relating to land arises from the basis of compensation. It is clear that objections to compulsory purchase would be far fewer if compensation were always assessed at not less than market value. It is not part of our terms of reference to consider and make recommendations upon the basis of compensation. But we cannot emphasise too strongly the extent to which these financial considerations affect the matters with which we have to deal. Whatever changes in procedure are made dissatisfaction is, because of this, bound to remain.[1]

The rules for calculating the compensation payable are to be found in the Land Compensation Act 1961. The most important rule is that the value of the land shall 'be taken to be the amount which the land if sold in the open market by a willing seller might be expected to realise'.[2] Of course the land is not being sold in the open market and the seller is not 'willing' (though the buyer is), but the valuer (and this is work for valuers not lawyers) has to say what a likely figure would be in those hypothetical circumstances. There may be no market for the land for the particular purpose for which it is used – say as a chapel – in which case, if there is a genuine intention to reinstate that use elsewhere, compensation will be assessed on the basis of the reasonable cost of 'equivalent reinstatement'. These are but two of the rules.

20 As fn 17.
21 [1994] 1 All ER 97.
  1 Cmnd 218, para 275. See p 118 above.
  2 Section 5. See further on this topic generally, Davies *Law of Compulsory Purchase and Compensation*.

We consider, *second*, the case where a person's enjoyment of land is injuriously affected (as by noise, vibrations or smells) by activities being carried on under statutory powers on neighbouring land. In *Metropolitan Asylum District v Hill*[3] neighbours obtained an injunction to prevent the building of a hospital. But in *Hammersmith and City Rly Co v Brand*[4] the plaintiff's house was affected by noise, smoke, vibration etc from a railway on adjoining land. The House of Lords held that the Acts empowering the building of the railway could not be interpreted so as to enable a person whose land had not been taken for railway purposes to recover statutory compensation from the railway company in respect f damage or annoyance caused by the passing of the trains, even though the value of the property had actually depreciated thereby. What the plaintiff suffered was the necessary consequence of the ordinary working of the railway whose construction had been statutorily approved. Notice that the plaintiff (unlike the plaintiff in *Hill*) was not trying to stop the railway from running (by means of an injunction), but was only asking in effect that the damage suffered by him should be regarded as part of the costs of running the railway, to be borne by the company's customers and shareholders. The Land Compensation Act 1973 deals with some of the problems. It provides for compensation to be paid, in certain circumstances, where the value of an interest in land is depreciated by 'physical factors caused by the use of public works'. Three points arise from this phrase. The 'physical factors' are noise, vibration, smell, fumes, smoke and artificial lighting, and the discharge on the land of any solid or liquid substance. Second, compensation is by these rules paid only in respect of the use, not construction, of works. And 'public works' means any highway, any aerodrome, and any other works on land provided or used in the exercise of statutory powers. Third, section 1(6) is of interest. It provides that compensation is not to be paid (except in respect of a highway) unless immunity from actions for nuisance in respect of the use in question is conferred (expressly or impliedly) by a statute relating to the works. In other words, a claim for compensation will fail if the authority show that they have no statutory immunity against an action in nuisance: in which case the claimant's remedy is to bring an action for the nuisance. The Act goes on to provide, in section 17, that if in those circumstances an action in nuisance is brought, the authority cannot blow hot and cold: they cannot then allege that they have that statutory immunity which they previously said they did not have.

The Act contains rules as to how the compensation is to be assessed. Disputes are referred to the Lands Tribunal. The compensation is payable, in respect of a 'highway' claim, by the highway authority; otherwise by the person managing the works.

The *third* case to note is this. The Town and County Planning Act 1990 provides that planning permission is required for the development of land, and 'development' is widely defined. If planning permission is granted,

3   (1881) 6 App Cas 193: see p 476 above.
4   (1869) LR 4 HL 171.

the land will probably have a higher value. If it is refused one fails to gain that increase in value. Compensation is not payable for that failure. There are some cases, though, where compensation is payable. One is that where planning permission is revoked, compensation is payable in respect of loss directly attributable to the revocation: the gain achieved is taken away and has to be compensated. And where the refusal of planning permission has particularly severe consequences for the applicant, over and above those which normally flow from a refusal of planning permission, compensation may be payable as where refusal of permission means that the land has become incapable of reasonably beneficial use in its existing state.

It will be noted that it is not the general rule that, where the value of one's land is *increased* by public works on a neighbouring land, as for example where a derelict site is turned into a park, any contribution to the cost of those works is required.[5]

All the examples considered relate to the use of land. Compensation may be available in very different circumstances, to the victims of riots,[6] of criminal injuries,[7] of a miscarriage of justice,[8] and of vaccination.[9] It may be payable for the unjustifiable seizure of goods,[10] for an unreasonable prohibition notice,[11] for an unnecessary or disproportionate direction,[12] or for injury caused by the emission of ionising radiation.[13]

There are non-statutory provisions for the payment of compensation. The concern of Ombudsmen for the payment of adequate compensation to those affected by maladministration is noted below.[14] And some departments and other public bodies have policies for the payment of compensation where delay occurs in the provision of certain services; it is important that the public is aware of them and the criteria applied.

Vicarious liability

The liability of public bodies carrying out statutory duties for the torts of their servants was established by the House of Lords in *Mersey Docks and Harbour Board Trustees v Gibbs*.[15] Who is a servant for this purpose is determined by the ordinary law of tort. But there are some special problems affecting the liability of public authorities. In *Fisher v Oldham Corpn*[16] the defendant was held to be not liable for the act of a police

5 But see eg Coast Protection Act 1949, s 6; Highways Act 1980, Pt XI.
6 Riot (Damages) Act 1886.
7 From the Criminal Injuries Compensation Board: see pp 150 above.
8 Criminal Justice Act 1988, s 133.
9 Vaccine Damage Payments Act 1979. See p 143 above.
10 Consumer Protection Act 1987, s 34.
11 Merchant Shipping Acft 1984, s 5.
12 Prevention of Oil Pollution Act 1971, s 13.
13 Nuclear Installations Act 1965. And see Building Act 1984, s 106.
14 See ch 16.
15 (1866) LR 1 HL 93. See p 479 above.
16 [1930] 2 KB 364.

officer when making an allegedly wrongful arrest for the reason that when so acting he was fulfilling his duty as a public servant and officer of the Crown, not as a servant of the local authority. Whether or not that decision was right, the law on that point is now different. The Royal Commission on the Police (1962) recommended that police authorities should be made vicariously liable, but the Police Act 1964, section 48, attaches such liability to the chief constable, on the ground that it is to his orders rather than those of the authority that the policeman is subject. Damages or costs awarded against the chief constable are paid out of the police authority's funds.

The *Fisher* case had followed *Stanbury v Exeter Corpn.*[17] In that case an action was brought against the defendant for the negligence of an inspector acting under the Diseases of Animals Act 1894. That Act put a duty on local authorities to appoint inspectors for enforcing the Act. The Ministry could remove incompetent inspectors. Ministerial regulations put a certain duty on inspectors, and it was while acting in pursuance of that duty that the negligence was alleged to have occurred. The court rules that the defendant was not liable. The inspector was not acting in the performance of duties imposed on the defendant, but in the performance of duties imposed directly on him. (It is not clear whether the whole of the inspectors' functions were defined by statutory regulations, so that the defendant would not, on the basis of that decision, be liable for anything he did, or whether in some respects the inspector might have been acting as the agent of the defendants so as to involve them in liability.)

In *Ministry of Housing and Local Government v Sharp*[18] Lord Denning likened the position of the local land charges registrar acting under the Land Charges Act 1925 to that of the inspector in *Stanbury v Exeter Corpn.* In *Sharp* the clerk to the local authority had been appointed registrar.

But in this respect he does not act as a servant of the council. He acts as a public officer in his own right. His duties are prescribed by statute. It is he who is responsible for their due performance not the council.

Whether or not the registrar could be sued depended on the terms of the statute in question. Although the certificate signed by the registrar had (incorrectly) stated that there were no charges against the land in question, the negligent search of the register had been made not by the registrar but by another employee of the council. The council did not wish to take the point that when searching the register that employee, though their servant, was then acting not under their orders but under the registrar's – with the result that he, not they, would have been liable for his negligence – but accepted liability for it.

If, in cases such as *Stanbury* and *Fisher* the local authority is not liable vicariously for the acts in question, the actual tortfeasor may of course be personally liable but is this satisfactory to either party.[19] It might be possible for a court today to arrive at a different view as to the liability of

17 [1905] 2 KB 838.
18 [1970] 2 QB 223, [1970] 1 All ER 1009. See p 492, above.
19 See Robinson *Public Authorities and Legal Liability*.

the local authority, and in any event it is not necessarily the case that an employer cannot be vicariously liable for the acts of a person whom he is bound to employ, nor that he cannot be liable for the acts of someone who is dismissible by a third party.[20]

The liability of the Crown in such circumstances is referred to below.

Personal immunity and indemnity

The immunity expressly, or by judicial interpretation, enjoyed by bodies exercising public power from liability in tort has been referred to. Personal immunity may also be provided for. Section 265 of the Public Health Act 1875, re-enacting earlier legislation, provides that nothing done, and no contract entered into, by a local authority (and certain other authorities specified) or by any member or by any officer of such authority, shall, if the thing is done 'bona fide for purpose of executing this Act' subject any of them ie members or officers personally to any action, liability, claim or demand whatsoever (though liability of a member to be surcharged was excepted). This section was extended to National Health Service authorities by section 72 of the National Health Service Act 1946.[1] In *Bullard v Croydon Hospital Group Management Committee*[2] it was argued that the effect of section 72 was to exempt the Committee from liability in negligence (the allegation was of negligence by a doctor, the Committee being vicariously liable). The court was not prepared to give the section that interpretation. As to section 265, the court thought that it had to be considered in conjunction with section 308 of the 1875 Act which provided (significantly) for the payment of compensation to persons affected by action taken under the Act. Section 265 has been extended by various other Acts to things done under those Acts, and now it has been extended to anything done for the purpose of any public, general or local Act.[3]

Section 139(1) of the Mental Health Act 1983 provides that 'no person shall be liable ... to any civil proceedings ... in respect of any act purporting to be done in pursuance of this Act ... unless the act was done in bad faith or without reasonable care'. The purpose is to provide those concerned with mentally disordered patients some protection against unjustified actions at law for damages. It does not protect against judicial review.[4]

The Banking Act 1987[5] exempts certain persons (and bodies) from liability in damages (but not judicial review) unless they acted in bad faith.

(Protection of a different kind is provided (to an authority) by section 144 of the Customs and Excise Management Act 1979 by which, if a plaintiff is successful in certain proceedings against the Commissioners

20 See Atiyah *Vicarious Liability*, p 77.
1 See now National Health Service Act 1977, s 125.
2 [1953] 1 QB 511, [1953] 1 All ER 96.
3 Local Government (Miscellaneous Provisions) Act 1976, s 39; Building Act 1984, s 115.
4 *R v Gardner, ex p L* [1986] QB 1090, [1986] 2 All ER 306.
5 Section 1(4), 2(7). Also Financial Services Act 1986, s 187.

of Customs and Excise, he will nevertheless not be entitled to recover any damages or costs if the court certifies that there were reasonable grounds for the action taken by Customs and Excise which is the subject of the proceedings.)

Where proceedings are brought against a public employee he may be able to claim an *indemnity* as against his employer. Every servant may claim to be indemnified by his employer against liabilities incurred by him in consequence of obedience to orders or incurred by him in the execution of his authority or in reasonable performance of the duties of his employer. In addition to this common law right there are many statutes empowering public authorities to indemnify their employees. For example, section 26 of the Health and Safety at Work etc Act 1974 provides that where an action has been brought against an inspector employed by the Health and Safety Executive for any act done in purported execution of the health and safety legislation and the circumstances are such that he is not legally entitled to require the Executive to indemnify him, the Executive may do so in whole or in part if it is satisfied that the inspector honestly believed that the act complained of was within his powers and that his duty as inspector required or entitled him to do it.

Liability of the Crown in tort

'The King can do no wrong'. Thus at common law the Crown itself could not be sued in tort before the Crown Proceedings Act 1947 came into force except that a few government departments could be sued under certain statutes.

Now where an employee commits a tort in the course of his employment and thereby injures a third person, that person will be able to sue not only the employee but also the employer, for the rule is that an employer is vicariously liable to third parties for torts committed by his employees in the course of their employment. The Crown's immunity in tort meant that unlike other employers it was not vicariously liable for the torts of its employees. With the Crown as a major employer this was an important defect in the law. Nor was one Crown servant vicariously liable for the torts of another. In *Bainbridge v Postmaster-General*[6] the plaintiff B sued C, a Post Office engineer, for damages suffered through the negligent relaying of a footpath. B sought to make the Postmaster-General, a body corporate, liable as C's employer, but the court held that C was not in his employment. 'Being equally servants of the Crown they are not servants of each other.'

The fact that 'The King can do no wrong' did not mean that an employee of the King could do no wrong. Thus a Crown servant who committed a tort could be made personally liable even if the tort was done in the course of Crown employment. The fact that it was so done was, and is, no defence, nor does the law acknowledge the defence that the act was done on superior

6 [1906] 1 KB 178.

orders or in pursuance of state policy or executive necessity. If damages were awarded against a Crown servant the Crown might pay them. But difficulties arose if it was not possible to identify the actual wrongdoer or if the Crown itself were the actual tortfeasor, as where an employee injured whilst working in an ordnance factory wished to sue the occupier, that is, the Crown. To get round these difficulties the practice grew up of a government department concerned providing the plaintiff with the name of a Crown servant as defendant and indemnifying him against any damages awarded. This nominated defendant may not in fact have had any responsibility for the damage in respect of which the action was brought. The courts revolted against this fiction and refused to hold the defendant liable where his personal responsibility for the damage could not be shown.[7]

The revolt hastened the passing of the Crown Proceedings Act 1947. A similar bill had been prepared in 1927 but had not been proceeded with. The Committee on Ministers' Powers had criticised what is called this *lacuna* in the law.[8] Notice that the Act does not simply assimilate the Crown's liability in tort to that of a person of full age and capacity, it rather provides for its liability in a number of specified matters, that is, it is liable only in so far as the Act provides.[9]

Vicarious liability

Section 2(1) of the Crown Proceedings Act 1947 reads, in part:

Subject to the provisions of this Act the Crown shall be subject to all those liabilities in tort to which, if it were a private person of full age and capacity, it would be subject:

(a)   in respect of torts committed by its servants or agents;
(b)   [see p 504 below];
(c)   [see p 504 below].

This provision leaves untouched the liability of the actual tortfeasor: to his liability is added the vicarious liability of the Crown. The personal liability of public officials for their tortious acts has long been regarded as an important aspect of the rule of law, but now that the Crown is vicariously liable for its servants it is unlikely that the victim of a tort will choose to sue the servant to the exclusion of the employer. Does this mean that the personal liability of the public official is now meaningless? Lawson wrote:

The effect of personal liability in preventing the growth of a hierarchical spirit and in persuading public officials to keep scrupulously within their powers has probably survived where personal liability has became illusory. Moreover the liability to appear publicly in court, even if not as a defendant, and submit to cross-examination on one's personal conduct, is still a powerful deterrent to

---

7 *Royster v Cavey* [1947] KB 204, [1946] 2 All ER 642, CA; *Adams v Naylor* [1986] AC 543.
8 Cmd 4060, p 112.
9 *Trawnik v Gordon Lennox* [1985] 2 All ER 368, [1985] 1 WLR 532. See G L Williams *Crown Proceedings Act 1947*; Street *Government Liability*.

officials who might be tempted to injure their fellow citizens under cover of statutory powers.[10]

The word 'servant' is not defined in the Act, and therefore the normal rules of the law of tort apply in determining whether a person or body is a servant of the Crown.[11] However, even assuming that he is a Crown servant, the Crown's liability for his acts is limited by section 2(6) of the Act which says:

No proceedings shall lie against the Crown by virtue of this section, in respect of any act, neglect or default of any officer of the Crown, unless that officer has been directly or indirectly appointed by the Crown and was at the material time paid in respect of his duties as an officer of the Crown wholly out of the Consolidated Fund of the United Kingdom, moneys provided by Parliament, the Road Fund, or any other Fund certified by the Treasury for the purpose of this subsection or was at the material time holding an office in respect of which the Treasury certify that the holder thereof would normally be so paid.[12]

The word 'officer' will be noticed. Section 38(2) of the Act says that it 'includes any servant of His Majesty'.

Section 2(1) (a) also refers to the Crown's liability for the acts of its *agents*. Section 38(2) says that 'agent' includes 'independent contractor'. Section 30(2) (d) also provides that the Act does not subject the Crown to any greater liabilities in respect of the acts or omissions of any independent contractor than it would be subject to in respect of such acts if it were a private person.[13]

The proviso to section 2(1) (a) must now be considered. It reads:

Provided that no proceedings shall lie against the Crown by virtue of paragraph (a) of this subsection in respect of any act or omission of a servant or agent of the Crown unless the act or omission would apart from the provisions of this Act have given rise to a cause of action in tort against that servant or agent or his estate.

Whatever may have been the intention behind the proviso,[14] it means that if you are to sue the Crown under section 2(1) (a) you must show that you have a right of action against the Crown servant who was responsible for the act complained of or, at least, that if it is shown that the act would not have given rise to an action against the servant, the action will fail. The only case which appears to have raised directly the meaning of the proviso is *Corney v Minister of Labour*.[15] C sued B, an official at a Labour Exchange for assault, and joined the minister as defendant. Previous criminal proceedings by C against B in the magistrates' court had been dismissed with the result that civil proceedings against B were barred. But C continued his action against the minister, who pleaded the proviso.

10 'Dicey Revisited' (1959) 7 Political Studies 124. Cf Sedley (1994) 110 LQR 287.
11 See ch 2, above for reference to public corporations as Crown servants.
12 This had particular relevance to torts committed by the police. For present position see Police Act 1964 and p 499 above.
13 Eg *Darling v A-G* [1950] 2 All ER 793.
14 See *Williams* and *Street*, fn 9, above.
15 [1959] PL 170.

The county court held that the action against the Crown could continue; the servant committed an act which 'gave rise to' an action at the time the act was done, so that the Crown was liable as employer even though proceedings against the servant were barred. (C lost on the facts.)

The nature of the Crown's liability under section 2(1) (a) is illustrated by *Home Office v Dorset Yacht Co Ltd*.[16] Borstal trainees escaped from the custody of Borstal officers and damaged the company's property. Lord Reid said, 'It is admitted that the Home Office would be vicariously liable, if an action would lie against any of these officers.' Lord Morris said, 'The allegations of fact are such that if there is any liability in the Home Office, it is on the basis of vicarious liability for the acts or omissions of the officers as their servants or agents.'

The Crown's liability under section 2(1) (a) is vicarious not personal. It would seem therefore that if the Crown was the defendant in the factual situation that existed in *Carmarthenshire County Council v Lewis*[17] it would not, unlike the local authority in that case, be vicariously liable, as there the employee was not negligent but the employer was. Further, it would seem that the argument put forward by Denning LJ in *Cassidy v Minister of Health*[18] (that a hospital authority's liability may be personal not vicarious) would not avail where the Crown was the defendant.

It has been suggested that the basis of the Crown's liability in tort is such that if, for example, a citizen suffers loss through the delay in the issue to him of a licence, he, in order to sue the Crown successfully, would have to show that apart from the Act he would have been able to sue the official.

And so the issue which the courts may have to examine in cases of this sort is not as to the duty of the Ministry but as to the duty of the ministry's official, and that may sometimes be a very different matter indeed.[19]

Liability to its servants
The Crown is, by section 2(1) (b) of the Crown Proceedings Act, also liable as if it were a private person of full age and capacity, for 'breach of those duties which a person owes to his servants and agents at common law by reason of being their employer'. The Crown must therefore, for example, take reasonable care for the physical safety of those persons.

Liability as the occupier of property
By section 2(1) (c) of the Act the Crown is subject as if it were a private person to liabilities:

in respect of any breach of the duties attaching at common law to the ownership, occupation, possession or control of property.

16 [1970] AC 1004, [1970] 2 All ER 294. See p 480 above.
17 [1955] AC 549, [1955] 1 All ER 565.
18 [1951] 2 KB 343, [1951] 1 All ER 574.
19 MacDermott *Protection from Power under English Law*, p 107. Complaints of this nature have been investigated by the Parliamentary Commissioner (see ch 16 below) and compensation paid.

It will be noted that by both section 2(1) (b) and section 2(1) (c) the Crown is subject to common law and hence not to statutory liabilities. Further, section 2(6) (p 503 above), does not apply to these two subsections, for it limits the Crown's vicarious liability which is imposed by section 2(1) (a), whereas section 2(1) (b) and (c) impose a direct and not a vicarious liability on the Crown.

The Defective Premises Act 1972 binds the Crown, but does not bind the Crown in tort further than it is made liable by the Crown Proceedings Act 1947.

Action for breach of statutory duty

Where a statutory duty is imposed on a person, and another is injuriously affected by its exercise, that other may have a right of action against him for breach of statutory duty.[20] Section 2(2) of the Crown Proceedings Act provides:

Where the Crown is bound by a statutory duty which is binding also upon persons other than the Crown and its officers, then, subject to the provisions of this Act, the Crown shall, in respect of a failure to comply with that duty, be subject to all those liabilities in tort (if any) to which it would be so subject if it were a private person of full age and capacity.

The limits imposed by this subsection are considerable. First, in accordance with principle, the Crown is bound by a statutory duty only where the Act in question so provides. Second, the Crown is liable by this subsection only where the duty is binding also on other persons. It is not therefore liable where the duty binds only itself. This rule does not apply to public authorities other than the Crown and there seems to be no good reason why it should exist in respect of the Crown.

Examples of statutory duties which, as a result of section 2(2), binds the Crown, are those under the Factories Act 1961, the Offices, Shops and Railway Premises Act 1963, and the Occupier's Liability Act 1957.[1] The borstal service has a statutory basis, but the claim in *Home Office v Dorset Yacht Co Ltd*[2] was not based on breach of statutory duty, thus evading the limits of section 2(2).[3]

Liability where function is imposed on officers of the Crown

In the light of *Stanbury v Exeter Corpn*[4] it might be thought that where statute or common law imposes a function on an officer of the Crown rather than on the Crown itself, the Crown would not be liable for torts committed by him in discharge of that function. However section 2(3) of the 1947 Act provides that in such cases the liability of the Crown shall be the same as if the function had been imposed solely by virtue of

20 See p 488 above.
1 See North *Occupiers' Liability*, p 34.
2 [1970] AC 1004, [1970] 2 All ER 294; p 480 above.
3 For tort action for breach of duty not to finance Channel Tunnel, see Channel Tunnel Act 1987, s 2(7).
4 [1905] 2 KB 838. See p 499 above.

instructions lawfully given by the Crown, so that it may be liable despite the fact that the function was imposed on the officer not the Crown.[5]

Judicial acts
Section 2(5) of the Act reads:

No proceedings shall lie against the Crown by virtue of this section in respect of anything done or omitted to be done by any person while discharging or purporting to discharge any responsibilities of a judicial nature vested in him, or any responsibilities which he has in connection with the execution of judicial process.

The word 'judicial' is not defined in the Act. In *Jones v Department of Employment*[6] J's claim for unemployment benefit was disallowed by the adjudication officer (AO). He submitted further evidence to the Department which affirmed the AO's decision. J then sued the AO and the Department alleging their negligence in disallowing the claim. The defendants argued that the AO's function was judicial. The Court of Appeal, relying on *R v Deputy Industrial Injuries Comr, ex p Moore*,[7] held that it was not, but the defendants escaped liability on other grounds.[8] In *Welsh v Chief Constable of the Merseyside Police*[9] it was held that the recording by the Crown Prosecution Service of the fact that an offence had been taken into consideration was an administrative not a judicial act and was not therefore protected by this provision.

Would the exemption provided by the section apply to the acts of inspectors holding public local inquiries, and of members of tribunals? But notice that before the Crown could in any case be made liable under this section it would have to be shown that the person discharging judicial responsibilities, etc was a Crown servant, and that he himself could have been sued. On that last point it will be appreciated that a degree of immunity from suit is given to certain persons exercising judicial functions.

Intellectual property rights
Section 3 of the 1947 Act now provides[10] that civil proceedings lie against the Crown for an infringement committed by a servant or agent of the Crown, with the authority of the Crown, of a patent, a registered trade mark, design right, copyright etc.

Joint liability
The law as to indemnity and contribution between joint and several tortfeasors and as to contributory negligence is made binding on the Crown by section 4 of the 1947 Act. The Civil Liability (Contribution) Act 1978 binds the Crown without prejudice to section 4.

5 See *R v HM Treasury ex p Petch* [1990] COD 19: Prime Minister not 'The Crown' for purposes of s 2(2) but an 'officer of the Crown' within s 2(3).
6 [1989] QB 1, [1988] 1 All ER 725.
7 [1965] 1 QB 456, [1965] 1 All ER 81. See p 159 above.
8 See p 484 above.
9 [1993] 1 All ER 692.
10 See Copyright, Designs and Patents Act 1988, Sch 7, para 4.

The armed forces

By section 10 of the Crown Proceedings Act 1947, the Crown is not liable in tort for death or personal injury caused to one member of the armed forces while on duty or on Crown premises by an *act* done by another member of those forces while on duty. The person who did the act is also exempt from liability. Nor can the Crown or an officer of the Crown be sued for death or personal injury suffered by a member of the armed forces in consequence of the nature or condition of *property or equipment* used for the purposes of the armed forces. These exceptions from liability only apply if the Secretary of State for Social Security certifies that the injury suffered is attributable to service for the purpose of entitlement to a pension. In other words where the injury entitles a man to a pension, he cannot sue for damages. But consider *Adams v War Office*.[11] The plaintiff was killed when on a training exercise by a shell fired by another member of the forces. The ministry said that his death would be attributable to service for purposes of a pension. It was later decided that no pension was in fact payable (to his parents). Nevertheless the attribution of his death to service exempted the Crown from liability in an action for negligence.

The exemptions provided by this section only apply to acts causing death or personal injury. There is therefore no immunity under it for eg defamation.

There are very few cases on the operation of the section. In one, a soldier injured in barracks was treated initially at the army medical centre and then transferred to a civilian hospital where he died.[12] In another a serviceman alleged that he had suffered injury through exposure to radiation while nuclear weapons were being tested some 30 years before.[13] However in the face of increasing criticism, section 10 was repealed by section 1 of the Crown Proceedings (Armed Forces) Act 1987.

But it is still necessary to know about section 10, as section 2 of the 1987 Act provides that section 10 may be revived in whole or in part by ministerial order when it is thought necessary to do so because of any imminent national danger or great emergency or for the purposes of a warlike operation. As long as section 10 remains repealed the possibility has been opened up of claims being made against members of the armed forces in person (the Crown itself could also be sued for its vicarious liability). The government has said that it would stand behind any member sued by another for alleged negligence in the course of his duties.[14]

The Post Office

Section 9 of the Crown Proceedings Act exempted the Crown from being sued in tort for anything done in relation to a postal packet. The Post Office is now however a public corporation, and section 9 has been repealed. The extent of the Post Office's liability is dealt with below.

11 [1955] 3 All ER 245, [1955] 1 WLR 1116.
12 *Bell v Secretary of State for Defence* [1986] QB 322, [1985] 3 All ER 661.
13 *Pearce v Secretary for Defence* [1988] AC 755, [1988] 2 All ER 348.
14 See Boyd [1988] PL 237.

Some cases noted

Reference to these actions in tort against the Crown may be of interest. In *Brazier v Ministry of Defence*[15] the plaintiff, a diver employed by the defendant, was being given an injection by a Royal Navy sick berth attendant, when the needle broke inside him. He was unable to make good his allegation of negligence. An action would have lain against the sick berth attendant.

Tramontana II (Owners) v Ministry of Defence and Martin[16] was an action against the minister and a Queen's Harbourmaster, alleging negligence in the marking of a wreck whereby the plaintiff's power-boat was damaged. It was held inter alia that the defendants having in the exercise of that statutory power assumed responsibility for marking the wreck, owed a duty to all persons lawfully using the port to act with reasonable care and skill. The action failed on the facts.

In *Bright v A-G*[17] a county council acting as agents for a government department employed their workmen to remove double white lines from a road. The work was done negligently causing ridges to be formed on the road surface. The plaintiff motor cyclist was injured. The council was liable for the workmen's negligence, and the Crown as the council's principal.

In *Churchill v Foot*[18] the plaintiff, a former SOE agent, sued the author of a volume of the official History of the War series *(SOE in France)* and HMSO, the publishers, for libel. The action was settled on the payment of damages.

Postal and telecommunications services

The Crown Proceedings Act 1947 made the Crown generally liable in tort. One of the exceptions excluded liability for anything done or omitted to be done in respect of a postal packet or a telephonic communication by any person while employed as a servant or agent of the Crown. Defending this exemption the Attorney-General said that no commercial firm would undertake to pay damage for the negligent loss of a letter in return for the mere cost of the stamp: it would exclude its liability by contract. The 1947 Act also provided that the actual tortfeasor was not to be civilly liable except at the suit of the Crown. This changed the previous rule of personal liability. Defending this change the Attorney-General said that actions against officials personally were 'very rare and quite valueless' unless the Crown stood behind the official. As the Crown was not prepared to accept responsibility, it would, he said, be unfair to officials to leave them exposed when the Crown was not liable.[19]

15 [1965] 1 Lloyd's Rep 26. And see *Barrett v Ministry of Defence* (1995) Independent, 3 January, breach of duty of care to drunken serviceman.
16 [1969] 2 Lloyd's Rep 94.
17 [1971] 2 Lloyd's Rep 68.
18 (1969) Times, 28 January.
19 439 H of C Official Report (5th series) cols 2616, 2620.

The exemptions from liability in tort were continued and extended by the Post Office Act 1969, section 29. Since the enactment of the British Telecommunications Act 1981 the Post Office is concerned with postal services; responsibility for telecommunications has been transferred to British Telecommunications. The services must be considered separately therefore. The position with regard to the former is that section 29 of the 1969 Act provides that no proceeding is to lie in tort[20] against the Post Office in respect of any loss or damage suffered by reason of anything done or not done in relation to anything in the post, or failure to collect the mail, and no officer or servant of the Post Office or person who, not being such an officer or servant, is a sub-postmaster, is subject, except at the suit of the Post Office, to any civil liability for any loss or damage in respect of which Post Office liability is excluded, as just explained. Further, no person engaged in or about the carriage of mail, and no officer, servant, agent or sub-contractor of such person, is subject to any civil liability for any loss or damage for which Post Office liability is excluded except, again, at the suit of the Post Office.

However, a measure of liability is imposed on the Post Office by section 30 of the 1969 Act (as amended by section 70 of the British Telecommunications Act 1981). The liability is imposed in respect of any 'inland packet' in respect of which the Post Office accepts liability under that section in pursuance of a scheme made under section 28 of the 1969 Act.[2] Liability arises in so far as the loss of or damage to the packet is due to any wrongful act done or any neglect or default committed by an officer, servant or agent of the Post Office while performing his functions as such while dealing with the packet. In any proceedings it is to be presumed, until the contrary is shown, that the loss or damage was due to such wrongful act. Proceedings must be begun within twelve months of the day on which the packet was posted.

The amount recoverable under these provisions is not to exceed the market value of the packet at the time when the cause of action arises (and this does not include the market value of any message or information which it bears); or the maximum amount payable, under a scheme made under section 28 of the Act, by way of compensation for a packet of that description.

As for telecommunications services, section 23 of the British Telecommunications Act 1981 provided that no proceedings were to lie in tort against British Telecommunications in respect of any loss or damage in providing, a telecommunications service etc. However the statute which denationalised British Telecommunications also removed its immunity in tort (and contract).[3]

---

20 Including an action for breach of bailment or of statutory duty: *American Express Co v British Airways Board* [1983] 1 All ER 557, [1983] 1 WLR 701.

1 For status of sub-postmaster see *Hitchcock v Post Office* [1980] ICR 100 EAT; *Tanna v Post Office* [1981] ICR 374, EAT.

2 For Post Office schemes see p461 above.

3 Telecommunications Act 1984, Sch 7. The company's *Offer for Sale* stated: 'In the opinion of the Board, it is not possible accurately to assess the likely effect of removing the immunity from legal proceedings in contract or tort previously enjoyed by British

A note on criminal liability

What follows is no more than a reference to some aspects of the criminal liability of public authorities and employees.[4]

Who can be prosecuted?

The Crown is not bound by an Act of Parliament in the absence of express words or necessary implication. Even if the Crown is, by that rule, bound by an Act, it cannot, it is said, be prosecuted. The arguments were considered by the High Court of Australia in *Cain v Doyle*.[5] Employers were by statute under a duty to reinstate in their employment persons who had done war service, and not to dismiss them. Offenders were liable on summary conviction to be fined. Other sections of the Act provided, for other offences, for fines and imprisonment. The Act stated that it bound the Crown. The defendant, manager of a government factory, terminated the employment of a person protected by the Act, and was prosecuted for procuring the offence. If the Crown could not be convicted of the offence, Doyle could not be guilty of procuring it. Latham CJ dismissed as unacceptable in principle the idea that the Crown can commit a criminal offence. His objections were: that the fundamental idea of the criminal law is a prosecution of offences against the King's peace; that the Crown itself would have to be the prosecutor in the case of serious offences; that the government would have to pay a fine to itself; and that where imprisonment was at least an alternative penalty the Crown could not be included as it could not be imprisoned. Dixon J, with whom Rich J agreed, did not regard the imposition of criminal liability on the Crown as a theoretical impossibility, but thought that there was the strongest presumption against such an interpretation of any statute, and in the circumstances of this case, as for example that there was no court with summary jurisdiction over the Crown and that the Treasury would pay the fine to itself, did not think the presumption was displaced. Two judges dissented. Starke J for example said that sovereign bodies may create rights and obligations against themselves and submit the determination of those rights and obligations to the courts, and provide means for enforcing them.

In *Canadian Broadcasting Corpn v A-G for Ontario*[6] the Corporation, an agent of the Crown, was prosecuted for breach of a Sunday Observance Act. Four of the seven judges comprising the court took the view that it was possible to impose criminal liability on the Crown, but to do so it must be clear beyond question; and that the Act in question did not. In a New Zealand case *Southland Acclimatisation Society v Anderson and the*

Telecom. However, the Board is of the opinion, as far as it can presently judge, that, having regard to, inter alia, the insurance arrangements made by the Company, it is unlikely that the financial position of British Telecom will be adversely affected to a material extent by the removal of the immunity'. 20 November 1984.

4   See also p 113 above.
5   (1946) 72 CLR 409.
6   (1959) 16 DLR (2d) 609.

Minister of Mines[7] the minister was prosecuted for failing to comply with a condition on which he held a statutory water right. Quillam J accepted the line taken by the majority in the cases mentioned: that the Crown may be criminally liable but that it is in every case a problem of statutory interpretation. In this case the expression 'every person' in the section which created the offence was not enough to include the Crown; the offences were summary offences, and the only machinery provided for bringing them before the court was that provided by an Act which did not bind the Crown: it followed that the magistrate had no jurisdiction to entertain the information. Discussing *Cain v Doyle* Friedmann argued[8] that there is no reason either of theory or of practice why the Crown ought not and could not be made liable in respect at least of what are called public welfare offences such as infringements of legislation relating to safety at work, pure food etc.[9]

The Road Traffic Act 1972 provides an interesting procedure for imposing criminal liability in respect of Crown vehicles. Where the driver only is responsible for the offence, no problem arises. But what of offences imposing liability on the person (here the Crown) permitting the vehicle to be used? The 1972 Act permitted proceedings to be brought against a defendant nominated for the purpose by the Department. *Barnett v French*[10] uncovered the problems raised by that device: they were dealt with by an amendment to the Act by section 64 of the Transport Act 1982.

The distinction between the Crown, its employees, and the Queen personally in the matter of criminal liability is illustrated by section 54 of the Food Safety Act 1990. It provides, first, that the Act binds the Crown. It goes on to say that no contravention by the Crown of the Act is to make the Crown criminally liable, but that the High Court may declare unlawful any act by the Crown which constitutes such a contravention. Next, despite that rule, the Act says that its provisions apply to persons in the public service of the Crown as it applies to other persons. And finally it says that nothing in the section is to be taken as affecting Her Majesty in her private capacity.

Public authorities other than the Crown are subject to the criminal law. For example in *West Mersea UDC v Fraser*[11] the local authority was convicted for failure to give a water supply, and in 1974 Leominster Borough Council (and its clerk and surveyor) were each convicted of an offence under section 55 of the Town and Country Planning Act 1971, in connection with the demolition of the Town Hall.[12] In 1982 the London Borough of Southwark was fined £2000 for the public nuisance of leaving

---

7 [1978] 1 NZLR 838.

8 (1950) 13 MLR 24.

9 Some years ago the Navy Army and Air Force Institutes was prosecuted for selling dried fruit under weight. It stated that it did not claim Crown status as it was clearly at fault but might have done so if the evaporation which caused the deficiency in the stock had been caused by the exigencies of the service.

10 [1981] 1 WLR 848, [1981] RTR 173.

11 [1950] 2 KB 119, [1950] 1 All ER 990. *York District Council v Poller* (1975) 73 LGR 522.

12 Leominster and Bromyard Gazette, 16 October 1974.

an unguarded pile of sand in the road which caused a man's death.[13] However, in *Leeds City Council v West Yorkshire Police*[14] the House of Lords refused to impose on the Council criminal penalties available against a guardian of a child charged with an offence. And in *R v Horseferry Road Magistrates Ct, ex p Independent Broadcasting Authority*[15] the court declined to imply a criminal sanction in respect of the Authority's duty not to transmit subliminal images.

Crimes against the public administration

The concept of crimes against the State is familiar – treason, sedition etc. Some crimes could be said to be imposed for the protection of the system of public administration. These might include crimes against the public revenue;[16] those imposed for failure to supply the administration with information it needs for its proper purposes;[17] the obstruction of certain categories of employees;[18] the unlawful assumption of the powers of certain employees;[19] the deceiving of a person responsible for a public duty into doing something he would not have done.[20] Crimes aimed at preventing corruption fall under this heading also.[1] The common law offence of misbehaviour in a public office will also be noted.[2] The offence can be committed by wilful neglect to perform one's duty. Culpability is not restricted to corruption or dishonesty; the misconduct impugned must be of such a degree as to injure the public interest to an extent that calls for condemnation and punishment.

Defence of reliance on advice

How far is it, or should it be, a defence to a criminal charge that one relied on advice from a competent administrative authority? In considering this question Glanville Williams has noted that very occasionally express rules of law confer immunity for acts done under official advice, but these are rare exceptions. 'The cases show that almost always our courts apply the insensitive and unjust rule that misdirection by a public officer ... constitutes no defence to a criminal charge, even though it led the defendant to believe, reasonably, that his conduct was lawful, or at any rate would not be made the subject of prosecution ... Some of these cases could have been decided otherwise if the courts had applied the doctrine of estoppel.'[3] He concluded that the law should allow a defence of

---

13 (1982) Times, 3 December.
14 [1983] 1 AC 29, [1982] 1 All ER 274.
15 [1987] QB 54, [1986] 2 All ER 666.
16 See p 114 above.
17 See p 112 above.
18 Eg Weights and Measures Act 1979, Sch 2, para 6.
19 Eg Customs and Excise Management Act 1979, s. 13.
20 *R v Terry* [1984] AC 374, [1984] 1 All ER 65.
1 Eg Prevention of Corruption Act 1906, Public Bodies Corrupt Practices Act 1889.
2 *R v Llewellyn-Jones* [1968] 1 QB 429, [1967] 3 All ER 225; *R v Dytham* [1979] QB 722, [1979] 3 All ER 641. R v Bowden (1995) Times, 6 March: local authority employee.
3 'The draft code and reliance upon official statements' 9 LS 177.

reasonable reliance upon information as to the penal law given by any public officer in respect of matters with which he is concerned – with such exceptions as may be determined.

Chapter 15

Discovery of documents: public interest immunity

As part of the pre-trial preliminaries of ordinary civil proceedings either party can ask the other to make a list of all documents which are in his possession and which are material to any question in issue in the action, and to allow him to inspect and take copies of these documents. This is known as discovery of documents. A party can refuse to disclose on certain grounds: a dispute between the parties is determined by the court. The court is not to order disclosure unless it is of opinion that the order is necessary either for disposing fairly of the cause or matter, or for saving costs.[1] The court can also be asked to order the other party to answer on oath questions submitted by the applicant. These are called interrogatories.

In this matter it used to be said that the Crown enjoyed 'Crown privilege', in that it could, on certain grounds, refuse to disclose any document or to answer any question where to do so would be injurious to the public interest. Oral evidence of privileged documents could not be given, and 'Crown privilege' could also be claimed for evidence of oral communication.

This is an area of law where there have been important changes, wholly brought about by judicial decision. The story starts with *Duncan v Cammell, Laird & Co Ltd*,[2] decided in 1942. The submarine *Thetis* built by the defendant under contract with the Admiralty sank while undergoing trials. In an action for negligence the plaintiff, the widow of one of those drowned, sought discovery of certain documents, including plans of the submarine. The Admiralty claimed Crown privilege for them and the House of Lords upheld the refusal of the judge to order their discovery. It laid it down that Crown privilege could be claimed for a document on two alternative grounds: (a) that the disclosure of the *contents* of a *particular*

---

1 RSC Ord 24. Discovery is also available in judicial review proceedings – see p 524 below. The requirements of Ord 24 apply. For discovery in criminal proceedings and special considerations that arise there see *R v Horseferry Road Magistrates Court, ex p Bennett (No 2)* [1994] 1 All ER 289, *R v Clowes* [1992] 3 All ER 440.
2 [1942] AC 624, [1942] 1 All ER 587.

document would injure the public interest, for example, by endangering national security or prejudicing good diplomatic relations; (b) that the document falls within a *class* which must be withheld from production to ensure *the proper functioning of the public service.*

The claim to Crown privilege on ground (a) above was generally regarded as acceptable, as matters touching security, defence and foreign affairs are properly left in the hands of the political rather than the judicial arm of government. A claim on ground (b) that is, that the document, whatever its contents, should be withheld because it belonged to a *class* of documents, was regarded by critics as less easy to justify.[3] It was argued that there is a public interest not only in the 'proper functioning of the public service' but also in the doing of justice, and that the doing of justice may be hindered or made impossible where documents are withheld. The government view was that a matter involving the 'proper functioning of the public service' was for the minister to decide, that a judge would consider the claim to privilege according to the contents of the document and its relevance to the particular action, so that the same kind of document would sometimes be protected and sometimes disclosed, and this, it was said, would destroy the whole basis of class privilege, which was *the need to secure freedom and candour* within or without the public service, which desiderata might be not attained if officials feared that the confidential nature of their reports might at some time be destroyed by disclosure in litigation.

The government view of the proper way to strike a balance between the needs of litigants and of the administration, was to reduce as much as possible the classes for which privilege would be claimed. Accordingly in 1956 and 1962 it was stated that in future privilege would not be claimed for certain classes of documents.[4]

The House of Lords achieved a breakthrough in *Conway v Rimmer*.[5] The plaintiff had been a probationary constable. He had been prosecuted for theft from a colleague but was acquitted and thereupon sued a police superintendent for malicious prosecution. The documents of which discovery was sought, and which were admittedly material to the action, were (a) four reports made on the plaintiff during his probationary period and (b) a report by the defendant to the chief constable of his investigation into the plaintiff's alleged offence. Production was, be it noted, desired by both parties, but resisted by the Home Secretary on the ground that they fell into the *classes* of, as to (a), reports by police officers relating to the conduct of individual officers, and as to (b), investigation into the commission of crime. The ground of refusal was simply stated to be that 'production would be injurious to the public interest'.

3 See eg *Ellis v Home Office* [1953] 2 QB 135, [1953] 2 All ER 149.
4 These included reports of government employees about accidents on the road, on government premises or to government employees, medical reports of the health of civilian Crown employees, doctors' reports where the Crown or the doctor is being sued for negligence etc: see 197 HL Official Report (5th series) col 741; 237 ibid col 1191.
5 [1968] AC 910, [1968] 1 All ER 874.

The House of Lords agreed in the result that the principle that the minister's refusal to disclose could in no circumstances be overridden, could no longer stand, (though some of their Lordships regarded themselves as overruling *Duncan v Cammell, Laird & Co Ltd*, whilst others were content to show that the principle of that case did not apply to the very different circumstances of *Conway v Rimmer*). They were unanimous that it is constitutionally entirely proper for the judiciary 'to hold the balance between the public interest, as expressed by a minister, to withhold certain documents or other evidence, and the public interest in ensuring the proper administration of justice', as Lord Reid put it. They were also equally firmly of the view that the greatest weight must be given to the minister's view in every case, thus, to quote Lord Reid again, 'if the minister's reasons are of a character which judicial experience is not competent to weigh, then the minister's view must prevail'. It would, in the House of Lords' opinion, be very rarely proper to override the view of a minister that it would be against the public interest to make public the *contents* of a *particular* document – an example would be the plans of a submarine as in *Duncan v Cammell, Laird & Co Ltd* itself. Some *classes* of documents probably ought never to be disclosed, whatever their contents might be, for example, cabinet minutes,[6] foreign office despatches, and documents relating to appointments to offices of importance.

The government put the argument, noted above, that the basis for the *class* privilege was the need not to discourage candour within the public service. However the House thought that that was not a good reason for not disclosing documents. Lord Reid preferred this reason:

To my mind the most important reason is that such disclosure would create or fan ill-informed or captious public or political criticism. The business of government is difficult enough as it is, and no government could contemplate with equanimity the inner workings of the government machine being exposed to the gaze of those ready to criticise without adequate knowledge of the background and perhaps with some axe to grind.[7]

He went on to say that that applied not only to the documents of the kind referred to but also to:

all documents concerned with policy making within departments including it may be minutes and the like by quite junior officials and correspondence with outside bodies. Further it may be that deliberations about a particular case require as much protection as deliberations about policy.

But the courts, the House held, would look more critically at a claim to privilege for routine or trivial documents; in such cases they are well placed to perform the task of weighing the two aspects of public interest involved. If the judge thought the minister's reasons for withholding

---

6   'It is quite clear that no court will compel the production of cabinet papers in the course of discovery in an action': per Lord Widgery in *A-G v Jonathan Cape Ltd* [1976] QB 752, [1975] 3 All ER 484. But cf Lord Fraser in *Air Canada v Secretary of State for Trade (No 2)* [1983] 2 AC 394 [1983] 1 All ER 910: Cabinet papers have a high but not complete degree of protection. See Eagles, 'Cabinet Secrets as Evidence' [1980] PL 263.
7   Lord Reid had been a minister.

evidence were not clearly expressed he could require him to clarify them. If he thought the documents ought to be produced he should see them before ordering production. Thus their Lordships, while firmly asserting the existence of the courts' right to overrule the minister, clearly did not envisage that this power would be lightly or frequently exercised.[8]

Referring to the documents in issue in *Conway v Rimmer* itself their Lordships thought that no harm to the public interest could result from the production of the probationary reports, or at least that the possibility of harm (that those making such reports would in future be less candid because of the possibility of their production) was out-weighed by the prejudice to the public interest from their being withheld. There was more doubt as to whether the report by the defendant of his investigation into Conway's alleged offence should be produced, as the consideration that the police should not be impeded in their work should be given great weight. However, Conway had been acquitted and the document could have a vital bearing on the issue in question – malicious prosecution. It too was therefore ordered to be produced for inspection. Following their inspection Lord Reid announced that he could 'find nothing in any of them and disclosure of which would in my view be in any way prejudicial to the administration of the Cheshire Constabulary or to the public interest'. Disclosure was therefore ordered.[9] (The action then proceeded but the plaintiff lost.)

In two later House of Lords decisions[10] the use of the expression 'Crown privilege' to justify non-disclosure was criticised. It was 'not accurate', ' a misnomer', 'apt to be misleading', 'wrong'; or generally disapproved of. Privilege on the ground of public interest or 'public interest immunity' is now the accepted terminology.

Now it will be agreed that the facts of *Conway v Rimmer* hardly involved high matters of state policy or any degree of policy making, or touched, to adopt a phrase of Lord Reid, the 'inner workings of government'. The documents in that case were, in that light, trivial and routine. The documents in *Burmah Oil Co Ltd v Bank of England*[11] were towards or at the other extreme. The facts were that in 1974 the Burmah Oil Co ('Burmah') was in grave financial difficulties. Unless a rescue operation could be mounted it might go into liquidation. Discussions took place between Burmah, the Bank of England, and the government. Burmah's assets included some 78 million stock units in British Petroleum Ltd. The Bank acting throughout on government instructions[12] offered to buy these at £2.30 per unit. The government *did not agree with the Bank's view* that Burmah should be able to share in any profit on a resale of the

8 See Clark, 'The Last Word on the Last Word' (1969) 32 MLR 142.

9 [1968] AC 996, [1968] 2 All ER 304n. For comment on impact of case on civil service see Kerry (1986) 64 Pub Admin 163.

10 *Rogers v Home Secretary* [1973] AC 388, [1972] 2 All ER 1057; *Alfred Crompton Amusement Machines Ltd v Customs and Excise Comrs* (No 2) [1974] AC 405, [1973] 2 All ER 1169.

11 [1980] AC 1090, [1979] 3 All ER 700, case note by Williams 39 CLJ 1.

12 See p 36 above.

stock by the Bank. The sale was agreed. By the following year the value of the stock had more than doubled. Burmah brought an action against the Bank seeking to set aside the sale on the grounds that it was unconscionable, unreasonable and at an undervalue. The Bank's list of documents in the litigation included documents which disclosed the part played by the government in the transaction and the advice received by it. The Bank was willing to disclose them, but at government request, objected to discovery of sixty-two of those documents. The certificate from the minister responsible, the Chief Secretary to the Treasury, stated that he personally had formed the opinion that the production of the documents would be 'injurious to the public interest'. The documents were in three categories. Category A consisted of communications between ministers and minutes of meetings attended by ministers. These were said to relate to the formulation of government policy, and the relevant policy considerations were noted in the certificate. Category B consisted of communications between and minutes of meetings of government and Bank officials, relating to the policies referred to in category A. It was in the minister's view necessary 'for the proper functioning of the public service' that A and B documents should be withheld. They all fell within the *class* of documents relating to formulation of government policy at the very highest level. The remarks of Lord Reid concerning the need to protect the inner workings of government from the common gaze were referred to in the certificate.

There was another category of documents, C, consisting of notes of meetings etc between representatives of other oil companies and of government, which recorded information given in confidence by the former. These too were sought to be withheld. It was argued that it was important for government to receive information relevant to its management of the country's financial affairs, and if such information, given in confidence, could be publicly produced, it would be less likely to be forthcoming, and this would be detrimental to the public interest. By the time the matter got to the House of Lords, Burmah was seeking disclosure of only ten of the sixty-two documents. They fell within categories A and B, not C.

The House applied *Conway v Rimmer*;[13] there is no rule that a claim by the Crown on the grounds of public interest for immunity from production of a class of documents is conclusive. A court may balance the public interest in the administration of justice with that of preventing harm to the state, to which the certificate alone refers, even in respect of a document dealing with the inner workings of government. On the facts, Lord Wilberforce regarded it as 'a plain case of public interest immunity properly claimed on grounds of high policy on the one hand in terms which cannot be called in question; of nothing of any substance to put in the scale on the other'. Discovery, or prior inspection by the court to decide whether there should be discovery, should not therefore be ordered he said. The majority took a different view on the facts, and inspected the documents. Each of the majority was influenced by different considerations, but the

13 [1968] AC 910, [1968] 1 All ER 874.

following factors were amongst those relied on (whilst acknowledging on the other hand that a good prima facie claim to withhold had been made out): the documents were admittedly relevant; what was in issue was not the government's reason for undertaking Burmah's rescue but the terms of the agreement between Burmah and the Bank and the Bank was known to have expressed a view as to the unfairness of those terms; it was not mere conjecture that the documents would give some support to Burmah – it was likely, or there was a reasonable possibility of relevant material emerging; this was a class, not a contents claim, but not even a contents claim could now be said to be conclusive against disclosure; and the 'need for candour' argument which, it will be recalled, was not welcomed in *Conway v Rimmer* was not acceptable. On that last point although Lord Wilberforce thought that 'candour' as a ground for immunity had received 'an excessive dose of cold water', Lord Keith thought that it had 'little weight, if any' and he continued:

The notion that any competent and conscientious public servant would be inhibited at all in the candour of his writings by consideration of the off-chance that they might have to be produced in a litigation is in my opinion grotesque. To represent that the possibility of it might significantly impair the public service is even more so. Nowadays the state in multifarious manifestations impinges closely on the lives and activities of individual citizens. Where this has involved a citizen in litigation with the state or one of its agencies, the candour argument is an utterly insubstantial ground for denying him access to relevant documents.[14]

The documents having been inspected, it was ruled that they did not contain material necessary for fairly disposing of the case: disclosure was not ordered.[15]

Later in his judgment Lord Keith added, more generally, and as a welcome counterblast to Lord Reid's view:

There can be discerned in modern times a trend towards more open governmental methods than were prevalent in the past. No doubt it is for Parliament and not for courts of law to say how far that trend should go. The courts are, however, concerned with the consideration that it is in the public interest that justice should be done and should be publicly recognized as having been done. This may demand though no doubt only in a very limited number of cases, that the inner workings of government should be exposed to public gaze, and there may be some who would regard this as likely to lead, not to captious or ill-informed criticism, but to criticism calculated to improve the nature of that working as affecting the individual citizen.[16]

In his judgment in the case Lord Scarman questioned whether, except in documents which concerned national safety etc there was anything so important in 'secret government' that it must be protected at the price of injustice in the courts.[17]

14 [1980] AC 1090 at 1133.
15 The action proceeded; Burmah lost: (1981) Times, 4 July.
16 [1980] AC 1090 at 1134, cf Lord Reid, p 516 above.
17 It has been held that the court will not inspect documents once an actual or potential risk to national security is demonstrated in a ministerial certificate: *Balfour v Foreign and Commonwealth Office* [1994] 2 All ER 588.

An important explanation of the court's role came in yet another House of Lords case, the *Air Canada* case[18] – 'a case of the very greatest importance to the Government'.[19] Landing charges at Heathrow Airport were fixed by the British Airports Authority (BAA), which was subject to the financial supervision of the Secretary of State. Eighteen airlines (AC) alleged that the Secretary of State had unlawfully directed BAA to increase the charges (having used his power for an improper purpose). At the discovery stage the Secretary of State produced to AC documents that had passed between him and BAA concerning the increased charges, but refused a class of documents comprising communications which had passed between ministers, and memoranda prepared for their use, all of which related to the formulation of government policy regarding BAA, the public sector borrowing requirement, and ministerial power to control BAA's borrowing. The judge ordered the documents to be produced for his inspection and, subject to that, to AC. His reason for doing so was that, even if the documents were not likely to assist the plaintiff's case, and might even harm it, they would substantially assist *the court* in eliciting the true facts of the case and would thereby affect the court's decision: this demonstrated a sufficient public interest in the production of the documents on the ground of the due administration of justice outweighing the public interest in their non-disclosure. In this sense, the judge said, (referring to RSC Ord 24)[20] the documents were necessary for 'fairly disposing of the case'. The House of Lords said that this was to misunderstand the court's role. In an adversarial system such as ours, the court's duty is to dispose of the case on such evidence as the parties choose to make available; there is no additional duty to seek some independent truth. Discovery may be ordered to make evidence available, not to the court but to the other party. If discovery is resisted on the public interest ground, the burden is on the person seeking discovery to show that it is 'likely' or that there is a 'reasonable probability' that the documents support his case; that is, there must be something beyond speculation or, according to Lord Fraser, it must be shown that the documents are 'very likely to contain material that would give substantial support' to his contention. If he meets that burden, the court will order discovery, and inspect the documents.

The above cases establish the principles; the following provides a further illustration. In *Williams v Home Office (No 2)*[1] the plaintiff, a prisoner, brought an action claiming that the Home Office had acted ultra vires in respect of his detention in an experimental 'control unit' set up within the prison system. In the course of discovery the Home Office disclosed documents amounting to 6,810 pages,[2] but objected to the disclosure of

18 *Air Canada v Secretary of State for Trade (No 2)* [1983] 2 AC 394, [1983] 1 All ER 910.
19 Lord Mackay 'Development of the law on public interest immunity' (1983) CJQ 337 at 345.
20 See p 514 above, fn 1.
 1 [1981] 1 All ER 1151.
 2 See comment of Lord Templeman on 'masses of documents of no or doubtful relevance or materiality' in *R v Chief Constable of the West Midlands Police, ex p Wiley* [1994] 3 All ER 420 at 423, [1994] 3 WLR 433 at 436.

twenty-three documents on the ground that they consisted of communications to and from ministers and records of meetings between
ministers and officials, all of which related to the formulation of policy on
the control unit. Privilege was claimed on the ground that the documents
came within the *class* of documents relating to the formulation of
government policy, and that it was necessary for the 'proper functioning
of the public service' that they be withheld from production, as production
would inhibit freedom of expression between ministers, and by officials
in advising ministers. McNeill J ruled that immunity was not to be
granted on the 'freedom of expression' or 'candour' ground; that the
plaintiff had an arguable case that his rights had been unlawfully
interfered with, and that there was more than a reasonable probability
that the disputed documents were likely to contain material relevant
to his case. That had to be balanced against the fact that disclosure
might lead to ill-formed criticism of the Home Office (a matter that
had worried Lord Reid in *Conway v Rimmer*), although some protection
against that would be given by the implied undertaking imposed on a
party to whom documents were disclosed that they are not to be used
for any purpose other than the action.[3] There was therefore a case for
inspecting the documents. Having done so, the judge ordered six
documents to be disclosed.

A number of cases have raised the question of whether information
given to a public authority should be disclosed to a third party or withheld.
This may raise the question of confidentiality. In *Rogers v Home Secretary*[4]
R applied to the Gaming Board for a certificate of consent (which would
enable him to apply to the magistrates for a licence under the Gaming
Act). In pursuance of its duty to consider R's character the Board made
enquiries of the police. In response, the chief constable C wrote to the
Board about him. A certificate was refused. R instituted proceedings
against C for criminal libel alleging that the libel was contained in C's
letter to the Board. Two witness summons were issued by a magistrate,
one against C, the other against the Secretary to the Board, requiring the
former to produce a copy of the letter and the latter to produce the letter
itself. The House of Lords held that neither letter nor copy should be
produced not on the ground of their *content* but because they belonged to
a *class* of documents which should be protected. It was well established
that certain evidence is inadmissible on the ground that its adduction
would be contrary to the public interest; for example, evidence that would
disclose the source of information obtained by the police. If such evidence
was required to be given in court, the source would be likely to dry up. So
here the Board could not adequately perform its duty of controlling gaming
unless it could preserve the confidentiality of communications to it
concerning applicants for consent.

3   Documents read out in court later shown to journalist who wrote critical article: contempt
    of court by solicitor: *Home Office v Harman* [1982] 2 All ER 532; leading to change in
    law in RSC Ord 24 & 14A; friendly settlement in Convention proceedings (1987) Times,
    24 August.
4   [1973] AC 388, [1972] 2 All ER 1057.

The immunity granted the Gaming Board was extended in *D v National Society for the Prevention of Cruelty to Children*.[5] Someone, 'X', informed the Society (NSPCC) that the plaintiff D was ill-treating her child. The information was false. D wished to know X's name: the NSPCC refused to give it. D then commenced proceedings against NSPCC claiming damages for failure to exercise reasonable care in investigating the complaint, and an order that the Society should disclose documents which would have revealed X's identity. The NSPCC sought an order that it should not have to disclose such documents. The refusal was based on the public interest in maintaining the confidentiality of the information given to the Society. It is important to appreciate the Society's status. It is a voluntary, chartered, body whose general purpose is indicated in its name. One of the principal methods of protecting children was by instituting care proceedings in a juvenile court. Such proceedings could be brought only by a local authority, the police, or an 'authorised person'. The only such authorised person was the NSPCC, which invited the help of the public in telling it of any case of child abuse. The invitation gave a guarantee of confidentiality without which the Society's ability to learn of such cases would be much reduced. The House of Lords held that the information required by D should be withheld. The rule giving immunity to police informants should be extended to those giving information about child abuse to the NSPCC: its effective functioning would otherwise be damaged. The Court of Appeal had rejected the privilege plea on the ground that the 'public interest' was equivalent to *Crown* privilege and that was confined to the effective functioning of *central* government of which the NSPCC is not a part. But the House of Lords said that the public interest as a ground for non-disclosure was not so confined.

As to the Category C documents in *Burmah Oil* which recorded information given in confidence to the government,[6] Lord Salmon took the view that they could be protected from production on the principles laid down in *Rogers v Home Secretary* and *D v National Society for the Prevention of Cruelty to Children*. Lord Edmund-Davies on the other hand was not satisfied that in the light of the latter case, the claim for non-disclosure could be maintained. The disclosure of those documents was not of course in issue.

Where the government gets information from the citizen for one purpose under compulsory powers, it cannot use it for another purpose. Thus, for example, public interest immunity attached to documents in the hands of the Inland Revenue relating to a taxpayer's tax affairs in the absence of consent to disclosure by the taxpayer. The court will therefore only order production of such documents if the public administration of justice outweighs the public interest in preserving the confidentiality of such documents.[7]

In *Alfred Crompton Amusements Machines Ltd v Customs and Excise Commissioners*[8] information had been given voluntarily to the

5   [1978] AC 171, [1977] 1 All ER 589, case note by Tapper 41 MLR 192.
6   See p 518
7   *Lonrho plc v Fayed* (No 4) [1994] 1 All ER 870.
8   [1974] AC 405, [1973] 2 All ER 1169.

Commissioners but could have been got compulsorily. In order to try to fix, for tax purposes, the wholesale value of the gambling machines made by Cromptons, the Commissioners got information from their customers. In proceedings between the parties the Commissioners claimed privilege for those documents. The House of Lords held that the fact that the information had been entrusted in confidence *was not in itself a ground for non-disclosure*, but confidentiality might be a very material consideration when privilege was claimed on the ground of public interest. In this case knowledge that the Commissioners could not keep the information secret might harm the working of the scheme.[9] The case for and against disclosure was evenly balanced, but the claim to 'privilege on the ground of public interest' should be upheld. The head of the department should be trusted to do what he could to mitigate the ill-effects of non-disclosure.

A case in which production was ordered was *Norwich Pharmacal Co v Customs and Excise Comrs*.[10] NP owned patents covering a chemical compound. Statistics published by the Commissioners showed that thirty consignments of the compound had been imported into the UK during a four year period. None of them had been licensed by NP and each therefore involved a tortious infringement of NP's patent. NP could not find out who the importers were. The Commissioners had their names but refused to give them to NP. NP then brought an action against the Commissioners claiming discovery of the names. A ground on which discovery was resisted was that the names had been given in confidence and under statutory duty. The House of Lords said that even if the Commissioners were right in treating the information as confidential there was no statutory provision prohibiting the court from ordering discovery if the public interest in the administration of justice required it. It did so require it here: discovery was ordered.

In *Gaskin v Liverpool City Council*[11] the proper functioning of the child care service required the confidentiality of the relevant documents to be preserved: and the judge was quite right not to inspect them, the Court of Appeal said. But contrast *Campbell v Tameside Metropolitan Borough Council*.[12] A teacher suffered severe injuries as a result of an assault by a pupil. In proceedings against the defendant she sought discovery of reports made on the pupil by psychologists as part of the defendant's statutory functions. She contended these would show the defendant's knowledge of the pupil's violent nature. The court held that the disclosure of such reports would not cause those who make them to be inhibited in doing so; further, there was a real risk that the teacher would be denied justice if the

9 See p 514, fn 14 below.
10 [1974] AC 133, [1973] 2 All ER 943.
11 [1980] 1 WLR 1549, CA. This was an application for an order under s. 31 of the Administration of Justice Act 1970. See now Supreme Court Act 1981, s. 33. The council later decided that records should be made available if the contributors to the files consented. The European Court of Human Rights ruled that this involved a breach of the European Convention on Human Rights and awarded Gaskin damages: *Gaskin v United Kingdom*, 1989.
12 [1982] QB 1065, [1982] 2 All ER 791.

documents were not disclosed. The case, though involving a child, was quite different from child-care cases, and was more like an injury caused by defective school equipment, when there would be no question of there not being discovery.

There was a group of cases relating to the immunity from disclosure of statements taken by the police when investigating, under section 49 of the Police Act 1964, complaints against police officers (The question of immunity arose in actions in tort against the police arising out of matters the subject of the complaint.) In *Neilson v Laugharne*[13] the Court of Appeal said that disclosure would impede the purpose of the inquiry, and that exemption should be granted on the class basis. This decision was extended in later cases. However in *R v Chief Constable of the West Midlands Police, ex p Wiley*[14] the House of Lords said that that decision was insupportable; there was no factual justification for its view as to the effect of disclosure. A class claim to public interest immunity did not therefore attach generally to all documents coming into existence in consequence of an investigation of a complaint against the police: a contents claim might apply.

Discovery in judicial review proceedings

Discovery (etc) is available in judicial review proceedings.[15] Order 24 (p 514 above) applies. Factors peculiar to judicial review should be noted. (a) The court may regard itself as limited to ordering discovery only where there is reason to think, from material before the court, that the respondent's affidavit is not accurate. (b) Where the ground of challenge is *Wednesbury* unreasonableness, a restricted approach is taken to a request for an order for discovery, on the ground that the applicant may only be on a 'fishing expedition' – hoping to find some more specific defect in the decision from the disclosed documents. (c) In the typical case nearly all the relevant evidence is in the hands of the respondent, and a restrictive attitude to discovery disadvantages the applicant.

The Law Commission notes these limitations and the dangers involved. It does not, however, see any need to change the Rule as the limitations are not inherent in it. It suggests that a Practice Direction may be the best way to deal with the situation.[16]

13 [1981] QB 736, [1981] 1 All ER 829.
14 [1994] 3 All ER 420.
15 For judicial review see ch 11 above.
16 See the Commission's Report on Administrative Law: Law Com No 226.

Chapter 16

Ombudsmen, auditors and others

Ombudsmen

The last thirty years have seen the world-wide adoption, from its origins in Scandinavia, of the concept of the Ombudsman. Ombudsmen can now be found in many countries at national, regional or local level. So attractive does the institution, or the name, appear, that it has been extended from the governmental to the private sector.

Crichel Down

In 1938 the Air Ministry bought 725 acres of poor chalk downland at Crichel Down in Dorset for use as a bombing range, including 328 acres belonging to the 17,000 acre Crichel Estate. Compulsory powers were used to acquire 15 of the acres belonging to another owner.[1] Ten years later, and the war over, the land was handed over to the Ministry of Agriculture. It was later decided by the Conservative minister, in the interests of maximising food production, to equip the whole unit as a modern farm, and let it to a tenant farmer capable of showing what could be done by the new farming methods then coming into use. The successor to the Crichel Estate wanted to buy back the 328 acres it had sold – he could not of course insist in law on doing so – but the decision was adhered to. The owner pressed his objections and various allegations were made against the civil servants concerned. The minister agreed to the holding of a public inquiry into the matter and appointed to conduct a lawyer (a former Conservative parliamentary candidate). The terms of reference were to inquire into the procedures adopted in respect of the disposal of the land to the tenant, but excluding all questions of government policy. The report of the inquiry showed that there was no corruption on the part of the civil servants (which had not been alleged) but at worst an excess

---

1   See I F Nicolson *The Mystery of Crichel Down*, from which the facts as summarised here are taken.

of zeal for the policy decided on, which had caused them to deal less than fairly with the complainant.[2] There had been a good deal of criticism of the minister from his own party, and feeling his position untenable, he resigned.[3] (A few years later he was given a peerage.)

About a year later the government announced the appointment of the Franks Committee.[4] Its terms of reference required it, as we have seen, to consider the working of statutory *tribunals* and of such administrative procedures as include the holding of an *inquiry* on an appeal or as a result of objections or representations. The *Crichel Down* affair did not involve a statutory tribunal but it did include the holding of an inquiry, and one might have thought that such inquiries were within the competence of the Franks Committee to consider. The committee, however, interpreted its terms of reference as excluding informal procedures and purely ad hoc inquiries, and as relating only to inquiries which are an obligatory part of the procedure in question.

It follows therefore that the celebrated case of *Crichel Down*, which is widely regarded as a principal reason for our appointment, itself in fact falls outside the subjects with which we have been asked to deal.

The *Crichel Down* inquiry resulted from the fact that those who objected to the decision were able to press their case so hard through such means as letters to the press, public meetings etc, in addition to the usual parliamentary methods, and were sufficiently influential, that the minister had to give way and agree to an independent inquiry. It resulted, in the words of the Franks Report 'from the exercise of ... informal methods of raising objection'.[5]

This reference to informal methods of raising objection brings us to an important distinction in the way disputes between an individual and authority may be resolved. There may be on the one hand some statutory procedure to be observed, involving either a court or a tribunal decision or the holding of an inquiry, matters we have considered in earlier chapters. On the one hand there may be no statutory procedure for objecting. 'But over most of the field of public administration no formal procedure is provided for objecting or deciding on objections.'[6]

The *Justice* Report

There was some dissatisfaction that this wide field of public administration had not been subjected to examination from this point of view, and in

2   Cmnd 9176.
3   The outcome was that the whole was sold back to the Crichel Estate subject to the tenancy already agreed. For government policy of offering back to former owner land compulsorily acquired but no longer needed see H of C Official Report, 5th series, vol 530, col 1178.
4   See p 3, above.
5   Franks Report, Cmnd 218, para 15. For reason for exclusion of *Crichel Down* case, see Nicolson, op cit, p 283.
6   Ibid, para 10.

1960 *Justice*, the law reform and research body, initiated an inquiry into the matter. Its report,[7] which was published in 1961, stated that there are two types of complaint to be considered. First, there are those cases where an individual alleges that a decision affecting him was wrong, and secondly, there are complaints of maladministration.

Dealing first with allegations of wrong decisions (that is, where the merits of a decision are disputed), we know that in many cases where the individual thinks the decision was wrong he can appeal to a tribunal, eg social security tribunals.[8] But in other cases no such right of appeal is provided.

The *Justice* Report suggested that in this type of case

the guiding principle should be that the individual is entitled to have an impartial adjudication of his dispute with authority unless there are overriding considerations which make it necessary in the public interest that the Minister should retain responsibility for the final decision.[9]

This would mean the extension of the jurisdiction of existing tribunals or the creation of new ones. The report suggested the setting up of a 'General Tribunal' to deal with miscellaneous appeals from discretionary decisions. Nothing has come of this, unlike its suggestions for dealing with complaints of maladministration.

Complaints of maladministration are vitally different, the *Justice* Report said, from the former kind in that they involve an accusation against some part of the administration of inefficiency, delay, negligence, bias, unfair preference or dishonesty. The then existing means of seeking redress – litigation, Parliamentary action of various kinds – were in its view inadequate or inappropriate for the investigation of the kinds of matters in question. The Report then considered the Scandinavian office of Ombudsman. (This has existed in Sweden since 1809, in Denmark and Norway for about forty years.) Though differing in detail as between these countries it has, the Report said, certain common characteristics. These are that the Ombudsman is an impartial person independent of the government, appointed by and acting on behalf of Parliament in his work of investigating complaints of maladministration made to him by members of the public against any person acting in the service of the state. The *Justice* Report recommended the establishment here of an institution along the lines of the Ombudsman to be called, perhaps, the 'Parliamentary Commissioner'.

The Conservative government rejected the proposal on the ground that the procedures available for dealing with maladministration were adequate, but the Labour party espoused it, and when in government caused to be enacted the Parliamentary Commissioner Act 1967 which provided for the appointment of a Parliamentary Commissioner for Administration

7 The Citizen and the Administration: the Redress of Grievances: The Whyatt Report. For an account of the work of the *Justice* committee, see Gwyn ' "Justice" and the Ombudsman' in *Perspectives on Public Policy-Making* eds Gwyn and Edwards, *Tulane Studies in Political Science*, Vol XV.
8 See ch 5, above.
9 As fn 7, above, at p 27.

for England, Wales and Scotland. In 1969 the Ombudsman principle was extended to Northern Ireland, in 1973 to the National Health Service, and in 1974 to local government. All these are popularly referred to, and by the Commissioners themselves, as Ombudsmen.

The appointment here of the Ombudsman had been preceded by the creation in New Zealand of the office (by that name) in 1962. Ombudsmen, at various levels of government, are now to be found in Canada, Australia, the United States, Mauritius[10] etc. A somewhat similar office, that of the Médiateur,[11] was imported into the quite different constitutional structure of France in 1973, and has been followed in Italy, Austria, Spain etc.

The Parliamentary Commissioner

The office

The Parliamentary Commissioner for Administration (PCA) is appointed by the Crown (in effect by the Prime Minister) after consultation with the Leader of the Opposition and the Chairman of the Select Committee on the PCA (referred to below). The Select Committee thinks that his appointment should be by the Crown but on the Address of the House of Commons, the motion to be made by the Prime Minister with the agreement of the two office-holders mentioned.[12] He holds office during good behaviour and may be removed by the Crown in consequence of addresses from both Houses of Parliament. He must retire at sixty-five.[13] He cannot be a member of the Commons; he is an ex officio member of the Council on Tribunals. He can appoint such staff as he needs to assist him, with the approval of the Civil Service Department as to numbers[14] and conditions of service. There is a staff of about 115 (including that of the Health Service Commissioner). The investigative staff are drawn from the civil service on secondment for a period of about three years.[15]

The first Commissioner had been before his appointment the Comptroller and Auditor General, the second and third, senior civil servants. These appointments were criticised by some because of the appointees' previous experience.[16] The fourth and fifth appointees were lawyers; the present one was a civil servant.

10 See Statutory Instruments 1968, p 1871 at 1931.
11 Brown and Lavirotte 'The Mediator: A French Ombudsman?' (1974) 90 LQR 211.
12 Cf Comptroller and Auditor General, p 560 below.
13 He may also be removed on grounds of incapacity for medical reasons; cf Supreme Court Act 1981, s 11(8). Notice that he is not appointed for a fixed term of years with the possibility of reappointment. He does not therefore have to bear in mind the possibility of non-reappointment.
14 Refusal to approve the number the Commissioner needs could hamper his work (as it could in the case eg of the Council on Tribunals). This does not seem to have happened.
15 For benefit of this see Clothier, 'The Efficacy of the Parliamentary Ombudsman' in *Parliament and the Executive*, RIPA.
16 For a case where a complainant alleged that the Commissioner was less critical of a department than the facts warranted because of his previous association with it, see First Special Report from the Select Committee on the Parliamentary Commissioner, 1975–6, HC 166.

The House of Commons appoints a Select Committee on the Parliamentary Commissioner. As will be seen it plays an important role in the development and work of the office.

Who can be investigated?

By section 5(1) of the Act the PCA 'may investigate any action taken by or on behalf of a government department or other authority to which this Act applies'.[17] To which bodies does the Act apply? It applies to departments and authorities *listed in the Second Schedule to the Act*. These include the usual departments – the Home Office, Treasury, Department of the Environment, the Foreign Office, the Ministry of Defence,[18] etc. (The Cabinet Office and Law Officers Department are amongst those not included.) Note that Executive 'Next Steps' Agencies (p 19 above) are part of the relevant department. Reference to a department includes reference to ministers.[19] It follows that a decision is not outside the Commissioner's jurisdiction simply because it is taken by a minister.

In addition to departments, bodies for which there is a measure of ministerial responsibility have been included since the creation of the office in 1967. Thus are included the Inland Revenue, the Royal Mint, the Charity Commission and others. In 1985 the Select Committee suggested that a considerable number of other non-departmental public bodies could be brought within the Commissioner's jurisdiction, though they excluded advisory bodies and tribunals. The government agreed. As a result, just over one hundred and forty bodies are now listed as within the Commissioner's jurisdiction, including the Arts Councils, various Research Councils, Tourist Boards, urban development corporations, the National Rivers Authority and the Directors-General of privatised utilities industries.

The Schedule can be amended, by an Order in Council, by altering, removing or inserting an entry. An entry may be inserted (a) if it relates to a government department or a body whose functions are exercised on behalf of the Crown; (b) if it relates to a body established by a minister all or some of the members of which are appointed by the Crown and at least half of whose revenues derive directly from money provided by Parliament. But in respect of bodies within (b), no entry is to be made of a body operating in an exclusively or predominantly commercial manner, or a corporation carrying on an industry or undertaking under national ownership. (This would include a commercial company whose shares are owned by the government.) This way of going about it means that as new departments are created etc the Schedule has to be amended. The Select Committee has said that the assumption should be that the Ombudsman's jurisdiction should run through all areas of government unless there are

17 Note the 'may': he cannot be compelled at the instance of a complainant to do so: *Re Fletcher's Application* [1970] 2 All ER 527n, HL.
18 Thus action taken by the *armed* forces is not excluded. Complaints of noise from low flying aircraft on training exercises have been investigated.
19 Section 4(4).

strong reasons to the contrary; and the Act should be amended to specify exclusions, not as at present, inclusions.[20]

Complaints against a wide range of public bodies have been rejected on the ground that they are not listed in the Second Schedule. Examples are the Gaming Board, the Parole Board, local authorities, the courts, the nationalised industries, and the police. The actions of such bodies will however be referred to by the PCA in his reports where necessary to provide a full account of matters which have been investigated. But where a body is not listed in the Second Schedule it is possible to investigate a complaint against it where it acted in the matter complained of 'on behalf of' a Second Schedule body (see that phrase in section 5(1), above). Examples are the Bank of England acting on behalf of the Treasury, and a local authority or a University[1] acting on behalf of a department. A complaint of maladministration by a public sector contractor is within jurisdiction as he is acting 'on behalf of' the Second Schedule body he is in contract with.[2] Where a department acts on behalf of a body not listed in the Second Schedule, the actions of the agent department can be investigated but not those of the principal.

It is sometimes the case that a person employed as a civil servant within a department has functions conferred directly on him by statute. It may then follow that when exercising such functions he is acting independently of the department and so outside the Commissioner's jurisdiction. The Commissioner has ruled that inspectors appointed by the Department of Trade to investigate the affairs of a company are not subject to his jurisdiction as they are not responsible to any Second Schedule authority; and he has ruled, for the same reason, that he cannot hear complaints against government-nominated directors of registered companies.[3]

Action that can be investigated: administrative functions only
We have just considered the bodies which can be investigated. Action taken by these bodies can be investigated (and action includes failure to act)[4] provided it is 'action taken in the exercise of administrative functions of that department or authority'.[5] This formulation might have been intended to exclude the investigation of complaints about the exercise of legislative and judicial functions.

With regard to the exclusion of the *legislative*, a complaint about the provisions of an Act of Parliament cannot be investigated. In one case a pensioner who had retired early because of ill-health received invalidity benefit until he was sixty-five, and a retirement pension thereafter. He

20 Select Committee on the Parliamentary Commissioner 1993–94 HC 33–1, First Report on the Powers ... of the Ombudsman.
 1 Was University acting as agent of DHSS when medical technicians wrongly destroyed deceased's organs, thereby prejudicing widow's claim to pension? First Report of the Commissioner, 1974, HC 2, p 47.
 2 Annual Report for 1993, Session 1993–94, HC 290.
 3 See also Transport and Works Act 1992, s 23(10).
 4 Parliamentary Commissioner Act 1967, s 5(1).
 5 Ibid, s 12(1).

complained that whereas the former was tax-free, the latter was not. But an Act of Parliament provided for that: the complaint was not therefore about the department's administrative activities.[6] The interpretation of legislation by a department is, however, an administrative function which can be and has been criticised. We have considered in an earlier chapter whether the making of delegated legislation is an administrative or legislative function.[7]

With regard to the exclusion of the *judicial*, judicial functions are normally exercised by courts or tribunals, whose actions are of course not within the PCA's jurisdiction. What of the actions of official of courts or tribunals who are on the staff of a department? There was for some years a dispute between the PCA (and the Select Committee) and the Lord Chancellor about this. The outcome was an amendment to the Act which provides that administrative functions exercised by court staff employed by the Lord Chancellor are deemed to be administrative functions of the Lord Chancellor's Department, but excluded from the PCA's remit is any action taken by court staff at the direction or on the express or implied authority of any person acting in a judicial capacity or as a member of a tribunal.[8] This did not apply to other tribunal staff, but further legislation provided for this.[9] Again some departmental functions can be classified, at least for some purposes, as judicial. But whatever judicial element there may be in public inquiries held by a department, for example, does not exclude them from his jurisdiction.[10] (We have noted in an earlier chapter that the Council on Tribunals (of which the PCA is an ex officio member) also has a role in respect of inquiries. Some cases have been investigated by both Council and PCA.[11])

The PCA has investigated a complaint that a statement made by a minister in the Commons about government support for a company, misled its customers and caused them financial loss. He must be satisfied therefore that that statement was in the exercise of administrative functions.[12] He has also criticised answers given to Parliamentary Questions as 'less frank' than they should have been.[13]

The allocation of time for party political broadcasts is made by an All-Party Committee. Asked to investigate a complaint about the arrangements for the allocation of time for such broadcasts the PCA found that the considerations determining the minister's action were 'essentially political' and therefore, although this was action taken in the exercise of administrative functions, he discontinued his investigation.[14]

6 Annual Report for 1974, p 19.
7 See p 105 above.
8 Courts and Legal Services Act 1990 s 110.
9 Parliamentary Commissioner Act 1994.
10 See p 125 above and Foulkes [1974] PL 1.
11 For a case illustrating their respective roles see Selected Cases 1980, vol 1, HC 351, p 11.
12 Fifth Report of the Parliamentary Commissioner 1975–5, HC 498.
13 Sixth Report of the Parliamentary Commissioner 1974–5, HC 529, p 181.
14 Second Report of the Parliamentary Commissioner 1971–2, para 15. For such broadcasts see now Broadcasting Act 1990, s 36.

Action is not excluded from investigation merely because it is taken under the prerogative rather than under statute.[15]

Action that cannot be investigated

(a) *Court or tribunal proceedings available.* By section 5(2) of the Act the Commissioner shall not conduct an investigation into 'any action in respect of which the person aggrieved has or had a right of appeal, reference or review to or before a tribunal ... [or] a remedy by way of proceedings in any court of law'. Thus where a person *had* appealed to a tribunal against a Ministry decision on an application for benefit, the PCA could not investigate the decision. And where a complaint was made to him about the valuation of property for rating purposes the PCA refused jurisdiction because of the *possibility* of appeal to the Lands Tribunal, etc.

But the Commissioner may conduct an investigation despite the availability of such a right or remedy 'if satisfied that in the particular circumstances it is not reasonable to expect the complainant to resort or have resorted to it'. The Commissioner does not seem to have acted under his proviso when there was a right of appeal to a *tribunal*, but has done so when there was a possible remedy before the *courts*, as where the law was not clear, or the complainant could not afford to sue.[16]

The exercise of the discretion to investigate a complaint when there is a possible remedy in the courts is of particular interest, 'and in fact very many of the complaints investigated could be presented as a cause of action known to the law'.[17] Where, for example, a complaint is of arbitrary action, of negligent advice, or of a lack of natural justice, is the PCA excluded? 'This is an area in which the courts also have a function and I have not found it easy to define the borderline between their jurisdiction and mine.'[18] So wrote one of the earlier Commissioners, but Commissioner Clothier, a lawyer, expressing himself strongly about the defects of litigation,[19] wrote that while a good many of the complaints might theoretically be actionable in law, when the probable dimensions of the loss were modest it was manifestly unreasonable to expect the citizen to undergo the expense and anxiety of a lawsuit against the state.[20]

A complaint may be put to the PCA in the hope that his investigation will uncover information which will justify the commencement of legal proceedings. Where he suspects that to be the case, he may refrain from investigating, or he may require an undertaking from the complainant not to resort to litigation, but the undertaking would not seem to be enforceable by the defendant. Where, after he has started his investigation,

15 Selected Cases 1985, vol 1, p 45.

16 Foulkes (1971) 34 MLR 377.

17 Clothier, 'Legal Problems of an Ombudsman', Law Society's Gazette, 1984, p 3108. The present PCA Reid, takes legal advice from Counsel to the Speaker.

18 Annual Report for 1976, HC 116 of 1976–7.

19 'Delay, expense, bitterness ... humiliation': Select Committee on the Parliamentary Commissioner, 1978–9, HC 251, Minutes of Evidence.

20 A similar exclusion found in the legislation relating to the local government Ombudsman has been judicially considered – see p 554 below.

legal proceedings are brought in respect of the matter being investigated, he will terminate his investigation. Where he has completed an investigation, the complainant is not debarred from bringing legal proceedings against the department in respect of the matter investigated.[1]

(b) *Third Schedule exclusions.* The Third Schedule to the Act excludes from the Commissioner's jurisdiction matters that would otherwise be within it. This Schedule may be amended by Order in Council so as to exclude (but not add to) items in it. The exclusions are as follows:

(a)   Action taken in matters certified by a minister to affect relations or dealings between the UK government and any other government or international organisation. Under this the Commissioner has been debarred from considering a complaint about payment for service in the Shanghai Police.

(b)   The commencement or conduct of civil or criminal proceedings before any court of law in the UK. Thus a complaint about a decision to institute or not to institute proceedings or about the conduct of proceedings by counsel could not be investigated.[2]

(c)   Any exercise of the prerogative of mercy. A Home Office decision not to grant remission of a prison sentence was therefore outside the Commissioner's jurisdiction.[3]

(d)   Action taken on behalf of the minister by a Regional Health Authority, a District Health Authority and Family Health Service Authorities. This paragraph excludes from the PCA's jurisdiction everything done by them, but it does not exclude action taken by the minister himself in relation to them. Thus the PCA has investigated a complaint against the minister's decision to confirm the closure of a hospital casualty unit. The work of the Health Service Commissioner must of course now be considered in this connection. It is dealt with later in this chapter.

(e)   Action taken in matters relating to contractual and other commercial transactions. Thus the PCA was unable to investigate a complaint about action taken in connection with guarantees under section 7 of the Shipbuilding Industry Act 1967.[4] Complaints about a department's tendering procedures are, it would seem, excluded.
(Transactions relating to the acquisition of land compulsorily or in circumstances in which it could be acquired compulsorily and to the disposal as surplus of land so acquired are not excluded from his jurisdiction by this paragraph.)

The justification given for this provision is that the PCA is concerned with relations between government and governed, and that he is therefore excluded from areas in which the government appears in a different

1   Clothier, 'The Efficacy of the Parliamentary Ombudsman' in *Parliament and the Executive*, RIPA.
2   See case C624/82, Fourth Report for 1984–85, HC 528, p 89.
3   A complaint about delay in reviewing a conviction for murder was not excluded. The Home Office was severely criticised: Fourth Report for 1983–84, HC 191.
4   Annual Report for 1977, HC 157, para 67. See p 457 above.

guise – as a trader. It is also argued that any change would place departments at a commercial disadvantage; that departments are already subject to scrutiny (an argument that would justify doing away with the Comm-issioner altogether); that any change would create an unjustifiable administrative burden. The Select Committee has argued that because the government disposes of so much money its position is unique, and if its purchasing policies were the subject of complaint they should be investigated, particularly if any government were to use the award of contracts as a political weapon.[5]

(f) Personnel matters, that is action taken in respect of civil and military employment under the Crown. Thus complaints by a civil servant's widow as to pension entitlement, by a member of the armed forces as to the termination of his service, and by a civil servant as to the way his department had dealt with an accident he had suffered at work could not be considered. The arguments advanced by governments for this exclusion are: first, that (as with the previous exclusion) the PCA is there to deal with relations between government and governed, and not therefore between government as employer and its individual employees; second, that adequate machinery exists to deal with grievances of civilian employees. They have refused to modify this exclusion also.[6] The Select Committee has said that some matters, such as dismissal, are justifiably excluded but that others eg recruitment, could be included.

(g) The grant of honours and charters. Investigation of a complaint as to the unreasonable withholding of a long service medal was thus debarred.

(h) Action taken by or with the authority of the Secretary of State for the purposes of investigating crime or of protecting the security of the State, including action so taken with respect to passports.

Notice that where a complaint includes a matter excluded from the Commissioner's jurisdiction, he may nevertheless investigate any aspect of the complaint not so excluded.

One provision in the Third Schedule has been amended on the Select Committee's recommendation so as to extend the Commissioner's jurisdiction. It relates to action taken abroad by consular officials. The position now is that the Commissioner can investigate the actions of career (that is, not honorary) consular officials abroad in the performance of their duties towards United Kingdom citizens who have a right of abode in this country.[7]

---

5 Cmnd 8274. Is the government a mere trader? See p 439 above. For contracts as political weapon, see p 451 above. Note that government contracting procedures re subject to scrutiny by departmental and other committees: see p 561.
6 Annual Report for 1979, paras 103–106; Cmnd 7449; Cmnd 8274.
7 See Parliamentary Commissioner Act 1967, Sch 3, para 2, amended by SI 1979/915; For 'right of abode' see Immigration Act 1971, s 2.

The complaint

(a) *Who can complain?* By section 6(1) of the Act a complaint may be made by an individual or by any body of persons, corporate or unincorporate, but not by:

a local authority or other statutory body constituted for purposes of public service or of a local government or for the purposes of carrying on under national ownership any industry or undertaking.

or by:

any other authority or body whose members are appointed by Her Majesty or by any Minister of the Crown or government department, or whose revenues consist wholly or mainly of moneys provided by Parliament.

Public authorities can of course resort to the law but the Ombudsman machinery is denied them. The reason is that the Office is seen as existing to protect the citizen, private person or individual. (Commercial organisations are not, as such, excluded as complainants.)

By section 6(2) the complaint must be made by 'the person aggrieved himself'. This means that if an injustice is done to X, only X can complain, not Y. ('Whistle blowers' have no locus.) However, the person aggrieved can authorise another to submit a complaint on his behalf, such as a solicitor, accountant, law centre, or trade union official. Complaints submitted by bodies such as Residents Associations, Conservation Societies etc. will also be investigated. Where a complainant has died or is unable to act for himself, the complaint may be made by someone on his behalf.

The complainant must be resident in the UK, or the act complained of must have been taken while he was present in the UK.[8] The mere fact of being a foreign national does not therefore prevent one from complaining.

A prisoner is not denied access to the Ombudsman – who has said that prisoners' complaints are examined 'with very particular thoroughness'.[9]

(b) *How is a complaint to be made?* By section 5(1) the PCA can investigate action taken by bodies within his jurisdiction where:

(a) a written complaint is duly made to a member of the House of Commons by a member of the public who claims to have sustained injustice in consequence of maladministration in connection with the action so taken and
(b) the complaint is referred to the Commissioner, with the consent of the person who made it, by a member of that House with a request to conduct an investigation thereon.

Thus a complainant does not have direct access to the Commissioner: he must approach him through a member of the Commons.[10] The reason

---

8 But see Parliamentary Commissioner (Consular Complaints) Act 1981 permitting complaints to be made by UK citizens with a right of abode in the UK about the actions outside the UK of career consular officials.

9 Annual Report for 1978, HC 205, para 31.

10 Not the House of Lords. The Act does not require the complainant to go to his own MP. It is a parliamentary convention that an MP does not deal with another MP's constituency business, but the Select Committee has said that the convention should be interpreted flexibly with regard to reference of cases to the Commissioner.

for refusing the citizen direct access to the Commissioner can be gathered from this quotation from the White Paper which preceded the Bill:

In Britain Parliament is the place for ventilating the grievances of the citizen ... It is one of the functions of the elected member of Parliament to try to secure that his constituents do not suffer injustice at the hands of the Government ... Members are continually taking up constituents' complaints ... We do not want to create any new institution which would erode the functions of members of Parliament in this respect ... we shall give members of Parliament a better instrument which they can use to protect the citizen, namely, the services of a Parliamentary Commissioner for Administration.[11]

But from the beginning the Ombudsman has received as many complaints direct from the public as through MPs.[12] Complainants were advised to approach their MP. In 1977 the then PCA introduced a system of *indirect access* by which he offers to send a complaint which appears to be within his jurisdiction to the constituent's MP saying that he is prepared to start an investigation should the MP wish him to do so. This leaves the complainant free to decide whether or not to proceed. If he has no objection, this spares him the need of starting the process of complaining again from scratch, while the MP has the opportunity either to discuss the matter with the constituent or to consent to the Ombudsman's investigation.[13] The Select Committee recently decided against removal of the MP filter.[14] The PCA has reiterated his view that it deprives members of the public of possible redress. His practice now on receiving a complaint from an MP is to deal with the complainant direct while keeping the referring Member in touch. The UK PCA is thus an exception to the rule of direct access which applies in all Ombudsman systems except in France.

By section 6(3) a complaint must be made to a member of the Commons not later than twelve months from the day on which the complainant first had notice of the matter alleged, but the PCA can waive this.

Notice that underlying these rules about how a complaint is to be made is a basic point that the PCA can act only on receipt of a complaint: that is, he cannot act of his own motion. (He could, however, in respect of some publicised event, make public his willingness to consider a complaint should one be submitted to him and has done so.) The Select Committee thinks that the PCA should be able to initiate an investigation when it so recommends.

No fees of any kind are payable. There are no lawyers to be hired and paid for. And there is no liability for costs should the complaint turn out to be unjustified.

(c) *The substance of the complaint.* Section 5(1) provides that the complaint is to be made by a person who *claims* to have sustained *injustice* in consequence of *maladministration*.

'Claims.' The complainant does not of course have to *prove* but *claim* injustice caused by maladministration. It is not enough for the complainant

11 Cmnd 2767.
12 See Cohen 'The Parliamentary Commissioner and the "MP Filter" ' [1972] PL 204.
13 Annual Report for 1977, HC 157.
14 Select Committee on the Parliamentary Commission Session 1993–94, HC 33–I.

to allege that he suffered injustice; while he does not have to specify the maladministration, he must produce some prima facie evidence of it.[15]

'Injustice in consequence of maladministration'. The Act does not define these words. On the second reading debate the minister, Mr Crossman, said that the government had deliberately refrained from trying to define 'injustice' by using such words as 'loss' or 'damage', for these have legal overtones which could be held to exclude 'one thing which I am particularly anxious shall remain within the meaning of the word – the sense of outrage aroused by unfair or incompetent administration even where the complainant has suffered no actual loss'. 'Maladministration', he suggested, might include such things as 'bias, neglect, inattention, delay, incompetence, ineptitude, perversity, turpitude, arbitrariness, and so on'. This is known as the 'Crossman Catalogue'. The meaning of both words would, he thought, 'be filled out by the practical processes of case work'.[16] The 'maladministration' must cause 'injustice'.[17]

What meaning has then been given to 'injustice' and 'maladministration' by the Commissioner's decisions? *Injustice* clearly includes financial loss caused by, for example, refusal to make a grant or an ex gratia payment, delay in paying a grant, issuing a licence, settling an estate, injury to livestock, etc. It also includes being deprived of an opportunity to object to or appeal against a decision, and being deprived of an amenity by the closure of a museum or a railway line, or the loss of a view. Loss of privileges through being wrongly classified as a convicted rather than an untried prisoner constitutes injustice, as does the loss of access to a child through an error in the Passport Office which enabled a complainant's divorced wife to take the child abroad. To cause a person (but not chickens)[18] avoidable concern, distress, confusion, inconvenience or uncertainty, or to impugn his honour – these too constitute injustice. However, injustice has not been suffered by a person or group who think that others have been favourably discriminated.[19]

What of *maladministration*? One Commissioner said that the word

might imply some major administrative failure. But in practice I look upon 'maladministration' as including any kind of administrative shortcoming[20] ... the term 'maladministration' is certainly imprecise. But it has been interpreted with great flexibility both by my predecessors and myself. Moreover the so-called 'Crossman catalogue' ... surely provides a very broad definition.[1]

---

15 Select Committee on the Parliamentary Commissioner 1978–9, HC 251, Minutes of Evidence.
16 734 H of C Official report (5th series) col 42.
17 See Gregory & Drewry [1991] 192, 408 for an account of the major *Barlow Clowes* investigation.
18 Annual Report for 1978, para 92.
19 See Clothier, 'Legal Problems of an Ombudsman' Law Society's Gazette 1984, p 3108. This was in relation to a complaint by taxpayers about the way other taxpayers were treated, and led to the 'Mickey Mouse' case p 355 above.
20 Annual Report for 1973, HC 106, para 14. See Marshall 'Maladministration' [1973] PL 32; 'Techniques of Maladministration' (1975) Political Studies 183.
 1 Annual Report for 1977, HC 157, para 19.

Commissioner Reid adds[2] the following fifteen defects to the Crossman catalogue: rudeness (though that is a matter of degree); unwillingness to treat the complainant as a person with rights; refusal to answer reasonable questions; neglecting to inform a complainant on request of his or her rights or entitlement; knowingly giving advice which is misleading or inadequate; ignoring valid advice or overruling considerations which would produce an uncomfortable result for the overruler; offering no redress or manifestly disproportionate redress; showing bias whether because of colour, sex, or any other grounds; omission to notify those who thereby lose a right of appeal; refusal to inform adequately of the right of appeal; faulty procedures; failure by management to monitor compliance with adequate procedures; cavalier disregard of guidance which is intended to be followed in the interest of equitable treatment of those who use a service; partiality; and failure to mitigate the effects of rigid adherence to the letter of the law where that produces manifestly inequitable treatment.[3]

Notice that in ruling against a department the Commissioner will not necessarily use the word 'maladministration'; and even though he finds that there was no maladministration he may say that he is, for example, left with a 'feeling of unease' about departmental administration.

Section 12(3) of the Act 'drafted by the formidable pen of the Lord Chancellor himself'[4] must be considered at this point. It reads:

It is hereby declared that nothing in this Act authorises or requires the Commissioner to question the merits of a decision taken without maladministration by a government department or other authority in the exercise of a discretion vested in that department or authority.

The first Commissioner took the view that this meant that he could investigate the administrative process *leading to* a discretionary decision: if there was a defect in those processes he would inquire into the prospect of a remedy by way of review of that decision, but if he found no such defect, he was not competent to question the quality of the decision even if it had resulted in manifest hardship. It was acknowledged by him that that distinction was unsatisfactory and often unclear. It is no longer applied. While the correct procedure may have been followed the decision itself may have 'reflected an error of judgment', been inequitable or caused hardship, for example.[5]

What then does section 12(3) mean? Nothing very much, it seems. It provides that the Commissioner is not to question the merits of a decision taken without maladministration, to which one says, 'of course not. If no maladministration is alleged, or if maladministration is not found, that is the end of it.'[6] If he does find maladministration he can 'question' the

2   Annual Report for 1993, HC 290 1993–94, para 7.
3   Cases decided by or principles applied by the Commissioner are referred to at the following pages above – 105, 112, 115, 116, 137, 139, 210, 231, 233, 234, 265, 271, 281, 310, 325, 457, 493 and 504.
4   Compton (1968) 10 JSPTL 101.
5   See Gregory & Drewry [1991] PL 192, 408. And see HC 490 of 1971–2 p 209, the *Dollar Land* case.
6   The Local Government Act 1974 has in s 34(3) in relation to Local Ombudsman the same provision as s 12(3). See p 554 below.

decision by displaying its defects whether of the procedure or of the decision itself – that is what he is there for. But, as we shall see, even in that case, he cannot reverse, overrule or quash the decision.

The investigation

By section 7(1) where the PCA proposes to make an investigation he must give the principal officer of the department concerned, and any other person alleged to be concerned, an opportunity to comment on the allegations. The investigation must be in private, but apart from that rule the PCA can (by section 57(2)) proceed as he thinks fit. He may obtain information from such persons and in such manner and make such inquiries as he thinks fit. His procedure is therefore inquisitorial: he is neither a judge nor an arbitrator arriving at a finding on the basis of evidence put before him by the parties: he ascertains by his own inquiries inside the department and elsewhere what the actions were which give rise to the complaint.

Notice that where the PCA undertakes an investigation, this, by section 7(4) 'shall not affect any action taken by the department ... or any power or duty of that department to take further action with respect to any matters subject to investigation'.

The PCA decides whether any person may be represented legally or otherwise in an investigation carried out by him. One has taken the view that legal representation would be proper if an investigation got to the stage where it appeared that reputations were at stake. A few formal hearings have been held where irreconcilable conflicts of evidence have arisen on a central issue which the investigators had been unable to resolve, with evidence taken on oath, and legal representation paid for by the Commissioner's office.[7]

To enable him to get at the facts section 8 of the Act says that he can require any person who in his opinion is able to furnish information or documents, to do so: he has the same powers as the High Court in this respect. This duty to assist the Commissioner overrides any obligation to maintain secrecy which is imposed by the Official Secrets Act or by any other rule of law. Furthermore, Crown privilege does not avail the departments:

the Crown shall not be entitled in relation to any such investigation to any such privilege in respect of the production of documents or the giving of evidence as is allowed by law in legal proceedings.[8]

These powers are particularly important in view of the citizen's difficulties in getting at official documents.

The only limit to this wide-ranging power is that secrecy is maintained for Cabinet proceedings and papers by the terms of section 8(4) which provides that:

---

7 Clothier, op cit at 3110.
8 Section 8(3). For 'Crown privilege' see p514 above.

No person shall be required or authorised by virtue of this Act to furnish any information or answer any question relating to proceedings of the Cabinet or to produce so much of any document as relates to such proceedings; and for the purposes of this subsection a certificate issued by the Secretary of the Cabinet with the approval of the Prime Minister and certifying that any information, question, document or part of a document so relates shall be conclusive.

A certificate under the subsection was issued in the Court Line case.[9] The Select Committee on the Parliamentary Commissioner has suggested that the Commissioner should have access to all papers etc, except where the Attorney-General certifies that access would prejudice the safety of the state, or would otherwise be against the public interest. The government's response was that in no case has the Commissioner said that his investigations were less than complete because of this provision; that there is no evidence that it causes difficulties for him. It could not therefore agree to the suggestion.

If any person obstructs the Commissioner (as by, for example, withholding or destroying relevant documents) or is in contempt of him the matter may be reported to the High Court which may deal with the matter as if that person had been guilty of contempt of court (section 9).[10]

Notice the PCA's discretion, by section 5(5) to discontinue an investigation. The discretion to investigate,[11] to refrain from investigating and to discontinue investigating is an aspect of his independence from government. He will not necessarily discontinue an investigation because the complainant wishes him to. 'I will invariably decide to continue my investigation where serious allegations have been made against a government department ... It seemed to me only fair to the Inland Revenue that the allegations of secretiveness, deviousness and misrepresentation should be fully explored ...'[12]

The reports
Section 10 requires that whenever the Commissioner conducts an investigation he must send on to the MP who raised the matter with him a report of the result of his investigation or, where he decides not to investigate, a statement of his reasons for not doing so. Where he does carry out an investigation he must also send a report to the principal officer of the department concerned and to any other person alleged to have been concerned. He is not required to and does not normally make reports of individual investigations available to the press, though it is open to the MP or complainant to do so. By section 10(4) he has to lay an annual report before Parliament, and may lay such other reports from time to time. It is his practice to lay quarterly reports of Selected Cases and occasional reports of cases of particular interest. If he finds that in

9 Gregory 'Court Line, Mr Benn and the Ombudsman' (1977) Parliamentary Affairs 269. Cf the attitude of the courts to the production of Cabinet papers in discovery: p 516 above.
10 Cf Health Service Commissioners Act 1993, s 16.
11 See p 529 above, fn 17.
12 Seventh Report, Session 1983–84, HC 548, p 56.

any particular case injustice has been done and has not been or will not be remedied he may under section 10(3) lay a special report before Parliament. Only one such report has been laid so far.

With regard to the contents of his reports, it is the Commissioner's practice to anonymise cases in his annual and quarterly reports. They do not therefore identify complainant, MP, civil servant or minister involved (though his other reports do so).[13]

By section 11(3) the PCA can be prevented by a certificate issued by a minister from disclosing in a report or otherwise, any document or class of document to any person. This does not mean that he may not examine it and take account of what is in it. Such a certificate, which prevented him from disclosing whether or not certain documents existed, has been issued. It referred to a tax matter.[14]

The view is taken that the personal standing of the Ombudsman and his ability to be personally involved with investigations is important to the success of the office. (The latter point is given as a reason for not extending his jurisdiction too widely.) A former Ombudsman said that, like his predecessors, he saw each case at least three times and approved the report.[15]

A note on the work load. In recent years the Commissioner has been receiving about 900 complaints a year through MPs. Of that number, remarkably low as it may seem, just under one-third fall within his jurisdiction. The main reasons for exclusion are that the authority complained of is outside the Commissioner's jurisdiction; that the complaint is simply of disagreement with the merits of the decision; that there was a right of appeal to a tribunal. Of the 208 investigations carried out in 1993, in 61 per cent the complaint was wholly justified, in 35% partly justified. The authorities most frequently complained against are the Department of Social Security and the Inland Revenue.

The remedies

It is essential to appreciate that even if the PCA finds maladministration causing injustice he cannot order the department to halt or delay or speed up action, to change a decision, to pay money, or to do anything else.[16] To report on the result of his investigation seems to be the extent of his power. This inability of the Ombudsman to enforce his decisions causes many to question the value of the office. The following points may put the matter in a different perspective. Commissioner Clothier said, 'It would be inappropriate ... to give an Ombudsman the power to enforce his own

13 See First Report from the Select Committee on the parliamentary Commissioner, 1976–7, HC 282.
14 Annual Report for 1971, p 7. The Commissioner referred to the minister's view that the working of the Customs and Excise and Inland Revenue Departments depends enormously on confidentiality, and that a great degree of reliance is put on it by persons giving evidence to the department, p 523 above.
15 Annual Report for 1977, HC 157, para 3.
16 For a private member's bill seeking to provide machinery for parliamentary implementation of the Commissioner's recommendation see 925 H of C Official report (5th series) col 1457.

decisions without some mechanism for appeals ... The power of enforcement quite properly rests with parliament and not with me'.[17] And, 'Never ... has there been the slightest intention of giving a Parliamentary Ombudsman anywhere in the world the power to implement his own decisions by some sort of directly enforceable order'.[18] It has even been suggested that one of the reasons for the success of the New Zealand Ombudsman has been the very lack of power that is complained of.[19]

The fact that the PCA cannot 'enforce' his decision does not mean that the complainants do not get their injustices remedied. In the first place he will expect the department to find a remedy. Sometimes if the department say they cannot find a remedy he will ask them to think again, or if he thinks the proposed remedy is inadequate he will say so. Second, the report of his investigation goes to the principal officer of the department – the senior civil servant. It is his job to see that his department is properly run. He will be concerned about the existence of maladministration in his department and should welcome an opportunity to put things right. Third, the PCA reports to Parliament which will hold the minister responsible for what he does and what his department does.

The Commissioner's reports do in fact result in a wide range of remedies being made available. Financial payments ranging from 25p to £30,000 have been made. A tax demand for £57,000 has been withdrawn.[20] He has prevailed on departments to extend the scope of a concession so as to include the complainant, to pay thirty years' arrears of war pension, to refund tax paid, to spread the payment of tax due over a longer period, to review an application from the complainant for a licence or for compensation in the light of further information put before it, to speed up a decision, to issue a conditional licence having previously refused to issue one at all, and to offer an apology. In one case he brought about a further review of a decision taken by ministers and on the basis of advice to be drawn up by different officials from those previously involved: their recommendations had been accompanied by subjective judgments backed by no convincing evidence.[1] In addition it sometimes happens that the PCA investigation will throw up entitlement by the complainant to some benefit he did not know about, and the PCA will draw his attention to it. Even where a matter is outside his jurisdiction the PCA will, where possible, suggest to the complainant where he might go for help or advice. And even where a matter is outside the PCA's jurisdiction the department may realise the error of its ways and remedy the injustice.

Sometimes, in the nature of things, no remedy is possible, (other than an apology) as in the case of error made by the Passport Office referred to at p 537 above. An apology may seem small satisfaction, but sometimes that is all the complainant wants – it proves his complaint was justified.

17 Annual Report for 1983, HC 322, para 12.
18 Clothier, *Parliament and the Executive*, RIPA.
19 Wood, 'New Zealand's Single Chamber Parliament', (1983) Parliamentary Affairs, p 346.
20 Sixth Report, Session 1983–84, HCP 388, p 82.
 1 Annual Report for 1976–7, HC 116, Appendix B.

And if a department apologises it is perhaps an indication of its willingness to remedy the defect found by the Commissioner.

It is clear from a reading of the Act that the first function of the PCA is to get redress for the individual who had a justified complaint. But 'the achievement of redress for the individual, though vital, is only part of the story'.[2] Where it is clear that others have suffered injustice similar to that uncovered by the PCA he will expect the department to identify those others and propose a remedy for them.[3] Numbers affected can run into thousands. And it is not only those who have suffered in the past who may benefit, as the elimination of the faults in an administrative scheme discovered by the PCA will be of future benefit to those affected.

To be particularly noticed is the publication of the results of an internal study of the way administrative practices may infringe legal entitlements.[4] This study was undertaken as a direct result of a PCA report in which he found that officials had failed to act as they had been legally advised to do. 'This has provided an excellent example of how, very properly, the investigation ... of one individual complaint can lead to a major re-examination by the Civil Service of a particular area of administrative practice.'[5] (Following the publication by the PCA of the report of his investigation, the matter was referred to the Director of Public Prosecutions to consider whether a charge of conspiracy to defraud should be brought against the officials concerned.)

If it is a credit item to uncover maladministration, it is also a credit item to find good administration and on occasions the PCA praises a department for their handling of a case (and he will not refrain from criticising an unreasonable complainant). Another credit item has been explained thus:

One of the satisfactions of the job was to explain at some length to the aggrieved citizen why things were as they were, why the law imposed certain requirements on all, but could not take account of the personal predicaments of all: and then to receive an acknowledgment that the explanations were satisfactory and that the citizen was in effect reconciled, if somewhat grudgingly, with his Government.[6]

Possible debits, such as the increased work put on departments, and a disinclination to give advice lest it turn out to be wrong, are of little or no significance when weighed against the beneficial effects of the office.[7]

The Citizen's Charter and the PCA

The Citizen's Charter, published by the government in 1991, lays down certain targets. Complaints of failure to meet these targets may be made

2 Annual Report for 1993, Session 1993–94, HC 290, para 5.
3 See eg HC 519 of Session 1992–93.
4 Legal Entitlements and Administrative Practices: a report by officials, 1980 (HMSO).
5 Annual Report for 1979, HC 402, para 15. See Harlow 41 MLR 446.
6 Clothier [1986] PL 204.
7 Compton (1968) 10 JSPTL 101; Clothier, op cit.

to the PCA, who has said that if targets are expressed as mandatory, or a promise has been given that the citizen has an expectation to compensation should they not be met or should they be missed by a specified period, the case for compensatory redress is strong. Otherwise targets are to be taken as indicators of satisfactory or unsatisfactory performance rather than a firm commitment: it would not follow that to miss such a target would give an entitlement to compensation. Nor would the achieving of a target necessarily mean that the department was free of fault: each case would be considered on its merits.

In pursuance of the Citizen's Charter the government issued in 1993 a Code of Practice on Access to Government Information. This commits certain public bodies to publish certain information. Which bodies? – those under the jurisdiction of the PCA. Complaints that information which should have been provided has not been, are first to be made to the body in question. If the applicant remains disappointed, complaint may be made, via an MP, to the PCA; he will investigate it in accordance with the 1967 Act under which he functions. (There are therefore no legally enforceable rights of access to information under this arrangement). The PCA has observed that while it is the Code and not him which says what information is and is not to be made available, 'I regard it as very much my task to see that access to official information which is in principle supported by the Code is not narrowed in practice. More than that, if ... I conclude that the line has been drawn too restrictively in places I shall make my views known.'[8]

The Select Committee on the Parliamentary Commissioner

The work of this Committee has already been noted at various places. It is regarded by the PCA as crucial to the effectiveness of his office. The Committee's formal terms of reference are to examine the Commissioners' reports which are laid before the House, and matters connected therewith. Each year the PCA's annual report is reviewed in a series of meetings, and specific meetings are held to deal with particular subjects of concern which emerge. Witnesses are summoned. The Committee does not act as a court of appeal from the PCA's findings on any particular investigation but considers important points of principle brought to light by his reports. It pays particular attention to cases where he has found maladministration but no satisfactory remedy has been provided. If the Committee backs the Commissioner, which it nearly always does, a remedy will almost invariably be provided by the Department. The Committee has encouraged him to take a broader view of the meaning of maladministration and it has repeatedly criticised the exclusion of various matters from his jurisdiction. It has examined the possibility of non-departmental bodies being brought within his jurisdiction. It has examined the extent to which the various Ombudsmen in the United Kingdom provide a comprehensive,

8   As fn 2 above, at para 3.

accessible and effective Ombudsman service in this country.[9] It has recently produced a major report on the 'Powers Work and Jurisdiction of the Ombudsman'.[10]

The Health Service Commissioners

The National Health Service Reorganisation Act 1973 created two Health Service Commissioners, one for England and one for Wales. The National Health Service (Scotland) Act 1972 had created the office of Health Service Commissioner for Scotland. The legislation was consolidated in the Health Service Commissioners Act 1993. All these offices have, since their inception, been held by the Parliamentary Commissioner, who thinks that is right: it gives economies of scale, cross-fertilisation, and consistency of practice.

The principal bodies subject to the HSC jurisdiction are (in England) Regional and District Health Authorities, Family Health Service Authorities and NHS Trusts referred to hereafter as 'health service bodies' (HSBs).[11]

A Health Service Commissioner (HSC) may investigate (a) an alleged failure in a service provided by a HSB, (b) an alleged failure of an HSB to provide a service it was its function to provide; (c) maladministration connected with any other action taken by or on behalf of an HSB. He may investigate a complaint where it is made, by or on behalf of a person, that he has sustained *injustice* or *hardship* in consequence of the 'failure' or 'malad-ministration' referred to.

As in the case of the parliamentary Commissioner, a HSC cannot investigate an action where there was an alternative remedy before tribunal or court (though he has the same discretion as the Parliamentary Commissioner to do so); he cannot investigate action taken by persons providing general medical, dental etc services under contract with a Family Health Service Authority; action taken by a FHSA under its disciplinary functions; nor action taken in connection with the diagnosis of illness or the care or treatment of a patient being action which in the Commissioner's opinion was taken solely in consequence of the exercise of clinical judgment.

In addition, he cannot investigate action taken in respect of appointments and other personnel matters. Matters relating to contractual or other commercial transactions are beyond him – except for matters relating to NHS contracts and matters arising from arrangements between a HSB and a body which is not a HSB for the provision of services for patients by that body.

A complaint may be made by an individual or body of persons whether incorporated or not, other than by a public authority (as defined).

9 See Gregory 'The Select Committee on the Parliamentary Commissioner for Administration 1967–1980' [1982] PL 49.
10 HC 33 of Session 1993–94.
11 For NHS bodies see p 25 above.

In contrast with the Parliamentary Ombudsman system a complaint does not have to go through a member of the Commons. The argument for not requiring this is that members do not, in respect of the actions of the authorities in question, occupy that constitutional position which they occupy in respect of the actions of departments. However, although a complaint may be made direct to a HSC, he cannot investigate it unless it was first brought to the notice of the HSB, and it was given reasonable opportunity to investigate and reply to the complaint.

The complaint has to be submitted in writing, and within twelve months, 'by the person aggrieved himself'; but if he is unable to act for himself (and this may well be the case with these complaints) or has died the complaint may be submitted by a member of his family or by any 'body or individual suitable to represent him'. This could include an employee of the authority or the Community Health Council.[12] Furthermore an HSB can itself refer to the HSC a complaint made to it. (It might welcome an independent inquiry into a serious allegation.)

Like the Parliamentary Commissioner, a HSC cannot act except on a complaint. One view is that this limit on his jurisdiction 'appears to conflict with the public interest'.[13] Like the PCA, the HSC cannot look at generalised complaints, such as staffing levels, but he is as concerned as the PCA about systemic faults disclosed by individual complaints.

The HSCs get somewhat more complaints than the PCA. About three-quarters of them are outside jurisdiction the biggest category being those which involve 'clinical judgment'.[14] (Of those investigated some 50% are justified in whole or in part.) The 'clinical judgment' exclusion excites particular interest – after all, it is for the exercise of clinical judgment that the NHS exists, everything else is peripheral. However, it should be noted that there are other procedures for dealing with complaints of clinical judgment. For hospital services there is a three-stage procedure agreed between departments and the professions. There are other procedures for non-clinical judgments. Health authorities are required by the Hospital Complaints Procedure Act 1985 to tell complainants that they have the right to go to the HSC if local investigation leaves them dissatisfied.[15]

The HSC has the same powers to get at the facts as the Parliamentary Commissioner. He must send a report of the results of an investigation to the complainant, to an MP who assisted the complainant, to any person who is alleged to have taken the action complained of, to the HSB, and also to the authority to which that HSB is accountable (eg where the complaint was against the Regional Health Authority, to the Secretary of State). Where the Commissioner thinks that injustice or hardship has been sustained and has not been and will not, be remedied, he may make a special report to the Secretary of State, who is to lay a copy before each House of Parliament. In addition to the annual report which the Commi-

12 For CHCs see p 30 above.
13 Annual Report for 1979–80, HC 650, para 29 for case.
14 The HSC construes the exclusion narrowly: HC 82, 1991–92.
15 See *Being Heard* a report on NHS complaints procedures, pub Dept of Health 1994. Legislation is being prepared. The HSC's jurisdiction is to be extended.

ssioner is required to make to Parliament, he publishes reports of Selected Cases investigated by him.

Cases investigated include, in relation to Family Health Service Authorities, complaints about the closure of a branch surgery, the absence of pharmaceutical services and the informal procedure adopted by a FHSA for dealing with a complaint. In relation to hospitals, cases investigated include complaints about delay in admission, failure to provide ambulance transport, inadequate investigation of a complaint by a hospital, inadequate records of an accident happening to a patient, the giving of treatment without a patient's consent, illegal detention of a mental patient, the failure of a consultant to attend his clinic, improper disclosure of medical records, serious shortcomings in the administration of waiting lists for infertility treatment, wrong advice as to whether the complainant, a foreigner, was entitled to free treatment, the standard of accommodation and services provided for patients who pay for private accommodation in NHS hospitals, discharge from hospital with inadequate advice, and the operation of the review procedure referred to above.

The Commissioner has reported that authorities have generally granted remedies he has proposed (although in many cases all that can be offered is an apology) but in some cases it has required severe pressure by the Select Committee on an authority and its employees. He has said as when wearing his PCA hat, that while remedies obtained for individuals are valuable, 'even more important in the long run are those which result in those changes in policies and procedures which should reduce the risk of others suffering similar hardship or injustice'.[16]

The Local Ombudsmen

The main problem here was to adapt the Parliamentary Ombudsman system to the different constitutional relationship that exists in local government. In local government there is no government-Parliament dichotomy. Unlike MPs, local authority members *are* the executive.

The Local Government Act 1974 provided for the appointment of Local Commissioners: at present there are three for England, one for Wales.[17] In addition there are two Commissions for Local Administration, one for England, and one for Wales. Each consists of the Local Commissioner(s) for the country together with the Parliamentary Commissioner and persons appointed to act as advisers.[18] But the Commission's main function is only to make the necessary administrative arrangements by acquiring premises, appointing staff etc. It is the Commissioner, not the Commission who, with his staff, investigates complaints. Unlike the Parliamentary

16 Annual Report for 1983–84, HC 537 containing a review of the first ten years of the office.
17 See Foulkes 'The Work of the Local Commissioner for Wales' [1978] PL 264; for Scotland, see Local Government (Scotland) Act 1975, as amended.
18 For the last mentioned, see Local Government and Housing Act 1989, Pt II.

and Health Commissioners, the Local Commissioner's staff is employed not on secondment but on a permanent basis. The staff totals about sixty-five.

The authorities subject to investigation include any local authority, any board the constituent authorities of which are all local authorities, an urban development corporation and any police authority other than the Secretary of State. As to *matters* that can be investigated, the Local Government Ombudsman (LGO) can investigate a complaint by a person who claims[19] to have sustained injustice as a consequence of maladministration in connection with action taken by or on behalf of the authority, being action taken in exercise of its administrative functions. The complainant must '[specify] the action alleged to constitute maladministration'. The Court of Appeal has acknowledged that the complainant 'of necessity cannot know what took place in the Council Offices ... Suffice it that he specifies the action of the local authority in connection with which he complains there was maladministration'.[20] As with other Commissioners, there is to be no investigation of a matter where there is an alternative remedy before a tribunal or court, and in addition, where there was an appeal to a minister (again subject to the LGO's overriding discretion). Another exclusion is in respect of action affecting 'all or most of the inhabitants of the area of the authority concerned'.

A number of additional exclusions are to be found in Sch 5 to the Act (they can be added to or excluded by ministerial decision). They include:

(a)   Action taken in matters relating to contractual or other commercial transactions, including the operation of public passenger transport and of markets. The government has resisted the deletion of this exclusion, on the same ground as in the case of the Parliamentary Commissioner. It has, however, acknowledged that in, for example, the allocation of market stalls, the commercial aspect of the decision may be secondary, thus suggesting that it may fall within the LGO's jurisdiction.

(b)   Personnel matters. Again, as in the case of the PCA, the government has resisted bringing these within the Local Commissioners' jurisdiction.

(c)   Certain education matters. The effect of this is to leave within the Commissioner's jurisdiction such matters as school catchment areas, grants, and school bus transport, but to exclude matters relating to school curriculum and discipline.

How is a complaint to be made?   Under the 1974 Act a complaint could not be made direct to a Local Commissioner: it had to be made, in writing, to a member of the authority complained of and then referred by that

19 The Advertising Standards Authority upheld a complaint against the English Commission which said in a recruitment advertisement that LGOs investigated complaints 'by people who have suffered injustice ...' – Local Government Chronicle, 21 Jan 1977, p 46; and see p 536 above.

20 *R v Local Comr v for Administration, ex p Bradford Metropolitan Council* [1979] QB 287, [1979] 2 All ER 881, per Lord Denning.

member to the Ombudsman, though if a member had been asked to refer a complaint to the Ombudsman and had not done so, the Ombudsman could act on the direct request of the complainant. However the Local Government Act 1988 now permits a complaint to be submitted direct to a Local Commissioner as an alternative to the procedure provided by the 1974 Act. Ninety per cent of complaints are 'direct'.

The complaint must be made to the LGO or a member within twelve months from the day on which the person aggrieved first had notice of the matter complained of; but the LGO may investigate an out-of-time complaint if he considers it reasonable to do so.

About 4,000 complaints a year are made to the English Commissioners, of which about one-fifth are within jurisdiction.

A Local Commissioner has the same powers of investigation as the Parliamentary Commissioner.[1]

The report and the remedy

What if the Commissioner finds injustice caused by maladministration – what can he do about it? Under the 1974 Act the most he can do is to 'report' and, if dissatisfied with the authority's response, publish a 'further report'.[2] Now in the case of the Parliamentary Commissioner, effect *is* given to his views, even though all he too can do is to report. Some local authorities have declined to accept the Commissioner's adverse findings (though happy to accept favourable ones). The English Commission took the view that unless a voluntary solution could be quickly achieved, legislation should enable a *citizen* to seek a remedy in the County Court where the authority fails to remedy the injustice. Another possible device would be to make the report binding and enable the *LGO* to seek a judicial remedy, or to give the *Secretary of State* power to direct local authorities to provide a remedy. The Widdicome Committee on the Conduct of Local Authority Business[3] was in favour of the proposal made by the English Commission. The Select Committee on the Parliamentary Commissioner took the view that the five per cent cases of failure to provide a remedy for maladministration was of special concern to it, (though it is concerned with the *Parliamentary* Commissioner) as a lack of effectiveness of some Ombudsmen reflects on the system as a whole. The level of refusal to implement reports it found to be 'wholly unacceptable': some change was essential. Their conclusion was that 'the best method of providing support

---

1 Local Government, Planning and Land Act 1980, s 184 remedies the interpretation given to s 32(3) of the Local Government Act 1974 in *Re a Complaint against Liverpool City Council* [1977] 2 All ER 650, [1977] 1 WLR 995.
2 The authority has to make available for three weeks, for public inspection and copying copies of the report of any investigation into a complaint against it; and any one can require a copy of the report, on payment. When the LGO finds maladministration which involves a member breaching the National Code of Local Government Conduct he is to name the member unless satisfied it would be unjust to do so. For the Code see Local Government and Housing Act 1989, s 31.
3 Cmnd 9797.

for local Ombudsmen's reports would be for our remit to be extended to allow the possibility of our calling recalcitrant local authorities to account'. If this did not have the necessary effect, serious consideration should be given to the judicial enforcement of Ombudsmen's reports. It was obviously going to be difficult to get acceptance of the idea that a Committee whose job it is to call central government to account should have jurisdiction over local government, and the government rejected it. The judicial enforcement of an Ombudsman report may look attractive, but the contrary arguments are weighty:[4] if the report were to be the basis of a court order this would have a considerable impact on the fact-finding procedure of the Ombudsman, making it more lengthy, legalistic and costly; and the authorities would be less willing to co-operate with the Ombudsmen. The government accepted these counter-arguments. The position now is as follows.[5] If the LGO reports that injustice has been caused through maladministration, it is the duty of the authority in question to consider (not merely to 'note') the report and within three months from receiving the report, it is to notify the LGO of the action it has taken or proposes to take. If he does not receive that notification, or is not satisfied with the action taken, or does not within three months receive confirmation from the authority that they have taken the action they proposed to take, then he is to 'make a further report setting out those facts and making recommendations' – the latter being the action which the Commissioner thinks the authority should take to remedy the injustice 'and to prevent similar injustice being caused in the future'.

If this 'further report' is not acted on the Commissioner may require the authority to publish a statement in a newspaper circulating in their area. This may include a statement by the authority of their reason for not implementing the recommendations made. If the authority fails to publish the statement, the Commissioner may do so. The government has said that if this is ineffective, there will be legislation to make recommendations legally enforceable.

Like the Parliamentary and Health Service Commissioners, a Local Commissioner's primary function is to investigate individual complaints of maladministration, and to report. But as in their cases, his reports may lead to general improvements in administrative practice. In particular, the Local Ombudsmen regard it as a secondary objective to encourage local authorities to develop and publicise their own procedures for the fair settlement of complaints and to settle as many as possible themselves; and to encourage the local settlement of complaints made to the Ombudsman.[6]

The monitoring officer
There is an obligation on a local authority to appoint a 'monitoring officer'. It is his duty to report to the authority, with a copy for each member,

---

4　*Judicial Teeth for Local Ombudsmen*, University of Edinburgh 1985.
5　Local Government and Housing Act 1989, s 26. See Marshall [1990] PL 489.
6　Note the role of the Commissions in providing advice and guidance about good administrative practice, ibid, s 23.

where any proposals, decision or omission by the authority has given or may give rise to maladministration or injustice (within the meaning of the legislation relating to the Local Commissioner). The authority must consider his report within 21 days; implementation of a proposal or decision reported on is meanwhile suspended.[7]

Relationship between the Commissioners: a unified system?

We have then, in England, Scotland and Wales a tripartite Ombudsman system, for central government, the health service, and local government. The separate institutions are, we have seen, linked in various ways – for example the Parliamentary Commissioner is a member of the Local Commissions for England and Wales and they maintain informal contacts. Now a complaint may well involve more than one of the three branches of the system; for example a complaint about town and country planning may involve central and local government, and a complaint involving both health care and housing will concern a health authority and a local authority.[8] How are such composite cases, as they are called, dealt with? The Acts provide that if at any stage in an investigation a Commissioner finds that the complaint relates partly to a matter which could be the subject of an investigation by another Commissioner, he must consult with him about the complaint, and must let the complainant know how to initiate the machinery for ensuring that that other aspect of his complaint is considered by the appropriate Commissioner.[9]

This way of dealing with composite cases clearly has disadvantages. The Parliamentary Commissioner has referred to the 'considerable procedural problems' facing a complainant and has said that 'in the long term ... it will be important to consider how a more co-ordinated total system, more directly related to the interests of members of the public, can be brought about'.[10] The Select Committee has since looked at the problem, but legislation will be necessary if a unified system is to be brought about.

Northern Ireland's Ombudsmen

The Parliamentary Commissioner Act 1967 did not apply to Northern Ireland but an Act of 1969 of the Northern Ireland Parliament created

---

7 Local Government and Housing Act 1989, s 5.
8 For a complaint involving Parliamentary Health Service and Local Commissioner, see Fourth Report from the Parliamentary Commissioner, 1976–77, HCP 413, p 53. Note too that some authorities are subject as to some of their functions to the Parliamentary Commissioner, and as to others to the Local Commissioner eg National Rivers Authority, and Urban Development Corporations.
9 See Parliamentary Commissioner for Administration Act 1967, s 11 (as amended), s 11A. Health Service Commissioners Act 1993 ss 17, 18.
10 Annual Report for 1975, para 55.

the office of *Northern Ireland Parliamentary Commissioner for Administration*. The Act is in all material respects identical with the 1967 Act except that the Commissioner can investigate personnel matters relating to service in government departments in Northern Ireland. (This was provided for as part of a package to deal with political and religious discrimination in the Province.) Complaints are referred to the Commissioner by members of the Westminster Parliament (by the Northern Ireland Assembly when it existed). He submits an Annual Report to Parliament, and is overseen by the Commons Select Committee on the Parliamentary Commissioner.

In addition the Commissioner for Complaints Act (Northern Ireland) 1969 provided for the appointment of a *Northern Ireland Commissioner for Complaints*.[11] The same person holds both offices and the office operates as a single entity. He can investigate action taken by any 'local body' and by the public bodies listed – the latter include Health and Social Service authorities, the Tourist Board and other bodies. Complaints about commercial transactions are not excluded. A complaint of injustice in consequence of maladministration may be made direct to the Commissioner on the payment of a fee which cannot be more than £5. This can be waived and may (and if the complaint is found to have been justified, shall) be returned.

The following provisions distinguish this Ombudsman from others in the UK. One of the purposes of the Complaints Commissioner's investigation is expressly stated (by section 7) to be (where it appears to him to be desirable), 'to effect a settlement of the matter complained of or, if that is not possible, to state what action should in his opinion be taken by the body against whom the complaint is made to effect a fair settlement thereof, or ... to remove ... the cause of complaint'.[12]

Where the Commissioner reports that the complainant has suffered injustice, the complainant can apply to the county court which on giving notice to the body complained of, may award the complainant damages to compensate him for expenses and loss of opportunity of acquiring the benefit he may reasonably be expected to have had but for the maladministration. If that court thinks that justice can be done only by directing the body in question to take or refrain from taking certain action, that court may grant the necessary injunction.

Furthermore, where the Commissioner, on finding injustice, thinks that the body in question has previously engaged in conduct similar to that condemned by him as maladministration and is likely to engage in such conduct in future, he can request the Attorney-General to apply to the High Court for an injunction.

The Ombudsman system is now well established. It has proved to be a major and welcome constitutional innovation. The system, it has been suggested, was

11 Poole 'The Northern Ireland Commissioner for Complaints' [1972] PL 131.
12 The Commission for Local Administration for England has suggested that it be given this power, but the government did not agree: Annual Report for 1979, Appendix 9.

designed to afford not so much remedies in the strict sense of the term as facilities for obtaining independent and impartial scrutiny of action by public bodies about which an individual believes that he has cause for complaint, even though the action may have been within the body's legal powers.[13]

But it can and does provide not only scrutiny but what the complainant might regard as a remedy. And the remedy may by administrative action be extended to other citizens; and the procedure is 'cheap, private, relatively quick, and final'.[14]

The role of the office has to be considered in relation to the operation of other institutions and procedures – Parliament, the Council on Tribunals, the courts etc. The relationship to the courts may seem one of contrast – legality versus administrative propriety.

Principles of good administration may look different from the rules of law to which we are accustomed and are likely to be phrased in terms of duties imposed on the administration. But just as the courts can protect the citizen's right to enforcement of the law in matters which directly affect him, so can the Ombudsman be a valuable means of protecting the citizen's interest in, or right to, good administration.[15]

The success of the Ombudsman is suggested by its rapid extension in both public and private sectors. This is referred to below.

Judicial review of Ombudsmen's decisions

The Ombudsmen are creatures of statute. In principle, therefore, their actions are subject to judicial review. In debate on the Parliamentary Commissioner Bill a minister said that the possibility of judicial review to test the Commissioner's jurisdiction had deliberately not been excluded.[16] There have now been a number of cases, first, in respect of the Local Commissioners. The extent of a Commissioner's power to require the production of documents was considered in *Re a complaint against Liverpool Council*;[17] the limited interpretation given there to his power was removed by statute. *R v Local Comr for Administration, ex p Bradford Metropolitan City Council*[18] was an unsuccessful attempt to obtain an order of prohibition to prohibit the Commissioner from proceeding with an investigation because of an incompetent complaint. In *R v Local Comr for Administration, ex p Eastleigh Borough Council*[19] the challenge was

13 Report of the Select Committee on a Bill of Rights 1978, HL Minutes of Evidence, p 31.
14 Clothier [1986] PL 204 at 209.
15 Bradley, 'The Role of the Ombudsman in Relation to the Protection of Citizens' Rights' [1980] CLJ 304. In *Gaskin v Liverpool City Council* [1980] 1 WLR 1549, at 1553 and in *R v City of Birmingham District Council, ex p O* [1982] 2 All ER 356 at 360, Lord Denning suggested that the plaintiff should have gone to the Local Ombudsman. For sequel to *Gaskin* see p 523 above. For proposed enactment of principles of good administration see 'Administration under Law' pub Justice 1971.
16 See Foulkes 34 MLR 377 at 392.
17 [1977] 2 All ER 650, [1977] 1 WLR 995.
18 [1979] QB 287, [1979] 2 All ER 881.
19 [1988] 3 All ER 151.

directly to the legality of the Commissioner's report. The commissioner found maladministration and a majority of the Court of Appeal said that in law he was not wrong to do so. (The minority view was that he had transgressed the Act in questioning the merits of a decision taken without maladministration.) The Commissioner went on to say that the maladministration had caused injustice, but a (different) majority thought that his report did not justify that finding. In the result a declaration as to the illegality of the report on the 'causal' point was granted.

In his judgment the Master of the Rolls expressed the view that it would be rare for Ombudsmen's reports to be challenged by judicial review, but within a few months came *R v Local Comr for Administration, ex p Croydon London Borough Council.*[20] Parents appealed against the decision of Croydon as to the school their daughter should attend. The appeal was heard by the education appeal committee,[1] and dismissed. A complaint was made to the LGO about that decision. The LGO concluded that there was maladministration causing injustice and Croydon sought judicial review of this report. The following points were raised.

(i) Was the committee exercising an administrative or a judicial function? The LGO being confined to the former. Woolf LJ did not 'find it at all easy' to say, but noted that the matters which the Commissioner criticised were within his jurisdiction to consider – that the committee acted on inadequate evidence, and that in reaching its decisions it applied a policy to the exclusion of the merits of the particular case before it.

(ii) Was the Commissioner's jurisdiction excluded by the availability to the complainant of a remedy before the courts?[2] He said that the possibility of a remedy was so remote as to be theoretical only, and that he did not consider the matter. Woolf LJ said that the effect of that provision is that the general rule is that where a complainant has a remedy in the courts he should resort there rather than to the Commissioner. The test the Commissioner should apply is not whether the court proceedings would succeed, but, whether a court of law 'is an appropriate forum' for investigating the subject matter of the complainant. And, while the court may not seem the appropriate forum when *beginning* an investigation the Commissioner must bear in mind throughout his investigation the possibility of a legal remedy and of his discontinuing his investigation. The Commissioner should have realised that possibility, but as he now said that if he had considered it he would have concluded that it was unreasonable to expect the complainant to pursue a legal remedy, the court would not grant a remedy on that basis.

(iii) With reference to the grounds on which the Commissioner found maladministration ((i) above), the court found that the committee *had* adequate evidence, and its decision *was* based on merits. A declaration was granted to the effect that there was no basis for a finding of maladministration.

20 [1989] 1 All ER 1033. See M Jones [1988] PL 608.
 1 See p 152 above.
 2 See p 548 above.

The following will be noted: (a) the court's decision as outlined in para (ii) above would seem inevitably to apply to the Parliamentary and Health Service Commissioners also (b) where there is an overlap of jurisdiction as between the courts and the Commissioner, the *Croydon* case would clearly relegate the Commissioner to the lesser position; (c) the more extensive the courts' reach into the matters of public administration, the less room is there for the Ombudsmen; (d) Commissioner's reports are not statutes or judgments, as the Master of the Rules observed. They were nevertheless subjected to detailed and microscopic examination by the courts. In future the Commissioners must write their reports with this in mind.

The above cases were brought by the local authorities complained against, and concerned the extent of the LGO's powers. In *R v Parliamentary Commissioner for Administration, ex p Dyer*[3] the applicant was the complainant, and concerned the exercise by the PCA of his discretion. The PCA had investigated D's complaint and found it justified, but she was dissatisfied with his report on a number of points. The first question was whether the court had any jurisdiction over the PCA in the exercise of his discretions. It was suggested that it had not in view of his relationship with Parliament. This was 'unhesitatingly' rejected, as was the argument that by analogy with the *Nottinghamshire* case[4] the court had a very restricted power. Nevertheless, the court would not readily be persuaded, in view of the language of sections 5(5) and 7(2),[5] and the degree of subjective judgment involved, to interfere in the exercise of the PCA's judgment: it would be difficult to prove *Wednesbury* unreasonableness[6] (as it would in the case of LGOs). On the facts of *Dyer* the court held that the PCA was entitled to limit the scope of his investigation, and that once he had reported, he was functus officio,[7] so could not re-open his inquiry without a further reference.

Other Ombudsmen

The Ombudsmen so far considered may be classified as public sector Ombudsmen, as they oversee the public sector. They are creatures of statute. There is now a considerable number of private sector Ombudsmen, which may or may not have a statutory basis. The *Legal Services Ombudsman*, created by the Courts and Legal Services Act 1990 investigates allegations made to him and which relate to the manner in which a complaint made to a legal professional body was dealt with by that body. He may recommend the action to be taken. The *Building Societies Ombudsman* operates through a statutory scheme set up under the

3 [1994] 1 All ER 375.
4 See p 255 above.
5 See pp 539, 540 above.
6 See p 239 above.
7 See p 232 above.

Building Societies Act 1986, to which all such societies belong.[8] This Ombudsman may *direct* the steps a society is to take, and order it to pay compensation. When the complainant accepts the Ombudsman's decision it becomes binding on the society: such a binding decision 'shall be final and conclusive and shall not be questioned in any court of law'. But the Ombudsman may be required to state a case for the court on a point of law. The *Banking Ombudsman* scheme, on the other hand, (itself in many respects modelled on the *Insurance Ombudsman* scheme) is a voluntary scheme which is constituted as a company headed by a board of directors appointed by the banks. The Social Security Act 1990 created the office of *Pensions Ombudsmen* to provide a means for resolving grievances of members of pension schemes. In investigating complaints he can determine disputes of fact and law, and make directions binding upon the managers of the scheme. Remarkably, such decisions are enforceable in a county court as if it were a judgment of that court.[9]

Other complaints procedures

Under the Financial Services Act 1986, eg Sch 2 para 6(1), certain financial institutions 'must have effective arrangements for the investigation of complaints'.

Every local education authority is to make arrangements for the consideration and disposal of any complaint to the effect that the authority or the governing body of a school maintained by it have acted unreasonably in the exercise of any power conferred or duty imposed relating to the curriculum.[10]

The Data Protection Registrar receives about 1,000 complaints a year on matters falling within his jurisdiction. He describes his work in handling them as 'Ombudsman work' and has explained how they may assist in establishing good data protection practice.[11]

The Revenue Adjudicator deals with the sort of complaints about the handling of a tax-payers affairs that could otherwise be dealt with by the PCA. This is not a statutory appointment: the official gets his powers – his recommendations are not binding but will normally be followed – from agreement between adjudicator and the Board of Inland Revenue.[12] (His role has been extended to cover Customs and Excise.)

Under Schedule 7 of the Cardiff Bay Barrage Act 1993 the Independent Groundwater Complaints Administrator can, ultimately, require the Development Corporation to take the steps specified by him to resolve the matters complained of.

---

8 See *Halifax Building Society v Edell* [1992] 3 All ER 389 at 398 for 'maladministration' in context of this scheme.
9 SI 1993/1978, and p 149 above.
10 Education Reform Act 1988, s 23.
11 Fourth Report, HC 570, 1987–88. For Registrar, see p 40 above.
12 See Oliver [1993] PL 407.

The Broadcasting Act 1990 provides for both a Broadcasting Complaints Commission and a Broadcasting Standards Council. Both can deal with complaints made to them, but the latter must also draw up a code for the guidance of broadcasters on certain matters. In addition it has to monitor programmes and may itself issue complaints – which it may then have to adjudicate on.[13]

Auditors

All public bodies have internal audit procedures,[14] but in addition are subject to external audit of their financial transactions.

Local government audit

A system of 'Auditors for the District' – the district audit system – emerged in a recognisably modern form in 1844 in connection with the administration of the Poor Law. During the nineteenth century it was extended to most types of local authority. The law required the accounts of local authorities to be audited by either the district auditor – a civil servant – or an 'approved auditor' (a firm of professional accountants whose appointment was approved by the Secretary of State).

An important change was made by the Local Government Finance Act 1982. That Act created the *Audit Commission,* a non-Crown body corporate whose members are appointed by the Secretary of State, and which must carry out any directions given to it by him. The Act provides that the accounts of local authorities are to be audited, and that the Commission is to appoint the auditors to do the job. (The functions of the Commission have now been extended to cover the health service.)[15] It may appoint either 'an officer of the Commission' (the Commission took over the employment of the former 600 or so district auditors) or 'an individual who is not such an officer or a firm of such individuals' (paralleling the former approved auditors these are firms of accountants). Certain rights and duties (referred to below) are put on the auditors, not the Commission, thus ensuring their operational independence. The Commission has to prepare a Code of Audit Practice prescribing the way auditors are to carry out their functions within the prescribed statutory limits – which are now considered.

The 1982 Act continues but extends the duties put on auditors by the former law.[16] The auditor must satisfy himself that the accounts comply with all relevant statutory provisions; and that the authority has made

13 See Coleman [1993] PL 448. See *R v BCC, ex p BBC* (1995) Times, 24 February.
14 For local government see SI 1983/1761; for central government, see *Government Internal Audit Manual.*
15 National Health Service and Community Care Act 1990 s 20; the Commission is now the Audit Commission for Local Authorities and the National Health Service.
16 See Radford 'Auditing for Change' (1991) 54 MLR 912.

proper arrangements for securing economy, efficiency and effectiveness in its use of resources.[17] The latter – the value for money (VFM) audit – was a new statutory requirement though auditors had for some time been concerning themselves with VFM audits. Such an audit does not require the auditor to consider the political merits of decisions; it is rather concerned to draw attention to consequences of decisions, and to alternative courses of action available for consideration, and to publicise the best practices. Additionally the auditor is to consider whether, 'in the public interest', he should make a report on any matter coming to his notice in the course of the audit so that it may be considered by the body concerned and brought to the attention of the public. The report has to be considered by the authority reported on, and is available to the public and press. Topics dealt with in such reports include arrears of rates, failure to charge for services, the need for competitive tendering. He has to consider whether the public interest requires the publication of an 'immediate' report, rather than at the conclusion of the audit.[18]

The publication of independent reports on the activities of a public body is a common and useful device. The auditor's function goes on beyond this. From the earliest days of the district audit the auditor was required to disallow items of account *contrary to law* and to surcharge the amount of any expenditure disallowed upon the person responsible. An important change was made in the Local Government Act 1972 and again in the 1982 Act: the auditor can no longer himself surcharge, but where he thinks an item is contrary to law, he can apply to the court for a declaration to that effect[19] (unless the expenditure is sanctioned by the Secretary of State).[20] Where the court makes such a declaration, it may order repayment by those responsible, and disqualification for local authority membership if the amount is over £2,000. Few such applications to the court are made.

The auditor has another power available to him. Where, under section 20, it appears to him that any person has failed to bring into account a sum which should have been included, or where it appears that a loss or deficiency has been caused by the wilful misconduct of any person, he must certify that the sum or deficiency is due from that person. The auditor and the body in question may recover that sum for the benefit of the body in question. Where there is wilful misconduct and the sum certified exceeds

---

17 *Effectiveness* means providing the right services to enable the authority to implement its policies and objectives. *Efficiency* means providing a specified volume and quantity of service with the lowest level of resources capable of meeting that specification. *Economy* means ensuring that the assets of the authority and services purchased are procured and maintained at the lowest possible cost consistent with a specified quality and quantity – Audit Commission, *Performance Review in Local Government*. See Education Act 1993, s 8 for 'VFM' studies.

18 See Local Government Finance (Publicity for Auditors' Reports) Act 1991.

19 *Hazell v Hammersmith and Fulham London Borough Council* was such a case: [1992] 2 AC 1, [1991] 1 All ER 545.

20 This sanctioning does not make the expenditure lawful but puts it beyond reach of the auditor. It is of long standing and is used only in the case of unwitting illegality – see Jennings *The Law relating to Local Authorities*, p 299.

£2,000 there is mandatory disqualification for local authority membership for five years. There is an appeal to the court against the certificate and against a failure to certify.[1]

To enable him to do his job the auditor is given access to all relevant documents and information and must be provided with every facility he needs.

A new power was given to the auditor by the Local Government Act 1988. Under the provisions just considered the auditor can take action only after the accounts have been audited. Under this new power he can take preventive action, thus – he can issue a *prohibition order* if he has reason to believe that the body (or one of its officers) whose accounts he is charged with auditing (a) is about to make or has made a decision which involves or would involve the body incurring unlawful expenditure; or (b) is about to take or has taken a course of action which if pursued, would be unlawful and likely to cause a loss or deficiency; or (c) is about to enter an item of account the entry of which is unlawful. The order will specify which of these paragraphs is being relied on, and will require the body to which it is addressed to desist from making the decisions etc in question; but it will not have effect unless the auditor gives his reason for his belief as to the matter in question. So long as a prohibition order has effect, it is not lawful for the body concerned, or its officers, to make or implement a decision etc (and it has effect until revoked by the auditor). There is a right of appeal, by the body concerned, against the order, to the High Court.[2]

Furthermore, an auditor may, with leave of the court, apply for judicial review of any decision of, or failure to act on the part of the body whose accounts he is auditing, when it is reasonable to believe that the decision or failure would have an effect on the accounts of that body. The availability to the auditor of his other powers are not to be regarded by the court as a ground for refusing leave to apply, or the application.

Consider now *public rights* in the audit. At each audit (the holding of which is publicly notified) any person interested may *inspect* the accounts to be audited, and all books, contracts etc, relating to them and may make copies. A local government elector for the area may also *question* the auditor about the accounts. This is to assist an elector who is considering whether to exercise the right to make *objection* to (a) any matter as to which an auditor could seek a declaration of illegality or could recover money not accounted for; or (b) any matter that could be the subject of an auditor's report. There is no specified procedure for dealing with objections, but it is well established that an auditor, when considering them, must observe the rules of natural justice. The hearing is not required to be in public. Few objections succeed.[3]

1 It was under this section that the auditor acted in *Lloyd v McMahon* (p 291 above). Forty-seven councillors were debarred from office and £106,103 was certified as due.
2 For obligation on local authority to appoint a 'chief financial officer' and his duty in connection with prohibition order see Local Government Act 1988, Pt VIII.
3 See Foulkes 'From District Audit to Audit Commission' [1983] Camb LR 34. In 1987 there were 613 questions and 98 objections. See Commission's Annual Reports.

Comptroller and Auditor General

The law relating to the office and functions of the Comptroller and Auditor General[4] (C & AG) was amended by the National Audit Act 1983, and can now be described thus. The office of C & AG was created by statute in 1866. It is a Crown appointment exercisable on an address presented by the House of Commons, the motion for the address being made only by the Prime Minister acting with the agreement of the Chairman of the Committee of Public Accounts. The C & AG is expressly stated to be an officer of the House of Commons; he can be removed from office only on an address by both Houses.[5] He has a staff of some 900 (who are neither officers of the House nor civil servants). The C & AG and his staff together comprise the *National Audit Office*.

The C & AG is designated by statute the auditor for government departments and of a wide range of public bodies. In addition he audits by agreement a large number of miscellaneous bodies, in particular certain non-governmental bodies which carry out government functions and which derive all or most of their income from public funds, such as the Sports Council and the British Council. The accounts of universities are open to his inspection as are those of health authorities and fund-holding practices.[6] The C & AG has never audited the accounts of the nationalised industries. (He audits the Audit Commission.) In addition the C & AG may carry out examinations into the economy, efficiency and effectiveness with which certain bodies have used their resources (that is VFM audit) namely, government departments, and any body whose members are appointed by or on behalf of the Crown and which in any year receives more than half its income from public funds[7] and certain other bodies (and universities in respect of their money which is paid by way of government grant). He is however expressly forbidden to 'question the merits of the policy objectives' of any such body.

The C & AG is given by statute 'complete discretion in the discharge of his functions' in particular whether to audit and how to do it, though, in deciding, he must take into account any proposals made by the Public Accounts Committee.[8]

---

4 See Harden 'Money and the Constitution' (1993) 13 LS 16, McEldowney in *The Changing Constitution*, 3rd edn, Jowell and Oliver.
5 The independence of external central government auditors is assured by statute. What of its internal auditors? The Treasury view is that they must be sufficiently independent to allow the auditor to perform his duties in a manner which allows professional judgments and recommendations to be effective and impartial. The NAO said that to achieve this the Head of Internal Audit should be graded at a similar level to the departmental Heads of Divisions on whose activities they report.
6 See p 30 above.
7 For relevance of government funding to legality of beating schoolchildren see Education (No 2) Act 1986, s 47.
8 For account of debates leading to National Audit Act 1983 see notes by Foulkes on Act in Current Law Statutes.

The Accounting Officer

We have noted the requirement that statutory authority for expenditure has to be obtained under the Appropriation Act by votes. In addition, the Treasury is required to appoint an Accounting Officer for each vote. Because of the principle that financial and administrative responsibility cannot be separated, the practice was established of appointing the Permanent Head of each Department as its Accounting Officer, (though in some large departments there may be two or more Accounting Officers). He is personally legally responsible for ensuring that funds voted by Parliament are spent for the approved purposes.[9] His responsibility extends to the efficient and economic administration of the department as a whole.

The importance of the role of the Accounting Officer and his personal responsibility is emphasised by the rule that where he disagrees with his minister on a matter of importance affecting the efficient and economic administration of the department he is expected to place on record his disagreement with any decision he would have difficulty in defending before the Public Accounts Committee. Having done so, he must of course accept the minister's decision. Where the disagreement involves the Accounting Officer's personal accountability on a question of safeguarding public funds or the regularity of expenditure, he is required to state his objection in writing and to carry out the minister's decision only on a written instruction from the minister overriding his objection.[10] As may be imagined, this happens very rarely.

Parliamentary Committees

We have looked in some detail at the work of the various Committees on Delegated Legislation[11] and the Select Committee on the Parliamentary Commissioner.[12] The work of the Public Accounts Committee must now be mentioned. It has the reputation of being the most important and effective of the Parliamentary Committees. It was first set up in 1861 with the intention of giving Parliament better control over the expenditure of public funds. It has some fifteen members: by convention the chairman is from the Opposition. It examines subjects raised by the Comptroller and Auditor General in his reports to Parliament on departmental and other accounts, and from time to time issues which the Committee itself thinks important. The most traditional field for PAC inquiries almost from its inception has been contracts and various support schemes for industry.

---

9 For the difficulties of decentralising functions (to NHS authorities) because of this personal responsibility see Ninth Report from the Public Accounts Committee, 1976–7, HC 352, Minutes of Evidence, p 19. For NHS see p 25 above. For serious breach of principle of personal financial responsibility, see HC 390 of 1984–85 re Defence Procurement.

10 Government Accounting, Section C (HMSO).

11 Chapter 3, above.

12 See p 544 above.

It examines the Accounting Officer and other officers, and on occasions private persons. It expects the Accounting Officer to satisfy it that the policy approved by Parliament has been carried out with due regard to economy. The Committee has the expert assistance of the C & AG and his staff. It reports to Parliament. Its reports may lead to important changes in departmental practice. This link between the C & AG and Parliament in the shape of the Public Accounts Committee is, as in the case of the Parliamentary Commissioner, of great importance. The C & AG has commented that experience in countries which have no comparable Parliamentary arrange-ments seem to be that the impact of the C & AG's reports is much reduced.

The two volumes of *Epitomes of the Reports from the Committee of Public Accounts*[13] form a body of precedents to guide departments. Examination of the *Epitomes* will show, for example, the extent of the C & AG's and the Committee's investigation into government contracts. Thus the need for Treasury sanction has been emphasised for, for example, payments in contravention of the terms of a contract, for compensation for suspension of a contract, and for a bona fide mistake in tendering. The right of the Comptroller to see rejected as well as accepted tenders has been asserted and the need to avoid competition between departments emphasised. Inexperienced departments have been reminded of the need to seek advice from major contracting departments in handling building contracts. Departments have been criticised for failing to insert or to enforce penalty clauses, and for entering into formal contracts without legal advice on the effect of the terms agreed to.

In addition to the above committees there were a number of other Select Committees, for example on Science and Technology, on the Nationalised Industries, and on Overseas Development, and the Expenditure Committee. However in 1979, following a recommendation from the Select Committee on Procedure, a major change took place in the structure of House of Commons Committees. There was introduced system by which a Select Committee was appointed in respect of each major government department. Each Committee thus 'shadows' a department[14] A further distinction is that the new committees are provided for by Standing Order and not merely on a sessional basis, and members are appointed for the duration of a Parliament. (Committees have an average of eleven members. Membership is proportionate to the strength of parties in the House: thus the government has a majority on, but not the chairmanship of, all committees.) There is thus a comprehensive and continuing mechanism

13 1937–8, HC 154; 1969–70, HC 187. And see its report. 'The Proper Conduct of Public Business', HC 154 of 1993–94.
14 Until 1992 there was no committee shadowing the Lord Chancellor's Department. Lord Chancellor Hailsham took the view that the committee would threaten the independence of the judiciary and the judicial process. The scrutiny of the Home Affairs Committee was extended in 1992 to include that Department and its associated offices including the Law Officers Department and the Council on Tribunals. Its scrutiny excluded consideration of individual cases and appointments, but includes the work of staff doing the administrative work of courts and tribunals.

for the scrutiny of departments. A further advantage is that more money has been made available for the employment of advisers by committees. (But notice that the committees referred to in the first paragraph have not been affected: each of them deals with matters which are the concern of more than one department.) And a Liaison Committee has been set up with the job of considering general matters relating to the work of all the departmental committees. The departmental Committees are entitled to examine the expenditure, administration and policies of the department in question and of its 'associated public bodies.' They are free to seek evidence from whomsoever they please. An official who appears before a Committee does so on behalf of his minister and subject to his instructions.[15] Officials are told to be 'as helpful as possible' to Committees but there is a substantial list of matters they should not give evidence about and topics they should not discuss. Example: advice given to ministers should not be disclosed, nor information about the level at which decisions were taken, or the manner in which a minister consulted his colleagues. And 'there is a well-established convention that the advice which Law Officers give to Ministers is confidential'.

A Select Committee on the work of this select committee system reported that it has proved a valuable and cost-effective addition to the ability of the House to perform its proper function of holding departments to account.[16]

Tribunals of Inquiry (Evidence) Act 1921

A tribunal can be appointed under this Act when both Houses of Parliament resolve that it is expedient to do so to inquire into 'a definite matter of urgent public importance'. So far, tribunals have been appointed on twenty occasions. The matters they have been concerned with have been very varied. Five have been concerned with complaints against the police. There have been inquiries into the disclosure of budget secrets, the loss of a submarine whilst on diving trials, corruption in municipal affairs in Glasgow, the bribery of ministers and public servants over the issue of building licences, the disclosure of a change in bank rate, the circumstances in which a spy, Vassall, was able to operate undetected in the Admiralty for many years, the causes of the 1966 Aberfan disaster, the collapse of the Vehicle and General Insurance Company,[17] and the activities of the Crown Agents.[18]

A tribunal has all the powers of the High Court in the matter of enforcing the attendance of witnesses and compelling the production of documents. Witnesses have the same immunities and privileges as in the High Court, so that they cannot be sued in slander for anything said in evidence, and

15 Memorandum of guidance for officials appearing before Select Committees, March 1988, Cabinet Office.
16 HC 19 of Session 1989–90.
17 The Parliamentary Commissioner had commenced an investigation into this but on the appointment of the Tribunal discontinued it.
18 See Segal [1984] PL 206.

are privileged from disclosing their sources of information to the same extent as before the High Court. The tribunal must sit in public unless it thinks it is against the public interest to do so, and it can authorise a person appearing to it to be interested to be legally represented before it. The tribunal usually consists of a lawyer as chairman with two other appropriately qualified persons to assist him. These tribunals may therefore seem akin to courts of law but there is no *lis*. The evidence on which a court decides is presented to it by the parties to the action: it weighs against one another the cases put to it, whereas a tribunal under the 1921 Act pursues its own inquiries in its efforts to seek the truth of the matters it was set up to consider. It is therefore inquisitorial, and not as the courts are, accusatorial. It is an inquiry, not a tribunal. It cannot impose any penalty or order the payment of damages. It merely reports its conclusions to the appropriate minister. Whether or not any further action is called for depends on the circumstances.

Certain features of these tribunals caused disquiet and a Royal Commission was appointed to consider their working. It reported in 1966.[19] Further, at the time of the Aberfan inquiry, criticism was made about the application of the law of contempt to these tribunals. A committee was appointed to inquire into that question. It reported in 1969. In 1973 the government published its views on the recommendations of the Commission and of the committee.[20] They include the following.

(a)   The most difficult question is the protection of persons liable to be involved as a result of allegations made against them by other witnesses in an inquiry. Before a tribunal hears evidence from a witness it should be satisfied that there are circumstances which affect him and which the tribunal propose to investigate. Whenever practicable, the tribunal should inform any person called as a witness who is likely to have allegations made against him of the nature of those allegations so far as they are known and of the substance of the evidence in support of them.

(b)   The 1921 Act should be amended so that anyone called as a witness should have the right to be legally represented, and so that the tribunal should have the power to make orders for costs out of public funds not after the inquiry but at such time as would enable the witness to rely on it before making arrangements for his representation.

(c)   The committee made recommendations as to the application of the law of contempt to these tribunals. That matter is now dealt with by section 20 of the Contempt of Court Act 1981.

(d)   There should be no appeal from a tribunal finding. Dissatisfaction with tribunals' findings will focus on whether any strictures in the report are warranted. This should be left, 'not to an appeal body but to Parliament, to which the reports are presented and by which it is customary for them to be debated'.

19 Cmnd 3121.
20 Cmnd 4078 and 5313.

(e) Normally the Parliamentary Commissioner is the person best equipped to deal with allegations of maladministration. But there may be circumstances in which an allegation of maladministration is of such gravity that the appointment of a tribunal is necessary.

The application of the principles recommended by the Royal Commission was considered by the tribunal which carried out a wide-ranging and complex inquiry into the affairs of the Crown Agents.[1]

Because of these various difficulties these tribunals are regarded as having fallen into disuse. The Scott Inquiry into the export of arms to Iraq, due to report in 1995, was non-statutory.

---

1 See the Tribunal's Report, HC 364 of 1981–2. Of particular interest in this chapter on Ombudsmen are the Tribunal's observations on the difficulty of defining what is meant by a lapse from accepted standards of public administration – see ch 2 of the Report.

Index